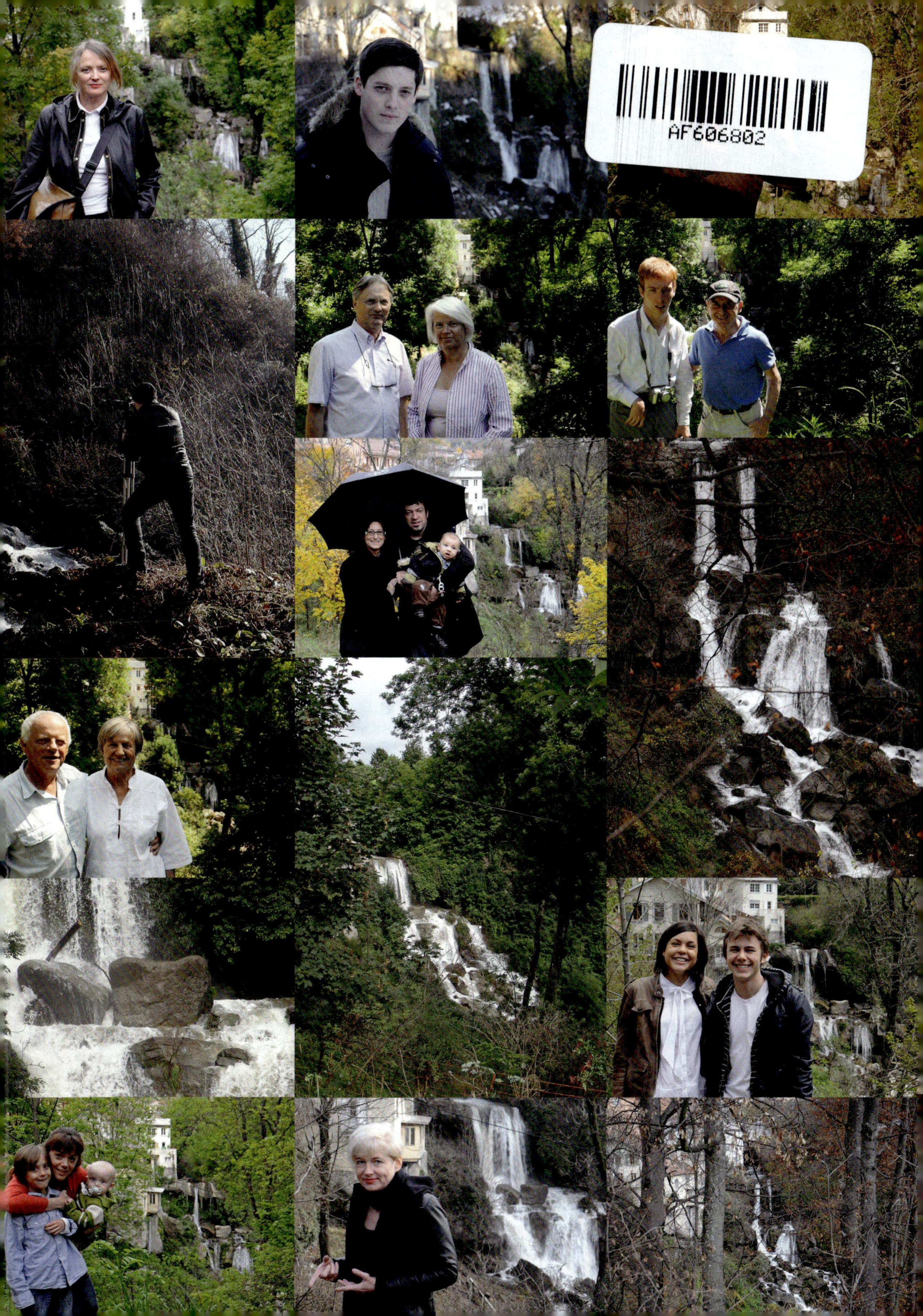

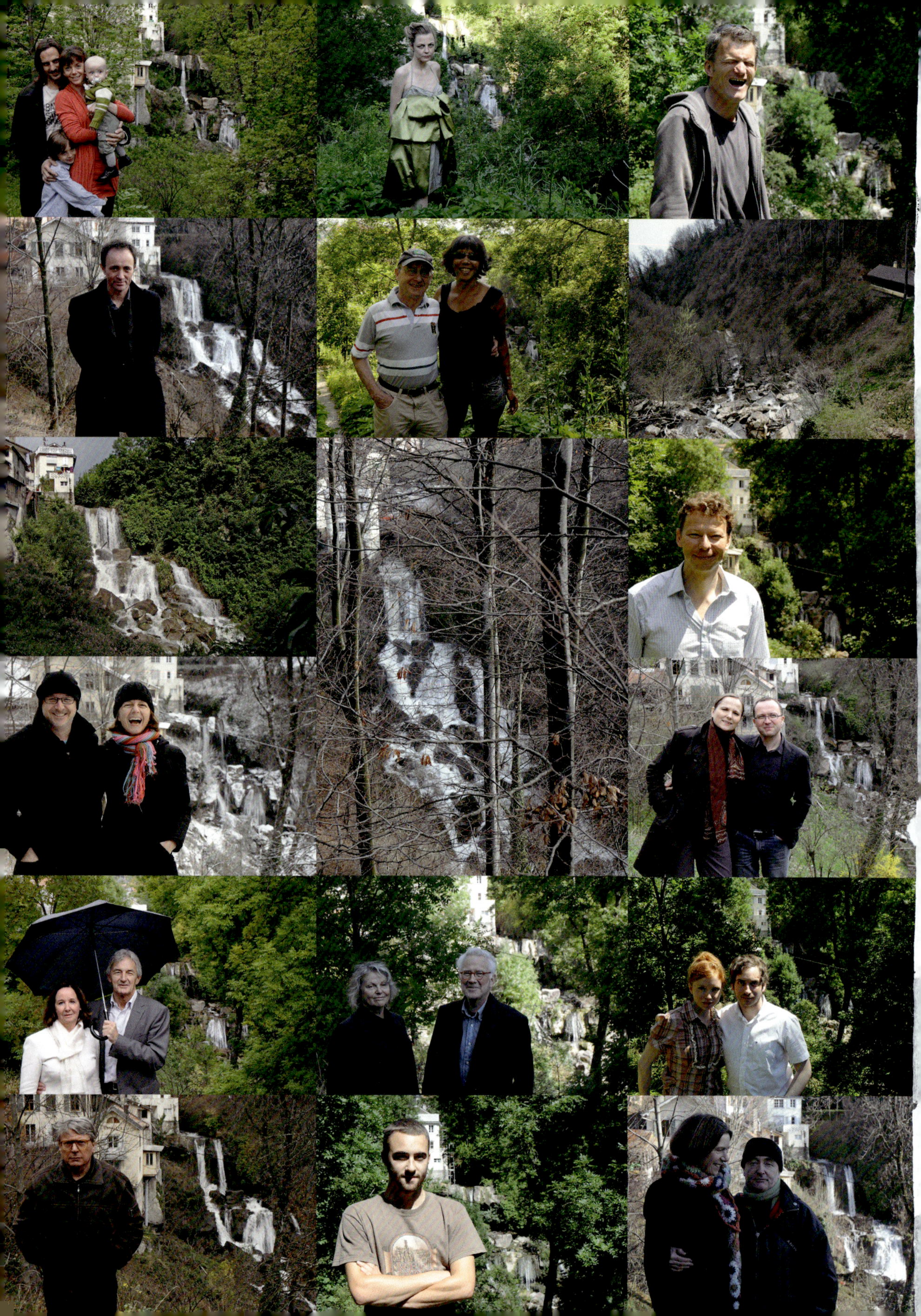

Edited by Stefan Banz

Marcel Duchamp and the Forestay Waterfall

Symposium – Concert – Intervention – Exhibitions

Salle Davel
Kunsthalle Marcel Duchamp
Galerie Davel 14
The Forestay Waterfall

May 6–9, 2010 / May 6–June 13, 2010
Cully and Bellevue-Chexbres, Switzerland

JRP|Ringier

In memory of

Antoinette Bachmann
Juan Antonio Ramírez
Serge Stauffer

http://www.bxb.ch/kunsthalle/
Organized and curated by Stefan Banz and Caroline Bachmann

Supported by
Philadelphia Museum of Art, Swiss Federal Office of Culture Berne, Swiss National Fonds, Loterie Romande, ECAL/University of Art and Design Lausanne, ECAV/Academy of Arts Sierre, Fondation Leenards, Stanley Thomas Johnson Foundation, Canton du Valais, Ville de Lausanne, Etat de Vaud, Ernst and Olga Gubler-Hablützel-Foundation, Migros Kulturprozent, Coop Switzerland, Kunstbetrieb Münchenstein, Likeyou.com, Zap-Design Cully, Kanton Luzern, Stadt Luzern, Commune de Cully, and private sponsors

Figures pages 4 & 5: **Marcel Duchamp, *Étant donnés: 1° la chute d'eau, 2° le gaz d'éclairage*** (Given: 1. The Waterfall, 2. The Illuminating Gas), mixed media assemblage, 242.5 x 177.8 x 124.5 cm, 1946–66. Philadelphia Museum of Art. Gift of the Cassandra Foundation. Page 4: **Exterior view.** Page 5: **Interior view.**

Marcel Duchamp and the Forestay Waterfall
Symposium – Concert – Intervention – Exhibitions

Welcome to the Event
Thursday, May 6, 2010, 18:00
Andreas Glauser plays *Sonitus Errans* after Marcel Duchamp's *Musical Erratum*
Concert at Salle Davel, Cully

Opening
Thursday, May 6, 2010, 19:00
Ecke Bonk
50cc Eau de Forestay, 110gr Auer von Welsbach ... et quelques rayons cosmiques
Inaugural exhibition at Kunsthalle Marcel Duchamp, Cully, designed by Melanie Althaus
May 7–June 13, 2010

Opening
Thursday, May 6, 2010, 20:00
I Want to Grasp Things with the Mind the Way the Penis is Grasped by the Vagina
Exhibition with works and documents by John Zorn, Tadanori Yokoo, Stephan Wittmer, Rolf Winnewisser, Martin Widmer, Wang Xingwei, Aldo Walker, Michael R. Taylor, Harald Szeemann, Denis Savary, Jukka Rusanen, Sam Rosenthal, Peter Roesch, Jason Rhoades, Jean-Michel Rabaté, Céline Peruzzo, Mimosa Pale, Mark Nelson/Sarah Hudson Bayliss, Olivier Mosset, Charles Moser, Gudrun Meier, Line Marquis, Le Forestay, Konrad Klapheck, Felix Kälin, Pierre Keller, Jing Wei, Richard Jackson, Fabrice Hyber, Erwin Hofstetter, Herzog & de Meuron, Erwin Grünenfelder, Goldfrapp, Jean-Claude Forest, Étant donnés, Marcel Duchamp, Anke Doberauer, Jacques Derrida, Basil Debraine, Rosemary Cel, Jacques Caumont, Ecke Bonk/Antoine Monnier, Monica Bonvicini, Rudolf Blättler, Georg Baselitz, Fritz Balthaus, Francis Bacon, Caroline Bachmann/Stefan Banz, and Ai Weiwei, at Galerie Davel 14, Cully, May 7–June 13, 2010

Symposium
Friday, May 7 to Sunday, May 9, 2010, 09:00–17:00 daily
Marcel Duchamp and the Forestay Waterfall. With papers by Hans Maria de Wolf, Philip Ursprung, Michael R. Taylor, Dominique Radrizzani, Molly Nesbit, Mark Nelson, Francis M. Naumann, Stanislaus von Moos, Herbert Molderings, James W. McManus, Bernard Marcadé, Michael Lüthy, Dalia Judovitz, Kornelia Imesch, Antje von Graevenitz, Paul B. Franklin, Luc Debraine, Lars Blunck, Étienne Barilier, and Stefan Banz, at Salle Davel, Cully

Special Opening Reception
Friday, May 7, 2010, 18:00
Roman Signer
Installation: Intervention in the Forestay Waterfall, Bellevue-Chexbres

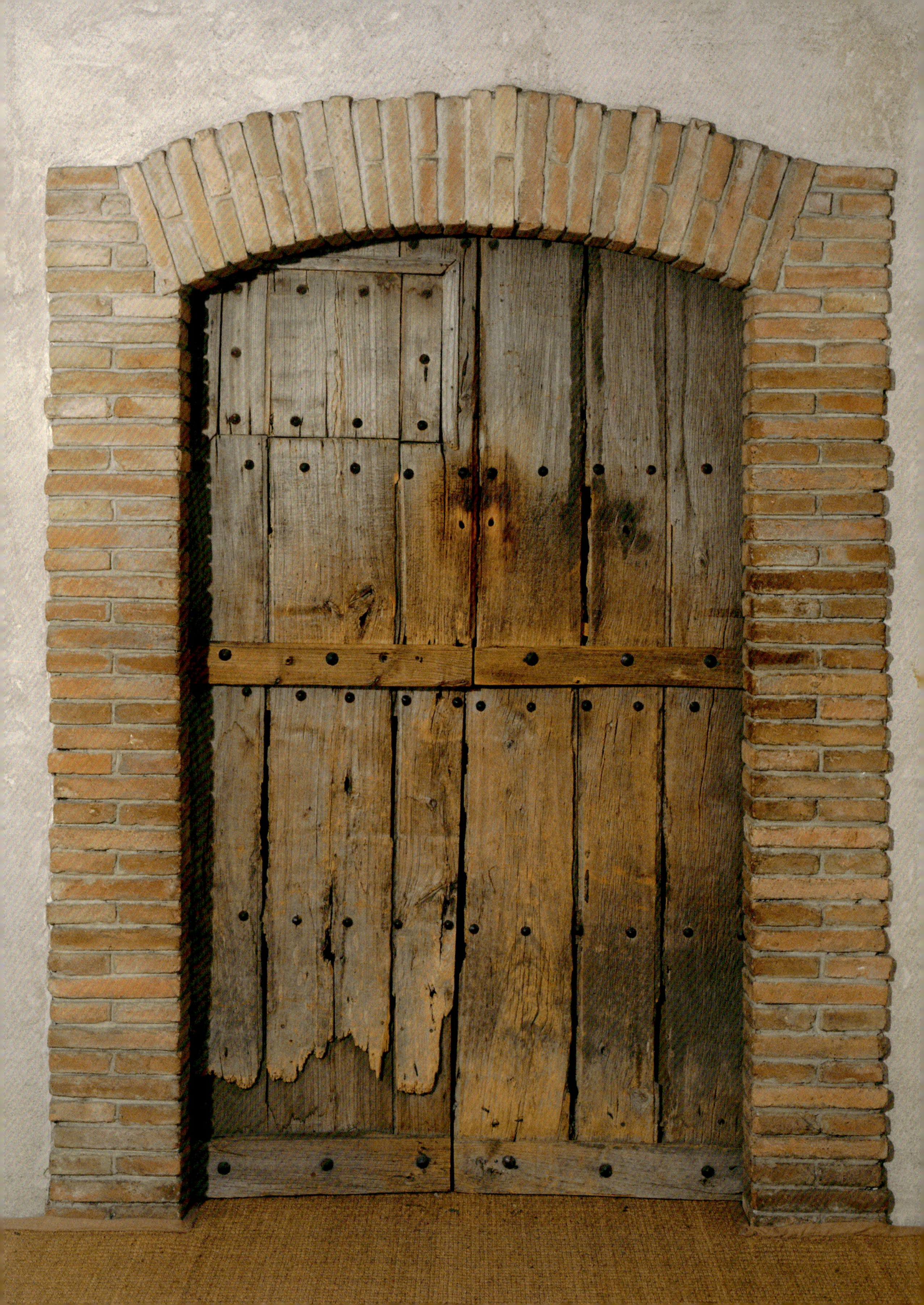

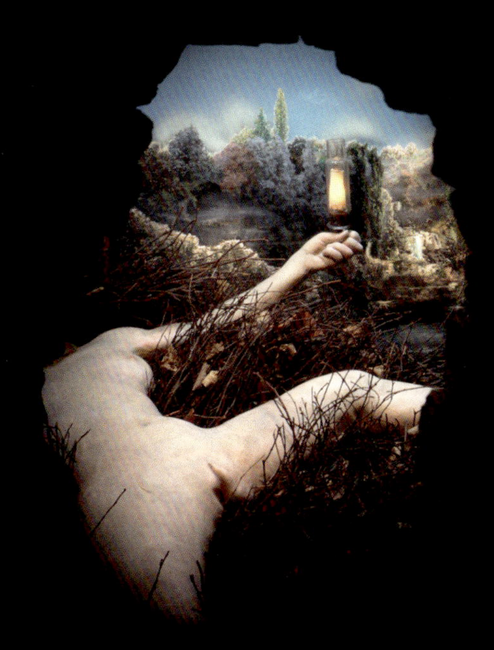

Contents

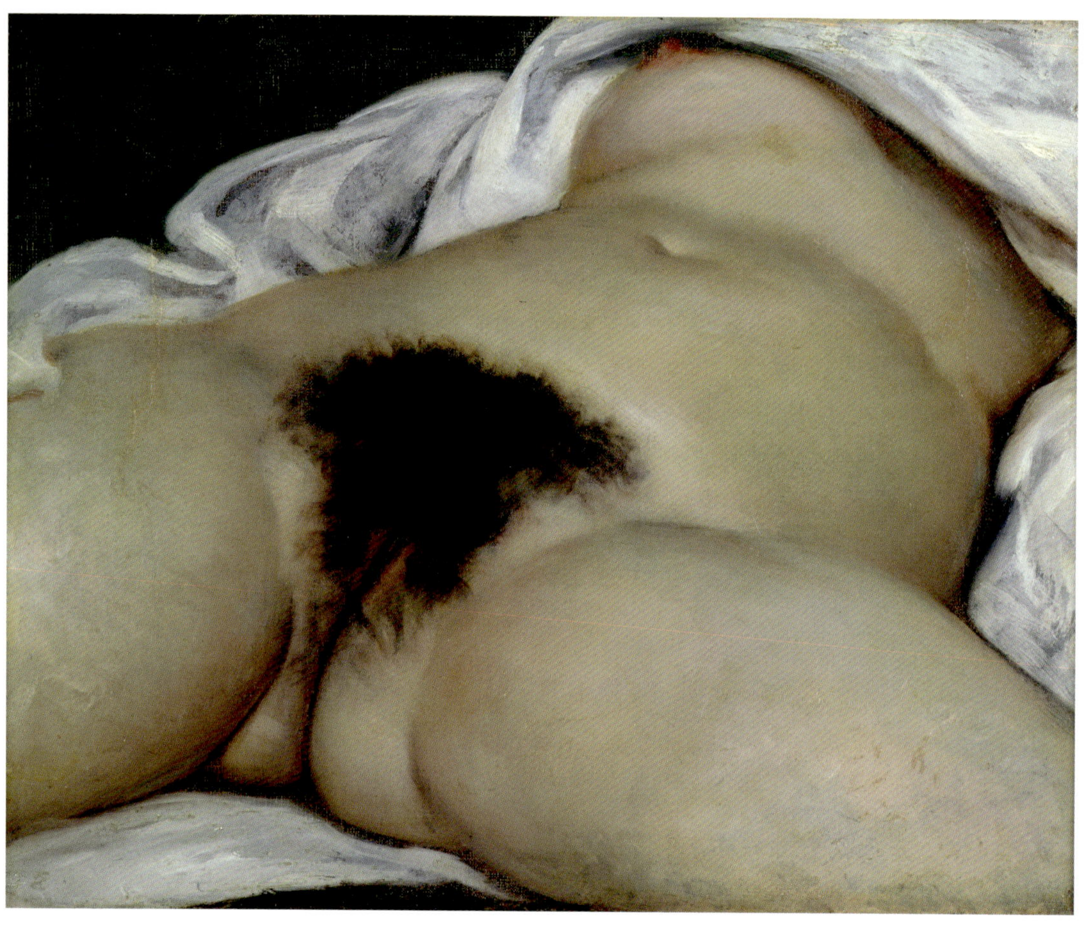

1 Gustave Courbet, *L'Origine du monde* (The Origin of the World), oil on canvas, 46 x 55 cm, 1866. Musée d'Orsay, Paris

Introduction

In April 2006, Caroline Bachmann and I moved to Cully, Caroline's almost fairytale birthplace where she grew up on Lake Geneva, with the intention of deepening our artistic collaboration that had begun in Lucerne. We were working at the time on various aspects of painting, and an important question for us was in what circumstances might a copy—a cover version—become an original. And so, we decided to do an oil painting of Marcel Duchamp's diorama *Étant donnés, 1° la chute d'eau, 2° le gaz d'éclairage* (1946–66, Philadelphia Museum of Art, Gift of the Cassandra Foundation, pp. 4–5).

On the mysterious conception of this installation, in particular the insurmountable paradox of the prostrate, naked, pubic-hairless woman in it—who, on one hand, holds a bec Auer lamp in the air, full of self-confidence and decisiveness; and on the other, presents the viewer with a strangely deformed vagina[1] and gives the impression of having just been the victim of a crime[2]—has always puzzled, touched, and fascinated us. Because this work cannot be shown in exhibitions due to its complex and fragile construction, all interested parties as well as the curious with a yen to see it "live" must make the journey to Philadelphia, almost like a religious pilgrimage. For this reason many perhaps only know it as a reproduction in catalogues and art periodicals, so the manner in which it is perceived and received is seriously distorted. This particularly affects the waterfall, for in reproductions it loses its "physical" presence. Whereas in the diorama it is a central subject (explicitly mentioned along with lighting gas in the title), photography reduces it to a pretty prop in the background of the highly charged scene. Seen "live," it is the only element that moves. Its shimmer as it flows not only gives the composition the suggestion of a gently remote idyll, it also, as it were, breathes a strange, silent, breezy "liveliness" into it.

Thus the photographic reproductions of *Étant donnés* basically show a work that—although everything remains visible—has little in common with the original. Its unique spatial organization is not only reduced to a flat, reproducible surface, but an entirely new form of reality is created. However, what happens if—as in our painting—a new unique work results, a classically hand-made painting?

A new original derived from a source picture is created, as when Gustave Courbet photographed the vagina of a woman lying before him and then painted a picture of it (see *L'Origine du monde,* fig. 1). In other words, an independent work comes into existence.

Though I had taken a keen interest in Duchamp as a student some twenty-five years earlier, this unusual insight moved me to undertake new, scholarly research in order to better understand the mystery of *Étant donnés*. Reading Calvin Tomkins's *Marcel Duchamp: A Biography* at the very beginning of my investigation, I came upon an unusual observation. In the chapter entitled "Maria,"[3] Tomkins mentioned that the artist had photographed the waterfall in *Étant donnés* in Switzerland, somewhere on Lake Geneva, which immediately piqued my curiosity in a different, rather more specific direction. Since the author had never been there, his description lacked sufficient detail for the identification of the exact location. I managed to find it nonetheless—thanks to the two large blocks of stone in the bed of the stream clearly seen in any reproduction, which reveal, with a little bit of imagination, a D and an M ([D]uchamp, [M]arcel, fig. 9, p. 29)—close to Bellevue exactly on the border between the communities of Chexbres and Puidoux, and identified it as the Forestay waterfall.

One can imagine that this discovery caused me a distinctly euphoric feeling, enhanced by a dash of serendipity. For in searching for the Original in the Copy I had come unexpectedly on something that was until then unknown in Duchampian circles, but surely must have been of primordial significance for his final masterpiece. And as my continuing research confirmed, nothing in the way of further research—apart from a short, precise description in "Ephemerides" by Jennifer Gough-Cooper and Jacques Caumont[4]—into the Forestay had taken place.

So my curiosity was aroused, and the question of why the artist had, in 1946, taken this particular waterfall and not another as the point of departure for *Étant donnés* began to seriously preoccupy my thoughts. There must—if we are to take his artistic thinking seriously—have been a quite specific reason; or at least chance, concept, and observation must have coincided so compellingly on that visit to Bellevue that there was for him no avoiding starting his last and most ambitious project with this waterfall. The present publication documents the results of this inquiry, and others.

And yet, one more important question remained unanswered: who actually found the Forestay waterfall for Duchamp research? In Eric Muller's book *Puidoux au coeur de Lavaux,* which appeared in 1982, I came upon the following clue:

> By a whim of chance, the municipality of Puidoux received a request in the spring of 1980 for information sent to every township in Switzerland by a resident of the canton of St. Gallen.
> The letter included a photograph and requested its recipients to identify, if at all possible, the landscape reproduced therein.
> It was child's play for Messrs the Councillors [of Puidoux] to recognize at once in the purveyed image the waterfall of Forestay, located near the watermill of Chexbres, at the border between the two townships.
> A few weeks later, a French couple turned up at the municipal registry with a similar photograph in hand, inquiring about a certain painter named Marcel Duchamp, one of whose works represented the site in question.
> Mr. Jacques Caumont, Director of the Académie de Muséologie Evocatoire of Yvetot (France) and his wife, biographers of the painter and shrewd commentators on his work, knocked on every door suggested to them in the hope of finding someone who might enlighten them, but in vain: no one had heard of the painter Marcel Duchamp, despite his international notoriety in the art world, nor was anyone able to provide any information on the supposed visit or stay of this artist in the region.[5]

I asked the township of Puidoux if they could show me this letter, so that I might eventually trace the sender. Unfortunately no such document could, to our surprise, be found in their archives. Despite this setback, I proceeded on the assumption that this mysterious tale must have something to do with Serge Stauffer, at that time the best-known Duchamp expert in Switzerland. In addition, the idea that Jacques Caumont and Jennifer Gough-Cooper, then living in France, sent letters from St. Gallen to every community in Switzerland seemed to me more than improbable. Some time later, Ecke Bonk told me that in the late eighties Serge Stauffer had given him a photograph of the Forestay waterfall. A few months later, on April 7, 2010, he sent me a scan of that photograph. On the back is the following dedication: "*'Étant donnés …' in Mar. 1981 / 12.4.88 / m. d. only used the upper part looking from the left / for ecke from serge (who took the picture).*" Serge Stauffer had, however, never lived in St. Gallen.

And as often happens in life, wonderfully enriching events followed in quick succession: on the very same day, I received in the mail an old, dusty, black and white art magazine entitled *Umsturz* (p. 384), with nearly the same photograph reproduced on the cover. In the imprint appeared: "Editor and Distributor: Felix Kälin, Felsenstrasse 36, 9000 St. Gallen." The package also included a little note:

- further information on the 1981 (Umsturz) project
- further copies are available from:
Wolfgang Steiger
Aschenwies
9103 Schwellbrunn
wolf.steiger@bluewin.ch

Wolfgang Steiger told me on the phone that he had visited the waterfall with Felix Kälin (fig. 2) and Serge Stauffer in the spring of 1981, after Kälin had found it at the end of a long and exhaustive search. He said that he and Kälin had been big Duchamp fans at the time and became fast friends with Stauffer, who from 1978 until 1981 ran an "art lab" at the Handelshochschule (business school) in St. Gallen and gave long lectures on Duchamp. I tracked down Felix Kälin's phone number and called him up. He told me that Wolfgang Steiger had visited the Philadelphia Museum of Art in 1976 and had returned with the small volume of *Étant donnés: 1° la chute d'eau, 2° le gaz d'éclairage: Reflections on a New Work by Marcel Duchamp* (1969), by Anne d'Harnoncourt and Walter Hopps. Reading the book in April 1979, Kälin explained that the authors' comment that Duchamp had taken the photo of the waterfall in that publication[6] somewhere in Switzerland immediately piqued his interest. He thereupon asked Serge Stauffer whether he knew where this waterfall was located. When Stauffer said he didn't, Kälin, among other things, wrote letters to Anne d'Harnoncourt (p. 372), Arturo Schwarz (p. 373), and Robert Lebel. Nobody knew where the waterfall was.

Inspired by Wim Wenders' much-discussed road movie *Alice in the Cities* (1974), Kälin drew up a four-phase plan to find the waterfall. He called them: (a) the tourist phase, (b) the bureaucratic phase, (c) the occult phase, and (d) the analytical phase. In September 1979, he began the first phase with Katharina Heusser, his girlfriend at the time; in a Volkswagen (*faux vagin*) they took an extensive tour of Switzerland, inquiring about the waterfall with the aid of the reproduction. They especially followed the course of the Doubs River, which

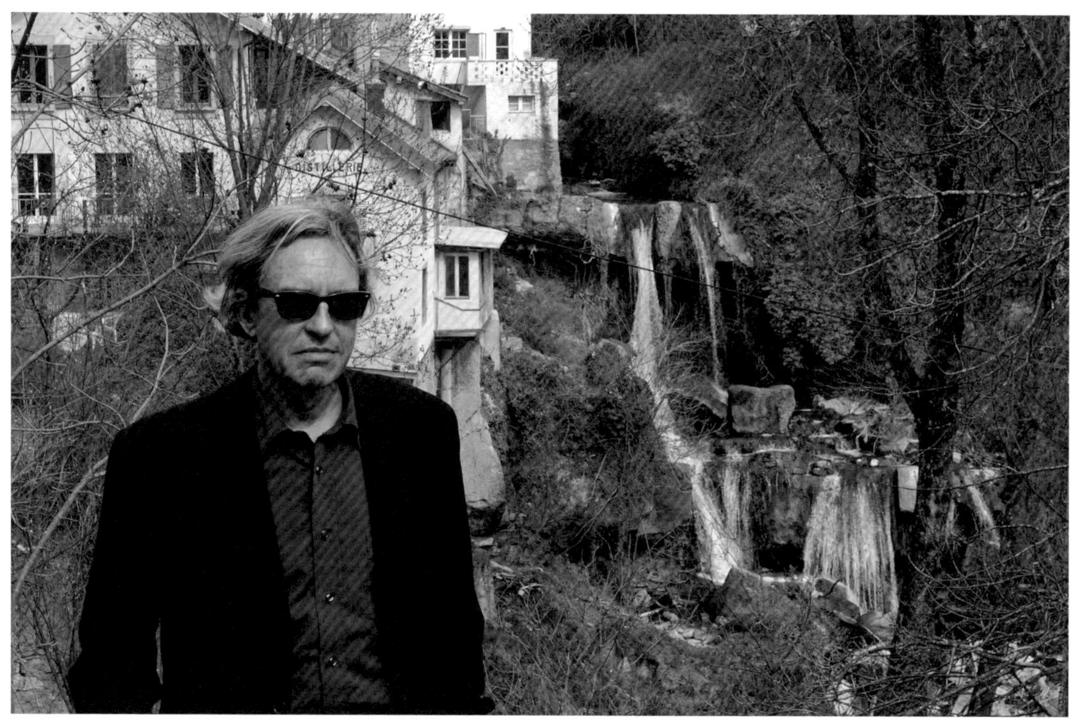

2 Felix Kälin in front of the Forestay waterfall, April 15, 2010. Photograph by Stefan Banz

during a particular stretch in the Jura forms the French-Swiss border, and whose Saut du Doubs is a spectacular tourist attraction. After searching for a time without success, in December 1979 Kälin decided to initiate the second phase and, as reported in Muller's book, write to all the Swiss townships. With the help of his girlfriend he dispatched a total of more than two thousand letters. Between the 5th and the 14th of May 1980, he at last received replies from the communities of Chexbres (p. 376), St-Saphorin (p. 377), Montreux, Ecublens, and Epesses (but not from Puidoux as Eric Muller erroneously wrote in his book!), confirming that the Forestay waterfall near Chexbres was indeed the one in question.

On June 8, 1980, Felix Kälin and Katharina Heusser drove to Chexbres. They took a number of Polaroids and photographs of the waterfall, of the surrounding houses and the fifty-meter shooting range that at that time was still standing though not in use, and of the little bridge over the Forestay river (p. 381). Three days later, on June 11, 1980, Kälin finally wrote a letter to Anne d'Harnoncourt in which he attempted to trade his discovery for six months' employment as a museum guard in the Duchamp section of the Philadelphia Museum of Art (pp. 374–75 & 378–79). To his disappointment, the young curator did not take up his suggestion, and the documents pertaining to this new information were soon gathering dust in his cellar.

Felix Kälin, along with Wolfgang Steiger and Serge Stauffer, then visited the waterfall for a second time in March 1981, at which point Stauffer took numerous photos (p. 383). It was one of these photos that Kälin used for the cover of his by himself called "overground" magazine *Umsturz* (p. 384). Seven years later, as I mentioned earlier, Stauffer gave another photograph to Ecke Bonk.

Oddly, Stauffer's photograph shows a rather unusual perspective of the waterfall, bearing little relation to Duchamp's view of the Forestay. Perhaps the hint of the lake in the background on the lower right of the work was what caused this particular problem; one imagines that he and his friends looked for and hoped to document the exact stretch of water in the stream bed of the Forestay that, in reality, was of Duchamp's own invention.[7] Stauffer could not have known—without seeing behind the scenes in the making of *Étant donnés,* and with no closer knowledge of Duchamp's special process for producing the photographed, collotyped, and colored landscape collage—that this suggestion of a lake did not exist and was an invention of the artist.

It is also astonishing that Stauffer, who was one of the world's most experienced Duchamp experts, did not pursue the question of why, in 1946, the artist chose precisely the Forestay and not another waterfall as a point of departure for his masterpiece.[8] In fact, one has the feeling that Duchamp scholars have not given due significance to this waterfall explicitly mentioned in the title of *Étant donnés* as *1° la chute d'eau.* With this in mind as you peruse the documents and texts in this publication, you will be surprised by just how perfectly the Forestay, its surroundings, and the symbolic narrative inherent in them fit not only with Marcel Duchamp's final work but also with many of his artistic concepts.

Stefan Banz, April 2010

Notes

[1] See Francis Naumann, "Notre Dame des désirs: Gynomorphism in Marcel Duchamp's *Chat Ouvert,"* in this volume.
[2] See Mark Nelson, "Surrealism and the Black Dahlia Murder," in this volume.
[3] Calvin Tomkins, *Marcel Duchamp: A Biography,* New York 1996, pp. 358–73.
[4] Jennifer Gough-Cooper and Jacques Caumont, "Ephemerides on and about Marcel Duchamp and Rrose Sélavy, 1887–1968," in *Marcel Duchamp,* exh. cat. Palazzo Grassi, Milan 1993, unpaginated.
[5] Eric Muller, *Puidoux aux coeur de Lavaux,* Puidoux 1982, p. 219.
"Au gré d'une nouvelle fantaisie du hasard, la Municipalité de Puidoux recevait, au printemps 1980, une demande de renseignement diffusée dans toutes les communes de Suisse par une personne du canton de Saint-Gall.
"Cette circulaire était illustrée d'une photographie, et l'expéditeur demandait à ses correspondants s'il leur était possible d'identifier le paysage reproduit.
"Ce fut un jeu d'enfant pour Messieurs les Conseillers de reconnaître immédiatement dans l'image transmise la chute du Forestay, au Moulin de Chexbres, à la limite des deux communes.
"Quelques semaines plus tard se présentait au greffe municipal un couple français enquêtant, photo semblable en main, sur un certain peintre Marcel Duchamp, dont une œuvre représentait le site en question.
"M. Jacques Caumont, directeur de l'Académie de muséologie évocatoire d'Yvetot (France) et sa compagne, biographes du peintre et commentateurs avisés de son œuvre, heurtèrent à toutes les portes qui leur furent suggérées pour éclairer leur lanterne, mais en vain: personne ne connaissait le peintre Marcel Duchamp, malgré sa notoriété dans le monde international des arts, et ne pouvait donc donner le moindre renseignement sur un éventuel passage ou séjour de cet artiste dans la région."
[6] Anne d'Harnoncourt and Walter Hopps, *Étant donnés: 1° la chute d'eau, 2° le gaz d'éclairage: Reflections on a New Work by Marcel Duchamp,* Philadelphia Museum of Art 1969 (reprinted 1987), p. 60.
[7] See Stefan Banz, "Paysage fautif: Marcel Duchamp and the Forestay Waterfall," in this volume.
[8] Felix Kälin, on the other hand, told me on a visit on April 15, 2010, that a theory of Serge Stauffer's referred particularly to the dead branches Duchamp's female figure was lying on. He was of the view that the whole thing was an ironic metaphor for the self-immolation of a witch. One had to imagine that this woman could not hold this lamp in the air forever, and that fatigue would consequently cause her to herself ignite the branches she was lying on.

Acknowledgments

We are particularly grateful to Michael R. Taylor, the Muriel and Philip Berman Curator at the Philadelphia Museum of Art and a deeply versed expert on *Étant donnés,* for actively following and supporting our project. Without his generous support it would not have been possible to mount the event in its ambitious form. Michael Taylor and his assistant Claire Howard came to Cully for two days in April 2009 in order to visit the waterfall with us. That we were able to make contact with Mr. Taylor was indirectly due to Barbara and Herbert Molderings, Cologne, who visited us for a few days in the summer of 2008, and had themselves photographed standing in front of the waterfall, and Francis M. Naumann, New York, who was kind enough to send our research directly to Michael. To them we offer our heartfelt thanks. Without their curiosity and openness we would most likely not have mustered the courage to turn our plans into reality.

We wish to thank Jacqueline Matisse-Monnier, Antoine Monnier, Paul B. Franklin, and Dona Hochart, Association Marcel Duchamp, Villiers-sous-Grez, for their deep interest, support, and generosity; and Felix Kälin for his enthusiasm in finding—with the aid of Katharina Heusser and the assistance of Wolfgang Steiger and Serge Stauffer—the Forestay waterfall between 1979 and 1981, to the lasting benefit of Duchamp research, and bringing its lost history to light again for our ventures.

We also offer our sincere thanks to Étienne Barilier, Lars Blunck, Luc Debraine, Paul B. Franklin, Antje von Graevenitz, Kornelia Imesch, Dalia Judovitz, Michael Lüthy, Bernard Marcadé, James W. McManus, Herbert Molderings, Stanislaus von Moos, Francis M. Naumann, Mark Nelson, Molly Nesbit, Dominique Radrizzani, Michael R. Taylor, Philip Ursprung, and Hans Maria de Wolf, who delivered papers at the symposium and to all the participating artists for their friendly collaboration. Particular thanks go to Ecke Bonk, Andreas Glauser, Peter Roesch, Roman Signer, and Tadanori Yokoo for their contributions specifically created for the individual events—concert, intervention, and exhibitions—and to Melanie Althaus for her extraordinary architectural design of the newly founded Kunsthalle Marcel Duchamp—an *hommage à la boîte-en-valise*—where we will be organizing regular exhibitions.

We owe a great debt of thanks to Antoinette Bachmann († 2009) and François Bachmann, Cully, for generously supporting our project from the start. And for their generous help we also thank Urs Staub, Director of Art and Design, Federal Office of Culture, Berne; Dominique Radrizzani, Director, Musée Jenisch, Vevey; Pierre Keller, Director, ECAL/ University of Art and Design, Lausanne; Georges Pfründer, former Director of the ECAV/ Academy of Arts, Sierre; Luc Debraine, Cully; and André Demaurex, Aldo Zoppi, Philippe Hierholtz, and Kidiste Degaffe, Chexbres. In addition we offer many thanks to our helpers for their indefatigable commitment to the realization of our event.

Our deep gratitude goes to Céline Peruzzo, Zurich, who helped us solve every little but important detail during the whole project; to Jonathan Fox for his excellent copyediting work; and to Lionel Bovier, Salome Schnetz, and Aurelia Gressel from JRP|Ringier for their support and advice on the editing and publication of this book. Additionally, we offer quite particular thanks to Carmilla Schmidt and Danielle Debraine, Cully; Line Marquis, Céline Burnand, and Adeena Mey, Lausanne; Mark Nelson, New York; Catherine Schelbert, Hertenstein; and to Claire Howard, Holly Frisbee, Jennifer Ginsberg, and Conna Clark, Philadelphia Museum of Art, for their help and cooperation.

Cordial thanks also to Uli Sigg, Mauensee; Dubravka Stojan, and Bruno Weber, Zurich; Ruth and Jürg Nyffeler, Erstfeld; the Musée Jenisch, Vevey; Parkett art magazine, Zurich; and the Association du Vieux Lavaux, Chexbres, who were all prepared to be parted from their works for the duration of the exhibition that accompanied the symposium.

And last but not least we owe a great debt of thanks to our patrons and sponsors: the Philadelphia Museum of Art; the Swiss Federal Office of Culture Bern; Loterie Romande; Swiss National Fonds; ECAL/University of Art and Design Lausanne; ECAV/Academy of Arts Sierre; Fondation Leenards; Stanley Thomas Johnson Foundation; Canton du Valais; Ville de Lausanne; Etat de Vaud; Ernst and Olga Gubler-Hablützel-Foundation; Migros Kulturprozent; Coop Switzerland; Like-you.com; Kanton Luzern; Stadt Luzern; Zap-Design, Cully; Kunstbetrieb, Münchenstein; Commune of Cully; Commune of Chexbres; Commune of Puidoux; Les routiers de Puidoux-Chexbres; Marion and Vincent Gétaz, Valentine Kunz, and Anne-Christine Bovard, Cully, and to the private sponsors who wish to remain anonymous.

Caroline Bachmann and Stefan Banz

Seven Photographs of the Forestay Waterfall by Marcel Duchamp

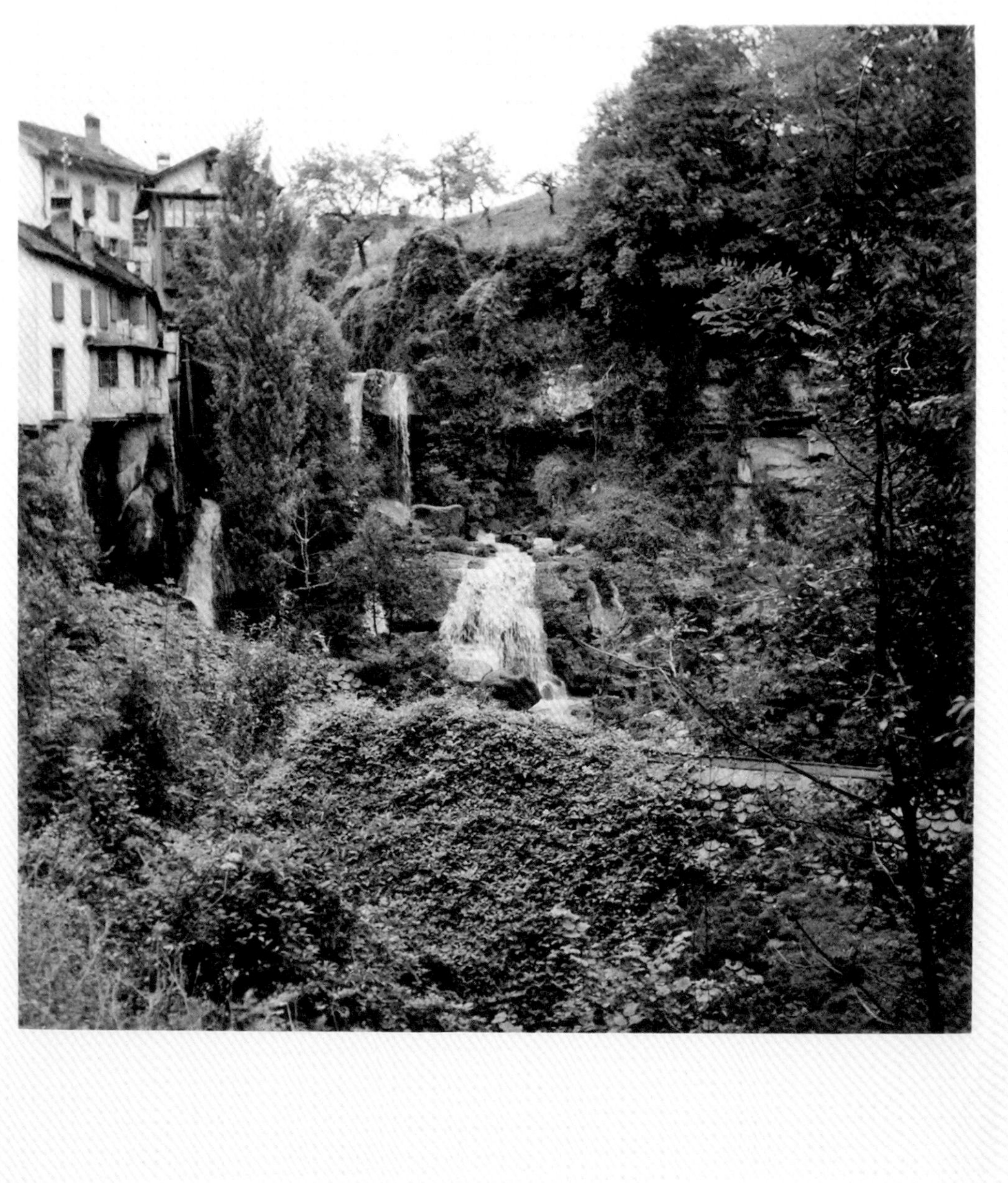

1 Marcel Duchamp, The Forestay Waterfall, Bellevue-Chexbres, Switzerland, copy print after 1946 original, printed c. 1973, silver gelatin print, 18.9 x 19.2 cm. One of seven photographs taken from August 5th to 9th, 1946; this from just above the shooting range after a rainy day, with lots of water. Philadelphia Museum of Art, Archives, Anne d'Harnoncourt Records.

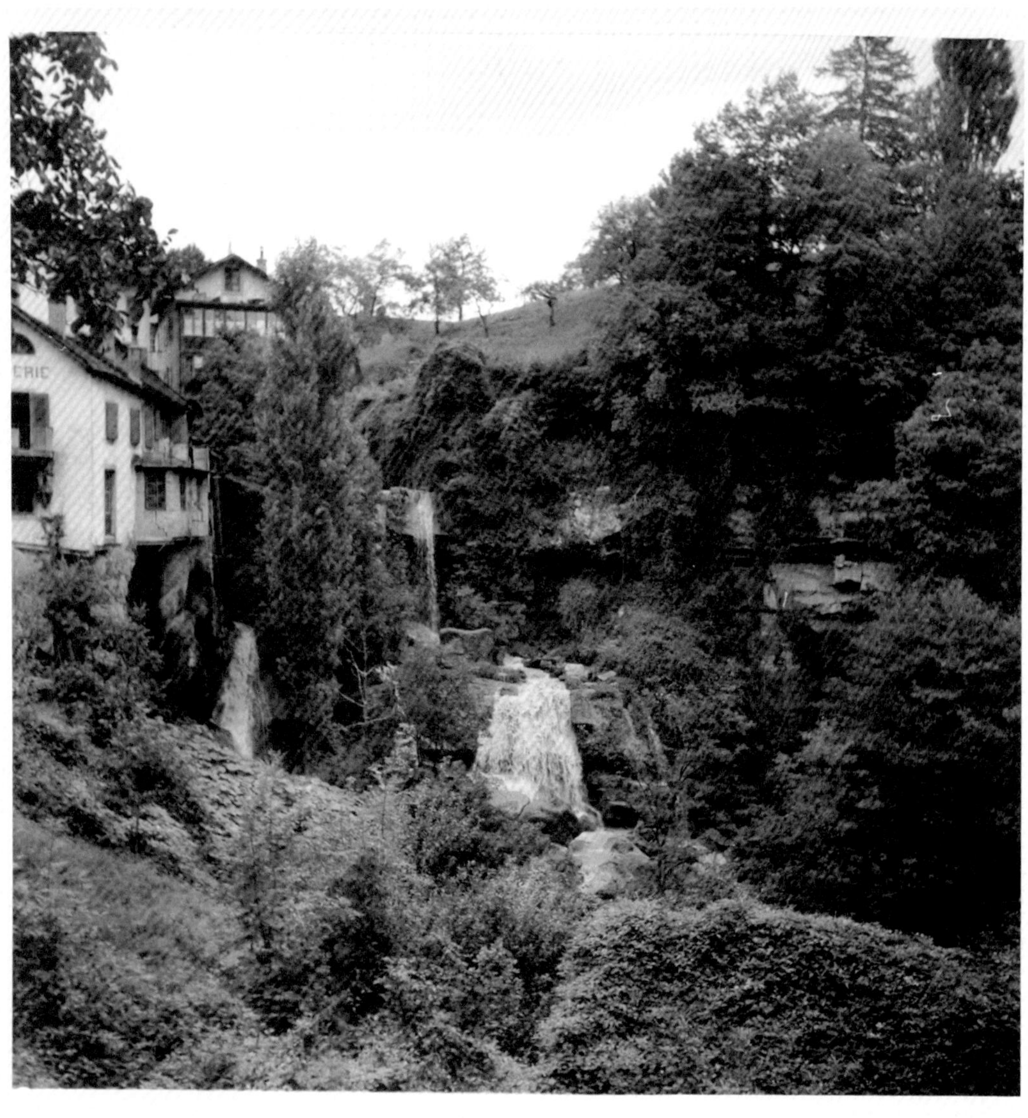

2 Marcel Duchamp, The Forestay Waterfall, Bellevue-Chexbres, Switzerland, silver gelatin print, 18.1 x 17.1 cm. One of seven photographs taken from August 5th to 9th, 1946; this from above the shooting range after a rainy day, with lots of water. Philadelphia Museum of Art, Archives, Anne d'Harnoncourt Records.

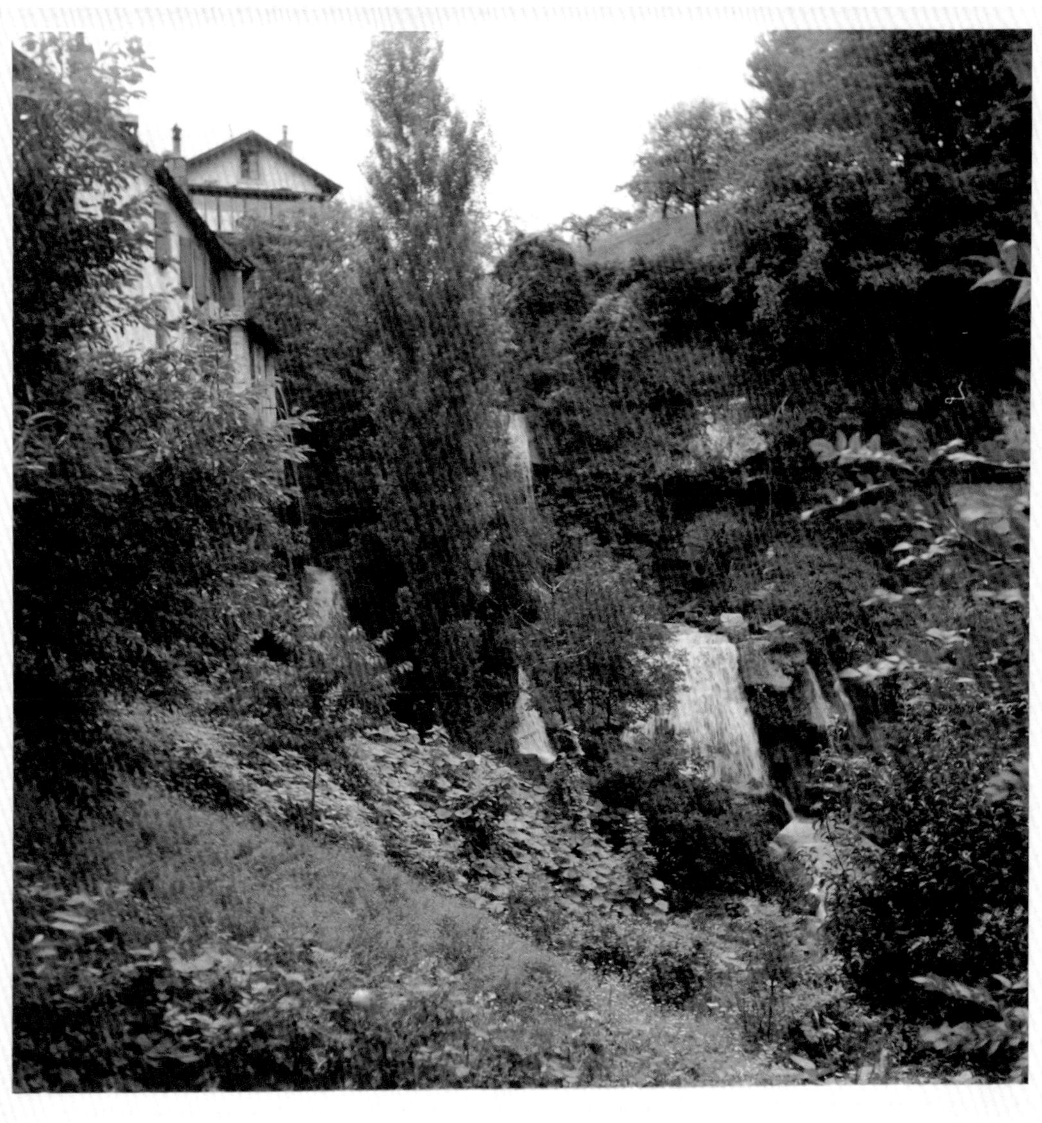

3 Marcel Duchamp, The Forestay Waterfall, Bellevue-Chexbres, Switzerland, silver gelatin print, 18.1 x 17.1 cm. One of seven photographs taken from August 5th to 9th, 1946; this from the shooting range after a rainy day, with lots of water. Philadelphia Museum of Art, Archives, Anne d'Harnoncourt Records.

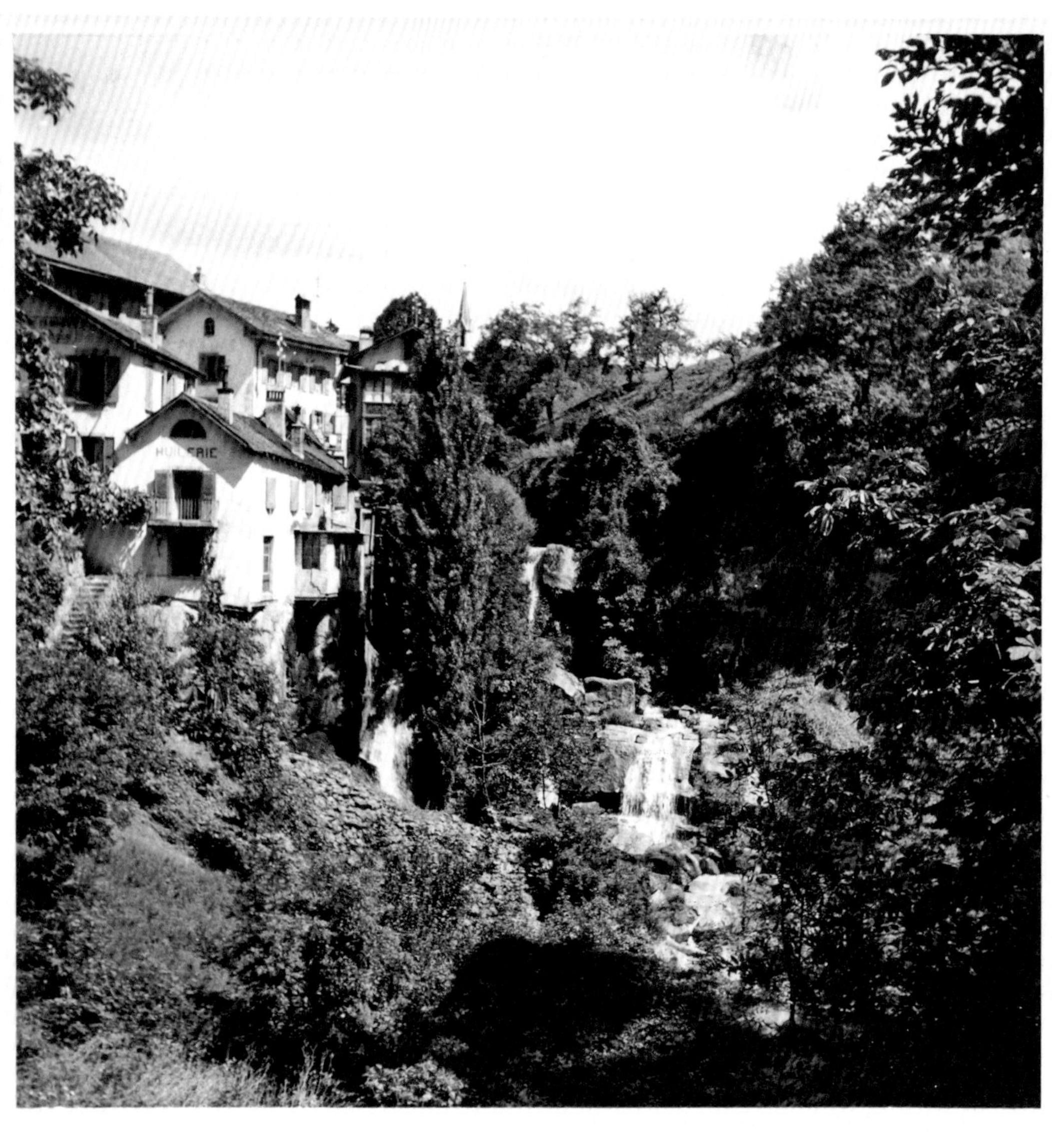

4 **Marcel Duchamp, The Forestay Waterfall**, Bellevue/Chexbres, Switzerland, silver gelatin print, 18.1 x 17.1 cm. One of seven photographs taken from August 5th to 9th, 1946; this from above the shooting range on a sunny day, with "less" water. Philadelphia Museum of Art, Archives, Anne d'Harnoncourt Records.

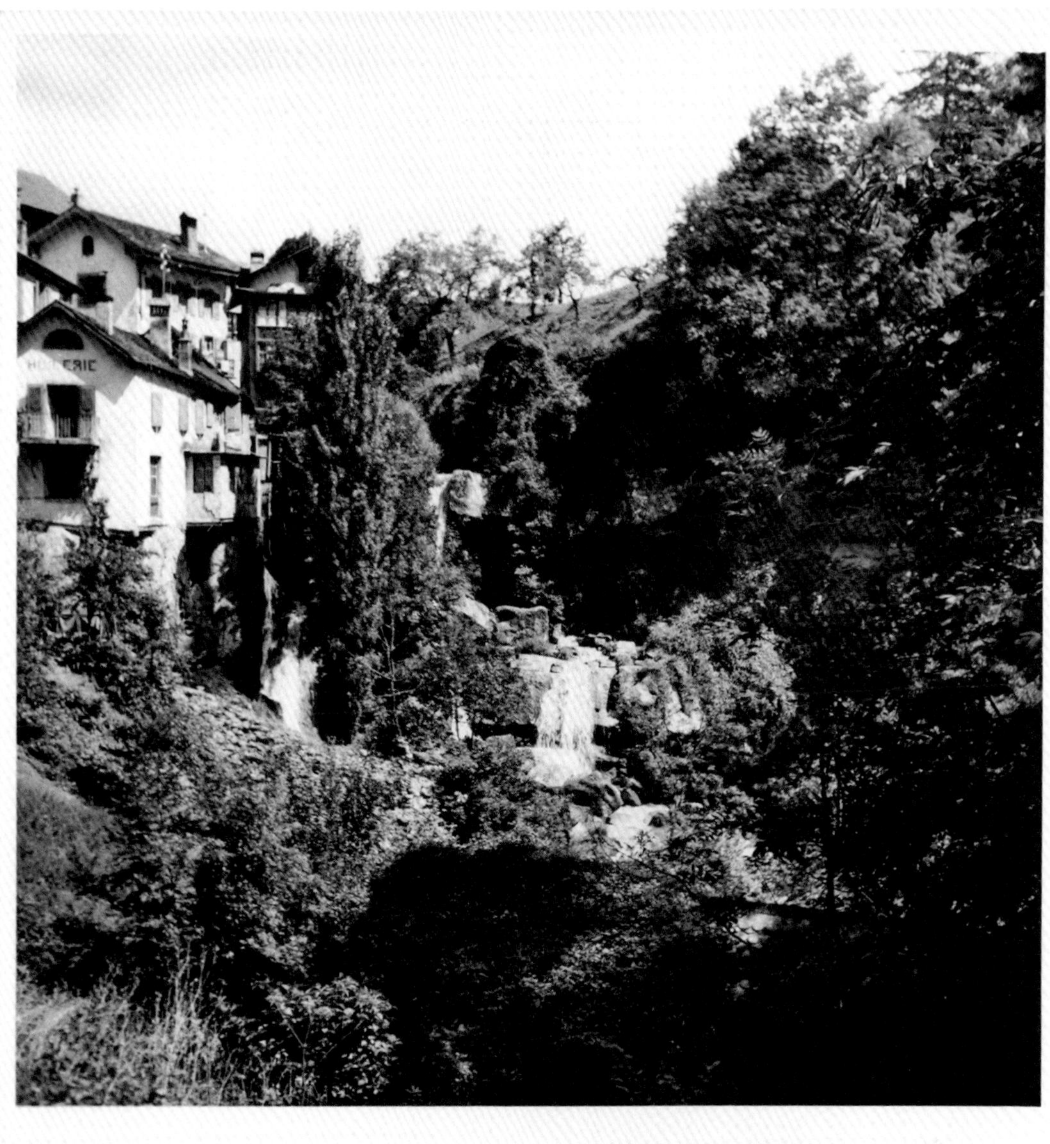

5 Marcel Duchamp, The Forestay Waterfall, Bellevue/Chexbres, Switzerland, silver gelatin print, 18.1 x 17.1 cm. One of seven photographs taken from August 5th to 9th, 1946; this from just above the shooting range on a sunny day, with "less" water. Philadelphia Museum of Art, Archives, Anne d'Harnoncourt Records.

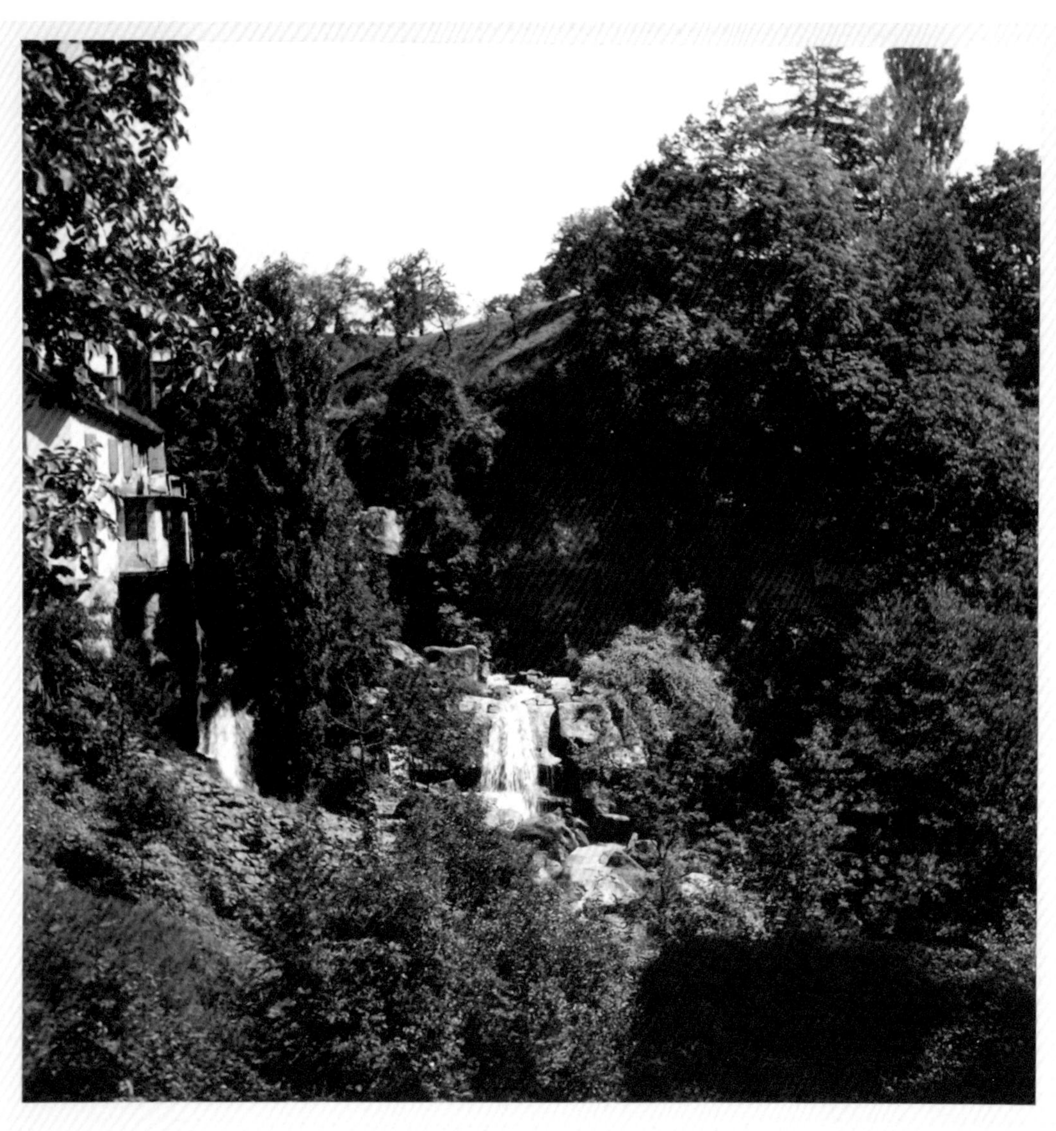

6 Marcel Duchamp, The Forestay Waterfall, Bellevue/Chexbres, Switzerland, silver gelatin print, 18.1 x 17.1 cm. One of seven photographs taken from August 5th to 9th, 1946; this from just above the shooting range on a sunny day, with "less" water. Philadelphia Museum of Art, Archives, Anne d'Harnoncourt Records.

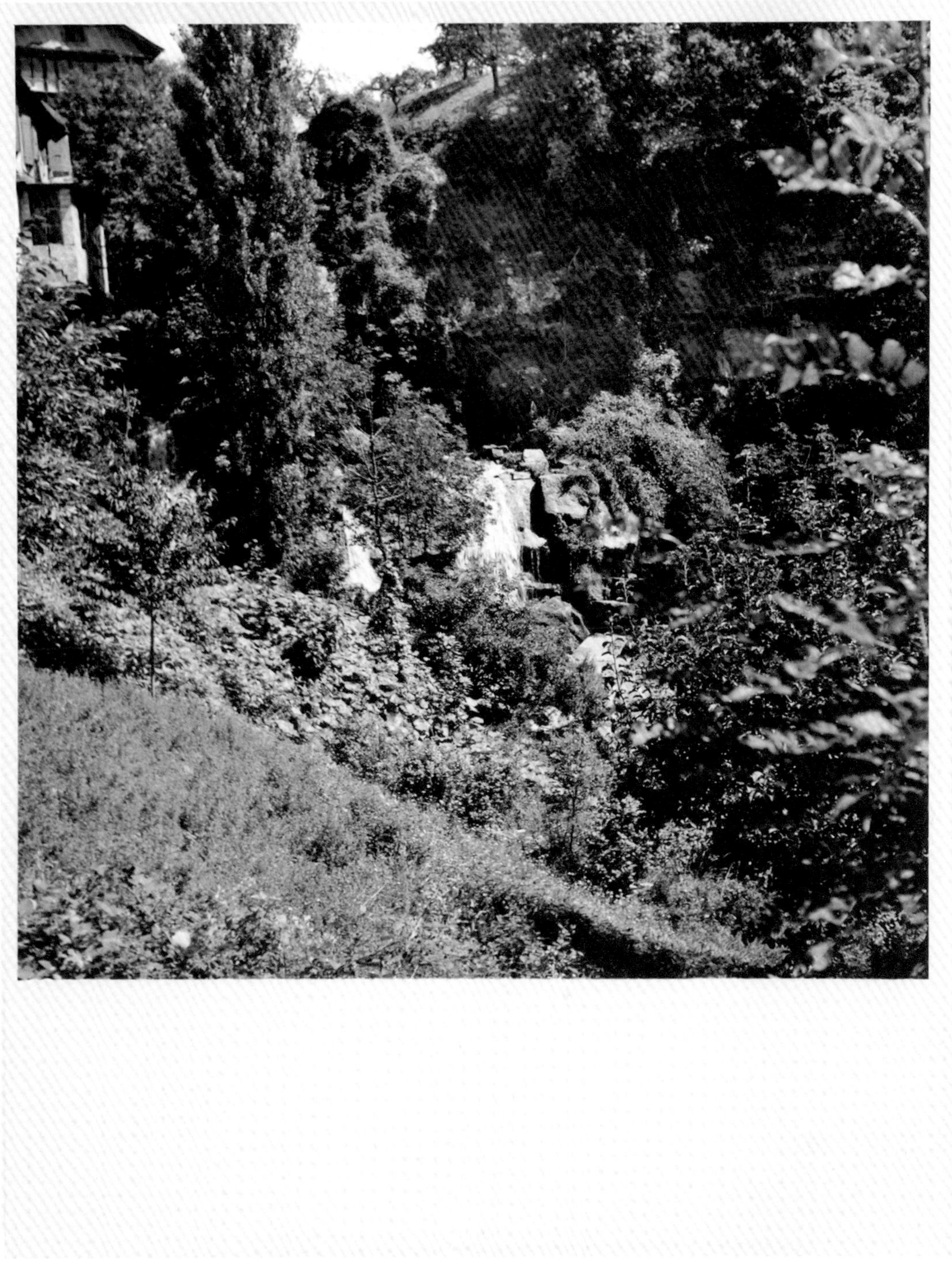

7 Marcel Duchamp, The Forestay Waterfall, Bellevue/Chexbres, Switzerland, silver gelatin print, 18.1 x 17.1 cm. One of seven photographs taken from August 5th to 9th, 1946; this from the shooting range on a sunny day, with "less" water. Philadelphia Museum of Art, Archives, Anne d'Harnoncourt Records.

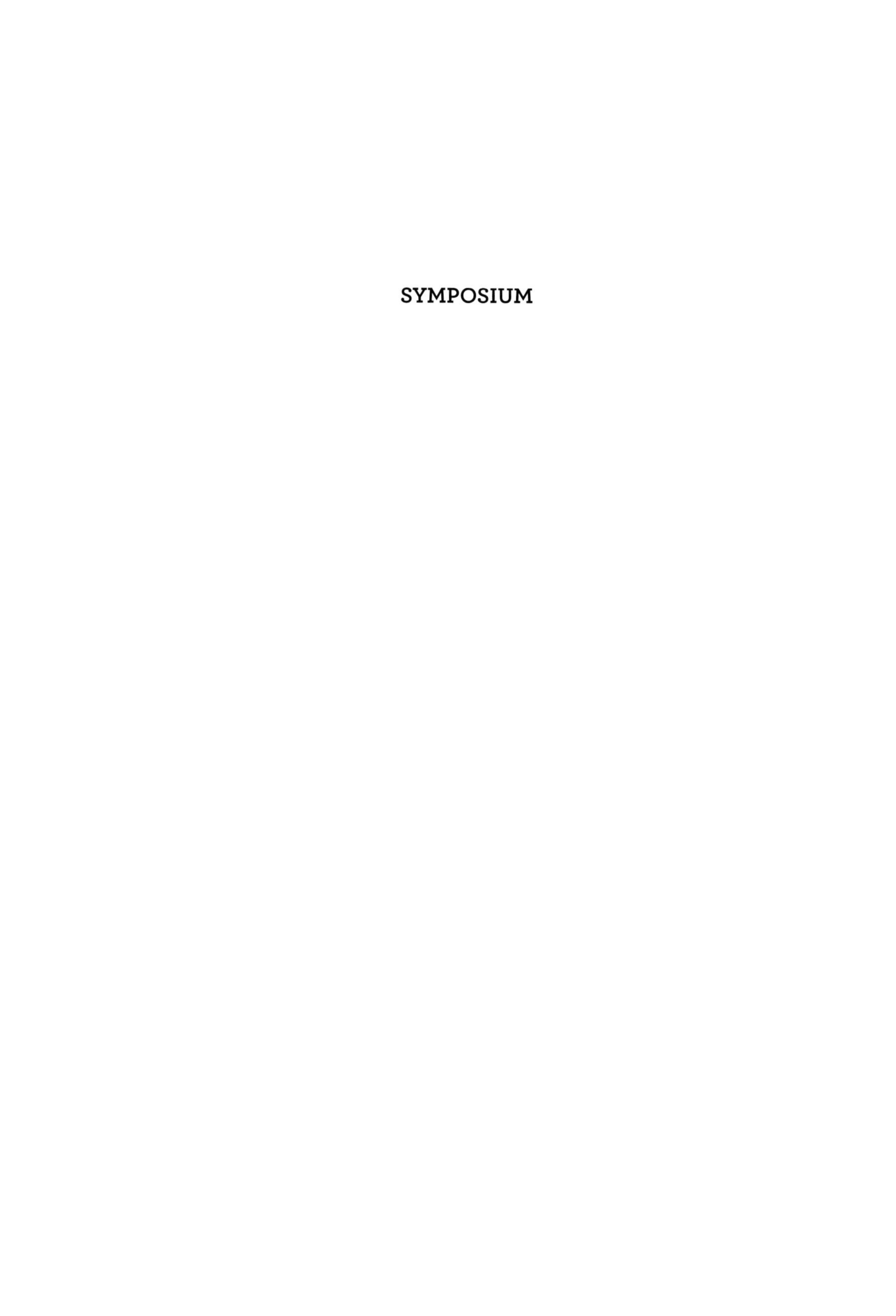

SYMPOSIUM

THE WATERFALL – THE LANDSCAPE

Stefan Banz

Paysage fautif
Marcel Duchamp and the Forestay Waterfall

One day during the preparations for the exhibition in Pasadena 1963 Walter Hopps asked Marcel Duchamp: "Assuming there is a secret work you have been working on for quite some time. Do you think this would be the time and place to show it?"
Duchamp answered: "If there were such a thing, the answer would be: No."[1]

The Waterfall and Its Environs

In 1946 Marcel Duchamp spent five weeks in Switzerland with his longtime lover, Mary Reynolds, including approximately twenty days on Lake Geneva.[2] There, in the exact center of the Lavaux Vineyards, since designated a world heritage site by UNESCO, they first took up residence from the 5th to the 9th of August at Hotel Bellevue (now Hotel Le Baron Tavernier) in Bellevue near Chexbres (figs. 1 & 2). The hotel, situated on the so-called Corniche route, offers one of the most striking panoramas in the region with a magnificent view of the lake flanked in the background by the mountains of Vaud, Valais and Savoy and the chain of the Jura Hills. On clear days, one can see almost the entire lake from Villeneuve to Geneva, an expanse so vast that it looks like an immense gulf (figs. 3 & 4).

The Corniche runs through the extraordinary vineyards of the region, linking Chexbres with the villages of Epesses, Riex and Cully. Hotel Bellevue is also about 100 meters away from a spot popularly known as the *Balcon du monde* (balcony of the world), which affords a spectacular view of the lake and dramatically conveys the steepness of the local vineyards that produce the Dézaley wine. The steep terrain also explains the presence of a waterfall between Bellevue and Chexbres. The topography is rocky as well, with the water gushing out from under the buildings in Chexbres, as if it were coming out of the buildings themselves, and then cascading down towards the lake, marking the border between Chexbres and the township of Puidoux, to which Bellevue belongs (figs. 5 & 6). Le Forestay, as the waterfall is called, slows down for a moment before gathering momentum again and crashing onto the back of the Dézaley hills below. From there it is contained in a brook for a few hundred meters until finally gushing out over another cliff near the historical village of Rivaz and plunging into Lake Geneva, where the shoreline is at its deepest, most perilous and most exciting.

Hotel Bellevue is situated not far from the first step of the Forestay waterfall. Duchamp must have heard the thundering waterfall sunder the idyllic silence every night, the sound of its cascading waters resembling the incessant din of ocean surf. The waterfall is also slightly hidden away, in reverse proportion to the imposing panorama of the lake. It cuts

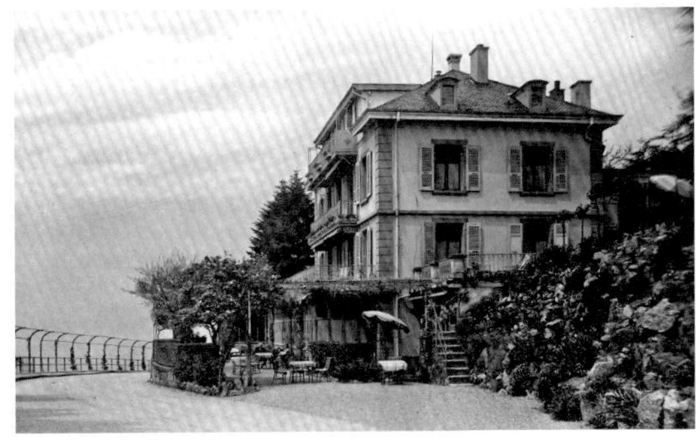

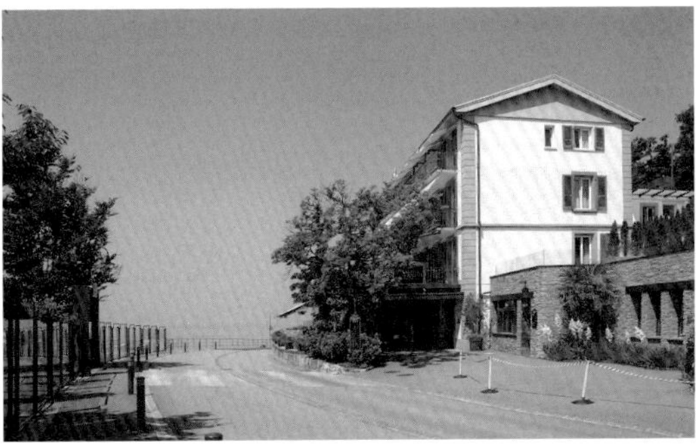

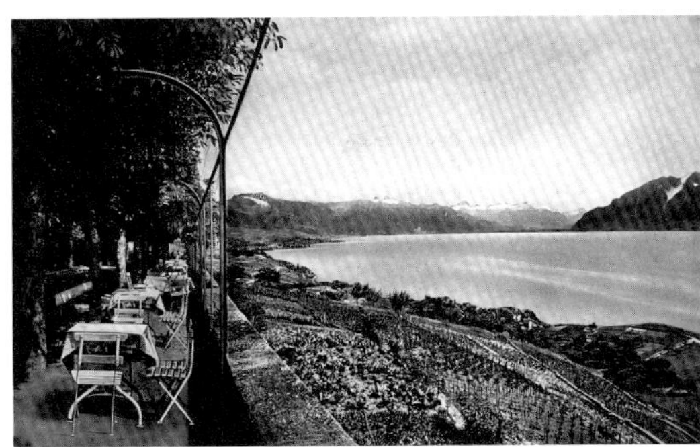

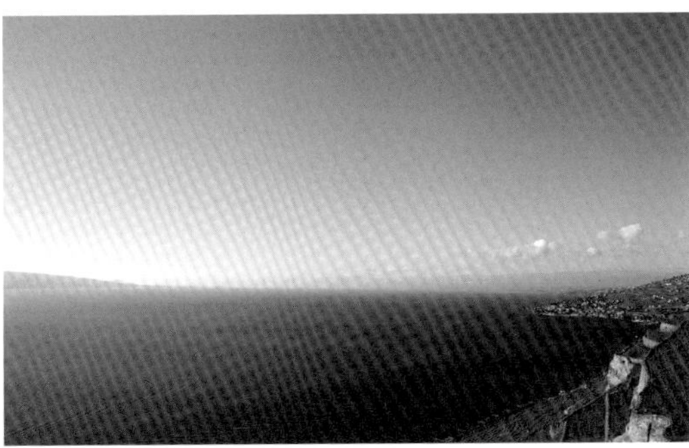

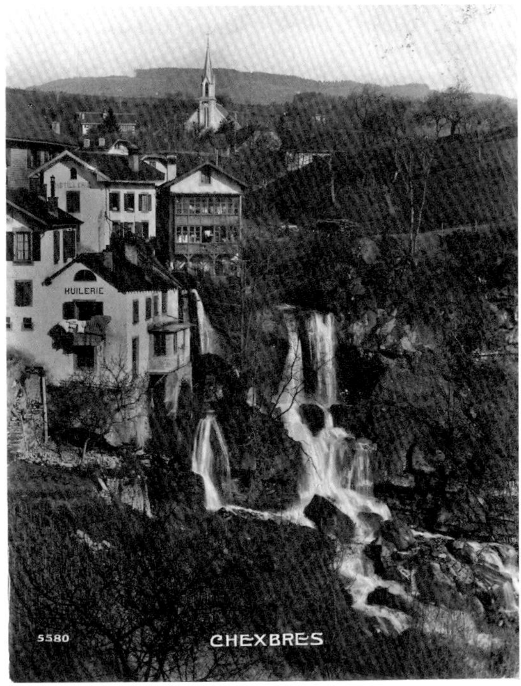

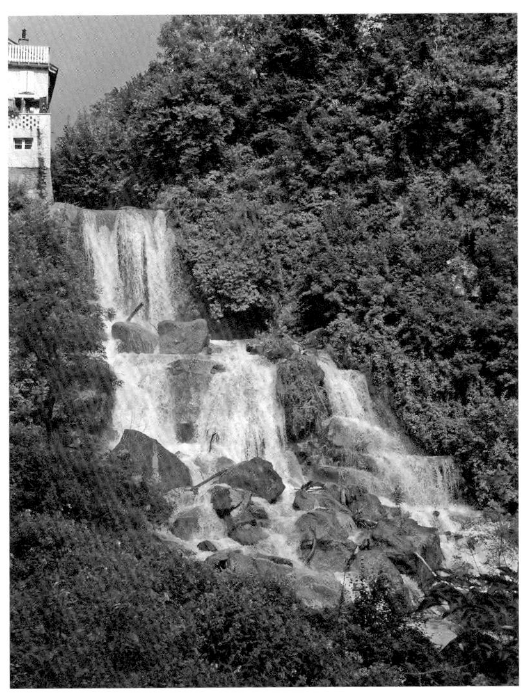

1 **Hotel Bellevue** in Bellevue near Chexbres, Switzerland, postcard, 9.1 x 14.1 cm, c. 1945. Collection Association du Vieux Lavaux, Chexbres. 2 **Hotel Bellevue** (now Hotel Le Baron Tavernier), July 1, 2008. 3 **View from Hotel Bellevue** across the Dézaley on Lake Geneva in the direction of Villeneuve with the Vaud, Valais and Savoy mountains, postcard, 9.2 x 14.2, 1935. Collection Association du Vieux Lavaux, Chexbres. 4 **View from Hotel Bellevue,** across the Dézaley on Lake Geneva in the direction of Geneva, December 7, 2008. 5 **The Forestay Waterfall** near Chexbres, postcard, 14 x 8.9 cm, c. 1924. Collection Association du Vieux Lavaux, Chexbres. 6 **The Forestay Waterfall,** August 12, 2007. Photographs (2, 4, 6) by Stefan Banz.

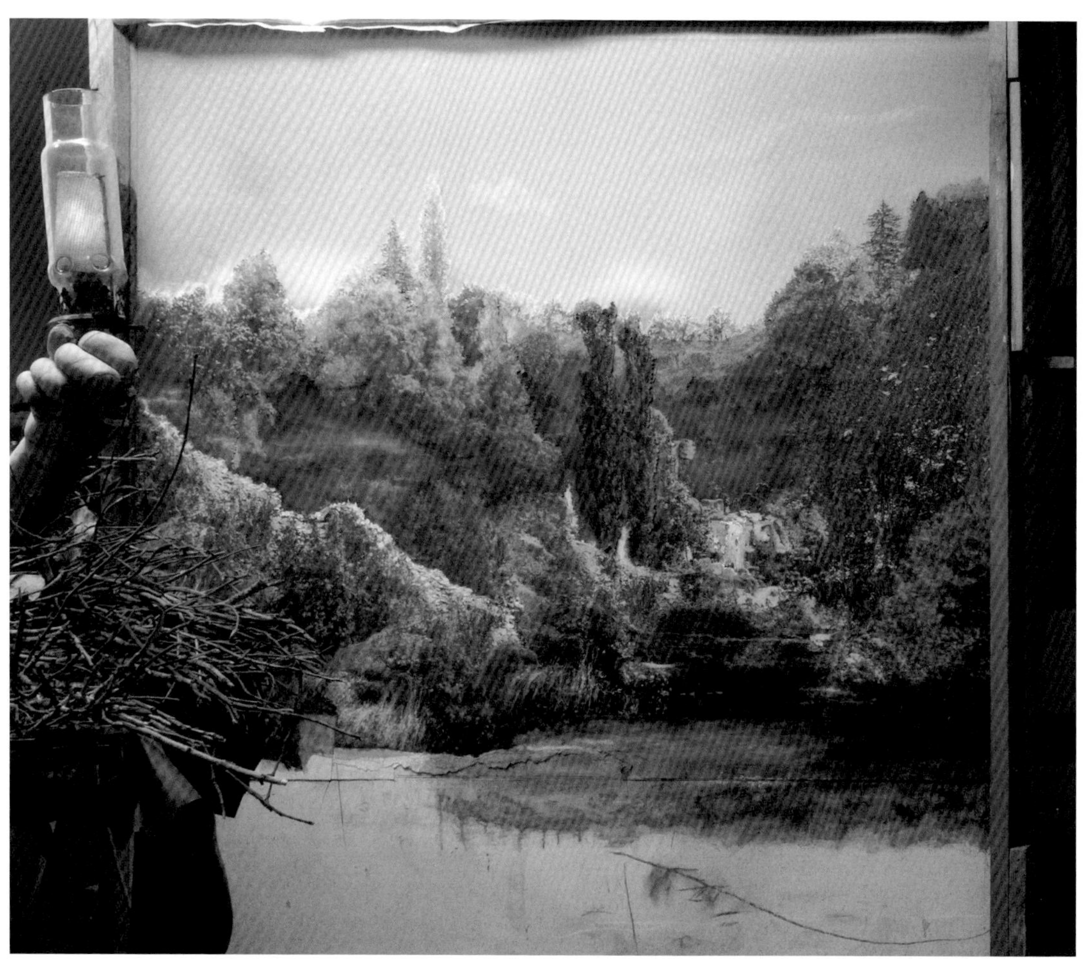

7 Marcel Duchamp, Le Forestay, in *Étant donnés: 1° La chute d'eau 2° Le gaz d'éclairage* (Given: 1. The Waterfall, 2. The Illuminating Gas), colored print (collotype) of a photo-collage, 63 x 89 cm, 1959. Philadelphia Museum of Art. Photograph by Philadelphia Museum of Art.

through the landscape of the vineyards, carving a vulva-like path between the splayed flanks of the terrain, where it is concealed among trees and bushes (fig. 8). Duchamp took seven pictures of it from different vantage points (pp. 16–23), one of which he selected for the landscape in his last great masterpiece, the diorama *Étant donnés: 1° la chute d'eau, 2° le gaz d'éclairage* (pp. 4–5). He had the photograph enlarged several times, cut out or duplicated parts of it, and reassembled them on a piece of plywood. He then had the resulting photographic collage of Le Forestay copied as a black-and-white collotype at Salvador Dali's home in Port Lligat near Cadaqués. He completely colored the collotype, outlining or enhancing various details in black and colored pencil, and adding elements such as the lake underneath the falls (fig. 7).[3] Duchamp used this extraordinarily complicated and elaborate procedure to create the background that pictures the waterfall mentioned in the title of his work *(1° la chute d'eau)*. Le Forestay and its environs are therefore both the conceptual point of departure as well as the visual objective of a provocative and disturbing

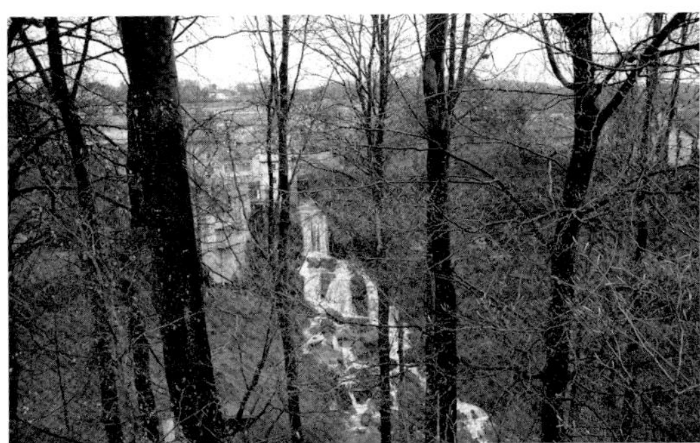

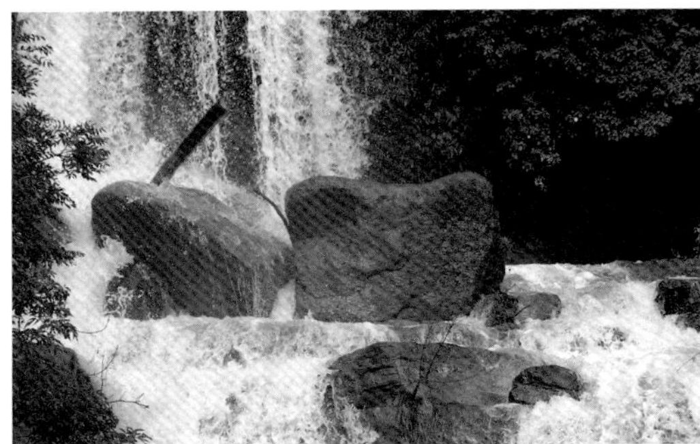

8 The Forestay Waterfall secluded by trees, April 20, 2008. **9 The Forestay Waterfall,** rock boulders on the cataract (with a little imagination they incorporate the letters *D* and *M* for Duchamp Marcel), August 12, 2007. Photographs by Stefan Banz.

three-dimensional artistic legacy on which he worked in secret for twenty years from 1946 to 1966. The work was not revealed to the public until 1969, a year after his death, by the Philadelphia Museum of Art, where it has since been permanently installed.

About 100 meters away from Hotel Bellevue on the route de la Corniche, there are steps and a narrow path descending to where the falls still look almost exactly as they do in Duchamp's photographs, although the environs of Bellevue and Chexbres have obviously changed over the past sixty years. Next to the small stand of trees and the houses around the waterfall, we can still see two large boulders in the middle of the riverbed below the first plateau: one figures prominently in Duchamp's photographs while the other is covered by shrubbery (fig. 9).

Remarkably, Duchamp may well be the first and only major artist in history to visit the spectacular region of Lavaux without taking inspiration from the lake and the mountains, as did such famous colleagues as Gustave Courbet, Ferdinand Hodler (fig. 10), Félix Vallotton, and William Turner. He did, however, append a note to a letter Mary Reynolds wrote the day after they arrived in Chexbres to the then French ambassador in Switzerland and his wife, Henri and Hélène Hoppenot: "The weather has a hand in it and every hour the lake changes her gown."[4] Nonetheless, Duchamp chose to focus his attention on the opposite direction: he gazed deep into the vineyards and captured the effluence gushing from within the earth's crevasse—this orgasm that feeds into the imposing lake and contributes to making it an overwhelming visual experience.

The artist's photolithographic, hand-colored landscape collage has also synesthetically rendered the sounds that we hear long before we catch a glimpse of the cataract through the trees and bushes. Duchamp captures what is concealed and converts it, in *Étant donnés,* into moving time, into all that irresistibly drives and fulfills the course of life. It is the center and, at the same time, the unobtrusive duplication of the naked woman with no pubic hair, holding a gas lamp in her hand. We are initially struck by the hairless vagina, oddly misshapen like an open incision. But as soon as we move beyond this penetrating visual intrusion, an almost inconspicuous bulge is seen in the artificially modified landscape, which is powered by a special, invisible mechanism behind the picture.[5] We assume the water is squirting out of a vagina in the midst of boulders and pine trees without perceiving the signs of civilization that are in reality present around Le Forestay. It is most extraordinary that Duchamp glued the waterfall to the print as a semipermeable, translucent relief of hardened glue, as a kind of *infra-mince* art object (to which we shall return), where it covers the hole behind which he installed the tin can with its rotating light mechanism (fig. 11). The movement of the light behind the waterfall itself makes it look like a vagina, out of which an almost sperm-like liquid is flowing. But it also seems to embody the transition between ice and water, that very moment, prior to freezing, when the water has begun to change into countless needles that still crack and give way to the pressure of a hand plunging into it.

On peering through the two small holes in the wooden door and seeing something visibly flowing out of the static photograph, one seems to hear the water burbling, to smell the liquid pouring out of the cleft—in 1946 the people of Chexbres still disposed of their garbage and feces in the waterfall, a circumstance that Duchamp recorded in a sketch describing the colors of Le Forestay (fig. 12)—and to see the bright and colorful bushes, alive and moving. Finally, we look at the bundled layers of dead twigs and hear the breathing of the woman lying in them, her leg bent at the knee exposing her sex while the gas lamp that she holds aloft, in an energetic yet oddly disturbing fashion, bathes the waterfall in light.

The Waterfall and Duchamp Research

It is astonishing that no one to date has investigated why Marcel Duchamp chose to photograph this particular waterfall. Presumably few researchers have visited this unique location on Lake Geneva.[6] Nor will they have realized that Duchamp had a direct view from Hotel Bellevue of the little town of La Tour-de-Peilz (fig. 13), where Gustave Courbet, the painter of *The Origin of the World* (fig. 14), spent the last years of his life. In Duchamp's words:

To imagine the future, we should perhaps start from the more or less recent past, which seems to us today to begin with the realism of Courbet and Manet. It does not seem in fact that realism is at the heart of the liberation of the artist as an individual, whose work, to which the viewer or collector adapts himself, sometimes with difficulty, has an independent existence.[7]

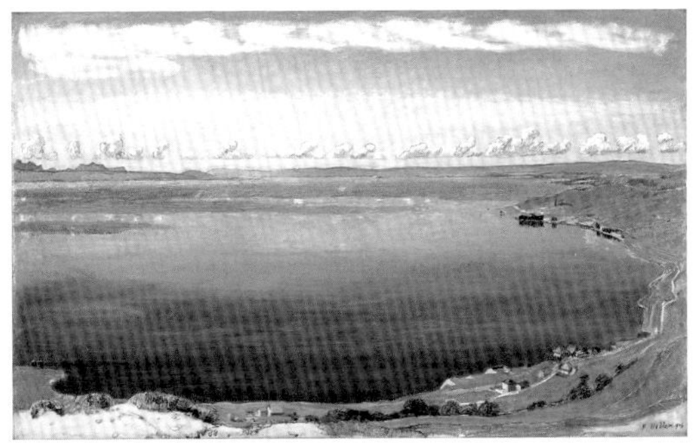

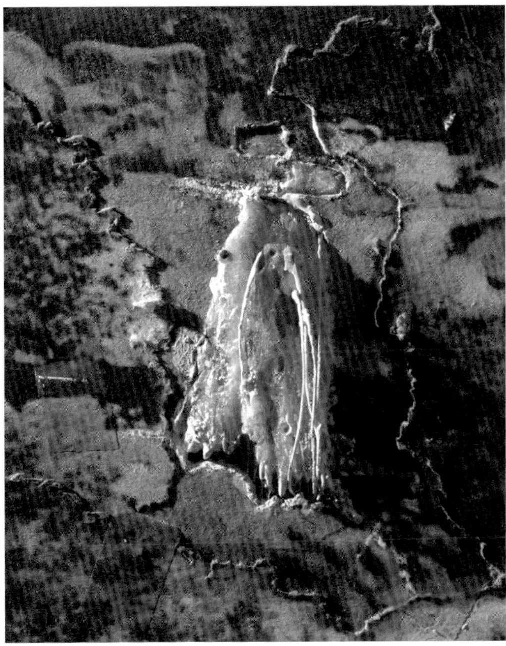

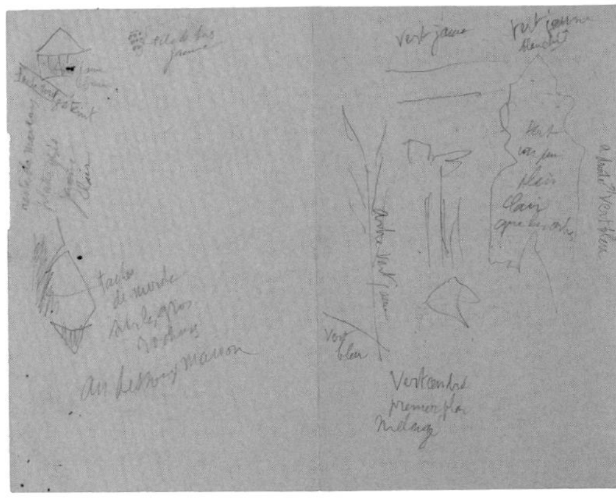

10 Ferdinand Hodler, *Bleu Léman,* oil on canvas, 70.2 x 108 cm, 1904. Musée cantonal des Beaux-Arts, Lausanne. Photograph by J. C. Ducret. **11 Marcel Duchamp, *Étant donnés,*** detail of the waterfall area in ranking light, showing the plastic form with painted threads and sections of pressure-sensitive tape applied to the adjacent collage elements. Photograph by Philadelphia Museum of Art. **12 Marcel Duchamp, One side of the double-sided note,** recording the colors of the Forestay waterfall, the landscape, and the feces on the big rocks under the *Huilerie* (oil mill), 1946. Philadelphia Museum of Art, Archives, Anne d'Harnoncourt Records.

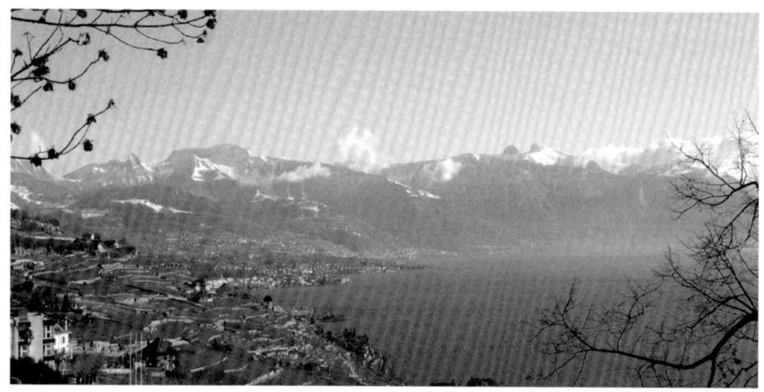

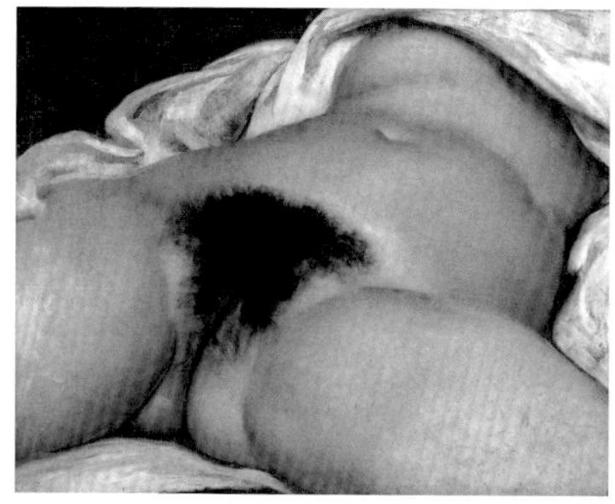

13 View from Hotel Bellevue to La Tour-de-Peilz, where Gustave Courbet died on December 31, 1977. Photograph by Stefan Banz, July 9, 2008. **14 Gustave Courbet, *L'Origine du monde*** (The Origin of the World)**,** oil on canvas, 46 x 55 cm, 1866. Musée d'Orsay, Paris.

I wanted to get away from the physical aspect of painting. I was much more interested in recreating ideas in painting. For me the title was very important. I was interested in making painting serve my purpose, and in getting away from the physicality of painting. For me Courbet had introduced the physical emphasis in the nineteenth century.[8]

Everything since Courbet has been retinal ... you look at a painting for what you see, what comes on your retina ... You would add nothing intellectual about it ... You should look and register what your eyes would see; that's why I call them retinal.[9] *By "retinal" I mean that the aesthetic pleasure depends almost entirely on the impression on the retina, without appealing to any auxiliary interpretation.*[10] *Since Courbet, all the Impressionists were retinal, all the Fauvists were retinal, the Cubists were retinal, and even ... well, the Surrealists did change a bit of that, and Dada also, by saying "Why should we be only interested in the visual part/side of a painting ..."* [11]

I was interested in ideas—not merely in visual products. I wanted to put painting once again at the service of the mind. And my painting was, of course, at once regarded as "intellectual," "literary" painting. It was true I was endeavoring to establish myself as far as possible from "pleasing" and "attractive" physical paintings. That extreme was seen as literary.[12]

As these quotations clearly demonstrate, Duchamp censured Gustave Courbet's understanding of the arts, primarily because he considered him too sensual, too physical, too retinal, a painter interested only in aesthetics. However, as we shall see, there was a great deal more to it than that. For one thing, Duchamp's concerns were not that dissimilar from those of his predecessor and we shall take a closer look at them in connection with *Étant donnés*. What's more, Courbet not only authored one of the world's most unambiguous representations of a woman's genitals in his famous *The Origin of the World*—an incontestable source of inspiration for *Étant donnés*—he also painted numerous waterfalls and springs in the course of his artistic career that allude directly to a woman's sex (fig. 15). In paintings like *The Source* (1862, Metropolitan Museum of Art, New York, p. 81), he even explicitly united the female nude and the waterfall. So we may assume that it was not mere happenstance that made Duchamp alight on Le Forestay in 1946 as the point of departure

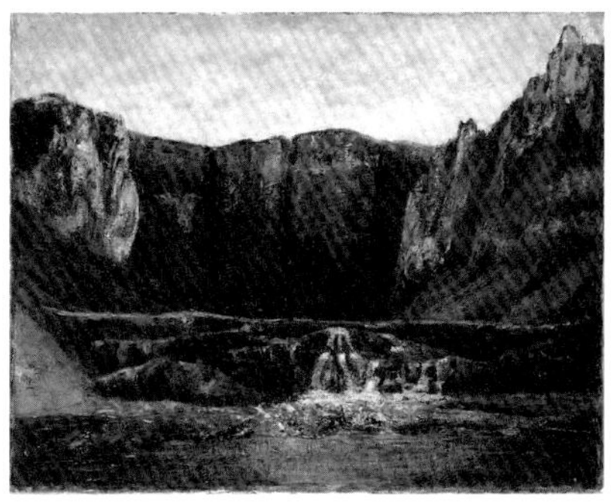

15 Gustave Courbet, *Paysage du Jura* (Jurassic Landscape), oil on canvas, 32 x 46 cm, after 1866. Musée des Beaux-Arts, La Chaux-de-Fonds. **16 Les tours d'Aï** (a.k.a. La tour de Mayen and La tour d'Aï), Winter 2004. Photograph by Stefan Banz.

for his masterpiece. From there he was also able to gaze upon La Tour-de-Peilz, the town in which his artistic predecessor died and, at the same time, on Les tours d'Aï, two mountains in Vaud, towering well over 2,300 meters into the sky, like exposed and provocative breasts (fig. 16). The name "La Tour-de-Peilz" evokes multiple associations: in French, "la tour" means the tower and is a phallic metaphor, while in English, we have the obvious connection of "tour" and "touring." "Peilz," though a proper name, phonetically contains the French words "pet," "paix," and "paie"—fart, peace, and payment—and by way of further association, the English verb "to pet." Given Duchamp's penchant for complex and sophisticated work titles and plays on words, the potential of these various semantic associations is of great interest and particularly significant with regard to his choice of location. The entire area around Le Forestay becomes a charged and richly allusive place of complex, multiple perceptions between the landscape and the names it has been given. Interpretations may even go so far as to include "tout se paie"—everything has a price. Duchamp also turned his back to the lake to photograph a waterfall in another village nearby, with an equally redolent name: Cully. The French word "cul" combined with the Swiss German diminutive "li" or "ly" means "little ass." Moreover, the visual similarity between "Cully" and "gully"—a gutter, a sinkhole, a ditch—evokes both erotic and fecal associations.

As mentioned, the waterfall eloquently named Le Forestay is embedded in the landscape so that it not only pours out between two clearly accentuated flanks (thighs) but can also be seen from the hotel through trees and shrubbery—like a vulva through pubic hair. The word "Forestay" is derived from the word "forel," which comes in turn from "forêt"—the forest that was reserved in the Middle Ages for the exclusive use of the Lord of the Manor and thus, metaphorically speaking, for God.[13] The remains of a water mill, in use until the 1950s, can still be seen next to the building to the left of the waterfall (figs. 17 & 18). The mill is a crucial motif in Duchamp's oeuvre, and in his first key work, *The Bride Stripped Bare by Her Bachelors, Even,* also known as *The Large Glass*. It represents the drive to grind one's "chocolate" oneself. Moreover, in Duchamp's day the building was used to produce oil out of walnuts, as indicated by the word "huilerie" (oil mill) then painted on the façade (it now reads "distillerie"). In connection with *The Large Glass* and Courbet's paintings, this can be interpreted as a metaphor for painting as aesthetic self-pleasuring. From his room in Hotel Bellevue and beyond the garden (where perhaps his companion

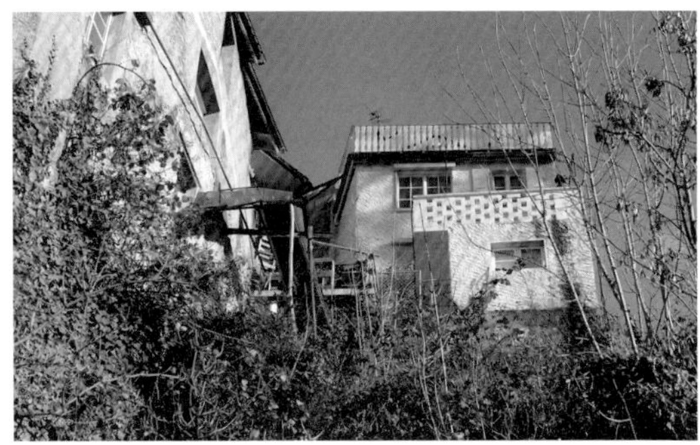

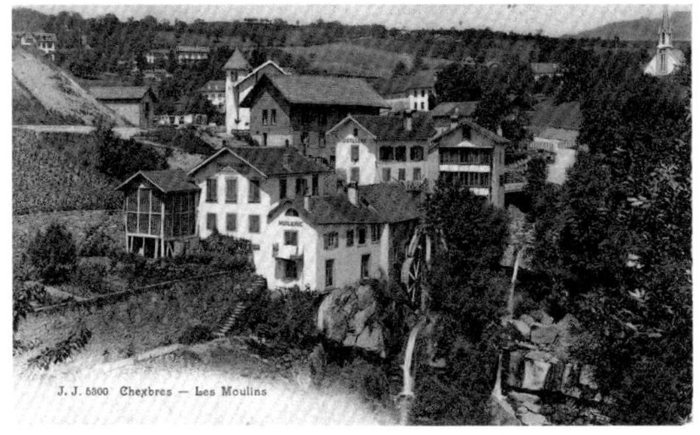

17 Remains of the water mill, Le Forestay, January 12, 2009. Photograph by Stefan Banz. **18 Water mill and huilerie,** Le Forestay, postcard, 8.8 x 13.8 cm, c. 1908. Collection Association du Vieux Lavaux, Chexbres.

Mary Reynolds was sunbathing in a deck chair?), the artist will have enjoyed a direct view of the waterfall (fig. 8). What we have here is perhaps a seminal inspiration of *Étant donnés.*

What's more, Duchamp took two of the seven photographs (p. 19 & p. 23) from a small wooden shed directly next to the waterfall (fig. 19). At the time, the building was the shooting stand of the Société de tir au pistolet Chexbres, Palézieux et environs. Not only is the association between "shooting a photograph" and "shooting a bullet" noteworthy, but also the fact that when marksmen from Puidoux used the stand, they were shooting across Le Forestay toward the territory of Chexbres (fig. 20).

These observations give an entirely new turn to the content and meaning of *Étant donnés.* Not only are important metaphorical preferences in early works brought into play again; the work also proves to have an even greater affinity with the so-called retinal painting of Gustave Courbet, which Duchamp persistently shunned.

The nature of this paradoxical affinity will be subjected to closer scrutiny in the arguments that follow. Both visible and invisible elements in the photographic collage of the diorama, such as trees and bushes, waterfall, mill, oil mill, boulders, shooting stand, mountains, vineyards, Lake Geneva, Courbet, landscape painting—in other words the significance of Le Forestay and its surroundings—will be investigated with a view to the conception, the content and the reading of *Étant donnés.* I should like to begin by taking a look at the two crucial works, *The Large Glass* and *Étant donnés,* as two distinct visual approaches to what is visible and, thus, nameable, identifiable and interpretable, and what we do not see although it is present.

The Visible and the Invisible

Everything in the *Large Glass* essentially refers to something we do not see. The crucial elements—the bride, the waterfall, the vapors—are not really visible. We have to imagine and envision them ourselves. In other words, we are compelled to move from interpretation, from the abstraction of the visible, to the concrete and physical, in order to understand what the work means. At the same time we are driven by the wish to look through the *Large Glass* to make everything we see transparent and realistic. And then we mustn't

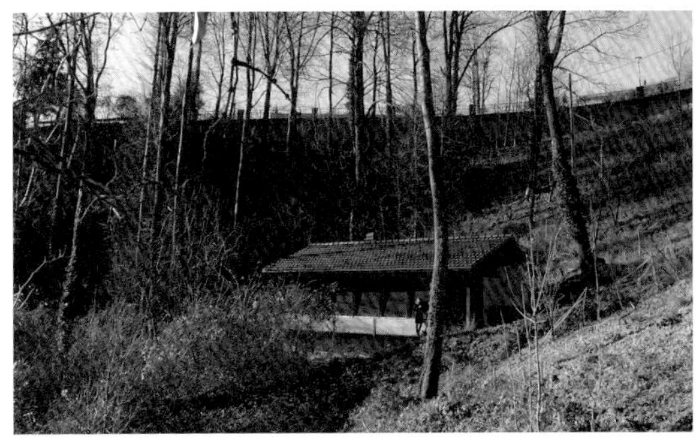

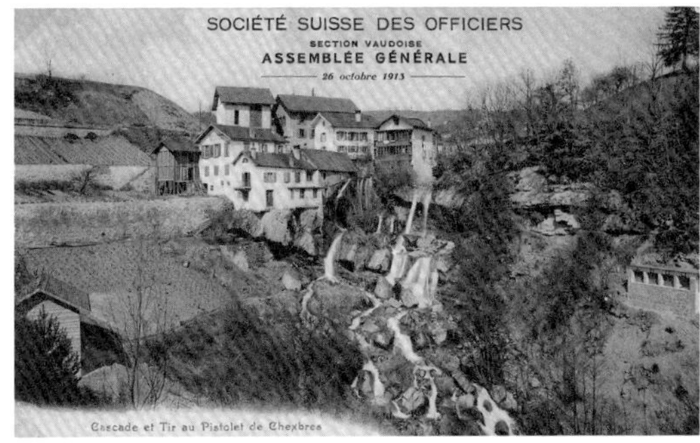

19 Shooting range near Le Forestay, December 8, 2008. Photograph by Stefan Banz. **20 Shooting range and targets** at Le Forestay, postcard, 9.1 x 14 cm, October 26, 1913. Collection Association du Vieux Lavaux, Chexbres.

forget the ninety-six loose sheets in the *Green Box* full of countless disparate text fragments and notes that are meant to be consulted while looking at *The Large Glass*; they are like a product catalog of ideas.[14] In Duchamp's words:

I wanted that album to go with the Glass, and to be consulted when seeing the Glass because, as I see it, it must not be "looked at" in the aesthetic sense of the word. One must consult the book, and see the two together. The conjunction of the two things entirely removes the retinal aspect that I don't like. It was very logical.[15]

In *Étant donnés,* the situation is reversed. As in *Las Meninas* by Velázquez, we see everything. It is all there—as obvious and visible as a snapshot. But then, another world opens up behind the first one—a mystery that inevitably plunges us into a sea of symbols and metaphors. It is then that we penetrate the invisible, the hidden world of abstraction and meaning in order to fathom the philosophical underpinnings. What is obviously there has to stand for something that is not visible even though it is there in reality.

Just what does that mean?

Duchamp initially discovered Le Forestay and its environs more or less by chance because Henri and Hélène Hoppenot had told him about this incredible spot on Lake Geneva, and his friend, the Neuchâtel writer Denis de Rougemont, had extolled the extraordinarily beautiful region of the Lavaux.[16] The accidental nature of his visit to the region is underscored by the fact that twenty-two years later, approximately half a year before he died, he was no longer able to find the waterfall. He had wanted to show it to his wife Teeny in 1968, during an excursion from Lucerne to Lake Geneva in a Volkswagen *(faux vagin).*[17] However, when he first saw the spot in 1946, he instantly recognized the incredibly distilled and concentrated potential it had in connection with his thoughts about art. He did not select the landscape for *Étant donnés* as if it were a readymade; it was not a gesture of indifference; nor was it an act of deliberately assumed unconcern or uninvolved selection. Instead, as in the *3 Standard Stoppages* of 1913, the choice was the consequence of pure happenstance of the kind that comes of a conceptual form of concentration. In retrospect, it could be compared to the *Unhappy Readymade* (fig. 21). While there the wind is the agent that

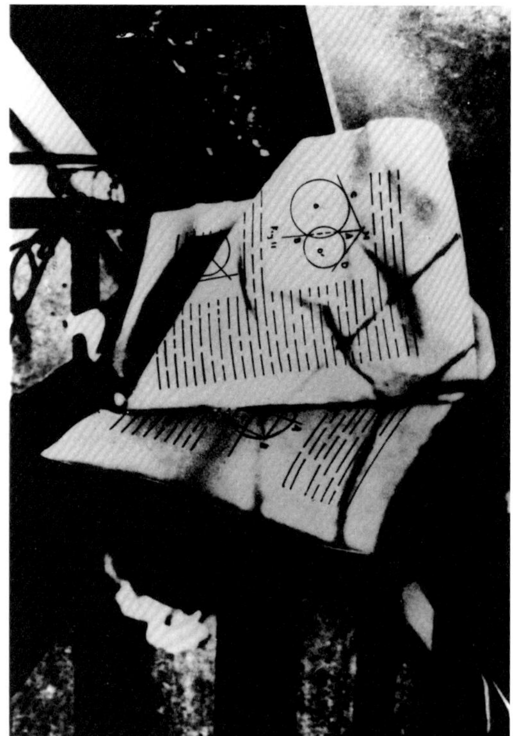

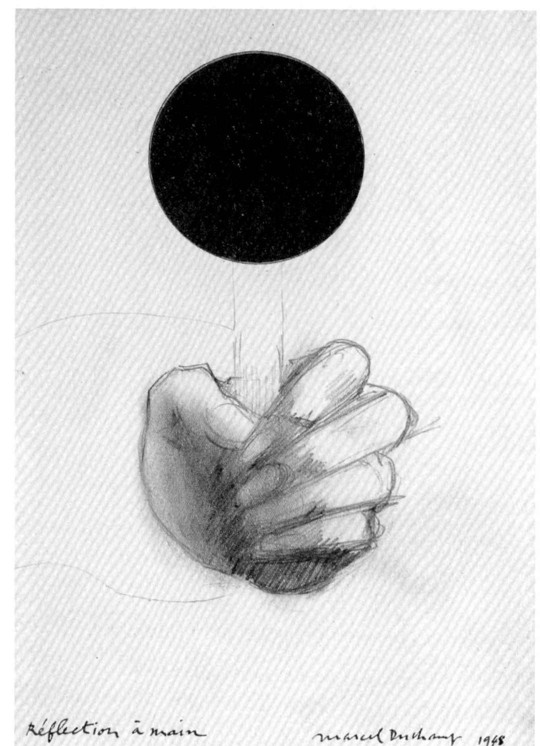

21 Marcel Duchamp, *Readymade malheureux* (Unhappy Readymade), telegram from Buenos Aires as a birthday present for Suzanne Duchamp in Paris, 1919; geometry textbook hung outside and exposed to the elements, lost. **22 Marcel Duchamp, *Réflection à main*** (Hand Reflection), original drawing from the deluxe edition *Boîte-en-valise* (The Box in a Valise), *de ou par Marcel Duchamp ou Rrose Sélavy*, no. 18/20, pencil on paper with collage of a circular mirror covered by a circular cutout of black paper, mounted under Plexiglas, 23.5 x 16.5 cm, 1948. Private Collection.

erases all the knowledge in the suspended book, Duchamp and later visitors to Le Forestay have the opportunity to learn everything that is worth knowing by reading the landscape.

Étant donnés is a trompe l'oeil in the sense of an illusionist arrangement skillfully staged in space to depict an actually visible reality and, simultaneously, another imagined reality that is equally present but not visible. As Herbert Molderings puts it in his book *Marcel Duchamp, Parawissenschaft, das Ephemere und der Skeptizismus*, "In all of the important works created after 1913, Duchamp worked with a subtle visualization of absence. That lends them their typical ambiguity and indeterminacy. The dialectics of concealing and revealing, of hiding and exposing, is an artistic device and, at the same time, the structure that underlies sexual fetishism."[18] And Duchamp's artist's journal of 1917, *The Blind Man,* notes, "But is it the art of Mr. Mutt since a plumber made it? I reply simply that the Fountain was not made by a plumber but by the force of an imagination."[19] It is precisely that imagination that is brought to bear in *Étant donnés,* and we shall examine it more closely here.

Most of the important ideas, subject matters and elements that Duchamp toyed with and gave shape to in *The Large Glass* between 1913 and 1923 converge quite naturally in Bellevue/Chexbres. They are historically embedded in the grand iconographic sweep of art history, with a particular bow to Duchamp's "sparring partner," the great Gustave Courbet. Duchamp looked down on the place, not far from the waterfall, where the retinal painter died a few vineyard terraces below against the visual backdrop of an exquisitely intoxicating landscape.

Quite possibly, Duchamp had long been brooding about a second masterpiece of an import comparable to that of *The Large Glass*, or indeed surpassing it in richness and complexity. When he saw Le Forestay with all of its ingredients, he might have been struck by the blinding realization that the new work had to begin not just with a waterfall, but with this particular waterfall. It was, in fact, the subject matter that he initially entertained for *The Large Glass*, but then abandoned, possibly to avoid succumbing to the tradition of landscape painting. Apparently the time had come to deal with the issue of the retina—which he consistently analyzed in terms of his favorite scapegoat Courbet—conceptually as a voyeuristic construction. Three years later, basically as an expression of his gratitude for this unexpected chance meeting, he gave the Hoppenots *The Box in a Valise*, no. 18/20 along with the study *Réflection à main* (fig. 22), which prefigures another important element of *Étant donnés*—the hand holding the gas lamp.[20] Duchamp's choice of a gift for his friends was very precise: we as viewers see ourselves reflected in the mirror and indulge our own narcissism, as it were, but in reference to the landscape of Le Forestay we see the lake in the background or the waterfall when facing the lake. When we look at ourselves in the mirror, we always see part of what is present, while other parts that are also present remain invisible. It is this unusual optical phenomenon, comprehensible only if viewed in terms of the philosophy of perception, that Duchamp proceeded to elaborate and apply to his entire installation: not only to the landscape collage, but also to the naked figure of the woman and, indeed, the entire spatial concept of the diorama.

We may be able to make better sense of the way in which Duchamp engaged perception on various levels of reality when we realize, as Molderings tells us, that he treated every

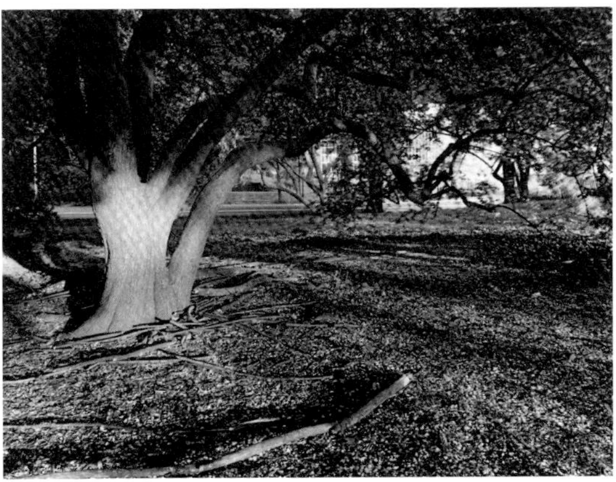

23 Joel Sternfeld, "On This Site, no. 1," color photograph, 47 x 58.4 cm, May 1993. Courtesy of the Artist and Luhring Augustine, New York. "Jennifer Levin and Robert Chambers were seen leaving Dorrian's Red Hand, an Upper East Side bar, at 4:30 A.M. on August 26, 1986. Her body was found beneath this crab apple tree in Central Park (north of the Obelisk, behind the Metropolitan Museum of Art), at 6:15 A.M. that same morning. An autopsy revealed that she had been strangled. She was eighteen years old when she died. Chambers, who was nineteen at the same time of the crime, pleaded guilty to first-degree manslaughter."

word, every gesture, every step in life as a philosophical artistic message, attuning its impact to the public, i.e., to the small circle of artists and millionaires who appreciated his work.[21] For instance, the fact that Duchamp's last studio in New York,[22] where he created *Étant donnés,* had previously housed the Majestic Optical Company confirms how important not only every single detail was to Duchamp but also the surroundings in which his works or their components were created. His approach might be compared with the fifty-part work *On this Site* (fig. 23) by the American photographer Joel Sternfeld, in which a murder is historically inscribed in the scene of the crime, that is, in the subject matter of the picture though it is factually invisible in the photograph. Sternfeld returned to the site of the crime to shoot a photographic record of past events, now invisible but nonetheless present and inscribed in history.

Duchamp goes several steps further: in his case, the real environs of Le Forestay are inscribed in *Étant donnés* not only as a historical but also as a metaphorical site, simultaneously recurring not to a real event but rather to the representation of his thoughts on art. The neighborhood of the waterfall, the waterfall itself, the water wheel, the oil mill, the fecal matter, the shooting stand, shooting a photograph, Bellevue, the mountains, the lake, Cully, La Tour-de-Peilz, Gustave Courbet, Les tours d'Aï: to him, these are all real, mutually related and meaningful symbols, or, to put it differently, in concert they acquire a specific meaning. Even the fact that, after the war, people suffering from tuberculosis believed they would be healed by standing under the falls[23] acquires great symbolic value in this context. And we cannot help wondering whether the famous pipe and cigar smoker, who described himself as a *respirateur*, secretly suffered from a respiratory disease. In 1954 he wrote to Monique Fong:

Several things isolated me for a while
1 – marriage
2 – appendicitis (operated)
3 – pneumonia (cured)
4 – prostate (operated)
which I am now leaving behind—and, by the way, in the best of health[24]

An unusual relationship emerges between the real location of Le Forestay, which has clearly undergone change in the course of time, and the work of art *Étant donnés,* which has no doubt aged and acquired a patina but essentially remains unchanged and "frozen" as an exemplary set piece. For example, although Gustave Courbet's place of death can be seen from the hotel, it is not shown in the printed and colored photo-collage. But it is still there, its existence underscored by the presence of the story. It is invisible and yet present and, in a sense, it is part and parcel of the entire work and its significance.

Now the above-mentioned paradox may make more sense to us. At first sight we have the impression that *Étant donnés* reveals everything—like a snapshot. We are instantly drawn into what confronts us with almost brazen blatancy, but then, almost as quickly, we find ourselves plunging into the invisible and the symbolic, and ultimately taking an entirely different direction. For this reason, it is essential to immerse ourselves in the study of the

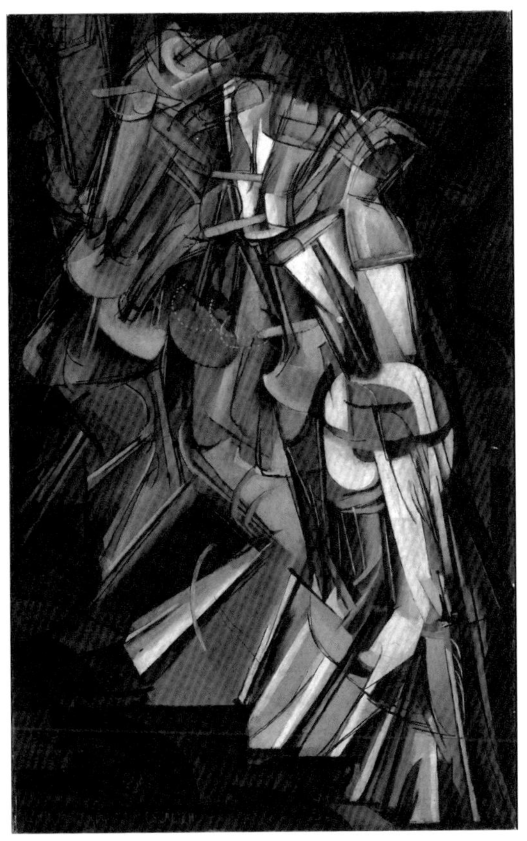

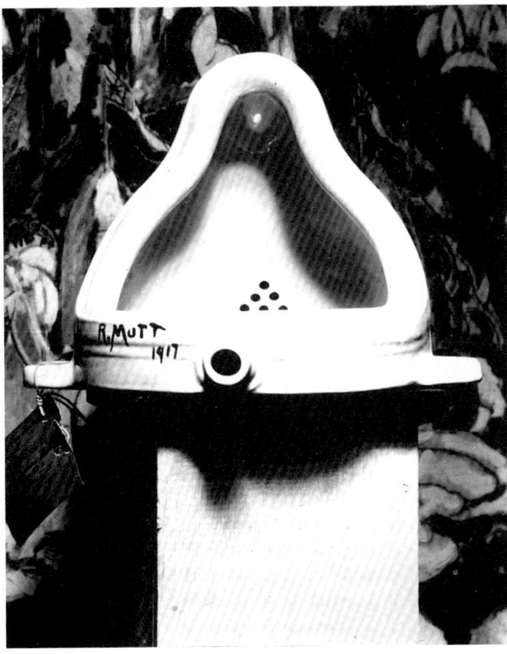

24 **Marcel Duchamp, *Nude Descending a Staircase, No. 2,*** oil on canvas, 146 x 89 cm, 1912. Philadelphia Museum of Art, Louise and Walter Arensberg Collection. 25 **Marcel Duchamp, *Fountain,*** readymade, height 60 cm, 1917. Philadelphia Museum of Art, Louise and Walter Arensberg Collection. Photograph by Alfred Stieglitz.

elements inscribed in the history of the place but not captured by the limited range of the camera eye or deliberately covered up by the hand of the artist: the shooting stand as the place of simulation; the oil mill as the mold of the oil, that is, as the form giver of the painting; the unquenchable energy of the water, ceaselessly flowing and regenerating, as a symbol of life; the vineyards as the mother of wine; and the wine itself as the imagination accelerator, as the colored material that fills the glass bottle *(bouteille de bénédiction, porte-bouteille)* and the wine glass (the gas lamp). Duchamp incorporated all of this into the background of his picture—the place where defecation and feces share the same territory with shooting and oil making. For the real waterfall is also covered by trees and bushes and we have to peer through them in order to see the essentials.

In this respect the landscape pictured in *Étant donnés* is much more than a simple manual combination of photography, collage, print, drawing, painting and object. The photograph does, of course, betoken the distance measured by the light and the liquid transparency of the developing bath, and the print is marked by the metallic touch and impenetrably solid blackness of the printer's ink.[25] But at the same time, Duchamp uses cotton for the clouds in the sky and renders the waterfall as a relief-like play of light, explicitly stating in his *Manual of Instructions*[26] that the clouds and the brightness of the flowing waterfall are the only elements of the work that may be changed or replaced, in other words, precisely those natural elements that are constantly changing in reality and that we perceive with the greatest immediacy. In consequence what we have is a constant back-and-forth between present/visible and present/invisible.

Similarly, in *Nude Descending a Staircase, No. 2* (fig. 24), we do not see what the title describes. The same discrepancy applies to the readymade *Fountain* (fig. 25), which shows

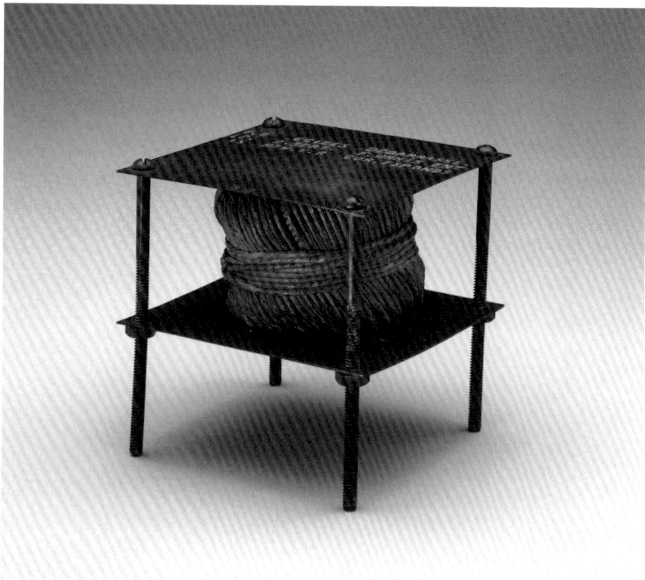

26 Marcel Duchamp, *À bruit secret* (With Hidden Noise), assisted readymade, 12.9 x 13 x 11.4 cm. Philadelphia Museum of Art, Louise and Walter Arensberg Collection.

neither the spray of water from a fountain nor the fountain itself. What we see is a urinal. In both cases, our first impression is that the information in the titles is visible in the works. Nonetheless, what we consider essential to them is not visible, even though it is bound up with reality and therefore present. This is illustrated especially well by the optimized or assisted readymade *With Hidden Noise* (fig. 26). Duchamp describes it as:

A ball of twine between two brass plates joined by four long screws. Inside the ball of twine Walter Arensberg added secretly a small object that makes a noise when you shake it. And to this day I don't know what it is, nor, I imagine does anyone else. On the brass plaques I wrote three short sentences in which letters were occasionally missing like in a neon sign when one letter is not lit and makes the word unintelligible. [27]

What better demonstration could there be of how to make what is vital to a work unmistakably present and yet invisible at the same time. Just as in Jacques Derrida's philosophy of *différance* where we can read the "a" although we cannot hear it, in *With Hidden Noise* we do not see the object that generates the hidden noise; we only hear the sound, and, what's more, only when we as viewers actively interfere by touching the ball of twine, by picking it up and shaking it. *With Hidden Noise* is a readymade, a reproducible object, which Duchamp has reinvested with Benjamin's aura[28] by way of Arensberg's "hidden" intervention.

This fundamental distinction between *The Large Glass* and *Étant donnés* is also reflected in the two titles. *The Bride Stripped Bare by Her Bachelors, Even,* the provocative and poetic title of *The Large Glass*, precisely describes what we are to imagine or envision on the basis of what we see while Duchamp's matter-of-fact title of his diorama, *Given: 1. The Waterfall, 2. The Illuminating Gas,* simply lists some of the things that are actually there. The fact that the list is only partial indicates that in order to understand the work we must hone our awareness of what is not visible by studying what actually is visible. We are reminded of how other works are titled, like *Fountain, Bottle Rack, Bicycle Wheel* and *Tu m'*. The descriptive nature of the title of *Étant donnés* can best be compared with the *Nude Descending a Staircase,* with one difference: the nude cannot be specifically identified as such in the work itself. As Duchamp recalled:

This final version of the Nude Descending a Staircase, *painted in January 1912, was the convergence in my mind of various interests among which the cinema, still in its infancy, and the separation of static positions in the photochronographs of Marey in France, Eakins and Muybridge in America [*sic*].*
Painted, as it is, in severe wood colors, the anatomical nude does not exist, or at least cannot be seen, since I discarded completely the naturalistic appearance of a nude, keeping only the abstract lines of some twenty different static positions in the successive action of descending.[29]

To return to Duchamp's landscape collage, one wonders why he didn't simply mount an enlargement of the selected photograph in the diorama? Why did he go to such lengths to produce his "backdrop," taking a black-and-white photograph of an intensely colorful

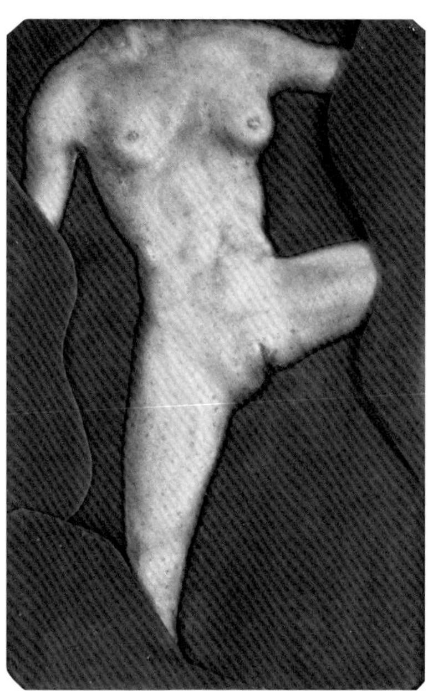

27 Marcel Duchamp, *Study for Étant donnés: 1° La chute d'eau 2° Le gaz d'éclairage,* pigment and graphite on leather over plaster with velvet, 50.2 x 31.1 cm, c. 1946–48. Moderna Museet Stockholm, gift 1985, dedicated to Ulf Linde from Thomas Fischer.

landscape, then modifying it by means of collage, transferring it to another medium and finally coloring it again and further modifying it by painting, drawing, and assemblage? This is an extremely painstaking technical and manual process of alienation in which, to our surprise, we can still immediately identify the point of departure even though an entirely new and self-contained reality has been generated in the result.

This "nonsensical" and even paradoxical mode of production between chance, readymade, and handmade reinforces the increasingly compelling impression that the content of a picture (in our case Le Forestay) is subject to constant change, even upon its completion. Duchamp's approach was similar when he made his figure of the woman in the foreground of the final tableau. The perhaps initial idea of "depicting" Mary Reynolds morphed into an imprint of his lover Maria Martins and, in the end, contained certain explicit ingredients of Teeny Duchamp. As mentioned, it was with Mary Reynolds that Marcel Duchamp went to Le Forestay in 1946. The artist placed his first three-dimensional study of the nude in and on a leather frame inspired by Mary Reynolds (fig. 27). And while the actual cast of the body is that of Maria Martins, the use of parchment to imitate skin was again inspired by Mary Reynolds' use of materials; she was an exceptional and well-known bookbinder. Duchamp later gave the "leather study" to Martins with the dedication, "This lady belongs to Maria Martins, with all my affection, Marcel Duchamp 1948–49."[30] And finally, the left arm and the blond hair of the figure in *Étant donnés* are indebted to Teeny, Duchamp's wife as of 1954. After an unusually hot summer in New York in 1959, the left arm, the one that was holding the bec Auer gas lamp, broke off. During a subsequent stay in Cadaqués, Duchamp used Teeny's arm to make a new cast.[31] A rather odd connection between body and limb resulted when the arm was screwed on again, evoking the title of his famous snow-shovel readymade, *In Advance of the Broken Arm*. In addition, the skin of the figure cracked in the heat and the cracks can still be seen through the peepholes, establishing an imaginary connection to the delicate cracks in *The Large Glass*.[32]

Étant donnés also alludes to another woman who played an important role in Duchamp's life: Beatrice Wood. She was the co-author of the two issues of *The Blind Man* (1917), and Duchamp was occasionally intimate with her. An artistic reinvention of this unusual relationship is incorporated in his readymade *Pliant ... de voyage* (Traveller's Folding Item), the cover of a typewriter that could also be interpreted as a woman's skirt. Wood was a writer and the typewriter was an Underwood, as seen in the lettering on the cover. Moreover, in *Étant donnés*, the woman is lying on wood—on dead twigs. This "woman with the open pussy," as Duchamp lovingly and ironically described it in a letter to Maria Martins,[33] also provoked an array of art historical comparisons with the likes of Hans Baldung Grien,[34] Gustave Courbet, and Hans Bellmer, among others. It was further related to the Hollywood universe of erotic thrillers and to actual crimes, like the murder of Elisabeth Short, famously dubbed the Black Dahlia, whose body was found mutilated in a painfully bizarre and bestial fashion in January 1947 in Los Angeles. In their most recent publications, Mark Nelson and Sarah Hudson Bayliss, and Jean-Michel Rabaté have advanced arguments to support their thesis that there was an indirect connection via Man Ray to George Hodel, one of the main suspects in the still unresolved murder.[35]

The technically complex mutation of the landscape image and the multiple modifications of the female figure in relation to its models undoubtedly testify to Duchamp's personal artistic mode of representing the eternally, inexorably changing appearance and, thus, meaning of all existence affected by time, thereby also drawing attention to the changing meaning of what he suggestively presents to us via the detour of the voyeur-cum-viewer. In an interview with Ulf Linde he said:

Rembrandt could never have expressed all the thoughts that are found in his work. In the age of religion, he was the greatest religious painter; another era discovered in him a profound psychologist, another a poet and still another—the most recent one—a master craftsman. This proves that people give more to pictures than they take from them. No one could possibly be both a profound psychologist and a great religious preacher at the same time. Whatever Rembrandt may have meant—if he's great, then he's great in spite of everything.[36]

Duchamp enlists the widespread strategy of appropriating art history for his own interests, as he had already done in his 1919 Dadaist sendup of the Mona Lisa: *L.H.O.O.Q.* In a letter to Jean Mayoux, Duchamp wrote:

I am a great enemy of critical writing as all I see in these interpretations ... is just an opportunity to open up the floodgates of words.... Every 50 years El Greco is revised and adapted to the tastes of the day, either overrated or underrated. The same goes for all surviving works of art. And this leads me to say that a work is made entirely by those who look at it or read it and make it survive by their claim or even their condemnation.... I refuse to think of the philosophical clichés rehashed by each generation since Adam and Eve in every corner of the planet. I refuse to think about it or to talk about it because I don't believe in language. Language, instead of expressing subconscious phenomena, in reality creates thought through and after words (I readily declare myself a "nominalist," at least in this simplified form).[37]

Duchamp implicitly incorporates these thoughts in the construction of his landscape image. And he does so because he is convinced that the survival of an historical picture is indebted to an "antiquarian spirit" that loves to see something old as beautiful and, furthermore, that there might always be something lost that is even better.[38] In other words, to put it in pointed terms: only those who have actually seen the location, the real landscape—in this case, Le Forestay—are the "true" beholders or voyeurs capable of perceiving and understanding the work in all its displacement and complexity.

Manual of Instructions

On applying these insights to Duchamp's *Manual of Instructions*[39] (figs. 28), one cannot help wondering whether the artist actually prepared it specifically for the dismantling of *Étant donnés* in his studio in New York and its reconstruction at the Philadelphia Museum of Art. As we now know, Duchamp did not intend to have the work exhibited only after his death. Upon its completion in 1966, he had made every effort to have it transferred and set up at the Philadelphia Museum of Art with the help of the Cassandra Foundation, but he died before the logistic and legal formalities had been completed and the installation actually reached Philadelphia.[40]

Is the *Manual of Instructions*, in fact, a great deal more than just a simple aid and a set of visual instructions? Since we already have *The Green Box*, which is conceptually and substantially related to *The Large Glass*, we are, of course, tempted to assume that the *Manual*

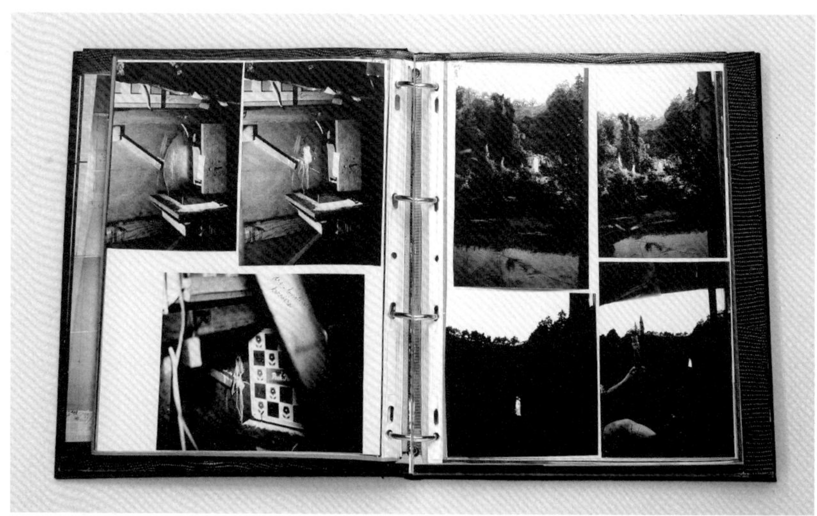

28 One double-page of **Marcel Duchamp's *Manual of Instructions*** *for the assembly of Étant donnés: 1° La chute d'eau, 2° Le gaz d'éclairage*, 1966. Philadelphia Museum of Art 1987 (English version 2009), unpaginated. Photograph by Stefan Banz.

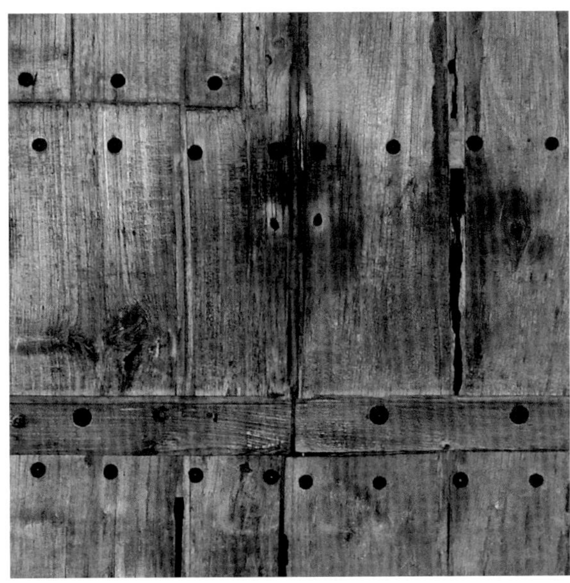

29 Marcel Duchamp, Detail of the wooden door of *Étant donnés*. Photograph by Stefan Banz, March 2008.

plays a similar role. However, in contrast to *The Green Box*, the *Manual of Instructions* is in chronological order and contains only technical and descriptive data on the construction and assembly of the diorama, which could lead to the deceptive conclusion that it provides no added value for the understanding and idea of *Étant donnés*. However, taking into account the above-detailed strategies of the visible and the invisible, it is perfectly obvious that the *Manual* makes a substantial contribution to our understanding of *Étant donnés:* it describes with great precision what is unmistakably present even though we do not see it on peering through the two eyeholes, namely, the entire, elaborate construction, the work's complete and invisible inner life, the very conditions that ensure the existence of *Étant donnés* as a whole. The *Manual of Instructions* literally reveals the discrepancy between what we see and what we do not see. It is through this document that Duchamp's work becomes a statement about appearance and being—a perfectly staged production on one hand and chaotic bricolage on the other.

The Mask of the Viewer

Over the decades, in an infinitely slow, imperceptible process, the faces of all the visitors who have peered through the two peepholes have left the imprint which looks like a mask on the double door (fig. 29).[41] This phenomenon is a striking reminder of the extent to which *Étant donnés* addresses and involves the viewer. Like a voyeur, we gaze at a disconcerting scene while other visitors watch us watching without realizing as yet that we are looking at something deemed improper. But what does "improper" mean? We are in a public museum where every exhibit placed on display is meant to be looked at, appreciated, and studied. Does *Étant donnés* perhaps only pretend to address and involve the viewer? Or should the viewer, in fact, be equated with the artist?

I want to grasp things with the mind the way the penis is grasped by the vagina.[42]

When *Étant donnés* was still in the New York studio, two nails with broad heads filled the two holes that Duchamp had drilled into the two wings of the wooden door he'd found in Cadaqués.[43] The viewer had to pull them out—like a penis out of a vagina—in order to see the diorama. The nails were removed after installation at the Philadelphia Museum of Art, as it would have been too complicated for the guards to take them out and put them back every time a visitor wanted to look at the work. In addition, the museum feared that the two little pointed objects might be stolen. Duchamp's original design ensured that the voyeur had to take the initiative in order to see what was invisible but present, that is, visibly hidden behind the visible door. This heightened the disturbing feeling of doing something indecent but it also made it perfectly clear that nothing would be revealed unless the viewer took action. Denis Brown Hare, who photographed *Étant donnés* in Duchamp's New York studio before it was dismantled, explained the ambivalence of her feelings about the nails: "The physical act of taking them out was so exciting, and very much a part of the erotic thrill of the piece for me, as they implicated you in the work, since you have the choice not to look, but you looked anyway."[44] And in 1969, John Russell, the art critic for the *Sunday Times* in London, wrote that "every museum is in essence a peepshow and every one of its visitors an eavesdropper: a sneaky sort of fellow who presumes to peer at the secret life of works of art."[45]

As mentioned, Duchamp put a great deal of thought into the significance and the activity of the viewer. In a 1967 television interview he declared that "there are too many people in the world who are looking. The number of those looking has to be cut down."[46] His approach to the viewer is clear-cut and unambiguous and yet indifferent as well. On one hand, for Duchamp a work of art doesn't exist without the viewer for which reason he considers the viewer as significant as the artist;[47] on the other hand, he spoon-feeds his audience, not only prescribing their angle of vision but also how the work should be viewed. He even wants to prevent crowding, to dictate numbers as it were, which is why he came up with the idea of a diorama with peepholes. Because Duchamp was convinced that the viewer completes the work, he became more and more interested over the years in controlling and defining his audience's vantage point as well as the relationship between what they see and what they do not see.

Jean Starobinski speaks about the orientation of art towards the encounter with a gaze, which means that the artist has to give up what he has made and abandon his work to an outside witness.[48] Writing about Duchamp's *In the Manner of Delvaux* (fig. 30), one of the works that prefigured *Étant donnés*, Michael Taylor observes that "the viewer/voyeur enters a conspiratorial relationship with the artist, and together they instigate an act of visual penetration."[49]

To my mind, both views must be taken into account to do justice to Duchamp's intentions, but, whatever the case, *Étant donnés* rules out a clear-cut separation of artist and viewer. In a tape-recorded interview of 1959 with Richard Hamilton, Duchamp acted like a compromised viewer himself when he linked the words "naked exposed" directly to the death and resurrection of Christ. It is not clear, however, whether he really was surprised at his own words about his work or whether he was intentionally putting on a show of ambivalence:

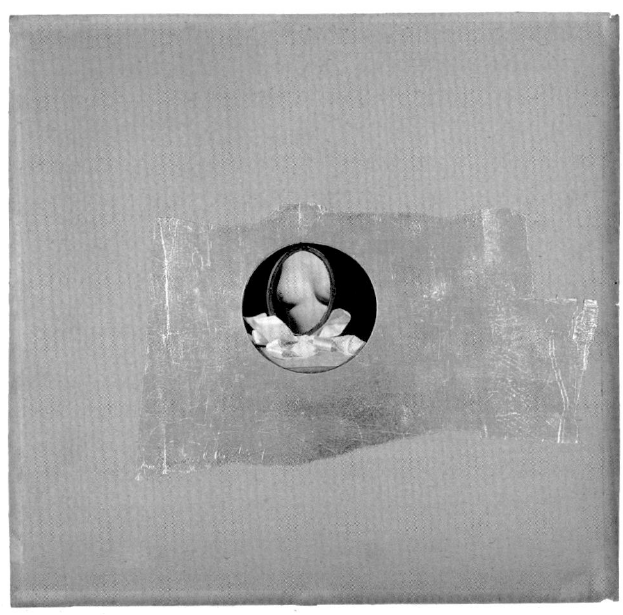

30 Marcel Duchamp, *À la manière de Delvaux* (In the Manner of Delvaux), collage on tinfoil and photograph on cardboard, 34 x 34 cm, 1942. Israel Museum, Jerusalem, Vera and Arturo Schwarz Collection of Dada and Surrealist Art.

There it is, naked exposed ... it is a form of fantasy, it also has a little bit to do with ... naked exposed was probably ... it even had ... an almost indecent association with Christ ... with Christ ... Christ was naked and exposed ... and it is ... it was an indecent means of introducing eroticism and religious ... I am ... I am ashamed about what I'm saying.[50]

If we apply these stuttering remarks to *Étant donnés*, we suddenly discover that we are in a religious grotto with a view, where Rrose Sélavy is represented as a female incarnation of Christ: the waterfall and the illuminated gas become the erotic symbols of life—the resurrection. Let there be light in the waterfall of tenderly sparkling temptation! For only those who "see" will understand what is hidden behind the "revelation." Once again, this is not about anything factually visible but, as in *The Blind Man*, about mental, cerebral seeing. The blind man becomes the seer because he sees in the urinal a *Fountain* of allusions and semantic references, as underscored by Duchamp himself in his famous lecture "The Creative Act," which concludes as follows:

All in all, the creative act is not performed by the artist alone; the spectator brings the work in contact with the external world by deciphering and interpreting its inner qualifications and thus adds his contribution to the creative act. This becomes even more obvious when posterity gives its final verdict and sometimes rehabilitates forgotten artists.[51]

Étant donnés is therefore intentionally, indeed deceptively designed as an optical illusion, in which the landscape collage of Le Forestay and the modified cast of the naked woman's body refer to themselves only inasmuch as the essential is invisibly present; it is only through them, as visible entities, that the essential becomes accessible. In one of his interviews,

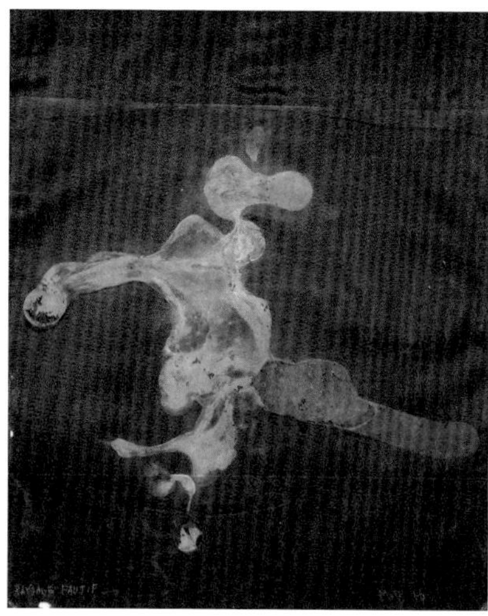

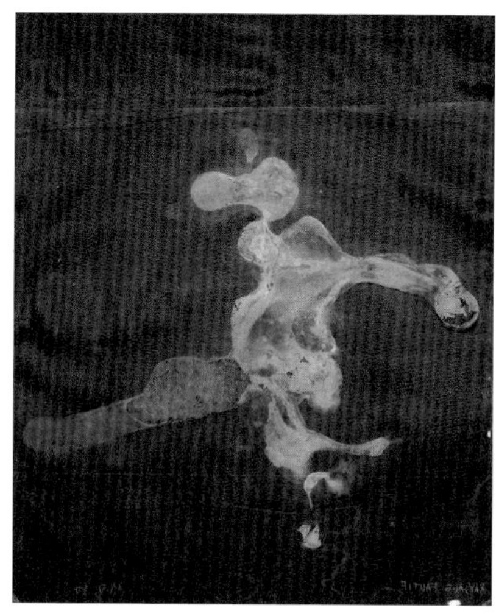

31a Marcel Duchamp, *Paysage fautif* (Faulty Landscape), original painting from the deluxe edition of the *Boîte-en-valise* (The Box in a Valise), *de ou par Marcel Duchamp ou Rrose Sélavy*, no. 12/20, seminal fluid on Astralon backed with black satin, 21 x 16.5 cm, 1946. Museum of Modern Art, Tokyo. **31b Marcel Duchamp, *Paysage fautif,*** reversed.

titled "I like breathing better than working" (1967), Pierre Cabanne asked Duchamp, "What personal definition of eroticism would you give?" To which the artist replied:

I don't give it a personal definition, but basically it's really a way to try to bring out in the daylight things that are constantly hidden—and that aren't necessarily erotic—because of the Catholic religion, because of social rules.[52]

Paysage fautif

When Marcel Duchamp gave his adored and beloved Maria Martins the special edition no. 12/20 of *The Box in a Valise*, he included an original abstract picture titled *Paysage fautif* (fig. 31a). He also gave her an edition of *The Green Box* in which he placed a folded piece of thick drawing paper with the personal dedication, "pour Maria, enfin arrivée."[53] The material Duchamp used to "paint" the picture was an unknown for many years until, for an exhibition, the Menil Foundation in Houston, Texas, conducted a scientific investigation with the help of the FBI and determined that it was semen.[54] That fact adds a new and unmistakable semantic thrust to the dedication—*enfin arrivée*. Historically, it is worthy of note that Duchamp sprayed his "pigment" onto the picture support about a year before Jackson Pollock introduced his drip painting and, what's more, he made the painting in 1946 just before he began working on *Étant donnés*.[55] If we look at the work in mirror image (fig. 31b) more or less the way Duchamp turned his back to the overwhelming panorama of Lake Geneva[56] to gaze into the origins of the earth in Bellevue, we notice that the abstract pattern suddenly becomes concrete, acquiring the shape of his "Lady of Desire" with outstretched arm and bent leg.[57] The "sinful" seminal landscape thus translates, almost naturally, into *Étant donnés*, and the waterfall and illuminating gas once again coalesce into one single whole: *The Origin of the World*—Les tours d'Aï—waterfall—oil mill—drip painting—masturbation—feces—urine—photograph—shot—print—*Paysage fautif*.

The Origin of the World

Tellingly, the story of Gustave Courbet's *The Origin of the World* is also an infinite and dazzling exchange between showing and hiding. The presentation of the painting consistently involved hiding it behind something visible—it was always there but not visible, to avoid provoking or taxing the public by the intimacy of the representation. It was commissioned by its first owner, the Turkish-Egyptian diplomat Khalil Bey, domiciled in Paris at the time, who sequestered it behind a green curtain in his personal dressing room. When Edmond de Goncourt saw the work at Antoine de la Narde Gallery in 1889, it had been hidden behind another Courbet painting, which the French art critic described as a painting of a village in the snow, today presumed to have been *Le château de Blonay* (fig. 32). The castle is situated just a few miles away from La Tour-de-Peilz and, to the visitor's great astonishment, it too can be seen directly from Hotel Bellevue. Michael Taylor describes the painting as "an innocuous winter landscape featuring a castle that the dealer had housed in a false-bottomed frame within a locked tabernacle or cabinet, which when opened revealed Courbet's erotic masterpiece below. The unremarkable landscape hangs today in the Museum of Fine Arts in Budapest, having been removed by another owner of *The Origin of the World*, the Hungarian-Jewish art collector Baron Ferenc Hatvany, who sold the covering panel to his brother-in-law, Baron Mór Lipót Herzog, who in turn donated the work to the museum in 1959."[58]

The Origin of the World was officially considered lost in June 1889 and did not reappear until 1955 at an auction, where it was acquired by the psychoanalyst Jacques Lacan and his wife Sylvia Bataille Lacan for 1.5 million French francs. The Lacans also concealed the painting behind another in their home. Sylvia Lacan commissioned her brother-in-law, the well-known Surrealist artist André Masson, to paint a picture (fig. 33), which slid into the frame and could be pulled aside *(glissière!)* to reveal Courbet's masterpiece for a select public.[59]

These unusual forms of presenting one of the most obvious paintings in the history of art once again underscore the fact that we must keep (re)discovering the enigmatic

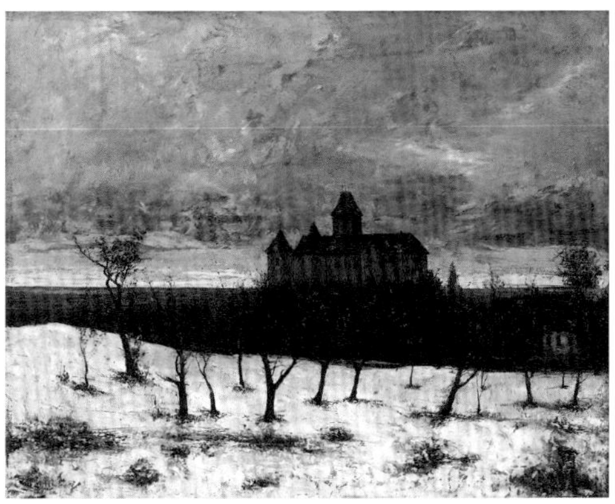

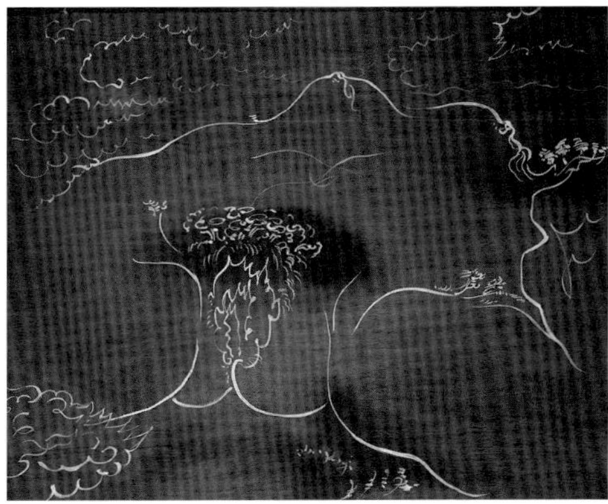

32 Gustave Courbet, *Le château de Blonay* (The Castle of Blonay), oil on canvas, 50 x 60 cm, c. 1875. Szépmuvészeti Múzeüm, Budapest. **33 André Masson, *Masque de l'Origine du monde*** (Mask of the Origin of the World) a.k.a. ***Terre érotique*** (Erotic Landscape), oil on wood, 44 x 66 cm, 1955. Private Collection.

phenomenon of simultaneous absence and presence. On September 21, 1958, Marcel and Teeny Duchamp were invited for dinner by the Lacans at their country house La Prévôté in Guitrancourt near Mantes-la-Jolie, and we may assume that the artist delighted not only in the painting but also in the special form of its presentation in spite of the fact that he could not tolerate body hair.[60] In contrast to Courbet's lushly hirsute depiction, his "woman with the open pussy" has skin, shaved as smooth as possible.

Shooting an Image

From the moment of its making, Gustave Courbet's painting suffered the risk of being a target of potential scandal, a threat that its owners assiduously sought to avoid by taking exceptional measures, possibly not only because such a scandal would have endangered the existence of the painting but also because it would have curtailed the beholders' pleasure. The Philadelphia Museum of Art was beset with similar misgivings regarding Duchamp's *Étant donnés*. In his book *Marcel Duchamp Etant donnes,* Michael Taylor describes in detail the logistical considerations that led up to the definitive move of the installation to Philadelphia, culminating in the notorious decision to strictly prohibit any visual reproduction of the interior of the diorama.[61] For fifteen years, the only visuals the media were permitted to publish were pictures of the wooden door: the actual content of the three-dimensional tableau was taboo and officially invisible the entire time. In symbolic terms, therefore, both *The Origin of the World* and *Étant donnés* are "targets" to be aimed at through a sight (holes) before pressing the release (ejaculation).

We also know that in *The Large Glass* Duchamp constructed a special device to shoot paint at the bride. Nine "bullet holes" can be seen in the upper half of the work at the lower right-hand corner of the bride's "halo." Moreover, his artistic beginnings can be linked to the art of marksmanship. In 1967 Pierre Cabanne remarked, "I believe your first important artistic adventure, which took place in 1905, was a course in printing in Rouen. It gave you a genuine printer's competence." To which the artist replied:

That's a funny episode. Expecting to serve, under the law, two years of military service, I felt, being neither militaristic nor soldierly, that I must still try to profit from the "three-year law"; that is, do only one year by signing up immediately. So I went through the steps necessary to find out what one could do without being a lawyer or doctor, since these were the two usual exemptions. That's how I learned that there was an examination for "art workers," which allowed one year's service instead of three, under the same conditions as those of a lawyer or doctor. Then I wondered what kind of art worker I might be. I discovered that one could be a typographer or a printer of engravings, of etchings. That's what they meant by art worker.[62]

As Georges Didi-Huberman in his book *La ressemblance par contact: Archéologie, anachronisme et modernité* specifies, it was not the first time that Duchamp presented a fateful necessity as a product of chance, as *tyche*. To avoid pulling the trigger of a gun, he decided to pull etchings. Later, incidentally, he united the two meanings of the word "pull" in a work—namely on the cover of a catalog published in New York in 1942, *First Papers of Surrealism,* its cover showing a wall at which Duchamp shot five times (fig. 34).[63]

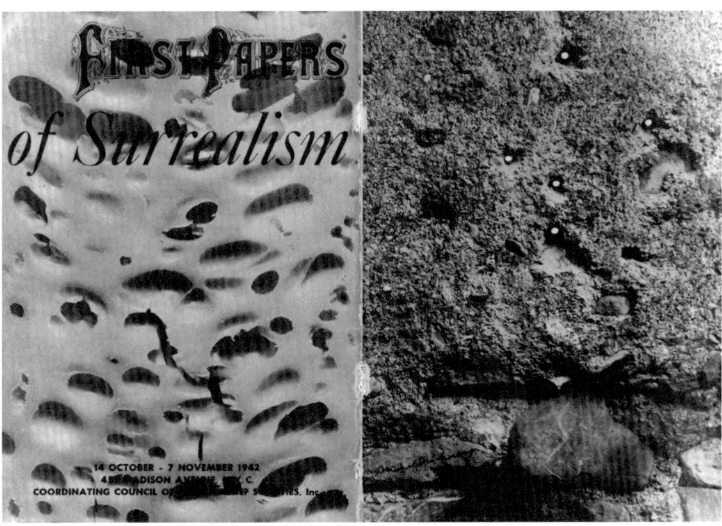

34 Marcel Duchamp, Covers of the catalogue, *First Papers of Surrealism* (back/front), Coordinating Council of French Relief Societies, New York, October 14–November 7, 1942, organized by André Breton and Marcel Duchamp. Private Collection.

In keeping with Didi-Huberman's argument, one might interpret the figure of the woman and the landscape collage in *Étant donnés* as complex and elaborately prepared pullings and prints; something equivalent is generated, a symmetrical opposite, and yet there is a tendency to negate, to separate, to destroy. The double generated by pulling a print therefore also functions as dissimilarity.[64] Duchamp's pullings successfully engage the dialectic act of breaking with classical imitation without entirely negating similarity.[65] And that raises another question: why does Duchamp's female body have such a dissimilar, deformed vagina in comparison to reality?

The Female Body

It is almost as if Maria Martins' genitals had fallen victim to the professional blunder of a cosmetic surgeon, but, whatever the case, the moment we walk up to the door and peer through holes, the odd malformation instantly undermines the voyeuristic, retinal character of *Étant donnés* and challenges our gray cells to start thinking about the weird anomaly.[66] This is what decisively distinguishes Duchamp's work from Courbet's *Origin of the World*. Subsequent modification of the cast of Maria Martins' body—especially with regard to her genitals—is so invasive that it makes the figure look utterly artificial and indeed bizarre. *Untitled* (fig. 35) and *Étant donnés: Maria, la chute d'eau, et le gaz d'éclairage* (fig. 36)—the first two studies for *Étant donnés*—prefigure this curious ambivalence. We cannot really tell which position the artist has chosen to represent, and the odd way in which the figure spreads her legs, simultaneously bending up the left limb, shows her as a giant above Le Forestay, unmistakably demonstrating that the topography of the waterfall resembles a woman's bent thigh, with water ceaselessly flowing out of the middle: the origin of the earth. This insight led to the artist's decision to represent the nude lying on a bed of twigs in his three-dimensional tableau, a decision possibly also inspired by Hans Bellmer's photographs (fig. 37). To my mind, it is only then that he made the relief-like, leather version, *Study for Étant donnés: 1° la chute d'eau, 2° le gaz d'éclairage* (fig. 27), to

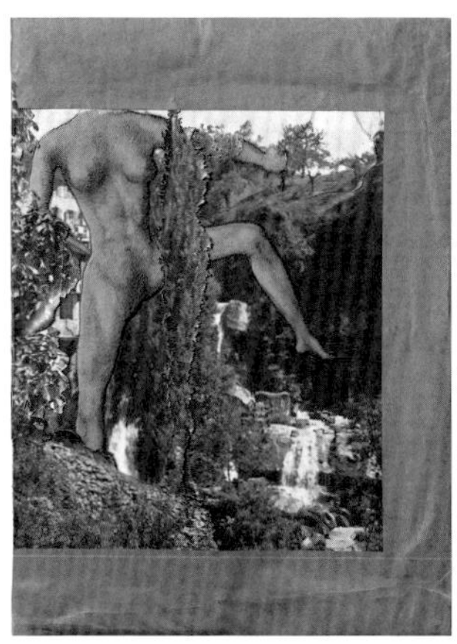
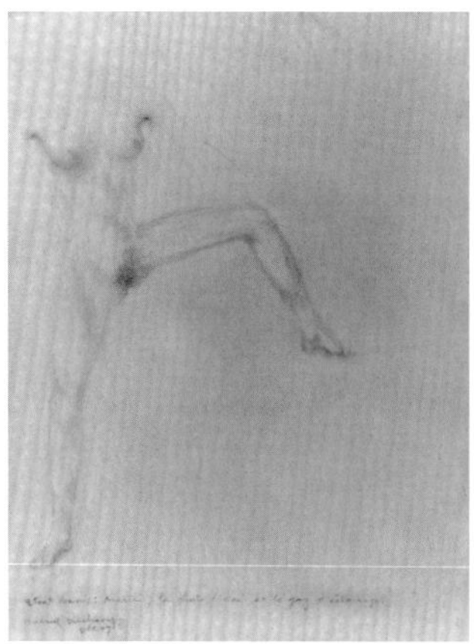
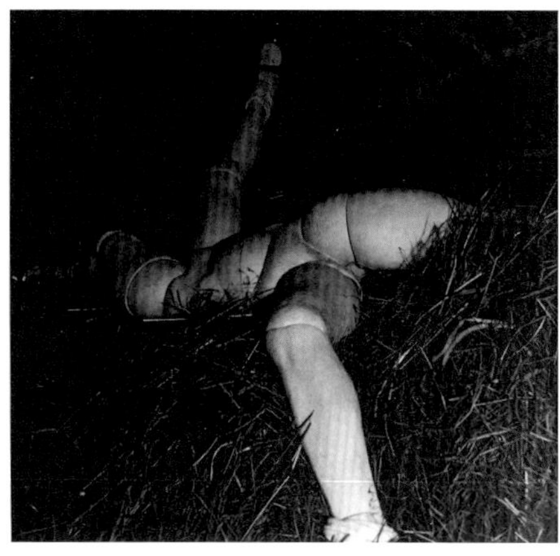

35 Marcel Duchamp, *Untitled* (photo-collage landscape study for *Étant donnés: 1° La chute d'eau 2° Le gaz d'éclairage*), textured wax, pencil and ink on tan paper and cut gelatin silver photographs, mounted on board, 43.2 x 31.1 cm, c. 1946. Private Collection. **36 Marcel Duchamp, *Étant donnés: Maria, la chute d'eau, et le gaz d'éclairage,*** pencil on paper, 40 x 29 cm, signed December 47. Moderna Museet Stockholm. Gift 1985, dedicated to Ulf Linde from Thomas Fischer. **37 Hans Bellmer, *La Poupée*** (The Doll), Black-and-white vintage gelatin silver print, blind stamped by the artist's estate, 14.2 x 14.5 cm, 1936–38. Courtesy Ubu Gallery, New York, and Galerie Berinson, Berlin.

find out whether—as in *The Large Glass*—it might not be more interesting after all to find a solution without the "naturalistic illustration" of the waterfall. Michael Taylor suggests that the pencil drawing was made in 1946 and was the first *Étant donnés* study, although the dedication reads "December 47." I would question that since the waterfall arguably determines the woman's unusual position, in which case it would follow that the *Untitled* collage was the introductory idea that shaped the composition.

From the start, Duchamp no doubt gave painstaking thought to how he would present the cast of Maria Martins, which shows an affinity with Courbet but is also extremely far removed from him, entering a zone of curiously tense indifference. For the naked woman that we perceive is neither unmistakably dead nor unmistakably alive despite the lively determination with which she is holding up the gas lamp. In other words, what is missing in the figure is absent but nonetheless visible and what she does have cannot be explained by its visibility alone.

Inframince

In his legacy of forty-six notes (1934–45),[67] Duchamp coined the word *infra-mince* to designate a barely perceptible but still significant difference, comparable, for example, to that between the landscape collage in *Étant donnés* and the environs of Le Forestay, or between the reclining nude and Maria Martins' body. If we have never seen the waterfall, or visit it many years later, we are as hard put to distinguish the difference between it and the collage as we are between Duchamp's sculpture of the woman and Maria Martins herself, whom we do not and cannot know personally. *Infra-mince* also means the difference between the visible and the invisible that is present in the visible, whose existence can be perceived only under certain circumstances. Duchamp seeks to demonstrate that the sameness of two things does not make them the same. In *The Green Box*, he writes:

... to separate the mass-produced readymade from the readyfound—The separation is an operation.[68] *To lose the possibility of recognizing, identifying 2 similar objects—2 colors, 2 laces, 2 hats, 2 forms whatsoever to reach the Impossibility of sufficient, visual memory, to transfer from one like object to another ...*[69]

And in note 35: *Infra-thin separation ... Two men are not / an example of identicality / and to the contrary move away / from a determinable / infra-thin difference—but there exists the crude conception / of the deja vu which leads from / generic grouping / (2 trees, 2 boats) / to the most identical "castings" / It would be better / to try / to slip / into the / infra-thin / interval which separates / 2 "identicals" than / to conveniently accept / the verbal generalization / which makes / 2 twins look like 2 / drops of water.*[70]

The assisted readymade, *Air de Paris,* is a case in point: the container of glass is the *infra-mince* (infra-thin) difference between the Parisian air enclosed inside and the air in New York, where the work was sent and preserved. Didi-Huberman writes that this readymade was technically meant to represent a cast of the air, in other words, to give the air in Paris a shape and to make this shape transportable, indeed personally portable, as a work of art. *Pulled at Four Pins* of 1917, a chimney cowl that rotates in the wind, is similar in effect. Duchamp reconstructed this lost readymade as precisely as possible in a drawing made almost fifty years later.[71] The drawing might be compared to *Étant donnés* inasmuch as its source—the chimney cowl—is lost but still exists somewhere just as Maria Martins and the waterfall were lost for Duchamp and yet still exist. This is a touching revelation. As Didi-Huberman explains, the Greek word *tyche* is a word related to touching. If we say that something happens or occurs by chance, that means that we are touched by it, like being unexpectedly injured by a stray arrow.[72] Both Maria Martins and Le Forestay accidentally touched Duchamp like Cupid's arrow. And he linked this accident with his own idiosyncratic approach to technical precision. Just as plaster takes shape in a mold, he is of the opinion that it is dallying *(retard en verre)* that makes significant works of art.[73] Dallying is infra-mince; dallying also enhances a woman's orgasm; and in *Étant donnés,* Duchamp was clearly dallying with the infra-thin difference between *regard* (gaze) and *retard* (delay).[74]

Four-Dimensionality

According to Herbert Molderings, "If a shadow is the projection of a three-dimensional object onto a two-dimensional plane, Duchamp argues that by analogy the three-dimensional object is the projection of a four-dimensional object in three-dimensional space. Everything that exists in the three-dimensional world is only the 'projection,' the 'depiction,' the 'reflex' of things that exist invisibly in another world with a higher dimension. Since our organs of perception are confined to three dimensions, that other world is forever beyond our ken. The concept of the 'fourth dimension,' which is crucial to Duchamp's para-scientific speculations, serves to designate this hypothetical reality. All objects are pictures of other, invisible objects, which are in turn pictures themselves. For even 'in its fourth dimension,' the world is not the real, true world."[75]

Then where or in which dimension does the real world exist? In none? In all of them? The projections, or rather that which is depicted by them and is not visible as such, must be viewed as the "real, true world." In other words: we have to invent a certain form of representation in order to refer visually or spatially to the fourth dimension since it is beyond our ken. One possibility would be the metaphor, another would be movement (time), and still another the conceptual relationship of artwork and viewer, of visible and invisible, of what is actually happening in a place even though it is not visible in the representation. "In Duchamp's imagination, the world is an endless tunnel of mirrors, projections and optical illusions."[76] On the other hand, knowledge, reflection, and appreciation intrinsically entail reduction by one dimension, and it is for that very reason that the title *Étant donnés: 1° La chute d'eau, 2° le gaz d'éclairage* is a reference to the fourth dimension. Combining the waterfall and the illuminating gas produces a "chemical" mixture that generates the idea of a four-dimensional reality. And the subsequent combination of three different spaces in *Étant donnés* gives this idea a visual counterpart: the empty, darkened room with the door, as the viewer's space, the utterly black space in between with no dimensions, as it were, where our gaze overcomes the immeasurability of the darkness, and, finally, the sight—through the hole in the brick wall—of a third illuminated zone of total illusion containing figure, lamp and waterfall.

The idea of a fourth dimension in *Étant donnés* is reinforced by the creation of a philosophical metaphorics, tailored to the space, where Duchamp directly links gaze, light, illusion, and the gray cells of the viewer to the magic of the paradoxical. Duchamp anchored the idea by simultaneously fixing the viewer's standpoint and the direction of his/her gaze. Were there several vantage points, the four-dimensional space would be overwhelmed by infinite possibilities of representation. His fourth dimension emerges by lining up three spaces that fuse and acquire new shape in the mind of the viewer.

Synthesis

Not only did Duchamp find an artistic means of visualizing the fourth dimension in his *Étant donnés,* he has also left us with a complex artistic rendition of what art is capable of achieving in extremis. Through an optical arrangement that sparks off an instantaneous retinal shock, he introduces small shifts and dislocates our notion of reality, moving away from the retinal and activating our gray cells. Interestingly, the work resembles a film set in which the printed and colored landscape collage of Le Forestay functions like the famous matte paintings, used in filmmaking in combination with various live elements to conjure the illusion of new realities (fig. 38). In this respect, *Étant donnés* is the total illusion of reality as art or the total illusion of art as reality and, what's more, it is the epitome of Duchamp's entire artistic vision and, indeed, of all erotic representations in the history of art. And let us not forget that the artist had already created seminal examples of that vision in such works as *Tu m',* *The Bride Stripped Bare by Her Bachelors, Even,* and *The Box in a Valise.* Duchamp's "nostalgia" began with *Tu m'* and came to a grand, spectacular climax in *Étant donnés.* This work is, to my mind, a legitimate descendent of Jan van Eyck's *Arnolfini Wedding* and Diego Velazquez's *Las Meninas.*

Translated from the German by Catherine Schelbert

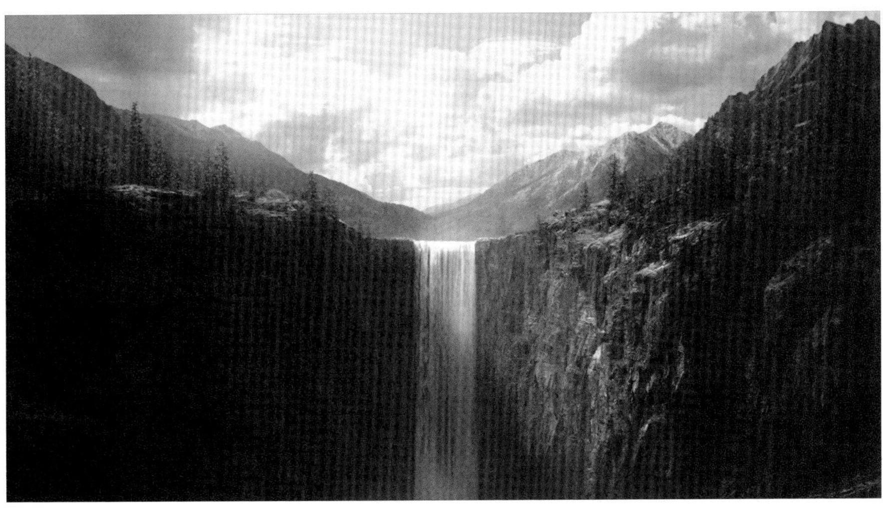

38 Matte painting for Guinness beer commercial, *Bring it to Life*, directed by Johnny Green, 2009.

Notes

The point of departure for the present study is my article *Warum nicht der Niesen, Monte Rosa? Das ist das Leben!* in Peter Fischer, Christoph Lichtin and Susanne Neubauer, eds., *Top of Central Switzerland. Zeitgenössische Kunst aus der Zentralschweiz,* Kunstmuseum Luzern 2007, pp. 32–40.

[1] Walter Hopps in a cable conversation with Ecke Bonk, May 9, 1988, in *The Box in a Valise de ou par Marcel Duchamp ou Rrose Sélavy, Inventory of an Edition by Ecke Bonk,* Munich, New York and London 1989, p. 186.
[2] See Marcel Duchamp's letter to Ettie Stettheimer, August 9, 1946, Chexbres, Switzerland, in Francis M. Naumann and Hector Obalk, *Affectionately, Marcel: Selected Correspondence of Marcel Duchamp,* Ghent 2000, pp. 254–55. See also the chapter "Marcel Duchamp in Switzerland 1946 and 1968" in this publication, pp. 387–90, based on Jennifer Gough-Cooper and Jacques Caumont, "Ephemerides on and about Marcel Duchamp and Rrose Sélavy 1887–1968," in *Marcel Duchamp,* Milan 1993, unpaginated.
[3] See Beth A. Price, Ken Sutherland, Scott Homolka and Elena Torok, "Evolution of the Landscape, The Materials and Methods of the *Étant donnés* Backdrop," in Michael R. Taylor, *Étant donnés,* Philadelphia 2009, pp. 262–81.
[4] See Gough-Cooper and Caumont, "Ephemerides," August 6, 1946 (note 2); and in this publication, p. 388.
[5] See photographs of the mechanism in Marcel Duchamp, *Manual of Instructions for Étant donnés: 1° La chute d'eau, 2° Le gaz d'éclairage ...,* Philadelphia Museum of Art 1987, revised and translated 2009, unpaginated.
[6] For the first published reference to Le Forestay, see Eric Müller, *Puidoux au coeur de Lavaux: Chronique d'une commune vaudoise,* Puidoux 1982. On page 219, in the chapter titled "Un Forestay surréaliste," he details the following interesting finding: "Another painter, affiliated with the less appealing school of Surrealism, used a third site in this region to create a work of art the grasp of which requires, truth be told, a degree of artistic appreciation generally beyond the reach of us ordinary mortals. Who and what are we talking about?
"By a whim of chance, the municipality of Puidoux received a request in the spring of 1980 for information sent to every township in Switzerland by a resident of the canton of St. Gallen. The letter included a photograph and requested its recipients to identify, if at all possible, the landscape reproduced therein. It was child's play for Messrs the Councillors [of Puidoux] to recognize at once in the purveyed image the waterfall of Forestay, located near the watermill of Chexbres, at the border between the two townships.
"A few weeks later, a French couple turned up at the municipal registry with a similar photograph in hand, inquiring about a certain painter named Marcel Duchamp, one of whose works represented the site in question.
"Mr. Jacques Caumont, Director of the Académie de Muséologie Evocatoire of Yvetot (France) and his wife, biographers of the painter and shrewd commentators on his work, knocked on every door suggested to them in the hope of finding someone who might enlighten them, but in vain: no one had heard of the painter Marcel Duchamp, despite his international notoriety in the art world, nor was anyone able to provide any information on the supposed visit or stay of this artist in the region." Translated from the French by Anthony Allen.
[7] Marcel Duchamp, "Where do we go from here?" Lecture at a symposium at the Philadelphia Museum College of Art, March 20,

1961, translated by Helen Meakins. Quoted from Gloria Moure, *Marcel Duchamp: Works, Writings, Interviews,* Barcelona 2009, p. 121.

[8] James Johnson Sweeney, *Eleven Europeans in America,* Bulletin of the Museum of Modern Art, vol. 13, nos. 4–5 (1946), p. 20, quoted from *The Writings of Marcel Duchamp,* ed. Michel Sanouillet and Elmer Peterson, New York 1973, p. 125.

[9] "BBC Interview with Marcel Duchamp," *The Late Show Line Up*, BBC Television Post-Production Center, London; interview conducted by Joan Blakewell, June 5, 1968, in Francis M. Naumann, *Marcel Duchamp: The Art of Making Art in the Age of Mechanical Reproduction,* New York 1999, p. 300.

[10] Duchamp, "Where do we go from here?" (note 7).

[11] "BBC Interview" (note 9), p. 300.

[12] Johnson Sweeney, *Eleven Europeans* (note 8).

[13] "Forel: Forêt dont l'usage était réservé au seigneur. Etymologie: Bas-latin forestis, tiré de forum, 'cour juridique'; la forme primitive du mot est forest; la graphie moderne n'apparaît que vers 1300." In Maurice Bossard and Jean-Pierre Chavan, *Nos lieux-dits: Toponymie romande,* Bière 2006, p. 126. In *Puidoux au coeur de Lavaux,* Eric Müller writes, "Forestay (rivière). De l'adjectif forestai, forestier, entouré de bois." (note 6), p. 305.

[14] "Eine Art 'Warenkatalog' von Ideen." See Herbert Molderings, *Marcel Duchamp: Parawissenschaft, das Ephemere und der Skeptizismus,* 3rd revised edition, Düsseldorf 1997, p. 80.

[15] Pierre Cabanne, *Dialogues with Marcel Duchamp, with an appreciation by Jasper Johns,* New York 1987, pp. 42–43.

[16] See August 2, 1945, in Gough-Cooper and Caumont, "Ephemerides" (note 2). See also Serge Stauffer, *Marcel Duchamp, Interviews und Statements,* Ostfildern-Ruit 1992, p. 30; and Luc Debraine, "Champ, Contrechamp, Duchamp: A Poetic Volte-Faced Homage," in Caroline Bachmann and Stefan Banz, *What Duchamp Abandoned for the Waterfall,* Zurich 2009, p. 7.

[17] "Lucerne, Saturday, June 1, 1968: On a card illustrated with a view of the lake and the alps in the distance, Marcel writes to Brookes Hubachek: 'We left Paris a week ago with just enough gas to make Basel ...' He and Teeny have been staying in Lucerne, far from the turmoil reigning in Paris. 'We hope that France will be all right again soon.' On an excursion in their Volkswagen one wet day to Lake Geneva, Marcel searches unsuccessfully for the waterfall at Chexbres, which inspired him for the setting of *Étant donnés.* But although he would like to have shown it to Teeny, the landscape of the water mill is now hidden in its overgrown ravine by tall trees." Quoted from Gough-Cooper and Caumont, "Ephemerides" (note 2).

[18] Molderings, *Marcel Duchamp* (note 14), p. 64. Translated from the German by CS.

[19] *The Blind Man, No. 2,* 33 West 17th Street, New York, May 1917, p. 6.

[20] Bonk, *The Box* (note 1), p. 170.

[21] Molderings, *Marcel Duchamp* (note 14), p. 32.

[22] *Étant donnés* was on the fifth floor of 210 West 14th Street until 1965 and, as of January 1, 1966 (two months before completing *Étant donnés*), on the fourth floor of 80 East 11th Street (room 403), with a separate entrance on 799 Broadway. From 1959 to 1968, Duchamp lived at 28 West 10th Street.

[23] As mentioned by Dr. Michel Badan, Cully, during a medical consultation, October 12, 2009.

[24] Monique Fong, *Duchamp des oiseaux,* Paris 2008, p. 56. Translated from the French by CS.

[25] See Georges Didi-Huberman, *La ressemblance par contact: Archéologie, anachronisme et modernité,* Paris 2008, p. 207.

[26] Duchamp, *Manual* (note 5), unpaginated.

[27] Anne d'Harnoncourt and Kynaston McShine, eds., *Marcel Duchamp,* Museum of Modern Art, New York 1973, Munich 1989, p. 280.

[28] See Walter Benjamin, *The Work of Art in the Age of Its Technological Reproducibility and Other Writings on Media,* Cambridge, Mass. 2008 (first published in 1936).

[29] d'Harnoncourt and McShine, *Marcel Duchamp* (note 27), p. 256.

[30] "Cette Dame appartient à Maria Martins / avec toutes mes affections / Marcel Duchamp 1948–49." Quoted in ibid., p. 306. In 1966 Maria Martins loaned the work for Richard Hamilton's exhibition *The Almost Complete Works* ... at Tate Gallery London, where it was on view before anyone had ever heard of *Étant donnés.*

[31] Taylor, *Étant donnés* (note 3), p. 94.

[32] In 1926, after its public debut at the Brooklyn Museum, *The Large Glass* was returned to its owner Katherine S. Dreier in Connecticut. The two panes of glass, placed on top of each other in the van, broke during transport. The damage was not discovered until six years later. When he repaired the work, Duchamp incorporated the damage as a new artistic element.

[33] "Besides which, as we have always said, the way out is your sculpture and my woman with the open pussy." From a letter to Maria Martins of April 7, 1949, in Taylor, *Étant donnés* (note 3), p. 409. Duchamp also called her his "Lady of Desire(s)"; see the letters of April 3, 1950 and October 25, 1951, ibid., pp. 417 and 423, and note 57 below. See also the excerpts reprinted in this publication, pp. 391–93.

[34] Ibid., p. 51. Taylor points out that, in the catalog *First Papers of Surrealism* (1942), Duchamp placed his work, *In the Manner of Delvaux,* beneath an etching by Hans Baldung Grien. Directly under the etching there is a Hegel quotation: "The history of the Fall sheds light on the universal theme of the birth of spiritual life." According to Taylor, the placement of the two works along with the quotation prefigures *Étant donnés.* The Hegel quotation specifically alludes to the waterfall and the light as a spiritual indication of what lies behind the visible.

[35] See. Mark Nelson and Sarah Hudson Bayliss, *Exquisite Corpse, Surrealism and the Black Dahlia Murder,* New York and

Boston 2006; and Jean-Michel Rabaté, *Given: 1° Art 2° Crime, Modernity, Murder and Mass Culture,* Brighton and Portland 2007.

[36] Ulf Linde, *Samtal med Marcel Duchamp,* quoted in Stauffer, *Marcel Duchamp* (note 16), pp. 123–24. Translated from the German by CS.

[37] Letter to Jean Mayoux of March 8, 1956, quoted in Naumann and Obalk, *Affectionately* (note 2), p. 348.

[38] Ana Dimke, *Duchamps Künstlertheorie: Eine Lektüre zur Vermittlung von Kunst,* Diss. Münden 2001, p. 28

[39] See Duchamp, *Manual* (note 5).

[40] Taylor, *Étant donnés* (note 3), p. 133. In the third chapter of his book (pp. 128–89), Taylor describes in detail the transport of *Étant donnés* to Philadelphia and its installation by the stepson of Paul Matisse in room 1759 at the Philadelphia Museum of Art.

[41] See Ursula Panhans-Bühler, *Gegeben sei: die Gabe; Duchamps Flaschentrockner in der vierten Dimension,* Hamburg 2009, p. 165.

[42] See Arturo Schwarz, *The Complete Works of Marcel Duchamp,* New York 2000, p. 114.

[43] On the history of the wooden door, see Taylor, *Étant donnés* (note 3), pp. 115–18.

[44] Denise Brown Hare in an interview with Michael Taylor, July 12, 1996, ibid., p. 145.

[45] John Russell's second article about the installation of *Étant donnés* at the Philadelphia Museum of Art, in *Sunday Times,* October 5, 1969, quoted from ibid., p. 177.

[46] Quoted from Stauffer, *Marcel Duchamp* (note 16), p. 229. Translated from the German by CS.

[47] Dimke, *Duchamps Künstlertheorie* (note 38), p. 31.

[48] Jean Starobinski, *Largesse,* Paris 2007, quoted in Panhans-Bühler, *Gegeben sei* (note 41), p. 163.

[49] Taylor, *Étant donnés* (note 3), p. 49.

[50] George Heard Hamilton and Richard Hamilton, "Marcel Duchamp Speaks." BBC Broadcast, 1959, cassette tape, *Audio Arts Magazine,* vol. 2, no. 4, London 1976; quoted from Stauffer (note 16), p. 81. Translated from the German by CS.

[51] "The Creative Act," in *The Writings of Marcel Duchamp* (note 8), p. 140.

[52] See Cabanne, *Dialogues* (note 15), p. 88.

[53] See Taylor, *Étant donnés* (note 3), p. 30.

[54] Bonk, *The Box* (note 1), p. 282.

[55] *The Box in a Valise* is signed, "pour Maria ce no. XII de vingt boîtes-en-valise contenant chacune 69 items et un original et par Marcel Duchamp, New York, April 6, 1946." The work itself is signed, "MD 1946." Ibid.

[56] On this subject, see the first chapter in the present text and the artist book *What Duchamp Abandoned for the Waterfall,* by Caroline Bachmann and Stefan Banz (note 16).

[57] See postscript of a letter to Maria Martins (April 3, 1950): "Our Lady of Desire is now flesh-pink: I am struggling against an overly fondant candy color." And in another letter to Martins (October 25, 1951), Duchamp writes, "As for Our Lady of Desires, I can manage to soften the paraffin and apply it to perfection (while still a little hot); I have obtained a mold that is perfect enough for what I want to do with it." Taylor, *Étant donnés* (note 3), p. 417 and p. 423.

[58] Ibid., pp. 112–13. For the source of his information, see his footnote 222, p. 127: Konstantin Akinsha, "The Mysterious Journey of an Erotic Masterpiece," *Art News,* vol. 107, no. 2 (February 2008), p. 94.

[59] Thierry Savatier, *L'Origine du monde. Histoire d'un Tableau de Gustave Courbet,* Paris 2006, pp. 115–20.

[60] About Duchamp's invitation by the Lacans see Bernard Marcadé, Marcel Duchamp. *La vie à crédit,* Paris 2007, p. 442. About the body hair, see Lydie Fischer Sarazin-Levassor, *Un échec matrimonial: Le coeur de la mariée mis à nu par son célibataire même,* Dijon 2004.

[61] Taylor, *Étant donnés* (note 3), pp. 128–89.

[62] Cabanne, *Dialogues* (note 15), pp. 19–20.

[63] Didi-Huberman, *La ressemblance* (note 25), p. 213.

[64] Ibid., p. 239.

[65] Ibid., p. 275.

[66] See Francis M. Naumann, "Notre dame des désirs: Gynomorphism in Marcel Duchamp's *Chat Ouvert*" in this publication. Naumann's new and very interesting research describes in detail this odd malformation.

[67] Marcel Duchamp, *Notes,* trans. Paul Matisse, Boston 1983, unpaginated.

[68] *The Bride Stripped Bare By Her Bachelors, Even, a typographic version by Richard Hamilton of Marcel Duchamp's Green Box,* trans. George Heard Hamilton, Stuttgart, London, and Reykjavik 1976, unpaginated (p. 104).

[69] Ibid. (p. 110).

[70] Note 35 (recto and verso), in Duchamp, *Notes* (note 67).

[71] See Didi-Huberman, *La ressemblance* (note 25), p. 288.

[72] See ibid., p. 301.

[73] See ibid., p. 304.

[74] See ibid.

[75] Molderings, *Marcel Duchamp* (note 14), pp. 46–47. Translated by CS.

[76] Panhans-Bühler (quoting an idea of Henri Poincaré), *Gegeben sei* (note 41), p. 39. Translated by CS.

Dominique Radrizzani

"The lake changes its dress every hour"
Marcel Duchamp in Vevey

The waterfall was rediscovered thanks to the Swiss Felix Kälin, who identified the site in early May 1980 (with the help of the municipalities, pp. 376–77). Some of the credit also goes indirectly to Serge Stauffer, the researcher, essayist, and photographer who knew, studied, and translated Duchamp and who gave an art seminar in spring 1979 at the Handelshochschule (business school) St. Gallen Kälin attended. Stauffer had no idea where the Swiss landscape that Duchamp photographed was located, and that was all it took to set Kälin on a quest that led him to this little piece of Swiss countryside.[1]

I was very glad to see a photograph by Stauffer (in the exhibition of the event, p. 383), who accompanied Kälin to the Forestay waterfall in March 1981. Not that his image has anything to do with this essay, but Stauffer, who indirectly invented the Forestay, was a key figure in my early childhood. He was a close friend of my parents (we would swap apartments during the holidays) and is part of my own family legend, and I would like to take this opportunity to pay tribute to his memory.

Marcel Duchamp and Mary Reynolds arrived at the Hotel Bellevue near Chexbres on August 5, 1946. The date is uncertain, but on around August 9 they moved to another hotel in Chardonne, which confusingly is also called Hotel Bellevue (pp. 366–70). We know that they visited Vevey on August 5 from a message they sent to the Hoppenots the next day:[2] "Ideal holiday thanks to you / both, dear Hélène, dear Henri. / The weather is doing its part and the lake / changes its dress every hour. / We loved Vevey yesterday, / Lausanne tomorrow we / hope with you. / We are looking forward to your phone call / and are impatient to / see you again / Affectionately / Marcel." In the postscript written by Mary Reynolds: "We are looking for a property for / you at the 'Régie Flouck' in Vevey."[3]

"A property for you." The couple is on an official mission for the Hoppenots, whose dream is to buy a small house in the region. On August 22 "Mister Flouck" takes Duchamp and Reynolds to visit a property in Chexbres. This Mr. Flouck, Mr. Edouard Flouck, who founded the Régie Flouck in 1941 (I include a copy of the advert that Duchamp often saw in the *Feuille d'avis de Vevey* when at the Hotel Bellevue, and a property-wanted advert published on August 22, possibly written by Duchamp [figs. 1 & 2]). I tracked down Edouard Flouck, the man who met Duchamp in Chexbres in 1946, but unfortunately I was just a little too late: he died on April 15 last year, nearly a centenarian (born in 1915, he was thirty-one in 1946). My consolation was that his daughter-in-law told me that a great artist Duchamp was never mentioned at Flouck family gatherings, and that Edouard Flouck probably never knew the importance of the man he met. Thanks to Mary Reynolds' detailed report,[4] and the invaluable help of regional experts,[5] we can identify the small property visited on August 22 as "La Folie" (fig. 3), the house at number 16, route de Chardonne (again, too late: the house was demolished in 2005). In 1946,

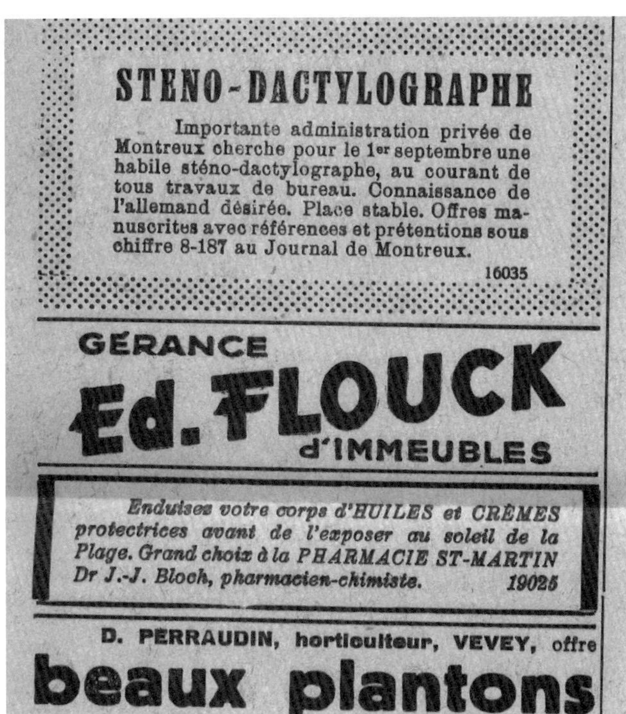

STENO-DACTYLOGRAPHE

Importante administration privée de Montreux cherche pour le 1er septembre une habile sténo-dactylographe, au courant de tous travaux de bureau. Connaissance de l'allemand désirée. Place stable. Offres manuscrites avec références et prétentions sous chiffre 8-187 au Journal de Montreux.

16035

GÉRANCE

Ed. FLOUCK

d'IMMEUBLES

Enduisez votre corps d'HUILES et CRÈMES protectrices avant de l'exposer au soleil de la Plage. Grand choix à la PHARMACIE ST-MARTIN Dr J.-J. Bloch, pharmacien-chimiste. 19025

D. PERRAUDIN, horticulteur, VEVEY, offre

beaux plantons

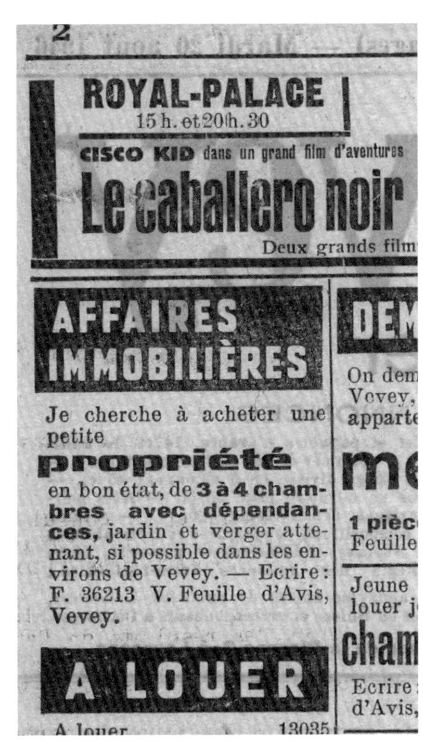

2

ROYAL-PALACE

15 h. et 20 h. 30

CISCO KID dans un grand film d'aventures

Le caballero noir

Deux grands film

AFFAIRES IMMOBILIÈRES

Je cherche à acheter une petite **propriété** en bon état, de **3 à 4 chambres avec dépendances,** jardin et verger attenant, si possible dans les environs de Vevey. — Ecrire: F. 36213 V. Feuille d'Avis, Vevey.

A LOUER

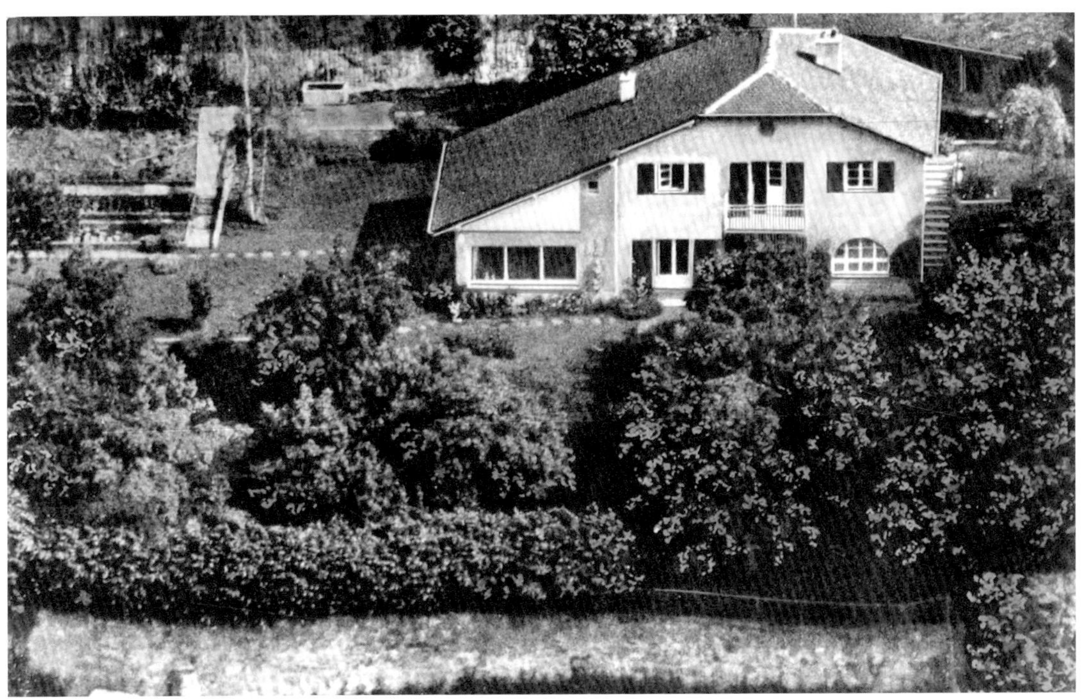

1 **Edouard Flouck, Advertisement,** *Feuille d'avis de Vevey,* Monday August 5, 1946, p. 2. Archives communales de Vevey. 2 **Property-wanted advertisement (Marcel Duchamp?),** *Feuille d'avis de Vevey,* Tuesday August 20, 1946, p. 2. Archives communales de Vevey 3 **Photograph of "La Folie,"** route de Chardonne 16 in Chexbres, 1970s. Françoise Nicod Collection.

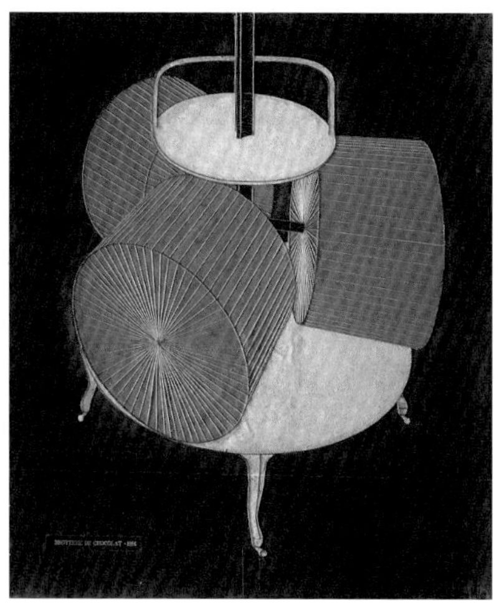

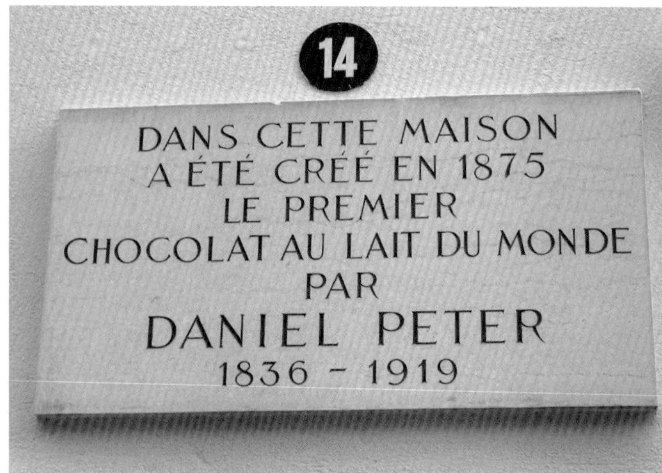

4 Marcel Duchamp, *Broyeuse de chocolat II* (Chocolate Grinder II), oil and thread on canvas, 65 x 54 cm, 1914. Philadelphia Museum of Art, Louise and Walter Arensberg Collection. **5 Chemin des Bosquets 14, Vevey.** Photograph by Dominique Radrizzani.

it was rented by "a doctor," Jean-Charles Biaudet (1910–2000), a future professor of history who ended up buying the house.

There was a heat wave in August 1946, with very hot days ending in magnificent sunsets. In the *Feuille d'avis de Vevey* of August 15, Duchamp would have read: "These mid-August days have a moving beauty about them. For anyone who is privileged enough, or duty-bound, to rise very early, the spectacle of nature is wonderful. At dawn, the light of the full, pale golden moon still reflects on the lake as a faint glow floats just above the Alpine skyline. Then / 'the dawn in the east unties / the golden hair that veils the cheek from him' [l'aurore matinale à l'orient dénoue / la chevelure d'or qui lui voile la joue] / and the sun's first rays replace the clear light of the moon, which slowly turns into a polished tin disk. / The air becomes so clear and transparent that the jagged outline, relief, and undulations of the closest and more distant mountains are all clearly visible to the naked eye from Vevey, as are the houses in Evian or the windows of the homes on the slopes of Mont Pèlerin. / All the colors are intense, the green foliage, the azure blue sky, the Prussian blue lake. On the horizon, the vineyards' leaves are already turning, and their fawn shade contrasts sharply with the deep, darkly wooded hilltops."[6]

In Vevey—though Duchamp didn't know it—was ground the "first chocolate in the world" (figs. 4 & 5). Also in the region (above Montreux), had just settled Paul Morand, who was asked by Duchamp in 1926 to write a preface for the *Brancusi* exhibition at the Brummer Gallery in New York. And one of *Rrose Sélavy's*[7] puns twisted Morand's famous *Ouvert la nuit* (Open All Night) into *Ovaire toute la nuit* (Ovary All Night).

Sacred and profane love

Did Duchamp push open the door of the Musée Jenisch when in Vevey? If he did, he would have discovered several Courbets, mostly dating from the painter's exile in La Tour-de-Peilz: *Portrait of Max Buchon* (1854), *La Dame à la mouette, poésie* (1875), *La Terrasse de Bon-Port* (1876), and particularly *Coucher de soleil sur le Léman* (Sunset over Lake Geneva, 1874) (fig. 6)—in my opinion one of Courbet's most beautiful landscapes, blending the fire of the setting sun with the liquid emerald of the lake, a point that will be of particular importance as we will see below. Fifteen years later, some of these works will find Duchamp; this time as they will travel to Philadelphia for the major *Courbet* retrospective in 1959.[8] In Vevey, Duchamp crossed paths with the ghost of Courbet, who had died seventy years earlier in La Tour-de-Peilz.

Much has been said about Duchamp's complex relationship with Courbet (fig. 7). On the one hand, Duchamp violently rejected Courbet as the father of what he called retinal art and all its ensuing abomination. At the same time, he is drawn to the realist painter's audacity. Several motifs seem to be taken from Courbet: the waterfall, the female nude with open legs.

Long before the work was created, the formulation *Étant donnés: 1° La chute d'eau, 2° Le gaz d'éclairage* appears as a preface to his notes for *La Mariée* (1912–15), published in *La boîte verte* in 1934. The expression dates from 1914–15 at the latest. In other words, the waterfall dates back at least thirty years before the Forestay, and before serving as a background to a "realist" installation it had already appeared in *La mariée mise à nu par ses célibataires, même* (The Bride Stripped Bare by her Bachelors, Even) (fig. 8). Its existence here is virtual, just like the waterfall in *Glissière contenant un moulin à eau en métaux voisins*. Duchamp said, "The wheel ... is supposed to be turned by a waterfall, which I did not bother depicting, to avoid 'falling into the trap of landscape painting.'"[9] It is treated as a hydraulic force over the mill. This is an important point, because the Forestay's location is known as "Sur le Moulin" (On the Mill) (p. 351–52).

Contrary to what has been often written, Duchamp had not seen Courbet's *L'Origine du monde* (The Origin of the World, fig. 1, p. 8), of which no reproduction existed and which only reappeared on the market in 1955. He was however familiar with *La femme aux bas blancs* (The Woman with White Stockings) from the Barnes collection, which he would

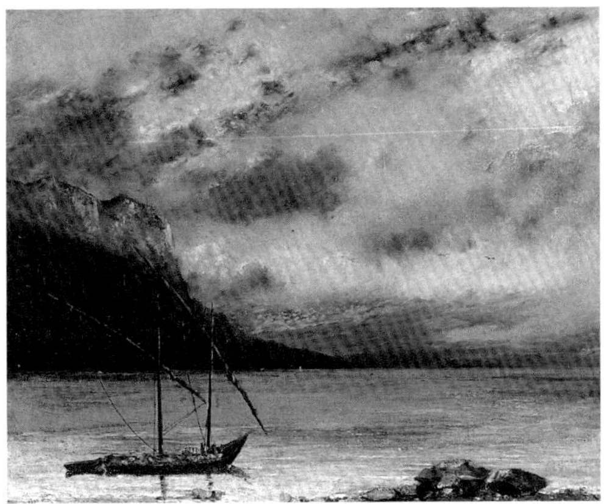

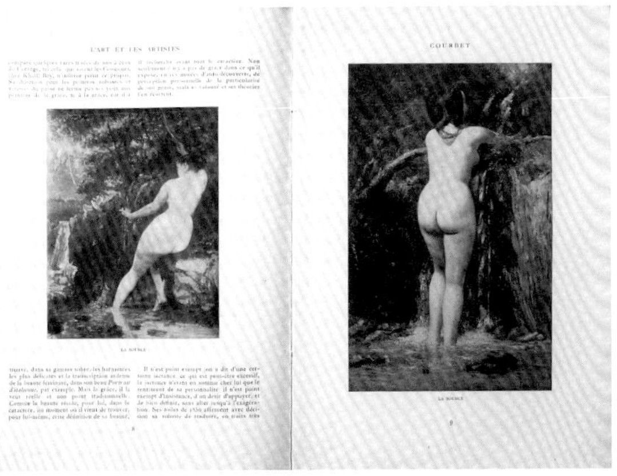

6 Gustave Courbet, *Coucher du soleil sur le Lac Léman* (Sunset on Lake Geneva)**,** oil on canvas, 54.5 x 65.4 cm, 1874. Musée Jenisch, Vevey. **7 Double page about Gustave Courbet** in Gustave Kahn, *L'art et les artistes*, no. 80 (October 1927), pp. 8–9.

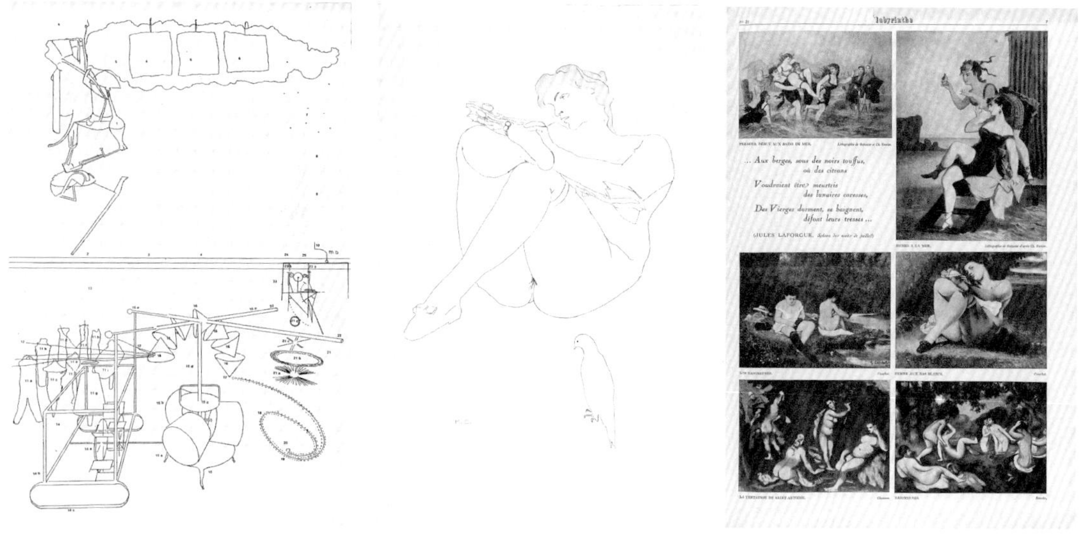

8 Marcel Duchamp, *The Large Glass Completed,* colored etching on Japan vellum, 50 x 33 cm, 1965. Private Collection. Diagram of *The Large Glass* showing the waterfall under the figure 13. **9 Marcel Duchamp, *Morceaux choisis d'après Courbet*** (Selected Details After Courbet), etching and aquatint, 42 x 25.5 cm, 1968. Philadelphia Museum of Art. Gift of Mme Marcel Duchamp. **10 *Labyrinthe,* no. 21** (July–August 1946), p. 7. Bibliothèque cantonale et universitaire, Lausanne.

quote in his *Morceaux choisis d'après Courbet* (Selected Details After Courbet) in 1968 (fig. 9). It is precisely in August 1946 that a reproduction of this painting appeared in Skira's Swiss journal *Labyrinthe* (fig. 10), the same journal in which André Breton has published two of Duchamp's works (including *La Mariée*) a few months before to illustrate his article on the origins and artistic perspective of Surrealism.[10] There is every reason to believe that *Labyrinthe* may have temporarily distracted Duchamp from the *Feuille d'avis de Vevey* during his holiday in Switzerland.

The July–August edition contains *The Woman with White Stockings* alongside a verse from Jules Laforgue's "Spleen des nuits de juillet": "Aux berges, sous des noirs touffus, où des citrons / Voudraient être meurtris des lunaires caresses, / Des Vierges dorment, se baignent, défont leurs tresses" (On the banks, under dense [bushy] blacks, where lemons / wait to be ravaged by lunar caresses / Virgins are sleeping, bathing, untying their braids). Courbet and Laforgue, the coincidence is just too much. Duchamp adores Laforgue. In 1912, he derived his *Nu descendant un escalier* (Nude Descending a Staircase) from one of Laforgue's poems.

As an illustration of the "co-intelligence of contraries," the Philadelphia installation combines and contrasts two antinomic styles of art: realism and allegory; realism because this nude in a landscape inevitably evokes Courbet and his brutality; allegory because the nude is carrying a lamp. Let us now look at this *gaz d'éclairage* (illuminating gas), this lamp burning pointlessly in broad daylight.

"Étant donnés" (Given) is an expression used in chess, in mathematical theory, and in criminology to expound a situation, a conjunction, a combination of several elements.

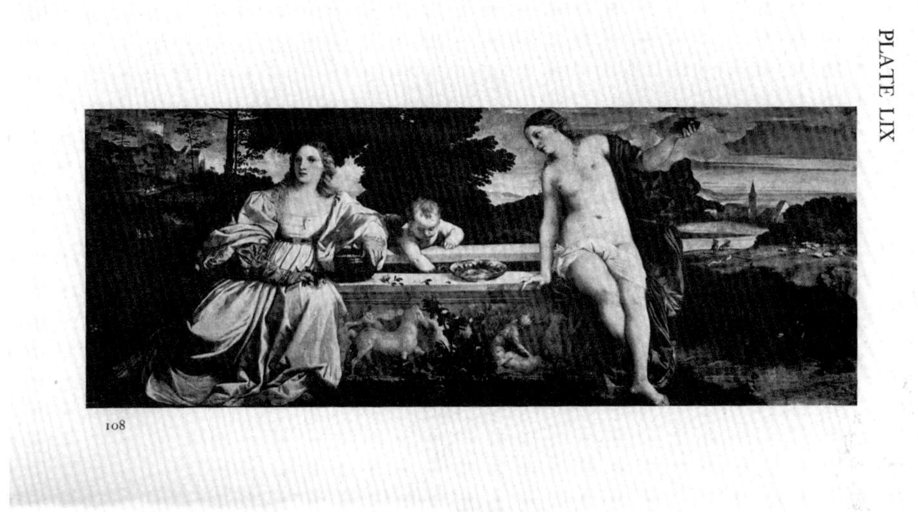

11 Titian, *Sacred and Profane Love,* oil on canvas, 118 x 270 cm, 1514. Galleria Borghese, Rome, in Erwin Panofsky, *Studies in Iconology*, New York 1939, pl. 59.

Strangely, while critics writing about Duchamp generally exercised little restraint, they appear to have avoided mentioning Erwin Panofsky. Perhaps because Panofsky was an art historian who embodied an accursed discipline and an artistic past from which Duchamp wished to break. Although both lived in the United States—Panofsky immigrated there in 1933—Duchamp and Panofsky didn't know each other or move in the same circles. Yet they shared common interests (perspective, iconology, image). Panofsky's essay on cinema, "Style and Medium in the Moving Pictures," was published in 1937 in the same edition of *Transition* (no. 26) with a cover by Duchamp.[11] Two years later, his *Studies in Iconology* was in every bookstore and Duchamp must have know of it since one of the chapters concerns Piero di Cosimo, his favorite among the Old Master painters.[12]

In this book, Panofsky detailed his theory on the three levels of understanding a work of art: (1) the motif (or different elements of the painting); (2) the theme, given the elements in the painting, say for example a waterfall and a lamp; and (3) the symbolic content. He included an extensive explanation of Titian's *Sacred and Profane Love* (1514) in the Galleria Borghese (fig. 11): "The nude figure is the 'Venere Celeste' symbolizing the principle of universal and eternal but purely intelligible beauty. The other is the 'Venere Volgare', symbolizing the 'generative force' that creates the perishable but visible and tangible images of Beauty on earth."[13] In all that has been written about the iconographic sources of *Étant donnés,*[14] the Venetian painter's masterpiece deserves mention as one of the rare examples of a Renaissance work on love involving a combination of water and a lamp lit in broad daylight (figs. 12 & 13).

On the same allegory, Panofsky outlined a theory on perception, holding that "it is the scholar, rather than the 'naïve beholder' who finds it difficult to interpret."[15] The "naïve

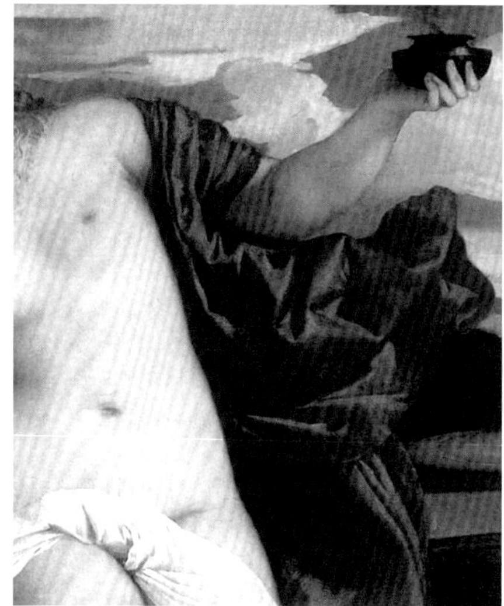
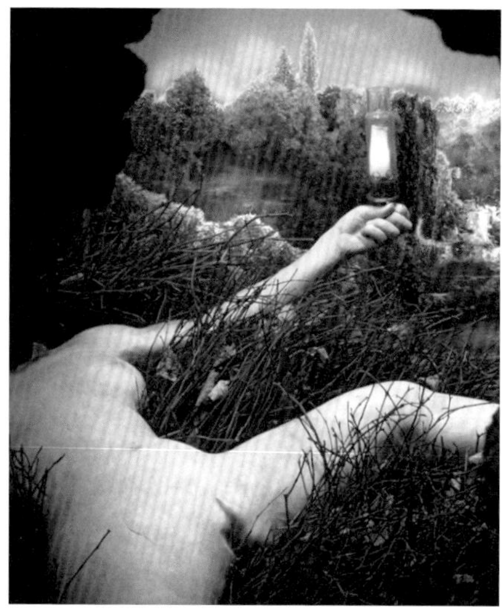

12 Titian, *Sacred and Profane Love* (detail), oil on canvas, 118 x 270 cm, 1514. Galleria Borghese, Rome. **13 Marcel Duchamp, *Étant donnés*** (detail), installation, 242.6 x 124.5 x 177.8 cm, 1946–66. Philadelphia Museum of Art. Gift of The Cassandra Foundation. **14 Marcel Duchamp, *Untitled*** (photo-collage landscape study for *Étant donnés: 1° La chute d'eau 2° Le gaz d'éclairage*), textured wax, pencil and

beholders" are the ones who hold the key to the puzzle. They are the naïve beholders or, simply put, the "regardeurs" who make the painting.

The point of the Green Ray in the full August sun

Lake Geneva is one of the most beautiful landscapes in the world, and hence an inexhaustible source of paintings (fig. 6). On February 14, 1877, Courbet sought to lure Whistler there: "I am here in a charming region, the most beautiful in the whole world, on the banks of Lake Geneva, surrounded by huge mountains. You would like the space here. There is the sea and its horizon, it is better than Trouville, because of the landscape."[16] Victor Hugo beautifully described the ocean-like Lake Geneva and its infinite horizon as a "moire immense." "Towards Geneva," he wrote, "the horizon imitated the ocean."[17]

At the risk of disappointing the reader, I doubt the waterfall really surpassed the lake. I doubt that Duchamp resolutely and stoically turned his back on the lake and its magnetic power.[18] This explicit confession should suffice: "The lake changes its dress every hour."

I find it quite unique and significant that the artist worked on two photo-collages at the same time, one of the waterfall (fig. 14) and another of a seascape (fig. 15): numbers 527 and 524, respectively, in the catalogue raisonné,[19] which demonstrates that they were created simultaneously. At the *International Surrealist Exhibition* in July 1947 at the Galerie Maeght in Paris, Duchamp presented his *Rayon vert* (The Green Ray), which was installed by Frederick J. Kiesler under Duchamp's direction from New York.

Through a circular, porthole-shaped opening, the viewer observed a sea with an intermittent Green Ray across its horizon. We know of this work, now lost, thanks to Herbert

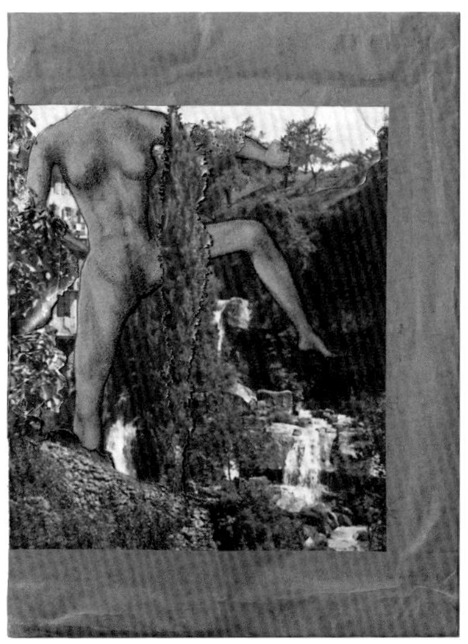

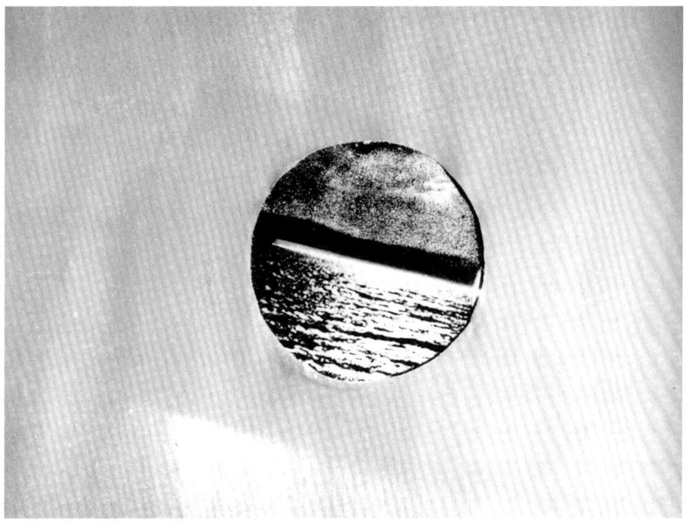

ink on tan paper and cut gelatin silver photographs, mounted on board, 43.2 x 31.1 cm, c. 1946. Private Collection. **15 Marcel Duchamp, "Un hublot laisse passer le rayon vert de Marcel Duchamp"** (A porthole lets Marcel Duchamp's Green Ray pass through it), exhibited in *Le Surréalisme en 1947,* Galerie Maeght, Paris 1947, destroyed. Photograph by Denise Bellon, © les films de l'équinoxe-fonds photographique Denise Bellon, Paris.

Molderings,[20] who correctly linked it to the Jules Verne novel of the same name. The central character in this novel is a bride (fig. 16). The very attractive Scottish heroine, Miss Helena Campbell, lives with her uncles and guardians Sam and Sib, who are determined to marry her off:

> "I marry? I!" exclaimed Miss Campbell, and her pretty lips parted with the most musical laughter that had ever resounded through the great hall.
> "Do you not want to be married?" asked her Uncle Sam.
> "Why should I?"
> "Never?" inquired Sib.
> "Never!" replied Miss Campbell, assuming a serious air, which her smiling lips quite contradicted. "Never, uncles—at least, not till I have seen—"
> "Seen what?" cried the brothers.
> "Until I have seen the Green Ray"[21]

That very morning in the *Morning Post,* Miss Campbell had read: "Have you sometimes observed the sun set over the sea? Have you watched it till the upper rim of its disk, skimming the surface of the water, is just about to disappear? Very likely you have; but did you notice the phenomenon which occurs at the very instant the heavenly body sends forth its last ray, which, if the sky be cloudless, is of unparalleled purity? No, perhaps not. Well, the first time you have the opportunity, and it happens but rarely, of making this observation, it will not be, as one might think, a crimson ray which falls upon the retina of the eye, it will be 'green,' but a most wonderful green, a green which no artist could ever obtain on his palette, a green which neither the varied tints of vegetation nor the shades of the most limpid sea could ever produce the like! If there be

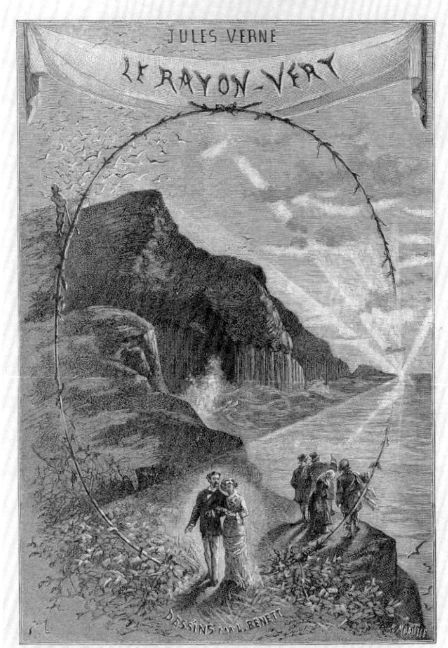

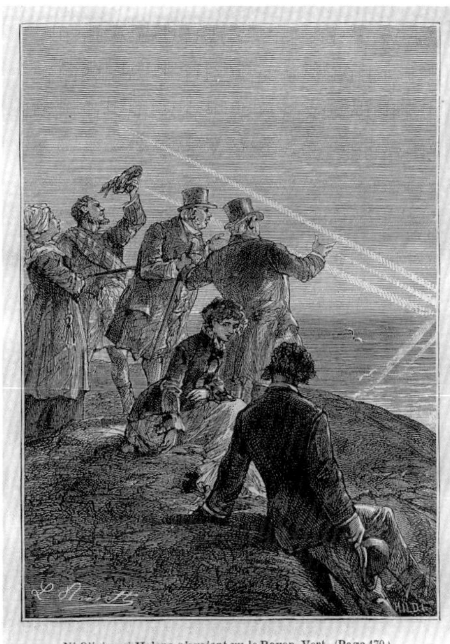

16 Frontispiece of *Le Rayon vert* (The Green Ray) by Jules Verne, drawing by Léon Benett engraved by Fortuné Méaulle, Hetzel, 1882. **17 Illustration from *Le Rayon vert* (The Green Ray) by Jules Verne,** drawing by Léon Benett engraved by Hildi (Henri Théophile Hildibrand), Hetzel, 1882.

green in Paradise, it cannot but be of this shade, which most surely is the true green of Hope!"[22]

This article and Miss Campbell's whim are the starting point for one of Jules Verne's spectacular journeys in which the young Scotswoman grows increasingly apart from her betrothed, the scholarly, priggish Aristobulus Ursiclos, and soon meets Olivier Sinclair.

Olivier Sinclair is a painter, Olivier Sinclair is single, Olivier Sinclair is Marcel Duchamp. From an amusing physics experiment involving the bride, he manages to create a surrealist composition that disconcerts his era, because the legendary Green Ray finally did appear, but the young lovers, too absorbed in each other, fail to see it (fig. 17). Sinclair-Duchamp nevertheless owes his life's masterpiece to it: "Although Oliver Sinclair had not seen the much-sought-after phenomenon, he was determined to have a souvenir of the last evening spent on Staffa. So one day he exhibited a remarkably fine sunset, in which a particular effect of a green ray of extreme intensity, as though it had been painted with liquid emerald, was very much admired. This picture aroused at the same time admiration and discussion; some said it was a natural effect marvelously reproduced, others ... maintained that it was purely imaginative and that nature could never produce such an effect."[23]

Was this comment the catalyst for Duchamp? To reconstitute a legendary painting based on an optical effect in the air that would generate controversy and address the question of Surrealism in scientific terms. To obtain his liquid emerald and the flash effect (again, according to Verne's text, the phenomenon allegedly lasts between a fifth and a quarter of a second[24]), Duchamp used an electric light placed behind gelatin films that cut the photograph at the horizon and provided the green.

Closer to Duchamp, we have Raymond Roussel,[25] an unconditional admirer of Verne who had already used *The Green Ray* on several occasions. Thus, *The Green Ray* appears in *Nouvelles impressions d'Afrique,* and was already spoken of in relation to its photographic reproduction: "a tripod, / When the *Green Ray* goes"[26] (note the presence of a tripod in the initial plans of assembly for *The Green Ray*;[27] see fig. 5, p. 242). In *Comment j'ai écrit certains de mes livres*—we know how much this book influenced Duchamp—the demonstration of the writing process is bathed in "matrimonial light," since "La peau de la raie sous la pointe du crayon vert" (The skin of the parting beneath the point of the green pencil) comes from the line "La peau de la raie sous la pointe du Rayon-Vert miroitait en plein soleil du mois d'août" (The skin of the skate beneath the point of the Green Ray gleaming in the full August sun).[28]

Did Duchamp's knowledge of his sources betray him? He certainly did not respect the conditions necessary for the optical phenomenon to occur. He placed us before a coastline with a dark mass obscuring the horizon, when it is the sun setting "on a clear horizon," the line where sky and sea meet, that must be observed.[29] It is a horizon of the sea and a perfectly pure sky that Verne's heroes are looking for.

It is extremely tempting to suppose that Duchamp is making fun of us with his seascapes, and that out of sheer laziness he used a photograph from his stay in Chexbres, developed at the same time as the waterfall (one of the rare moments in his life when he has a camera at his disposal, loaned to him by the Hoppenots). Molderings is correct to stress "the very calm surface of the water."[30]

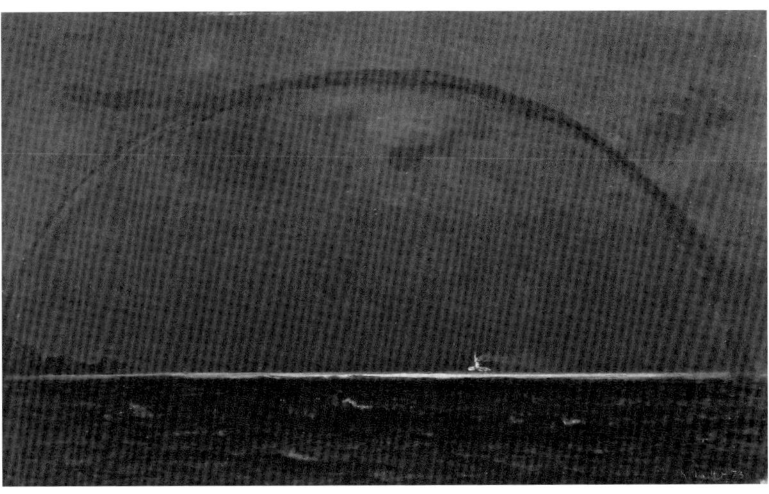

18 François Bocion, *L'Arc-en-ciel* (Rainbow), oil on cardboard, 21.5 x 31.5 cm, 1873. Private Collection, Pully.

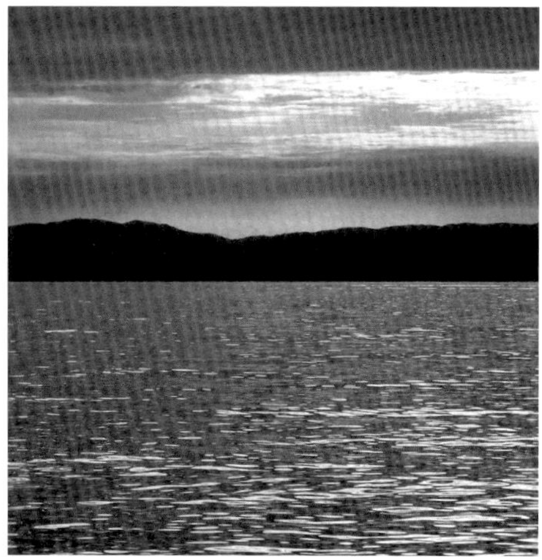
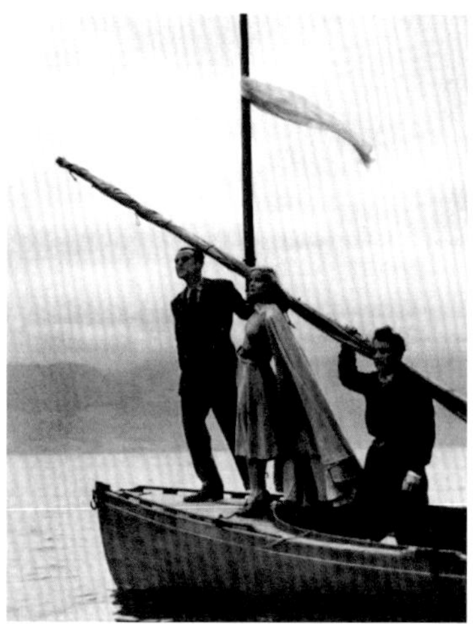

19 View of Lake Geneva, August 10, 2010 at 19:26. Photograph by Dominique Radrizzani. **20 Photograph from the set of *L'Éternel Retour* by Jean Cocteau,** 1943. Claude Séférian Collection.

The porthole shape is enough to make us forget the fresh water. Far from undermining our theory, the fact that Duchamp would have produced his sea using inappropriate and unconventional material, i.e., a Swiss lake of which he happened to have a photograph, was just like him. On top of the chromatic dispersion effects, Fata Morganas, rainbows (fig. 18), mirages, and all the optical phenomena observed and described by the scholar F.-A. Forel in his impressive *Monographie limnologique* on Lake Geneva,[31] Duchamp added a new one: *The Green Ray!*

Even the position of the sun corresponds to Lake Geneva, as the sun sets behind the Jura mountains in August as seen from Vevey or the Pointe de Rivaz, not far from the point where the Forestay flows into the lake (fig. 19). Given firstly the body of water and secondly the illuminating gas, *Le rayon vert* may well be one of the most beautiful portraits of Lake Geneva of the mid-twentieth century, alongside Cocteau's *The Eternal Return* (1943) (fig. 20), Hergé's *The Calculus Affair* (1954) (fig. 21), and Kokoschka's paintings.

The weather conditions in August 1946 produced spectacular paintings. And, for just one evening, the shores of the lake or the deck of the paddle steamer may have become the plateau of Staffa.

Translated from the French by Suzanne Kobine-Roy and Amélia Tarzi

Notes

[1] See Stefan Banz's introduction to this volume.

[2] On Duchamp and Reynolds' relations with the Hoppenots, see Paul B. Franklin, "Confidences: Un dialogue à travers les lettres de Mary Reynolds et le journal intime d'Hélène Hoppenot," *Étant donné Marcel Duchamp,* no. 8 (2007), pp. 106–45.

[3] Quoted in ibid., p. 119.

[4] Letter from Mary Reynolds to the Hoppenots, Chardonne, August 23, 1946; ibid., pp. 120–21.

[5] Thank you to the Chexbres municipality, Marjolaine Guisan, and Françoise Nicod (she identified the house beyond all doubt) for their assistance.

[6] *Feuille d'avis de Vevey,* Thursday August 15, 1946, p. 4.

[7] Marcel Duchamp, *Rrose Sélavy,* Paris 1939.

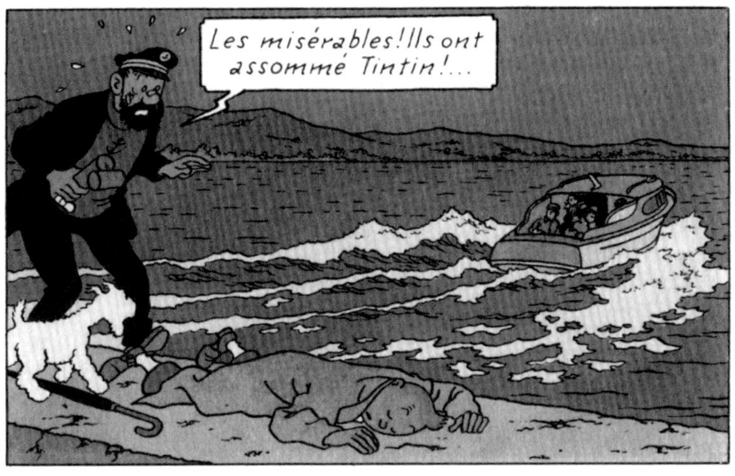

21 Hergé, *L'Affaire Tournesol,* Tournai 1954, p. 30.

[8] *Gustave Courbet,* foreword by Henry Clifford, exh. cat. Philadelphia Museum of Art / Museum of Fine Arts, Boston 1960, cat. no. 18 (*Max Buchon,* 1854) and cat. no. 85 (*La Terrasse de Bon-Port,* 1876). A few years earlier, the commissioner of the exhibition installed the Arensberg Collection at the Philadelphia Museum with Duchamp.
[9] "Apropos of Myself," notes written by Marcel Duchamp for his lecture at the City Art Museum of St. Louis (Missouri) on November 24, 1964.
[10] André Breton, "Genèse et perspective artistiques du surréalisme," *Labyrinthe,* no. 5 (February 15, 1945), pp. 10–11.
[11] Thank you to Molly Nesbit for this information.
[12] Marcel Duchamp, *Entretiens avec Pierre Cabanne* (1967), Paris 1995, p. 88.
[13] Erwin Panofsky, *Studies in Iconology,* New York 1939, p. 152.
[14] See in particular: Patrice Quéréel, "Rouen : le lac des signes," *Étant donné Marcel Duchamp,* no. 3 (2001), pp. 72–77; Herbert Molderings, "Un cul de lampe : réflexions sur la structure et l'iconographie d'*Étant donnés,*" ibid., pp. 106–9.
[15] Panofsky, *Studies in Iconology* (note 13), p. 152.
[16] Gustave Courbet, *Correspondance de Courbet,* ed. Petra ten-Doesschate Chu, Paris 1996, p. 526; see Dominique Radrizzani, "Bonjour Monsieur Bocion!" in *François Bocion. Au seuil de l'impressionnisme,* ed. Dominique Radrizzani, exh. cat. Musée Jenisch Vevey, Milan 2006, pp. 91–92.
[17] Victor Hugo, *Le Rhin* (letter 39, dated September 21, 1839, entry in the 1845 edition), Strasbourg 1984, p. 421.
[18] Caroline Bachmann and Stefan Banz published an artist's book ironically called *What Duchamp Abandoned for the Waterfall,* text by Luc Debraine, Zurich 2009.
[19] *The Complete Works of Marcel Duchamp,* 2. vols., ed. Arturo Schwarz, 3rd revised and expanded ed., New York 1997.
[20] Herbert Molderings, "Object of Modern Skepticism," in *The Definitively Unfinished Marcel Duchamp,* ed. Thierry de Duve, Cambridge, Mass. and Halifax 1991, pp. 257–61, 267–75.
[21] Jules Verne, *The Green Ray,* trans. M. de Hauteville, Holicong, PA 2003, p. 11. Originally published as Le *Rayon vert* in Paris in 1882.
[22] Ibid., p. 16.
[23] Ibid., p. 123.
[24] Ibid., pp. 22 and 122.
[25] See Michel Carrouges, *Les Machines célibataires* (1954), Paris 1976, pp. 54–78; René Radrizzani, "Roussel explorateur de nouveaux mondes," in *Junggesellenmaschinen / Les Machines célibataires,* ed. Jean Clair and Harald Szeemann, Venice 1975, pp. 144–55.
[26] Raymond Roussel, *Nouvelles Impressions d'Afrique,* Paris 1932, p. 69. Translated by GB/JF.
[27] Quoted in Molderings, "Object of Modern Skepticism" (note 20), fig. 6.11, p. 269. At the same *International Surrealists Exhibition* in 1947, Marcel Duchamp installed a billiard table in the Salle de la Pluie, possibly a reference to the same Roussel and to the "old billiard table" in *Comment j'ai écrit certains de mes livres* (1935).
[28] Raymond Roussel, *Comment j'ai écrit certains de mes livres,* Paris 1935, pp. 354–60.
[29] Jules Verne, *The Green Ray* (note 21), p. 17.
[30] See Herbert Molderings, "The Green Ray: Duchamp's Lost Work of Art," in this volume; originally titled "Le bonheur même. A la recherche du 'Rayon Vert' de Marcel Duchamp," delivered at the "Marcel Duchamp and the Forestay Waterfall" symposium, Cully, May 7, 2010.
[31] F.-A. Forel, *Le Léman. Monographie limnologique,* 3 vols., Lausanne 1892–1904: vol. 1, 1892; vol. 2, 1895; vol. 3, 1904; see the chapter "Optique" in vol. 3, pp. 408–571. See also Radrizzani, *François Bocion* (note 16), p. 93.

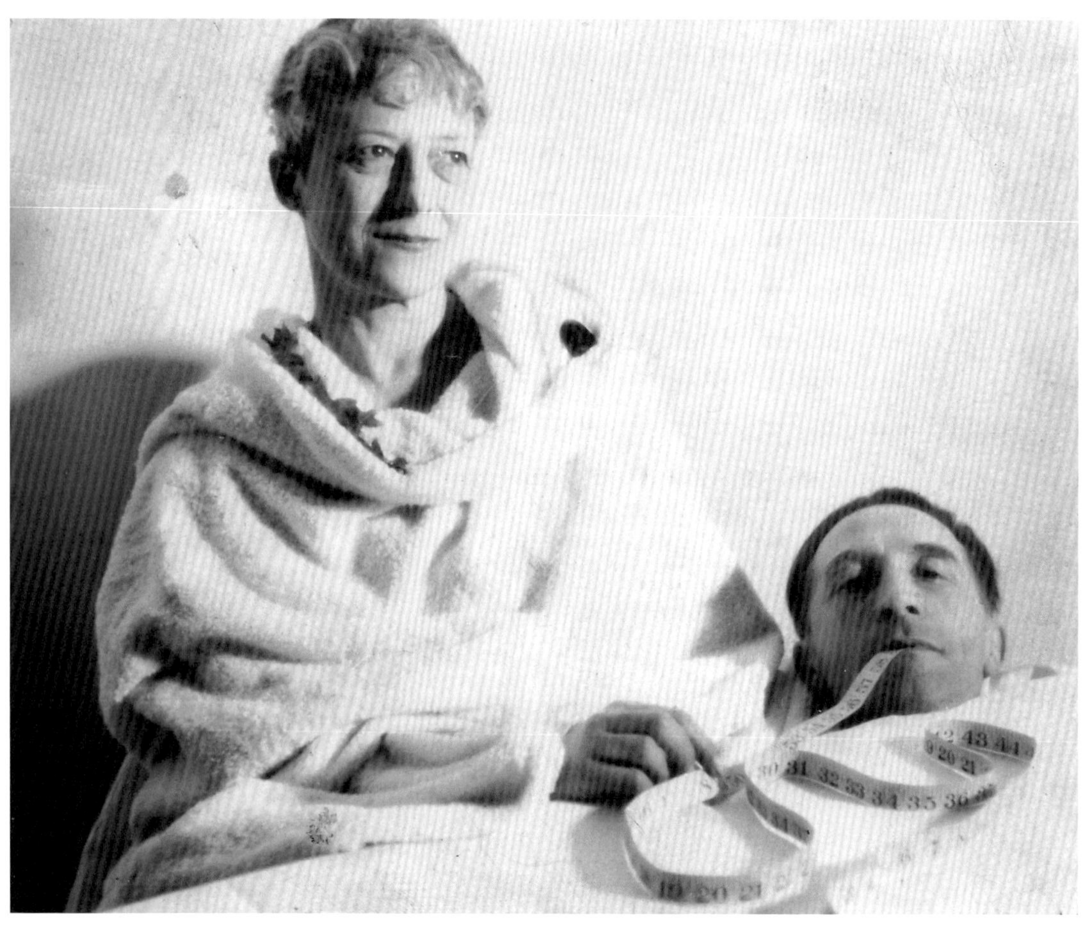

1 Konstantinos "Costa" Achilopulu, Mary Reynolds and Marcel Duchamp in London, gelatin silver print, 12.5 x 15 cm, 1937. Archives Marcel Duchamp, Villiers-sous-Grez.

Paul B. Franklin

In the Beginning, There Was Mary
Marcel Duchamp, Mary Reynolds, and the Landscape Backdrop of *Étant donnés*

Twenty years before Marcel Duchamp began his notorious romance with Maria Martins, and thirty years before he married Alexina "Teeny" Matisse, he fell for Mary Reynolds (fig. 1). As Henri-Pierre Roché wrote in his diary on July 3, 1924, "As a butterfly goes to certain flowers, so Marcel makes a beeline for beauty. He could not fail to be drawn to Mary."[1] From late 1923 or early 1924, when they commenced their relationship, until Reynolds's sudden death in September 1950, she and Duchamp were a couple. Pierre Cabanne asked Duchamp in 1966, "What importance did your meeting with Mary Reynolds have for you?" The artist replied, "That of a great friendship. Mary was a very independent woman.... It was a true liaison, over many, many years, very agreeable; but we were not hitched, in the 'married' sense of the word."[2]

Who *was* Mary Reynolds? Even if scholars systematically mention her in discussions of Duchamp's life, they usually do so only in passing, and rarely with specific reference to his work. My desire to explore this question—and augment the historical record in the process—inspired me in 2007 to devote an entire issue of *Étant donné Marcel Duchamp* to the Frenchman and his liaison with Reynolds, the longest he had with any woman. Delving anew into the archival material gathered for this volume, I want to pose a related question: What impact did Duchamp's relationship with Reynolds have on the conception and execution of *Étant donnés*? While Duchamp left tangible traces of both Maria Martins and Teeny Duchamp in his elaborate three-dimensional assemblage, references to Reynolds are more metaphorical. This is most clearly evident in the work's lush landscape backdrop.

Mary Louise Hubachek was born on October 19, 1891 into a bourgeois family in Minneapolis, Minnesota. She was the older of two children. Her father was a lawyer, and her younger brother, Frank Brookes Hubachek, followed in his footsteps. After graduating from Vassar College in Poughkeepsie, New York, in 1913, Mary enrolled in graduate school at the University of Minnesota, where she met Matthew Givens Reynolds Jr. They relocated to Greenwich Village in 1915 and married on July 24, 1916. The bohemian culture of Lower Manhattan, with its mix of artists, writers, actors, sexual and political radicals, and assorted nonconformists, greatly appealed to Mary.

Soon after the United States entered World War I, Matthew Reynolds enlisted in the army. He managed to survive the trenches, but died of influenza on January 10, 1919. While her husband was on the battlefield, Reynolds began an affair with Laurence Vail, a writer, artist, and the future husband of Peggy Guggenheim. He recorded details of their encounter in his unpublished autobiography: "She was so easy to be with, and also entertaining; I liked the way she talked and gossiped, the teasing, the quaint little jokes, the wicked twinkle in her eye, but always soft voiced, when she made malicious remarks about most of the people we knew in the Village. In spite of her long strong figure—she was fond of violent wrestling, she was cosy [*sic*] as well as ardent to sleep with. It was an odd figure, the smooth round robust calves, the concave stomach and small breasts, the long neck, the sharp but gentle birdlike face; she had a graceful awkwardness, like a girl in a picture by Cranach."[3] One day in 1917 or 1918, during an outing at the Lafayette Hotel at University Place and East 9th Street in Greenwich Village, Vail pointed out Duchamp to Reynolds.[4]

Unwilling to yield to parental pressure to remarry and start a family, and eager to leave behind her middle-class, Midwestern roots, Reynolds left the United States in spring 1921. After six months in Rome, she landed in Paris in November and took up residence near the Eiffel Tower in an apartment building at 14 rue de Monttessuy. She spent most of her time in Montparnasse, which had displaced Montmartre as the artistic and literary epicenter of the French capital. Reynolds survived thanks to her husband's modest military pension and regular funds from her father. In Montparnasse, she reconnected with Vail, who introduced her to Djuna Barnes and Peggy Guggenheim. The latter recalled, "Mary was dark with a beautiful figure. She was tall and elegant and had soft eyes. Her widow's peak was her great attraction. She was the only person in Bohemia with any money, and yet she was always broke because she lent it or gave it away the minute it arrived from America."[5] Generous, affable, charismatic, and carefree, Reynolds had a penchant for dancing and imbibing, and quickly became a local fixture in Montparnasse. In addition to Barnes and Guggenheim, she counted Samuel Beckett, Kay Boyle, Constantin Brancusi, Mary Butts, Alexander Calder, Jean Cocteau, Janet Flanner, Man Ray, Virgil Thomson, and many others among her intimates. The latter crowned Reynolds "the queen of American Montparnasse," while James "Jimmie the Barman" Charters—an ex-boxer from Liverpool who became the most popular bartender in the neighborhood—aptly described her as "the girl with the Mona Lisa smile."[6] The American writer Robert McAlmon similarly recalled: "Mary Reynolds was handsome and Mary Butts called her 'the world's most charming woman.' She was, indeed, too charming, and that is dangerous when accompanied by a striking head set magnificently on a fine neck above as fine a pair of shoulders and as beautiful a back as Aphrodite. She drank with, and was friends with, all of the better people of each type [in Montparnasse], artist, gigolo, drunk, scrubwoman, *poule,* or parasite, and generally she paid the bills of them all. Her friends of longer standing tried to prevent her from stranding herself by giving away her money to everyone."[7] Reflecting on her life in Montparnasse in the 1920s, Reynolds unabashedly admitted, "*I* had a good time!"[8]

Keen on perfecting her French, sometime between the summer of 1923 and early 1924, Reynolds hired Duchamp to give her language lessons. Their romance began soon thereafter. With her tall lithe physique and bobbed hair, the independent, cigarette-smoking, shy but hedonistic Reynolds resembled a New Woman, that sexy, liberated breed that captivated Duchamp when he first arrived in New York. As he confessed to an American journalist in September 1915, "The American woman is the most intelligent woman in the world today—the only one that always knows what she wants, and therefore always gets it."[9]

The first few years that Duchamp and Reynolds spent together were turbulent, due to his jealous attempt to guard his freedom and keep their love affair a secret. By the late twenties, however, he and Reynolds settled into a comfortable domestic existence. In 1929,

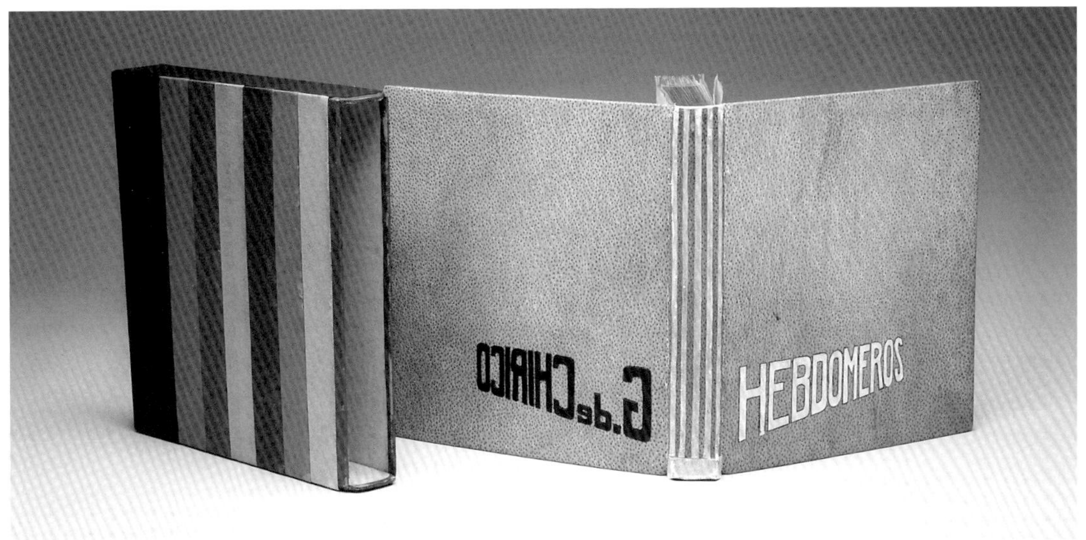

2 **Marcel Duchamp and Mary Reynolds, Binding for *Hebdomeros* by Giorgio de Chirico** (Paris: Éditions du Carrefour, 1929), executed c. 1936–39, unidentified leather, calf, Niger goatskin doublures, silk endpapers, and cardboard slipcase collaged with strips of colored paper. Mary Reynolds Collection, Ryerson and Burnham Libraries, Art Institute of Chicago.

she apprenticed with Pierre Legrain and learned bookbinding. Duchamp encouraged her in this pursuit, as Reynolds's niece remembered: "He was very influential in getting her organized and started. And I think he was quite interested in bookbinding himself.... I think she and Marcel did it together, and it meant something to both of them. It was highly personal."[10] Reynolds made a name for herself with her innovative creations, incorporating atypical materials—readymade objects like a thermometer, leather gloves, toad and snake skins, the handle of a teacup, a corset stay—as well as nontraditional methods of fabrication. Her enthusiasm for the craft, however, remained strictly noncommercial. Nearly all the books Reynolds bound were gifts from or to her artist and writer friends. As word of

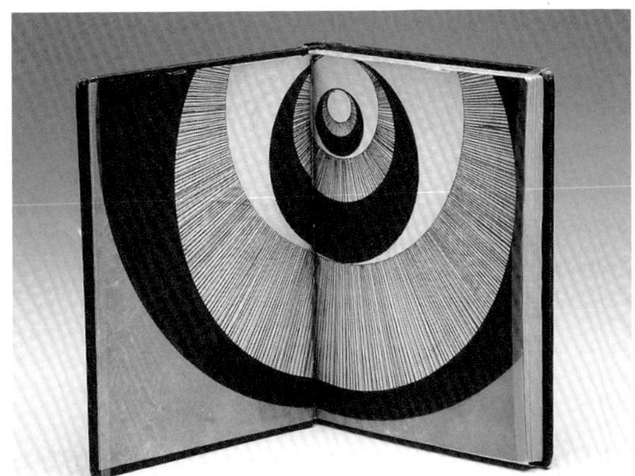

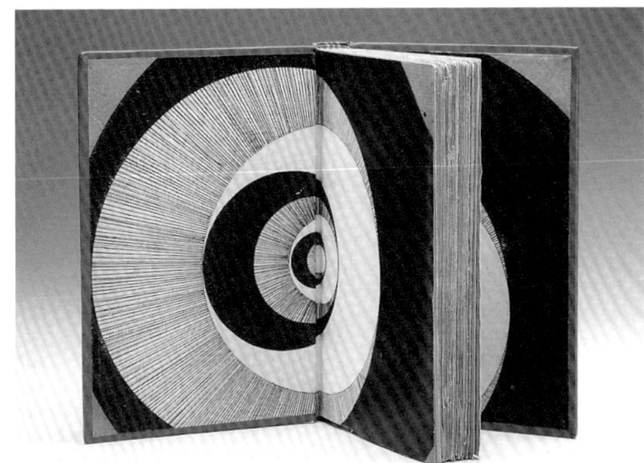

3 **Mary Reynolds, Endpapers of *Night Flight* by Antoine de Saint-Exupéry** (Paris: Crosby Continental Editions, 1932) **and *Loin de Rueil* by Raymond Queneau** (Paris: Gallimard, 1944) consisting of color proofs of *Corolles*, the first of Marcel Duchamp's twelve *Rotoreliefs (disques optiques)*, 1935. Mary Reynolds Collection, Ryerson and Burnham Libraries, Art Institute of Chicago.

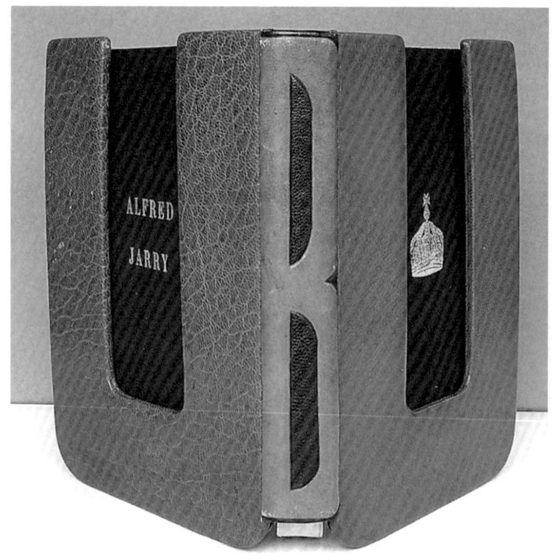

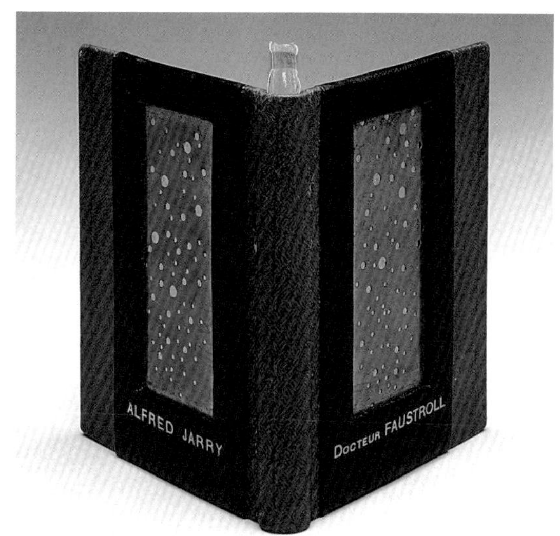

4 Marcel Duchamp and Mary Reynolds, Binding for *Ubu Roi: drame en cinq actes* by Alfred Jarry (Paris: Librairie Charpentier, 1921), executed 1935, morocco, levant, and Niger goatskin with silk and glassine endpapers. Archives Marcel Duchamp, Villiers-sous-Grez, formerly collection of Jacques Villon. **5 Marcel Duchamp and Mary Reynolds, Binding for *Gestes et opinions du docteur Faustroll, pataphysicien* by Alfred Jarry** (Paris: Librairie Stock, 1923), executed

her talent spread, many of these same individuals solicited her to bind their personal copies of the books they had written or illustrated. In the fall of 1940, when Duchamp realized that the design he had devised for a portable suitcase of miniature reproductions and replicas of his oeuvre was too fragile and unstable, he turned to Reynolds for help. Thanks to her bookbinding experience, they devised a new outer container with a back wall that folded down flat and to which the lid remained attached.[11] In acknowledgment of his companion's assistance, Duchamp presented Reynolds with the first copy of his redesigned deluxe edition of the *Boîte-en-valise* (1935–41) when it was completed.

From the mid-thirties to the early forties, Reynolds and Duchamp collaborated on a handful of bindings. As he informed his friend, the art dealer Julien Levy, on February 18, 1936, "Mary and I are going to London for a show of bookbinding (made by Mary)__ If you have any clients for bookbindings more or less deluxe ... let us know. I might design a cover if the book appeals to me."[12] In 1935, Duchamp conceived the binding for a 1921 edition of Alfred Jarry's *Ubu Roi,* and Reynolds executed three similar examples (fig. 4). In the late thirties, he designed another for *Hebdomeros* by Giorgio de Chirico, which Reynolds also produced (fig. 2). The title and author's name recede in perspective on the covers, an idea that Duchamp appropriated from his 1932 chess treatise *L'Opposition et les cases conjuguées sont réconciliées.* He and Brancusi had perfected the design for the latter in September 1931 while vacationing with Reynolds in a villa she had rented in Villefranche-sur-Mer on the French Riviera. Around 1935, Duchamp offered Reynolds several color proofs of *Corolles,* his first *Rotorelief (disque optique)* (1935), which was destined for the front cover of *Minotaure.* She eventually employed them as endpapers in her copies of *Night-flight* (1932) by Antoine de Saint-Exupéry and Raymond Queneau's *Loin de Rueil* (1944) (fig. 3). In the early forties, Duchamp and Reynolds also collaborated on the binding of

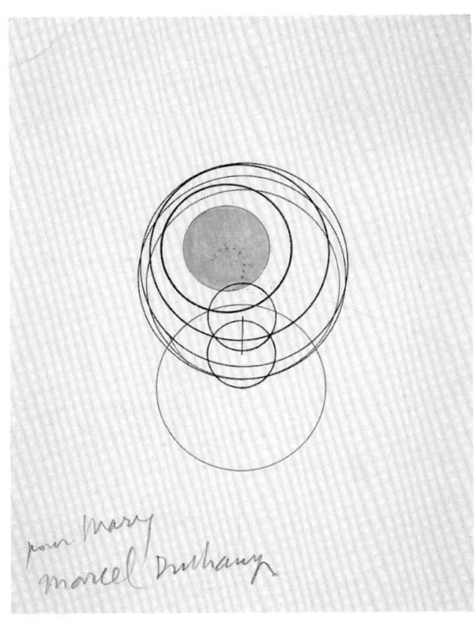

c. 1930–45, brown leather stamped in herringbone pattern, black morocco, perforated copper plates, and green glassine endpapers. Mary Reynolds Collection, Ryerson and Burnham Libraries, Art Institute of Chicago. **6 Marcel Duchamp, *Œuf à la coque*, prototype for the second *Rotorelief (disque optique)*,** pencil and red, blue, black, and orange ink on paper, 14 x 10.8 cm, c. 1935. Art Institute of Chicago. Gift of Frank Brookes Hubachek Sr.

her copy of his 1939 book of puns and spoonerisms entitled *Rrose Sélavy*. He supplied her with two castoff pieces of gray cardboard on which trial impressions of the title of his miniature museum in a suitcase had been stamped using a letterpress block. She mounted the two boards on the front and back covers over luxurious sienna, beige, and rose-colored goatskin, punched holes at each corner, and framed them in humble twine. For the endpapers, Reynolds drew an ant, mosquito, and leaf insect over stenciled fern fronds. The twine and insects both call to mind Duchamp's celebrated spider-web-like installation of string for the exhibition *First Papers of Surrealism* (October 14–November 7, 1942) held at the Whitelaw Reid Mansion in New York.

One additional binding that Duchamp and Reynolds probably conceived together is that for a 1923 edition of Alfred Jarry's *Gestes et opinions du docteur Faustroll, pataphysicien* (fig. 5). A worn copy of the same book, one of Duchamp's favorites, was discovered in his studio with *Étant donnés* after his death.[13] This binding echoes his preoccupation with peepholes. Over brown leather stamped with a herringbone pattern, Reynolds laid black goatskin. She then cut rectangles out of the front and back covers and fitted them with sheets of copper perforated with small holes of various sizes. Translucent green glassine endpapers partially obscure one's view through the many tiny openings, which seem to necessitate poly-ocular vision. While this binding harks back to Duchamp's interest in windows, like *Fresh Widow* (1920) and *La Bagarre d'Austerlitz* (1921), the pierced covers foreshadow the peepholes in the wooden door of *Étant donnés*, and evoke his cover design for the catalogue of *First Papers of Surrealism*. Furthermore, Reynolds owned Duchamp's paper prototype for his *Rotorelief* entitled *Œuf à la coque* (circa 1935) (fig. 6). Both the study and the round offset color lithograph upon which it was based are comprised of overlapping pairs of circles reminiscent of the openings in the door of *Étant donnés*.

In their essays in the catalogue of the recent exhibition devoted to *Étant donnés*, Michael R. Taylor and Melissa S. Meighan convincingly argue that Reynolds's bookbinding activities probably guided Duchamp in his decision to cover the body of the nude female figure in his tableau-construction in parchment, a material that Reynolds frequently utilized.[14] The couple also traveled to Denmark for two weeks in mid-July 1937, where they purchased leather, no doubt for their binding projects.[15] During this same voyage, Duchamp started jotting down his ruminations regarding what he termed the "inframince," a decidedly corporeal concept definable almost exclusively by way of example and largely perceivable through the senses. One of his notes on the subject, composed in the late thirties or early forties, includes several doodles of what appears to be a human figure with its knees bent and legs spread-eagle like Gustave Courbet's *Femme aux bas blancs* (circa 1861), which Duchamp saw on December 3, 1933 at the Barnes Foundation in Merion, Pennsylvania. The accompanying text reads: "Toiles d'araignée comme exemple d~~e~~'isolement / ~~d~~'<u>nat</u>ural' d'une <u>carcasse</u> / pseudo-géometrique / d'inframince" (Spider web as example of '<u>nat</u>ural' isolation of a <u>carcass</u> / pseudo-geometric / of inframince).[16] As Molly Nesbit has astutely observed, this drawing is an antecedent to the nude in *Étant donnés*.[17] Such a confluence of circumstances also suggests that Duchamp's note and the notion of the inframince in general may bear some relationship, however elusive, to Reynolds herself. Duchamp, in fact, articulated several of his initial thoughts on the inframince with regard to pairs and the infinitesimal differences between them, the archetype being the human couple.

From July 30 to September 2, 1946, Duchamp and Reynolds took a second trip that had a decisive impact on the creation of *Étant donnés*. At the invitation of Hélène and Henri Hoppenot, a French couple in Bern, they sojourned in Switzerland, where Henri Hoppenot was the French ambassador. Both he and his wife had artistic leanings. Hélène Hoppenot took up photography in 1918, producing two little-known portraits of Duchamp in the 1960s. Henri Hoppenot was an accomplished poet and best friends with Paul Claudel and Saint-John Perse (né Alexis Leger), two other literary luminaries in the French diplomatic corps. The Hoppenots also collected modern art by the likes of Georges Braque, Fernand Léger, Pablo Picasso, and Calder. Reynolds first met the diplomatic duo in New York in spring 1943, shortly after she escaped occupied France, where she had served with their daughter, Violaine, in the French Resistance. Coded reports from Violaine Hoppenot concerning atrocities committed during the Nazi occupation drove her father to resign from the Vichy government in October 1942. He was subsequently appointed General Charles de Gaulle's representative to the Provisional Government of the French Republic in Washington, D.C.

The Hoppenots adored Reynolds, and Hélène Hoppenot became one of her closest confidants. Soon after their introduction in New York, Reynolds presented them to Duchamp, and the two couples socialized regularly. Thanks to the Washington diplomatic circuit, the Hoppenots also knew Maria Martins and her ambassador husband. In her diary, on February 20, 1944, Hélène Hoppenot dismissed the work of Duchamp's new lover: "Dinner with the Martinses at the Brazilian Embassy. Maria is a sculptor (under this name) and creates works where mammary glands of every dimension spring forth on all sides. Obsession with breasts and poor imitations of works by Lipchitz, who was her teacher."[18] In years to come, through her eyewitness testimony, Hélène Hoppenot revealed that Reynolds was fully aware of Duchamp's affair with the Brazilian artist, which at moments deeply distressed her. On September 7, 1947, Hélène Hoppenot reported, "Mary herself is hardly cheerful, and I sense that her instability derives from what she calls 'Marcel's desertion.'... She has learned that Marcel has been seeing a lot of Maria Martins.... I tell her: 'I don't think that she presents a great danger for you.' I think to myself that it is [Maria's] extreme animalism that attracts the one-hundred-percent intellectual who is Marcel Duchamp."[19]

Through diplomatic channels, Henri Hoppenot obtained a visa for Reynolds in spring 1945 so she could return to Paris. At the same moment, he was named ambassador to Switzerland, moving to Bern. After the war, Reynolds corresponded regularly with the Hoppenots and saw them often. On New Year's Day 1946, Hélène Hoppenot mentioned in her diary, "To Lausanne with Mary Reynolds. Speaks of Marcel Duchamp. Praises his sensitivity, intelligence, totally original, but complains of his complicated character.... 'Obviously,' she sighs, 'our liaison is far from perfect. But life with Marcel is nonetheless preferable to life without Marcel.' Her suffering also comes from his having stopped creating, painting, before he even met her, ... but Marcel's friends, for whom she remains 'the American,' accuse her, in permitting him to live comfortably like a bourgeois, of having sterilized him at the same time."[20]

Duchamp followed Reynolds back to Paris in May 1946, and they invited the Hoppenots to dinner on June 30. The French couple suggested that they spend their summer vacation in Switzerland. Hélène Hoppenot remarked in her diary a month later, "Arrival of Mary and Marcel [in Bern]. A bit uncomfortable to find themselves in an official embassy without being married, living, as Mary says, 'in sin.' They also want to go settle into a small hotel."[21] After several days with their hosts, Duchamp and Reynolds traveled to Chexbres, a small Swiss village some ninety-two kilometers southwest of Bern nestled atop a steep, rocky landscape dotted with vineyards and overlooking Lake Geneva. On Hélène Hoppenot's recommendation, they took a room at the nearby Hôtel Bellevue in a tiny hamlet of the same name, where she had stayed as a girl. Duchamp and Reynolds remained there from August 5 to August 9. Remarkably situated along a cliff road, the Hôtel Bellevue offered a breathtaking panoramic view across Lake Geneva onto the Alps, a scene that previously had enchanted artists like Courbet, Félix Vallotton, and Ferdinand Hodler. Duchamp, however, preferred the frothing waterfall visible from the other side of the Hôtel Bellevue. Known as the Forestay, this cascade flows from Lake Bret, rushing down a boulder-strewn ravine that separates Chexbres and the neighboring village of Puidoux, to which Bellevue belongs and whose residents were known as "les Amoureux" (the Lovers), a nickname that must have delighted Duchamp.[22] At the turn of the twentieth century, the view of the waterfall from the Hôtel Bellevue was even more dramatic, as period postcards confirm.

Enthralled with the pastoral countryside, Reynolds wrote the Hoppenots the day after their arrival at the Hôtel Bellevue and announced, "We are overflowing with gratitude for the hospitality of the Embassy of France under the sign of the Hoppenot's [*sic*]—and are still travelling under their star from Bellevue to Bellevue—This one is very pleasant as an initiation to Bellevue—Chardonne—which we anticipate as perfection." In a note

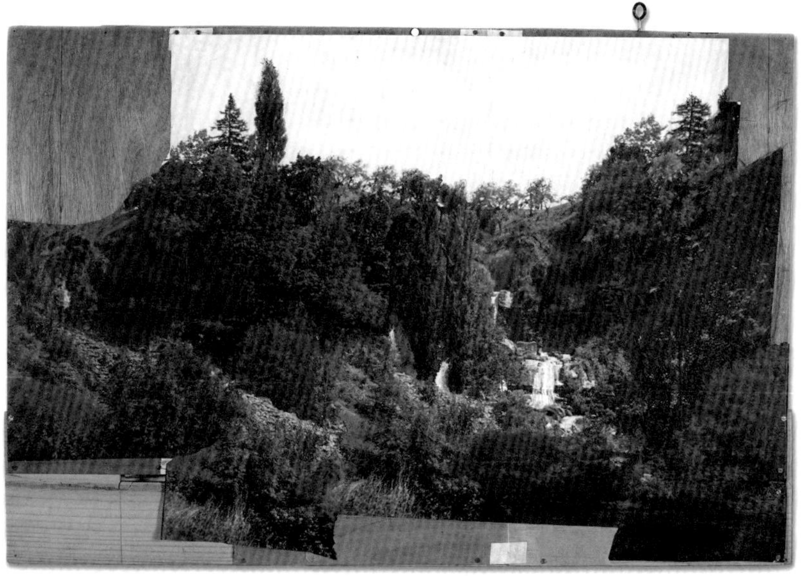

7 **Marcel Duchamp, *Landscape collage on plywood*** (study for landscape backdrop of *Étant donnés: 1° la chute d'eau, 2° le gaz d'éclairage*), collage of cut gelatin silver photographs over paper, with paint, graphite, crayon, ballpoint-pen ink, and adhesive on plywood, with pressure-sensitive tape, 67 x 99.4 cm, 1959. Philadelphia Museum of Art. Gift of Mme Marcel Duchamp.

appended to the same letter, Duchamp focused on the climate and the landscape: "'Vacation' ideal thanks to you two, dear Hélène dear Henri__ The weather is turning against us and the lake changes color every hour."[23] Before leaving the Hôtel Bellevue, Duchamp took a series of photographs of the Forestay and the craggy yet verdant terrain around it, looking toward Chexbres. These images formed the basis of the landscape backdrop of *Étant donnés,* a fascinatingly complex artwork that he produced through an intricate, labor-intensive process (fig. 7). On August 19, 1946, ten days after visiting Chexbres, Duchamp wrote James Johnson Sweeney from nearby Chardonne, where he and Reynolds stayed in a second Hôtel Bellevue: "Spending 4 nice weeks in Switzerland which is the model-country for those who hate politics and economy."[24]

Even though Duchamp lived apart from Reynolds through most of the late forties—he in New York and she in Paris—he remained in contact with the Hoppenots. In December 1949, just before he commenced work on the landscape backdrop of *Étant donnés,* he sent them no. 18/20 of the deluxe edition of his *Boîte-en-valise* as a Christmas present (fig. 8). On the inside lid, he inserted a 1948 pencil drawing entitled *Réflection à main.* With its combination of English and French spelling, the title is a neologism derived from *miroir à main,* or "hand mirror." In French, *miroir* is also a figurative term for "reflection," meaning a manifestation or result, such as a "reflection of reality." In this drawing on paper, Duchamp literally translated the double valence of his title. He portrayed the reflection of a human hand in the form of a realistic sketch of a fist clutching a round handle at the top of which he cut out a circular aperture. Behind the opening, he mounted a hand mirror. In looking at the drawing, one perceives *both* a hand and, through the aperture, the reflection of one's eye, as in René Magritte's three versions of *Objet peint: œil* (1936–37) (fig. 9) or his two paintings *Le Faux miroir* (1929 and 1935). Presenting a large human eye with clouds reflected on its surface, the latter canvases, the title of which translates as *The False Mirror,* strongly resonate with *Réflection à main.*

The verbal-visual pun of *Réflection à main* must have amused the Hoppenots, who, like Duchamp and Reynolds, were bilingual and had a great fondness for poetry. The drawing's particular relevance, however, surely eluded them. In retrospect, it is obvious that the composition prefigured the hand of the nude in *Étant donnés*. In his three-dimensional assemblage, Duchamp substituted the mirror for a bec Auer, strategically positioning the mannequin's appendage and her lamp on the same horizontal axis as the waterfall, as if to direct the viewer's attention to the glistening cascade. He did something similar in a photo-collage study for *Étant donnés* created around 1946 (fig. 10). In a pose reminiscent of Auguste Rodin's *Iris, messagère des dieux* (conceived 1890–91), the giant, erect, Gaia-like nude points to the diminutive chute with her left foot. In this study, Duchamp also wrapped both the collaged photographic elements and the blue strips of paper framing them around the edges of the board to which they are glued, much like a bookbinding.

When Duchamp gave *Réflection à main* to the Hoppenots, he conceded their role in his discovery of Chexbres and the nearby Forestay waterfall. In so doing, he also alluded to Reynolds as the instigator of this revelation, since she first presented him to the couple. The dialogue between *Réflection à main,* the hand in *Étant donnés* that grips the bec Auer, and Reynolds herself is even richer when one examines the derivation of her married name. In *An Etymological Dictionary of Family and Christian Names,* a tome first published in New

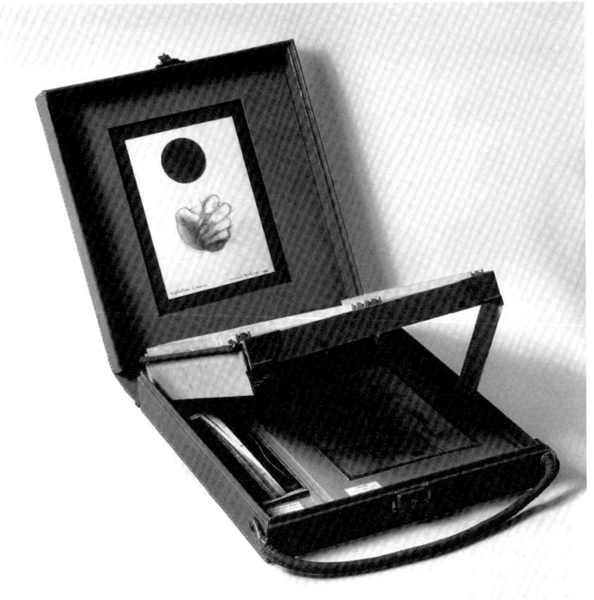

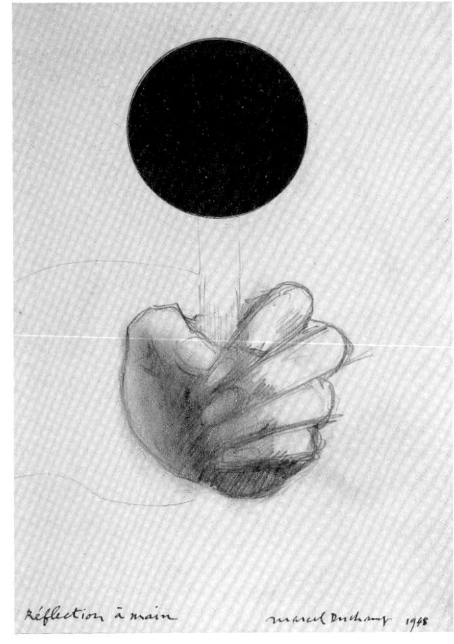

8 Marcel Duchamp, *Réflection à main* (Hand Reflection), pencil on paper with collage of a circular mirror covered by a circular cutout of black paper inserted on inside cover of deluxe edition no. 18/20 of the *Boîte-en-valise*, 23.5 x 16.5 cm, 1948. Private Collection, formerly Henri and Hélène Hoppenot Collection.

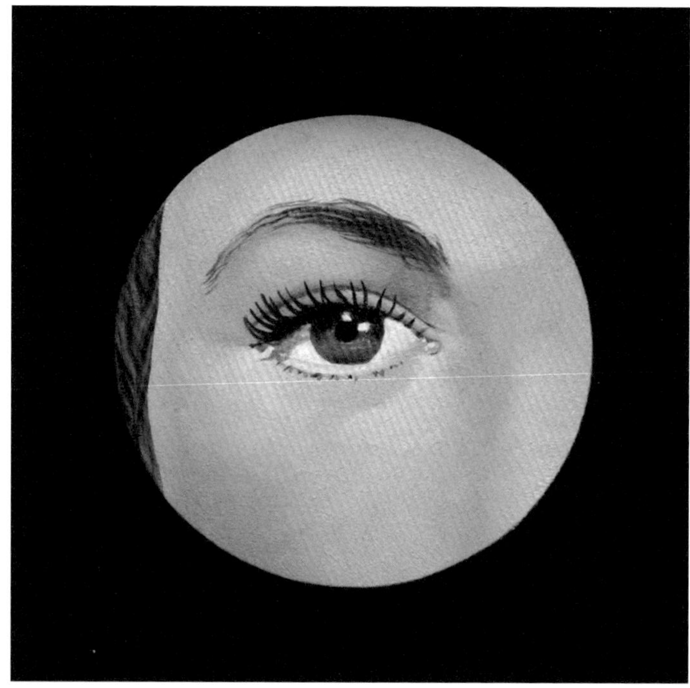

9 René Magritte, *Objet peint: œil* (Painted Object: Eye), oil on canvas, 27 x 24.8 x 14.4 cm, 1936–37. Art Institute of Chicago. Through prior gift of Arthur Keating. **10 Marcel Duchamp, *Untitled*** (photo-collage landscape study for *Étant donnés: 1° la*

York in 1857 but reprinted several times, most recently in 1990, William Arthur offers the following analysis of the surname Reynolds: "(Sax.) Sincere or pure love from, *Rhein,* pure, and *hold,* the old English for love. It also may signify strong or firm hold."[25]

The landscape background in *Étant donnés* was Duchamp's personal homage to Reynolds and the affectionate hold she had over him for nearly thirty years. As such, it extends that great tradition of woman as nature, and more specifically woman as waterfall, which reached its apogee in nineteenth-century France with such iconic and erotically charged canvases as *La Source* (1856) by Jean-Auguste-Dominique Ingres or Courbet's 1862 and 1868 paintings of the same title (fig. 11). A more contemporary precedent for *Étant donnés,* and one that scholars largely have overlooked, is André Breton's *Arcane 17,* written between August and October 1944 while he traveled on the Gaspé Peninsula on the majestic eastern coast of Quebec with his new lover, Elisa Claro (née Bindorff). He had met the brunette, blue-eyed Chilean beauty in Duchamp's presence the previous December at Larré's, a small French café and restaurant at 50 West 56th Street in Manhattan. Breton derived the title of his text from the seventeenth major arcanum in a deck of tarot cards. Identified as the Star, this trump card traditionally depicts a kneeling nude woman with one foot submerged in a body of water and the other on land. With a star blazing overhead, she grasps a jug in each hand, pouring the liquid from one into the pool and that of the other onto the ground. Her gesture signifies renewal. Roberto Matta repeated this same iconography in his illustration *Les Étoiles,* which appeared in the deluxe edition of *Arcane 17* published in New York in 1944 (fig. 12).

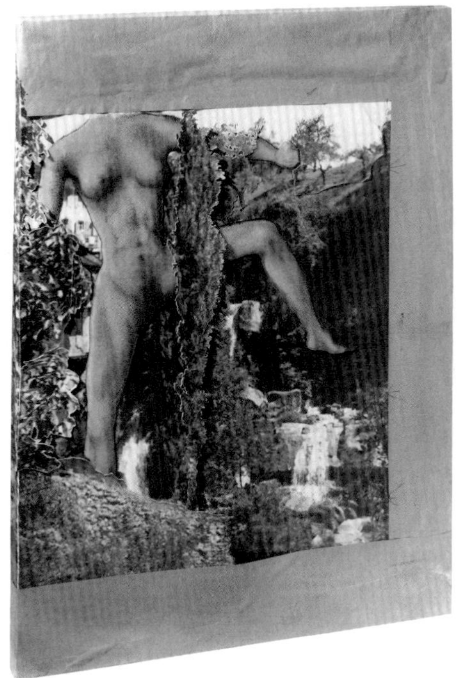

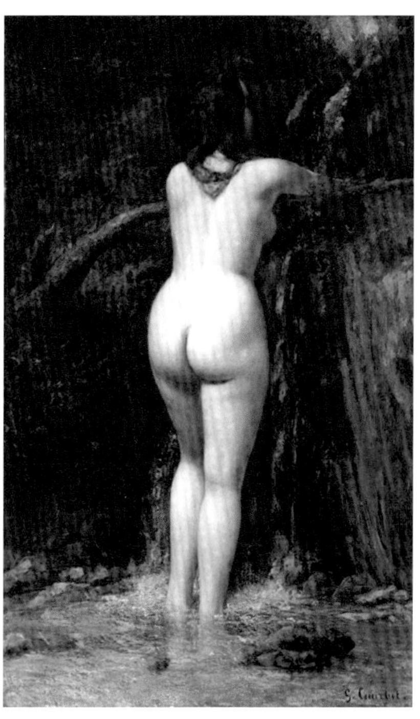

chute d'eau, 2° le gaz d'éclairage), textured wax, pencil, and ink on paper and cut gelatin silver photographs, mounted on board, 43.2 x 31.1 cm, c. 1946. Private Collection. **11 Gustave Courbet, *La Source*** (The Source), oil on canvas, 120 x 74.3 cm, 1862. Metropolitan Museum of Art, New York, H. O. Havemeyer Collection. Bequest of Mrs. H. O. Havemeyer.

The mystery, or arcanum, that Breton explored in *Arcane 17* is that of woman, the source and savior of life. As World War II drew to an end and the myriad atrocities that men had perpetrated against one another took on mounting significance, he proffered that the sole hope for humanity was the "*salvation of the earth by woman*."[26] With references ranging from ancient myths and esotericism to autobiography, philosophy, and historical commentary, *Arcane 17* was Breton's poetic meditation of his love for Elisa, who had given his life new meaning after his wife, Jacqueline, left him in 1943 for the American artist David Hare. As he had done in *Nadja* (1928), Breton singled out Melusine as the archetype of femininity. "She is the only one I see who could redeem this savage era," he proclaimed.[27] Appearing throughout *Arcane 17*, this at once monstrous and seductively phallic fairy figure from European folklore possessed a serpent- or fish-like lower body and personified the spirit of fresh waters. According to legend, Melusine's husband discovered her true identity when he covertly gazed through the peephole of a door and observed her bathing. Given the association of Melusine with water, it seems more than mere coincidence that the front cover of the French-Canadian school notebook in which Breton wrote *Arcane 17* features a color reproduction of one of Quebec's many streaming cascades.[28] Furthermore, the window display that Duchamp installed for *Arcane 17* in New York in April 1945 included a nearly nude female mannequin with a metal faucet attached to her right thigh, suggesting both the symbolism of the seventeenth major arcanum and that of Melusine.

The trip that Reynolds and Duchamp took to Switzerland in the summer of 1946 was their last vacation as a couple. In the years that followed, his relationship with Martins

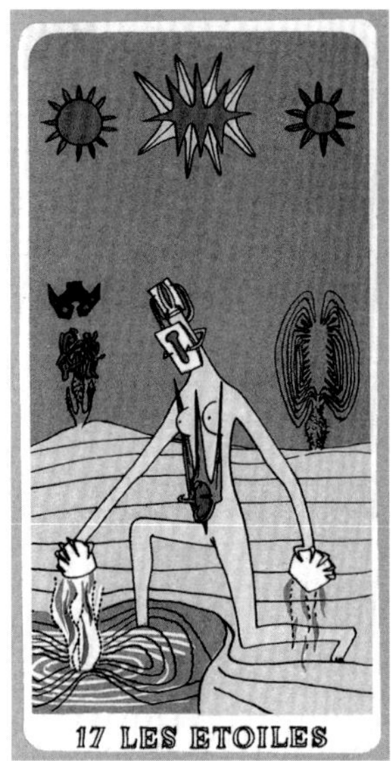

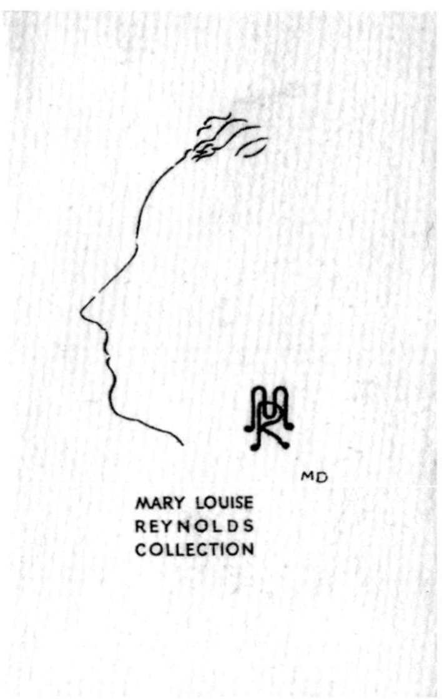

12 Roberto Matta, *Les Étoiles* (The Stars), color photolithograph for the deluxe edition of *Arcane 17* by André Breton, 12.7 x 7 cm, New York: Brentano's, 1944. **13 Marcel Duchamp, Bookplate for the Mary Reynolds Collection,** engraving, c. late 1953–early 1954. Mary Reynolds Collection, Ryerson and Burnham Libraries, Art Institute of Chicago.

intensified. On May 27, 1947, Reynolds lamented to Djuna Barnes, "Marcel [is] wedded to New York instead of [to] me."[29] Despite the distance that developed between them, when Reynolds fell seriously ill in spring 1950, Duchamp became quite concerned. As her health declined, Frank Brookes Hubachek asked him to return to Paris to be with his ailing sister. Duchamp obliged and was at her side on September 30, 1950, when she died of uterine cancer. The loss was a great shock, as he expressed to the Hoppenots on October 14: "A profound thanks for your letter and your sentiments regarding your close friendship with Mary, whose departure, at once so quick and so slow, remains an enigma."[30] Seven weeks later, he vented his anger to Man Ray: "The same thought of rage that I have had ever since the beginning of her illness haunts me now, since she herself, in a kind of unconscious suicide, refused all surgical procedures when in fact there perhaps would still have been time__ Nothing like a single death to bring home the damned stupidity of the rest of humankind."[31]

After Reynolds's demise, Duchamp remained in Paris for two months, living in her house. He settled her affairs and shipped her possessions to her brother in Chicago, keeping only three mementos for himself: two unfinished bindings for books by Jarry and an ornate silver necklace made by Calder, whom he met in 1931 thanks to Reynolds. The emotional toil was intense, compounded by the fact that Martins had abandoned him several months earlier, returning to Brazil with her retired husband and children. As Duchamp wrote to Martins from Paris on November 19, 1950, "Everything seems to be more and more tangled, and I am almost suffering physically from my stay here, despite the very great kindness shown me by my family and a few friends."[32] The loss of both Reynolds and Martins within such close proximity to one another may have instigated Duchamp to change the orientation of the nude figure in *Étant donnés*.[33] For personal as well as technical reasons, around 1950, he decided that the towering giantess who had dominated the landscape in his photo-collage of circa 1946 and who thereafter had been modeled in plaster based on casts of Martins' body now would lie recumbent.

From summer 1938 until her death, Reynolds rented a small house at 14 rue Hallé on a quiet cul-de-sac in southern Paris. Over the years, she and Duchamp decorated the interior, and in her workshop off the kitchen, they bound books. Behind the house was a private garden in which the couple entertained countless friends and family, many of whom attested that this tranquil parcel of nature was a refuge from the hurly-burly of Paris. Jean Suquet, who visited the house in summer 1949, recalled, "The space seemed quite vast because the neighboring gardens were not closed off by high walls. And further afield, a convent added to the greenery."[34] Reynolds was deeply attached to her unpretentious corner of paradise, and so was Duchamp, who spent most nights there when in Paris. Immediately after Reynolds's death, he encouraged the Hoppenots to buy the property for their daughter and her family, assuring them in a letter of October 14, 1950, "At whatever price, this house is a jewel and can easily be transformed for little money."[35]

For Duchamp, 14 rue Hallé and its bucolic garden were laden with memories, which undoubtedly resurfaced as he elaborated the backdrop for *Étant donnés,* a project he began in the early fifties only *after* Reynolds died. The association of Reynolds with Arcadian landscapes may explain the palette he chose for the backdrop. Even though he photographed the waterfall between Chexbres and Puidoux in the thick of summer, he ultimately depicted it in the blistering colors of early autumn, the season of Reynolds's untimely death. As he was methodically constructing the backdrop for *Étant donnés,* Duchamp also was working closely with the Art Institute of Chicago and Reynolds's brother to catalogue her library and bindings, which the latter had donated to the museum. Duchamp designed the bookplate for the collection in 1951, featuring a profile portrait of Reynolds wearing monogrammed earrings that Calder had fashioned (fig. 13), supervised the layout of the 1956 catalogue, and wrote the introduction. In his text, the Frenchman championed his departed companion as "a great figure in her modest ways."[36] During this busy period, he also visited the rustic country estate of Frank Brookes Hubachek on Basswood Lake in the wilderness of northern Minnesota, a remote region that Reynolds had known well. Duchamp discovered here yet another picturesque landscape associated with her, and one that once again wedded water and vegetation. As a thank you to his host, on August 21, 1953, he produced on site a highly impressionistic sketch of Basswood Lake beneath the moonlight, using blue blotting paper, ink, pencil, crayon, talcum powder, and chocolate (fig. 1, p. 87). The aqueous countryside boasts a marked resemblance to the backdrop of *Étant donnés.*

At first glance, Duchamp's work can appear hermetic and impenetrable. Once one delves into the details of his life, however, one realizes that much of his art emanated from the pleasures or sorrows of his daily existence. *Étant donnés* is no exception. William Copley, who purchased the artwork and donated it to the Philadelphia Museum of Art, said it best: "It is ... 'frank' in the sense that it is a monument to certain actions between men and women that some editors still delete if called by a certain four-letter word. But we are willing to use a four-letter word, *life,* and wink slyly."[37] In June 1966, when a Belgian journalist asked Duchamp, "What have you done with your life?" he retorted, "I used painting, art, to establish a modus vivendi, a way of understanding life. That is to say, probably, to try and make of my life itself a work of art, instead of spending my life making works of art.... One could very well make of one's life—the way one breathes, behaves, reacts to things or to people—one can easily understand it as a painting, if you will, a tableau vivant, even a cinematic picture."[38] A labor of love, *Étant donnés* is the silent, virtually motionless, but nonetheless entrancing, Technicolor film of Duchamp's passionate relationships with Mary Reynolds, Maria Matins, and his wife, Teeny.

I would like to thank Jack Perry Brown, director of the Ryerson and Burnham Libraries at the Art Institute of Chicago, and Jacqueline Matisse Monnier for their assistance in obtaining illustrations for my text.

Notes

[1] Henri-Pierre Roché, "Amours croisées: extraits d'un journal intime, 1924–50," *Étant donné Marcel Duchamp,* no. 8 (2007), p. 232. Unless otherwise noted, all translations are my own.

[2] Pierre Cabanne, *Entretiens avec Marcel Duchamp,* Paris 1967, p. 125.

[3] Laurence Vail, "Here Goes," unpublished autobiography, circa 1945, p. 60. I am grateful to the Estate of Laurence Vail for allowing me to quote from this document.

[4] Ibid., pp. 98–99.

[5] Peggy Guggenheim, *Out of This Century: Confessions of an Art Addict,* preface by Gore Vidal, intro. Alfred H. Barr Jr., New York 1979, p. 28.

[6] Virgil Thomson, *Virgil Thomson,* New York 1966, p. 110; and James "Jimmie the Barman" Charters, *This Must Be the Place: Memoirs of Montparnasse,* ed. Morrill Cody, intro. Ernest Hemingway, London 1934, p. 115.

[7] Robert McAlmon, *Being Geniuses Together, 1920–1930,* revised with supplementary chapters by Kay Boyle, New York 1968, pp. 103–4.

[8] Quoted in Charters, *This Must Be the Place* (note 6), p. 295.

[9] [Henry McBride], "The Nude-Descending-a-Staircase Man Surveys Us," *New York Tribune,* September 12, 1915, sec. 4, p. 2.

[10] Paul B. Franklin, "Remembering Aunt Mary: An Interview with Marjorie Hubachek Watkins and Frank Brookes Hubachek Jr.," *Étant donné Marcel Duchamp,* no. 8 (2007), p. 11.

[11] Ecke Bonk, *Marcel Duchamp, the Box in a Valise: De ou par Marcel Duchamp ou Rrose Sélavy, Inventory of an Edition,* trans. David Britt, New York 1989, p. 159.

[12] Marcel Duchamp, letter to Julien Levy, February 18, 1936, Julien Levy Papers, box 11, folder 31, Philadelphia Museum of Art Archives, Philadelphia Museum of Art, Philadelphia.

[13] Michael R. Taylor, "The Genesis, Construction, Installation, and Legacy of a Secret Masterwork," in *Marcel Duchamp: Étant donnés*, exh. cat. Philadelphia Museum of Art, Philadelphia and New Haven 2009, p. 145.
[14] Ibid., p. 76; and Melissa S. Meighan, "A Technical Discussion of the Figure in Marcel Duchamp's *Étant donnés*," in ibid., pp. 245–47.
[15] See Marcel Duchamp, letter to Henri-Pierre Roché, July 26, 1937, Carlton Lake Collection of French Manuscripts, box 60, folder 2, Harry Ransom Humanities Research Center, University of Texas, Austin, Texas.
[16] Marcel Duchamp, *Marcel Duchamp, Notes*, preface Pontus Hultén, arrangement and trans. Paul Matisse, Centre national d'art et de culture Georges Pompidou, Paris 1980, n.p., note 24.
[17] Molly Nesbit, "Last Words (Rilke, Wittgenstein) (Duchamp)," *Art History* 21, no. 4 (December 1998), p. 547.
[18] Mary Reynolds and Hélène Hoppenot, "Confidences: un dialogue à travers les lettres de Mary Reynolds et le journal intime d'Hélène Hoppenot," *Étant donné Marcel Duchamp*, no. 8 (2007), p. 114.
[19] Ibid., p. 124.
[20] Ibid., pp. 117–18.
[21] Ibid., p. 119.
[22] See *Dictionnaire géographique de la Suisse*, ed. Charles Knapp and Maurice Borel, Neuchâtel 1903, vol. 2, p. 125.
[23] Reynolds and Hoppenot, "Confidences: un dialogue" (note 18), p. 119.
[24] Marcel Duchamp, letter to James Johnson Sweeney, August 19, 1946, Estate of James Johnson Sweeney, Raith House, Newport, County Mayo, Ireland.
[25] William Arthur, *An Etymological Dictionary of Family and Christian Names*, New York 1857, p. 224.
[26] André Breton, *Arcane 17*, ed. and presented by Henri Béhar, Paris 2008, p. 176.
[27] Ibid., p. 186.
[28] See the facsimile of the notebook's front cover in ibid., p. 253. While Béhar (ibid., p. 16) claims that the cascade is "probably the Montmorency Falls," which at eighty-four meters high are the most impressive in the province, the size and shape of the chute, not to mention its escarpment, belie such an identification. It is more likely one of the several waterfalls in Mont-Tremblant National Park, Quebec's oldest and second largest provincial land reserve, containing six major rivers as well as four hundred lakes and streams.
[29] Mary Reynolds, letter to Djuna Barnes, May 21, 1947, Djuna Barnes Papers, series II, box 14, folder 21, Literary Manuscripts, Archival and Manuscript Collections, Special Collections, Hornbake Library, University of Maryland, College Park, Maryland.
[30] Reynolds and Hoppenot, "Confidences: un dialogue" (note 18), p. 140.
[31] Marcel Duchamp, Mary Reynolds, and Man Ray, "A Friendship in Words and Pictures," *Étant donné Marcel Duchamp*, no. 8 (2007), p. 201.
[32] "Marcel Duchamp's Letters to Maria Martins, 1946–1967/68," trans. Paul Edwards, in *Marcel Duchamp: Étant donnés* (note 13), p. 419.
[33] During discussion following the presentation of this essay at the Duchamp symposium in Cully, Herbert Molderings first suggested the connection between Mary Reynolds's death and the reorientation of the nude figure in *Étant donnés*.
[34] Jean Suquet, "14 rue Hallé," *Étant donné Marcel Duchamp*, no. 8 (2007), p. 202.
[35] Reynolds and Hoppenot, "Confidences: un dialogue" (note 18), p. 140.
[36] Marcel Duchamp, "The Mary Reynolds Collection," in *Surrealism and Its Affinities: The Mary Reynolds Collection*, comp. Hugh Edwards, Art Institute of Chicago, Chicago 1956, p. 6.
[37] William Copley, "The New Piece," *Art in America* 57, no. 4 (July–August 1969), p. 36.
[38] Marcel Duchamp, interview with Jean Antoine, filmed June 1966, *Signé: Marcel Duchamp*, Radio-Télévision belge de la communauté française, broadcast 1971.

Dalia Judovitz

Landscape as Ironic Causality in Duchamp's *Étant donnés*

> The air moves like a river and carries the clouds with it; just as running water carries all the things that float upon it. Leonardo, *Notebooks*

> The possible without the / slightest grain of ethics of esthetics / and of metaphysics. Marcel Duchamp, *Notes*

On the occasion of his first artistic retrospective at the Pasadena Museum of Art in 1963, Duchamp commented to Francis Roberts, "My landscapes begin where da Vinci's end. The difficulty is to get away from logic."[1] Did his comment imply a hidden reference to the landscape of *Étant donnés: 1° La chute d'eau, 2° le gaz d'éclairage* (Given: 1° The Waterfall 2°, The Illuminating Gas, 1946–66) (pp. 4–5), whose veristic outlook shocked the critics habituated to his more conceptual interventions? Duchamp's insistence that his incidental landscape *Moonlight on the Bay at Basswood* (1953) (fig. 1) be exposed along with his far better known works, and his production of two landscape drawings in 1959 that established explicit links between *Étant donnés* and *La mariée mise à nu par ses célibataires, même* (The Bride Stripped Bare by Her Bachelors, Even or The Large Glass, 1915–23) (fig. 2) not only back this contention, but also suggest the necessity of re-examining the role played by landscape in relation to vision in these works. However, such an analysis of landscape must take into account Duchamp's emphatic denial of returning to art, to the idea and genres of painting, drawing, or sculpture: "I can't do a painting, or a drawing, or a sculpture. I absolutely can't. I'd have to think for two or three months before deciding to do something which would have significance. It couldn't be simply an impression, an amusement. It would have to have a direction, a sense. That would be the only thing that would guide me. I'd have to find it, this sense, before I started."[2]

Made in the wake of the completion of *Étant donnés* in 1966, Duchamp's remark alerts the viewer that his return to landscape should not be understood simply as return to painting and the retinal. It cautions the viewer to consider Duchamp's appeal to visual semblance as a strategic move that would fuel conceptual speculation. This essay examines how the notion of landscape informs Duchamp's works, and in what sense it can be said to represent a completion of Leonardo's project. Does the depiction of landscape imply a return to ordinary perception and the retinal, given its apparent "verism,"[3] or does it also bring into play issues of logic and conceptual considerations? This paper will explore Duchamp's representation of landscape as an ostensible return to the physical laws that subtend its logic only to "strain" them a little through the introduction of irony. Landscape will be at issue as a hinge notion, whose transformations mark its modes of appearance in *The Large Glass* and *Étant donnés* and whose ironic character will serve to challenge notions of "reality" and "causality" as fundamental givens.

Duchamp's interest in landscape is surprising, since he explained to Roberts that his choice in *The Large Glass* to use glass rather than canvas was driven by the idea of doing

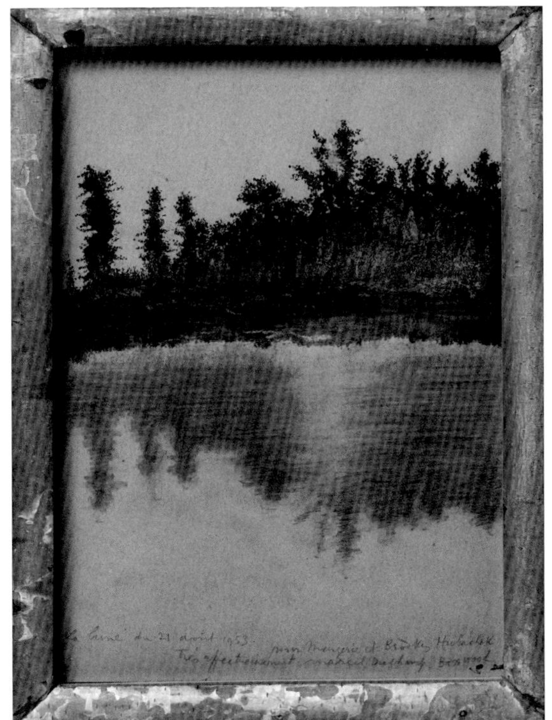

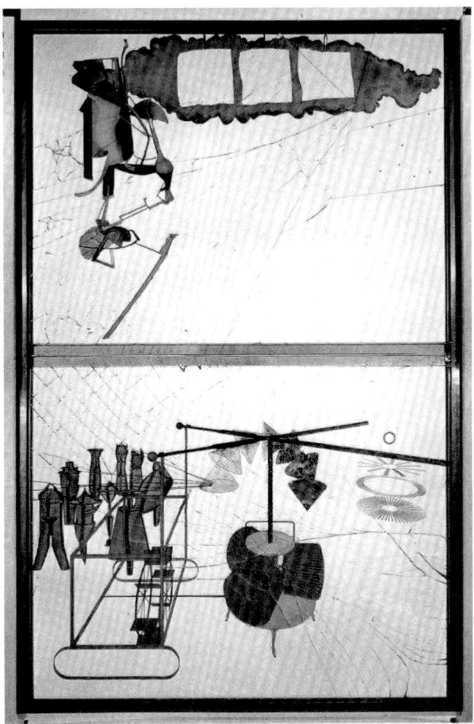

1 Marcel Duchamp, *Moonlight on the Bay at Basswood,* black ink, graphite pencil, wax crayon, talcum powder, and chocolate on blue blotting paper, 26.4 x 18.4 cm, August 21, 1953. Philadelphia Museum of Art. Gift of Frank Brookes Hubachek Sr.
2 Marcel Duchamp, *La mariée mise à nu par ses célibataires, même* (The Bride Stripped Bare by Her Bachelors, Even, or The Large Glass), oil, varnish, lead foil, lead wire and dust on two glass panels (broken), mounted between two panes of glass in an aluminum, wood, and steel frame, 272.5 x 175.8 cm, 1915–23. Philadelphia Museum of Art. Bequest of Katherine S. Dreier.

away with the pictorial background in order to concentrate on the figure: "The main point is the subject, the figure. It needs no reference. It is not in relation. All that background on the canvas that had to be thought about, tactile space like wall paper, all that garbage, I wanted to sweep it away. With the glass you can concentrate on the figure if you want and you can change the background if you want by moving the glass. The transparency of the glass plays for you. The question of painting in background is degrading for the painter. The thing you want to express is not in that background."[4]

Duchamp's focus on the figure in *The Large Glass* implied a strategy that detached it from its background, be it that of domestic space or exterior landscape. His emphasis on the figure reflected his strategic shift from a "visual" to an "ideatic" understanding of painting as inaugurated by the *Nude Descending a Staircase* painting series of 1911–18. His introduction of conceptual considerations would turn against the idea of painting in the background, summed up as "tactile space like wall paper" and reduced to "garbage" to be swept away. However, by using the transparency of glass as a medium in *The Large Glass,* Duchamp transformed the notion of pictorial background into a ready-made, one whose visual appearance would change according to the position of the glass. In so doing, Duchamp conceptually recast the relations between figure and background as no longer internal to the logic of the image, but as a product of the work's chance encounters with

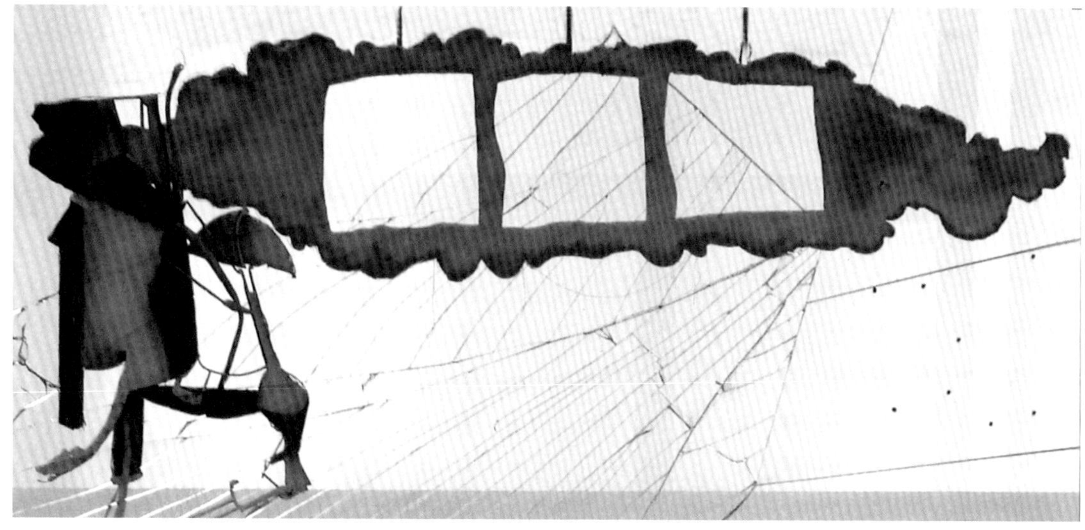

3 Marcel Duchamp, The upper Bride section of *The Large Glass* (for details see fig. 2, p. 87), 1915–23. Philadelphia Museum of Art. Bequest of Katherine S. Dreier. Photograph by Stefan Banz.

the world. Supervening the desire to escape landscape, he re-inscribed the landscape as a necessary effect of the work's contingent encounters with the world and produced by no design of his own, as it were.

Given Duchamp's denunciation of "landscapism" as a trap to be avoided in *The Large Glass,* why would he return to its detailed and laborious representation in *Étant donnés?* Despite Duchamp's denunciations of the painted background in favor of the figure in *The Large Glass,* the problems associated with landscape are alluded to conceptually even if they are not represented literally. In the upper Bride section of the *Glass,* in the top inscription (fig. 3) we find three apertures whose outlines were produced by taking three photographs of a hanging piece of one-meter-square gauze netting before a window whose shape changed when exposed to air currents. Entitled *Piston de courant d'air* (Draft Pistons, 1914) (fig. 4), these photographs associated artistic draftsmanship with drafts of air, there by inscribing allusions to the artist's abilities to draw on both landscape and chance: "I wanted to register the changes in the surface of the square, and use in my Glass the curves of the lines distorted by the wind. So I used gauze, which has natural straight lines. When at rest, the gauze was perfectly square—like a chessboard—and the lines perfectly straight—as in the case of graph paper. I took the pictures when the gauze was moving to the draught to obtain the required distortion of the mesh."[5]

The fact that the windows behind the netting are closed indicates, as with his later windows of the twenties, the shutting down of the ocular in favor of the optical.[6] Unlike Renaissance perspective windows which used a veil or gauze netting as a perspective generating device, the three *Draft Pistons* or *Nets* shut down visual reference only to activate the idea of the landscape in terms of the forces that govern it, such as wind, water, and time. Capturing the fugitive traces of the movement of air, the three photographic exposures trace the playful distortion of the geometrical logic of perspective, gently "straining its laws." They represent yet another instance of "sketching [or drawing] on chance"[7] that Duchamp first experimented with in *3 Standard Stoppages* (1913–14), his supposed joke on the meter. Resembling but inactivated as perspective-producing pictorial devices, these windows conceptually allude to landscape, visually imperceptible yet physically present in the movement of air drafts. By capturing the movement of air, Duchamp was bringing to completion the project started by Leonardo, who had discussed how to paint the wind and thus capture its subtle form.[8] The *Draft Pistons* or *Nets* carry out Leonardo's pictorial conceit as well as supply a conceptual perspective to *The Large Glass,* which Duchamp summed up as combining wind, skill, and weight.[9] He redefined the mechanics of *The Large Glass* as governed not just by eroticism and its libidinal determinism but also by physical laws whose determinacy he gently strained through the playful intervention of chance and the strategic play of irony.

The domain of the Bachelors in the lower half of the glass presents two additional references to landscape and to Leonardo. In the area of the seven Sieves, which recall cones for the production of perspective, Duchamp "raised" or "bred" dust over a period of four to six months. The dust was graded or pruned into a miniature landscape in relief, before being fixed in varnish and visually captured in Man Ray's photograph *Élevage de poussière* (Dust Breeding, 1920) (fig. 5). While "perspective resembles color"[10] insofar as it relies on the eye, it differs from it since it also entails a mental projection that enables the passage from a two-dimensional image to the third dimension. Drawing on Leonardo's observation that accumulated dust takes on the scenic disposition of a landscape, *Dust Breeding* privileges gray matter (a pun that associates the color of dust with mind's matter) in order to hold the visual bias of painting and the lure of color at bay through conceptual interventions. The sediments of dust trace the outlines of a landscape whose hills and valleys would capture visually the intervention of the invisible physical forces that shaped it: the movement of air, water, and the passage of time.

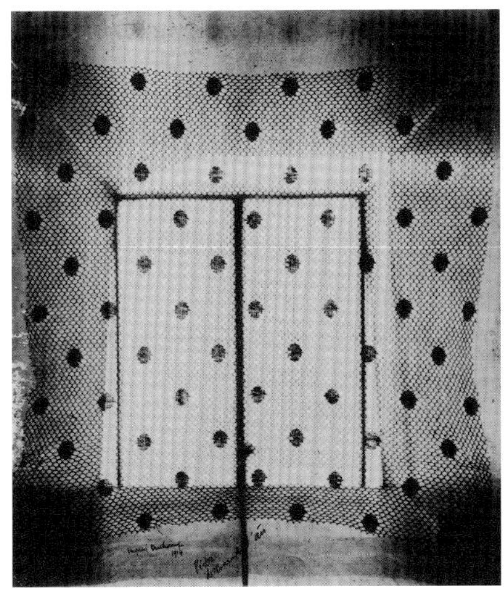

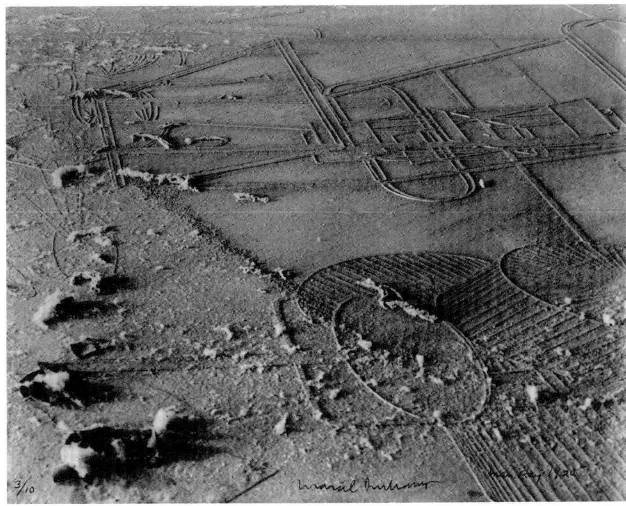

4 **Marcel Duchamp, *Piston de courant d'air*** (Draft Piston), gelatin silver print, 59 x 50 cm, 1914. Philadelphia Museum of Art. 5 **Marcel Duchamp, *Élevage de poussière*** (Dust Breeding), photograph (by Marcel Duchamp and Man Ray), gelatin silver print, 7.5 x 11 cm, 1920. Musée National d'art Moderne, Centre George Pompidou, Paris.

Speaking of the Water Mill in the Bachelor Apparatus in the lower half of the Glass, Duchamp explained: "The wheel which you see inside is supposed to be activated by a waterfall, which I did not care to represent to avoid the trap of being a landscape painter again."[11] However, his refusal to engage with the waterfall given its associations with traditional painting appears not only to give way but is in fact brought to the fore in *Étant donnés*. The invisible waterfall whose force drives the Water Mill in *The Large Glass* re-emerges as a key element in *Étant donnés,* as referred to in the work's title and as a defining element of the background landscape. Its preeminence also marks Duchamp's debt to Leonardo's extensive studies of the forces that shape the movement of water in waterfalls, vortices, and waves,[12] which combined empirical observation with speculative notations. It is interesting to note in this regard that the waterfall is the sole element of *Étant donnés* that moves, driven by an electric motor housed in a "Peek Frean" biscuit tin hidden behind the plywood backdrop. Alluding to the power pole in *Du Tignet* and *Cols alités,* this invisible motor attests to the ubiquity of electricity in *Étant donnés*. Duchamp's additional reference to landscape in his discussion of the *Chocolate Grinder* ends by suggesting that the presence of landscape could be ascribed to *The Large Glass* as a whole, hence its overarching subtitle: "Background of trees. (Ideal landscape!!!) ... *A world in yellow: general subtitle.*"[13]

The landscape of *Étant donnés* is comprised of wooded hills in green and reddish tones in the background. A waterfall meanders in their cleft, making its way into a small lake covered in a light mist, which recalls Leonardo's *sfumato* technique. A blue sky and a few requisite clouds complete the scene, whose simultaneous banality and unreality invite further inquiry. However, the visual illusionism and coherence of the background landscape has hidden from view its highly artificial, indeed contrived nature, along with the variety of media entailed in its production, including photography, printmaking, painting, drawing, sculpture, along with the kinetic element noted earlier.[14] Moreover, like many

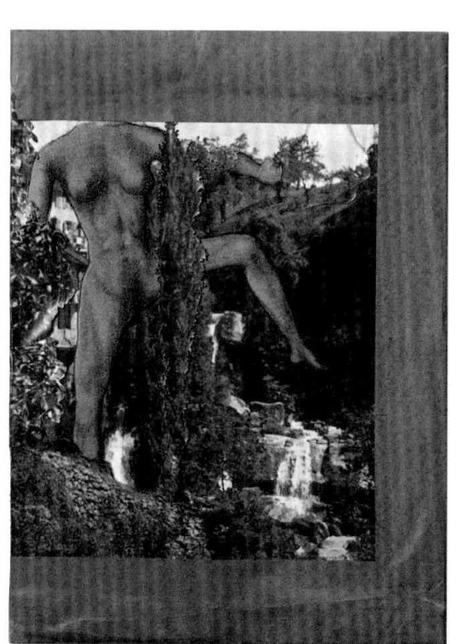

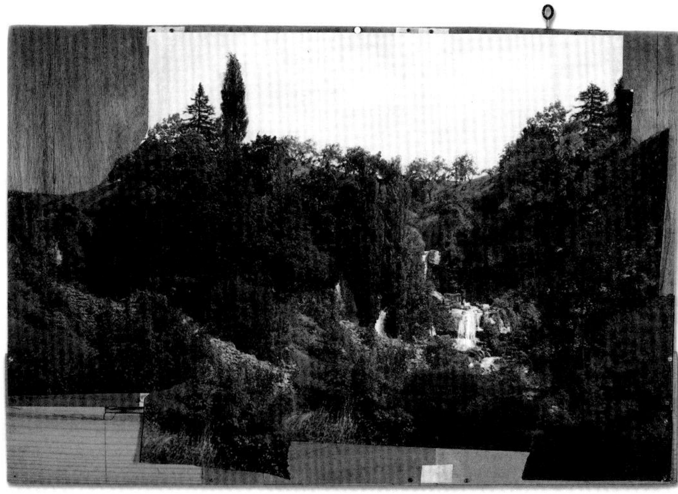

6 Marcel Duchamp, *Untitled* (photo-collage landscape study for *Étant donnés*), textured wax, pencil and ink on tan paper and cut gelatin silver photographs, mounted on board, 43.2 x 31.1 cm, c. 1946. Private Collection. **7 Marcel Duchamp, *Landscape collage on plywood*** (study for landscape backdrop of *Étant donnés: 1° la chute d'eau, 2° le gaz d'éclairage*), collage of cut gelatin silver photographs over paper, with paint, graphite, crayon, ballpoint-pen ink, and adhesive on plywood, with pressure-sensitive tape, 67 x 99.4 cm, 1959. Philadelphia Museum of Art. Gift of Mme Marcel Duchamp.

of Duchamp's prior works, the production of this landscape ranged through multiple iterations, starting with the initial small study, *Untitled* (photo-collage landscape study for *Étant donnés: 1° la chute d'eau, 2° le gaz d'éclairage*, c. 1946) (fig. 6), followed by the production in the early to mid-fifties of a working study mounted on plywood, *Landscape collage on plywood* (study for the landscape backdrop of *Étant donnés: 1° la chute d'eau, 2° le gaz d'éclairage*, 1959) (fig. 7). This photo-collage was based on cut-outs from the photographic enlargements of the Forestay waterfall which were assembled, expanded through repetition, and hand-colored so as to enhance the natural illusionism of the scene. Duchamp's coloring was based on his 1946 records that he kept of the greens, yellows, and browns at the scene, a strategy that recalls Leonardo's extensive studies of the variety of colors and shades that compose the look of a wooden landscape.[15] The final version of the backdrop of *Étant donnés* is a collotype reproduction of the working study, using a photomechanical printing process on acetate silk mounted on paper, that was further enhanced through cardboard padding to create volume and hand-coloring using paint and pencil.[16]

In his initial photo-collage working study for the landscape in *Étant donnés*, Duchamp deleted all elements associated with human habitation and inscription that were visible in the initial photographs of the Forestay waterfall, *Swiss Landscape with Waterfall* (1946, pp. 16–23), and that can still be perceived in the backdrop of the 1946 study. While this gesture may be seen to reflect a common artistic or aesthetic decision, especially in the case of landscape painting, it merits special scrutiny given Duchamp's highly speculative approach. His gesture is all the more significant since he could have taken pictures of two other waterfalls of the same stream above and below the Forestay which had a more "natural" look since they were not encumbered with traces of human habitation. In his photo-collage blueprint, he removed from the landscape the "Huilerie" building, the church spire at Chexbres, and the shingle rooftop of a pistol range. These details are quite telling in their own right since they establish a network of references to *The Large Glass*. The Huilerie building is an oil mill or distillery for the fabrication of vegetable oils. Recalling the Water Mill in *The Large Glass*, this mill would be involved in the processing of oil, a substance whose artistic connotations would bring in the specter of painting and the retinal while also affirming their deliberate exclusion from the landscape of *Étant donnés*.[17] The elimination of the roof of the pistol shooting range brings into play allusions to the toy canon used to shoot matches covered in paint, which was used in the production of the Nine Shots in the *Glass*. The idea of using *The Large Glass* as a target to take shots at would hold particular appeal for Duchamp, since it would mark yet again his efforts to take barbs at the sacrosanct status of art, as implied in his elimination of the church spire (Fr.: *flèche d'église*, literally church barbs or darts) from the background. These deliberate attempts to target the idea of art are further reinforced by his choice of landscape, a waterfall on the shores of Lake Geneva. The view of the waterfall requires that the spectator turn away from the lake, which had been a privileged object of artistic representation since Romanticism.[18] His gesture underlines his attempts to engage with landscape in terms that resist reduction to the conventions and traditions of art.

The removal of these visual references from the depiction of the landscape, which are still present in the 1946 sketch of *Étant donnés*, point to the deliberate artifice and reconstructed nature of its visual appearance. Their erasure points to the conceptual considerations that subtend the retinal illusionism of the background. The fact that this working study is mounted on plywood with a hinge mechanism that allows it to be folded, thus hindering visual access and enabling its portability for travel, reinforces the work's conceptual implications. Erasing all indices of human intervention and spoliation that would blight the view appropriately entitled "Bellevue," Duchamp restituted the landscape to its virginal/pristine condition, after the fact, as it were. Transforming the landscape into what it had been once but was no longer when the photo was taken, he redefined its "reality" as an effect produced after the fact (*après-coup*). Duchamp's gesture of restitution to an original condition also implies an ironic conceit, the suggestion that the "reality" of this landscape would also be seen as a function of *The Large Glass,* insofar as allusions to this work appeared to have already been embedded in the original Swiss landscape. Duchamp reversed the priority of the landscape as referent with an artistic representation that recast and undermined its status as origin, thus challenging notions of causality. By reversing the temporal and referential logic of the landscape in its relation to the original photograph (and the implied references to *The Large Glass*), the visual illusionism of the landscape in *Étant donnés* emerges as a function of logical and temporal scandals that scramble the priority of reference through a strategy of simulation.

What mandates and indeed drives this speculative insight is Duchamp's apparent return to landscape in a drawing entitled *Cols alités* (Bedridden Mountains, 1959) (fig. 8), whose title is a French pun on "causality." This drawing is a visual composite insofar as it superimposes an earlier drawing *Du Tignet* (1959) (fig. 9) on an outline of *The Large Glass. Du Tignet* represents a view of distant hills whose bucolic ordinariness is disrupted by the presence of an electrical pole with insulators in the foreground. This belated return to figuration inscribed in the *Glass* alludes to the blatant "landscapism" and hidden role of electricity in *Étant donnés,* which Duchamp was working on in secret at that time. Anne d'Harnoncourt and Walter Hopps suggest that *Cols alités* hints at the forthcoming landscape of *Étant donnés* while at the same time looking backward to its potential origins in Duchamp's earlier works. The latter possibility is figured through the bias of a superimposition in *Network of Stoppages* (1914), which was painted over an enlarged and unfinished version of an earlier landscape with figures entitled *Young Man and Girl in Spring* (1911).[19] Whereas Hellmut Wohl contends that *Cols alités* represents a break with the past, since it suggests that the concerns of the *Glass* can no longer be represented in schematic terms and require a new language anchored in the visual world of sense experience.[20] By showing that *Cols alités* enacts the ostensible completion of *The Large Glass* (which had been "definitively unfinished"), but in a paradoxical sense, I hope to demonstrate Duchamp's reconciliation of two radically opposed approaches to landscape. His introduction of figuration implies an appeal and possible return to a representational system whose perceptual procedures explicitly contradict the schematic conceptualism of *The Large Glass.* Duchamp's hooking up of the Bachelor Apparatus to a power pole and his introduction of the faint outlines of a landscape of hills, which is reprised in the bottom part of the Bride section of the *Glass,* generates a collision between two opposing systems of artistic representation. The viewer is stumped by being confronted with two ways of seeing incorporated in one work, that imply not just different perspectives or views, but

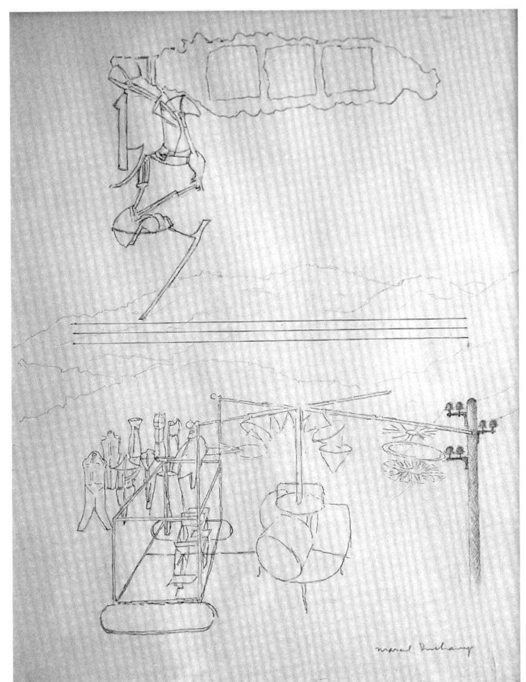

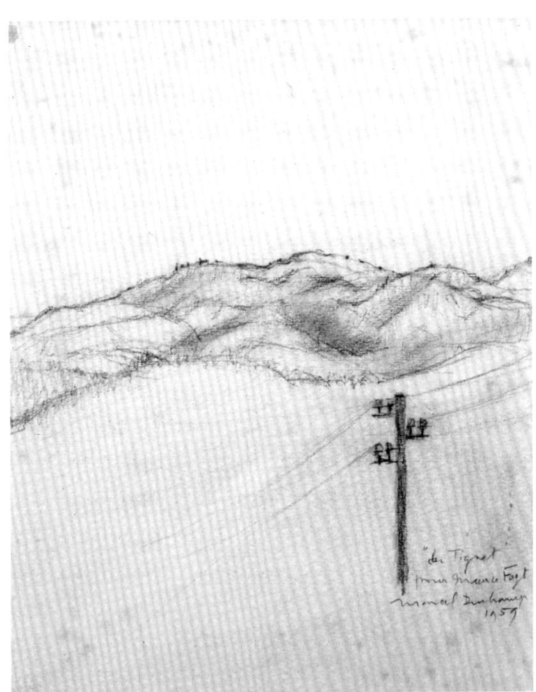

8 Marcel Duchamp, ***Cols alités*** (Bedridden Mountains), ink and pencil on paper, 32 x 24.5 cm, 1959. Private Collection.
9 Marcel Duchamp, ***Du Tignet*** (From Tignet), pencil on paper, 30.5 x 22.8 cm, 1959. Private Collection.

also mutually exclusive trends in the history of art. The evocation of causality in the work's title, *Cols alités,* adds to the viewer's confusion, making him or her wonder about the logical status of the implied claim regarding the possibility of an event having two opposing causes. Octavio Paz described *Cols alités* as a hinge between *The Large Glass* and *Étant donnés:* "the hinge is both the resolution of contradiction and its metamorphosis into another contradiction."[21] *Cols alités* restages contradictions in these works not in order to resolve them, but rather to transform them into a new set of contradictions. By juxtaposing references to *The Large Glass* and *Étant donnés, Cols alités* alludes to their capacity for disruption, for creating conundrums whose ironic character disrupts the seamlessness of representation. By persistently befuddling the spectator, these works attest to attempts to outwit rational consciousness in ways that confuse and disrupt logical, temporal, and visual registers.

The work's subtitle, "COLS ALITES/ Project for the 1959 model of 'The Bride Stripped Bare by her Bachelors, Even,'" represents yet another instance of Duchamp's deliberate scrambling of logical and temporal registers. Referring to the idea of causality, understood as an original event, the subtitle couples it to the idea of a project suggesting a future plan or design. By presenting this drawing as an update to the schematic design of *The Large Glass* with a figurative landscape, since it is ostensibly a later 1959 model of it, Duchamp suggests two things at once: that the figurative landscape is the hidden causal principle that underlies *The Large Glass,* and/or that this causality is merely an afterthought, a contingent effect produced after the fact. *Cols alités* challenges the idea of what exactly is given and to whom, and consequently what comes first in the causal sense of an origin. This work questions the givenness of the origin by disturbing its temporal logic and sequential order. By using the word "project" [*projet*] defined as project, plan, draft, or scheme, to describe *Cols alités,* Duchamp inscribes the possibility of a "future" into his redesign of *The Large Glass,* confusing the viewer with the double notion: he implies that this drawing is just a 1959 copy of the *Large Glass,* and/or that this work is the 1959 blueprint for a future prototype of the *Glass.* The question thus arises whether the landscape has already been there in *The Large Glass,* as an underlying causality whose figurative nature would haunt its conceptual schematism? Or rather, in an equally plausible sense, that the conceptual schematism of *The Large Glass* projected the possibility of its visual embodiment as "reality" to come, but after the fact, as it were.

Duchamp's introduction of landscape in *Cols alités* implies bringing back and thus seemingly returning to what he had attempted to get away from in *The Large Glass.* But in bringing the figurative landscape back was he only bringing forward something that had already been there given that he was working on glass and not canvas? The glass "delays" the viewer's gaze confronting him or her with the conjunction of two irreconcilable views: the first is figured through the schematic outlines on the glass and the other is a view across the glass, which brings into focus the surrounding room and the window across whose aperture provides an outlook on the landscape outside. Presented with two equally viable and yet opposing ways of seeing, the spectator is outwitted by Duchamp's ironic construction of the gaze. In addition to the temporal and logical contradictions already identified in *Étant donnés,* the viewer is faced with another disruptive detail, that of the burning gas lamp that illuminates a scene already flooded in blinding lights. The incongruous nature of this detail disrupts common sense, since it combines references to both night and day, and it suggests the necessity of further inquiry into this work's "reality" in relation to vision. Whereas in *The Large Glass* temporal delays interrupt and forestall the immediate gratification of the viewer's gaze, in *Étant donnés* the viewer is reduced to the position of a voyeur, whose eye is sped up, gaining full access all at once, in the pitiless immediacy of an instant. Lyotard contends that Duchamp attempts to outwit the logic of the gaze, be it by eliding the body as the object of its glare, hence its destiny of its persistent stripping in *The Large Glass,* or by deliberately exposing the body to its consuming grasp in *Étant donnés,* thus reducing it to a nudity so blatant as to court the opprobrium of obscenity. These mutually exclusive scenarios of temporality are hinged together in the "now," thereby challenging both the logic of temporality and the order of consciousness.[22] Thus the viewer of Duchamp's works finds him or herself outwitted by the work, that is, stripped of the norms of conventional judgment by the intelligence implied in the work.

The "reality effect" staged by *Étant donnés* considered as a portal and/or window draws on the idea of painting embodied in Leonardo only to undermine through simulation its referential logic. If in *The Large Glass* ambiguity "was achieved through transparency"[23] fueled by schematism, in *Étant donnés* ambiguity is sustained through opacity, through a conceptual appeal to the language of the senses and the forces of the physical world. By literalizing the mimetic impulses and conventions of painting in a three-dimensional installation, the scenic landscape of *Étant donnés* reveals its conceptual potential as a speculative device that puts reality into perspective, and/or perspective into reality, as it were. But let us be clear what we mean about perspective here, since according to Jurgis Baltrušaitis it entails a double move: perspective seeks to recreate through mathematical projection a reproduction of sensorial reality. It is an "art of illusion" that recreates visual semblance, but only in the wake of the intervention of science, "which fixes the exact dimensions and positions of objects in space."[24] Consequently, there is a fundamental opposition, indeed contradiction, at work at the heart of perspective insofar as it entails a double move: namely, the de-realization of visual appearance into geometrical schematism, followed by a re-realization, a counter move that restores to geometrical apparitions their visual semblance. Drawing on the idea of pictorial perspective as a transformative device, Duchamp plays out its ironic potential in *The Large Glass* and *Étant donnés*. He appeals to its machinations in order to make visible the contrived nature of "reality," undermining its referential force as underlying causality.

Duchamp's staging of these logical, temporal, and visual contradictions enabled him to uphold through irony two incompatible positions at the same time: "Always or nearly give, the why of the / choice between 2 or several solutions. (by /ironic causality)"[25] The irony of "ironic causality" is that in providing multiple solutions or reasons for any problem, it undermines the uniqueness of causality understood as originating principle. In an interview with Denis de Rougemont in 1945 at Lake George, Duchamp addressed the ideas of "reality" and "causality," thus providing important hints as to the direction of his thoughts in the period leading to the inception of *Étant donnés* in 1946. He explained the need to adopt a strategy that would enable artists to reclaim their creative freedom in the face of the masses which merely attempt to "consolidate what they call 'reality,' the 'material' world such as we suffer it."[26] And he concluded that "this is the world that science then observes, and on which it decrees its so-called laws."[27] Challenging the idea of reality as ultimate referent and cause, he suggested that its solidity and authority derives its weight from its public iteration as myth. In so doing, he resituated the force of reality as an effect rather than a cause, which is further reinforced through the complicity of science. Taking to task the "mythical authority of physics or mathematics," Duchamp concluded that their demonstrations rely on rules that are nothing more than tautologies that lead back to other myths. Thus their "reality" is no different from the conventions that govern the logic of games. Moreover, he also argued that the notion of "causality" as driving force and origin proved to be yet another foundational myth: "Take the notion of cause: cause and effect, different and opposite. It's quite indefensible. It's a myth from which the idea of God has been drawn considered as a model for all cause. If one doesn't believe in God, the idea of cause has no meaning."[28] His critique of "causality" exposed its mythic character, undermining its authority and hence its powers of explanation.

Duchamp's interrogation of the ideas of "reality" and "causality" help illuminate the puzzling nature of the title of *Étant donnés: 1° La chute d'eau, 2° le gaz d'éclairage* (Given: 1° The Waterfall, 2° The Illuminating Gas), since it combines references to concrete physical details with the logical format of a mathematical proof. There is irony at play, since the title appears to put forth an affirmation of the given nature of reality, only to invite queries that suggest that it should not be taken for granted. Duchamp's reliance on an ironic strategy served to undermine notions of "reality" and "causality" by straining the logic and conventions of both of art and science. He drew on Leonardo's speculative approach to landscape in his annotations on the movements of water and wind (gas), but he did so from an ironic perspective, insofar as water and gas later became the insignia of modernization, indeed of the commodification of the landscape through the development of utilities. Duchamp playfully alluded to this redefinition of the landscape when he produced a plaque *Eau & gaz / à tous les étages* (Water & Gas / on All Floors, 1958) (fig. 10), a ready-made that imitated plaques affixed to apartment houses at the beginning of the 1900s to indicate the presence of modern utilities. Like the visual depiction of landscape in *Étant donnés: 1° La chute d'eau, 2° le gaz d'éclairage,* the title holds out two opposing, indeed irreconcilable views: the first references a sense of the natural world ("the waterfall"), while the second points to its utilitarian aftermath in the modern period ("the illuminating gas") which is followed by the advent of electricity. Rather than representing a mere return to the landscape genre and its implied affirmation of the physical world, *Étant donnés: 1° La chute d'eau, 2° le gaz d'éclairage* takes to task its "reality" challenging its rational order through a strategy of irony that undermines causality by perpetuating contradictions. Duchamp's strategy seems particularly apt given his self-description as an "unfrocked Cartesian," since irony will enable him to continue to question the idea of landscape as a given rather than take for granted its visual manifestation and artistic meaning.

Notes

[1] Francis Roberts, "Interview with Marcel Duchamp: I propose to Strain the Laws of Physics," *Art News* 67, no. 8 (December 1968), p. 63.

[2] Pierre Cabanne, *Dialogues with Marcel Duchamp,* trans. Ron Padgett, New York 1987, p. 160.

[3] See Joseph Masheck's comments in his "Introduction: Chance Is zee Fool's Name for Fait," in *Marcel Duchamp in Perspective,* Englewood Cliffs, NJ 1975, pp. 22–24.

[4] Roberts, "Interview with Marcel Duchamp" (note 1), p. 46.

[5] "Ephemerides on and about Marcel Duchamp and Rrose Sélavy: 1887–1968," texts by Jennifer Gough-Cooper and Jacques Caumont in *Marcel Duchamp: Work and Life,* ed. and introduction by Pontus Hultén, Cambridge, Mass. 1993, n.p., May 21, 1915.

[6] For an analysis of Duchamp's critique of the ocular in favor of the optical, see my *Drawing on Art: Duchamp and Company,* Minneapolis and London 2010, pp. 5–28 and 37–48.

[7] *The Writings of Marcel Duchamp,* eds. Michel Sanouillet and Elmer Peterson, New York 1973, p. 187.

[8] *The Notebooks of Leonardo Da Vinci,* ed. and trans. Edward MacCurdy, London 1977, vol. 2, p. 263.

[9] Marcel Duchamp, *Notes and Projects for the Large Glass,* ed. Arturo Schwarz, trans. George H. Hamilton, et al., New York and London 1969, p. 138, note 89.

[10] *Writings of Marcel Duchamp* (note 7), p. 87.

[11] Anne d'Harnoncourt and Kynaston McShine, eds. *Marcel Duchamp,* exh. cat. Museum of Modern Art, New York 1973, p. 276.

[12] See Ernest H. Gombrich's analysis, "The Form of Movement in Water and Air," in *The Heritage of Apelles: Studies in the Art of the Renaissance,* Ithaca, NY 1969, pp. 39–56.

[13] Marcel Duchamp, *Marcel Duchamp, Notes,* ed. and trans. Paul Matisse, Boston 1983, note 114.

[14] For a comprehensive account of the genesis and production of the landscape, see Michael R. Taylor's seminal study in *Marcel Duchamp: Étant donnés,* exh. cat. Philadelphia Museum of Art, Philadelphia and New Haven 2009, pp. 67–69 and 82–92; and also his colleagues' technical analysis in the same volume, Beth A. Price, Ken Sutherland, Scott Homolka, and

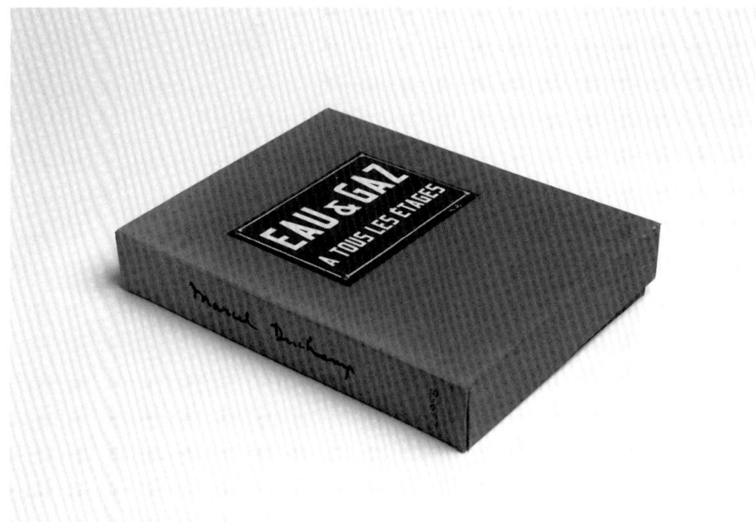

10 Marcel Duchamp, *Eau & gaz à tous les étages* (Water and Gas on All Floors), cover of deluxe edition of Robert Lebel's *Sur Marcel Duchamp*, linen-covered cardboard box with collotype-printed and stencil-colored plaque, 35 x 27 x 5.5 cm, 1959. Philadelphia Museum of Art. Gift of Henri Marceau.

Elena Torok, "Evolution of the Landscape: The Materials and Methods of the *Étant donnés* Backdrop," pp. 262–78.
[15] Leonardo, *Notebooks* (note 8) vol. 2, pp. 285–97.
[16] This collotype print was printed with the help of Salvador Dalí (who also signed the work) and issued in an edition of 35 copies. The purpose of this multiple edition remains unclear, although Michael Taylor suggested that it may have been a companion project to a book deal with Robert Lebel that had fallen through, see Taylor, *Marcel Duchamp: Étant donnés* (note 14), p. 91.
[17] See Stefan Banz's concept for the symposium (http://www.bxb.ch/images/public/3_Concept_Duchamp_Forestay_en_2.pdf), and his discussion on page 33 of this volume.
[18] See Caroline Bachmann and Stefan Banz's conceptual attempt to restore Duchamp's oversight in *What Duchamp Abandoned for the Waterfall*, Zurich 2009.
[19] Anne d'Harnoncourt and Walter Hopps, *Étant donnés : 1) la chute d'eau 2) le gaz d'éclairage*, Philadelphia 1973, pp. 27–28.
[20] Hellmut Wohl, "Beyond *The Large Glass:* Notes on a Landscape Drawing by Marcel Duchamp," *The Burlington Magazine*, no. 119 (November 1977), p. 767.
[21] Octavio Paz, *Marcel Duchamp: Appearance Stripped Bare*, trans. Rachel Phillips and Donald Gardner, New York 1978, p. 147.
[22] Jean-François Lyotard, *Duchamp's Transformers*, trans. Ian McLeod, Venice, CA 1990, pp. 198–99.
[23] Paz, *Marcel Duchamp: Appearance* (note 21), p. 136.
[24] Jurgis Baltrušaitis, *Anamorphic Art*, trans. W. J. Strahan, New York 1977, p. 4.
[25] *Marcel Duchamp, Notes* (note 13), note 68.
[26] Herbert Molderings examined Duchamp's comments in light of his understanding of art, see "Un Cul-de-lampe: Réflections sur la structure et l'iconographie d'*Étant donnés*," *Étant donné Marcel Duchamp*, no. 3 (Fall 2001), p. 93.
[27] Gough-Cooper and Caumont, "Ephemerides" (note 5), n.p., August 2, 1945.
[28] Ibid.

Bernard Marcadé

Water Leaking on All Floors

If we stick to the old Aristotelian categories of dry and moist, one of the more common (and persistent) themes when thinking about Marcel Duchamp is to consider him a dry artist: physically dry, sentimentally and morally dry, artistically dry. Perhaps it is a consequence of his legendary detachment from the inherent moistness of paint (and of course turpentine) and, more seriously, of his aesthetic discourse: "precision painting" and "the beauty of indifference" underlie the creation of *The Large Glass*. Thus, commenting on the execution of *Chocolate Grinder No. 1* (the first study of the lower section of *Bride Stripped Bare by Her Bachelors, Even*) using oil paint, Duchamp stated, "I couldn't go into the haphazard drawing or the paintings, the splashing of the paint. I wanted to go back to a completely dry drawing, a dry conception of art, and the mechanical drawing for me was the best form of that dry form of art."[1]

Looking a bit closer, however, we see running throughout Duchamp's work fluxes, streams, fragrances, discharges, and secretions, which, though not exactly spectacular, are nevertheless efficient and operative. In the name of the *co-intelligence of contraries*, Duchamp's art oscillates permanently between an aesthetic dryness and a consideration of processes such as flux and fluidity (in order for the machine to work, one must lubricate it), and more generally of the *future* (Duchamp declares himself more a follower of Heraclites—"everything flows," *panta rhei*—than of Parmenides). One must simply gather together all the marginal notes of the great machinery of *Bride Stripped Bare by Her Bachelors, Even,* to observe a vocabulary—perspiring, oozing—that one must accept in relation to the *mechanics of fluids;* that is, the classical study of the behavior of liquids and gases (fig. 1): "erotic liquid," "secretion of love gasoline," "dew of Eros," "Planes of Flow" "reservoir of love gasoline," "drop by drop," "liquefaction," "splashes"...

The words are there to signify operations or devices linked to an economy of fluxes and fluids. In this network of moist words, the waterfall has a key role (fig. 2); *La chute d'eau* is the first term of the programmatic exhibition of *The Large Glass* (the other term being *Le gaz d'éclairage,* the illuminating gas), the "driving force" of this great machinery. We will see how this signifier, linked to a natural phenomenon, subliminally (*infra-mince*) and metaphorically traverses Duchamp's work until it is finally found prosaically displayed (we are in a way celebrating his Swiss epiphany!) in his last work of art: *Étant donnés* (pp. 4–5). Duchamp wasn't necessarily a naturalist; in *The Large Glass,* the waterfall is a fall among others: "falls of the name brand bottles / fall in piano form / fall of the drops after compression" (note 91). These are almost certainly related to the "little wasted energies," among which are found "the fall of urine and shit" and "the fall of tears."

Concerning "the fall of urine," we need to look deeper into the famous *Fountain* of 1917 (fig. 3). The title of the readymade is not nearly as innocent as Duchamp would later claim.[2] Great lover of popular culture and racy slang that he was, Duchamp could not have been unaware that "fontaine" in *argot* refers to a woman's vagina (fig. 5). The fact that a urinal—the "passive" object par excellence, the receiver of men's urine—becomes a

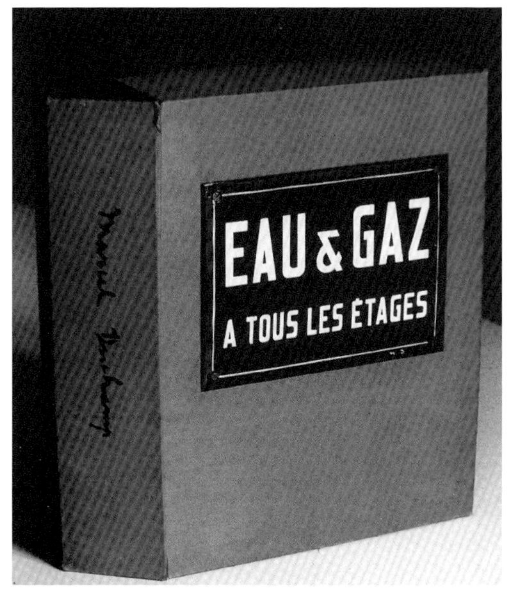

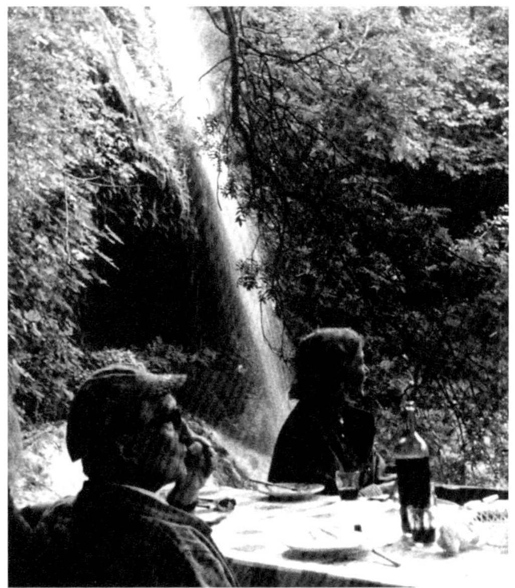

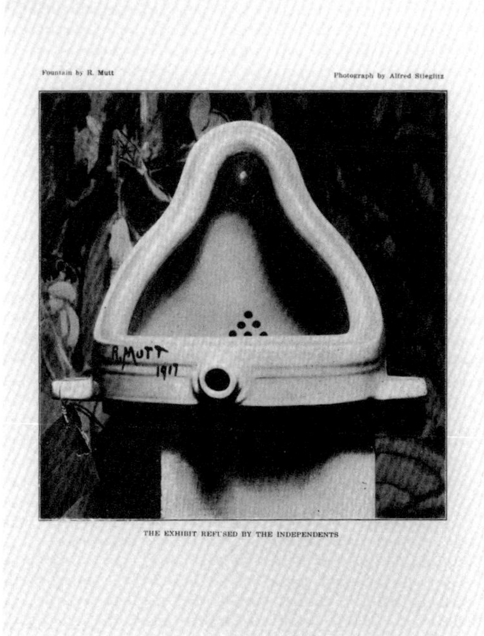
Fountain by R. Mutt

Photograph by Alfred Stieglitz

THE EXHIBIT REFUSED BY THE INDEPENDENTS

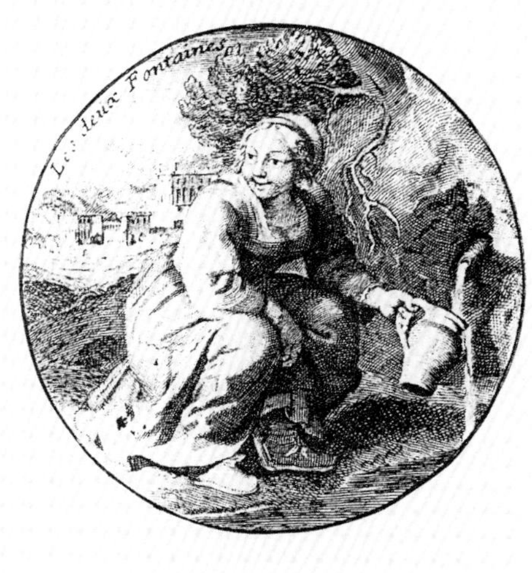

Bernard Picart The Two Fountains, 16th C

1 Marcel Duchamp, *Eau & gaz à tous les étages* (Water and Gas on All Floors, for details see fig. 10, p. 97). **2 Denise Brown Hare, Marcel Duchamp in engineer's hat with Teeny in front of La Caula waterfall,** Figueres, Spain, gelatin silver print, 25.4 x 20.3 cm, 1965. Philadelphia Museum of Art, Archives, Alexina and Marcel Duchamp Papers. Gift of Jacqueline, Paul, and Peter Matisse in memory of their mother, Alexina Duchamp. **3 Marcel Duchamp, *Fountain,*** readymade, height 60 cm, 1917. Philadelphia Museum of Art, Louise and Walter Arensberg Collection. Photograph by Alfred Stieglitz. **4 Bernard Picart** (1673–1733), ***The Two Fountains,*** gravure, undated.

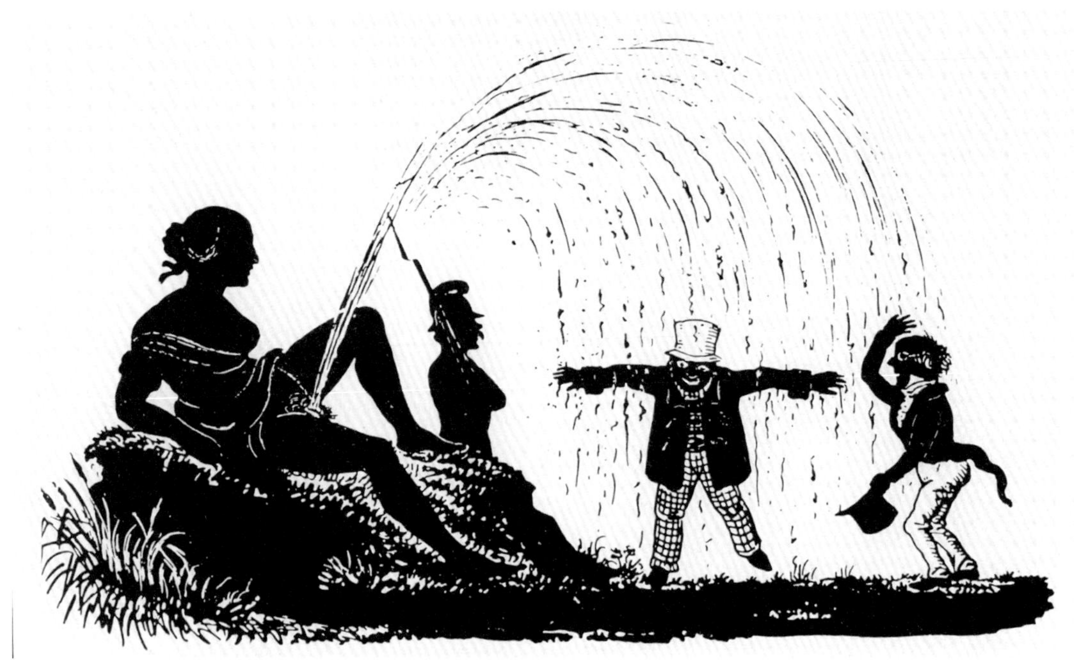

5 ***Femme fontaine,*** Anonymous caricature, 1847.

fountain—an "active" device—quite clearly shows the profound ambiguity/reversibility of the economy of liquids at work here (fig. 4). Duchamp's famous formula of 1914, "On n'a que: pour femelle la pissotière et on en vit" (One only has: for the female the urinal and one lives by it) here anticipates with his mocking crudeness the eminently sexual and scatological dimension of the readymade to come.

In this sense, *Fountain* might be thought of as the sanitary detour imagined by Duchamp to simultaneously show the female sex organ ("On n'a que pour femelle" [on a queue pour femelle: we've got dicks for woman]) and, by "mirrorical return," that of the man ("et on en vit" [et on envie: and we want]). In 1961, on a puzzle-shaped etching he dedicated to his friend Matta, he wrote, "TOUT-A-L'EGOUT SONT DANS LA NATURE" ("all tastes are in nature," but also "sewers are in nature"). This aphorism cheerfully combines the most banal statement with a play on words that could have come straight from the popular *Almanach Vermot,* providing a particularly suggestive idea about "things." (In Littré's dictionary, "nature" refers to "the parts used in reproduction, especially those of the female"). Jean Clair recognizes in this schoolboy "joke" the primitive cloaca figure, and, following the same logic, also sees the urologic fantasy of the fountain as a starting point for Duchamp's ambition, ruining ("ruiner, uriner") his career as a painter to establish the "paradigm of novelty in art."[3]

Arrose, c'est lavie

In one of the first scenes of *Entr'acte* (1924), a short film about which Francis Picabia said, "[it] respects nothing except the right to roar with laughter,"[4] Duchamp and Man Ray play chess on the roof of a theater (fig. 6). The wind picks up, some pawns fall over ... water falls

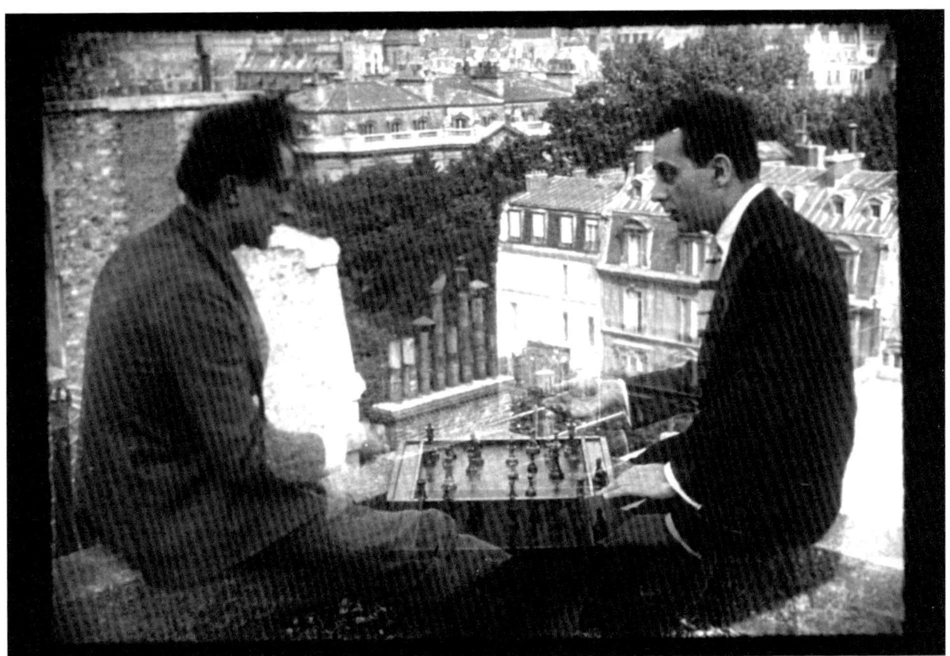

6 Marcel Duchamp and Man Ray in René Clair's *Entr'acte,* film still, 1924.

over the players (it was Picabia himself holding the hose). The two protagonists keep playing. Superimposed on top of the flooded chessboard appears the image of the Place de la Concorde, and then a small paper boat... This inundated scene, typical of Burlesque movies, is clearly associated with *Passage de Rose à Rrose,* made by Duchamp when he took part in Picabia's collective tableau in 1921. "The double R comes from Picabia's painting, you know, the *'L'Œil Cacodylate,'* ... it's the one Picabia asked all his friends to sign. I don't remember how I signed it.... I think I put *'Pi Qu'habilla Rrose Sélavy'*—the word 'arrose' demands two R's, so I was attracted to the second R—*'Pi Qu'habilla Rrose Sélavy.'*"[5]

Duchamp's life and work are *bursting* with facts and anecdotes related to his fondness for waterfalls and their jocular and scatological subtext. In this vain, Duchamp recounts an incident that occurred at the Arensbergs (most likely around the time of *Fountain*) during an evening *doublement arrosée* ("doubly soaked"). A guest with the sudden urge to relieve himself went upstairs in search of the bathroom. "A little because of the mounting pressure inside of his bladder, and a little in the spirit of a prank, he [the guest] pissed down the stairs. A little stream, bounce by bounce, step by step, found its way down to the front door and [to] the crowd of invited guests."[6] This unseemly scene that oddly combines a staircase and a strong urge to pee, certainly could not have left Duchamp indifferent...

In 1927, while visiting the city of Orange during their picaresque "honeymoon," Marcel Duchamp and Lydie Sarazin-Levassor attended a play in the city's famous old theater. Lydie told the story: "At intermission the spectators stayed in their seats because, not being numbered, they were worried about losing them. But many of the men with a dire need to relieve themselves went as close as they could to the vomitoria [exits] to empty

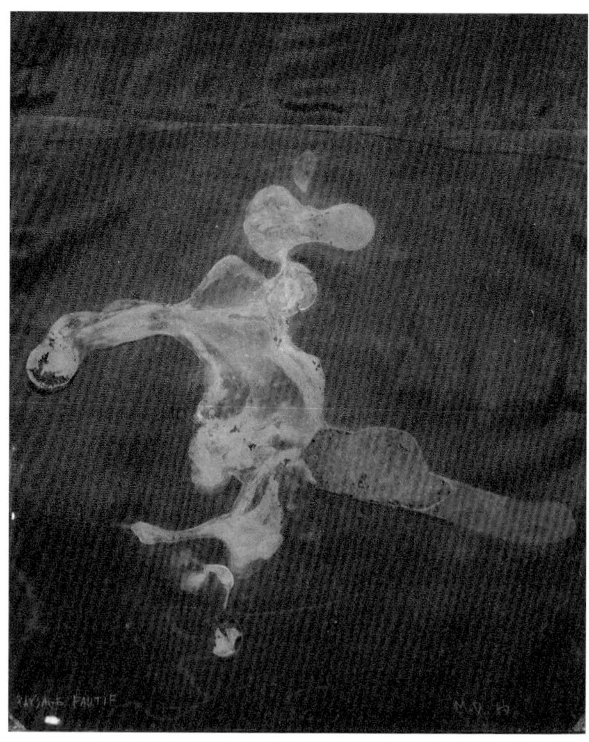

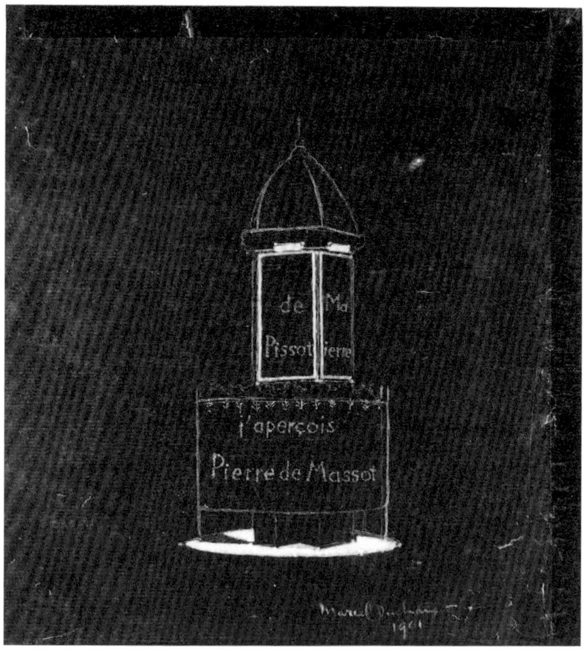

7 **Marcel Duchamp, *Paysage fautif*** (Faulty Landscape), original painting from the deluxe edition of the *Boîte-en-valise* (The Box in a Valise), *de ou par Marcel Duchamp ou Rrose Sélavy*, no. 12/20, seminal fluid on Astralon backed with black satin, 21 x 16.5 cm, 1946. Museum of Modern Art, Tokyo. 8 **Marcel Duchamp, *Anagramme pour Pierre de Massot,*** gouache on black paper covered by waxed paper on which is incised the outline of a street urinal, 21.1 x 19.2 cm, January 1961. Private Collection.

their bladders, transforming the old theatre into a gigantic urinal—much to Marcel's delight! I dared to point out to him the romantic, Hugoesque side of the contrast between the glorious spectacle of the act and the mess that followed. 'No,' said Marcel, 'I don't see it like that. You're free to see a romantic side if that's how you perceive it.... Personally, I see something else: on one side a bunch of sincere artists giving the best of themselves to convey emotion to the spectators, who, on the other side, show their gratitude by pissing on them. That is the public. It judges, and this judgment is what gives things their value. It is they that perform the performer."[7]

An economy of incontinence

Duchamp's economy of fluxes and fluids follows a more general economy (in an artistic and domestic sense) in which the artist has imagined a *transformer* of "little wasted energies." In the artist's notes (note 187) published by André Breton in his *Anthologie de l'humour noir:* "Transform all of the small, external manifestations of man's energy (in excess or wasted), as for example: the excess of pressure on a light switch, the exhalation of tobacco smoke, the growth of hair and nails, the fall of urine and shit, the convulsive movements of fear, fright, laughter, the fall of tears, demonstrative gestures of the hands, cold looks, arms which hand down along the body, stretching, expectoration of mucous or blood, vomiting, ejaculation (fig. 7), sneezing, the cow-lick or rebel hair, the noise from blowing one's nose, snoring, tics, fainting, whistling, yawning."[8]

Most of these "little wasted energies" and, oddly, the humors—the states of mind (saliva, sweat, tears, etc.)—are things, gestures, or events that the body *lets out*. Much has been written about the cerebral quality of Marcel Duchamp's visual thinking. He has been proclaimed the artist of control and self-control. But this ignores the particular attention Duchamp paid to events beyond his control [à son corps défendant], or his anti-authoritarian capacity to accept what happens: "There is something that undoubtedly exists; in other words, let the door open instead of trying to control through words our actions or desires. Explain nothing. Let go, let it be."[9]

Let it be; in other words, let the events lead us. "It's a sign of a noble heart dowered with patience, never to be in a hurry, never to be in a passion.... You must pass through the circumference of time before arriving at the center of opportunity." This maxim by Baltasar Gracian (*The Art of Worldly Wisdom,* maxim 55) about "knowing how to wait" takes us closer, perhaps, to Marcel Duchamp's desire, beginning in 1912, to "distend the laws of physics." "'There is an elastic side to time that changes everything, and that verifies my idea of not seeking out the truth or that false nowhere—*de laisser pisser le mérinos,* as they say.'"[10] *Laisser pisser le mérinos* (there, he said it!), obviously taking a certain pleasure in using an expression very much in the scatological, radically urophile, and even odinistic spirit of Duchamp's sense of humor ("Do Shit Again," "Ruiner: uriner," "Tout-à-l'égoût sont dans la nature," "De ma Pissotierre, j'aperçois Pierre de Massot.") (fig.8). *Laisser pisser le mérinos:* this old French expression has been traditionally attributed to Louis XVI who supposedly said this to an astonished royal court upon seeing a Merino sheep (of Spanish origin, known for the quality of its wool, then recently introduced to France) strangely and inappropriately urinating on his estate of Rambouillet.

Duchamp applies the expression to himself. In fact, there is a somewhat royal attitude to letting go, to stop holding in, to stop controlling, to letting things run free, to allowing oneself to linger in the voluptuousness of detachment. Duchamp confided in Pierre Cabanne: "Thanks to my luck, I was able to manage without getting wet. I understood, at a certain moment, that it wasn't necessary to encumber one's life with too much weight, with too many things to do, with what is called a wife, children, a country house, an automobile."[11] *Passer à travers les gouttes* ("getting away with it"), *Laisser pisser le mérinos:* Marcel Duchamp is the artist of detachment. The artist spent his life detaching himself from the tableau, from painting, from aestheticism, from women, from money, from work, and also from ownership.... *Ruiner, uriner.* Not to own, letting it be, letting it be said, is a way of not being attached, a way of not feeding the aesthetic and social machine. In this context, the "transformer of little, wasted energies" imagined by Duchamp in his notes constitutes a way to recycle his own incontinences. These *leaks,* no matter how thin, no matter how *hypophysical* they may appear, embody the most subversive explosions. There would be a lot to say on Duchamp's *incontinences,* on all the things he lets go, as he does not seem to be touching anything. To remain in the urologic framework, it is notable that with the exception of the heart murmur that prevented him from participating in World War I, his prostate was the cause of his only serious ailment.

Throughout his life Duchamp suffered discomfort as a result of his prostate. As early as 1929 he was sharing his health problems when he wrote to Katherine Dreier, "My bladder is beginning to speak."[12] On July 5, 1954, right after his first prostate operation, he wrote to his friend Henri-Pierre Roché: "I came out of the hospital yesterday and am resting in the country near Cincinnati to let the scab form after my scrape and disappear.... I must admit that being able to pee just like everybody else is a new-found and immense pleasure (one I haven't known for 25 years). The operation itself was something of an anticlimax as I had absolutely no after effects and no temperature (anesthetic: lumbar puncture). I got up from the operation table at 1 o'clock in the afternoon and at 7 o'clock in the evening I was smoking my pipe!! All this just to fill you in on the good sides of having an intra-urethral operation."[13]

Perhaps the relation between his problems urinating (which he enjoyed describing in humorous detail) and his exaggerated fondness for anything having to do with waterfalls and urine jokes is merely fortuitous. Nevertheless, let us add these documents to the dossier on the desk of the "ministry of coincidence" (the only legitimate ministry in Duchamp's eyes).

On displacement

At any rate, Duchamp's work forces us to go further, to move on. Duchamp is an artist of displacement, and *Fountain* the cardinal example. Let's move on to this "waterfall" around which we are in a way all gathered. I cannot resist recalling the context in which Duchamp and Teeny were photographed in front of the cascade of La Caula. The photographer Denise Brown-Hare gave a precise description of the event: "The photo must have been taken I believe in 1964 or 1965, near Figueres, on the other side of the mountains from Cadaqués, where Duchamp summered. [One day] after having run our errands, we

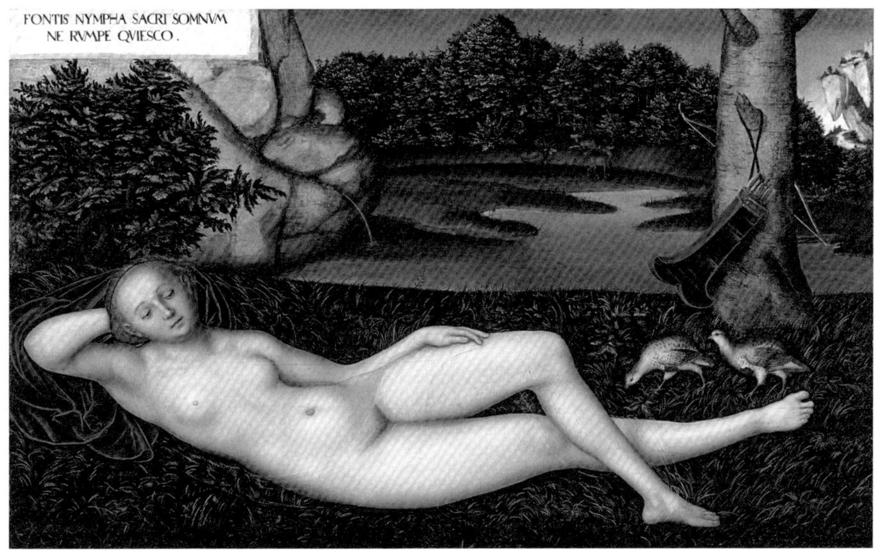

9 Lucas Cranach the Elder, *Reclining Nymph,* oil on panel, 75 x 120 cm, 1530–34. Museo Thyssen-Bornemisza, Madrid.

went to a rather modest restaurant with just a few tables outside covered in check tablecloths. We seemed to be the only clients except for a few scrawny dogs and two or three kids.... We were warmly greeted and the owner seemed to know Duchamp well. A bit later Marcel called to two young boys and took them aside to talk and gave them a few coins. I imagined that he sent them to buy his favorite cigars. We ordered a bottle of wine, they served us, and in the middle of lunch, a sudden and enormous quantity of water began to rush down the escarpment near our table. A real waterfall. Marcel didn't pay much attention and didn't say anything about it.... I happened to have my Minox in my pocket and I quickly photographed the sparkling curtain of water. It went on for some time and no one explained the mechanics of this scintillating sheet of water, but when we had finished our coffee, the waterfall suddenly stopped as quickly as it started. It was pure theater: the curtain rose and then it fell. In fact, there was a lake quite a ways above us that we couldn't see. Perhaps in other times it had a natural waterfall, but today they have constructed a dam that can be opened at will."[14]

This domestic decoy, discreetly staged by Duchamp, inevitably reminds us of the great staging of *Étant Donnés*. Could it be that it is also a decoy? Even if the device forces us to confront the body of the mannequin head-on, the peripheral elements—enhanced by the power of the work's title—are impressed upon us in spite of themselves. It is obvious that the woman-mannequin with no pubic hair is in itself a trap, a visual trap. Why, as in the dominant critical reception, should one continue to see this acephalous framing as if it were inspired by a morbid and mortified vision (a rape, a murder, etc.)? It is indeed the one looking who makes the art. And perhaps more here than anywhere else... Personally I cannot help but imagine (and here I am clearly projecting) another scenario. In this instance, I cannot stop seeing in this work the peepshow version of *La nymphe à la fontaine* by Lucas Cranach (an artist of reference for Duchamp, fig. 9). In this context, the waterfall

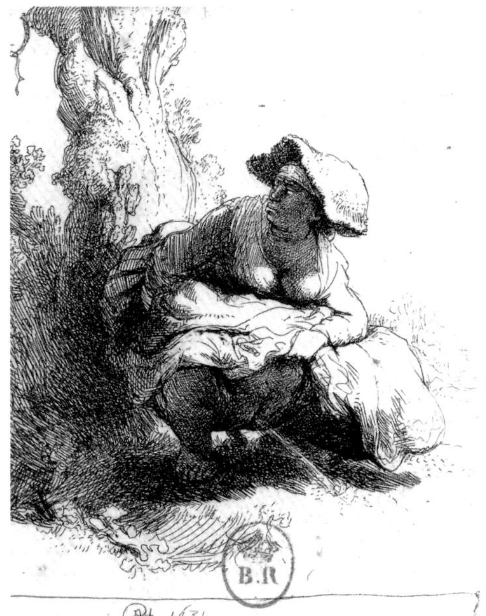

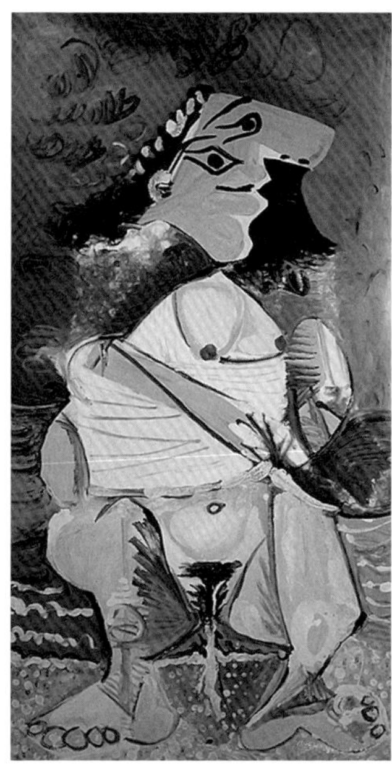

10 Rembrandt van Rijn, *Derrière l'arbre ou La femme cachée* (Woman Under a Tree), etching, 1631. **11 Pablo Picasso, *Woman Pissing,*** oil on canvas, 195 x 97 cm, April 16, 1965. Musée National d'Art Moderne, Centre George Pompidou, Paris. Donated by Louise and Michel Leiris, 1984.

indeed plays its "title role." The different versions painted by Cranach of this scene show the spring (the fountain) gushing into the softness of a hairless bush, to the extent that it becomes possible to detect in this series of works the diffracted (dismantled) and Mannerist figure of a *pisseuse*. Duchamp's version (p. 5)—this is our hypothesis (and it is as good as any)—is both more obscene (the genitals are not hidden behind a veil as with Cranach) and more subliminal, *infra-mince* (the waterfall is less explicit). Nevertheless, as with *Nude Descending a Staircase,* it is in fact the title that gives "an invisible color" to this device and leads our eyes elsewhere...

On this matter we can distinguish two schools: from Rembrandt (fig. 10) to Picasso (fig. 11), the figure holds a trivial frontal position; from Cranach to Duchamp, as well as Ingres (fig. 12) and Courbet (fig. 13), the figure is displayed more obliquely and displaced. A note from Duchamp seems to be a possible commentary on the enigmatic staging of *Étant donnés:*

> LHOOQ.
> Elle a chaud au cul comme des ciseaux ouverts
> à jet continue
> nage et continue
>
> (She has a hot ass like open scissors
> with a continuous stream
> spray and go on)[15]

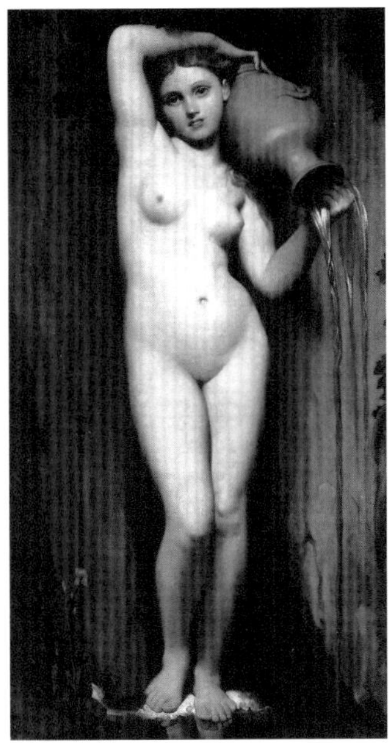

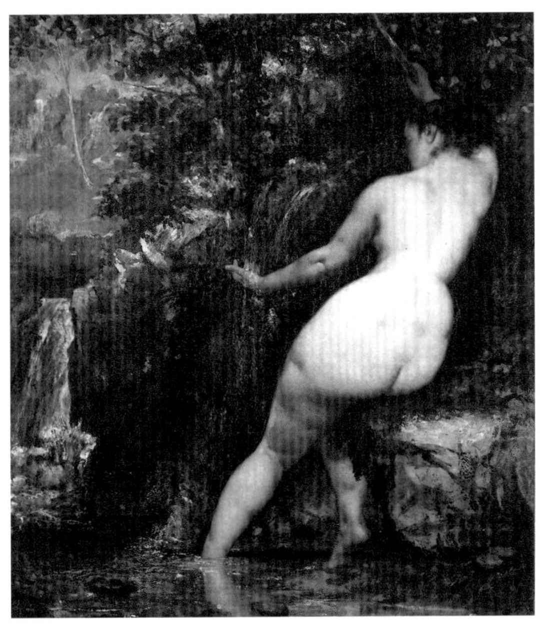

12 Jean Auguste Dominique Ingres, *La Source* (The Source), oil on canvas, 163 × 80 cm, 1820–56. Musée d'Orsay, Paris. **13 Gustave Courbet, *La Source*** (The Source), oil on canvas, 128 x 97 cm, 1868. Musée d'Orsay, Paris.

Yet in this work a displacement exists, perhaps of even greater consequence, for it puts into question the very way in which we look. *Étant donnés* is probably the first modern work of art whose device implies a unique spectator (Max Stirner) (fig. 6, p. 137.). One by one, one after the other, we are confronted with a scene that sends back to us the *thing that stubbornly looks at us*. And yet, this device flips around the *regard* once more, in a manner whereby we find ourselves in a position quite similar to that in which we are put by a popular object, the "Bourdaloue," the name of which takes us back to the famous Louis XIV-era preacher (fig. 14). During his sermons, "farsighted ladies hid a little vase in their muffs or petticoats that allowed them, when a certain pressing need came upon them, to remain in their seat."[16] These chamber pots became quite popular in the nineteenth century, their bottoms adorned with an eye and even at times reinforced with the inscription, "Je te vois" (I see you). We are reminded of Duchamp's vantage point when he saw his friend the poet Pierre de Massot: "De ma Pissotierre, j'aperçois Pierre de Massot" (From my urinal, I spy Pierre de Massot). Perhaps *Étant Donnés* similarly puts us in a position against our will [à notre corps défendant], a position that we must ultimately qualify as deliciously uncomfortable.

Translated from the French by Gaston Bertin and Jonathan Fox

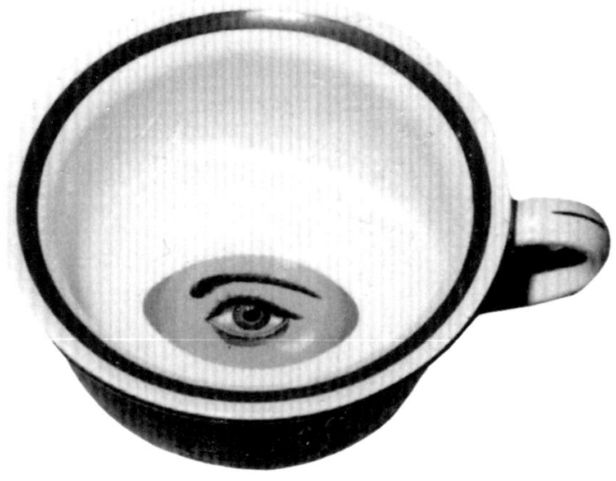

14 Chamber pot known as a “Bourdaloue,” 19th century.

Notes

[1] Marcel Duchamp, interview with James Johnson Sweeney, 1955, in *The Writings of Marcel Duchamp,* ed. Michel Sanouillet, New York 1973, p. 179.

[2] See interview of Marcel Duchamp by Otto Hahn (1 of 2), *Paris-Express,* no. 684 (1964); reprinted in *Étant donné Marcel Duchamp,* no. 3 (2001), p. 112: "My fountain-urinal comes was the product of an experiment I carried out on the question of taste: choosing the object that has the least chance of being loved. A urinal—there are very few people who will think that is marvelous. Artistic delight is the danger. But you can convince people of anything, and that is what happened."

[3] See Jean Clair, *Méduse,* Paris 1989, pp. 200–2.

[4] Francis Picabia, "Programme de Relâche," *La Danse* (November 1924); reprinted in *Écrits 2,* p. 165

[5] Marcel Duchamp, in Pierre Cabanne, *Dialogues with Marcel Duchamp,* trans. Ron Padgett, New York 1987 (orig. ed. London 1971), pp. 64–65.

[6] See Enrico Baj, "Marcel Duchamp and Plumbing," in Wouter Kotte, *Marcel Duchamp als Zeitmaschine,* Cologne 1987; quoted in Francis. M. Naumann, *New York Dada, 1915–23,* New York 1994, p. 47.

[7] Lydie Fischer Sarazin-Levassor, *Un échec matrimonial: le cœur de la mariée mis à nu par son célibataire même,* Paris 2004, p. 102.

[8] *Marcel Duchamp, Notes,* presentation and translation by Paul Matisse, Centre national d'art et de culture Georges Pompidou, Paris 1980, n.p., notes, pp. 115–17.

[9] Marcel Duchamp interviewed by Georges Charbonnier, *Entretiens avec Marcel Duchamp,* Marseille 1994, p. 29.

[10] Alain Jouffroy, *Marcel Duchamp, rencontre* [1961].

[11] Duchamp, in Cabanne, *Dialogues* (note 5), p. 15.

[12] Marcel Duchamp to Katherine S. Dreier, September 11, 1929, *Affectionately Marcel,* p. 170.

[13] Letter from Marcel Duchamp to Henri-Pierre Roché, July 5, 1954 in ibid., p. 339.

[14] Denise Brown-Hare, "Au sujet de l'atelier de Marcel Duchamp," *Étant donné Marcel Duchamp,* no. 3 (2001), p. 46.

[15] *Marcel Duchamp, Notes* (note 8), p. 143.

[16] Henry Havard, *Le Dictionnaire de l'ameublement et de la Décoration d'Havard,* Paris n.d. [1887–90].

ÉTANT DONNÉS

Michael R. Taylor

Resisting Courbet's Retinal Revolution
Marcel Duchamp's *Étant donnés* and the Erotic Legacy of Cubist Painting

In his introduction to the 1971 English-language edition of Pierre Cabanne's *Dialogues with Marcel Duchamp,* Robert Motherwell decried the fact that the artist never discussed *Étant donnés* (pp. 4–5) in any of the published interviews: "There is one 'deception,' of Duchamp's here," wrote Motherwell. "He never mentions, even when questioned about his having given up art, that for twenty years (1946–1966) he had been constructing a major work: *Given: 1. The waterfall, 2. Illuminating gas.*"[1] Writing in the immediate aftermath of the public unveiling of *Étant donnés* at the Philadelphia Museum of Art, the Abstract Expressionist painter pointed out that "this extraordinary achievement" revealed "how literal Duchamp had been in insisting that the artist should go 'underground'" in his recent interviews and public statements.[2] However, Motherwell's objection to Duchamp's apparent silence on the subject of *Étant donnés,* which he claimed took "the form of a deliberate omission," fails to take into account the numerous references, however subtle they may be, to the ideas embodied in the artist's three-dimensional tableau assemblage. Indeed, as I shall argue, Duchamp's interviews with Pierre Cabanne and other writers, journalists, artists, and art historians in the post-World War II era, especially those in which he explained his ideas on retinal art and the role of the spectator in the creative act, provide unique insights into his artistic and philosophical outlook at the time he was making *Étant donnés.*

When read in their entirety, these postwar interviews form a collective portrait of the artist and his creative thinking that was very different from the image of Duchamp already in the public domain by the end of the fifties, which largely came from the biographical accounts and personal interpretations of such friends and colleagues as André Breton, Robert Lebel, and Henri-Pierre Roché. In light of its important retroactive status for the understanding of *Étant donnés,* the information contained in these interviews needs to be carefully scrutinized and put in its historical context. For more than fifty years, Duchamp used the medium of the celebrity interview for his own ends. Radio, television, art journals, and the popular press became useful vehicles to promulgate his views on art and reach a wide audience, especially in the sixties, which was a self-defining and self-producing moment in which the artist kept the subversive nature of his earlier work alive in the era of Neo-Dada and Pop Art, while completing *Étant donnés* in secrecy.

Duchamp honed his public interview style shortly after arriving in New York in June 1915, where the scandal surrounding the display of his notorious *Nude Descending a Staircase* at the Armory Show two years earlier ensured that he was in popular demand. The resulting newspaper articles and humorous caricatures had made Duchamp a household name in the United States and his celebrity status ensured that a steady flow of articles and interviews appeared in the press soon after his arrival, including six interviews in the first year alone. Throughout these interviews, Duchamp maintained a curious silence on the subject of his own work and ideas, even when asked about them directly; preferring instead to discuss the beauty and independence of American women, his admiration for

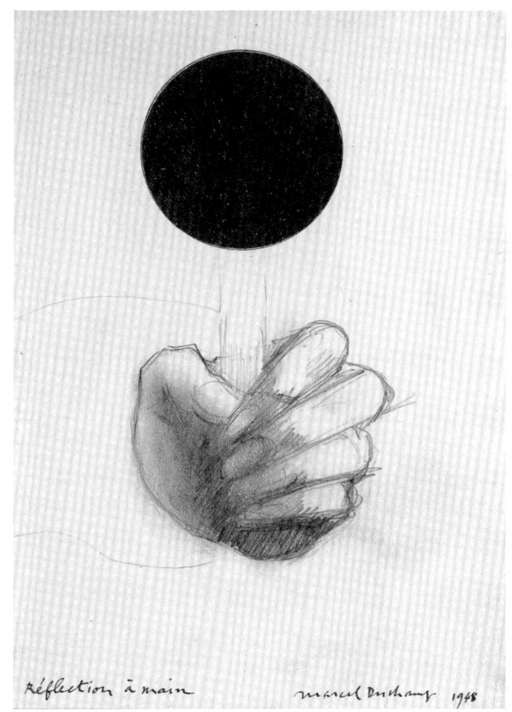

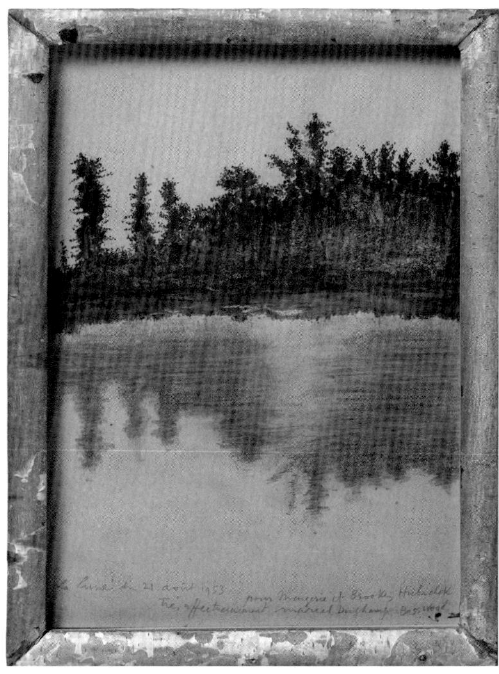

1 Marcel Duchamp, *Réflection à main* (Hand Reflection), original drawing from the deluxe edition *Boîte-en-valise* (The Box in a Valise), *de ou par Marcel Duchamp ou Rrose Sélavy*, no. 18/20, pencil on paper with collage of a circular mirror covered by a circular cutout of black paper, mounted under Plexiglas, 23.5 x 16.5 cm, 1948. Private Collection. **2 Marcel Duchamp, *Moonlight on the Bay at Basswood*,** black ink, graphite pencil, wax crayon, talcum powder, and chocolate on blue blotting paper, 26.4 x 18.4 cm, August 21, 1953. Philadelphia Museum of Art. Gift of Frank Brookes Hubachek Sr.

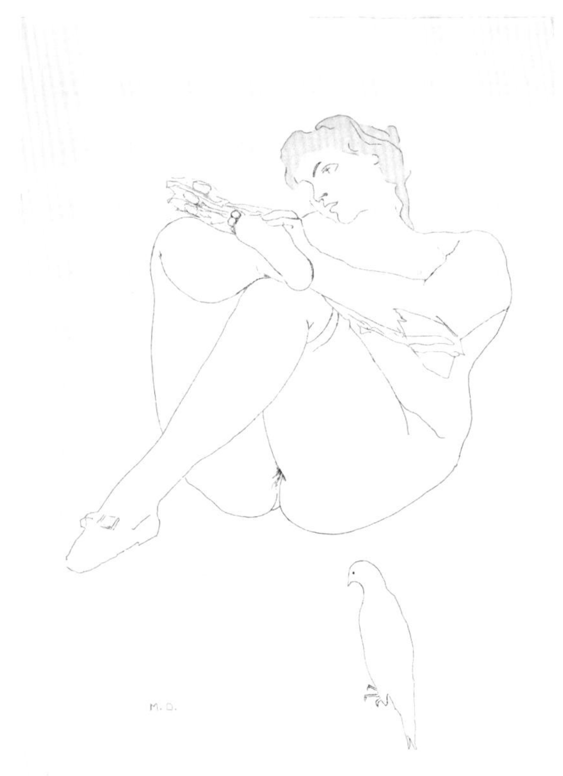

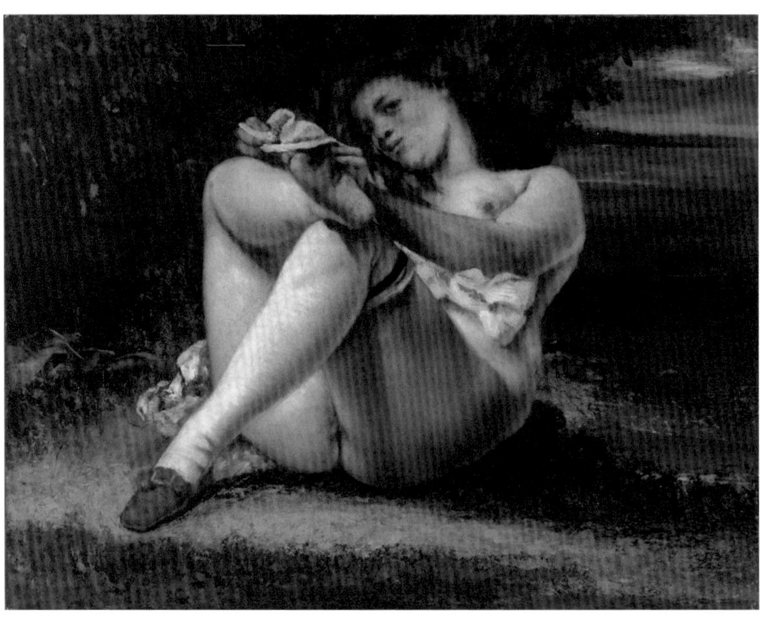

3 Marcel Duchamp, *Morceaux choisis d'après Courbet* (Selected Details After Courbet), etching and aquatint on paper, 42 x 25.5 cm, 1968. Philadelphia Museum of Art. Gift of Mme Marcel Duchamp. 4 **Gustave Courbet, *Woman with White Stockings,*** oil on canvas, 65 x 84 cm, c. 1861. The Barnes Foundation, Merion, Pennsylvania.

New York skyscrapers, and his firmly held belief that "America is the country of the art of the future."[3] These early interviews are deliberately evasive, revealing very little about Duchamp's artistic practice and intellectual pursuits during this period of intense experimentation. Far more compellingly, they tell you instead what Duchamp is like to interview. It would appear that Duchamp knew instinctively that people wanted to read about the artist, rather than the art work itself. The mass audience of a popular newspaper did not give a damn about a painter's theories, but if he or she had an opinion about the Woolworth Building then they wanted to hear it. As the British novelist Martin Amis has written on the art of interviews, "a personality is more palatable than a body of work, so all the faceting and detail of life and writing is subsumed into thumbnail approximation."[4]

This self-effacing attitude would change in the interviews that Duchamp gave after World War II, in which he expressed his personal philosophy of art, as well as his disdain for the current state of modern painting, especially Abstract Expressionism. When seen collectively, these postwar interviews provide a verbal counterpart to the visual allusions to *Étant donnés* that Duchamp had been making since the late 1940s, as seen in works like *Paysage fautif* (1946), *Réflection à main* (1948) (fig. 1), and *Moonlight on the Bay at Basswood* (1953) (fig. 2). These carefully chosen works of art can be read as symbols or hieroglyphs for the soon-to-be revealed diorama, which functions as an immense rebus of desire whose precise meaning is ultimately unfathomable. It is therefore not my aim here to speculate on the artist's intentions, which are unknowable, or put forth any radically new interpretation of the work, but rather to reflect upon the ideas expressed by the artist in these interviews, especially as they relate to *Étant donnés* and its related progeny, such as Duchamp's 1968 etching *Morceaux choisis d'après Courbet* (fig. 3), which appropriated the seated nude from Gustave Courbet's painting *Woman with White Stockings* (fig. 4) to allude to the secret tableau diorama. The artist also added a rather nondescript bird to create a delightful pun on *faucon* (falcon)—a pun that can also be read as *faux con,* or "false cunt." The etching can thus be understood as a subtle reference to the artificial nature of the female nude's hairless genitalia in *Étant donnés,* which are undeniably "false" in their strange oscillation between vagina and anus, but the reference to Courbet also irrefutably connects this work with the Duchamp's notion of retinal art, which he expressed in countless newspaper, magazine, radio, and television interviews conducted between 1945 and 1968.

The artist used the informal, conversational format of these interviews to repeatedly condemn what he perceived to be Courbet's pernicious influence on modern art since the nineteenth century, which had placed special emphasis on an artist's individual touch, or *patte* (literally "paw mark"), as the index of creative expression.[5] A highly ambitious, entrepreneurial artist seeking fame and fortune in Paris during the Second Empire, Gustave Courbet had created a number of anodyne, market-driven paintings in which the pure visual pleasure of luscious surface textures made up for a paucity of new ideas (fig. 4). His slickly painted female nudes reveled in the sensuousness of oil paint, with which the artist, through consummate control of his medium, was able to create the illusion of voluptuous flesh, while also deliberately provoking scandals that gained him public notoriety through the press. In his postwar interviews, Duchamp repeatedly insisted that his own work and ideas were antithetical to Courbet's approach, where "the emphasis has been on the eye, the retina. Colors and forms only, always on the surface."[6] According to Duchamp, the richly embellished surfaces of paintings by Courbet and his twentieth-century successors created art that appealed to the eye rather than the brain, since they downplayed cerebral ideas in favor of the seductive slickness of the oil paint medium. In 1968, Duchamp explained that "Everything since Courbet has been retinal ... you look at a painting for what you see, what comes on your retina, you see? You would add nothing intellectual about it."[7]

By the late 1950s, Duchamp had connected Courbet's retinal revolution with the work of the Abstract Expressionists, whose paintings he abhorred. "Abstract Expressionism was not intellectual at all for me," he said in 1965, "it is under the yoke of the retinal. I see no gray matter there."[8] For Duchamp, this anti-intellectual, commercial approach to painting, in which an artist's personal style was more important than his ideas, also had its origins in Courbet's work, as he explained in 1959: "Courbet's revolution was mainly visual. He insisted, without even mentioning it, that a painting is to be looked at, and only looked at, and the reactions should be visual or retinal, not much to do with the brain. A plain physical reaction in front of a painting. This is still in vogue today, if I might say so. Expressionism is the line, the form, the play of colors together and the more abstract the better."[9] Duchamp repeatedly outlined what he saw as the century-long trajectory of retinal art, beginning with Courbet and continuing in his own time through the gestural brushwork and tactile intensity of the Abstract Expressionists, whose work collectively constituted "a cult devoted to the material on the canvas—the actual pigment."[10] "Abstract Expressionism," Duchamp explained in 1962, "seems to have reached the apex of this retinal approach."[11]

Duchamp's remarks about Courbet and Abstract Expressionism in the interviews he gave between 1945 and his death in 1968 provide a broader context in which to understand his appropriation of the nineteenth-century painter's erotic works in the *Morceaux choisis* etchings, as well as the retinal aspect of *Étant donnés*. In fact, Duchamp's final project has frequently been understood as an effort to deconstruct Western regimes of representation through a demonstrably staged and artificial recapitulation of the modes and practices of modern painting since Courbet and Impressionism. What has often gone overlooked in this discussion, however, is the source for Duchamp's historical genealogy of retinal art, which comes directly from Albert Gleizes and Jean Metzinger's 1912 treatise *Du "Cubisme."*[12] The first chapter of this book begins with the following criticism of Courbet, whom the authors' argued—in terms that would later be recycled by Duchamp in his postwar interviews—had failed to move beyond the retina in order to penetrate the surface of the visible world:

"To evaluate the importance of Cubism," wrote Gleizes and Metzinger, "we must go back to Gustave Courbet. That master—after David and Ingres had magnificently brought an age-old secular idealism to a conclusion—instead of squandering himself in slavish repetition, following the example of Delaroche and Devéria, inaugurated an aspiration for realism in which all modern efforts participate. But he remained the slave of the worst visual conventions. Not knowing that, to discover a true relationship, one must sacrifice a thousand surface appearances, he accepted without any intellectual control everything his retina communicated to him. He did not suspect that the visible world becomes the real world only through the operation of thought, and that the objects that strike us more forcefully are not always those whose existence contains the greatest wealth of plastic truths. Reality is more profound than academic recipes, and more complex as well. Courbet was like one who contemplated the Ocean for the first time and who, diverted by the play of the waves, did not dream of the depths."[13] The retinal aspect of Impressionism also came under fire in Gleizes and Metzinger's summa of their artistic aims in 1912, as seen in the following passage, which again resonates with statements that Duchamp would make after World War II: "The art of the Impressionists is inherently nonsensical: through the diversity of color it attempts to create life, and it propagates a drawing that is feeble and worthless. The dress sparkles, marvelous; the forms disappear, atrophied. Here, even more than Courbet, the retina predominated over the mind; but the Impressionists were aware of this and, to justify themselves, they gave credit to the incompatibility of the intellectual faculties and artistic feeling!"[14]

What can account for Duchamp's return in the mid-1940s to the historical arguments first posited in 1912 by Gleizes and Metzinger in *Du "Cubisme"?* The simple answer may be that Duchamp probably re-read the book in 1945, when he entered into a series of lengthy interviews with James Johnson Sweeney, who was at that time working on a retrospective exhibition of the artist's work. Duchamp met Sweeney in October 1935 through their mutual friend Man Ray, and the two men had become close friends and frequent collaborators during the following decade on a variety of curatorial projects and avant-garde magazine publications, including *Transition* and *View.*[15] Duchamp's interviews with Sweeney coincided with his friend's short-lived tenure as director of the Department of Painting and Sculpture at the Museum of Modern Art, New York, a position that he held between 1945 and 1946. Duchamp was closely involved with the Museum of Modern Art during this two-year period, especially after March 1946, when he received a fellowship at the museum paid for by the Southern Educational and Charitable Trust.[16] In April 1946, while working on a memorial exhibition for his late friend Florine Stettheimer, Duchamp supervised the de-installation, packing, and safe return of his *Large Glass* to Katherine Dreier, who had placed the work on long-term loan at the Museum since September 1943.[17] He also advised Sweeney on numerous acquisitions for MoMA, including sculpture by Constantin Brancusi, and important early paintings by Robert Delaunay and Francis Picabia,[18] and it is surely no coincidence that the museum acquired an important 1912 painting by Duchamp during Sweeney's tenure as director of the Department of Painting and Sculpture. Indeed, as Calvin Tomkins has noted, Sweeney was "the prime mover behind the trustees' decision to purchase *The Passage from the Virgin to the Bride* from Walter Pach in December 1945—the painting, which had belonged to Pach ever since Duchamp gave it to him in 1915, was the first major work by Duchamp to enter a public collection."[19]

In his report to the Southern Educational and Charitable Trust in February 1947, Duchamp also mentioned that he had also "collected information and documents for the catalogue of a retrospective show" of his work at the Museum of Modern Art, and indicated his intention to closely study and edit the typescripts of his conversations with Sweeney in the near future.[20] Sadly, Sweeney resigned from his position at the Department of Painting and Sculpture in September 1946, after his administrative responsibilities were reduced by the appointment of a committee consisting of five staff members,[21] and he appears to have scrapped his plans for the Duchamp retrospective exhibition and its related catalogue by the end of the following year. Five years later, in a letter dated June 22, 1952, Fiske Kimball, the director of the Philadelphia Museum of Art, asked Sweeney if he had any interest in "getting back to your conversations with Duchamp and their publication. I suppose they were begun," Kimball continued, "when you were with the Museum of Modern Art and thought of an exhibition of Duchamp there. But now the Philadelphia Museum owns the central body of his work, and ought to be the one to make the exhibition. We would be proud if we *could* publish what you write in that connection."[22] Unfortunately, this Duchamp exhibition, which was scheduled for the fall of 1953 and was to have comprised his "entire *oeuvre*," along with a catalogue to be financed by Walter Arensberg, never materialized.[23] However, Sweeney's response, which the Philadelphia Museum of Art's director recorded in a handwritten note following a telephone conversation between the two men in July 1952, reveals that Sweeney declined Kimball's generous offer as he already had a verbal agreement with Albert Skira to publish a 250-page Duchamp monograph through his publishing house in Geneva, based upon his intensive interviews with the artist in the previous decade.[24]

Sweeney abandoned this book project shortly thereafter—a decision that possibly relates to his appointment as director of the Solomon R. Guggenheim Museum in October 1952, as well as his desire for "perfection,"[25] which he feared that Skira could not deliver on—but the interview transcripts in the archives of the Philadelphia Museum of Art provide invaluable insights into Duchamp's work and ideas at the inception of *Étant donnés*.[26] The fact that Sweeney originally planned to write his book in conjunction with a Duchamp retrospective exhibition at the Museum of Modern Art explains why the artist willingly participated in the grueling interview process, during which he participated in at least twenty-five formal conversations with Sweeney between February 1945 and March 1947. "I am telling my whole life to him like a confessor," Duchamp told Henri-Pierre Roché in August 1945, "and that has already lasted six months at the rate of two hours a week!"[27] Recounting the history of his work and ideas to Sweeney for his unrealized book project must have prepared Duchamp for his encounter with the Forestay waterfall in August 1946, since he had discussed the iconography of the *Large Glass* at great length with the museum curator in the previous year. In their fourteenth conversation, which took place on June 9, 1945, Duchamp addressed the "chute d'eau (donné)" and the "Moulin à eau" elements, and declared how delighted he was "to be able to introduce paysage [landscape] without having one there."[28]

In one of the most famous passages from his interview sessions with the artist, which Sweeney published in 1946 in his "Eleven Europeans in America" article, Duchamp explained how the retinal painting that had characterized modern art since the 1850s had downplayed intellectual ideas and contrasted this with his own efforts to create artworks that appealed to the brain, rather than the eye: "I was interested in making painting serve my purposes, and in getting away from the physicality of painting. For me Courbet had introduced the physical emphasis in the nineteenth century. I was interested in ideas—not merely in visual products. I wanted to put painting once again at the service of the mind."[29] Although Duchamp did not use the word "retinal" in the selections from the Sweeney interviews that were published in 1946 in the *Bulletin of the Museum of Modern Art*, he did discuss this concept at great length in their conversation on November 24, 1945. To the best of my knowledge, this is the first time that Duchamp used the term "retinal" in relation to modern art, so I am going to quote the entire passage, which like most of the Sweeney interviews takes the form of shorthand notations. These handwritten notes were transcribed by a third party after each interview, but the typed documents nonetheless capture the cadence of Duchamp's speech and the conceptual framework of his arguments:

> Rétinien painting rather than physical painting
> Mondrian is not rétinien, although abstract.
> Picasso in some paintings—most even in surrealist vein are rétinien
> Impressionist[s] pure rétinien
> Surrealists and even Dalí are non-rétinien.
> Has nothing to do with figurative and non-figurative.
> Things touch you on retina and need go no further.
> The minute you attach allegorical, literary or any other sense it becomes non-rétinien.
> Has nothing to do with values good or bad. I think this is important.
> Take a man like El Greco—we the inventor—we look at it with rétinien eyes.
> Painter makes rétinien work—Not intended to go beyond the retina.
> Brancusi and Lipchitz both rétinien, although both different.
> Maria [Martins] = non-rétinien and acoustical.
> Illuminates the situation today.
> There is a need for a change from predominant tendency toward the rétinien.

These fascinating remarks, which ultimately derive from Gleizes and Metzinger's anti-retinal position in *Du "Cubisme,"* represent the first articulation of Duchamp's idea that painting should be an intellectual rather than purely visual expression, which he would go on to articulate and develop in a large number of subsequent interviews. The fact that Gleizes and Metzinger's earlier writings informed Duchamp's repeated disparagement of retinal art in his postwar interviews does seem rather astonishing, since the artist had long expressed his intense loathing for the two French painters, whose narrow-minded definitions of Cubism had caused him to withdraw his *Nude Descending a Staircase, No. 2* from the 1912 Salon des Indépendents exhibition in Paris. As Duchamp later recalled, the painting was due to have been shown alongside other Cubist paintings, but Albert Gleizes, after conferring with other members of the hanging committee, including Jean Metzinger, Robert Delaunay, and Henri Le Fauconnier, rejected the work on the grounds that it had "too much of a literary title, in a bad sense—in a caricatural way. A nude never descends the stairs—a nude reclines you know. Even their little revolutionary temple couldn't understand that a nude could be *descending* the stairs."[30]

Ever since the publication of *Du "Cubisme,"* which had attempted to rationally explain Cubism to the general public, Duchamp's friend Francis Picabia had wittily labeled

Gleizes and Metzinger the "Bouvard et Pécuchet" Cubists, after the bumbling heroes of Gustave Flaubert's tragicomic novel of bourgeois life.[31] Picabia's derisory nickname for the hapless painters emphatically links their pedantic theorization of Cubism with the farcical attempts of Flaubert's copy-clerks to understand scientific theory, which baffles them with its continuous array of contradictory and ever-changing facts and findings. Flaubert's theme of bourgeois stupidity resonates, with cruel parallels, with Gleizes and Metzinger's derivative paintings and their humorless academic treatise on Cubism. For his part, Duchamp's published statements in New York in the 1910s reveal that he believed that Gleizes and Metzinger's crowd-pleasingly legible Cubist paintings were pale imitations of Pablo Picasso's work, thus turning the two French artists into "monkeys following the leader without comprehension of their significance."[32] The artist may even have had Gleizes and Metzinger, whom he regarded as professional painters working according to established formulas, in mind when he revived the nineteenth-century French saying, "bête comme un peintre" ("stupid as a painter") in his March 1945 interview with James Johnson Sweeney.[33]

Like Gleizes and Metzinger in *Du "Cubisme,"* Duchamp singled out Courbet's retinal revolution as the catalyst for a profound change in the history of painting. After Courbet, modern painting became a self-referential act, provoking a visual, rather than cerebral, response from the viewer. Artists were seduced by the slickness of wet paint and the olfactory sensations produced by pigment ground in linseed oil. He compared the "sensuous feeling" invoked by the colors and brushstrokes of these aesthetically pleasing paintings to taking a hot bath—a pleasant experience, but not conducive to expressing profound thought—"I got out of the bath."[34] It was the desire to go beyond the retina and create a work of art that would appeal to the brain that lay behind the highly intellectual planning and painstaking execution of the artist's enigmatic magnum opus *The Large Glass,* as well as Duchamp's concept of the readymade.[35] *Étant donnés* must also be read, on some level, as the artist's meditation on the legacy of retinal art, although by the time he completed the environmental tableau construction in 1966 his ideas on retinal art and what he called "the retinal shudder" ("le frisson rétinien!")[36] had moved well beyond their original source in Gleizes and Metzinger's *Du "Cubisme"* to become perhaps the most important and influential idea to come out of his work after World War II.[37]

Another recurring idea in Duchamp's postwar interviews and lectures was the important role of the spectator in the creation of works of art; an idea that can also be related to the posthumously unveiled *Étant donnés* project. As the artist explained in a lecture he gave in Houston in April 1957, "The creative act is not performed by the artist alone; the spectator brings the work in contact with the external world by deciphering and interpreting its inner qualifications and thus adds his contribution to the creative act."[38] Eleven years later, he elaborated on this idea in an interview with the Canadian journalist Robert Fulford, in which he again expressed his opinion that "the work of art is always based on the two poles of the onlooker and the maker, and the spark that comes from that bipolar action gives birth to something—like electricity. But the onlooker has the last word, and it is always posterity that makes the masterpiece. The artist should not concern himself with this, because it has nothing to do with him."[39]

Duchamp credited the notion of the onlooker's active participation in the creation of the work of art to the nineteenth-century French artist Georges Seurat, whose paintings were made up of small dots of primary colors that coalesced into the visual likeness of figures or objects in the mind of the viewer. Once again, this idea has its origin in Gleizes and Metzinger's 1912 treatise, *Du "Cubisme,"* where the pointillism of Seurat is described in the following terms: "A thousand little dabs of a pure color break down the white light, the synthesis of which must come about in the beholder's eye."[40] The notion that the finely divided colors that Seurat applied through small regular brushstrokes combined in the viewer's eye through an optical mixture was first proposed by the Italian-born art critic Félix Fénéon in a review that was published in June 1886. Relying on technical information supplied by another Neo-Impressionist painter, Camille Pissarro, rather than Seurat himself, Fénéon boldly claimed that Seurat's "colors, isolated on the canvas, recombine on the retina: we have therefore, not a mixture of material colors (pigments), but a mixture of differently colored rays of light."[41] By 1912, the year that *Du "Cubisme"* was published, the idea that Seurat's colors were reconstituted in the viewer's retina was widely accepted.

While Gleizes and Metzinger praised the systematic application of natural laws in the tessellated brushwork of Seurat and his follower Paul Signac for "boldly breaking with the age-long habit of the eye,"[42] they also criticized their "negation of living beauty,"[43] their blatant disregard for shading, and the restriction of their palette to colors predetermined by paint manufacturers. Indeed, as Peter Brooke has recently argued, *Du "Cubisme"* can be understood as Gleizes and Metzinger's respectful yet firm rebuttal of the ideas put forth in Paul Signac's 1899 treatise *D'Eugène Delacroix au Néo-Impressionnisme,* which was republished in Paris in 1911.[44] Metzinger had gone through an important Neo-Impressionist phase in his early career, but later grew dissatisfied with the results of its scientifically based theory of color. He was thus highly familiar with Signac's color theories, especially his insistence that a maximum luminosity could only be achieved through the use of primary colors, which the Cubists rejected through their formulation of a "new way of imagining light."[45]

Duchamp had first encountered Seurat's work in Paris in the spring of 1905, when he visited the artist's retrospective exhibition at the Salon des Indépendants. Seeing this show, which included the artist's monumental masterpiece, *A Sunday Afternoon on the Island of La Grande Jatte* (fig. 5), as an impressionable eighteen-year-old student at the Académie Julian undoubtedly contributed to Duchamp's lifelong admiration for Seurat. As the artist later explained to Calvin Tomkins, "the only man in the past whom I really respected was Seurat, who made his big paintings like a carpenter, like an artisan. He didn't let his hand interfere with his mind."[46] Duchamp's immense respect for Seurat helps to explain why he did not share Gleizes and Metzinger's reservations regarding the apparent failings and limitations of the artist's efforts to reconstitute light by the optical mixture of its components. Whether or not the artist's blending of colors in the eye of the viewer succeeded or not was beside the point for Duchamp, who was fascinated instead by the contingency of Seurat's method, as seen in the following *inframince* note: "The possibility of several tubes of color becoming a Seurat is the concrete 'explanation' of the possible as infra-thin."[47]

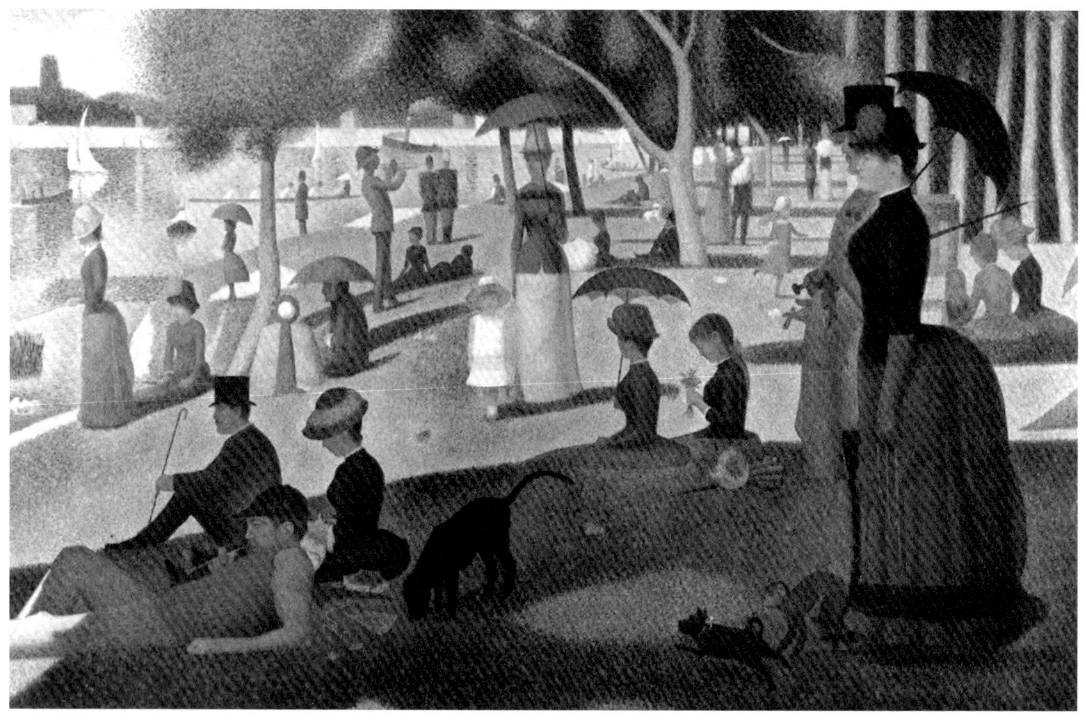

5 **Georges Seurat, *A Sunday Afternoon on the Island of La Grande Jatte,*** oil on canvas, 207.6 cm x 308 cm, 1884–86. Art Institute of Chicago.

Duchamp repeatedly praised Seurat's "cold" and "scientific" approach, which produced a cerebral, impersonal, and completely non-retinal approach to art. As early as September 1915, Duchamp described Seurat as "the greatest scientific spirit of the nineteenth century, greater in that sense than Cézanne," before predicting that "the twentieth century is to be still more abstract, more cold, more scientific."[48] The cold, scientific, intellectual Seurat represented the antithesis of the retinal art of Courbet and Impressionism, and thus remained for Duchamp a vital precursor to his own efforts to put art at the service of the mind. As his postwar interviews make clear, the artist was fully aware that Seurat's paintings invited the audience to collaborate in the creative process by allowing colors to blend and fuse together at a fixed viewing distance, this anticipating the viewing conditions of *Étant donnés.*

Drawing these arguments together suggests that Duchamp used the format of the celebrity interview to explore and test out ideas that were often simultaneously taking shape in three-dimensional form in the *Étant donnés* assemblage. The role of the spectator in this work, which actively solicits the viewer to develop his or her own verbal descriptions and scenarios as to its possible meaning, adds a cognitive dimension to *Étant donnés* that was discussed at length by the artist in his interviews, despite Robert Motherwell's claims to the contrary. What Motherwell overlooked in the Pierre Cabanne interviews was precisely Duchamp's ability to discuss the conceptual ideas behind *Étant donnés,* especially the co-operative efforts of the spectators and the retinal aspect of the viewing apparatus, without specifically addressing the work itself.

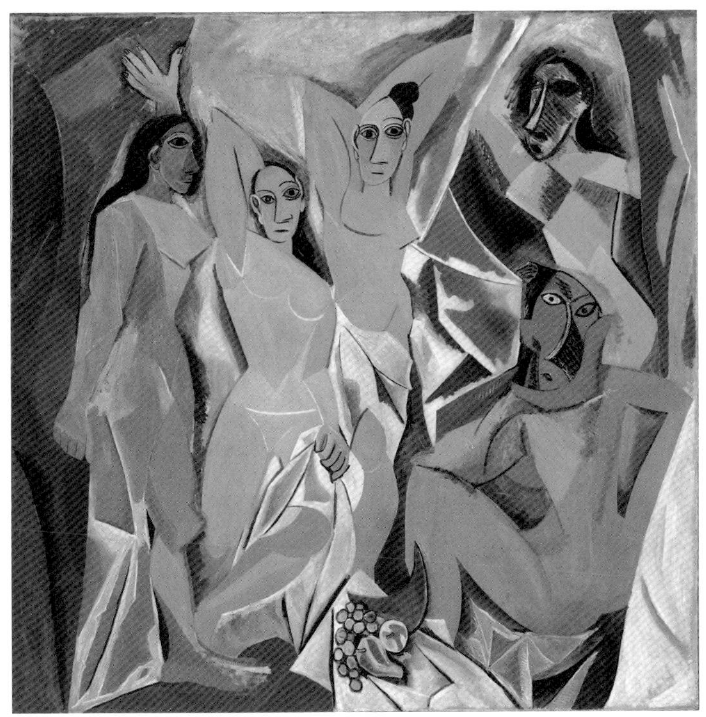

6 Pablo Picasso, *Les demoiselles d'Avignon,* oil on canvas, 245 x 235 cm, 1907. Museum of Modern Art, New York.

But what are to make of the fact that Duchamp reformulated many of these ideas from Gleizes and Metzinger's 1912 treatise on Cubism? Or, to put it another way, can one discern a Cubist dimension in *Étant donnés,* given the artist's return to the theoretical arguments of *Du "Cubisme"* in the mid-1940s? I would argue that the startling anatomical configuration of the nude's crotch area points in this direction, since it can be read simultaneously as a vagina and an anus, thus recalling the oscillation of erogenous zones within the splayed and squatting figure of the prostitute on the right-hand side of Picasso's *Les demoiselles d'Avignon* (fig. 6), who offers the viewer/client the promise that either hole is available for the right price. In *Étant donnés,* Duchamp presents the viewer with a symbiosis of world and vision that offers an encompassing trinity of earth, water, and sky. These elements combine to form a hyperrealistic natural setting in which to place his archetypal supine female form, following the centuries-old tradition of situating the female nude within an idealized landscape setting, as seen, for example, in the series of paintings by Lucas Cranach the Elder on the theme of *The Nymph of the Fountain* (fig. 7), where the seductive nymph reclines under a spouting fountain in a bucolic landscape setting. However, upon closer inspection, the implicated spectator is suddenly, and often uncomfortably, aware that the seemingly tangible reality of this illusionistic pastoral scene contains alternate corporeal visibilities that disrupt the unified field of vision through the presentation of multiple and simultaneous viewpoints akin to those found in Cubist painting and verbally paralleled by the well-known limerick:

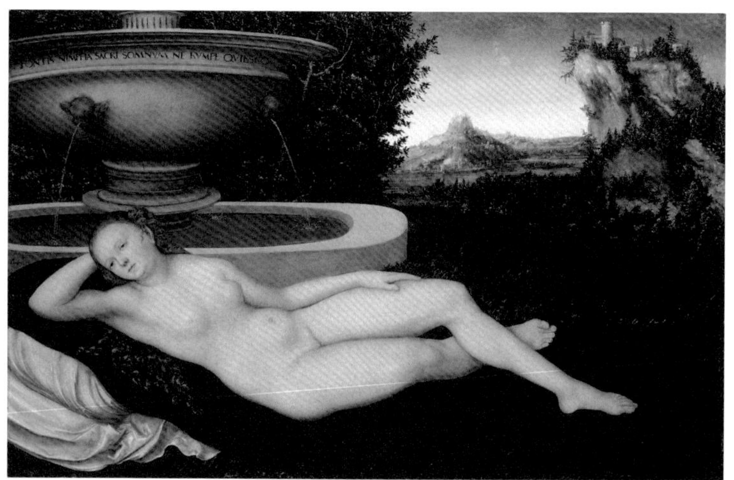

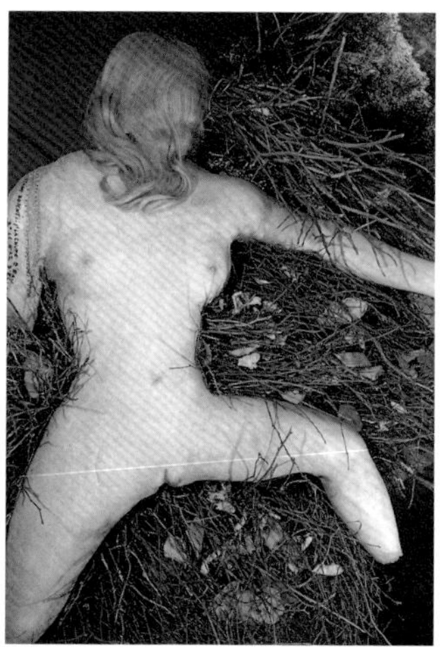

7 Lucas Cranach the Elder, *The Nymph of the Fountain,* oil on panel, c. 1515. Jagdschloss Grunewald (Stiftung Preussischer Kulturbesitz), Berlin. **8 Overhead view of the figure in *Étant donnés,*** showing reversed placement of blond wig.

There once was a man from Racine
Who invented a fucking machine
Concave and convex
It would fit either sex
With a bucket beneath for the cream[49]

This argument is supported by the fact that Duchamp placed the blond wig over the two pieces of plastic that form the *Étant donnés* mannequin's head (fig. 8) so that just a few wisps of hair would be visible from the peepholes. However, the wig was placed back to front, thus confirming the idea that the *Étant donnés* figure contains a degree of visual ambiguity, inherited from Cubism's simultaneous points of view, with the implication being that the nude can be seen and, on the level of erotic fantasy, be possessed both frontally and from behind, perhaps even at the same time. This notion indelibly links the work with Duchamp's playful investigations of the luminal spaces of the *inframince,* in which front becomes back, inside becomes outside, concave becomes convex, solid becomes void, female become male, and vice versa.[50] This can be seen again in the cover that the artist designed in 1956 for the first edition of *Le Surréalisme, même* (fig. 9), which turned the *Female Fig Leaf* (fig. 10) inside out by photographing it in a rotated and reversed position, and then retouching the negative, so that the convex cast crease of the labial slit would read as the concave opening of a pair of male or female buttocks. This inversion of body parts can also be discerned in the shellacked torso fragment (fig. 11) that bears the indexical trace of Maria Martins' genitals. Technical examination of this 1949 body cast has revealed that Duchamp aggressively chastened and filed-down the plaster surface with a rasp-like tool to heighten the visual ambiguity and reversibility of the sexual organs. As with the completed *Étant donnés* mannequin, we are no longer sure whether the sculpture's flesh-like protuberances relate to the external genitalia of the splayed female nude, or her buttocks and asshole; a corporeal ambiguity that may

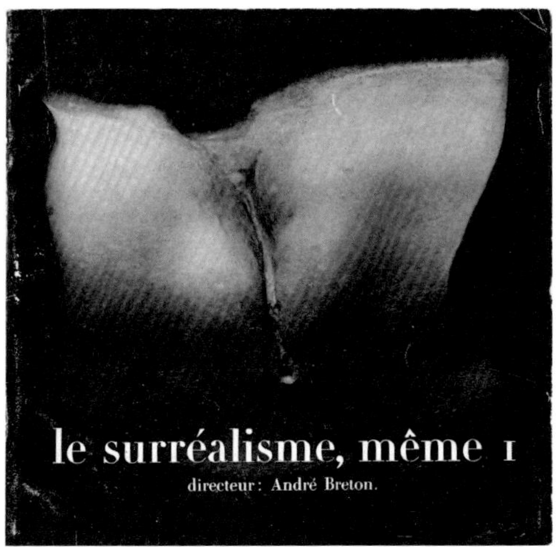

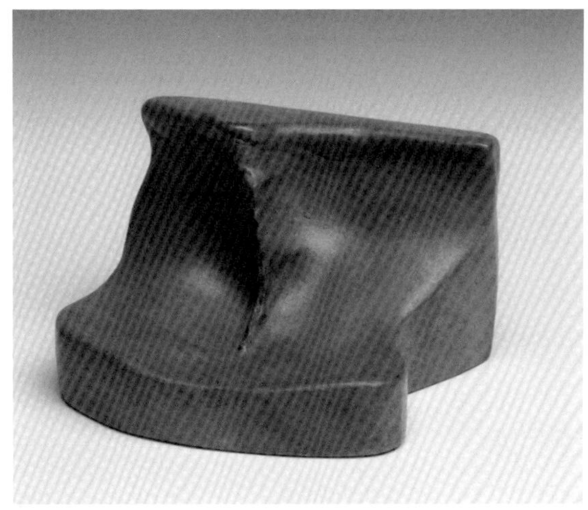

9 Marcel Duchamp, Cover design for *Le Surréalisme, même, no. 1*, paperbound exhibition catalogue, 19.6 x 19.6 cm, Winter 1956. **10 Marcel Duchamp, *Feuille de vigne femelle*** (Female Fig Leaf), painted plaster cast of 1950 copper-electroplated plaster original, 9 x 14 x 12.6 cm, 1951. Philadelphia Museum of Art. Gift of Alexina Duchamp.

have first suggested itself in the perspectival distortions that became apparent when Duchamp changed the mannequin's posture from a standing to recumbent position in the early 1950s (fig. 12). The shift in perspective that took place when the nude moved from an upright to a reclining pose also required additional body casting, which took place in the fall of 1951, when Maria Martins visited Duchamp's studio in New York.[51] It was probably at this time that the artist definitely replaced the hand-held mirror with the bec Auer gas lamp, perhaps as a way of memorializing his unrequited love for Maria, who by this time had permanently severed their relationship and returned with her husband and children to Brazil, as well as commemorating the memory of his late friend and companion Mary Reynolds, who died of uremia in September 1950.

By showing that the variables of recto and verso can cohabit in the same prone female body, Duchamp gave three-dimensional form to the one of the basic tenets of Cubism, namely the presentation of multiple aspects of a figure or object simultaneously, while at the same time revealing the heretofore suppressed erotic impulse in showing the same person from different angles. In *Du "Cubisme,"* Gleizes and Metzinger had predicted that in the future "the act of moving around an object to grasp in succession several of its appearances ... will no longer outrage reasonable people."[52] However, their work largely ignored the female nude in favor of the French tradition of landscape painting, which they updated by applying the cloak of geometric abstraction to the Arcadian visions of Nicolas Poussin or Pierre Puvis de Chavannes. The studious avoidance of the reclining female nude in their work after 1910 suggests that Gleizes and Metzinger were fully aware of the erotic implications of Cubism's multiplicity of perspectives and their fear of the inevitable scandal that would result from the public display of such a painting may explain their vehement rejection of Duchamp's *Nude Descending a Staircase, No. 2* in 1912. As Duchamp later explained to Pierre Cabanne, "In the most advanced group of the period, certain people had extraordinary qualms, a sort of fear! People like Gleizes ... found that this "Nude" wasn't in the line

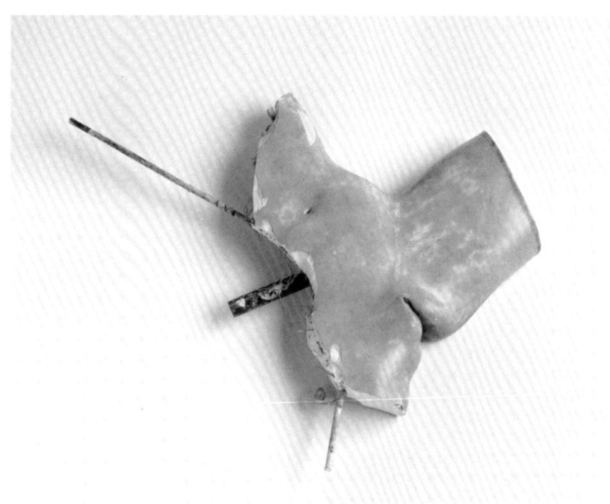

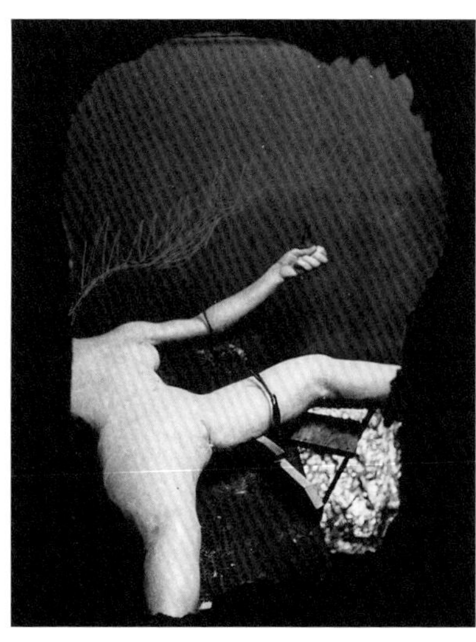

11 Marcel Duchamp, *Untitled* (Torso Fragment), plaster with iron and cloth armature, 55.2 x 44.5 cm, c. 1949. Philadelphia Museum of Art. Gift of Alexina Duchamp **12 Marcel Duchamp, Photograph of a plaster study for the figure in *Étant donnés,*** gelatin silver print with red crayon, 28.6 x 25.4 cm, 1959. Philadelphia Museum of Art, Archives, Alexina and Marcel Duchamp Papers. Gift of Jacqueline, Paul, and Peter Matisse in memory of their mother, Alexina Duchamp.

that they had predicted. Cubism had lasted two or three years, and they already had an absolutely clear, dogmatic line on it."[53]

Leo Steinberg, in his celebrated essay "The Algerian Women and Picasso at Large," argued that in its earliest manifestation Cubism had strived for but had not delivered on its promise of simultaneity, since Picasso and Braque's paintings of the 1910s inserted fragmented body parts "in a relief-like space where no hint of reverse aspects survives."[54] According to Steinberg, it was not until Picasso's post-Cubist variations on Delacroix's *The Women of Algiers* in the mid-1950s that the Spanish artist achieved the "unheard-of visualization of simultaneity."[55] Picasso's final painting in the *Women of Algiers* series, completed on February 14, 1955 (fig. 13), contains a chimerical reclining nude, whose body is comprised of schematic, interwoven parts, "like the shook fragments in a kaleidoscope," to borrow Steinberg's memorable description.[56] Like Duchamp's multi-aspected female figure in *Étant donnés,* Picasso's compound figure is endowed with interchangeable sexual organs that transcend the visual ambiguity of the squatting figure in *Les Demoiselles d'Avignon,* where the viewer was presented with the choice of seeing the prostitute either from the front or behind. In the culminating *Women of Algiers* painting, Picasso achieves the impossible by reshuffling human anatomy before our very eyes through the complex intermingling of front and back views into a single image. Steinberg ended his landmark essay by declaring that Picasso "had neither help nor companionship" in this enterprise, since there was "nothing in modern art that encouraged it."[57] As I hope to have shown in this paper, this statement no longer rings true, since the Spanish artist had in Marcel Duchamp an unlikely ally in his bid to release vision from retinal fixity by fulfilling the long-held promise of rendering the female nude through the simultaneous, mobile perspectives of Cubist painting.

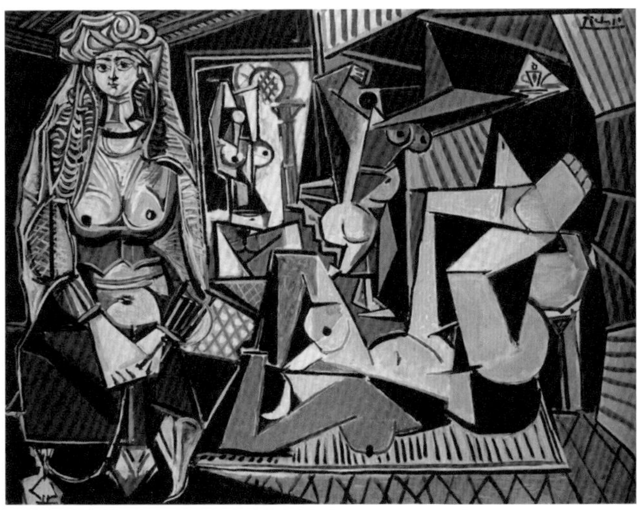

13 Pablo Picasso, *Women of Algiers (after Delacroix),* oil on canvas, 97 x 130 cm, February 14, 1955. Private Collection.

Notes

[1] Robert Motherwell, "Introduction," in Pierre Cabanne, *Dialogues with Marcel Duchamp,* trans. Ron Padgett, New York 1971, p. 11.

[2] Ibid, p. 12.

[3] [Henry McBride], "The Nude-Descending-a-Staircase Man Surveys Us," *The New York Tribune,* section IV, September 12, 1915, p. 2.

[4] Martin Amis, *Visiting Mrs. Nabokov and Other Excursions,* Harmondsworth 1993, p. 54.

[5] As Duchamp later explained to Calvin Tomkins: "There was never any essential satisfaction for me in painting. I just wanted to react against what the others were doing—Matisse and the rest. All that work of the hand. In French, there is an old expression '*la patte,*' meaning the artist's touch, his personal style, his 'paw.' I wanted to get away from '*la patte,*' and from all that retinal painting"; Marcel Duchamp quoted in Tomkins, "Not Seen and/or Less Seen," *The New Yorker,* vol. 40, no. 51 (February 6, 1965), p. 48.

[6] Marcel Duchamp, quoted in Anonymous, "Art Was a Dream...," *Newsweek,* vol. 54, no. 19 (November 9, 1959), p. 118.

[7] Marcel Duchamp, quoted in "BBC Interview with Marcel Duchamp," in Francis M. Naumann, *Marcel Duchamp: The Art of Making Art in the Age of Mechanical Reproduction,* Ghent 1999, p. 300. This television interview, which was recorded on June 5, 1968, was conducted by Joan Bakewell for the BBC *Late Show Line-Up.*

[8] Marcel Duchamp, quoted in Anonymous, "Pop's Dada," *Time,* vol. 85, no. 6 (February 5, 1965), p. 85. Duchamp's disparaging evaluations of Courbet and retinal painting in the late 1950s and early 1960s were not shared by the Abstract Expressionist painters, such as Willem de Kooning, Franz Kline, and Robert Motherwell, who admired not only the painterly facture of Courbet's landscapes, especially those where the variegated palette-knife work takes on abstract qualities, but also the physical energy of his frenzied paint application, which suggested to mid-twentieth-century viewers the elemental power of nature. De Kooning, for example, praised Courbet in a 1958 *Art News* interview, which posed the question, "Is today's artist with or against the past?": "I'm very interested in Courbet," declared the Dutch-born painter. "He could walk in a forest and see something, concretely, just the way it is; be obsessed by the bark on a tree. His painting is not tradition or nature or style, but there it is." Willem de Kooning, quoted in Thomas B. Hess, "Is Today's Artist with or against the Past?" *Art News* 57, no. 4 (Summer 1958), p. 56. Duchamp no doubt was aware of de Kooning's remarks on Courbet, since they were preceded by a negative comment about *L.H.O.O.Q.,* the artist's 1919 rectified readymade, in which he transformed a chromolithograph of Leonardo's *Mona Lisa* through the addition in pencil of an upturned mustache and rakish goatee. De Kooning viewed this iconoclastic gesture as exemplary of the fact that "Marcel Duchamp's just not an art lover"; ibid, p. 27.

[9] Marcel Duchamp, interview with George Heard Hamilton, BBC radio, January 19, 1959; reprinted in "Mr. Duchamp, if you'd only known Jeff Koons was coming?" *The Art Newspaper,* no. 15 (February 1992), p. 13.

[10] Marcel Duchamp, quoted in Katherine Kuh, "Marcel Duchamp," in *The Artist's Voice: Talks with Seventeen Artists,* New York 1962), p. 89.

[11] Ibid.
[12] Thierry de Duve was the first Duchamp scholar to link the artist's anti-retinal position with the arguments expressed by Albert Gleizes and Jean Metzinger in *Du "Cubisme,"* see de Duve, *Nominalisme Pictural: Marcel Duchamp, la peinture et la modernité*, Paris 1984, p. 109.
[13] Albert Gleizes and Jean Metzinger, *Du "Cubisme,"* (Paris 1912); reprinted in Mark Antliff and Patricia Leighten, eds., *A Cubism Reader: Documents and Criticism, 1906–1914*, Chicago 2008), pp. 418–19. Translation from the French by Jane Marie Todd.
[14] Ibid, p. 419.
[15] Marcia Brennan, *Curating Consciousness: Mysticism and the Modern Museum*, Cambridge, Mass. 2010, pp. 59–61.
[16] Jacques Caumont and Jennifer Gough-Cooper, *Ephemerides on and about Marcel Duchamp and Rrose Sélavy 1887–1968*, London 1993, unpaginated (entry for February 20, 1945).
[17] According to Paul Franklin, "Duchamp spearheaded the dismantling of the *Large Glass* at the Museum of Modern Art on April 1, 1946," see Paul B. Franklin, "The Travels of the *Large Glass*," *Étant donné*, no. 9 (2009), p. 236.
[18] Caumont and Gough-Cooper, *Marcel Duchamp and Rrose Sélavy* (note 16), unpaginated (entry for April 24, 1946). During his stay in Europe, between May 1946 and January 1947, Duchamp also investigated for Sweeney the possibility of arranging an exhibition in Paris entitled "Painting in New York, 1939–1945." Ibid.
[19] Calvin Tomkins, *Duchamp: A Biography*, New York 1996, p. 352.
[20] Caumont and Gough-Cooper, *Marcel Duchamp and Rrose Sélavy* (note 16), unpaginated (entry for February 20, 1947).
[21] In response to his resignation, several prominent artists wrote a letter to the *New York Times* expressing their support for Sweeney and protesting the Museum of Modern Art's handling of the affair, see "Artists Uphold Sweeney," *New York Times*, November 2, 1946, p. 72.
[22] Fiske Kimball, Letter to James Johnson Sweeney, June 22, 1952. I am most grateful to Sean Sweeney for sharing this important letter with me.
[23] Fiske Kimball, Letter to James Johnson Sweeney, July 2, 1952. Philadelphia Museum of Art Archives, Fiske Kimball papers. This letter was never sent, since Kimball's hand-written notes in pencil at the top of the page reveals that the two men discussed the matter on the telephone and had no need for further correspondence on the matter.
[24] Ibid.
[25] Ibid.
[26] The fact that Sweeney's book on Duchamp was shelved at some point in the early 1950s meant that the artist's admirers would have to wait until the appearance of Robert Lebel's monograph at the end of that decade to read a comprehensive account of his life and work. It is fascinating to note in this regard that Sweeney's review of *Sur Marcel Duchamp*, which appeared in the *New York Herald Tribune* in December 1959, chastises Lebel for making only a passing reference to the philosophical ideas of Max Stirner. Duchamp had discussed the German philosopher at length during his interviews with Sweeney, leading him to claim in his 1959 review that "in *The Ego and His Own* by Stirner we have probably the fullest key to the philosophy which has encouraged Duchamp over the years 'to depreciate our ordinary and tacitly accepted notions of value in order to exalt the strictly private and sovereign choice which is accountable to no one.' 'The minority,' as Stirner wrote, 'may occasionally err, but the majority is always in the wrong,' see James Johnson Sweeney, "Marcel Duchamp: The Career of an Influential and Enigmatic Artist," *New York Herald Tribune*, vol. 36, no. 21, December 27, 1959, p. 5. There is also a slight hint of jealousy and regret in Sweeney's review, since he knew that he could, and perhaps should, have completed "the fullest critical and historical picture of one of the most provocative figures in contemporary painting" more than a decade before Lebel's monograph, based upon his interview sessions with Duchamp in the mid-to-late 1940s. Marcel Duchamp, quoted in James Johnson Sweeney, "Eleven Europeans in America," *Bulletin of the Museum of Modern Art* 13, nos. 4–5 (1946), p. 20.
[27] Marcel Duchamp, letter to Henri-Pierre Roché, August 21, 1945, reprinted in Francis M. Naumann and Hector Obalk, eds., *Affectionately, Marcel: The Selected Correspondence of Marcel Duchamp*, trans. Jill Taylor, Ghent, Belgium, 2000, p. 251. Sweeney's miscellaneous notes for this book project also reveal that he had the full co-operation and enthusiastic support of Walter Arensberg in this endeavor. In an undated letter, probably written around 1945, Arensberg informed Sweeney that he was "so happy to hear that you are doing a book on Marcel. There is no one so well qualified, and there are comparatively few people in the world who realize, as you must, how much a real study of Marcel is needed. Anything you want of ours is yours for the asking," see Walter C. Arensberg, letter to James Johnson Sweeney, c. 1945, in Sweeney, "Miscellaneous Notes," p. 7, transcript in the archives of the Philadelphia Museum of Art.
[28] Marcel Duchamp, fourteenth conversation with James Johnson Sweeney, June 9, 1945, Philadelphia Museum of Art, Alexina and Marcel Duchamp Papers, reprinted with the permission of the Estate of James Johnson Sweeney.
[29] Marcel Duchamp, quoted in Johnson Sweeney, "Eleven Europeans in America" (note 26), p. 20.
[30] Marcel Duchamp, quoted in William Seitz, "What's Happened to Art? An Interview with Marcel Duchamp on Present Consequences of New York's 1913 Armory Show," *Vogue*, no. 4 (February 15, 1963), p. 112.
[31] Caumont and Gough-Cooper, *Marcel Duchamp and Rrose Sélavy 1887–1968* (note 16), unpaginated (entry for April 4, 1916).
[32] Marcel Duchamp, quoted in Anonymous, "A Complete Reversal of Art Opinions by Marcel Duchamp, Iconoclast," *Arts and Decoration* 5, no. 2 (September 1915), p. 428; reprinted in *Studio International* 189, no. 973 (January–February 1975), p. 29.
[33] Marcel Duchamp, quoted in James Johnson Sweeney, "Eleven Europeans in America" (note 26), p. 21. This remark was made in the previous year, see Marcel Duchamp, fourth conversation with James Johnson Sweeney, March 30, 1945, Philadelphia Museum of Art, Alexina and Marcel Duchamp Papers, reprinted with the permission of the Estate of James Johnson Sweeney. In his lecture, "Should the Artist Go to College—and Why?" which Duchamp delivered on May 13, 1960

at Hofstra University on Long Island, New York, he linked this expression with Henri Murger's 1851 novel, *Scènes de la vie de bohème*, which famously inspired Giacomo Puccini's 1896 opera *La Bohème*. It is perhaps no coincidence that Marcel, the dim-witted painter who appears in Murger's stories of bohemian life, shares Duchamp's first name. Based upon the French writer Jules Fleury, who would later achieve considerable fame under the name Champfleury, Marcel's aspirations in life were to live respectably and become a recognized artist in bourgeois society, much like Gustave Courbet, who also appears in the novel. Unfortunately, the only painting that Marcel manages to sell during the course of the novel ends up as a shop sign for a grocer and his status as an intellectually inferior pariah serves to highlight the dilemma of the poverty-stricken artist who struggles to achieve official recognition and financial security in an age when patronage from the monarch, state or church had been replaced by the cut-throat commercialism of the art gallery system. Duchamp probably read Murger's novel as a young artist and spent the rest of his life trying to dispel the notion that artists were devoid of intelligence. For more on the reception of Murger's novel, see Jerrold Siegel, *Bohemian Paris: Culture, Politics, and the Boundaries of Bourgeois Life, 1830–1930*, New York 1986, pp. 31–58.

[34] Marcel Duchamp, quoted in Dore Ashton, "An Interview with Marcel Duchamp," *Studio International* 171, no. 878 (June 1966), p. 245.

[35] In theorizing the readymade manifestation, the artist rejected the arguments put forth by Gleizes and Metzinger in *Du "Cubisme,"* which promoted good taste in modern art, whereas Duchamp set himself the challenge of removing personal taste from the creative act by selecting objects that would be neither attractive, nor ugly, but aesthetically neutral. For more on Duchamp's experiment with taste in the readymade gesture, see Michael R. Taylor, "Blind Man's Bluff: Duchamp, Stieglitz, and the *Fountain* Scandal Revisited," in *Mirrorical Returns: Marcel Duchamp and Twentieth Century Art*, ed. Yukihiro Hirayoshi, exh. cat. The National Museum of Art, Osaka 2004, pp. 206–13.

[36] Marcel Duchamp, quoted in Cabanne, *Dialogues with Marcel Duchamp* (note 1), p. 43.

[37] It is interesting to note that in 1966, the year the artist completed *Étant donnés*, he qualified his remarks to Otto Hahn by saying that he talked too much about retinal art in his public interviews: "I won't say retinal, I talk too much about that; in each interview I mention my rejection of retinal painting, which is concerned with the eye's reaction only..." Marcel Duchamp, quoted in Otto Hahn, "G255300 [Marcel Duchamp's United States Passport Number]," *Art and Artists* 1, no. 4 (July 1966), p. 9.

[38] Marcel Duchamp, "The Creative Act," 1957, *Art News* 56, no. 4 (Summer 1957), p. 29, reprinted in Michel Sanouillet and Elmer Peterson, eds., *Salt Seller: The Writings of Marcel Duchamp*, New York 1973, p. 140.

[39] Robert Fulford, "Marcel Duchamp, the Old Master," *The Toronto Star*, February 6, 1968, unpaginated.

[40] Gleizes and Metzinger, *Du "Cubisme"* (note 13), p. 426.

[41] Félix Fénéon, "Les Impressionnistes en 1886," *La Vogue* 1, no. 8 (June 13–20, 1886), pp. 261–75; reprinted in Norma Broude, ed., *Seurat in Perspective*, Englewood Cliffs, NJ 1978, p. 37. The scientific principle of "optical mixture" [mélange optique] was first elaborated in Charles Blanc's *Grammaire des arts du dessin (Grammar of Painting and Design)* of 1867, and the French physicist's notion was later endorsed by Ogden Rood in his *Modern Chromatics, Students' Text-Book of Color with Applications to Art and Industry* of 1879, which was published in French two years later as *Théorie scientifique des couleurs et leurs applications à l'art et à l'industrie*. In a statement that lay at the heart of Seurat's ideas and practice, Rood, a professor of physics at Columbia University, argued that "a quantity of small dots of two colors very near each other" would "be blended by the eye placed at the proper distance ... This method is almost the only practical one at the disposal of the artist whereby he can actually mix, not pigments, but masses of colored light, see Ogden Rood, *Modern Chromatics, Students' Text-Book of Color with Applications to Art and Industry*, New York 1879, p. 140. However, John Gage has pointed out that Rood developed his color theory in a laboratory situation in which surfaces are lit simultaneously by white and colored light, rather than the conventional light conditions of an artist's studio. This discrepancy led both Seurat and Fénéon to wrongly believe that Rood claimed that *every* material mixture was deficient in luminosity when compared to color achieved by optical mixture, see Gage, *Color and Meaning: Art, Science, and Symbolism*, Berkeley and Los Angeles 1999, p. 210. This misunderstanding resulted in colors in *Sunday Afternoon on the Island of the Grande Jatte* that Emile Hennequin, as early as 1886, correctly perceived to be "dusty and lusterless" and "almost entirely lacking in luminosity," see Hennequin, "Notes d'art: Exposition des artistes independents," *La Vie modern* (September 11, 1886), p. 581; reprinted in Broude, *Seurat in Perspective*, p. 42.

[42] Gleizes and Metzinger, *Du "Cubisme"* (note 13), p. 425.

[43] Ibid, p. 426.

[44] Peter Brooke, *Albert Gleizes: For and Against the Twentieth Century*, New Haven and London 2001, p. 33.

[45] Gleizes and Metzinger, *Du "Cubisme"* (note 13), p. 427. As Peter Brooke has observed, Gleizes and Metzinger "argue for the use of intermediary colours, such as the earth colours, and also for the luminosity of dark colours, including black. Signac had argued that, although primary colours mixed on the palette became muddy, the original brightness can be retained in the 'optical mix' of the same primary colours placed in small dots together directly on the canvas. The Cubists argue that the optical mix is likely to be as muddy as the mixture on the palette. And they call for a more discreet use of the law of contrasts (that colours are heightened by juxtaposition with their complementaries) than that recommended by Signac, or at least by some of his followers"; ibid.

[46] Marcel Duchamp, quoted in Tomkins, "Not Seen and/or Less Seen" (note 5), pp. 48, 50.

[47] This note was posthumously published in Paul Matisse, ed., *Marcel Duchamp: Notes, exh. cat.* Musée National d'Art et de Culture, Centre Georges Pompidou, Paris 1980), unpaginated.

[48] Marcel Duchamp, quoted in Anonymous, "A Complete Reversal," p. 428; reprinted in *Studio International* (note 32), p. 29.

[49] This limerick is cited in Robert Rosenblum, "Picasso and the Anatomy of Eroticism," in Theodore Bowie and Cornelia V. Christenson, eds., *Studies in Erotic Art,* New York 1970, p. 343.
[50] The concept of the *inframince* appears in several notes that Duchamp wrote during the 1930s and 1940s in which he describes, for example, the infinitesimal differences between two objects taken from the same mold. A thorough scholarly investigation into Duchamp's concept of the *inframince* has yet to be undertaken, although several books and articles on the subject have appeared in recent years that offer a useful, but by no means definitive introduction to this complex theme; see, for example, Yoshiaki Tono, "Duchamp et l'Inframince/Duchamp and Inframince," in *Duchamp,* ed. Gloria Moure, exh. cat. Fundació Joan Miró, Barcelona 1984, pp. 53–56; Molly Nesbit, "Last Words (Rilke, Wittgenstein) (Duchamp)," *Art History* 21, no. 4 (December 1998), pp. 546–64; and Cal Clements, "Duchamp's Infrathin," in *Pataphysica,* Lincoln, NE 2002, pp. 70–90.
[51] In October 1951 Duchamp explained to Maria Martins that he was "putting the skin on the severed leg while waiting for the rest of madame to dry out. The leg will be finished this week," see Marcel Duchamp, letter to Maria Martins, October 8, 1951, in Michael R. Taylor, *Marcel Duchamp: Étant donnés,* exh. cat., Philadelphia Museum of Art, Philadelphia and New Haven 2009, p. 421. Duchamp was referring in this letter to the detachable left leg of the mannequin, bent at the knee, which

had been cast in plaster from Martins' lower thigh, knee, and calf during her visit to New York in the early fall of 1951. The detachable left arm of the figure, which does not survive today, would have been cast on this same trip to enable Duchamp to adjust the position of the hand holding the mirror, which would no longer have been visible after the mannequin was placed on her back. This major re-adjustment to the work in the fall of 1951, as well as the poignant events in his personal life relating to the end of his affair with Maria and the death of Mary Reynolds, was probably the catalyst for Duchamp's decision to replace the mirror with the bec Auer lamp.

[52] Gleizes and Metzinger, *Du "Cubisme"* (note 13), pp. 431–32.

[53] Marcel Duchamp, quoted in Cabanne, *Dialogues with Marcel Duchamp* (note 1), p. 17.

[54] Leo Steinberg, "The Algerian Women and Picasso at Large," in Steinberg, *Other Criteria: Confrontations with Twentieth Century Art,* Oxford 1972, p. 155.

[55] Ibid.

[56] Ibid, p. 230.

[57] Ibid, p. 234.

Michael Lüthy

Étant donnés as a Form of Experience

In 1954, when Duchamp was supervising the installation of the Arensberg Collection at the Philadelphia Museum of Art, he also inspected and measured the room that he would later use to present his then nascent work *Étant donnés:* a long, narrow room at the far end of the eastern wing of the museum, where works by Kandinsky and Jawlensky were hung until 1969, when it was cleared for *Étant donnés.*[1] From this moment on, he not only knew where his installation was destined to appear, he also knew the exact spatial dimensions he had to plan for. He thus also knew that the installation that he was building in his atelier would only take up half of the space available to him in the museum. Actually, he was not able to set up the other half—that means the part not behind, but in front of the wooden door of *Étant donnés*—in his atelier to test its effect, because the atelier was far too small to accommodate it. Nevertheless, it can not be denied that Duchamp must have been absolutely clear about the fact that *Étant donnés* would be a two-room installation, consisting of a space that the viewer must cross through in order to be able to look into a peephole, and the space that would then be revealed beyond the peephole. Between these two halves of almost identical dimensions, serving as both their separation and their link, there is a wall with a wooden door, brick framing, and plaster—a wall which looks as if it were always there, but was only built for the installation of *Étant donnés* in 1969.

Surprisingly, there is hardly any mention of the front room in the extensive literature on *Étant donnés,* and up to now there has been no depiction of this space as a space in its own right; the image reproduced here (fig. 1) has been made only for this essay. In short, it is a blind spot in the reflection on Duchamp's final work. This is surprising given the fact that Duchamp planned *Étant donnés* specifically for this space and could therefore consider all aspects, not only of the work's production, but also of its reception; and given, on a more general level, that throughout his entire oeuvre Duchamp constantly reflected anew on how the viewer and the work encounter each other in space, concretely staging this aspect, for instance in 1938 at the *Exposition Internationale du Surréalisme,* where he designed the central "grotto" of the exhibition, or in 1942 at the exhibition *First Papers of Surrealism,* where he mounted a network of strings,[2] but also when installing his works in 1954 at the Philadelphia Museum of Art, creating a precise spatial viewing apparatus for the *Large Glass,* including an especially made door which opened to the eastern terrace of the Philadelphia Museum. My thesis is the following: that we must understand *Étant donnés* as a two-room installation, that is, that *Étant donnés* does not begin with the wooden door and the view through the peepholes, but already with entering the empty door frame, which separates the big, bright room where the *Large Glass* is exhibited from the significantly smaller and darker room that leads to the wooden door (fig. 2). In this essay, I will be speaking only about this first room in the two-room installation of *Étant donnés,* and I will use it to address certain aspects of the experience of Duchamp's last great work. In doing so, I will focus on two aspects: first I will thematize the particular emptiness of this space, as well as the specific way that it activates the viewer. In a second step, I will be speaking of *Étant donnés* as another of those "period rooms" for which the Philadelphia Museum of Art is so famous, asking what insights might be revealed by viewing this work

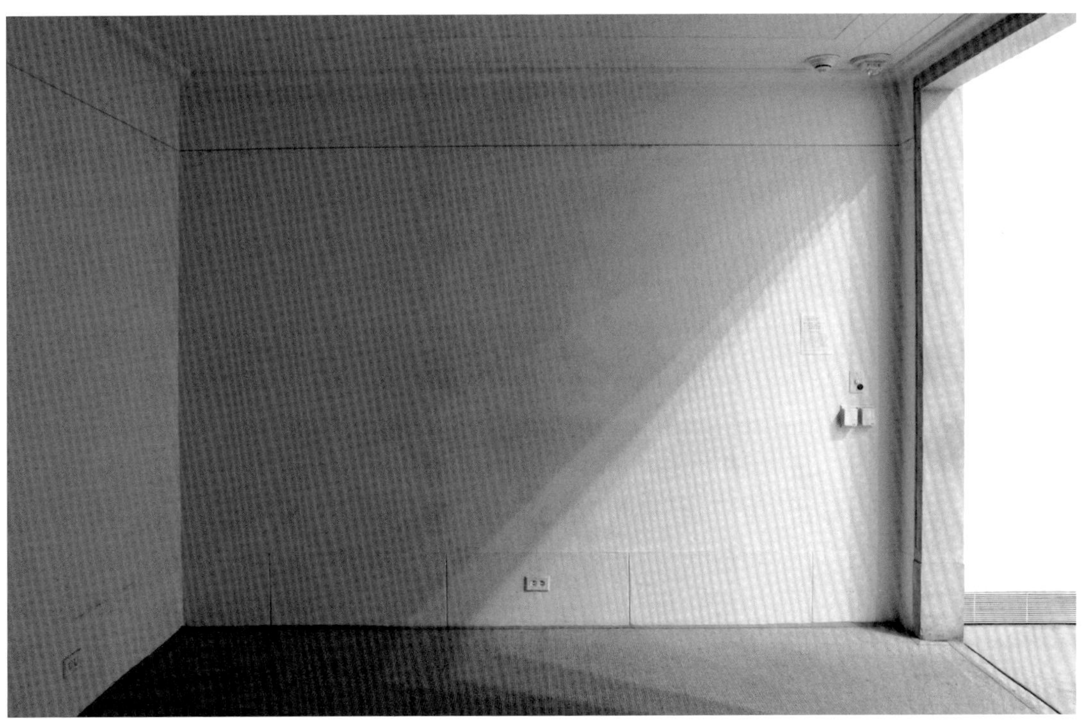

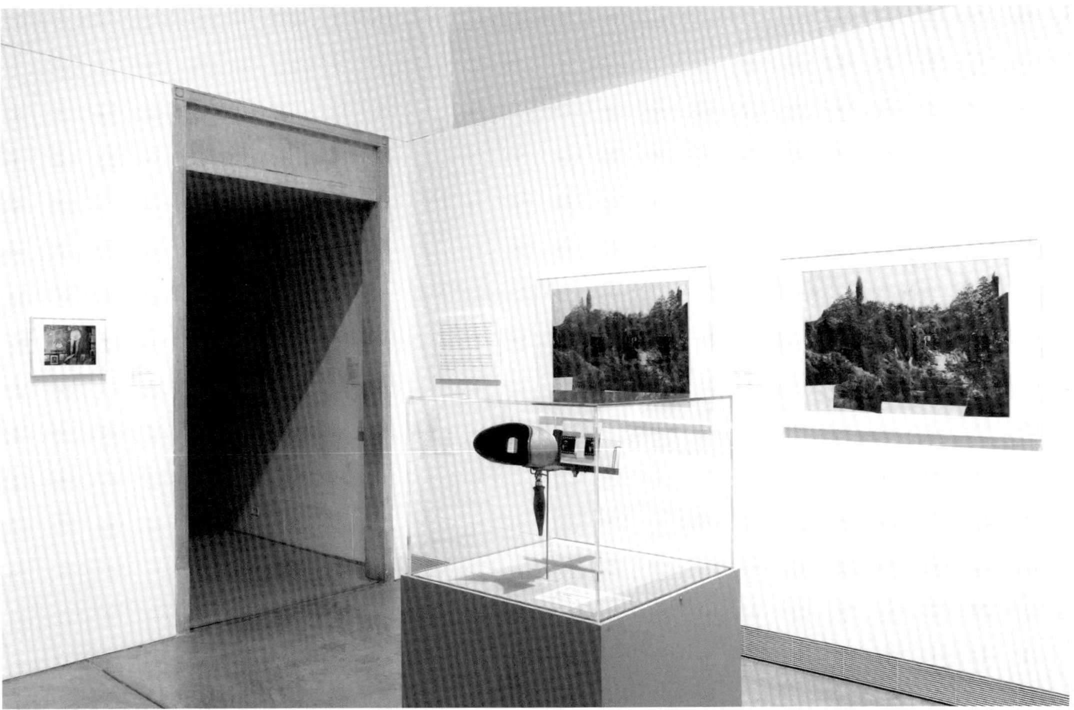

1 Marcel Duchamp, Empty room in front of the wooden door of *Étant donnés*, Gallery 182. Philadelphia Museum of Art. **2 Marcel Duchamp, Empty door frame** between Galleries 182 and 183, leading to the first room of *Étant donnés*. Philadelphia Museum of Art.

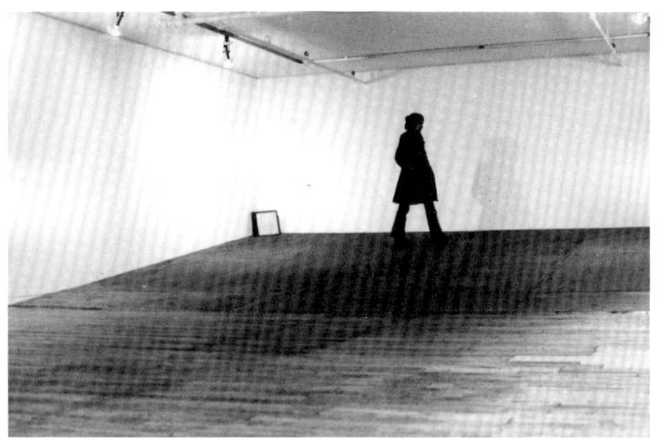
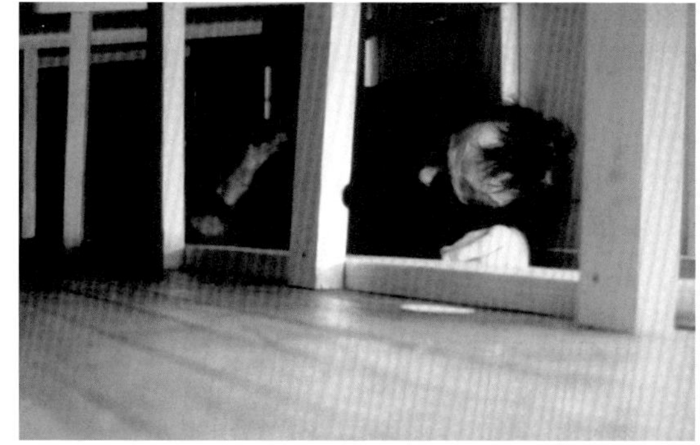

3 & 4 Vito Acconci, *Seedbed,* performance, Sonnabend Gallery, New York, January 15–29, 1972.

as another "period room." Here it will not so much be a matter of the emptiness of the room, but of what the room does contain: the plaster wall with the Spanish wooden door and its framing made of Spanish bricks, as well as the Sisal rug covering the entire floor.

1. Empty Space, Action, Situation

I come to the first aspect by which we can view the anteroom to *Étant donnés,* that of emptiness. In his later lecture "Where do we go from here," given in Philadelphia in 1961, Duchamp complained about the reification and commercialization of art, which had created the need for an ascetic revolution. His own artistic response to this was *Étant donnés,* which radically resisted the object status of the work, in the first place because it is not a movable art object, but instead a place where the viewer must go, and secondly because the experience of *Étant donnés* is less the experience of an art object and more the experience of a situation in which the viewer experiences him or herself as someone who productively takes part in the experience to be had here, which creates a connection between the experience of the work and experience of the self. Due to these qualities, and although Duchamp had been planning the work since the late 1940s, *Étant donnés* can be seen as having a specific currency at the time of its public exhibition in 1969. In 1969 it is a *contemporary artwork* in a quite particular way. But in what sense?

On the one hand, what *Étant donnés* shares with the neo-avant-gardes of the 1960s and '70s is the attempt to break through the boundaries of the particular arts and métiers to get to practices that could incorporate all kinds of materials and all artistic processes. On the other hand, it also shares that trait that Lazlo Glozer expressed with the famous formula "exit from the image."[3] With the formula of an "exit from the image," Glozer grasped a significant trait of those phenomena that marked the era, such as Installation Art, Performance Art, or Conceptual Art. What all of these phenomena had in common was an iconoclastic shift away from the conventional forms of the image, and this iconoclasm was applied to the image as an object of art as well as to the image as a model of representation. What was being sought on a broader front, and in the most varied forms, was an aesthetics of spatial and temporal actuality, the presence of bodies and materials, as well as the situational involvement of the viewer, precisely in order to resist that reification of art that Duchamp had also complained about in his 1961 lecture. In this quest to get beyond the boundaries of the image and into a situation that includes the viewer, the first room of *Étant donnés,* with its emptiness, is absolutely essential. I would like to clarify this by taking a slight detour to look at two performances—or performance spaces—that were created a few years after the presentation of *Étant donnés*. As far as I know, they were made totally independent of Duchamp's work, but share with *Étant donnés* the intention of undermining or overrunning the conventional triad of artist, artwork, and viewer.

The first of these performances is Vito Acconci's *Seedbed,* which he created in 1972 (fig. 3 & 4). One of Acconci's goals—in this performance but also more generally—consisted in simultaneously understanding and undermining the position of the artistic field of his time, which he experienced as the playing field of "exaggerated formalist criticism" and which he was skeptical about, much like Duchamp.[4] To this end, his performances thematized three central aspects of the field: the act of artistic production, the act of seeing, and the experiential space of the gallery. For *Seedbed,* Acconci had an inconspicuous ramp built in the New York Sonnabend Gallery, which caused the floor in the entire back half of the room to rise gradually to a height of seventy-five centimeters. Anyone coming in the gallery at first did not see much more than an empty room, in which no distinct object could be identified for viewing. Acconci was lying under the ramp, invisible to the spectators, for a total of nine days during the three-week exhibition.

When the spectators walked onto the ramp, he would begin to communicate with them by means of two loudspeakers set up in the room. He masturbated (or pretended to be doing so) and fantasized while the visitors walked around on the ramp above him. Thus, Acconci was confronting two very different spaces with each other: an empty room in which the viewers walked around, and a space separated from it where he himself was. In contrast to *Étant donnés,* here the two spaces are not behind one another, but on top of one another. Furthermore, in the space inaccessible to the viewer there was no life-sized female figure, but Acconci himself, and the contact between the two rooms was not optical, as was the case with Duchamp's peepholes, but acoustic. I am thus not interested in any direct analogy between *Seedbed* and *Étant donnés,* but in the structural relationships in the layout and in the processes of experiencing both works. This will be particularly clear when we consider the goals that Acconci was pursuing with *Seedbed*. For in a quite aggressive way, the performance reverses what Acconci described in an interview as the common and equally aggressive behavior of viewers in relation to artworks. They enter the exhibition space and single-mindedly let loose at the artwork; that is, they treat the artwork as if it were a target. In his own words, Acconci says:

"It seems like in any kind of art situation, viewer enters exhibition space, viewer heads towards artwork, so viewer is aiming towards artwork. Viewer is treating artwork as a kind of target, so it seems to me this is a kind of general condition of all art viewing, art experience."[5]

Seedbed is an answer to this instrumental way of seeing, since Acconci leaves the viewer looking at emptiness. The work was not an object on the wall or a sculpture in the room, but the situation as a whole—a situation in which the gallery visitor was simultaneously both inside and outside, part of the work and at the same time excluded from it. He or she could no longer approach the work frontally: the work was everywhere and nowhere. The slanted surface where the gallery visitor walked around becomes a symbol of the destabilized relations between the viewer, the artist, and the work, and at the same time the relations are slipping into the realm of the sexual.

The second performance that I would like to draw on is Bruce Nauman's *Body Pressure* from 1974 (fig. 5). In the Konrad Fischer Gallery in Düsseldorf, Nauman had an artificial wall built into the room and hung a notice next to it. The text directed the visitors to press their own bodies against this wall as hard as they could. Furthermore the text directed the viewers to imagine that they were themselves pressing back from the other side of the wall, that is, that they were not pressing against the wall, but against themselves. The final sentence in the directions, which revolves around this gradual, imaginary replacement of the wall by the double of one's own body, states that "This may become a very erotic exercise."[6] In the case of Nauman's *Body Pressure,* the artist himself is not present like in Acconci's *Seedbed,* but is instead using the printed notice to direct the visitor to carry out a specific activity. But here as well, the work is no isolated object on the wall or in the room, but a situation. The negation of the conventional work structure on the part of Acconci and Nauman is accompanied by the production of a spatial apparatus in which the visitor becomes activated as the co-producer of the work. One of the things this means is that the positions of subject and object overlap. The visitors are not only the subjects of an aesthetic experience that they are having in relation to the artwork. They simultaneously experience themselves as the objects of the artistic situation, which directs their movements and which forms their perceptions of other and self. While Acconci says that the viewers normally aim at the artwork like a target, in Acconci's *Seedbed* and Nauman's *Body Pressure* the situation is reversed and the artwork becomes something that aims at the viewer.

These dynamics and reversals are also provoked by *Étant donnés*. In this case, the deconstruction of the conventional forms of viewing artworks does not begin with what we see *beyond* the wooden door. It is already happening when we enter the first, front room. Upon entering, we initially see nothing more than a disturbingly empty and underlit room, illuminated only by the light coming in from the open door frame. Some viewers simply turn around and walk out after taking a short look around in this empty room, thinking there's nothing more to see. But even those who notice the door, its brick frames, and the plastered wall and move toward it to examine it more closely do not encounter any artwork in the conventional sense, which would call on us to contemplate it like a picture or sculpture. Until the viewer figures out what is here to see—that is until he discovers the peepholes—he walks around searching for it like on Acconci's ramp, and when he has discovered the peepholes, he has to press up against the wooden door like in Nauman's *Body Pressure* (fig. 6). But neither walking around nor pressing against a door are typical activities when dealing with art. Afterwards—as soon as one has looked through the holes in the wooden door—the experience of the first room of *Étant donnés* is altered once again. For at this moment it becomes clear that when we were walking around in this first room, we have been both in the artwork and outside of it, being already part of it and at the same time not yet knowing it.

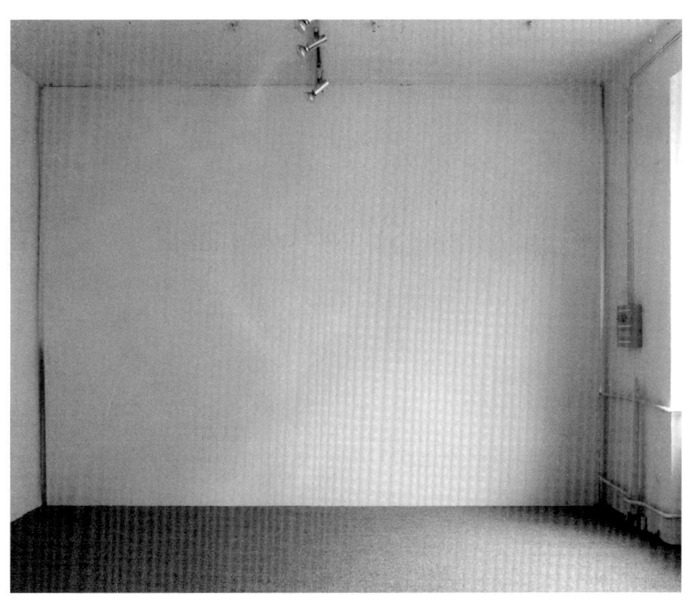

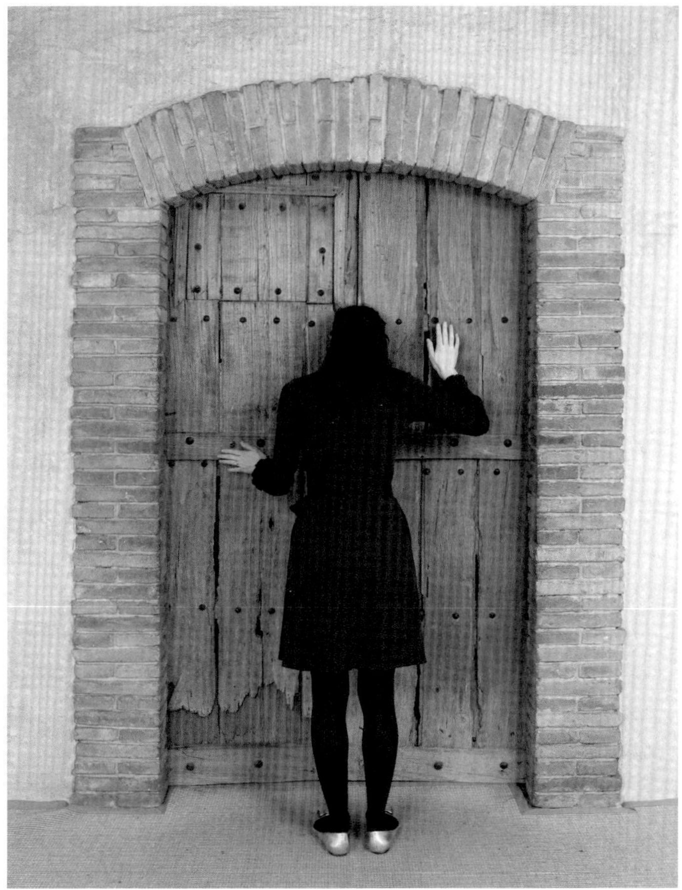

5 **Bruce Nauman,** ***Body Pressure,*** pink poster with text and freestanding wall, 345 x 260 cm, first shown as part of the exhibition *Yellow Room*, Konrad Fischer Gallery, Düsseldorf, February 4–March 6, 1974. Friedrich Christian Flick Collection, Berlin. Photograph by Dorothee Fischer. 6 **Marcel Duchamp,** ***Étant donnés,*** woman looking through the two peepholes.

I would like to end this comparison between Duchamp, Acconci, and Nauman by mentioning two more structural parallels. The first parallel is that all three works tend to individualize the viewer and produce a one-to-one relationship between the work and the viewer—in Acconci's case through the dialogue with the visitor, in Nauman's through the directions for a bodily encounter with the self, and finally in Duchamp due to the impossibility of two persons looking through the peephole at the same time. All three works thus prevent the art becoming the kind of mass spectacle that Duchamp saw coming and explicitly condemned. The second structural parallel is the following: As soon as one is looking through the peephole and is discovering the interior of *Étant donnés,* one becomes, as the viewer, an exterior element, who can be observed by other visitors. As awkward as it may be to be observed while walking around on Acconci's ramp, being the target of his fantasies, or to be observed pressing against the wall that Nauman had built, trying to have the erotic experience promised by him, it is equally awkward to turn around after looking through *Étant donnés*'s peepholes only to discover that one has been the object of view for other museum visitors.

What binds *Étant donnés* with other contemporary aesthetic projects is thus its concern with an apparatus of viewing,[7] which has striking parallels to the neo-avant-garde critique of the modernist understanding of art that defines art as an object that is perceived by a unbiased viewer, who unlocks its meaning and value with the appropriate knowledge. And it is this modernist and aestheticist understanding of art that has the tendency to turn artworks into fetishes not only of the contemplative gaze of the beholder, but also into fetishes of the art market. Instead Acconci and Nauman, and in a different way also Duchamp, follow another idea, which I called an aesthetic of spatial and temporal actuality, the presence of bodies and materials as well as the situational involvement of the viewer. Not only Acconci and Nauman, but also *Étant donnés* links seeing to the completion of an *action,* understood as a bodily activity carried out over a certain period of time, which in *Étant donnés* includes having to press one's body on a wooden door. At the same time, it links seeing with a *situation,* understood as a place at which this special action takes place.

This expansion of seeing into action and situation opens up the experience of art along a fault line that in a certain sense coincides with the wall set up in the room, which separates *Étant donnés* into two distinct spaces and at the same time links these spaces like a hinge. This hinge separates and links not only the two distinct spaces of *Étant donnés,* it simultaneously separates and links qualities that are commonly understood as oppositional: inside and outside, here and beyond, presentness and timelessness, materiality and immateriality, etc. Duchamp gave this hinge a name: he called it an *infra-thin.*[8]

2. A Kind of Period Room

The thematization of the wall that separates and connects the two spaces of *Étant donnés* like a hinge leads me to the second section of this essay. Here we are not concerned with the emptiness of the room, which is filled up as a space of action and situation, but with what is materially contained in this space and what it becomes through this. At the same time I am changing perspective. So far I have attempted to contextualize *Étant donnés* in *time,* not by situating the work in the chronology of Duchamp's work—as the summation

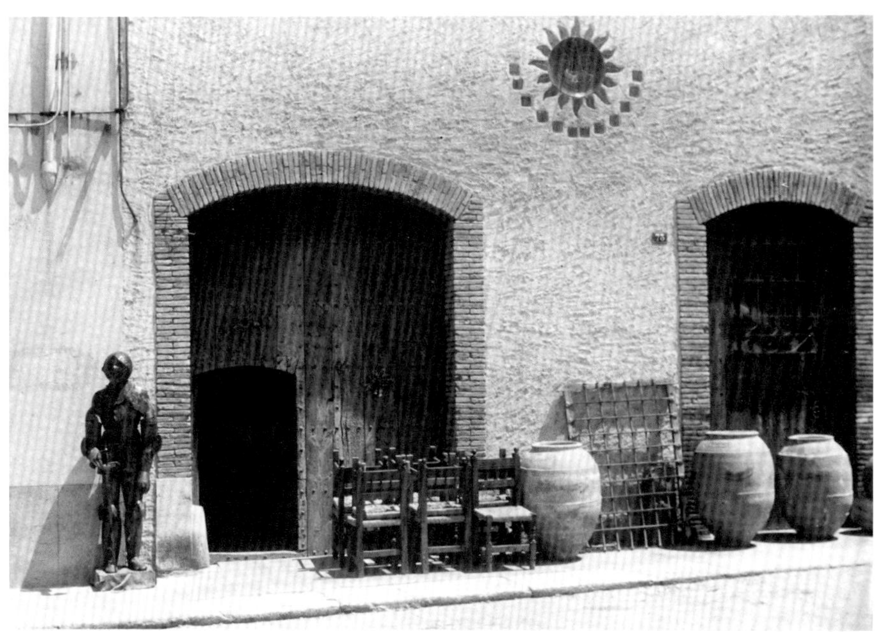

7 Marcel Duchamp, Photograph of plastered wall with brick-framed doors in La Bisbal d'Empordà, Spain, early 1960s.

of the oeuvre, as the continuation of the *Large Glass,* or the like—but by working out an aspect of its contemporary aesthetic qualities. Now I would instead like to contextualize it in terms of *space* by discussing *Étant donnés* in its aesthetic relation to the place for which Duchamp conceived the work: the Philadelphia Museum of Art.

Three of the four walls of that first room, which is my sole topic here, are empty; the fourth wall, however, which was constructed especially for the work, is a carefully executed artifact over its entire surface, consisting of a wooden door and a brick frame, for which Duchamp selected the raw materials in Spain and had them transferred to America, as well as the plaster surface covering the remainder of the wall. The design of this wall, which in its current form decidedly bears the stamp of Duchamp's stepson, the engineer Paul Matisse, is based on photographs that Duchamp had taken during his summer trips to Spain of similar doors and walls (fig. 7).[9] This combination of using original materials and artificially recreating a space in the context of the museum is precisely the aesthetic logic of the period rooms, which the Philadelphia Museum of Art already possessed in great number and was already famous for by the time Duchamp was working on *Étant donnés* and determined the space for it within the museum. The period rooms seek to merge individual elements that may not necessarily belong together in the way shown—pieces of furniture, elements of decor, artworks, etc.—into a complete aesthetic situation, which makes it possible for the viewer to go on a visual trip to another place and another time.

Interestingly, the fact that Duchamp's installation forms a bridge to the period rooms is one of the arguments that had to be made on January 15, 1969 at a decisive meeting of the Executive Committee of the Board of Trustees of the Philadelphia Museum in order

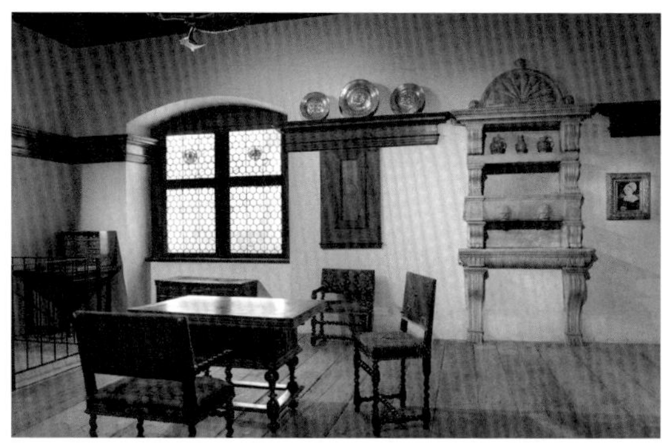

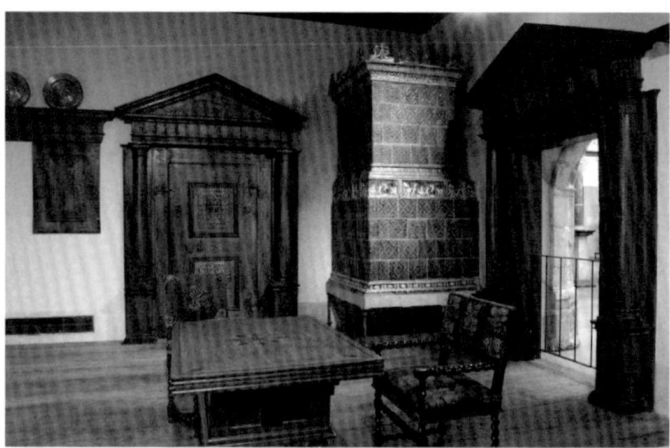

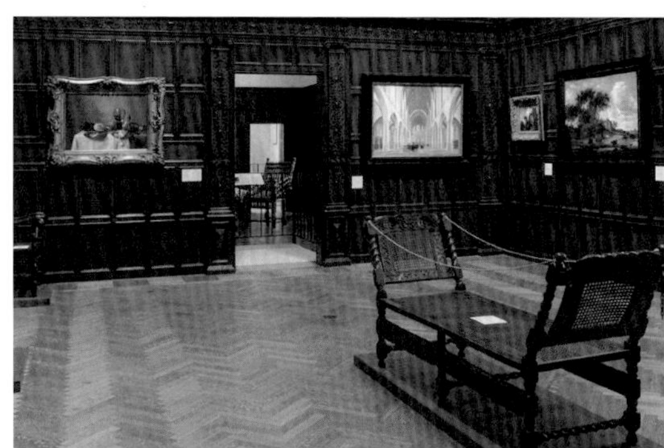

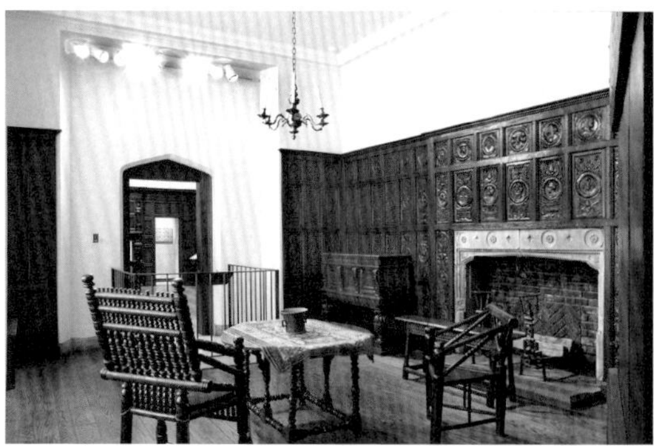

8 & 9 Gallery 256, room from the Stiegerhof near Villach, Austria, late 16th century. Philadelphia Museum of Art (in the museum since 1929). **10 Gallery 262,** Netherlandish paintings and English furniture of the 17th century. Philadelphia Museum of Art (in the museum since 1951). **11 Gallery 263,** paneling from a room in the Red Lodge, Langley Park estate, Kent, 1529. Philadelphia Museum of Art (in the museum since 1929).

to accept the endowment of Duchamp's posthumous work. As the third speaker, after the president and then the director of the museum, Henry Clifford, one of the Trustees and earlier a curator of painting, stressed that "in a Museum so rich in period rooms [*Étant donnés*] would add one of this century."[10] Clifford's remark is absolutely pertinent; but I suspect that the aesthetic point of Clifford's statement, that *Étant donnés* would be another "period room" in the museum, has not yet been sufficiently addressed.

Therefore I would like to draw our attention to another element of that first room of *Étant donnés:* to the Sisal carpet that fills the entire room, from the threshold at the entrance to this first room, up to the wooden door where one finally stands and looks. When I stood in this room for the first time, I found this Sisal carpet considerably disturbing. Why was it there? In the meantime I have been able to find out from Michael Taylor's extensive and precise catalogue, published in conjunction with the 2009 exhibition on *Étant donnés,* that it was the last element to be installed, shortly before the work was presented to the public. It cannot be traced back to any decision of Duchamp's, but was rather installed to hide the electronic sensors that had been built into the flooring, which caused the lights to go on behind the wooden door as soon as someone entered the first room of *Étant donnés*. In the meantime, however, the Sisal carpet has actually become unnecessary, as I was also able to find out from Taylor's catalogue. For in August 1998, the floor sensors were replaced with motion sensors installed in the ceiling of the room. Nonetheless, the carpet is still there and even gets replaced when it is too worn out.[11] We must therefore now ascribe to this carpet no longer merely a pragmatic function, but an aesthetic one. This aesthetic function, however, is significant. For in fact we also encounter this Sisal carpet at decisive spots in the museum's period rooms. There, they do not only have the pragmatic function of protecting the valuable flooring, but also a further aesthetic function. They mark that indeterminate space, both spatially and temporally, that you find yourself in when you stand in the viewing station from which you look into these period rooms which you can not enter. In figure 8 we see Gallery 256, the reconstruction of a room of the so-called Stiegerhof near Villach in Austria, built in the late sixteenth century. On the left is the viewing station with the Sisal carpet, from where one has the view shown in figure 9. Actually you stand on a section of the floor in the room that you are looking at, but at the same time you are elsewhere, as if there were an invisible wall separating you from what you are seeing. The situation becomes even more peculiar when two rooms that are temporally and spatially different are directly adjoined. In Gallery 262 with Netherlandish paintings from the seventeenth century, you can enter a viewing station from which you are looking into the adjacent room, originally part of a hunting lodge in Kent, England, made one century earlier, in 1529 (figs. 10 & 11). When you stand at this viewing station, you are still part of the first room's time-space, but are already looking into the second room's time-space, literally standing in a spatial-temporal nowhere.

A further element of the period rooms corresponds with this non-place of the viewing stations: the light falling through the windows that lights up the rooms, along with spotlights mounted in the rooms themselves that serve to draw attention to details in the furnishings. The light falling through the windows is not natural light, but artificial light simulating natural light. It falls completely evenly, free of the fluctuations that would be caused by the time of day or weather conditions, shining in through panes that are usually made of frosted glass. The period rooms are thus transformed into a constant present, which gives them a peculiar, somewhat surreal atmosphere. In Gallery 268, a salon from a Parisian town house, there is yet another dimension to this (fig. 12). A balcony railing is visible through the high windows. But of course we cannot walk out onto this balcony, nor even open the window, not only for reasons of conservation, but because we would not be able to look out onto the Rue Royale in Paris, where this palace was constructed shortly before the French Revolution, but onto an interior wall of the museum, complete with the neon lights that are the source of the light coming through the frosted glass. The balcony railing appears on this glass like fantasmatic shadows. In Duchamp's context, one is tempted to speak of this balcony railing as the three-dimensional shadows of that ungraspable four-dimensional spatial time in which this period room lives, somewhere between Paris and Philadelphia, between the French Revolution and the present. In the so-called Late Gothic Room, a late-fifteenth-century French interior, the viewing station and the windows are directly opposite one another (figs. 13 & 14). For anyone standing here after having seen Marcel Duchamp's *Étant donnés,* the impression is overwhelming. The view from the station into these windows is structurally the same as the view through Duchamp's door, only that here the door is missing, which makes this view over time and spaces all the more inscrutable. In short, the link between the position that one takes standing at the station with its Sisal-carpeted floor and the spaces that one looks at from there, is *infra-thin.* In precisely the way that I have just described them for the period rooms, the viewer in *Étant donnés* stands on the Sisal carpet and looks through the peepholes (fig. 6), at that female figure and that landscape that are bathed in an even, timeless light by an elaborate arrangement of spotlights and neon, which is installed above the strange diorama (fig. 15), hidden from the spectator and visible here only by way of the photographs Duchamp made for his manual of instructions for the dismantling and reassembly of *Étant donnés.*

In his lecture on the "Creative Act," Duchamp speaks of the fact that it is not only the artist that makes the work, but that the spectators, who come into the world later, contribute equally to it. The first room of *Étant donnés,* which was constructed in Philadelphia without having previously been dismantled in Duchamp's atelier in New York, is a space in which this programmatic statement becomes constructed reality. For it is as much conceived by Duchamp as it is added to by posterity, at least in its current form. It is marked by an irrevocable *différance* between Duchamp's intentions and the actual reality. In his lecture on the creative act, Duchamp claims that this difference is precisely the art-coefficient held in the work. It has been my wish to show that the art-coefficient of *Étant donnés* is closely connected with the hinge function of the wall that simultaneously separates and links the two very different spaces of *Étant donnés.* I wanted to show that this hinge function of the wall only becomes apparent if we take *Étant donnés* not as beginning with and beyond the wooden door, but conceive of it as a two-room installation, where the door with its peephole is not the delimitation of the installation, but is located in the *middle* of it. To end this essay by coming back to its title—*Étant donnés* as a Form of Experience—my argument sums up to this: *Étant donnés* is an apparatus which produces for the beholder a very special experience: the experience of the *infra-thin.*

Translated from the German by Daniel Hendrickson

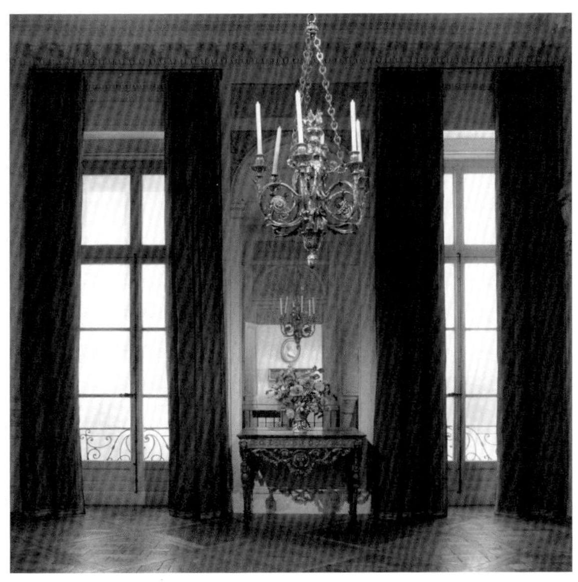

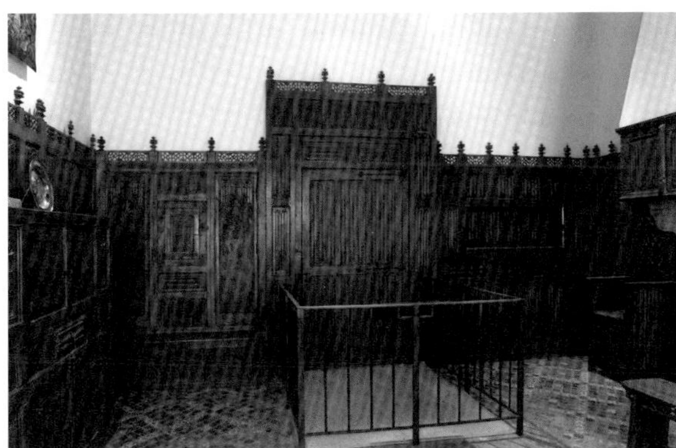

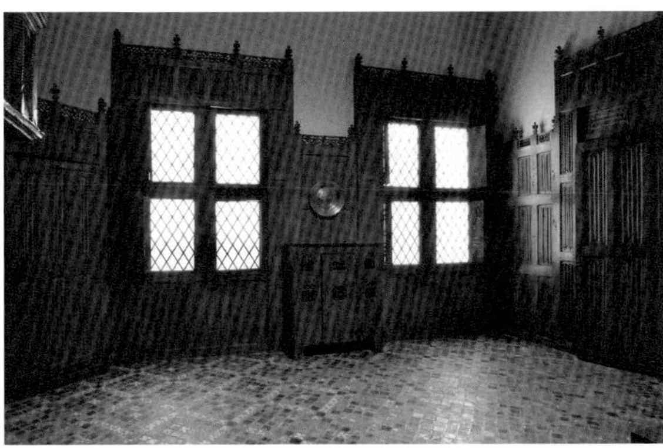

12 Gallery 268, Salon from Hôtel Le Tellier, 13, rue Royale, 1782–85, with modifications in 1789. Philadelphia Museum of Art (in the museum since 1928). **13 & 14 Gallery 214,** Late Gothic Room, composed of elements from several late-fifteenth-century Northern European, mostly French interiors. Philadelphia Museum of Art (in the museum since 1928). View of the entrance door and the viewing station (13) and view of the windows (14).

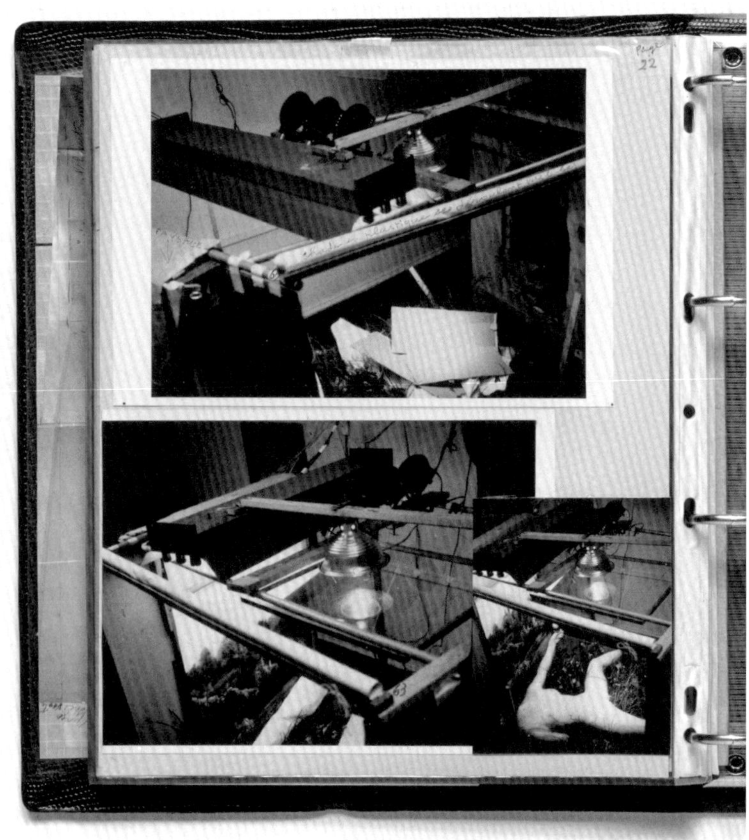

15 **Marcel Duchamp,** One page of ***Manual of Instructions*** *for the assembly of Étant donnés: 1° La chute d'eau, 2° Le gaz d'éclairage*, 1966. Philadelphia Museum of Art 1987 (English version 2009), unpaginated.

Notes

[1] Michael R. Taylor, *Marcel Duchamp: Étant donnés,* exh. cat. Philadelphia Museum of Art, Philadelphia and New Haven 2009, p. 89, giving the details and reproducing the relevant documents.
[2] For the details of these two environments, see Arturo Schwarz, *The Complete Works of Marcel Duchamp: Revised and Expanded Paperback Edition,* New York 2000, nos. 461 and 488.
[3] Lazlo Glozer, *Westkunst,* exh. cat. Museen der Stadt Köln, Cologne 1981, pp. 234ff. In the original text, written in German, the formula reads "Ausstieg aus dem Bild."
[4] "I was feverish to know the rules of the field—you know, the rules of the game. And it's funny because a lot of the stuff that meant a lot to me at that time was real exaggerated formalist criticism—Michael Fried, whatever. Not so much that I agreed with it, but it made a certain position clear—what I wanted to resist." Vito Acconci (in a retrospective statement from 1984), quoted in Christine Poggi, "Following Acconci/Targeting Vision," in *Performing the Body/Performing the Text,* ed. Amelia Jones and Andrew Stephenson, London and New York 1999, pp. 255–72, here p. 255.
[5] Vito Acconci, interviewed by Robin White at Crown Point Press (1979), quoted in ibid., p. 259.
[6] Janet Kraynak, ed., *Please Pay Attention Please: Bruce Nauman's Words,* Cambridge 2003, pp. 83–85. My usage of Nauman's work in this context is inspired by Amelia Jones, "Kunsthandeln. Bruce Naumans *Body Pressure* und das Scharnier," in *Kunsthandeln,* ed. Karin Gludovatz et al. Zurich and Berlin 2010, pp. 16–36. Jones already notes and convincingly discusses the connection between Nauman's and Duchamp's aesthetics of the hinge.
[7] See Dalia Judovitz's nuanced analysis of *Étant donnés* as an "apparatus of spectatorship" (Dalia Judovitz, "The Apparatus of Spectatorship: Duchamp, Matta-Clark, and Wilson," in *Drawing on Art: Duchamp and Company,* Minneapolis 2010, ch. 5, pp. 181–218). Judovitz argues, and I am in complete agreement with her, that *Étant donnés* is a reflection on the mechanisms of sight at play in the act of reception. While Judovitz is concentrating on *Étant donnés* as a peephole setup staging the spectator's "look" and at the same time disassembling it, I'm changing perspective by bringing the hinge-like wall and the empty front room of *Étant donnés* into focus. Judovitz discusses what my analysis is deliberately leaving out: what happens in that precise moment when the spectator is looking through the peepholes. In fact her and my arguments are like communicating vessels.
[8] For some examples by which Duchamp explains the principle of *infra-thin* (in French: *infra-mince*), see *Marcel Duchamp, Notes,* Paris 1999, pp. 21–24: "Le possible est un infra mince … Le possible impliquant le devenir—le passage de l'un à l'autre"; les "porteurs d'ombre représenté par toutes les cources de lumière (soleil, lune, étoiles, bougies, feu) … travaillent dans l'inframince"; "La chaleur d'un siege (qui vient d'être quitté) est infra-mince"; "Peinture sur verre vue du côté non peint donne un infra mince"; "La différence (dimensionnelle) entre 2 objets faits en série [sortis du même moule] est un inframince quand le maximum (?) de précision est obtenu." For Duchamp's notion of the *infra-thin,* see the contributions of Antje von Graevenitz and Molly Nesbit in this volume.
[9] Taylor, *Marcel Duchamp* (note 1), pp. 163–65.
[10] Ibid., p. 148.
[11] Ibid., pp. 167–68.

Francis M. Naumann

Notre Dame des désirs
Gynomorphism in Marcel Duchamp's *Chat Ouvert**

Anyone who peers into two holes in the center of an antique wooden door in a gallery at the Philadelphia Museum of Art and sees the interior of Marcel Duchamp's *Étant donnés* (pp. 4–5) for the first time is in for a surprise. If they knew nothing about the existence of this work beforehand, it is likely that they would find it difficult to reconcile the sight of a three-dimensional nude female figure—her legs spread apart to openly reveal her sex—within the normally hallowed walls of an art museum. Even if they knew about Duchamp and his work—as I had when seeing this work for the first time—they would likely find this bizarre scene aesthetically and conceptually incomprehensible. Within the context of the paintings and readymades by Duchamp that were on display in the surrounding galleries, it made no sense whatsoever, at least not to me. What exactly was this thing I was looking at? Somewhat bewildered, I began to seek help right away; eventually, I came across a museum label informing me that it was a work by Marcel Duchamp. That realization hit me almost as hard as my comprehension that an ordinary object could be considered a work of art, a lesson Duchamp's readymades had taught me just a few years earlier. Once I had accepted the fact that the same artist was responsible for this dioramic scene of a nude female figure lying in an outdoor setting, I went back for a more careful and studied look. Although I certainly kept asking myself questions about how this environmental tableau related to the artist whose revolutionary ideas I had come to embrace in my own work as an artist (and later, as an art historian, I came to understand its complex relationship to *The Large Glass*), there was a question that I kept quietly asking myself, but one that was simply too private and intimate to be voiced aloud. It is a question that has only been asked recently, and then only in the aftermath of Michael Taylor's phenomenal show devoted to the *Étant donnés* that was held at the Philadelphia Museum last year, and that is: What is wrong with the nude figure's vulva?[1]

Although I must confess that this is not a detail of a woman's anatomy with which I was intimately familiar during the time of my first viewing (I was only twenty-one years old at the time), I did realize that something wasn't quite right. To my eyes, it seemed misshapen. At first, I let the question pass, imagining that my lack of familiarity with this detail of a woman's body was responsible for my inability to fully comprehend the distortions I had perceived. After all, this portion of the female anatomy is usually covered with pubic hair, and what is visible is not enough—or at least not enough for me at the time—to be certain that everything was rendered in an anatomically correct fashion. Moreover, even though my experiences were limited, I knew enough to know that everyone is constructed differently

*N[otre]. D[ame]. *des désirs* (also at times: *de désir*) and *chat[te] ouvert* are the terms by which Duchamp referred to the *Étant donnés* in his letters to Maria Martins (translated by Paul Edwards in Michael R. Taylor, *Marcel Duchamp: Étant donnés*, exh. cat. Philadelphia Museum of Art, Philadelphia and New Haven 2009, pp. 402–25). The term "gynomorphism" is a neologism, but has been used in feminist literature since the 1970s (meaning, in this case, the morphology of the vagina). This essay was first presented in the form of a paper delivered as part of the symposium "Marcel Duchamp and the Forestay Waterfall," The Association Kunsthalle Marcel Duchamp, Cully, Switzerland, May 9, 2010.

(men and women alike), and perhaps what I was seeing was nothing exceptional, but rather simply something outside the purview of my personal experience, so I let the question slide.

In the forty years that have passed since I saw the *Étant donnés* for the first time (a period that has coincided with its public life), that question has not gone away, and although it was an issue that I was too timid to address then—and something that I have consistently avoided in my teachings and published writings on the artist—it is a question that continues to haunt me. As I have learned from friends and colleagues who have viewed this work, I am not alone in having perceived these distortions, although until now they, too, have either ignored this issue or dismissed it as something not really worthy of consideration. In my mind, however, the fact that it has persisted after all this time justifies its significance and, at the very least, warrants continued inquiry, however uncomfortable the topic might still be for some.

Before attempting to address this question, it is worthwhile to pause for a moment and ask another: Why did it take so long? Why is this question only being asked now? I believe it is due in part to the feminist revolution of the 1960s and 70s and, more specifically, to the courage of woman around the world—particularly lesbians—who have openly proclaimed their sexual identities within the public arena. An expression of that freedom came with *The Vagina Monologues,* a stage play written by Eve Ensler that premiered Off Broadway in 1995, but which gradually grew in popularity and has now reached an international audience. As the title suggests, the play consists of monologues spoken by four women (often one or more are well-known celebrities) on the subject of vaginas—theirs and everyone else's. For those who have seen the play (or read the book that was derived from it), absolutely nothing about the subject is considered taboo or off-limits. It was this play and book that inspired *The Visible Vagina,* an exhibition I organized with David Nolan that was held at our respective galleries in New York earlier this year. As I wrote in the introduction to the accompanying catalogue, "Ensler gave voice to countless women worldwide, honoring the complexity and mystery of their sexuality, encouraging them to consider their vaginas as powerful and expressive components of their physical selves, something not to be ashamed of, but to be proudly protected as an assertive and positive manifestation of their being."[2] The vagina has, of course, long been identified as a female sexual organ designed for procreation, while its capacity for erotic pleasure has been either ignored or avoided, or left instead to a new breed of psychiatrists who specialize in human sexuality. I believe that if we are to attempt a response to the question posed about perceived distortions to the vulva in Marcel Duchamp's *Étant donnés,* we must not only rely upon the expertise provided by gynecologists and sexologists, but perhaps even more importantly, upon the basic rudiments of logic and reasoning.

It might be instructive at this point to review the anatomy of the vagina, a process that feminists and lesbians long ago realized was essential if they were ever to understand the complexity of their own bodies and empower themselves to be in control of the sexual pleasures that could be derived from them (fig. 1). It is important to point out that although the term *vagina* is used interchangeably with *vulva* to refer to this portion of a woman's body, from a gynecological point of view, it is incorrect. The vagina is the internal

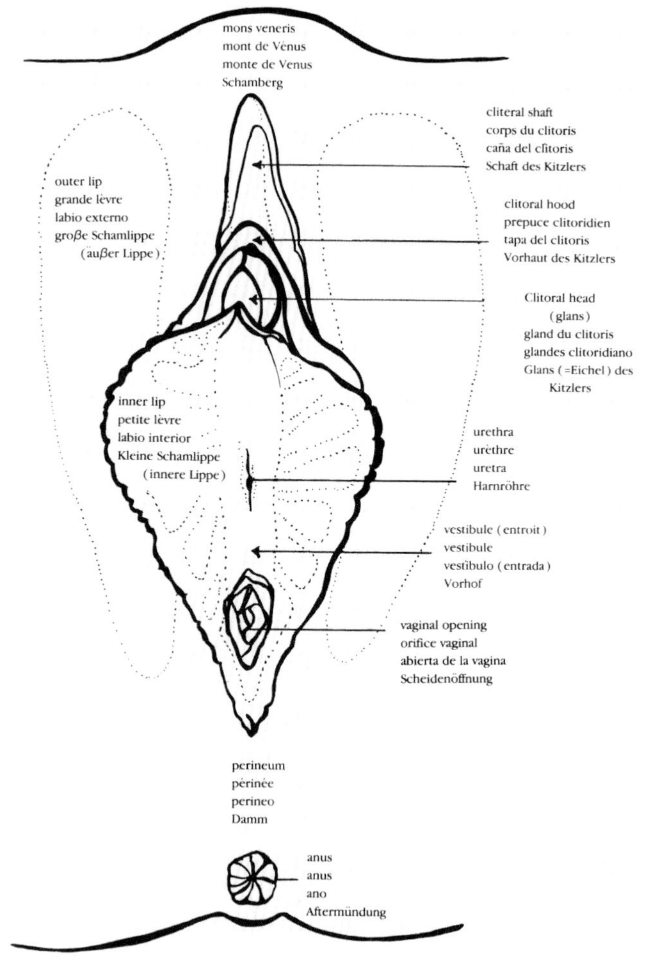

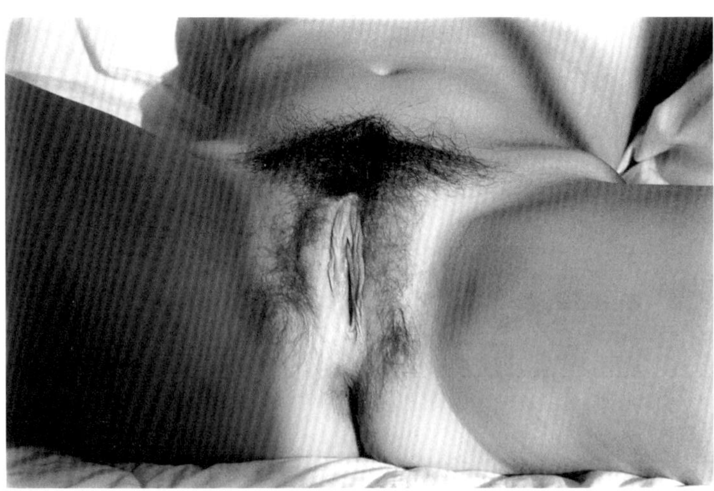

1 Tee Corrine, Diagram of a vagina, from her *Cunt Coloring Book*, 1973 (first published in 1975). **2 Gerard Malanga, *Shadow-Catching,*** black-and-white photograph, 40.5 x 50 cm, 1983. Private Collection, New York.

structure that leads from the exterior of the body to the uterus (the birth canal); what we are actually talking about here is the vulva, the external or visible portion of the female genitalia. Another term that is often used interchangeably with vulva is *pudendum,* which also refers to the same general area of a woman's body, but that term comes from the Latin meaning "shameful thing" and, as such, has largely fallen out of favor in modern cultures. In studying this portion of a woman's anatomy, it is most useful to consult a diagram, and I am here using the one Tee Corinne used in her *Cunt Coloring Book,* first published in the mid-1970s but which remains in print to this very day. For our purposes, we need only note how complex and intricate this organ is, giving special attention to those areas that seem missing in the figure of Duchamp's *Étant donnés,* particularly to what Corinne calls the "outer lip," but which is today called the *labia majora,* and the "inner lip," today called the *labia minora,* as well as the raised area at the summit, called the *mons pubis* or *mons veneris,* These same details can be readily identified in human form (fig. 2), and I am showing here a photograph taken by Gerard Malanga, another artist included in the *Visible Vagina* exhibition. This image, as they say, leaves nothing to the imagination. It is worthwhile contemplating that if it were Duchamp's intention to make this portion of a woman's anatomy visible, why did he not select a view similar to the one taken in this photograph? My guess is that because had he shown only this detail—particularly in such a blatant, in-your-face fashion as it appears in the Malanga photograph—then the image presented to the viewer would be so commanding and potentially offensive as to make any other element within the composition seem visually irrelevant or, at the very least, subordinate to the shock each viewer would experience in confronting such an overwhelmingly powerful image (particularly within the confines of an art museum).

While we are on the subject, it might be instructive to contemplate a variety of alternatives that Duchamp might have considered in his rendition of the exposed female body. There are a number of precedents in the history of art, beginning with Gustave Courbet's famous *L'Origine du monde* of 1866 (p. 8), to which the *Étant donnés* has often been compared. Ironically, art historians have only recently noted anatomical inaccuracies in Courbet's rendition of the female anatomy as well, anomalies explained by informing us that "Courbet's Realism has more to do with truth than reality."[3] The supporting proof of these inaccuracies is provided in the form of three stereoscopic photographs of a woman exposing herself to the camera taken by Auguste Belloc—two of which are shown here (fig. 3)—a mid-nineteenth-century French photographer whose work was deemed pornographic by the Préfecture de Paris and, in 1860 (six years before Courbet painted his picture), seized by the police. There is no proof that Courbet saw these photographs, but if not these, he likely saw others that were similar and, of course, he always had his own model to guide him. If we compare *L'Origine du monde* with the photographs, we will see that Courbet seems to have intentionally suppressed certain anatomical details, minimizing the existence of labia, but, with a single stroke of a brush, suggested the existence of what Michael Taylor might very well have been the first to identify as a clitoris. Although the existence of this painting was known, it was rarely seen; we know that when Duchamp began work on the *Étant donnés,* he had not seen it (and would not until 1958, long after the female figure in his tableau had already been made). The painting by Courbet that we know Duchamp had seen was *Woman with White Stockings* in the Barnes Foundation in Merion, Pennsylvania (fig. 4), which the artist visited in 1933. In attire, the woman in this painting—who is either putting on or removing thigh-length white stockings with a blue garter—is reminiscent of the model in the Belloc photographs, but, because she lies in an outdoor setting with the view of water in the background, the painting consists of elements that are closer to those contained within the *Étant donnés*. Although Duchamp would later use this very painting in an etching that he made in the last years of his life, we can readily see that little is visible between the woman's legs that could have helped him to articulate the vulva of the three-dimensional figure within his elaborate tableau.

So what exactly did Duchamp rely upon? I believe he learned a great deal from the body of Maria Martins, who, as we know, he sketched—probably in the privacy of his own studio (or perhaps hers)—in 1946 (fig. 5). Until now, it has been assumed that Maria was lying recumbent, but if we look carefully at the drawing we can see a faint tracing above her left thigh suggesting the position of her left forearm. This indicates that she is holding her leg up for support, because, in actual fact, she is in a standing position, her leg elevated so as to more readily reveal her sex (a detail of the anatomy that Duchamp clearly wanted to make the focal point of the *Étant donnés* project from the very beginning). Her foot rests on a ledge, radiator, desk, or some other piece of furniture that is not rendered within the image. We will also notice that her pubis is not shaven, a step in the process that I believe was taken only in preparation for casting her body, where, of course, the existence of pubic hair would have made the procedure more difficult (not to mention the potential for unnecessary pain in removing the solidified casting material from her hair). A black-and-white photograph discovered some years ago among the papers of Maria Martins records the earliest version of a plaster cast (fig. 6), where we can see the pubic hair has been removed and the vulva is, consequently, fully exposed. But even here certain anatomical anomalies are evident, but I believe these were caused, in part, by the casting process, for no matter how carefully a mold is prepared, the casting material pushes into the soft tissue of the body and causes it to distort. Of course there are other factors at play here as well, one being that Maria Martins was fifty-five years old at the time when this cast was made and had given birth to five children. It is also known that with the onset of menopause, hormone levels dramatically decrease and, as a result, all components of the vulva—the *mons pubis*, labia, and even clitoris—shrink considerably in size. Finally, in analyzing the plaster cast, it is clear that the model is no longer standing upright (as she was when posing for the drawing), but because the casting process takes considerably more time than a quick sketch, lies supine on some sort of flat surface. This causes her right leg to flatten, while her left leg, elevated somewhat, appears comparatively thinner. As for the area of the vulva, a mound of flesh accurately records the shape and position of the *mons veneris*, but the curved shapes echoing its form directly below are not actually a part of the vulva. They are, rather, a protrusion of the buttocks, an inevitable effect of gravity on an aging body, a situation compounded, to a degree, by the weight of heavy casting material. It is the relationship between these two curving shapes that appears to have been accentuated in the finished figure (fig. 7)—which is here represented by one of several colored photographs taken by Duchamp in 1965. I believe these distortions are compounded by the raking angle at which the spectator is forced the view the recumbent figure: from above and to the left of her outspread legs.

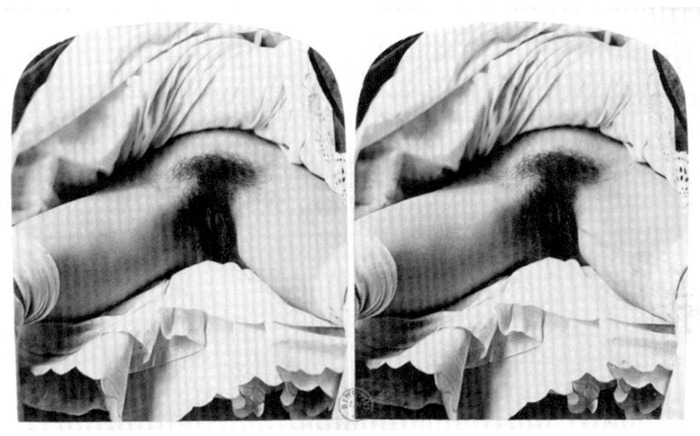

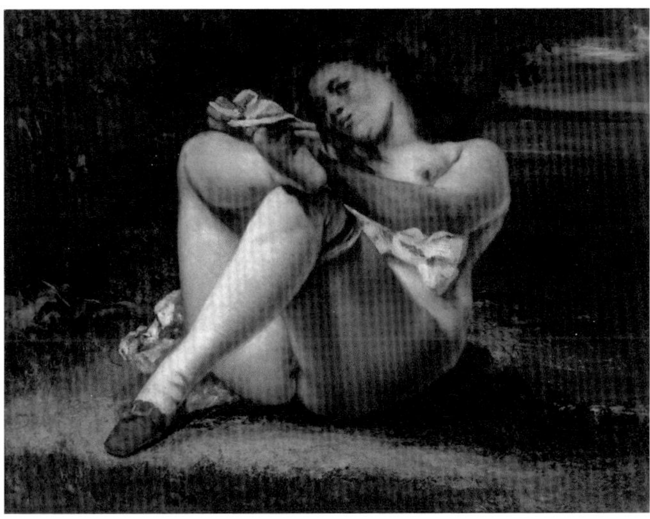

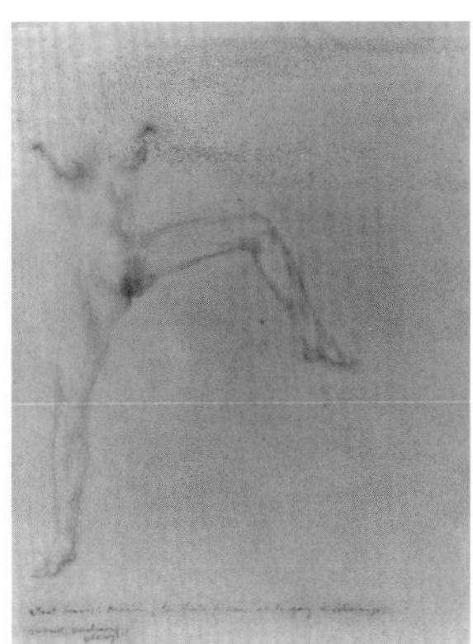

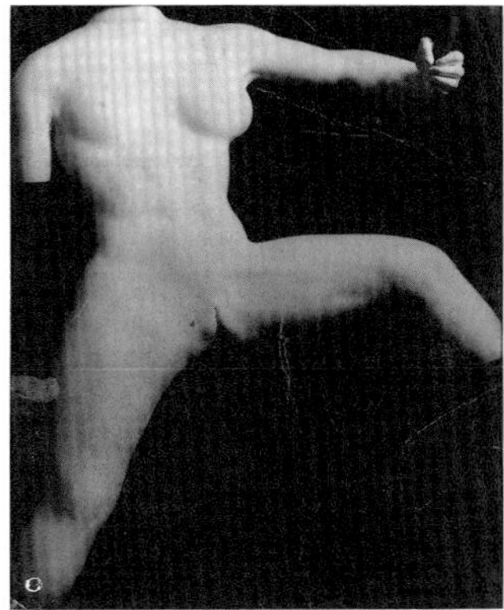

3 Auguste Belloc, Obscene photographs for the stereoscope, albumen prints from collodion negatives, colored with transparent ink, 8 x 7 cm each, c. 1860, Bibliothèque Nationale de France, Département des Estampes et de la Photographie, Paris. **4 Gustave Courbet, *Woman with White Stockings,*** oil on canvas, 64.1 x 81.3 cm, 1864. The Barnes Foundation, Merion, Pennsylvania. **5 Marcel Duchamp, *Étant donnés: Maria, la chute d'eau, et le gaz d'éclairage,*** pencil on paper, 40 x 29 cm, 1946. Moderna Museet, Stockholm. Gift 1985, dedicated to Ulf Linde from Tomas Fischer. **6 Marcel Duchamp, Plaster study for the figure in *Étant donnés,*** gelatin silver print, 23.5 x 19.1 cm, 1949. Norman and Norah Stone Collection, San Francisco. Courtesy of Thea Westreich Art Advisory Services.

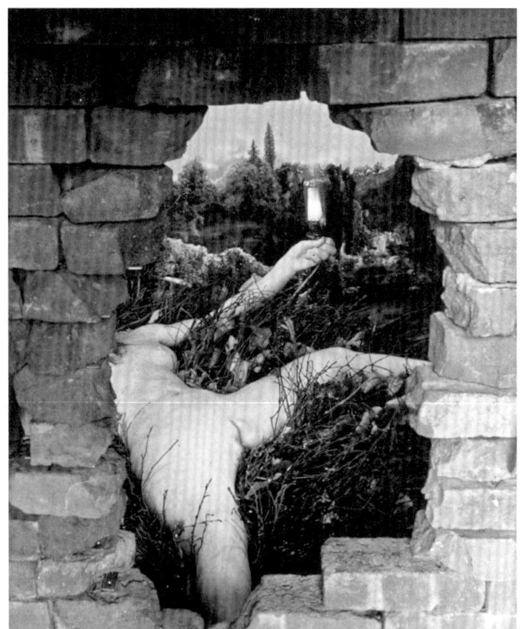

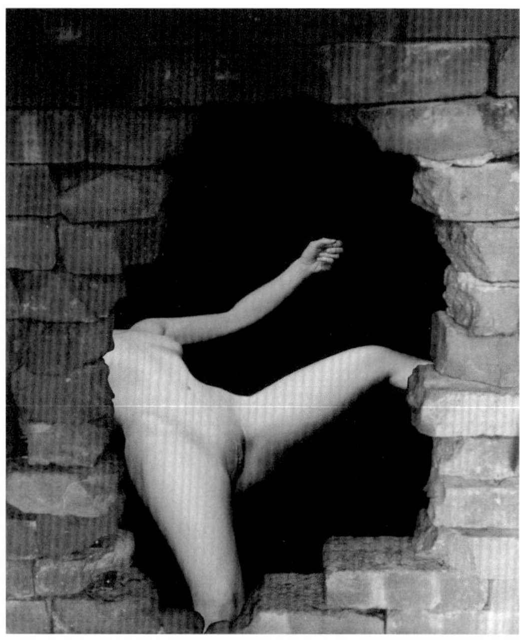

7 Color photograph of *Étant donnés,* 1946–66, taken by Marcel Duchamp, 1965. Philadelphia Museum of Art, Archives, Anne d'Harnoncourt Records. **8 Model in the position of the figure in Marcel Duchamp's *Étant donnés.*** Photograph by D. James Dee, 2010. Photoshop by Joy Whalen. Courtesy The Soho Photographer, New York.

At this point, in order to put things in perspective, we need to see exactly what the vulva of this figure would have looked like if not subjected to distortion, neither by the casting process, nor the point of view. It is for this reason that I engaged the photographic skills of D. James Dee, a professional photographer in New York who specializes in taking pictures of works of art, but whose creative work involves taking pictures of nude female models (some examples of these photographs were included in *The Visible Vagina*). After a considerable search, we located a model who was not only willing to assume the position of the figure in Duchamp's *Étant donnés,* but who agreed to shave her pubic hair, since we had planned to cast her body as well (a plan that failed disastrously, since the rubber mold detached from the plaster reinforcement and was, consequently, ruined). Nevertheless, with some effort, the model was able to approximate the position of the mannequin and, after the superimposition of surrounding bricks in Photoshop, we were able to attain an image that superficially resembles the color photograph taken by Duchamp (fig. 8).

If the two images up on the screen are compared, noteworthy differences are readily discernable. To begin with, it should be acknowledged that—at the age of 27—our brave model is considerably younger than was Maria Martins when she posed for Duchamp. Moreover, despite the flexibility that a younger body unquestionably possesses, she was unable to get into exactly the same position as the mannequin of the *Étant donnés*. Indeed, I would argue that nothing short of a professional contortionist could assume that position, for what we learned in this process is that it is absolutely impossible to raise a leg in this fashion—I am here speaking of the model's left leg (the one we see on the right)—without lifting it a considerable distance from the flat surface that supports the rest of her body (we were forced to insert a prop under the cloth to support the leg some eight to ten inches from the surface of the table on which she reclines). If we look at several photographs that Duchamp took of his mannequin disassembled (fig. 9), however, we can see that the plane of her body from one outstretched leg to the other is almost completely flat; it is only when we are forced to see it from an angle and from above—as we are in the finished tableau (p. 5)—that the leg recedes in view, allowing perspective—in effect—to correct the problem, whereupon we sense no distortion whatsoever.

Of course, no matter what point of view we take, there are major points of departure between the figure appearing in the *Étant donnés* and the live model (fig. 8), but none perhaps so prominent as those that exist with the vulva. To begin with, in life, this organ is positioned far lower on the trunk of the body, more directly between the legs, where it belongs in the case of all adult females. I say adult because in preadolescent girls the vulva is positioned more toward the front of the body, but, in puberty, it gradually descends (the equivalent in males of descending testicles) to a position that is, when standing, parallel to the ground. I am not suggesting for a moment that Duchamp used a teenage model, or, for that matter, that he even had any knowledge of this change that occurs in the bodies of young women, for that is the sort of information that only medical doctors—especially gynecologists—would be familiar with (or people like myself, who have read up on the subject). Rather, I believe Duchamp wanted to make sure we saw enough of this detail to register it in our minds as an opening, conforming in appearance with what our minds see, or at least what our minds tell us is a vulva, that is to say, a vertical slit in a woman's body that possess an orifice to allow for male penetration. That's enough. Anything more—like the image of the model on the right—is what kids today might call "tmi" (too much information). For Duchamp's concerns, we don't really need to see this body part in all of its resplendent glory, for any such display would only detract from the overall effect, which

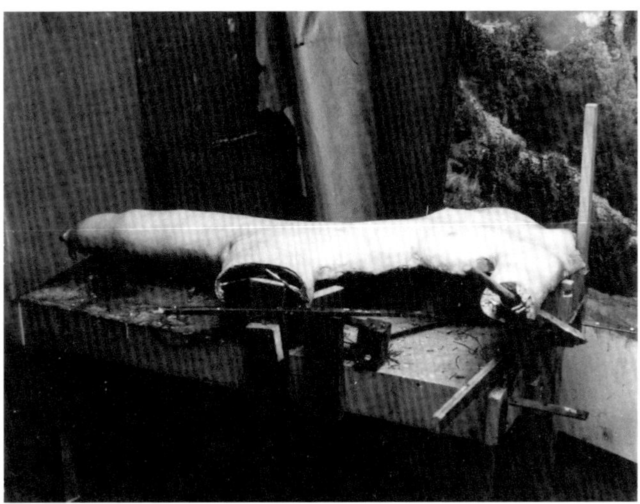

9 Black-and-white Polaroid of the *Étant donnés* mannequin (detail), taken by Marcel Duchamp, 1965. Philadelphia Museum of Art, Archives, Anne d'Harnoncourt Records.

is to allow the viewer to register the information in his mind, and then move on, to see whatever else the scene has to offer. If Duchamp had rendered everything with anatomical accuracy—the position, the *mons veneris,* the labia, etc.—we might very well not get too far beyond it. The average viewer would probably examine this area of the body and ask themselves if it conformed in appearance with what they had expected to see. With the exception of gynecologists, few people are sufficiently familiar with this part of a woman's body to know whether or not everything was rendered accurately.

Still, aside from the factors of viewpoint and an awareness of the knowledge possessed by each viewer, there is probably yet another factor that contributes even more significantly to the anatomical distortions that we perceive, and that is because they are genuinely there, the result of Duchamp's increased detachment from the subject of his inspiration. Upon the retirement of her husband from diplomatic service in 1950, Maria Martins returned permanently to Brazil, where she resumed her career as a sculptor and, with the exception of occasional trips abroad, remained for the last twenty-five years of her life. In a long and thoughtful review of the *Étant donnés* exhibition at the Philadelphia Museum, curator and art historian Helen Molesworth recently concluded that the distortions we see are caused by a slippage of memory. Referring to the figure, she writes, "Her muteness is compounded by our inability to remember her accurately, which is how I read the problem of the misplaced labia—as a physicalization of the distortions of memory."[4] To this I would suggest that Duchamp might very well have been aware of these distortions, for he knew that they were an inevitable product of the accumulative errors that occur when working on something over an extended period of time, especially when you no longer have access to the original object you are attempting to render. In the end, he knew that within the context of an art museum, any spectator would immediately realize that they were looking at a sculpture, and not an actual living, breathing human being on the other side of the door. Moreover, as time progressed, Duchamp became increasingly interested in the impression each viewer would receive upon seeing the work for the first time, and details such as the articulation of the vulva would have only been incidental to the overall effect. The same sort of attitude, it is worthwhile to point out, informed Duchamp when he first allowed replicas of his readymades to exist; if they were selected from the same generic type of object—without necessarily being identical to it (as when he allowed Sidney Janis in 1950 to select a urinal for him to replicate his *Fountain* of 1917), it was sufficient to convey his original intent. Only later, when the edition of readymades was made by Arturo Schwarz in 1964, did Duchamp insist that they conform in appearance to the originals, for by then he understood them as historical artifacts, objects that had to reflect the time and place of the original gesture. In the case of the *Étant donnés,* if the vulva conformed in appearance to what we generally understood to be the size and shape of a human vulva, that was enough—enough to convey, as Jasper Johns once expressed it, "something the mind already knows."

Finally, one last factor may have contributed to the somewhat artificial articulation of the vulva in ways that cannot be determined with any degree of certainty, and that is actions motivated by the unconscious mind. Stefan Banz was the first to describe the original Forestay waterfall—the scene from nature that appears as the background motif in *Étant donnés*—as having "cut through the landscape ... carving a vulva-like path down the hillside." Moreover, when viewed from a distance (as Duchamp could from the hotel where he was staying with Mary Reynolds in Bellevue near Chexbres, Switzerland, during the summer of 1946), the waterfall appears embedded "between two clearly accentuated flanks," which Banz likens to "thighs," making the whole scene conjure—as he says—the image of "a vagina through public hair."[5] Having visited the site he describes, I must confess that it was not this image that immediately popped into my mind. Nevertheless, something must be said for the unusual formation of the waterfall, which Banz also notes is not really a waterfall but a cascade that "consists of three steps" that "surge over the cliffs in Chexbres." The same triple, step-like pattern could be said to define the general shape and contour of the *Étant donnés* vulva, which, it should be noted, is positioned virtually parallel to the waterfall in the background. However, to what extant this formal rapport is purely coincidental or consciously employed is something we will probably never know for sure.

To recapitulate, I believe that there are no fewer than eight different factors that can be cited to account for the distortions that appear in the vulva of the figure in Duchamp's *Étant donnés:*

1) Everyone is constructed differently. Unless a nude photograph of Maria Martins should emerge in the future—and one that makes the articulation of her vulva visible—we will probably never know for certain the degree to which this particular body part was subjected to distortion (if any).
2) The age of the body and the degree of its flaccidity at the time the plaster cast was made are factors that could account for some of the distortion, as well as the imposing weight of the plaster cast itself.
3) The angle at which we are forced to view the figure through the two little peepholes—from above and to the left—compounds the distortions to which the vagina had already been subjected during the casting process.
4) Accumulative error. Even when an accurate impression is taken of a body part, the negative cast must then be converted into a positive three-dimensional sculpture. This is already two steps removed from the object being cast, and we can be fairly certain that even at this point, Duchamp intervened to make certain critical refinements. Beyond that, we know that he covered the figure with a thin layer of parchment that resembled flesh, which, in turn, he later painted. Every step in this process allows for potential errors, mistakes that would only be compounded as they accumulate over time.
5) Although this has not yet been mentioned, it is possible that once the figure was finished, Duchamp had intended to restore the pubic hair that was necessarily removed to facilitate the casting process. After all, he did exactly that to the armpits, and we know that when Duchamp's studio was cleared out, Denise Browne Hare, a writer and photographer who was then married to the Surrealist sculptor David Hare, recalls having found plastic envelopes that she believed were filled with body hair.[6] If Duchamp had planned to glue the pubic hair back in place, then the distortions that we perceive would have been less apparent, although at some point he seems to have decided that she would look better denuded.

6) As Duchamp no longer had access to the source of his inspiration—namely, Maria Martins—both his familiarity with this body part and his intimacy with its owner gradually diminished. Over time, he was forced to record more his memory of Maria than a depiction of Maria herself. Not only was love lost, but also the body that harbored it.
7) A loose formal rapport seems to exist between the articulation of the vulva and the three-step waterfall in the background, a formal reading that could have meaning, but, in my humble opinion, only in so far as we can attribute significance to the meanderings of the unconscious mind.
8) The rendering of this body part as an accurate reflection of human physiognomy was eventually deemed unimportant to Duchamp's intent. It was sufficient to present enough visual information—and not necessarily more than was required—to register in the minds of viewers that they were seeing a depiction of a nude female figure with her vulva exposed.

In the end, whether Duchamp got his rendering of this particular body part right or not is of little consequence to the overall meaning of the work, for although he had planned for the *Étant donnés* to be revealed after his death, he had also hoped that the identity of Maria Martins would never be made public. Certainly he had made every effort not to reveal this information in his lifetime, and why would he? The work was never intended to be the portrayal of a specific individual, but rather the representation of a deep and profound love that is both physically and emotionally unattainable, which is why spectators are forced to view the scene from the other side of an impenetrable door. If people wanted to come to terms with this work intellectually, they would have examples of his previous work to serve as a guide—not only the *Large Glass,* but also his notes for it, particularly the one that begins with the words *Étant donnés: 1° la chute d'eau, 2° le gaz d'éclairage,* the title given to this last great work. It is only when we think of the figure as being the depiction of a specific individual that the matter of her anatomical correctness becomes an issue, for within the context of Duchamp's work, she is meant to represent the bride of his dreams, or, as it relates to each viewer, a generic depiction of womankind. And who among us can stand in judgment and critique the accuracy of that vulva?

Afterword

After this paper was written, I was given the opportunity to examine a life-size reconstruction of the *Étant donnés* that was made in 1991 by the French artist Richard Baquié (fig. 10). Although this work is in the collection of the Musée d'art contemporain de Lyon, it was on temporary display at the Musée d'Art moderne de la Ville de Paris, where I viewed it in April 2010. If one examines the vulva of this figure, another unexplained anomaly appears: a small nub-like protrusion is visible attached to the lower portion of the vaginal opening. At first, this would seem to be a technical flaw introduced by the artist during the replicating process, until it is compared to the *Étant donnés,* where, it can be determined, this same protrusion exists. This detail is not visible in most photographs that reproduce the work (fig. 2), but is readily apparent when viewing the work itself, a result, apparently, of binocular vs. monocular vision. However, this does not explain how Baquié perceived and replicated this detail, for, so far as is known, he never saw the original *Étant donnés* in the Philadelphia Museum. As Michael Taylor has suggested to me, he may have learned about this anomaly when viewing the binocular reconstruction based on stereoscopic

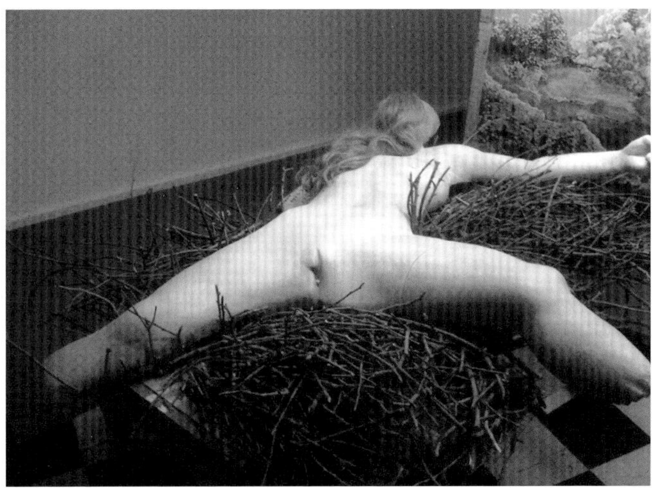

10 Richard Baquié, *Étant donnés: 1° la chute d'eau, 2° le gaz d'éclairage,* reconstruction after Marcel Duchamp, mixed media, 1991. Musée d'art contemporain, Lyon. Photograph taken by Francis M. Naumann in the Musée d'Art Moderne de la Ville de Paris, April 2010.

photographs taken by Babette Mangolte that was made for the Duchamp retrospective in Paris in 1977. It is still unknown exactly what this protrusion represents (unless, of course, Maria Martins was herself possessed of such an unusual physical abnormality).

Notes

[1] This very question was recently asked by the artist Carolee Schneemann at the close of a panel discussion devoted to *The Visible Vagina* that was held at the David Nolan Gallery, New York, on January 30, 2010 (for more on this exhibition, see the text that follows and the next note below); although I attempted a response to this question, the session was in the process of closing so it remained largely unanswered. In his catalogue essay on the *Étant donnés,* Michael Taylor does note that some viewers have described "the anatomical distortions of the nude's genitalia ... as a gashlike castration wound;" he also notes that Jean-François Lyotard argues that it is "part-anus, part vagina" (citing Lyotard, *TRANS/formers,* trans. Ian McLeod, Venice 1990; see Michael R. Taylor, *Marcel Duchamp: Étant donnés,* exh. cat. Philadelphia Museum of Art, Philadelphia and New Haven 2009, p. 193). It was Amelia Jones who described the vulva as "a castration wound," and she might very well have been the first to observe and put into print that the vulva is missing some critical components: "There are no 'labia major,' 'labia minora' in view; there is no vaginal vestibule or clitoris ... she has not a vagina leading into her interior, her womb, but a shallow crevice with no exterior lips at all. Aside from the beginnings of a small puckered hole like a puncture wound in the center of this crevice, there is, apparently, no deep internal orifice here." While accurately observing these anatomical anomalies, Jones does not provide an explanation for exactly why they occur, beyond telling us that they are among many details in works by Duchamp dealing with issues of gender and sexuality that "American discourses on postmodernism have refused to see" (Amelia Jones, *Postmodernism and the En-Gendering of Marcel Duchamp,* Cambridge, UK 1994, pp. 201–4). Finally, in a colloquium devoted to "Duchamp and Eroticism" held at the University of Orléans and at the Musée des Beaux-Arts in Orléans, France, in 2005, the subject of the *Étant donnés* came up often, but other than for passing references in the paper of Michael Taylor, the subject of the vulva never came up, with the exception of Elfriede Dreyer, who, in an analysis of color, described it as "the bland, almost de-sexualized, genital crevice" (for transcriptions of all the papers delivered in this conference, see Marc Décimo, *Marcel Duchamp and Eroticism,* Cambridge, UK 2007; for references cited, see pp. 41 and 193).

[2] Francis M. Naumann and David Nolan, "Introduction," *The Visible Vagina,* exh. cat. Francis M. Naumann Fine Art and David Nolan Gallery, January 28–March 20, 2010, New York, p. 5.

[3] L[aurence des C[ars]., *Gustave Courbet,* New York 2008, p. 382.

[4] Helen Molesworth, "My Funny Valentine: *Étant donnés,*" *Artforum* (January 2010), p. 168. Thus far, the only reviewer of this exhibition that mentions the vulva is that of Frédérique Joseph-Lowery, who described "her strange genitals" as looking like "a rictus" ("Marcel Duchamp et le Dahlia noir," *Artpress,* no. 363 [January 2010]).

[5] Stefan Banz, "Marcel Duchamp and the Forestay Waterfall: Chexbres on Lake Geneva," paper delivered on May 8, 2010, "Marcel Duchamp and the Forestay Waterfall" symposium (see prefatory note), Cully, Switzerland (Banz kindly provided me with a copy of the manuscript for his paper).

[6] Reported in Taylor, *Étant donnés* (note 1), p. 69.

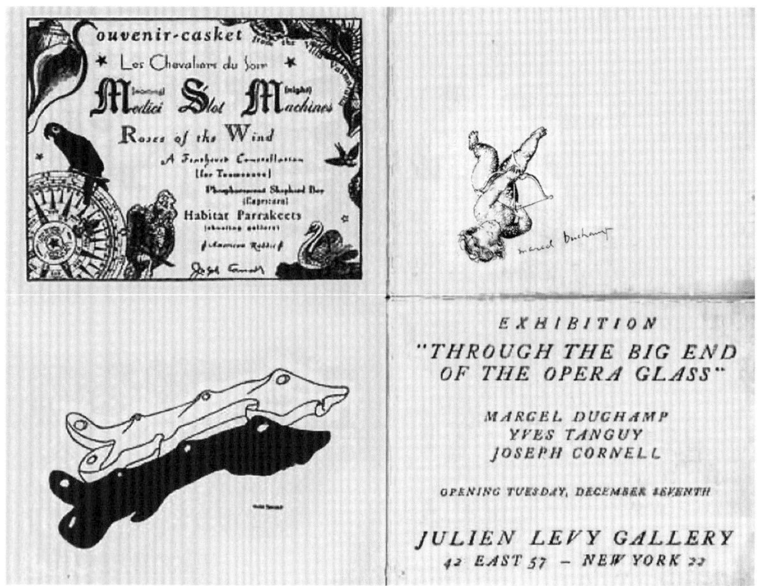

1 Julien Levy Gallery's exhibition announcement for *Through the Big End of the Opera Glass,* 1943, complete view of announcement, unfolded, recto.

In 1943, the gallery owner Julien Levy created a double-sided leaflet to announce an exhibit in New York (figs. 1 & 2):

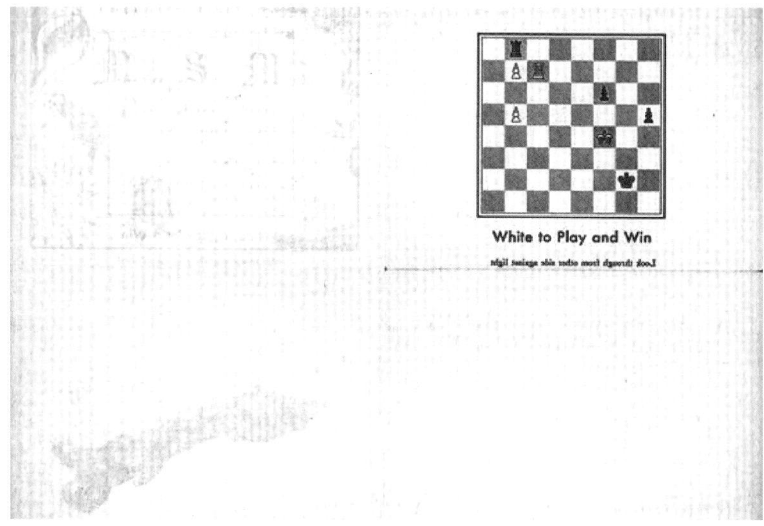

2 Julien Levy Gallery's exhibition announcement for *Through the Big End of the Opera Glass,* 1943, complete view of announcement, unfolded, verso.

On the upper right of the recto is the work of Duchamp who, as we can see, drew a Cupid upside down and holding a drawn bow. The arrowhead as an extension of Cupid's penis has great significance; to go straight to the point, this god of love is ready for action. Duchamp's signature is at the bottom of the drawing (fig. 3):

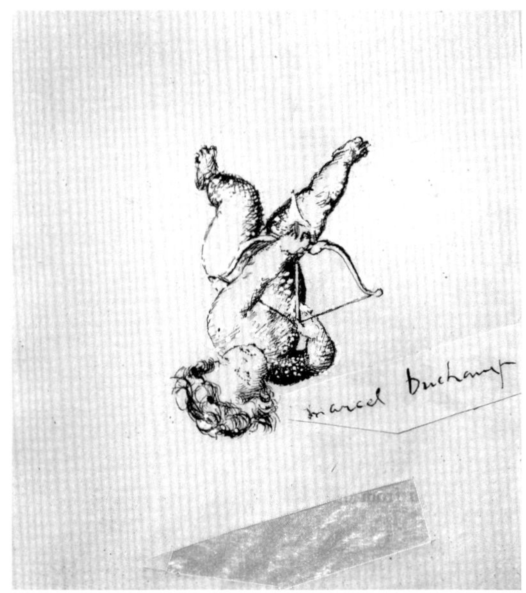

Fig. 3

On the verso, corresponding to the same position as Cupid, we find the diagram of a chess game with the notation, "White to play and win." Here is a closer look (fig.4):

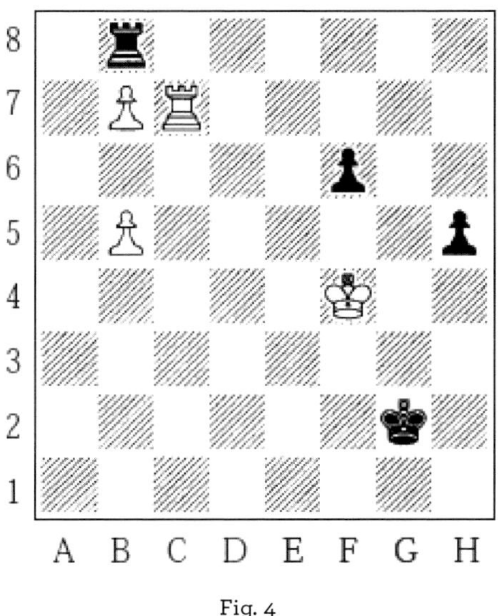

Fig. 4

In the chess lexicon, this notation indicates that we are dealing with a problem or study, or even an "endgame." It is Whites' move [ont le trait], and no matter how Black responds, White must win, i.e. checkmate the black king.

Duchamp, however, encourages us to hold the page up to the light; under the notation "White to play and win," he instructs us, "Look through from other side against light." And when we do, the two drawings—the diagram and the inverted Cupid—are superimposed, producing the image below (fig. 5):

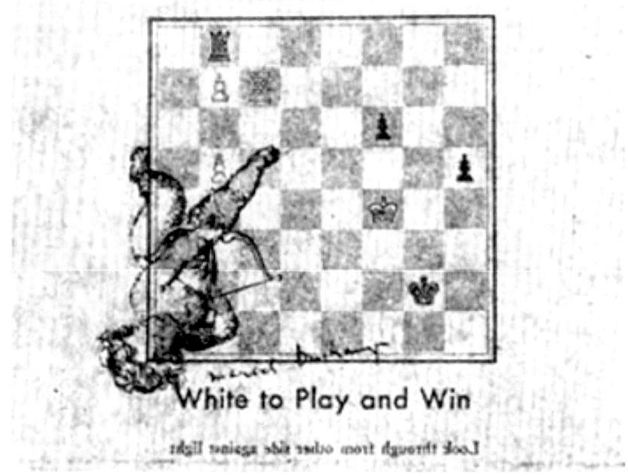

Fig. 5

How are we to understand this drawing or rather the superimposed drawings? We are aware that Marcel Duchamp was an avid chess player and dedicated years of his life to the game (we also know that for two decades his only artwork unrelated to chess was *Étant donnés*). We can therefore reasonably assume that the position he offers in this diagram is a real problem or study. Going further, we could even put forward the hypothesis that the superimposition of the Cupid and the chessboard is not insignificant, and that it might provide a clue to the next move to play in order to solve this chess problem. Observers, for example, have proposed moving the pawn at b5, as Cupid's arrow seems to be aiming at this piece.

But art historians are not necessarily experts in the game of chess. In order to resolve the problem presented by this diagram, they turn to the grand masters of the noble game, asking them which path to follow to find the solution. In other words: what move should White make to be assured of winning the game?

I should point out, for those who might be unfamiliar with the game of chess, that the possibilities are of such complexity that not even the most powerful computers are currently capable—or will be in the near future—of exhaustively analyzing all possible outcomes of a relatively complex position. Thus it is only by applying theoretical and strategic considerations that we are able to ascertain whether a position is a winning position or not.

After subtle and penetrating research into Duchamp's problem, great chess masters have come to an irrefutable conclusion: contrary to appearances (particularly the white pawn in b7, which seems rather close to being promoted to queen, and the position of the white king controlling the black pawns), it is simply impossible to resolve this problem. In other words, the Whites, no matter what move they make (in particular the move Cupid seems to suggest), will be incapable, in either the short or long term, of winning the game. Even a computer, no matter how powerful, no matter how many billions of calculations it might make, cannot find a path to victory for the Whites—a checkmate.

Thus, as described by Francis Naumann in the article he dedicated to this conundrum, Duchamp's parameters ("White to play and win") cannot be honored, and we face "a problem with no solution" (the title of his essay).[1] We are also well aware of Duchamp's love of wordplay, and there is no doubt that his goal with this conundrum was to "mate" potential investigators.

Yet many devotees of both Duchamp and the noble game could not admit defeat. They thought that if there were a solution, they would be obliged to change their approach in order to find it. Since we are asked to look at the page in transparency, wouldn't the problem simply resolve itself if we moved the chessboard in one way or other? You could, for example, create a mirror image; a1 would then take the place of h1 (fig. 6):

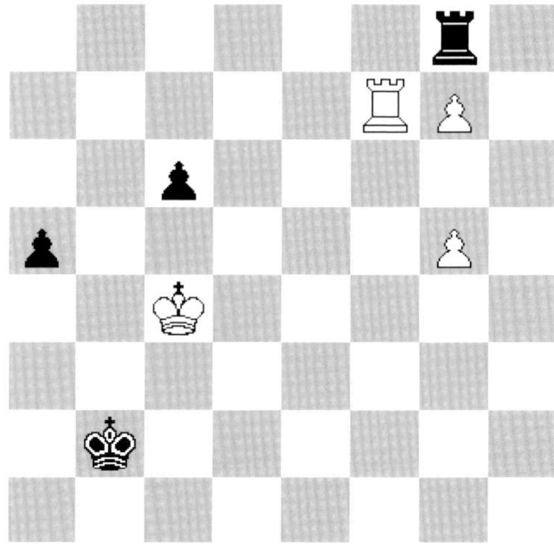

Fig. 6

Well, this does not work either; even thus transformed the position remains unsolvable for both humans and computers. So, continuing with the experiment, I asked myself if one would have more luck by inverting the colors of the pieces (fig. 7):

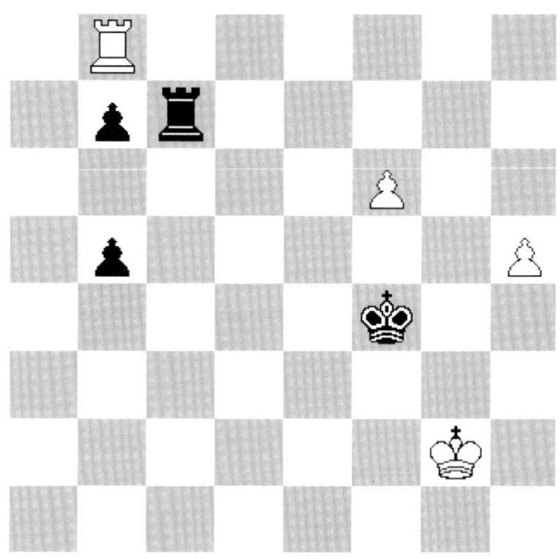

Fig. 7

Again, no luck; the problem remains sealed tight as an oyster. And if I flip the chessboard 180 degrees (fig. 8)?

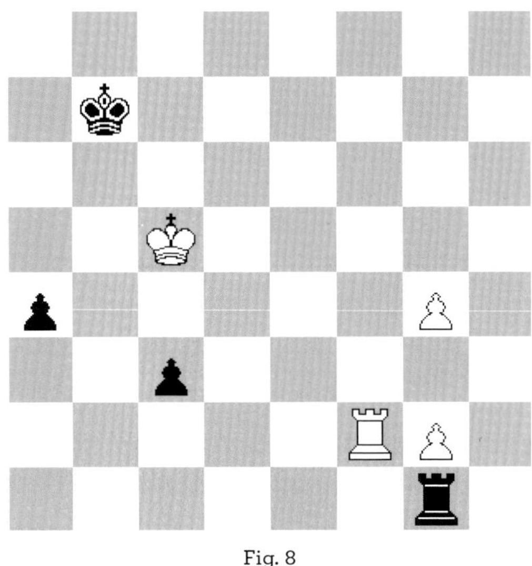

Fig. 8

Once again it is a lost cause; I am quite simply out of luck.
Unquestionably, no manipulation, no inversion, no optical illusion renders this famous problem solvable. "White to play and win." There is no way around it, Whites play but they do not win.

*

Never? Well, not really. I refused to give up. I kept on looking and I finally found a way, even two, for "White to play and win." And yet, I realized that these two methods, somewhat transgressive and somewhat poetic (at least I hope), could also be applied metaphorically to *Étant donnés* to give this enigma something resembling a solution (the reason we are here). But first off let me assure you that I do not really take my "solutions" to *Étant donnés* seriously, nor those I will provide to Duchamp's chess problem. These necessary transgressions might, however, provide great insight into the singular and perhaps unique frame of mind that Duchamp's work puts us in.

*

Before going into *Étant donnés,* I will first tackle the chess diagram. What can be done for "White to play and win"? Well, let's take a fresh look at the presence of Cupid and his sexual arrow. One must understand that Cupid is not, as we hastily assumed, pointing at a piece to play in the diagram, but is purely and simply *a piece of this diagram.* What leads me to believe this? Well, quite simply the fact that in the drawing Duchamp wishes us to see—the superimposed drawing—Cupid is actually *in* the chessboard. Next, I am reminded of a play on words I believe to be in the Duchampian spirit: "Cupid *to play*"

[Cupidon *a le trait*]: couldn't this have a double meaning? On one hand it could mean that he is holding the bow and the arrow (of which "trait" is a literary synonym in French), and on the other hand (in the chess lexicon) that it is *his turn to play*.
Now I only need to decide which chess piece best fits Cupid. It is obviously the bishop (in French *le Fou*, the madman): the motion of this piece follows or symbolizes an arrow's trajectory and the shape resembles its tapered form. Moreover, Cupid represents the madness of love, *amour*, and it is therefore *amour fou* (sung by the Surrealists). I now allow myself to put Cupid upon the chessboard, giving him the role of the bishop, *le Fou*. No sooner said than done, I replace Cupid on the diagram with a bishop, which I place in the lower left of the chessboard, in the general area occupied by the little god. I choose the square c3 (fig. 9):

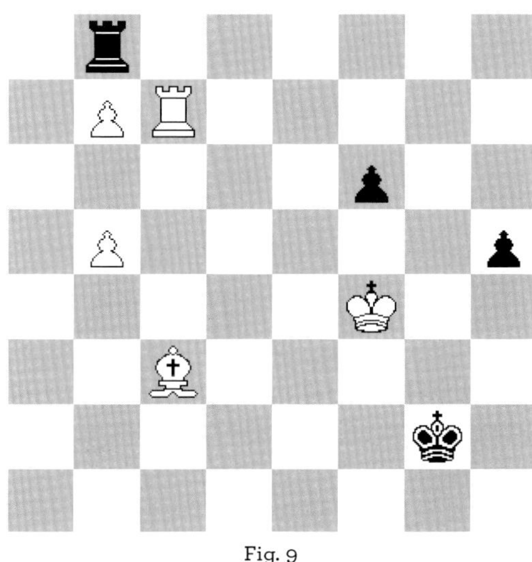

Fig. 9

Well, the miracle takes place! In this new position, Duchamp's stipulation, "White to play and win," becomes true! The bishop's arrow fits so well in the aforementioned position that not only is "White to play and win," but White will irrefutably achieve checkmate in exactly nine moves (the only possible first move being, 1. Fd4, as I learned from my computer after it had scanned over one billion positions).
Here is my first poetic idea, and my first transgression: Cupid is not *outside* the chessboard, he is *inside it;* and as a result, the problem can be solved. We will later see where this idea leads us when applied to *Étant donnés...*

*

My second poetic solution to the problem is both simpler and more radical. Rather than adding to the diagram a piece that is not explicitly there, the solution consists of creating an inversion or a mirroring, an operation apparently no one had previously thought of, perhaps because it is, as said, too simple and too radical. Rather than changing the color of the pieces or their position, the solution involves transforming the *directmate* into what is called the *helpmate*.

What are we referring to here? A word of explanation for those who are not familiar with the noble game: there is something called fairy chess in the universe of chess problems (we are no longer talking about games of chess), where novel rules dictate the movement of the pieces or the pieces are allowed to make new, *sui generis* movements. However, the *helpmate* device is not so complicated. It is an extremely simple innovation familiar to "problemists," which completely alters how chess players traditionally approach the game. Typically, for a player the aim of the game is for the Whites to beat the Blacks, and vice versa. It is understood that the Whites as well as the Blacks must devise moves that will allow them to defeat their opponents, that is, checkmate the opposing king.
In a chess problem or study, the notion of battle disappears. The essential is not whether the Whites or the Blacks "win" as in a traditional game, but rather for the "solutionists" to discover unusual, graceful, and subtle moves. Even when the problem is a *direct checkmate,* that is to say specifying White must checkmate the black king in x number of moves, the focus is not on the checkmate itself, but on the richness, the originality, the resourcefulness, the gracefulness of the moves that lead to the checkmate.
If the notion of battle no longer exists, it is tempting for problemists to take an extra step and imagine that the Blacks and the Whites, far from being in opposition, collaborate in finding ever more beautiful solutions. And this is where the *helpmate* comes in: as the name implies, the Blacks unreservedly *help* the Whites to achieve the basic objective of the problem. (By the way, I would like to point out that for makers of problems, it is much more difficult to design a helpmate than a directmate, because Blacks leave every conceivable path open to Whites for achieving checkmate, so that creating problems with *one* and only one solution is infinitely challenging.) But this is the essence of the *helpmate:* it is a type of problem in which—and this is key—it is the Blacks that *play first* [ont le trait] and help the Whites toward checkmate in a given number of moves.

I look again at the given conditions in Duchamp's diagram:

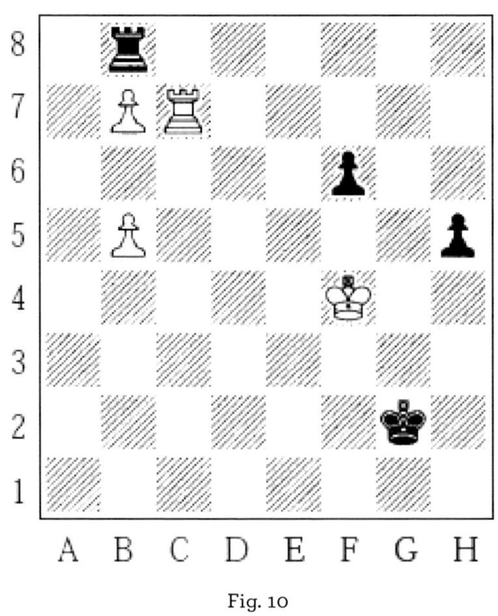

Fig. 10

I leave it untouched, but I consider that the stipulation is no longer "White to play and win," but "Blacks play and Whites win"; that is, in chess terms, "helpmate in x moves," with Blacks playing first. Well, the problem has not one solution, but five different ones (1. ... Rh3, f1, h1, g1, Tb8-a8) that produce almost immediate checkmates (in 2 moves)! Not only is Duchamp's problem no longer unsolvable, but without changing the pieces or the position of the chessboard, it immediately offers a plurality of extremely simple solutions!

*

I just showed you two ways to solve our strange diagram. But don't worry; let me repeat that I do not take them too seriously, if at all. I will let you know why later on. But let me now deal with *Étant donnés* (p. .5). Confronting this enigma, I realized it was possible to apply through metaphor the same poetic and transgressive solutions we used with the chess diagram.

Let us begin with the first solution, which considers Cupid not as a figure outside of the game indicating the next move to be played by aiming at the supposedly most effective piece, but rather as a piece in the chessboard and thus part of the game. Cupid had the opening move, he played first [avait le trait]; he was the sexual bishop [le Fou sexué] penetrating the diagram whose move will eventually enable the checkmate of the opponent.

How would this behavior apply in relation to *Étant donnés?* Well, confronted with this enigmatic work, I decided that my Cupid's eye, my covetous [cupide] eye (the eye of a man looking through a spyhole desiring a naked woman) is not merely outside the picture, but is part of the game. It can and must *penetrate the picture,* pass through the wooden door and transform the woman from an object of contemplation into an object of pleasure.

What I mean is something very simple, indeed trivial, if not even primitive. We noticed (it would have been hard not to) that *Étant donnés* is displayed exactly like a peep show, as staged voyeurism, or even that the artwork was suggesting or revealing the voyeuristic nature of all visual impulses, especially those that move us to look at art. Thus my transgressive and *literally primitive* thought is that *Étant donnés* should be taken at face value; it is not a work of art disguised as a peep show, but rather the opposite, a peep show disguised as a work of art, and the viewer—really the men—need not find any meaning there, just sexual arousal under the cover of artistic contemplation.

The (male) viewer must therefore *enter the piece* (and this is why it is three-dimensional) to effectively *checkmate* (in French *mater,* which also means to leer) the black king, or rather the white queen, the woman with her legs spread. In other words, the meaning of *Étant donnés* would be that it has *no* hidden meaning, *no* artistic meaning no matter how one defines art. It would be primarily, directly, uniquely, and strictly speaking a *peep show.* Voyeurs of this kind of show are often invited into the room where the woman as object performs, just as the bishop [le Fou] is invited into the chess diagram and, following the rules or the rules we envisioned, "penetrates" Cupid's position.

This was my first poetic and transgressive solution to *Étant donnés;* in reality more transgressive than poetic, I admit. But we are dealing after all with an operation that—it seems to me—is not entirely contrary to the Duchampian spirit. I am thinking of this famous haiku: "Pulling off / the wings of the dragonfly / a red pepper pod: adding wings / to the red pepper pod / a dragonfly." If an artwork typically leads us to see the dragonfly rather than the red pepper, this interpretation would simply lead us to look past the dragonfly to the red pepper pod.

*

After this first solution of the enigma, which was created by a direct, abrupt, and primitive intrusion of Cupid into the work, comes the second solution, the *helpmate*. What could this mean when applied to *Étant donnés* rather than to a chess problem? What it means is the most radical possible inversion. No longer substituting a literal interpretation for a figurative one, the solution entails subverting the very rules that govern the conversation between the artwork and the viewer.

An artistic equivalent to the *directmate* is the fact that the viewer *plays first,* meaning that he is the one who looks at the piece and searches for the solution, i.e. the meaning. The *helpmate* inverts this rule or this relationship: it is no longer the viewer who *plays first,* but rather the *show*. Metaphorically, it is no longer the museumgoer that is looking at the work, but the reverse. The artwork is no longer the object, but the subject. And if it is the work that is looking, what is it looking at? Everything but itself, everything in front of it—in short, everything behind rather than in front of the viewer. And Stefan Banz's discoveries tell us what is there: the landscape around Lake Léman (Geneva), the lake itself, the vineyards, the mountains and their almost infinite openness. In other words, if in conceiving *Étant donnés* Marcel Duchamp so completely turned his back on what his predecessors always saw in these Lemanic landscapes—the lake to start—is to suggest that the artwork is the true viewer. So, based on this interpretation (that follows the rules of *helpmate* and gives the move [le trait] to the work rather than to the viewers), *Étant donnés* is precisely what one should not look at, but rather is the thing looking.

Incidentally, the female sex organ in this sort of interpretation would be the *eye,* not in Georges Bataille's terms, the eye within the sex organ, but rather the eye that supplants the sex organ to become the one looking. And the woman as art, *object* in my first version, becomes *subject* in my second.

*

These are my two solutions in which I use—with the help of metaphors—the same transgressions I devised to solve Duchamp's chess problem. On the one hand, the intrusion of Cupid in the artwork, emptying it of all artistic substance and reducing it to the condition of a *peep show* that, though sophisticated, is nevertheless a *peep show;* and on the other, the alteration of the rules of looking that *give the opening move* [le trait] to the artwork, such that the artwork becomes not what is looked at, but the one looking, thus forcing us to turn our back to it.

I think I might justifiably claim that these two "solutions" in no way betray the Duchampian spirit since they employ the very processes of inversion or substitution he held so dear. Above all, they both essentially negate the existence of what art history conventionally calls a *work of art*. In my first solution, *Étant donnés* destroys the ideal of the artwork understood as a sublimation of desire, as it portrays itself as the site of pure sexual desire and as fundamentally non-sublimated. My second solution—more civilized perhaps but no less radical—subverts the notion of a work of art by shattering the very idea that an artist's work needs *to be looked at*. In the first instance, *Étant donnés* attracts the eye, but as a pure sexual object; in the second, *Étant donnés* is asking the eye to look somewhere else. It is Charybdis and Scylla. This double self-negation of the artwork, I believe, would not have displeased Duchamp.

*

Nevertheless, it is time that I give in and confess: the solutions I just offered to the problem of *Étant donnés* have a great weakness, just as, for that matter, the solutions I proposed to solve Duchamp's chess problem.

Allow me first to revisit the latter. Duchamp, the avid chess player, would not have approved of, much less have imagined them. For one thing, they possess little or no real value in terms of chess. I am not going to detail their weaknesses, as this would only interest chess enthusiasts, and particularly because it is not that Duchamp would have disapproved of my solutions for their value in terms of chess, but it is simply because *they are solutions,* and that the meaning, or rather the non-meaning of his problem and the given conditions is precisely their lack of solution.

When confronted with Duchamp's diagram, I was itching for a solution; I fell victim to Sherlock Holmes syndrome. But, I must admit: this chess game does not have a solution, that's all. Duchamp had no other intention than to provoke in me *the desire for a solution* by offering a diagram that looked like a problem but was not one. By doing so he remains faithful to his famous formula, which I am now compelled to respect: "There is no solution because there is no problem."

Returning to *Étant donnés* and the solutions I put forward for it: I must express the same reservations, make the same confession. The idea of introducing the viewer into the artwork that has now become purely and simply a *peep show,* or on the contrary diverting him from it to contemplate the Léman or nothing at all, were undoubtedly paradoxes that, in themselves, are not unsustainable in the Duchampian universe. But they become hard to sustain if I really want to present them as *solutions* for the artwork. Because *Étant donnés,* like the chess diagram, *does not have* a solution. *Étant donnés* does not have a solution because it is not a problem.

But then again, in such circumstances one might wonder: is it still possible to risk interpreting *Étant donnés,* whatever that might be? Are not all interpretations critics and art historians strive to provide incorrectly trying to explain something that rejects explanation, to gloss something that evades all gloss, to hold forth on something that forestalls all discussion?

To this I could answer that an *interpretation* is not a *solution.* An interpretation worthy of its name (contrary to what I proposed earlier in my little games) does not pretend to approach *Étant donnés* as a riddle, an enigma to be solved, a problem that has one, unique solution. What distinguishes interpretation from solution is that the artwork remains intact, taking away none of its substance but rather adding to it, enriching it; whereas a work of art with a so-called solution is reduced to a mere riddle, stripped of all value the moment a solutionist (as it is called in the chess world) decrypts it.

That said, and even if the *interpretation* is not as restrictive as the *solution,* it still assumes there is something to interpret. It assumes that the work of art, or what is called as such, contains, expresses, suggests what we call meaning or signification. From that point on, it is perfectly legitimate to explain in words and concepts the meaning enclosed in a work of visual art. Or is Duchamp—consciously and deliberately—deceiving us into thinking there is hope for a solution? Isn't he actually walling himself off from *interpretation* as much as *solution?*

"There is no solution because there is no problem." By asserting this isn't Duchamp also asserting that "*there is no interpretation because there is no meaning;* there is no discussion about the artwork because there is no artwork? Everything falls through: the artwork and its interpretation"? Don't you think he must be smiling in his grave to see fall flat so many explanations of something about which there is *nothing* really to be said.

True loyalty to Duchamp would then be silence. But that would also be the limitation of his artwork (that could no longer be called by that name). Even more so it would limit those who wish to take after Duchamp, for his artistic approach can only exist if it is unique. This leads us to the extreme situation in which both man and artist question where this search for meaning is taking us. After Duchamp, there is nowhere left to go.

*

"There is no solution because there is no problem." This formula appears to be a man's ultimate attempt to unburden himself of the human condition, because life is made, whether we like it or not, of problems if not solutions.

Please permit me a final word. There is a phrase that even Duchamp himself has never pronounced, because it would be too clearly contrary to the experience that man can and must have of reality. That phrase would be: "There is neither solace nor reassurance because there is no suffering." Perhaps there is no solace or reassurance, but there certainly is suffering. Who could deny this? Not even Duchamp.

At the very end of the aforementioned article by Francis Naumann on the "problem with no solution," the author points out that Duchamp composed this chess problem after having met Maria Martins, a Brazilian sculptor with whom he fell in love—but this woman, married and the mother of three, was unattainable. The lack of solution to the chess diagram [diagramme d'échecs] would then be, according to Naumann, a manner of illustrating or symbolizing this failure [échec] at love. Therefore, the least we can say is: if there are no solutions in life, *there are problems*. And Duchamp's experience had just reconfirmed this.

My intention is not to give his work, chess related or not, a straight biographical explanation, but rather to remind us of the obvious: there might not be solutions in life, but there are problems. There are problems since there is suffering. In life there is suffering; it is part of our human condition. And yet, amid the solaces and the reassurances, can't we include works of art? And who knows, there—against all odds and even perhaps against the artist's will—we might even find what I am tempted to call the *artwork* of Marcel Duchamp. At least this is what I would like to believe. Art has something to do with the suffering of life, and in a certain, mysterious way, it makes this suffering less insane. *Given* life [*Étant donné* la vie], there is art. I am thankful to all the artists, Duchamp included.

Translated from the French by Gaston Bertin and Jonathan Fox

Note

1 See Francis Naumann, "A Problem With No Solution," Toutfait.com, http://www.toutfait.com/online_journal_details.php?postid=47066#N_I_top (accessed March 30, 2010).

CONTEXTUALIZATION OF ÉTANT DONNÉS

Hans Maria de Wolf

Beyond Swiss Cheese and Bullet Holes – Part II*
And Some Other Elements in Duchamp's Notorious Endspiel, *Étant donnés*

During a prestigious symposium organized by Michael Taylor at the Philadelphia Museum of Art last September, I had the privilege to unfold for the first time in public a path I discovered that allows us to bridge the gap between Marcel Duchamp's two most ambitious enterprises: *The Large Glass* on the one hand, and the *Étant donnés* diorama on the other.[1]

Today I would like to retrace the essential elements of that argument, partly in order to commemorate the contribution of a small Swiss waterfall in the complex resuscitation of Duchamp's oeuvre throughout the 1940s and 50s, but also because I need them as a context, necessary to understand how a couple of other late pieces could possibly be integrated into Duchamp's monumental closing act.

The argument starts with the consideration that the banner under which this closing act is known also serves as a kind of prelude, written to open up the oeuvre as a whole. The title *Étant donnés* comes from a well known but difficult note, called "Préface" (fig. 1).[2] All this reminds us of the fact that Duchamp turned away from a traditional notion of the oeuvre being the list of all pieces attributed to the same artist and initiated a far more demanding idea of the oeuvre, being the formal part of an intense attitude, a way of life, that apparently evolved according to a circular logic. Every single element Duchamp consciously brought under our attention must be understood as a genuine part of the oeuvre to which he devoted an entire life.

In a certain sense, this conception of the oeuvre as an autonomous and self-regulating body of pieces, notes, and facts reflects for the first time in the visual arts one of Stéphane Mallarmé's central devices: that the world is meant to lead to one beautiful book and nothing more.[3]

If we now agree to adopt this notion of the oeuvre, we cannot but accept all its consequences, as for instance: that we will not be successful in understanding the ultimate raison d'être of the *Étant donnés* unless we succeed in determining its appropriate place within the oeuvre, as the last piece in an enormous puzzle. This then conducts us right away in the direction of the first major campaign: *La mariée mise à nu par ses célibataires, même,* better known as *The Large Glass* (fig. 2).

Time does not allow us to crank up here for the occasion the Bachelor machine, like Jean Suquet has done so many times ever since the appearance of his *Miroir de la Mariée* in

* The present article was conceived and written originally for the Duchamp conference in Cully in May 2010. However, a part of it, mainly concerning the *First Papers of Surrealism* exhibition catalogue, was also included in a lecture I gave in September 2009 in Philadelphia and later in Bonn. The reason for this overlap is obvious and is inspired by the specificity of Duchamp's oeuvre. At one point, my reading of *The Large Glass* offered two (or more) different directions to be continued.

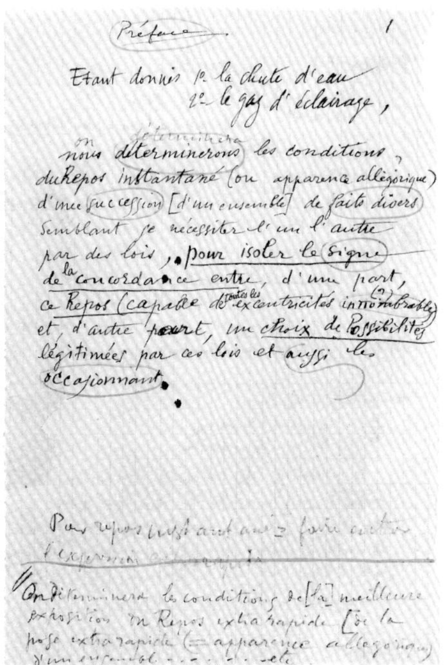
Préface 1

Etant donnés 1° la chute d'eau
2° le gaz d'éclairage,
on déterminera
nous déterminerons les conditions
du Repos instantané (ou apparence allégorique)
d'une succession [d'un ensemble] de faits divers
semblant se nécessiter l'un l'autre
par des lois, pour isoler le signe
de la concordance entre, d'une part,
ce Repos (capable de toutes les excentricités innombrables)
et, d'autre part, un choix de Possibilités
légitimées par ces lois et aussi les
occasionnant.

// On déterminera les conditions de [la] meilleure
exposition du Repos extra rapide [de la
pose extra rapide (= apparence allégorique)
d'un ensemble ... etc.

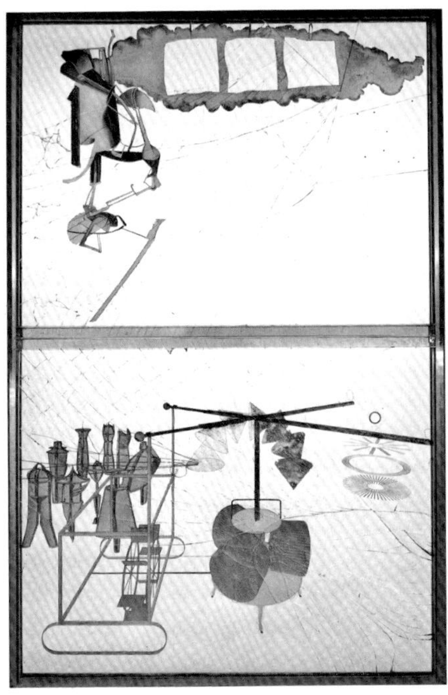

1 **Marcel Duchamp, *Préface: Étant donnés: 1° La chute d'eau, 2° le gaz d'éclairage*** (Given: 1. The Waterfall, 2. The Illuminating Gas), facsimile (collotype on paper) of manuscript note in *La mariée mise à nu par ses célibataires, même ou La boîte verte* (The Bride Stripped Bare by Her Bachelor, Even or The Green Box), 21 x 12.7 cm, 1934. Philadelphia Museum of Art. Louise and Walter Arensberg Collection. 2 **Marcel Duchamp, *La mariée mise à nu par ses célibataires, même ou Le grand verre*** (The Bride Stripped Bare by Her Bachelors, Even, or The Large Glass), oil, varnish, lead foil, lead wire and dust on two glass panels (broken), mounted between two panes of glass in an aluminum, wood, and steel frame, 272.5 x 175.8 cm, 1915–23.Philadelphia Museum of Art. Bequest of Katherine S. Dreier.

1974.[4] There are by now several manuals that explain in detail how a curious male gas is transformed through the Bachelor apparatus (visualized in the lower plate) into an explosive plasma, obsessed with the Bride. Neither will we open again on this occasion a confusing debate, as to what is exactly supposed to be hanging in the upper part of the Glass. For today just accept the idea that this is the domain of the Bride, an environment that obeys a set of rules that determines a purely speculative fourth dimension.[5]

Let me take you now to one of the most enigmatic parts of Duchamp's construction. As you can see, the whole vertical zone, between the nine shots and the three floating optical discs known as the oculist witnesses, is almost empty. And yet this is the area that was intended to host the final battlefield between the male and the female principles. So how can we explain the silence over there?

One of the answers could be that the hostilities do take place, but only within the *Green Box* (fig. 3), which, after all, bears exactly the same title.[6] Among this first selection of ninety-three notes we find several mechanical experiments that are clearly conceived to operate in this zone:

The large *Toboggan* that conducts the gas towards the basement (fig. 4)

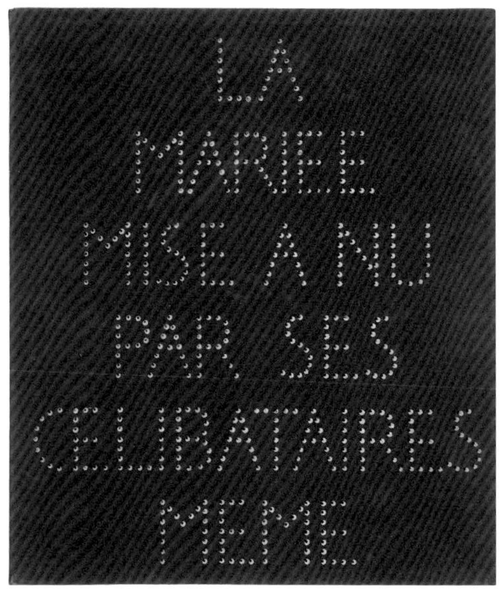

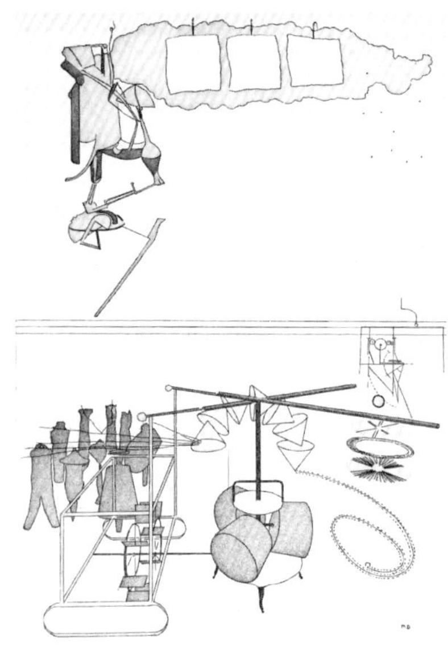

3 Marcel Duchamp, *La mariée mise à nu par ses célibataires, même ou La boîte verte* (The Bride Stripped Bare by Her Bachelor, Even, or The Green Box), ninety-three facsimile notes (photographs, drawings, handwritten notes [1911-15]) and a color plate, 33.2 x 28 x 2.5 cm each, 1934. Philadelphia Museum of Art. Louise and Walter Arensberg Collection. **4 Marcel Duchamp, *The Large Glass Completed,*** colored etching on Japan vellum, 50 x 33 cm, 1965. Private Collection.

> The *Mobile* that is supposed to be shaken off by the big scissors, in order to smash into the gas provoking its explosion (fig. 5)
>
> The *Boxing Match,* designed to strip off the Bride from her clothes (fig. 6)
>
> Or the *Manieur de gravité,* the handler of gravity, a curious little instrument that seems to penetrate the Bride's domain (fig. 7)

Jean Suquet integrated them all into his famous reconstruction (fig. 8), championing most of all the handler of gravity for bridging the gap between the Bride and her Bachelors after all.[7] But then, some important questions remain. Why is it that all those devices finally didn't succeed in reaching the final stadium; that is, to be added to the Glass? And what could be the reason for the oculist witnesses to be more successful? In the late 1980s Herbert Molderings came up with an important part of the answer when he argued that in around 1918 Duchamp's research for *The Large Glass* made a major shift from mechanical devices to optical ones.[8] We now understand that the entire engagement of Duchamp in the field of optics was inspired by his quest for workable solutions to the problems he was confronted with throughout *The Large Glass.* Although the optical experiments offered him a permanent place in the history of physics, they finally didn't result in convincing solutions for the Glass; so, asking why this specific zone remains that empty is asking why Duchamp finally stopped working on the glass in 1922, signing it as unfinished for ever. As he himself confessed, he ran out of ideas, or could it be that the project had reached such a degree of complexity that the artist finally got trapped in his own work ?

All that remained visible on the Glass from this period full of doubts and riddles are the oculist witnesses, a spying instrument carefully orientated towards the bride, and another small device that is always overlooked because its presence is so discrete: the Kodak lens.

If we now reconsider the fact that every development in Duchamp's work occurs according to the principle of the oeuvre, it then seems rather likely that the connections between *The Large Glass* and the *Étant donnés* diorama must take into consideration the unresolved problems in this specific zone. I suggest we take a closer look at a couple of elements from this area that eventually could play a major role in establishing those connections. The first is well known, the second has gone entirely unconsidered until now.

The nine shots are mainly understood as being the theatre for the closing act of the Bride's drama. It is her quintessential erotic area. It is in this part of her domain that the Bride's letters fade away, probably after having been exposed to reflections of the male gas coming from the world below. Rather irrational in its function in support of the female orgasm, the nine shots are nevertheless very physical, as they were drilled into the glass.

In an intriguing note from the *Green Box* (fig. 9), Duchamp describes the procedure that determined the placement of each shot on the Glass.[9] From a previously fixed place in space the artist fired by means of a toy canon, one after the other, nine matches towards the same point of the Glass. As they were all dipped in paint, they left a trace where they had touched the Glass.

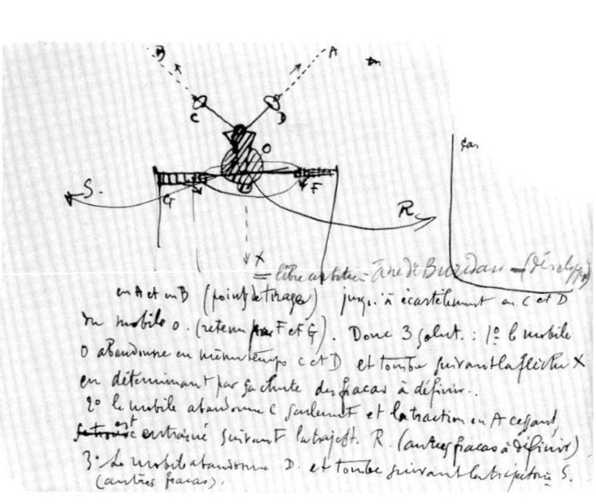

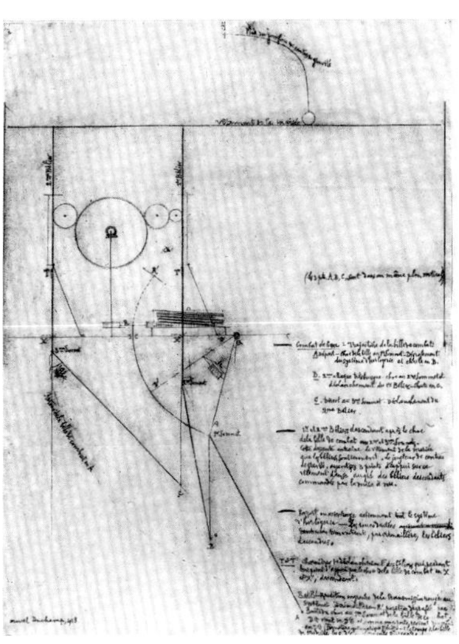

5 Marcel Duchamp, Mobile, facsimile (collotype on paper) of manuscript note in *La mariée mise à nu par ses célibataires, même, ou La boîte verte* (The Bride Stripped Bare by Her Bachelor, Even, or The Green Box), 1934. Philadelphia Museum of Art. Louise and Walter Arensberg Collection. **6 Marcel Duchamp, Boxing Match,** facsimile (collotype on paper) of manuscript note in *La mariée mise à nu par ses célibataires, même, ou La boîte verte* (The Bride Stripped Bare by Her Bachelor, Even, or The Green Box), 1934. Philadelphia Museum of Art. Louise and Walter Arensberg Collection.

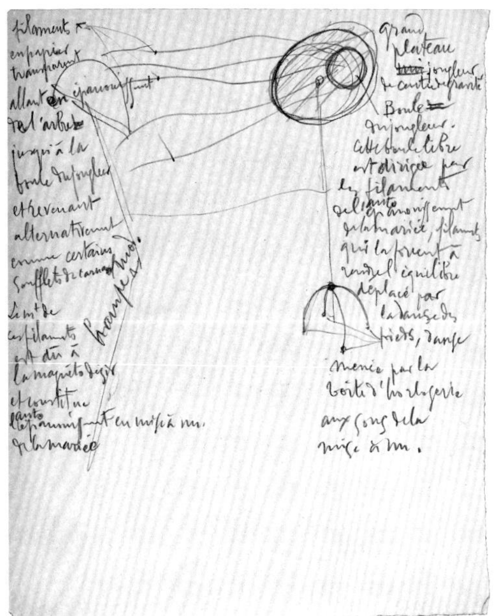

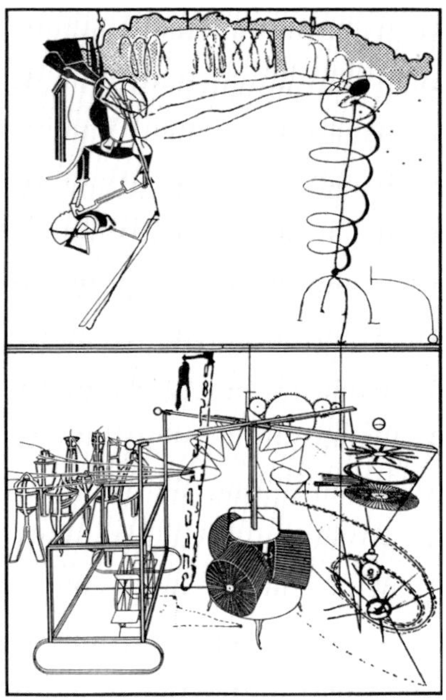

7 **Marcel Duchamp, Manieur de gravité,** facsimile (collotype on paper) of manuscript note in *La mariée mise à nu par ses célibataires, même, ou La boîte verte* (The Bride Stripped Bare by Her Bachelor, Even, or The Green Box), 1934. Philadelphia Museum of Art. Louise and Walter Arensberg Collection. 8 **Jean Suquet, Reconstruction of the Bachelor Machine,** in Jean Suquet, *Marcel Duchamp ou l'éblouissement de l'éclaboussure,* Paris 1998, p. 26.

With maximum skill, he remarks, the projection would be reduced to one point on the Glass, but since we only have ordinary skill, the projection became a de-multiplication of the target...

If the second element I would like to bring up went completely unconsidered until recently, then here it is not Duchamp who is to blame, but his loyal editor of the notes: Michel Sanouillet. The "Weight with Holes" (fig. 10), an important coupling in the Bachelor mechanism, was forgotten for many decades because Sanouillet edited the note under the title: "Témoins oculistes" in chapter 18 of his presentation of the *Green Box*.[10]

When we carefully examine the original note and the way Duchamp displaced the drawing and the text on the paper, we easily understand the origin of Sanouillet's mistake. The title of a following thought concerning the oculist witnesses was incorrectly linked to the drawing above as a subtitle. Even the correct displacement of Hamilton seems to suggest such a connection.

There is no such connection. What we see in the drawing is an original part of the Bachelor machine. It is nothing other than a circular stone riddled with holes. The note explains how at a certain point in the track of the gas it will move from position A (where it is now situated) to point B, where it has to be in time in order to collect the gas gliding down from the toboggan. Even the last of the seven cones is mentioned. So there can be no mistake:

the Weight is supposed to support the gas in finding the right direction on a vertical axis towards the Bride.

The drawing shows how, according to a sectional plan, the displacement from A to B will occur. So to help us understand the move, the plan cuts the weight in two, on the vertical axes A-B, the midpoint of the weight. Unfortunately this contributed to our condemnation to ages of ignorance.

So far for *The Large Glass*. I would like you to keep those two elements in mind.

The First Papers of Surrealism—A New Beginning

As I suggested, the fact that *The Large Glass* project finally got stuck as a consequence of its own tremendous ambition resulted in some brutal implications that probably could not be avoided: for several years the artist Marcel Duchamp seemed to have been condemned to complete artistic silence, and this in full conformity with the logics of the oeuvre.[11]

Now, another thought is very dear to me, namely the presumption that it may well have been the same logics of the oeuvre that engendered the conditions for lifting the blockade. A first step might have been the restoration of the destroyed *Large Glass* in Connecticut in early 1930.[12] Then, in 1934, followed the production of an open book containing ninety-three notes produced in facsimile as floating leaves, the so-called *Green Box*. We can imagine that during this elaborative editing work, dear souvenirs of the early days twenty-two years

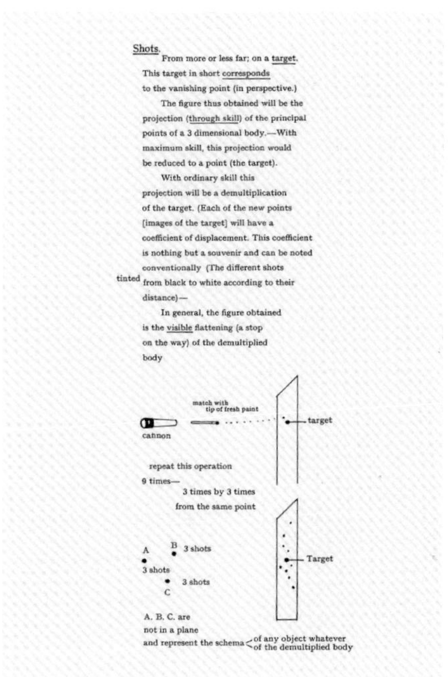

Shots.
From more or less far; on a target.
This target in short corresponds
to the vanishing point (in perspective.)
The figure thus obtained will be the
projection (through skill) of the principal
points of a 3 dimensional body.—With
maximum skill, this projection would
be reduced to a point (the target).
With ordinary skill this
projection will be a demultiplication
of the target. (Each of the new points
[images of the target] will have a
coefficient of displacement. This coefficient
is nothing but a souvenir and can be noted
conventionally (The different shots
tinted from black to white according to their
distance)—
In general, the figure obtained
is the visible flattening (a stop
on the way) of the demultiplied
body

match with tip of fresh paint
cannon
target

repeat this operation
9 times—
3 times by 3 times
from the same point

A
B 3 shots
3 shots
3 shots
C
Target

A. B. C. are
not in a plane
and represent the schema of any object whatever / of the demultiplied body

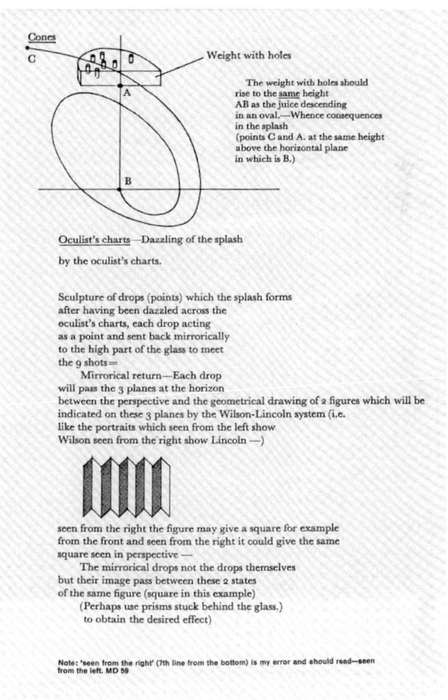

Cones
C
Weight with holes
A
B

The weight with holes should
rise to the same height
AB as the juice descending
in an oval.—Whence consequences
in the splash
(points C and A. at the same height
above the horizontal plane
in which is B.)

Oculist's charts—Dazzling of the splash
by the oculist's charts.

Sculpture of drops (points) which the splash forms
after having been dazzled across the
oculist's charts, each drop acting
as a point and sent back mirrorically
to the high part of the glass to meet
the 9 shots=
Mirrorical return—Each drop
will pass the 3 planes at the horizon
between the perspective and the geometrical drawing of 2 figures which will be
indicated on these 3 planes by the Wilson-Lincoln system (i.e.
like the portraits which seen from the left show
Wilson seen from the right show Lincoln —)

seen from the right the figure may give a square for example
from the front and seen from the right it could give the same
square seen in perspective —
The mirrorical drops not the drops themselves
but their image pass between these 2 states
of the same figure (square in this example)
(Perhaps use prisms stuck behind the glass.)
to obtain the desired effect)

Note: 'seen from the right' (7th line from the bottom) is my error and should read—seen from the left. MD 59

9 Marcel Duchamp, Shots, in *The Bride Stripped Bare by Her Bachelor, Even,* a typographic version by Richard Hamilton of Marcel Duchamp's *Green Box*, Stuttgart, London, Reykjavik 1960, 1963, and 1976, unpaginated. **10 Marcel Duchamp, Cones, Weight with Holes** (for details see fig. 9).

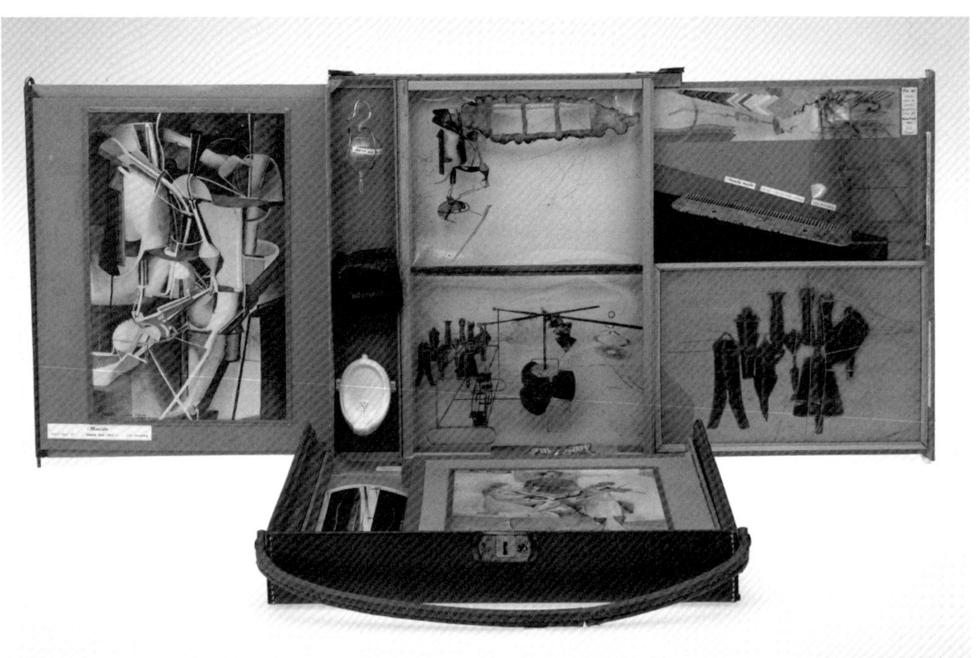

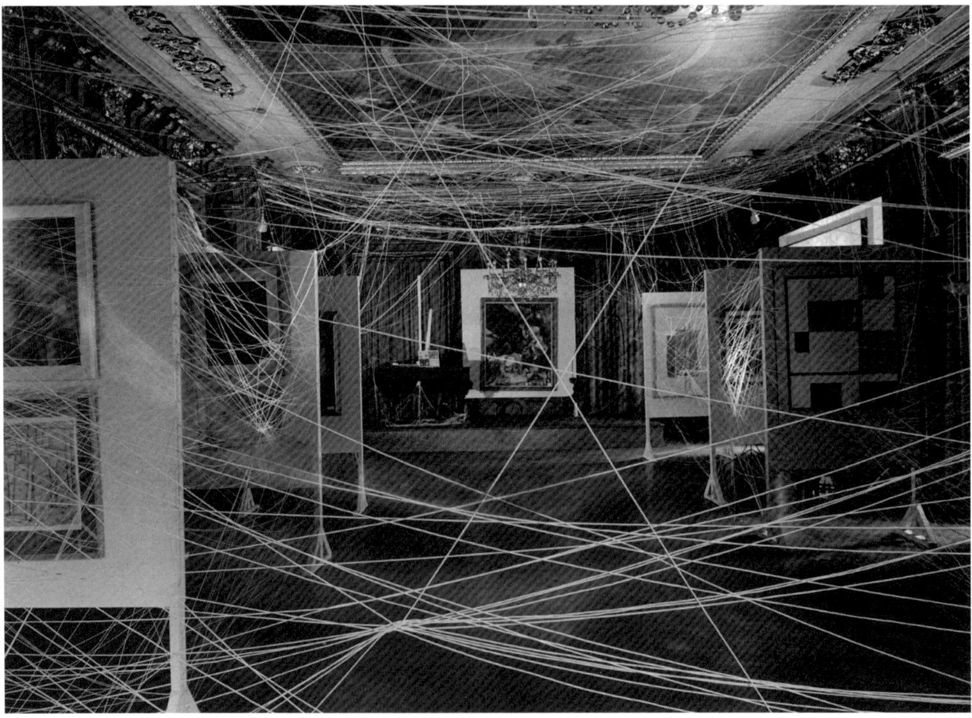

11 Deluxe edition of *The Box in a Valise (From or by Marcel Duchamp or Rrose Sélavy),* edition of 20, 1937–49. Museums and Private Collections. **12** Marcel Duchamp, ***Sixteen Miles of String,*** Installation in the exhibition *First Papers of Surrealism,* Coordinating Council of French Relief Societies, New York, October 14–November 7, 1942, organized by André Breton and Marcel Duchamp.

before, when it all started, might have come up. Only one year later, a new, even more ambitious plan was put in the pipeline. Working out a new general concept, Duchamp decided to recollect every single piece of the oeuvre, reproduced under the form of reproductions and scale models into one single box, the so-called *Boîte-en-valise* (fig. 11).[13]

In the early 1940s, Marcel Duchamp was again fully immersed in the universe of the Bride and her Bachelors. All the elements of the game were on his table in New York, where the portable musea were produced. I'm convinced that it is there and then that he finally found a way out. I will now try to illustrate how in a first move Duchamp wanted us, the spectator, to finally close down for ever *The Large Glass* chapter, in order to create the mental conditions for a new, radical plan that once again developed quickly into a complex endeavor.

According to Arturo Schwarz, the *Étant donnés* project started in 1946. I believe that this is much too late. Let's go back to a moment right in the middle of World War II when a bunch of European refugees, headed by André Breton, accompanied Marcel Duchamp to work on an exhibition of Surrealist art.[14]

The *First Papers of Surrealism* exhibition (fig. 12) has been the subject of several discussions over the past years. We all remember the pictures of an exhibition space transformed by Duchamp into a giant spider web. For our purpose, however, a short moment of concentration on the catalogue of the exhibition will do. As we will see, Duchamp did not hesitate for a moment to turn Breton's invitation to conceive the catalogue into an idea of himself.

Our short investigation of the catalogue will start with the cover (fig. 13). The first action Duchamp undertook as part of the project was to visit Kurt Seligman's farm Sugar Loaf, where he borrowed a gun and fired five shots into an old and eroded stone wall. He then photographed the zone where the result of this outburst of violence could be witnessed. It is this document, printed on yellow cardboard, that Duchamp chose for the cover. The marks of the bullet holes were replaced by real perforations. So every time a spectator opens the catalogue, five little spots light up, illuminated by the first white paper of the book. Optics and optics again.

As a matter of fact, the five little stars are supposed to be understood as a statement. Do they refer to a constellation that accompanies the new project, blessing a set of new ideas Duchamp secretly placed within the catalogue? And of course we do recall right away Duchamp's own prescription from the *Green Box* that resulted in the nine shots on *The Large Glass,* as we understand that he merely was a gunman of ordinary skill. We are reluctant nevertheless to choose, because if we privilege a reference toward the nine shots, why did the artist limit himself to five holes? Five is not a Duchampian figure.[15]

Now, if the cover seems to contain some female elements, such as an atmosphere lighted up by stars, the back of the publication is all the more prosaic. Here we encounter a close-up of Swiss cheese. How do these elements coincide? Strangely enough, and apparently despite all rules of editing, it was against this flat surface that the title of the exhibition

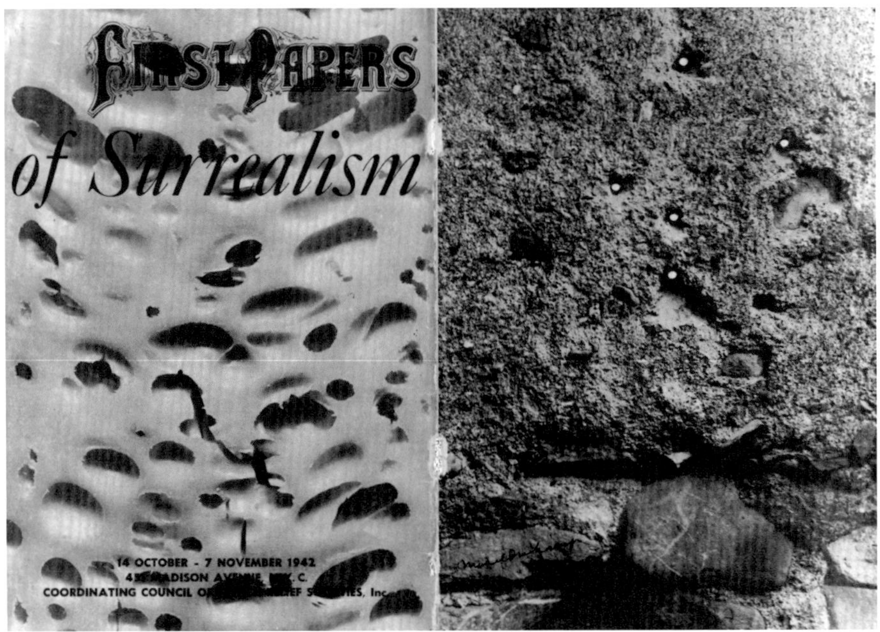

13 Marcel Duchamp, Covers of the catalogue, *First Papers of Surrealism* (back/front), Coordinating Council of French Relief Societies, New York, October 14–November 7, 1942, organized by André Breton and Marcel Duchamp. Private Collection.

was projected. Are we supposed to understand the image as an expression of merely male substance, producing its own specific smell? Or could it be a pun at the expense of his Surrealist friends lost in a new world?

I believe that with an artist such as Marcel Duchamp, the answer never lays in a pun or a reference alone. And I also believe that with this catalogue the artist pays a final farewell to *The Large Glass* and the second dimension that is linked to it. Every time a spectator picks up the publication and opens it, he symbolically is to bring about the destruction of the glass in its second dimension. And welcome in the third dimension. But how does that work?

Well, whoever picks up the publication doesn't find a title, only little holes, turns it around, bumps on a piece of cheese … is not executing actions that are normally related with the first approach to a catalogue. In fact, she or he just entered Duchamp's metaphysics: who could have had the strange idea to confront the stone with the cheese, and why? Vaguely alerted, looking for an answer, the catalogue is then turned around and put on a table. And that is what you get: one vertical image, a modern diptych in its own right, fully emancipated from the content of the catalogue. This is our starting point.

Strangely enough this is also exactly the way in which Duchamp's contribution to the catalogue is remembered in almost every publication in which it is mentioned, and no scholar ever seemed to have been intrigued by the fact that she or he has never published such a bizarre cover before.

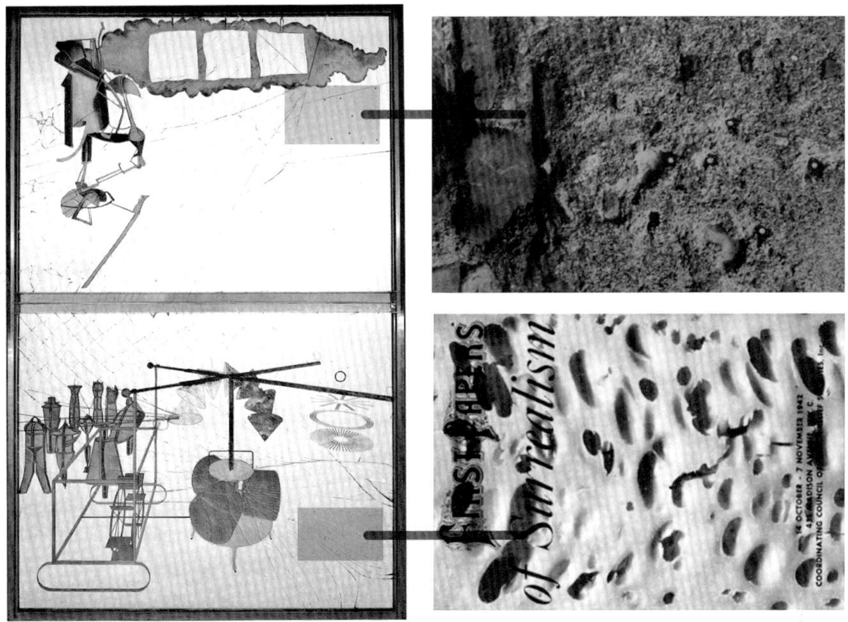

14 Hans Maria de Wolf, Schema with Marcel Duchamp's *Large Glass* and covers of the catalogue, *First Papers of Surrealism.*

Through the first operation in the closing procedure of the Glass, we now found an answer for a major editorial problem we mentioned before. The title of the exhibition has moved to the elegant left upper part of a coherent surface. Time to move on to a second manipulation of the image.

The discovery of a diptych as an autonomous image resulted in the manifestation of another tiny element that should not be overlooked. In fact, if we examine the picture attentively we clearly identify a small white line that separates both elements of the image, just as the horizon in *The Large Glass.* We can now make our final operation, ninety degrees left, in order to obtain a marvelous extrapolation of *The Large Glass* (fig. 14). Ninety degrees is what Craig Adcock used to call the simplest metaphor for a jump to the fourth dimension.[16]

As pieces of a puzzle that finally fit into the right hole, this second operation brings about the most logical answer to a couple of problems that remained unresolved. Now that we have identified the bullet holes as related to the nine shots, we understand that within the cover project Duchamp only needed a rectangular fragment that could refer to the idea "nine shots." The same goes for the cheese, whereby one cannot but consider that a massive wheel of Emmenthal is such an appealing alternative to the Weight with Holes.

Moreover it is interesting to find out that Duchamp not only selected two corresponding devices that belong to what we called the empty vertical zone of *The Large Glass;* even more interesting is the fact that these are the elements that are related to the final stadium

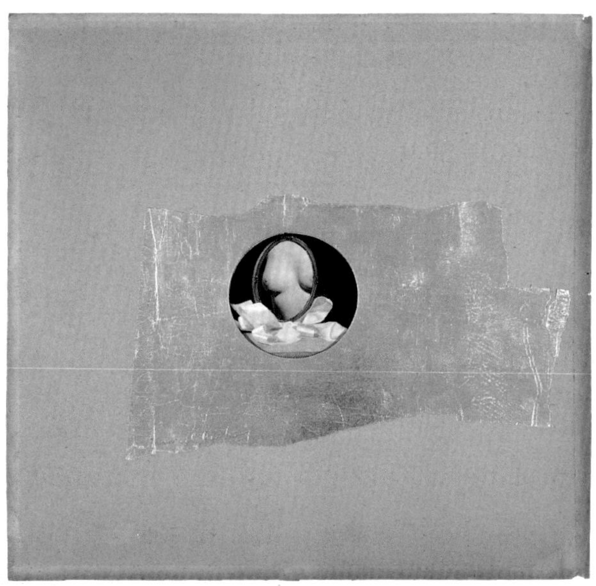

15 Marcel Duchamp, *À la manière de Delvaux* (In the Manner of Delvaux), collage on tinfoil and photograph on cardboard, 34 x 34 cm, 1942. Israel Museum, Jerusalem, Vera and Arturo Schwarz Collection of Dada and Surrealist Art.

of the female and male sexual release, that most probably never found each other within the context of *The Large Glass*.[17]

And this brings us to an unavoidable conclusion: however brilliant and original this construction may be, it only leads us into a dead end. This is the end. All *The Large Glass* still has to offer is a stone wall with some bullet holes for the female and the hard crust of a Swiss cheese for the male principles. By making the same moves in the opposite direction, we leave *The Large Glass* and get back to the catalogue. Five little holes are lighting up from the cover. Here, a new story starts. Only bits and parts of this new story have yet to be elucidated, but at least we now can affirm: as soon as we open the catalogue of the *First Papers of Surrealism* exhibition, we leave the second dimension behind. Again: welcome in the third dimension.

We will not collect here all the elements of passion and crime that were locked up within the catalogue. Let's turn over the pages one by one and find the pearl hidden inside. The most striking forerunner to the *Étant donnés* project is to be discovered here, in 1942, by means of a small, not to say modest little collage. For most obvious reasons, Duchamp called it *À la manière de Delvaux* (In the Manner of Delvaux) (fig. 15) and, how could we possibly not be susceptible to this piece of scenery, with a mirror, a woman's naked breast and, last but not least, that typical silk bow, à la manière de Delvaux?

It is in that bow that we got trapped again, probably under the influence of the image in the mirror. Although all the individual elements of the piece were glued carefully one on the other, *À la manière de Delvaux* is not supposed to be appreciated as a collage. It is a

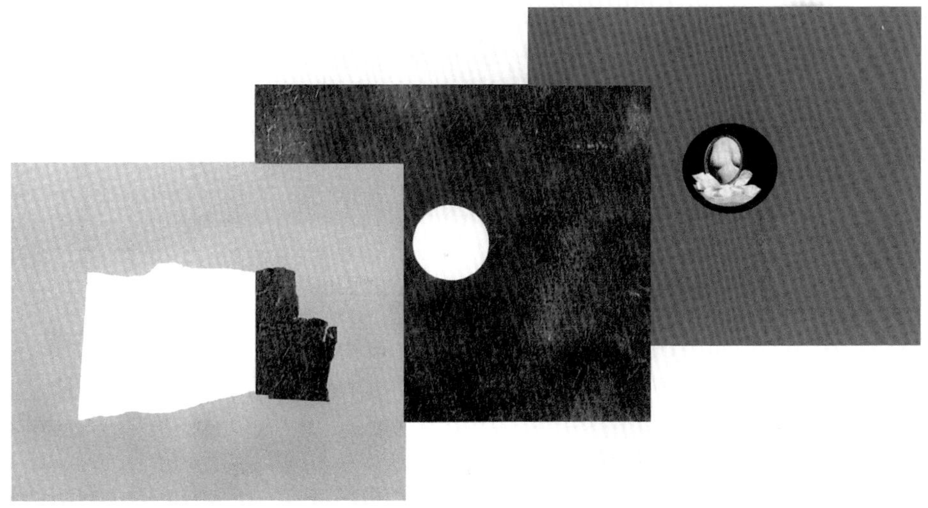

16 Hans Maria de Wolf, Reconstruction of *À la manière de Delvaux* (In the Manner of Delvaux).

model, a construction published in a catalogue, and waiting ever since to be de-constructed in order to reveal its ultimate significance.

Once de-constructed into its several components, the elements themselves appeal for another structure, another tension towards each other, and in doing so, a basic shift from a second to third dimension finally is consumed (fig. 16). So, that is what we then obtain: a kind of little nephew of the camera obscura, a tool that, as soon as it existed was used to spy upon the naked female body.

And we have now fulfilled our task as the spectator within the story, and it is indeed a touching moment. We just witnessed the construction in space of the first, somehow clumsy model for the new masterpiece that would eventually close Duchamp's oeuvre only twenty-seven years later (fig. 17). How could we not be struck by the evident similarities between our fragile de-construction of *À la manière de Delvaux* and a first cardboard model of the *Étant donnés* diorama?

The farm, the stable, the hole in the wall, the headless and naked female body, the silence and the anti-chambre in which the spectator becomes a privileged witness of a story that he can't control, a peeping tom… It's all in the picture. Only the water is still missing.

Sink Stopper

I hope you will now join me in my conclusion, namely that a crooked path leading from *The Large Glass* towards a new period of intense creativity indeed exists. This period would eventually culminate in the *Étant donnés* diorama. As I pointed out in

Philadelphia and Bonn, this also led to a final "no" to painting. Hence, there is still another way out. Let us now consider a couple of Duchamp pieces that never received much attention.[18]

In a detailed note Paul Matisse described how a little counter-weight called *Bouche-évier*, or *Sink Stopper* (fig. 18), came into being.[19] Confronted with the breakdown of the closing mechanism of the bathtub in his summer residence of Cadaqués, out of a number of options Duchamp chose an original solution in producing himself a device out of lead. It served for several years. When in the early sixties he got approached by a society of art collectors eager to include Duchamp in a series of artists medals, he offered the society (after having refused the offer for several years) *Sink Stopper*, that got multiplied as several noble metals, in an edition of 300 pieces.

Sink Stopper was never taken very seriously among Duchamp scholars. Bill Camfield integrated the medal in an exhibition focusing on the readymade *Fountain* on the basis of a most obvious positive-negative connection between the little holes in the famous urinal and the little circle of bulges that provides *Sink Stopper* all its elegance.[20]

However disconnected as it is in regard to its original function, this piece of metal continuously points towards a counter-form upon which it can impose its proper weight as a final and unique destination. Seen as an isolated object, every single bulge in the medal insists on this. Until recently, there was no such counter-form known in Duchamp's machinery. Now, having plugged in the Weight with Holes within the Bachelor apparatus again, we will have to reconsider *Sink Stopper* from a whole new perspective.

Let us first take a look at this rather unusual creative act. Confronted with a banal daily discomfort, Duchamp intervened by applying a material he was familiar with: lead. There is no doubt that the object as we know it today was created at that very moment. However, it received its status as an artwork only some years later, when Duchamp elected it as such. So, independently from the moment of its creation, there has been a second moment in time at which the artist chose this existing, already fabricated device to become an autonomous artwork. So apparently good arguments can be brought forward in order to include *Sink Stopper* to the list of readymades.

However, I am reluctant to do so. The creative act we are dealing with seems more complicated to me. The object combines two identities. In a first period it was nothing more than a utilitarian object, and it was used as such. Hence, compared to billions of other utilitarian objects, it always embodied a feature none of the others could ever claim: it is a unique object. Every summer Marcel and Teeny found it back in the bathroom, kept it in their hand, felt its weight. And then, suddenly, a transmutation took place, I quote:

> … through the change from inert matter into a work of art, an actual transubstantiation has taken place, and the role of the spectator is to determine the weight of the work on the aesthetic scale.[21]

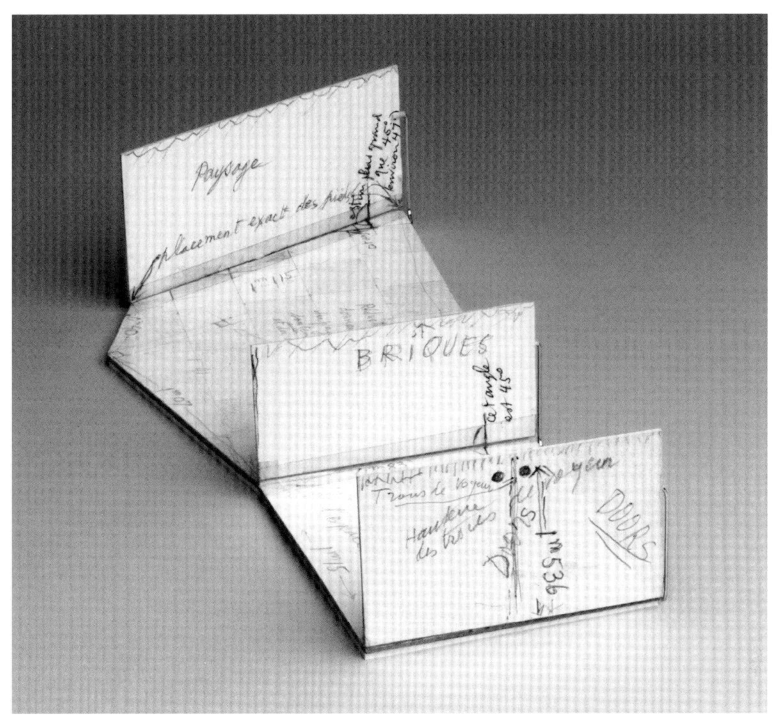

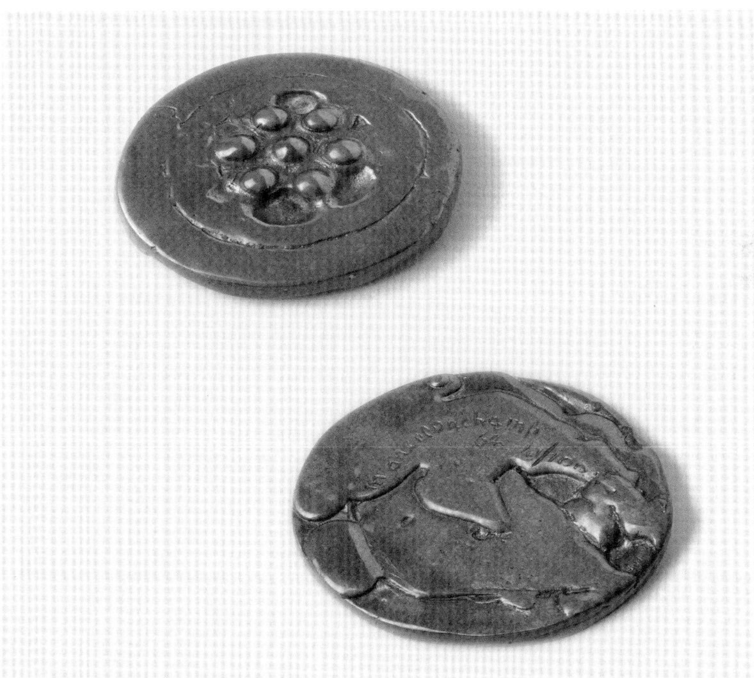

17 Marcel Duchamp, Folding model of *Étant donnés: 1° La chute d'eau, 2° Le gaz d'éclairage* (Given: 1. The Waterfall, 2. The Illuminating Gas), graphite and ballpoint-pen ink on cut cardboard assembled with adhesive and clear pressure-sensitive tape, inserted into page one of *Manual of Instructions for the assembly of Étant donnés: 1° La chute d'eau, 2° Le gaz d'éclairage*, 30.5 x 11.1 x 5.1 cm, c. 1966. Philadelphia Museum of Art. Gift of the Cassandra Foundation. **18 Marcel Duchamp, *Bouche-évier*** (Sink Stopper), recto (left) and verso (right), bronze, cast of 1964 lead original, 1 x 6.4 cm, 1967. Philadelphia Museum of Art. Gift of Carl Steele.

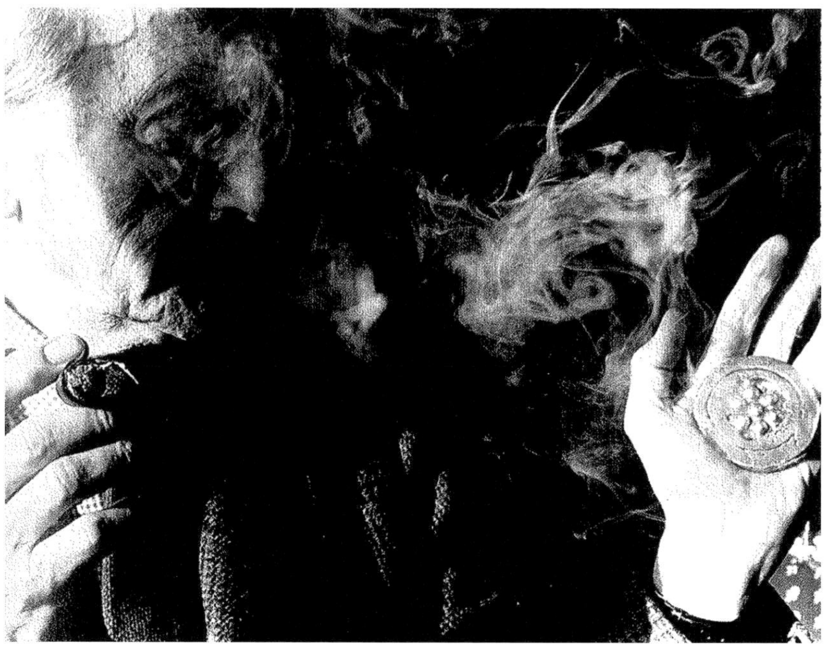

19 Marcel Duchamp, Cover of the sales brochure for *Bouche-évier,* published by the International Numismatic Agency, November 1967. Photograph by Bert Stern.

In all its complexity an idea has come through. Not without a certain delay, the object now obtains a second identity as a piece of art. All this implies that throughout the process Duchamp's role as a medium is over. It's our move now.

Once the creative act is initiated, Duchamp runs into another idea. He informs the directive of the International Collectors Society that he had changed his mind. His suggestion now is to use a piece of his, called *Sink Stopper,* as the master of their multiplication. However, the 300 multiples will be called "Art Medals" and will be distributed by the Society.[22]

It is notable that Duchamp immediately changed the name of the newly produced objects, as if he wanted to exclude any form of contamination between the world of material values (the medals were offered in noble steel, bronze, and silver), a world of collectors and dealers hoping to increase the return on their investment, and his own private universe.

We should not necessary read this as a judgment. The society offered what it stood for: the delivery of valuable objects of art to a select group of collectors. However, the most valuable piece of all remained in Duchamp's oeuvre. This one, called *Sink Stopper,* does not belong to the world. Moreover, it was founded in the most modest metal of all, lead, the metal of *The Large Glass,* the metal of the Bachelors.

One could argue that all this could also be understood as the practical joke of an elderly fox that—recuperated in his old age by a certain success within the art world—would not let this chance pass by: to take a collective of collectors by the nose. But then, in a beautiful brochure that was part of the sales strategy of the Society, we find this photograph of Duchamp holding the "Art Medal" (fig. 19) in a cloud of smoke. Here, there can't be any doubt. We are fully back in Duchamp's own metaphysics.[23]

It is time now to make a final connection with the Bachelor machine, and the Weight with Holes in particular. It seems clear by now that within that context the sink stopper is supposed to execute exactly what is in its name: it has to close the other weight, the one with holes.

In 1964 Duchamp was already a seventy-seven-year-old bachelor. In a small studio on West 14th Street, New York, he was about to complete his final statement, the *Étant donnés* diorama, that would not be unveiled until after his death. He had almost arrived at his final destination. It had been enough. No more passion. After almost eight decades of activity the Bachelor machine could now slowly be brought to a standstill.

So the Weight with Holes could be covered, and the Mona Lisa, whom he had disarmed in 1919 in completing her with a moustache and a goat, could now be shaved again.[24] A cheap reproduction of the famous Florentine bride, which he had turned by force into her gender opposite, but which through that operation became an original work of art, now achieved the status of cheap reproduction.

Those two pieces can be understood as closing statements in regard to the oeuvre. The *Sink Stopper* turns off the energy at a moment in which Lisa is liberated from a kidnapping that went on for almost half a century, and was mostly beneficial for the popularity of her kidnapper, Marcel Duchamp.

However, together they also represent a hinge point. Then, if we choose to give the *Sink Stopper* the value of colophon, closing down the book of the Bride and the Bachelors, then *L.H.O.O.Q. rasée* contains a major hint in the direction of the hidden masterpiece, the *Étant donnés*. Except for a handful of reliable friends, in 1965 nobody knew about it.[25]

So, it was not too bad after all that we had those "art medals" in silver, bronze, and noble steel.

By that time they must have been the property of a group of well-off people who considered themselves experts in the field of the visual arts. Those members of the society might have deeply cherished their private Duchamp, without considering for a single moment that they had invested in an active symbol representing the slow fading away of masculine sexuality. Tragic but funny at the same time.

And so we can imagine all those medals standing as heralds of a forthcoming state of impotence of the owners, among many other valuable objects, in a well-protected and well-visible environment. Every medal came with an oak stand. The society had taken care of that.

One year later, after a quiet evening in the company of Teeny and Robert Lebel, Marcel passed away with a peaceful smile on his lips.

Notes

[1] First Annual Anne d'Harnoncourt Memorial Symposium: "Marcel Duchamp: *Étant Donnés,*" Philadelphia Museum of Art, September 11–12, 2009.

[2] Marcel Duchamp, *Duchamp du signe suivi de Notes. Ecrits réunis et présentés par Michel Sanouillet et Paul Matisse,* Paris 2008, pp. 64–65.

[3] "Au fond, voyez vous, le monde est fait pour aboutir à un beau livre," in Stéphane Mallarmé, *Réponses à des enquêtes sur l'évolution littéraire, Oeuvre Complètes,* Paris 1945, p. 872.

[4] Jean Suquet, *Miroir de la mariée,* Paris 1974.

[5] Jean Suquet had no warm feelings at all for the bride as she is represented on *The Large Glass:* "Si la mise à nu doit découvrir une chair chaude, une fourrure éclaboussée de rosée, pourquoi Duchamp a-t-il fait la Mariée tellement laide, rébarbative, abstraite, promise à on ne sait quel misérable assez fou de solitude pour courtiser sa main?" in Jean Suquet, *In vivo, in vitro. Le grand verre à Venise,* Paris 1994, p. 30. What Suquet seems to ignore is the fact that Duchamp's presentation of the Bride on the glass is nothing more than a projection of that warm flesh of a real woman in three dimensions, called the Bride within a speculative fourth dimension.

[6] The so-called *Green Box* contains a first consistent selection of 93 notes accompanying *The Large Glass.* It was published in a facsimile edition of 300 in 1934, with an additional 20 pieces in a deluxe version. The *Green Box* bears the same title as *The Large Glass: La mariée mise à nu par ses célibataires, même,* In 1958, the notes became available in a pocket edition edited by Michel Sanouillet as Marcel Duchamp, *Marchand du sel,* Paris 1958.

[7] Suquet finds in the handler of gravity the ultimate instrument for a communion between Bride and Bachelors. See Jean Suquet, *Le Guéridon et la virgule,* Paris 1976.

[8] Herbert Molderings in Thierry de Duve, ed., *The Definitively Unfinished Marcel Duchamp,* Cambridge, Mass. 1991.

[9] Duchamp, *Duchamp du signe* (note 2), ch. 6, p. 72.

[10] Ibid., ch. 18, p. 100. In the most recent edition of Duchamp's notes—Marcel Duchamp, *Duchamp du signe suivi de Notes* (note 2)—this mistake is maintained. I presented the real nature of the "Weight with Holes," for the first time during the September 2009 colloquium on the *Étant Donnés* in the Philadelphia Museum of Art. During a six-hour-long interview with the Swedish Duchamp expert Ulf Linde, however, I learned that Linde had also understood correctly the functions of the

Weight with Holes. The interview with Linde was filmed and later edited by the French artist Franck Scurti into a 50-minute-long documentary. It will be released soon.

[11] In the catalogue raisonné, edited by Arturo Schwarz, we cannot find any trace of aesthetic production between 1927 and 1934, except for some small drafts for chess pieces. Seven years of inactivity is a rather long time for an artist. Arturo Schwarz, *The Complete Works of Marcel Duchamp*, New York 1997.

[12] After having been exhibited in the Brooklyn Museum of Art in 1927, *The Large Glass* got completely destroyed during transport back to Katherine Dreier's place in Connecticut. In 1936, Duchamp undertook the complete restoration on the work. This project followed the publication in facsimile of the notes of the *Green Box* in 1934.

[13] Ecke Bonk, *The Box in a Valise. De ou par Marcel Duchamp ou Rrose Sélavy*, New York 1989.

[14] Schwarz, *The Complete Works* (note 11), p. 865.

[15] Duchamp developed his own theory on numbers, holding one for the single, two for the dialectics, and three for everything else. Marcel Duchamp, *Ingénieur du temps perdu. entretiens avec Pierre Cabanne*, Paris 1967–77.

[16] "The fourth dimension is essentially ninety degrees from everything else." Craig Adcock in de Duve, *Definitively Unfinished* (note 8), p. 335.

[17] As to today, there is no consensus among Duchamp scholars specialized in *The Large Glass* concerning a possible contact between the upper and the lower part, between the Bride and the Bachelors. Jean Suquet has always been very positive about a necessity to meet, championing in particular the "handler of gravity" as the major go-between. In my forthcoming study on *The Large Glass*, I am much more reluctant in relation to the possibility of an eventual osmosis. Too much elements are separating both worlds; so many aspects of their functioning can go wrong.

[18] In the Philadelphia paper the focus goes further on certain procedures Duchamp develops during the creative process that leads to "à la manière de Delvaux." Those can be red as a last farewell to the notion of painting. Further emphasis is put on the little Kodak lens.

[19] Pierre Matisse, "Avant-propos," in Duchamp, *Duchamp du signe* (note 2), p. 256.

[20] William A. Camfield, *Marcel Duchamp: "Fountain,"* exh. cat. The Menil Collection, Houston 1987, pp. 110–12.

[21] Duchamp, *Duchamp du signe* (note 2), p. 180–81.

[22] Schwarz, *The Complete Works* (note 11), p. 843.

[23] In order to promote Duchamp's artists multiples, the International Collectors Society, New York edited a brochure that was distributed among its members. The publication was at least partly edited by Duchamp, who delivered the photograph that was used for the cover.

[24] Schwarz, *The Complete Works* (note 11), p. 849.

[25] It is obvious that the act of shaving a female figure (in this case the Mona Lisa) contains a direct reference to the last masterpiece.

Mark Nelson

Surrealism and the Black Dahlia Murder

Introduction

Making a case for evolutionary theory in his book *Why Darwin Matters,* Michael Shermer introduces us to what the nineteenth-century philosopher of science William Whewell called "the consilience of inductions," a scientific method that Whewell was first to describe. According to Shermer, "Whewell believed that to prove a theory, one must have more than one induction, more than a single generalization drawn from specific facts. One must have multiple inductions that converge upon one another, independently but in conjunction. Whewell said that if these inductions 'jump together' it strengthens the plausibility of a theory."[1]

In our book *Exquisite Corpse: Surrealism and the Black Dahlia Murder,* Sarah Hudson Bayliss and I argue that a notorious killing in Los Angeles in 1947 dovetails in time with the commodification and popular acceptance of the visual strategies of Surrealism; and that in some of its specific details the crime itself may have been patterned as a wildly distorted homage to Surrealist art. *Exquisite Corpse* cautiously supports some of the conclusions drawn by Steve Hodel in his book *Black Dahlia Avenger,* in which Hodel argues that his own father, a doctor named George Hodel, was responsible for the murder. We now know that George Hodel was a close friend of the artist Man Ray and that he personally identified with Surrealist ideology and aesthetics. In tracking the friendship of these two men, Sarah and I further suggest that Marcel Duchamp's posthumously revealed masterpiece *Étant donnés: 1° la chute d'eau 2° le gaz d'éclairage* (Given: 1° The Waterfall 2° The Illuminating Gas) (1946–66, pp. 4–5), may have been partly informed by the crime.

I would like to make clear at the outset that Sarah and I are not suggesting that Marcel Duchamp be implicated in the Black Dahlia murder. However, this paper will argue that inductions along six different lines form a consilience, or "jump together," to validate our inquiry with respect to the possible influence of art on this crime and, in turn, to the possible influence of this crime on art. These six lines of inquiry are: visual comparison, iconology, timeframe, social network, geography, and criminology.

Visual comparison

It is impossible to exaggerate the violence committed against Elizabeth Short, the woman who was murdered in 1947, at the age of twenty-two, and who became famous after her death as the Black Dahlia (fig. 1). Short's naked body was found on January 15 of that year on an undeveloped residential lot in the Leimert Park neighborhood of Los Angeles. Extensive lacerations and other injuries had been inflicted all over her body, and her wrists and ankles had ligature marks, indicating that she had been tied to endure torture.[2] After her death, at a still-unknown location, her body had been cut in two. The nature of the bisecting incision strongly suggests that her killer was familiar with surgical method. Short's body was then washed mostly clean of blood and moved to the Leimert Park lot, where its two parts were placed together on the ground, the lower half about a foot away

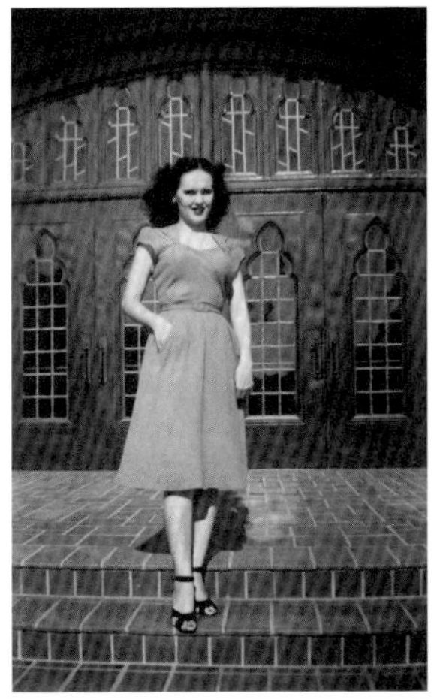
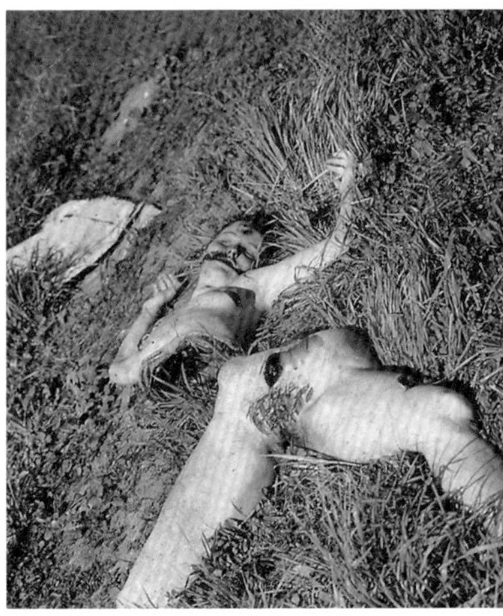
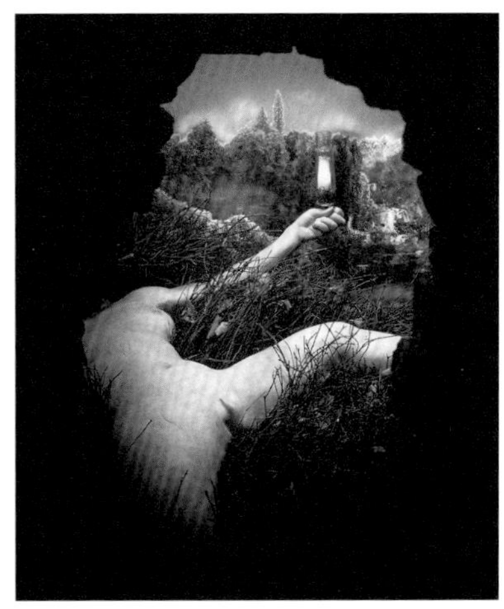

1 Elizabeth Short, photographed by Glen Kearns on the steps of Marshall High School, Los Angeles, California, October 22, 1946. Collection Steve Hodel. **2 A crime scene photograph of the Elizabeth Short (Black Dahlia) murder** taken on January 15, 1947, compared with **Marcel Duchamp's *Étant donnés: 1° la chute d'eau, 2° le gaz d'éclairage*** (Given: 1. The Waterfall, 2. The Illuminating Gas), interior view, 1946–66. Philadelphia Museum of Art. Gift of the Cassandra Foundation.

from the upper half. Her arms were bent at the elbows so that her hands were in line with her head, and her legs were opened wide to display her sexual organs.

After reading *Black Dahlia Avenger* and reviewing the crime scene photographs, I saw an uncanny resemblance to the figure in Duchamp's *Étant donnés* (fig. 2). Believing that this similarity deserved scrutiny, Sarah and I explored it in *Exquisite Corpse*. After our book was published, in September 2006, we found ourselves in a lively discussion that continues today and shows no sign of abating. We expected, of course, that the comparison of Short's horribly abused body to one of the most famous artworks of the twentieth century would meet with resistance. Indeed, one of my companions on this panel, curator Michael Taylor, has questioned the tendency among scholars in general to make associations between Duchamp's final work and misogynistic violence. In his book *Marcel Duchamp: Étant donnés,* Michael writes that Duchamp's "incorporation of body parts and materials relating to Mary Reynolds, Maria Martins and Alexina (Teeny) Duchamp [all women with whom Duchamp had emotional relationships] suggests that *Étant donnés* can be viewed as a grand summation of the artist's life, loves, and obsessions, rather than a violated corpse."[3] He describes a wide range of possible influences on *Étant donnés* but refutes the possibility that the Black Dahlia murder was one of them.

Michael devotes a section of his book to the work of four authors—Jean Michele Rabaté, Jonathan Wallis, Sarah, and myself—who have theorized on the possibility of such a relationship. He finds real issues to argue with in some of these writings, but the core of his critique, I think, is the idea that Duchamp could not have seen photographs of the Black Dahlia crime scene.[4] However, this possibility cannot be ruled out. The crime scene was extensively documented by both police and newspaper photographers. Many prints made from original negatives of their photographs have surfaced in recent years, leaving no doubt that copies of the crime scene images circulated outward from several points of origin immediately after the murder and in the years following.[5] The murder was of enormous public interest—a shocking, scandalous crime—and it is easy to imagine that well-connected members of the Hollywood community could have had both the desire and the means to get hold of such prints. One such resident—and one who maintained his own darkroom—was Man Ray, a close friend both of Duchamp and of George Hodel. Photography is the most transmittable of mediums, and we know that both police and press photographs of the Black Dahlia crime scene were no exception. Though no proof of this has so far emerged, it seems perfectly plausible that such photographs could have reached Man Ray, and through him Duchamp. Man Ray's prurient nature is more than enough to suggest he would have been interested, but the fact that his friend Hodel was openly tied to the case in the newspapers in 1949, and can be shown to have been discussing the fact that he was under investigation in that crime in 1950, makes such an argument even more compelling. Ironically, by acknowledging the relationship between Man Ray and Hodel in his book, Michael highlights the fact that there was but a single degree of separation between Duchamp and Hodel, a prime suspect then and now in the crime.

Of course the fact that two things look alike does not mean they are related, and the similarities between *Étant donnés* and the crime-scene photographs might be coincidence. The possibility of a relationship between them, though, is strongly suggested by a number of other elements of information and interpretation—by a "consilience of inductions." As we move farther into these six different areas, the first question to consider is this:

Given that Duchamp was a close friend of Man Ray, who was in turn a close friend of Black Dahlia murder suspect George Hodel; and given that Duchamp's *Étant donnés* shows striking resemblances to crime scene photographs of the Black Dahlia murder; what is the probability that *Étant donnés* bears some relation to those images?

Iconology

The motives for murder are usually fairly clear—money, jealousy, anger, and so on. Even deviant murder, however repulsive, seems to follow a limited number of scripts. This, I believe, is why the murder of Elizabeth Short is so haunting: killings both so violent and so calculated are rare. Equally rare is a killer with the means, motive, opportunity, technical skill, and audacity not only to commit this crime in the middle of a major city but also to escape detection and prosecution for more than half a century. In other words, what is so startling about this particular crime's execution is the apparent absence of precedent.[6]

Sarah and I suggest, however, that precedent for the murder may lie not only in other crimes but in the themes and motifs of Surrealism, which by early 1947 was widely known to the American public.[7] During the years leading up to the Black Dahlia murder, writings and photo essays on Surrealism appeared regularly in the popular press, rather awkwardly communicating the movement's intellectual underpinnings to the lay reader. A 1941 cartoon from the *Los Angeles Times,* for example, shows the upper half of a female manikin. Its caption reads, "Hello There! Latest Whimsey of Surrealist Salvador Dalí: 'Enchanting' a country estate by planting such things as show window manikins in

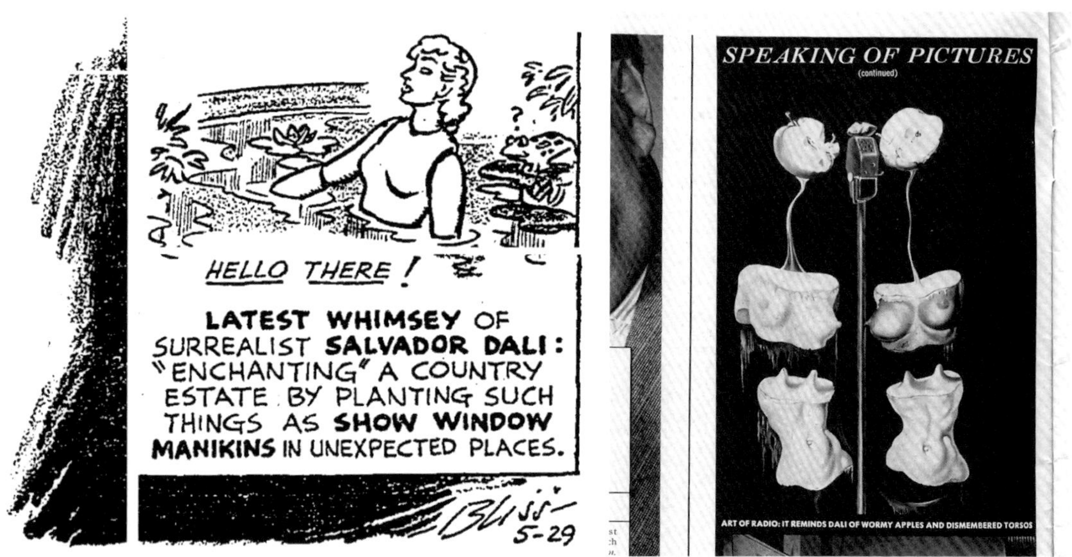

3 A cartoon from "Private Lives by Edwin Cox," in *the Los Angeles Times,* May 29, 1941. **4 Page detail from "Speaking of Pictures . . . Dali Paints the Seven Lively Arts,"** in *Life* magazine, January 1, 1945.

unexpected places" (fig. 3). In 1943 in the same newspaper, in an article titled "Surrealists Again Go Into Their Weird Act," the art critic Arthur Millier gave the movement a drubbing: "Surrealism," he wrote, "with its affectation of irrational attitudes, its pretense of enormous crimes and immoralities ... was an expression of people, who, having no conviction to sustain them, nonetheless felt they were doomed to undergo torture. Its prime hero was the Marquis de Sade, who experimented with torture."[8] A feature article on Salvador Dalí in *Life* magazine, published in 1945, includes a detail of his painting *Art of Radio,* which pictures two bisected female torsos (fig. 4).[9] It is a reminder of Dalí's own description of the distended, distorted, and disemboweled female figures common in his artworks. "The 'dismantle-able body,'" Dalí had written in a 1934 essay in *Minotaure* magazine, "is the aspiration and verification of feminine exhibitionism, which ... permits each piece to be isolated and separately consumable."[10]

Another feature in *Life,* on Hans Richter's Surrealist film *Dreams that Money Can Buy,* shows a publicity photo of one of the film's protagonists, Narcissus, brandishing a knife over a young woman lying in a hammock; the caption reads: "Narcissus debates briefly between kissing the girl and cutting her throat, an implication that all love is very close to hatred." This issue of *Life* was published on December 1946, six weeks before Elizabeth Short was found dead.[11] If, by the time of the Black Dahlia murder, the word "surreal" had been absorbed into the American lexicon, in popular usage its connotations were sometimes cruel or worse.

These accounts in the popular press may seem simplistic or exaggerated, but representations of sectioned, distorted, or disassembled female torsos aren't uncommon in Surrealist art. Here are just a few interpretations of the Surrealist model:

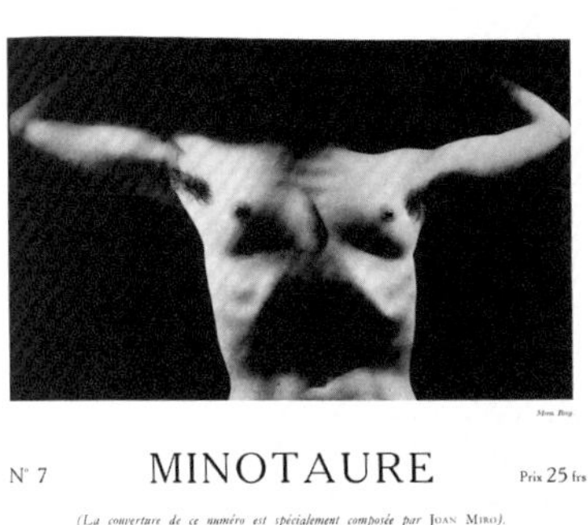

Man Ray

N° 7 MINOTAURE Prix 25 frs

(La couverture de ce numéro est spécialement composée par Joan Miro*).*

La peau de la peinture	E. Tériade.
Portraits de femmes	Man Ray.
Mimetisme et psychasthénie légendaire Documents photographiques de Le Charles.	Roger Caillois.
Un tout petit cheval	Henri Michaux.
La manière blonde. Eaux-fortes de André Beaudin pour l'illustration des « Bucoliques » de Virgile.	Jacques Baron.
Appliquée Illustrations de Bellmer et de Man Ray.	Paul Eluard.
Borès. Hors-texte en couleurs.	Maurice Raynal.
Nuits romantiques sous le Roi Soleil	Maurice Heine.
Le Jour est trop court	Young.
Il n'est pas encore trop tard Photographies de Brassaï et de Man Ray.	Young.

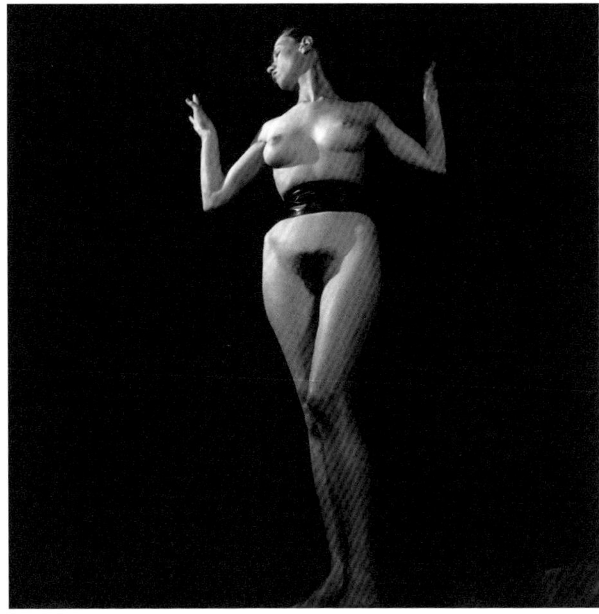

5 Page from issue 7 of *Minotaure* magazine—featuring Man Ray's *Minotaur*—published by Albert Skira, Paris, 1935.
6 Denise Bellon, *Nu* (Nude), gelatin silver print, 30 x 30 cm, 1936. Made from the original negative in 2004 by Laboratoire Cyclope, Paris. © les films de l'equinoxe-fonds photographique Denise Bellon, Paris.

1. Victor Brauner, *L'Éclair questionne,* 1930
2. Harry Carlsson, *Triumph of Love,* 1936
3. Denise Bellon, *Nude,* 1936
4. Richard Taylor, Cover of *The New Yorker,* January 9, 1937
5. Clarence John Laughlin, *The Eye That Never Sleeps,* 1946
6. Bruce Angrave, An illustration for "Miss Thing and the Surrealists," in John Kier Cross's *The Other Passenger,* 1946

The six images here are only a sampling of hundreds of artworks made in this vein in the two decades preceding the Black Dahlia murder. Denise Bellon's photograph, for example, is a remarkable compression of Surrealist symbology: the upraised arms familiar from Surrealist depictions of the minotaur, the closed eyes and softly bent neck familiar from a myriad of Surrealist "dream state" images, and the "sectioning" of the female torso pervasive in Surrealist artworks. Taken the year after Man Ray's circa 1933 photograph *Minotaur* was published as the frontis image of a 1935 issue of *Minotaure* magazine (fig. 5), Bellon's picture (fig. 6) neatly conveys one of the principal arguments of Sarah's and my book: that the murderer's treatment of Short's body strikingly reflects a mix of archetypal Surrealist tropes.

In discussing this idea, Sarah and I made no claim to speak for the intentions of Surrealist artists. Rather, we were interested in how Surrealist motifs and themes might have been interpreted by an unstable killer, albeit a highly functioning one. Murders in which the body is posthumously mutilated, moved, or posed are not unknown, but the details of the

Black Dahlia murder are a challenge to categorize neatly. I know of no other American murder so self-consciously meticulous in its display of sadistic technique. Put another way, no other murder looks so much like a work of art.

None of the pictures I've listed above are crucial in the history of Surrealism; I've made no attempt to pick especially powerful examples, let alone an example powerful enough to animate a murderous impulse. But that is exactly to the point: I am not suggesting that Short's killer saw a Surrealist picture and copied it. Instead I am raising the possibility that the killer's particular pathology was supplemented by his interest in Surrealism. With that idea in mind, let's look again at the *Los Angeles Times* cartoon, for while it reports on a specific event, it is also an eerie portent of the Black Dahlia murder: half of a female body "planted in an unexpected place."[12]

If the general argument intrigues, its specifics haunt. Consider Man Ray, who swings like a hinge between Duchamp and Hodel. Man Ray called Hollywood home from 1941 to 1951, in some way using the title "Surrealist" as a shield against the culture of the town. He and Hodel became close; their relationship spanned at least four years on each side of the murder.[13] A 1946 picture of Hodel, taken by Man Ray, in which the doctor cradles a statue of the Tibetan deity Yamantaka gives a glimpse into the nature of their friendship (fig. 7). At first glance the portrait seems relatively banal, but upon study it reveals subtle clues: what may not be immediately apparent to the casual viewer, for example, is that Yamantaka is engaged in intercourse with his concubine. Statues of this type are a genre in Tibetan art, and often show the couple's engorged sexual organs.[14] Look closely and you will see that Hodel's left thumb and forefinger lie at the backs of the concubine's thighs—he is symbolically opening her legs. Given what is known of the proclivities of both men, not much is needed here by way of explanation. In 1948, the year after the Black Dahlia

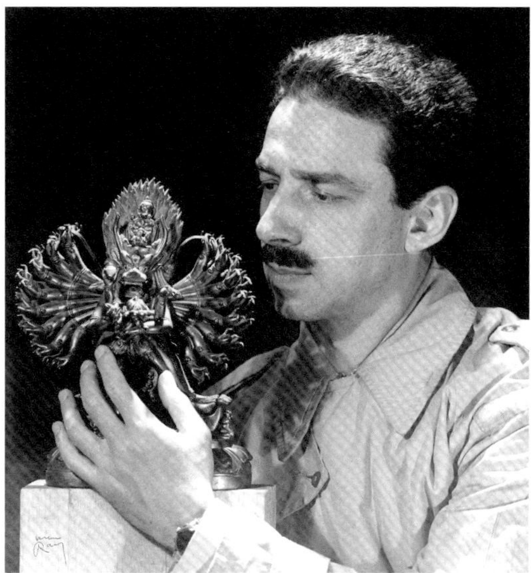

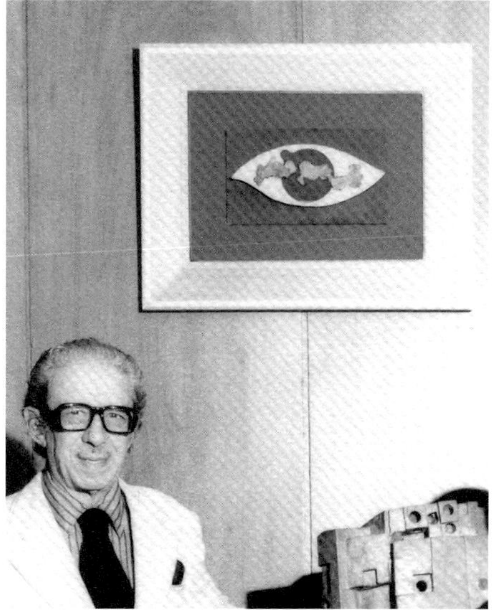

7 Man Ray, Portrait of George Hodel, 1946. Undated copy after signed original, 35 x 27 cm. **8 George Hodel in his penthouse apartment in the Philippines,** with Man Ray's 1944 work *L'Oculiste* (The Oculist), c. 1985. Both Collection of Steve Hodel.

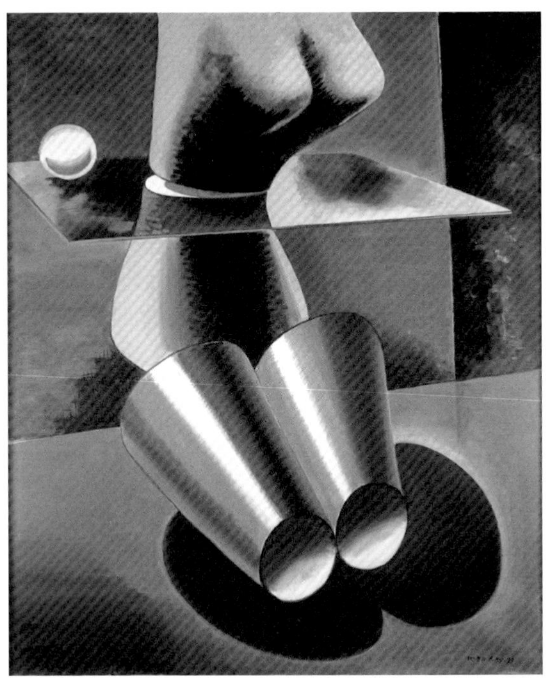

9 Man Ray, *La Jumelle* (The Twin), oil on canvas, 92 x 74 cm, 1939. Private Collection.

murder, Man Ray gave Hodel one of his own works, *Objet de mon affection—L'Oculiste* (Object of my Affection—The Oculist), which he had made in 1944 and exhibited in 1946 at the Circle Gallery in Los Angeles (fig. 8). Needless to say, the ocular theme figures prominently in the work of both Man Ray and Marcel Duchamp.

Man Ray, of course, was one of the earliest progenitors of the Surrealist archetype under discussion here. The darkness of his artistic themes, including his love of the Marquis de Sade and his objectification of women, has been discussed by many art historians.[15] Well before the Black Dahlia murder, Man Ray made artworks prefiguring the crime scene photographs. Consider again his famous photograph *Minotaur;* or his painting *La Jumelle* (The Twin) (fig. 9), of 1939; or his drawing *T-Square* of 1943—three of several Man Ray pictures in which a female torso is cut at the waist. Finally, consider his photograph *Juliet on the Couch at Vine Street* (fig. 10) from around 1945. Far from spontaneous, the image is heavily art-directed and thematically linked to a number of other Man Ray pictures.[16] These images beg the question:

A young woman's body is cut in half and readied for public discovery with her arms carefully positioned above her head. What is the probability that one will find a prime suspect with a close friend who had made many artworks incorporating those same motifs?

Timeframe, Social Network, Geography

A central part of Michael's critique of *Exquisite Corpse* is his speculative dating of two early artworks relating to *Étant donnés*. One of these works is a drawing of Maria Martins,

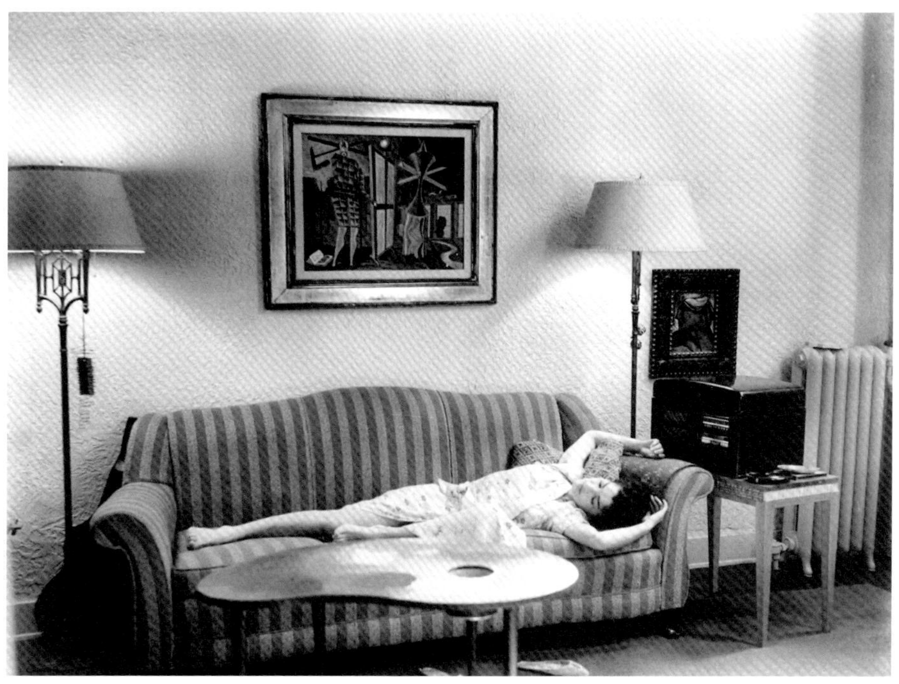

10 Man Ray, Juliet on the couch at Vine Street, gelatin silver print, 21.5 x 28 cm, c. 1945. Private Collection.

hand-dated December 1947 (fig. 36, p. 52); the other is a collage (fig. 35, p. 52), incorporating what appears to be a tracing of the drawing of Martins along with photographs Duchamp took of the Forestay waterfall near Chexbres, Switzerland, in August 1946 (pp. 16–23). If both of these works predate 1947, Michael argues, Duchamp must have had the final tableau fully in mind before the murder of Elizabeth Short.[17]

I claim no authority on the dating of the drawing of Martins, and I know that Duchamp did misdate some of his artworks.[18] But he is known to have been in Martins' company in December 1947, the date written on the drawing. This suggests, at the very least, the possibility that this date is correct.[19] As for the collage, the photographs in it are known to date from August 1946, when Duchamp and Mary Reynolds vacationed in Chexbres. Supposing that the drawing he traced for the collage was already in existence, as Michael argues, he could indeed have made the collage in the last four months of 1946, before the discovery of Short's body in mid-January of 1947. I would still argue for a 1947 date for the collage, however, since Duchamp is more likely to have made a piece like this one in his New York studio, where he would best have been able to maintain the privacy in which he worked on *Étant donnés*. Duchamp had returned to work there in late January of that year, after his extended European trip.

In any case, the dating of these two works is somewhat tangential to the theory I am proposing. Whether the drawing was made before or after the murder—and I'd like to point out here that I do think it may be too tender a work to relate to the Black Dahlia crime-scene photographs—I don't believe we can rule out the crime scene photographs

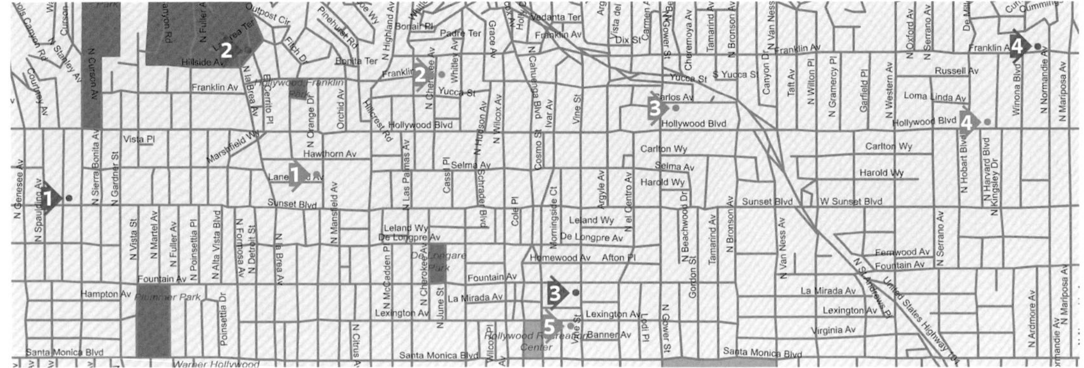

11 A partial map of Hollywood, California, showing the Circle Gallery (7623 West Sunset Boulevard—1) where Man Ray showed *The Oculist* in 1946; the home of Marcel Duchamp's major patrons Walter and Louise Arensberg (7065 Hillside Avenue—2), the home of Man Ray (1245 Vine Street—3); and the home of George Hodel (5121 Franklin Avenue—4). Five known Hollywood addresses occupied by Elizabeth Short in the last six months of her life are also shown, including: the Hawthorne Hotel (1611 North Orange Drive—1); the Chancellor Apartments (1842 North Cherokee Avenue—2); the Marc Hansen residence (6024 Carlos Avenue—3); the Guardian Arms Apartments (5217 Hollywood Boulevard—4); and the Hotel Brevoort (6326 Lexington Avenue). Note that U.S. Highway 101 which runs diagonally from top to bottom was not built until 1948.

as a source for *Étant donnés*. I'm certainly not claiming that the final tableau installed at the Philadelphia Museum of Art is a direct copy of the crime scene photographs, nor do I at all disagree with the idea that the work was informed by Duchamp's relationships with his lovers. However, the making of *Étant donnés* spanned twenty years; this alone should inhibit us from believing we can determine precisely what fits or does not fit some template that may have inspired it. Surely a work this complex wasn't fixed from the outset; surely Duchamp's fierce intellect made him open to change, whether in his inner ideas and or in his outward context. Indeed, various studies for *Étant donnés* document shifts in the moods, relationships, and resources of their creator over time.[20]

While noting that an artwork two decades in the making may have been influenced at many points in that history, I also recognize that *Étant donnés* had a sort of formative period: 1947 to 1951. That timeframe, it so happens, exactly overlaps the crucial years of the Black Dahlia murder investigation. During that same period, Duchamp felt a keen interest in Los Angeles, even though he did not live there, since many of his major works were in the Hollywood home of his patrons Walter and Louise Arensberg. He visited Hollywood twice during these years, in April 1949 and again in April 1950, as the disposition of the Arensbergs' collection was becoming an urgent issue. Whether he met George Hodel during his 1949 visit we do not know, but since both men were close to Man Ray, it is surely possible. It should also be remembered that George Hodel hailed from a prominent Pasadena family and can be linked, in various ways, to the same elite social circle that Duchamp mixed with when he visited Los Angeles. Only a month before Duchamp's 1950 visit, however, Hodel hurriedly left Los Angeles under police suspicion of the Black Dahlia murder. This remarkable development, coming on the heels of an unrelated criminal case a few months earlier in which Hodel was very publicly involved, would certainly have been much on Man Ray's mind.

In imagining Duchamp in Los Angeles during these years, we must also imagine the impact of the Black Dahlia murder locally. For longtime Angelenos it remains a defining moment in their city's history, an iconic entry point into myriad discussions of systematic police failure and tabloid culture. I interviewed two friends of Man Ray's during his Hollywood years, James and Barbara Byrnes, and both told me emphatically that the shock of the Black Dahlia murder was intensely felt by those who lived in the city at the time. "You couldn't go to a cocktail party for years afterward without discussing it," James Byrnes said.[21] Surely Duchamp was aware of the murder.

This collision of timeframe and social network is even more striking when one considers the geographical proximity of the principal characters in our narrative—including Elizabeth Short. In the months leading up to her death, Short seems to have been caught in a downward spiral in which she entrusted her safety to people she did not know well. During the last six months of her life, she lived in at least five different Hollywood apartments, including one that was less than two blocks from Man Ray's Vine Street apartment and another that was three blocks from the home of George Hodel (fig. 11).[22]

This web of connections continued long after the murder investigation wound down. I am convinced that the 1961 painting *Il est Minuit Dr. __* (It Is Midnight, Dr. __) by William Copley (fig. 12), harks back to the Black Dahlia case. In it, a doctor—his name left blank, to be supplied by the viewer—commands a grotesque assortment of surgical tools positioned over a recumbent nude woman. The reference seems specific and obvious: Copley had been living in Los Angeles at the time of the murder. Indeed, he had fostered great friendships with both Man Ray, dating back to late 1946, and Duchamp, dating to sometime in late 1947 or early 1948. Ultimately, it was Copley who donated *Étant donnés* to the Philadelphia Museum of Art.

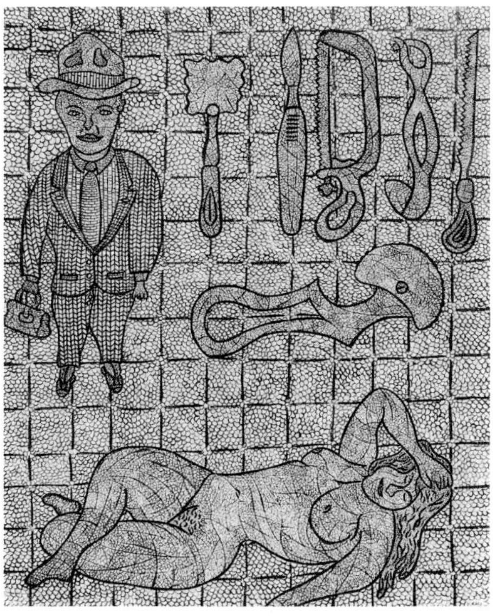

12 William Copley, *Il est minuit Dr. __* (It is Midnight Dr. __), oil on linen, 81.3 x 65.75 cm, 1961. Private Collection. Courtesy of the estate of William N. Copley / Copley LLC, New York.

In *Marcel Duchamp: Étant donnés,* Michael suggests that "future scholarship on the relationship between the Black Dahlia case and the visual arts" might look to Bruce Conner's 1959 assemblage *Black Dahlia* rather than to *Étant donnés*. What Michael does not mention is that Duchamp is likely to have seen this work before *Étant donnés* was finished: in 1963, it was owned by Walter Hopps, who had learned about art as a teenager in the Arensbergs' home and who that year organized Duchamp's first major retrospective, in Pasadena. In *Exquisite Corpse,* Sarah and I only briefly noted this possible reemergence of the Black Dahlia in Duchamp's experience, but Hopps's interest in Conner's piece reminds us again of the attention that the murder commanded, years after the crime was committed.

If two researchers set out to answer the question, "Is *Étant donnés* modeled to some degree on crime scene photographs of the Black Dahlia murder?," what is the probability they would find the two things so dramatically intersecting at the crossroads of time, social network, and place?

Criminology

The argument for the influence of the Black Dahlia murder on *Étant donnés* is not dependent on the guilt of George Hodel. In the context of a speculation on that influence, however, Duchamp's link to Hodel through Man Ray seems to call for the possibility of the doctor's guilt to be addressed here.

The case against Hodel is circumstantial but strong. That he had the surgical training and experience necessary to bisect a human body is borne out by his medical-school transcripts, applications for government posts, legal papers, and other personal documents.[23] Hodel was also desensitized to viewing crime scenes, having been exposed to them when he worked as a tabloid reporter in his early twenties. In an elegant but callous piece of writing for the *Los Angeles Record,* in which Hodel exercised the mellifluous diction for which he was known, he made wordplay of the name of a murder victim, Theresa Mors: "Death. Mors, mortis, morti—what gender is death? Feminine of course. It is of that declension. Yes, death is feminine."[24] This is but one example of Hodel's particularly mordant and removed personality.

At the time of the murder, Hodel owned and lived alone in the Sowden House, on Franklin Avenue in Los Angeles. Designed by Lloyd Wright, the son of the architect Frank Lloyd Wright, this impressive residence was modeled after a Mayan temple and built around an interior courtyard. The home's high, gated entrance and nearly windowless exterior clearly telegraphed privilege, wealth, and, most important in this connection, the ability to maintain privacy—qualities of Hodel's life not shared by most of the other suspects in the crime (fig. 13).[25]

A great variety of publicly accessible information suggests that Hodel engaged in a pattern of abuse and violence directed against women. On October 6, 1949, he was arrested on morals charges, accused of incest with his daughter Tamar. Three other people, including Hodel's friend the artist Fred Sexton,[26] were also accused of illegal sex acts. The

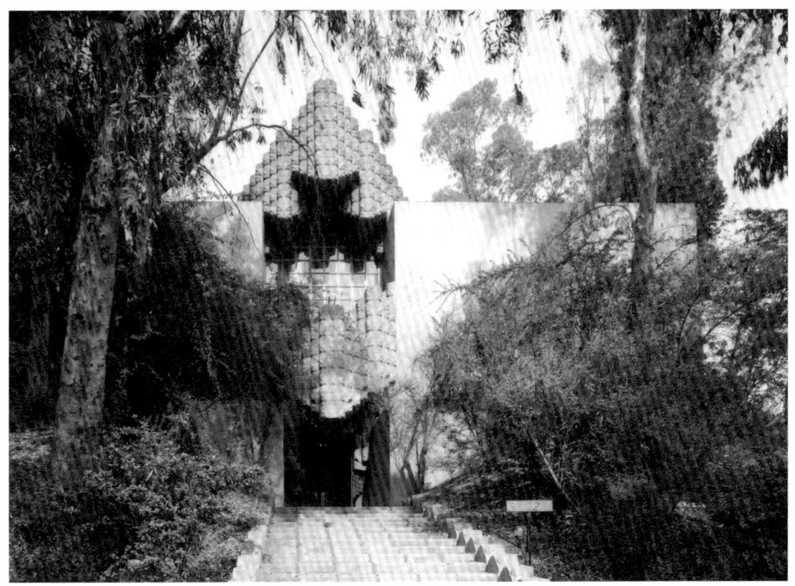

13 George Hodel's Hollywood home at 5121 Franklin Avenue, photographed by George Hodel himself, in 1950. Courtesy Steve Hodel.

following day, a doctor and an employee of Hodel's were arrested for allegedly performing an abortion on Tamar, a felony offense at the time. Hodel went on trial for incest in December 1949, and was acquitted. The abortion case was subsequently dismissed. It was during Hodel's trial that he was first publicly associated with the Black Dahlia murder, when one of his defense attorneys, Robert Neeb, suggested that Tamar had accused him of the crime, which only proved that she was a pathological liar.[27] To this day, Tamar Hodel maintains that the incest, pregnancy, and abortion did occur.

In January 1950, less than a month after Hodel's acquittal, he was involved in an altercation at his home with Lillian Lenorak, a woman who was spending time there. According to a letter to the Los Angeles district attorney's office from police officer Mary Unkefer, who had escorted Lenorak from the house, Lenorak had scratches and bruises on her forehead and arms. Her three-year-old son, John Farrow, Jr. (half brother of the actress Mia Farrow), told Unkefer that Hodel "knocked his mommie down and made mommie cry hard." Lenorak told Unkefer that Hodel had drugged her and cut her wrists to make it appear that she had attempted suicide; that she had been present at Tamar's abortion; and that she had perjured herself at Hodel's trial because he had threatened to have her child taken from her if she did not testify in his favor.[28]

It is unclear exactly when Hodel became a suspect in the Black Dahlia murder. Tamar Hodel maintains that the police were investigating her father as early as the summer of 1947, though no publicly available record supports this claim. By October 28, 1949, however, Hodel was a prime suspect, as a grand jury document makes clear.[29] For five weeks beginning on February 18, 1950, after the Los Angeles district attorney's office and police department secretly placed microphones in his home, he was under twenty-four-hour-a-

HODEL FILE - 126

8:00P	Meyer, LAPD, on duty. All qiet.
20-61 11:10P	Hodel and Baron (man with accent) came in talking low - can't hear (recording) only stays few minutes and leaves. I was wrong - was in bathroom. Sounded like Hodel said something about Black Daliah. Baron said something about F.B.I. Then talked about Tibet - sounded like Hodel wants to get out of the country. mentiond passport - Hodel giving Baron dope on how to write to Tibet. Hodel talking about Mexico - going down and take pictures and write a story. Hodel seems afraid about something. Hodel says his Sanatarium - if he got it started in Mexico - would be "Safe".
Spool 39	
12:00A	Spool ran out - changing - talking about women.
Mar 26,1950 0-50 12:07A	Not much talk - still recording. Hodel says he wants money and power - talking about China - talking about selling some of Hodel's paintings or something. Hodel talking about picture police have of him and some girl - thought he had destroyed them all - wire quit at 50 - new one going on - not much talk.
Spool 40 3-37 1:00A	Had trouble with one spool. Had to use another - still talking about selling paintings.
1:50A	Sounds like Baron left - don't know if there is anything on these records or not.
2:00A	Hodel at his desk - all else quiet - Good night.
3:00P	Hodel having party - about 8 people - party ends - someone
3:30P	listening to radio programs. Wean, LAPD, on duty.
5:00P	Woman and Hodel talking, but radio too loud to hear.

14 One page of many from the Los Angeles District Attorney's office surveillance logs showing George Hodel and the "Baron" (Ernst von Harringa) nervously discussing the Black Dahlia murder. LADA Archive. **15 View of Los Angeles looking north on Olive Street towards Pershing Square,** c. 1930–39 (detail). At approximately 10:00 p.m. on January 9,

day audio surveillance. Officers listening in made logs summarizing the conversations and movements of those in the house (fig. 14). Among the things these logs document is Hodel's interest in Surrealism. It is also clear from them that he was aware that he was under investigation, though not that his house was bugged. In the first log entry he seems to admit to having killed not only Short but also his secretary, Ruth Spaulding, in 1945. Though Spaulding's death had been ruled a suicide, it was Hodel himself who had brought her to Los Angeles Central Receiving Hospital, where she was pronounced dead. On March 2, 1950, Lieutenant Frank Jemison in the district attorney's office wrote a note arguing that Spaulding's death should be reinvestigated. The transcript of an interview he conducted on March 22 with Hodel's ex-wife, Dorothy Hodel, is one of many documents suggesting that investigators were building an aggressive case against Hodel.[30] On March 27, 1950, however, the home surveillance abruptly ended when Hodel left Los Angeles permanently for Hawaii, and later the Philippines, where he would live for most of the rest of his life. The investigation into Hodel was subsequently dropped—just why is not currently known.

When Sarah and I were writing our book, we tried to cross-check Steve Hodel's claims about his father against source material that did not originate from him. Although we cannot be certain that Hodel killed Short, we agree with Steve Hodel that he should be considered a strong suspect. Since the publication of *Exquisite Corpse,* two developments have furthered the case against him. First was the discovery, by Steve Hodel, of documents showing that just prior to the murder, his father had contracted with Lloyd Wright for some

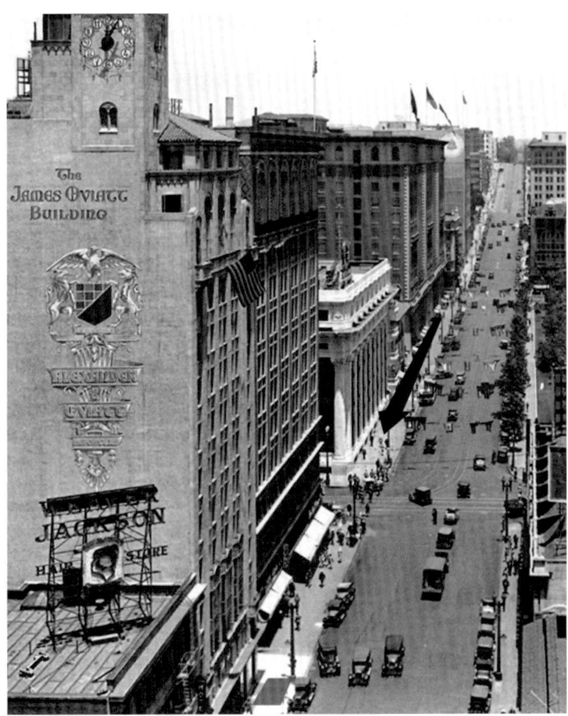

1947—the day Elizabeth Short famously went missing—she exited the Biltmore Hotel lobby (as indicated by the arrow) and began walking down the west side of Olive Street toward 6th street. The location of Ernst von Harringa's gallery in the Oviatt building is indicated by the gray square in the foreground.

cement work to be done on the house, entailing the delivery there of ten sacks of cement. This work was completed five days before Short's body was found on the Leimert Park lot; on the ground next to it was a bloodstained cement sack. In December 2008, Sarah and I published a paper detailing this discovery and our argument for its significance.[31]

Second, in February 2009 a reader of Steve Hodel's Internet blog, Jil Anderson, informed him that she had identified a mysterious "German Baron" who appears repeatedly on the surveillance logs, nervously discussing the Black Dahlia murder with Hodel. The logs misspell his name "Herringer," but Anderson had finally identified him as Ernst von Harringa,[32] an art dealer who owned and operated the Oviatt Galleries in downtown Los Angeles[33]—less than a block-and-a-half walk from the Biltmore Hotel, where Short was last seen alive and well, on January 9, 1947.[34] According to a Los Angeles Police Department report, Short was seen leaving the hotel and walking in the direction of von Harringa's gallery (fig. 15). In his book *The Unknown God: Wilfred T. Smith and the Thelemites,* Martin P. Starr describes von Harringa (fig. 16) as "an extreme individualist who believed that any effort for humanity was a waste."[35] This discovery reinvigorates the idea that perhaps more than one person was somehow involved in the crime, and further supports the idea that it bore a relation to art.

The usefulness of the surveillance logs as evidence is somewhat limited; filled with misspellings, and lacking the intonation of real voices, they are neither as accurate nor as

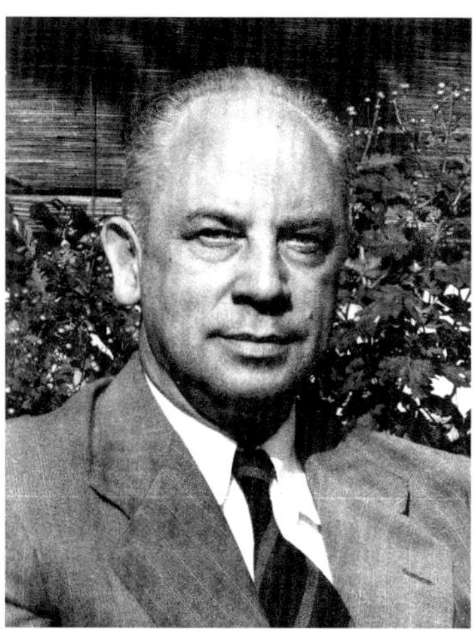

16 Ernst von Harringa, photographed at the Hollywood home of Wilfred Talbot Smith and Helen Smith. Courtesy of Martin P. Starr.

decipherable as a modern recording would be. As for Elizabeth Short's walk out the door of the Biltmore Hotel, she could have turned at the intersection, or walked past the Oviatt Galleries without stopping. The discovery of such suggestive, cross-referenced evidence, however, reminds us not only of the small joys of studying history but why there is no statute of limitations on murder.

By way of conclusion, I quote from William Copley's essay "The New Piece," one of the first and most heartfelt writings on *Étant donnés,* published in the Summer 1969 issue of *Art in America* magazine. Copley writes, "The materials for [*Étant donnés*] came from daily experience, endless and random." This quiet sentence leaves room for every reading of the artwork. Michael Taylor would agree with this, I think—in *Marcel Duchamp: Étant donnés,* he writes that a theory such as ours "can be defended on the ground that the artist himself believed it was the spectator who completed the work of art." Duchamp did believe that—but that is not the peg on which we hang our hats. Sarah Bayliss and I believe our theory is defensible because of a consilience of inductions: six distinctly different lines of evidence converge upon one another, independently but in conjunction.

Notes

[1] Michael Shermer, *Why Darwin Matters: The Case Against Intelligent Design,* New York 2006.

[2] The official autopsy report on Elizabeth Short is not publicly available. In its absence, the most reliable information on her body appears in "Summary of the Elizabeth (Beth) Short Murder Investigation," prepared by the Los Angeles Police Department for the Los Angeles District Attorney's Office in 1949. This document can be found in the Historical Evidence Collection of the Los Angeles District Attorney's Office. See also the sworn testimony of the Chief Autopsy Surgeon of Los Angeles County, Frederick D. Newbarr, in "Transcript of Inquest Held on the Body of Elizabeth Short at the Hall of Justice. Los Angeles, California, January 22, 1947 at 10:30 A.M." This document has been transcribed online at http://blackdahlia.info/modules/news2/article.php?storyid=1 (accessed June 21, 2010). In *The Encyclopedia of Unsolved Crimes,* New York 2004, Michael Newton reprints the information contained within the autopsy report, which he received from a former detective with the Los Angeles County Sheriff who copied the document by hand and then typed it.

[3] Michael Taylor, *Marcel Duchamp: Étant donnés,* exh. cat. Philadelphia Museum of Art, Philadelphia and New Haven 2009, p. 193.

[4] First addressing Jean-Michel Rabaté's description of "the macabre [Black Dahlia] photographs published in January 1947 and after throughout the United States, which seemed to top all the photographed horrors of the Second World War," Taylor

notes that in 1947 it would have been impossible to publish uncensored crime scene pictures in a newspaper (ibid., p. 194). Indeed, since no uncensored pictures of the crime scene appeared in print until after Marcel Duchamp's death, I agree with Taylor that this aspect of Rabaté's book, *Given: 1° Art 2° Crime. Modernity, Murder and Mass Culture,* Brighton et al. 2006, is problematic. Moving on to Jonathan Wallis's essay "Case Open and/or Unsolved: Marcel Duchamp and the Black Dahlia Murder," *Rutgers Art Review* (2003), Taylor takes issue with Wallis for "find[ing] it suspicious ... that Man Ray left Hollywood for Paris, shortly after the murder, possibly fearing an association with Hodel." If Man Ray was afraid of guilt by association, Taylor argues, wouldn't this fear "have prevented Man Ray from fraternizing with the conservative Los Angeles Police Department with the hope of obtaining lurid photographs in the immediate aftermath of the murder?" (ibid., p. 95). On the motives of Man Ray's trip to Paris in 1947, here too I agree with Taylor; in fact, in *Exquisite Corpse,* Sarah Hudson Bayliss and I note that Man Ray's correspondence shows no sign he was under the sort of duress one might equate with a murder investigation and clearly indicates that he was planning his Paris trip the previous year, before the murder occurred. Yet although the circumstances can only be surmised, the possibility cannot be eliminated that Man Ray could both have obtained crime scene photographs and have given them to Duchamp. In *Exquisite Corpse* we speculate on one such scenario: that a then-young William Copley, whom Man Ray instructed on how to contact Duchamp when visiting New York, could have brought them with him. Of this suggestion Taylor writes that "although [the meeting is] presented in a factual manner [our] use of ambiguous phases, such as 'it is conceivable' and 'or perhaps even,' ... underscore[s] the fact that this exchange is entirely fictitious." To this I can only respond that a great deal of art-historical writing uses similar language to bridge known facts and conjecture.

[5] Journalist RJ Smith begins "Living with the Black Dahlia: The Murder that Changed Los Angeles," his September 2006 article in *Los Angeles* magazine, "Her pictures collect in the shadows. They are everywhere. Say that you are writing a story about the murder of Elizabeth Short ... and people want to pull out their photos. They want you to see." Even a brief perusal of Black Dahlia–related materials makes this clear. The 1949 "Summary of the Elizabeth (Beth) Short Murder Investigation" notes that "Upon the arrival of Sgts. Brown and Hansen ... they found representatives and photographers from the newspapers. Pictures had been taken by the newspapers of the body." The official police photographs were made by Gilbert Laursen, R. L. Oliver photographed the scene for the *Los Angeles Times,* and Felix Paegel took pictures for the *Los Angeles Examiner.* One of Paegel's photographs of Short's body ran on January 16, 1947 in the *Examiner* in airbrushed form. At least six other local newspapers of varying means and influence—the *Los Angeles Daily News,* the *Los Angeles Evening Herald Express,* the *Hollywood Citizen-News,* the *Pasadena Star-News,* the *Saturday Pictorial Herald Express,* and the *Pasadena Independent*—competed aggressively for the story and ran front-page banner headlines on it. No fewer than eleven police officers of varying rank and specialty are named in the "Summary" as having been at the scene. Among the reporters known to have been present are Will Fowler, who later published pictures of the crime scene in his 1991 book *Reporters: Memoirs of a Young Newspaperman,* and Agnes (Aggie) Underwood. It is worth noting that Will Fowler's father, the screenwriter Gene Fowler, was a close friend and occasional writing partner of the director and screenwriter Rowland Brown (who, incidentally, was the lover of Dorothy Hodel, George Hodel's ex-wife); and that Will Fowler's older brother, Gene Fowler Jr., was a film editor for the director John Huston (who, incidentally, was Dorothy Hodel's ex-husband). Here, then, are two possible paths by which copies of the photographs could have traveled quickly into the elite Hollywood circle described in *Exquisite Corpse.* If we also take into account the myriad employees of the newspapers (editors, darkroom staff, etc.) and of the police department (beat officers, bureaucrats, etc.) who could have gotten hold of photographs and extrapolate outward to their friends, let alone to those willing to pay for the pictures, it seems far from impossible that Man Ray or Duchamp might have come across them.

[6] In suggesting "an apparent absence of precedence," we are not suggesting that the crime doesn't exist within the broad taxonomy of deviant murder, or that Elizabeth Short's killer did not positively display the internal rage generally ascribed to perpetrators of violent sex crimes. We are arguing that the killer's visual presentation of the body to a public meant to find it—which has confounded those who have studied it for more than sixty years—has an analog with the strategies of an art movement then in vogue. Of course, we can only speculate as to whether this influence would have been premeditated or an afterthought to the murder itself, but the fact that a prime suspect in a murder so distinctly resembling Surrealist artwork personally identified with Surrealism involves a certain statistical improbability.

[7] In the framework of our general argument, Sarah Bayliss and I do not distinguish between high art and low art. We understand that many Surrealistic images of the 1930s and 40s were products of fashion or reportage, but feel they participate equally in the zeitgeist of the period.

[8] Arthur Millier, "Surrealists Again Go into Their Weird Act," *Los Angeles Times,* August 15, 1943, p. C5.

[9] "Speaking of Pictures: Dalí Paints the Seven Lively Arts," *Life,* January 1, 1945, pp. 4–6.

[10] Salvador Dalí, "Les nouvelles couleurs du 'sex-appeal spectral,'" *Minotaure* 5 (1934), p. 20. Also quoted in Dawn Ades and Taylor with the assistance of Montse Aguer, *Dalí,* exh. cat. Philadelphia Museum of Art, Philadelphia 2004, p. 202.

[11] "Surrealist Movie: Six Ultramodern Artists Supply Dreams for New Film," *Life,* December 2, 1946, pp. 86–88.

[12] Edwin Cox, "Private Lives," *Los Angeles Times,* May 29, 1941, p. 15. This cartoon refers to Dalí's "enchanting" of Caresse Crosby's Hampton Manor, near Bowling Green, Virginia. Dalí's "necromantic labors" at Crosby's home had been detailed a month earlier in "Life Calls on Salvador Dalí," a feature article published in the April 7, 1941 issue of *Life* magazine. One photograph accompanying that article shows Dalí holding a manikin intended to be "a sleeping beauty in a bush." Another shows Dalí "plant[ing] a bare-busted manikin waist-deep in a frog pond." Dalí would use the same trope again for the "Night in the Surrealist Forest Ball," held on September 2, 1941 at the Del Monte Lodge Hotel in Pebble Beach, California. At that party, a benefit for artists trapped in Europe during World War II, the hotel's publicist, Herb Caen, arranged on Dalí's

behalf for twenty-four nude store mannequins to be scattered around the grounds. See Meredith Etherington-Smith, *The Persistence of Memory: A Biography of Dalí*, New York 1992, pp. 261–63, 268–71.

[13] After publishing *Exquisite Corpse*, Sarah Bayliss and I wrote a paper titled "Man Ray and George Hodel," which partially documents the relationship between the two men. This paper is available online at http://www.exquisitecorpsebook.com/GeorgeHodel_ManRay02.pdf (accessed June 21, 2010). In 2008, I also interviewed Hodel's grandson, Joshua Hodel Spafford, who further illuminated Hodel's friendship with Man Ray. Six recordings of the interviews are available online at www.exquisitecorpsebook.com.

[14] There is a statue of Yamantaka similar to the one in the photograph in the collection of the Museum of Natural History, New York. See also Maurice Heine, "Eritis Sicut Dii," *Minotaure* 11 (1938), pp. 30–33. In this profusely illustrated essay Heine directly equates the Yamantaka with the Minotaur.

[15] See, e.g., Merry Foresta, Stephen C. Foster, Billy Kluver, et al., *Perpetual Motif: The Art of Man Ray*, exh. cat. National Museum of American Art, Smithsonian Institution, Washington, D.C., New York et al. 1989), pp. 211–28.

[16] Man Ray composed this picture with several of his earlier works in mind. I refer specifically to photographs he took that juxtapose his painting *A l'heure de l'observatoire–Les Amoureux* (Observatory time—the lovers, 1932–34) with a nude woman, a clothed woman, or with half of a female bust. The picture can also be related to Man Ray's 1941 painting *La Femme et son poisson II* (The Woman and her Fish II). These works are reproduced often in monographs on Man Ray.

[17] Taylor, *Marcel Duchamp* (note 3), pp. 65–69, 194–96.

[18] Artists' misdating of their own work, whether deliberately or accidentally, is of course not unknown. Duchamp, for example, wrote "12" on his drawing *Once More to This Stair;* he later said the correct date was 1911. See Francis M. Naumann, "Frederic C. Torrey and Duchamp's Nude Descending a Staircase," in *West Coast Duchamp*, ed. Bonnie Clearwater, Miami Beach 1991, p. 22, note 7.

[19] On the evening of December 9, 1947, Duchamp and Maria Martins together visited the architect and artist Frederick Kiesler, at 56 Seventh Avenue, New York. See Jennifer Gough-Cooper and Jacques Caumont, *Marcel Duchamp: Work and Life/Ephemerides on and about Marcel Duchamp and Rrose Sélavy 1887–1968*, ed. and with an introduction by Pontus Hultén, Milan and Cambridge, Mass. 1993, p. 9 (December).

[20] Regardless of any discussion of the Black Dahlia murder, the dating of *Étant donnés* has been a preoccupation of scholars since the work was revealed. Duchamp certainly embedded allusions to his earlier works in *Étant donnés*, and he may well have been thinking of creating some sort of large-scale assemblage prior to 1946. However, my own belief is that the dates with which Duchamp signed the work, 1946–66, are accurate, reflecting the creation dates of each physical element in the tableau, with the photographs he took of the Forestay waterfall in 1946 being the earliest. I think the tendency to want to date the figure itself to 1946 comes largely from the fact that the signature lies on the figure's right arm. The placement of the signature, however, may be attributed to the figure's centrality; surely it makes sense that Duchamp should have signed the figure rather than, for instance, the lamp. I believe that Duchamp's dates denote the work in its entirety rather than the figure specifically.

[21] In a two-hour telephone conversation in April 2006, James Byrnes also told me, "We even nicknamed our car 'Dahlia-something,' though I can't remember if that had anything to do with the murder or not." Both James and Barbara Byrnes were intrigued by the possibility that the Black Dahlia murder might have been modeled after Surrealism, and neither seemed surprised by the idea that artists might have reinterpreted the crime in their work. The Byrneses graciously gave Sarah and me the right to print images from the estate of Gloria de Herrera in our book. Unfortunately, we were too close to our press date to relate any of their anecdotes from those years in the book.

[22] Among Short's confirmed addresses in Hollywood are the Hawthorne Hotel (1611 North Orange Drive), The Guardian Arms Apartments (5217 Hollywood Boulevard), The Chancellor Apartments (1842 North Cherokee Avenue), The Marc Hansen residence (6024 Carlos Way), and the Brevoort Hotel (6326 Lexington Avenue).

[23] See Nelson and Bayliss, "George Hodel, Surgical Experience and Practice," published online at http://www.exquisitecorpsebook.com/GeorgeHodel _Surgeon02.pdf (accessed June 21, 2010).

[24] "Words of Death," *Los Angeles Record*, August 14, 1924. Reprinted in Steve Hodel, *Black Dahlia Avenger: The True Story*, New York 2003/2004. The piece has no byline, but is among the clips of his own writing that George Hodel kept in his records.

[25] Drawings and photographs of the Sowden House are available on the Library of Congress Web site at http://hdl.loc.gov/loc.pnp/hhh.ca0267 (accessed June 21, 2010).

[26] Fred Sexton, an artist living in Los Angeles at the time of the murder, was given his debut exhibition by Earl Stendahl, an art dealer who was the next-door neighbor of Duchamp's patron Walter Arensberg. Sexton's work was collected by many prominent Angelenos, and he made the sculpture of the Maltese Falcon used in Huston's 1941 film of the same name. (Sexton, Huston, and George Hodel had been friends since their teenage years.) In *Black Dahlia Avenger*, Steve Hodel suggests that Sexton may have committed the Black Dahlia murder with George Hodel, and Rabaté, in *Given: 1° Art 2° Crime*, suggests that Sexton was actually the motivator of the crime. My own and Bayliss's research, however, yielded no information bearing this out. The fact that Sexton was a witness for the prosecution during Hodel's incest trial seems particularly antithetical to the idea that the two men had earlier participated jointly in a murder.
[27] See "Girl Accused of Trying to Pin Dahlia Murder on Dad," *The Los Angeles Daily News*, December 16, 1949, and "Girl's Story Is 'Fantasy,' Court Hears," *The Los Angeles Mirror*, December 16, 1949. Both quoted in Hodel, *Black Dahlia Avenger* (note 24), p. 96. Hodel's book mistakenly sites the date of both articles as December 17 in the text, and incorrectly lists only the former as February 17, 1949 in the bibliography.
[28] See Mary H. Unkefer, letter to the Los Angeles District Attorney's office, January 30, 1950, in the Historical Evidence Collection of the Los Angeles District Attorney's Office. It is also published in *Black Dahlia Avenger* (note 24), pp. 480–83. Here Unkefer further states that Joe Barrett, another Sowden House tenant, told her that Lenorak's claims were true and that Hodel had boasted to him of having given money to his attorney, Jerry Geisler, to be used to influence the district attorney during the trial.
[29] See Nelson and Bayliss, *Exquisite Corpse: Surrealism and the Black Dahlia Murder*, New York and Boston 2006, p. 118.
[30] The surveillance logs, interviews, and letter mentioned here all lie in the Historical Evidence Collection of the Los Angeles District Attorney's Office, along with many other papers relating to the possibility of George Hodel's involvement in the Black Dahlia murder.
[31] See Nelson and Bayliss, "George Hodel, Lloyd Wright, the Black Dahlia Murder, and the J.A. Konrad Bill for Cement Work," published online at http://www.exquisitecorpsebook.com/GeorgeHodel_CementSack01.pdf (accessed June 21, 2010).
[32] Jil Anderson's tentative identification of "Baron Herringer" as Ernst von Harringa was confirmed when Steve Hodel used Los Angeles voter-registration records to match the address of Mary Valla (owner of a 1936 Packard parked in front of George Hodel's home) to that of von Harringa. Valla was the mother of von Harringa's wife, Alene.
[33] The Oviatt Gallery was housed in the Oviatt Building, one of the most extravagant American buildings of the 1920s and the creation of James Zera Oviatt, haberdasher to film stars and the moneyed elite of Los Angeles. On this spectacular building see Seth Shulman's documentary *The Oviatt Building*, Puzzled Pictures, 2008, executive producer Marc Chevalier.
[34] On Tuesday, January 22, 1947, the Los Angeles Police Department posted a "Special Daily Police Bulletin" across the city seeking "information on Elizabeth Short Between Dates January 9 and 15, 1947." According to the bulletin, Short was "last seen January 9, 1947 when she got out of a car at Biltmore Hotel." Short had been dropped at the hotel by Red Manley, a married salesman who was initially a suspect in the crime but who was ultimately exonerated. The 1949 "Summary of the Elizabeth (Beth) Short Murder Investigation" states that Manley left Short seated in the Biltmore lobby at approximately 6:45 p.m., and that an employee of the hotel, a Mr. Studholme, saw her "get up from the lobby as if she had been signaled by someone on the outside, and walk out of the Olive Street entrance. He last saw her walking south toward 6th Street on Olive, on the west side of the street." The ensuing "missing week," as those who study the murder have called it, is hotly disputed; whether Short met her killer then or later is unknown. However, to find not only documents showing von Harringa nervously discussing the murder with Hodel, but also documents showing Short walking directly toward von Harringa's place of business on the very day she famously "disappeared," involves a certain statistical improbability.
[35] Wilfred Talbot Smith, the subject of Martin P. Starr's biography, was an adherent of Aleister Crowley's Ordo Templi Orientis and of its more public face, the Church of Thelema, esoteric initiatic religions whose culturally subversive central tenet was "Do what thou wilt shall be the whole of the Law." In an e-mail of March 30, 2010, Starr wrote to me that Ernst von Harringa "and Smith were close personal friends whose commonality was a sort of Nietzschean world view." Given that Hodel and von Harringa seem to have shared a similar outlook and social milieu, and given the salacious (though wildly misunderstood) reputation of the Ordo Templi Orientis, it is tempting to try to link Hodel with Smith. Starr and I spent several hours on the telephone discussing the overlap in our different narratives, however, and agree that although both Hodel and Smith were close to von Harringa, there seems little else to tie Smith or his church to the other characters discussed in *Exquisite Corpse*.

Lars Blunck

The Hermetic Work
Duchamp, *Étant donnés,* and Its Posterity

A few years ago, the German art historian Walter Grasskamp pointedly characterized Duchamp scholars as a "syndicate of decipherers" that has set itself to the task of "cracking codes," bringing out a contaminated secondary literature with "eccentric figures of thought" and a "comet's tail of interpretations."[1] One does not need to share Grasskamp's harsh judgment, but I totally agree with his opinion that Duchamp (and *Étant donnés* as well) ceaselessly entices with the "fragrance of inexhaustible enigmaticalness."[2] Even though Grasskamp's whole formulation may sound a little bit blunt, I think that it may lead Duchamp scholarship to the task of considering the issue of enigmaticalness in Duchamp's work and especially in *Étant donnés*.

In what follows I intend to consider *Étant donnés* as something one could call with Theodor Adorno a "hermetic work"; this means: not only a work of art that is enigmatic but an artwork that bears a decided enigmaticalness. In doing so I act on a suggestion made by Rudolph Kuenzli in 1987 when he asserted that "[t]he frustration, exasperation, and puzzlement of Duchamp interpreters seems to be due largely to their persistent but hopeless attempt to find something which does not exist: a consistent meaning in a work by Duchamp. In order to avoid this futile search, we might shift our focus from a fixation on meaning to an analysis of Duchamp's strategies, through which he precisely explodes the notion of a single meaning."[3] One could suspect the "explosion of the notion of a single meaning" and the plurality of perspectives on Duchamp, as well as the diversity of interpretations of *Étant donnés,* being due to an openness of Duchamp's works. Which leads me to my point of departure: Umberto Eco's famous book *The Open Work,*[4] first published as *Opera aperta* in 1962.

Eco's Notion of Openness

It is rather evident how much the title of this paper borrows from Eco's *The Open Work*. Although many readers may be familiar with Eco's notion of "openness," it is worth bringing Eco's argument back to mind, because its initial point has been often overlooked. Every artwork, says Eco, is open. Openness as a "fundamental ambiguity" would be "a constant of every artwork of any time."[5] Openness would be "the very condition of aesthetic pleasure," and "each form whose aesthetic value is capable of producing such pleasure is, by definition, open."[6] This is a kind of first degree of openness: openness as a constant of every artwork. But it is crucial for Eco's argument that there is also what he calls a "second degree of openness."[7] Because artists since the late 1950s would have, says Eco, subsumed openness "into a positive aspect of ... production, recasting the work so as to expose it to the maximum possible 'opening.'"[8] Openness thus became an "operational program."[9] And since the fifties, openness as a specific form of ambiguity would be one of "the assertive aims of the artwork."[10]

Thus, we have to distinguish at least two degrees of openness, and I think this has happened too little so far (Eco himself speaks of the "two kinds of openness"[11]): openness in a broader sense (as a basal ambiguity of every artwork) and openness in a narrow sense, namely openness as something which I would like to address as an aesthetic quality of the artwork. Because in open works (i.e., in artworks that bear a decided openness) the recipient would be, says Eco, "excited by the new freedom of the work, by its infinite potential for proliferation,"[12] the recipient could, Eco goes on, "at the very moment in which he abandons himself to the free play of reactions that the work provokes in him," go back "to the work to seek in it the origin of the suggestion and the virtuosity behind the stimulus" and is then "not only enjoying his own personal experience but is also appreciating the value of the work itself, its aesthetic quality."[13] According to Eco, this "aesthetic quality" of open works lies within the openness itself, an openness structurally borne within the artwork.

Taking into account Eco's notion of the duplicity of openness (openness as a "fundamental ambiguity" of all artworks and openness as a specific "aesthetic quality" of some artworks), I am reluctant to label *Étant donnés* as an "open work." Although, it is definitely still open insofar as its fundamental ambiguity is concerned, I wonder if its aesthetic quality lies within its openness.

Instead, I would prefer to label it a decidedly enigmatic work; that is (with Adorno), a hermetic work. The reason is very simple: while both openness and enigmaticalness are specific forms of ambiguity, openness means that works of art are specifically open to different interpretations (and are therefore intended to be decidedly open), whereas enigmaticalness means that artworks seem to subvert every attempt to grasp an assumed meaning (and are intended to do so: they are therefore decidedly enigmatic).

Adorno's Notion of Enigmaticalness

As may be known, enigmaticalness achieved its theoretical status through Theodor Adorno's *Aesthetic Theory* published posthumously in 1970. More precisely: through a chapter in his *Aesthetic Theory* that is devoted to the "enigmaticalness of art"[14] and the "enigmaticalness of artworks":[15] "All artworks—and art altogether—are enigmas.... Artworks that unfold to contemplation and thought without any remainder are not artworks.... The better an artwork is understood, the more it is unpuzzled on one level and the more obscure its constitutive enigmaticalness becomes."[16] In fact, understanding itself would be a problematic category "in the face of art's enigmaticalness."[17] Understanding as an alleged dissolution of the enigmaticalness does not, says Adorno, "extinguish the enigmaticalness." If need be, understanding would blank the enigmaticalness, but therewith suspend the most constitutive element of art, which is its basal enigmaticalness: "Even the felicitously interpreted work asks for further understanding, as if waiting for the redemptive word that would dissolve its constitutive darkening."[18] But such a "redemptive word" and a brightening elimination of the "constitutive darkening" would be impossible, otherwise the artwork would, says Adorno, stop being an artwork.

Adorno implies enigmaticalness as a historico-philosophical category, comparable to Eco's "first degree of openness." Artworks would have gained enigmaticalness gradually:

"The enigmaticalness of artworks remains bound up with history. It was through history that they became an enigma."[19] Whether one agrees with Adorno's historico-philosophical notion of a basal enigmaticalness or not, the important issue here is that he also delineates a second degree of enigmaticalness, structurally comparable to Eco's notion of openness, namely an enigmaticalness in the case of artworks intended to be enigmatic.

According to Adorno, a hermetic work is an artwork that implies significance, but subverts in itself every attempt to fix a meaning. Such an artwork would be, says Adorno, enigmatic in a double sense: it would be enigmatic in a historico-philosophical sense by virtue of being an artwork, and it would be enigmatic in an aesthetic sense because its subversion is to be acknowledged aesthetically. Thus enigmaticalness is an aesthetic quality of the artwork comparable to the aesthetic quality of decidedly open works. Enigmaticalness is, to put it in Eco's words, a "value of the work itself, its aesthetic quality."[20]

Duchamp's Notion of Posterity

Now, why do I consider *Étant donnés* to be a "hermetic work" in the sense just given? There are mainly two reasons leading to my assumption, directly connected to each other. First reason: Duchamp's calculated abstinence and his self-approved absence as far as the release of *Étant donnés* is concerned.

As Walter Hopps and Anne d'Harnoncourt have pointed out in their seminal essay on *Étant donnés*, Duchamp's last piece had been "carried out in the privacy of his studio with the assistance of his wife, who shared the secret."[21] *Étant donnés* was "intentionally kept hidden and secret,"[22] which in my point of view not only liberated Duchamp from the obligation to comment on his new masterpiece or explain its meaning but also allowed him to drop a time bomb. I wonder if, in fact, *Étant donnés* had not been (at a certain time) strategically intended to be published posthumously, in a way following the model of Raymond Roussel, who intended his book *How I Wrote Certain of My Books* "to secure an appreciation for his work in death that he was unable to accomplish in life."[23] If this is, as far as Roussel is concerned, true, one may wonder if Duchamp did not intend with the hyperrealism of *Étant donnés* to secure a refusal in death that he was unable to accomplish in his late life. Anyway, it almost seems as if Duchamp not only worked in secret on his last masterpiece like Balzac's Frenhofer did in *Le Chef-d'oeuvre inconnu,* but that even he himself, once again, intended *Étant donnés* to be published as his mysterious legacy. In a way he did not address it to his contemporaries but obscured its history and bequeathed it to posterity.

Duchamp knew that posterity would be, as he wrote in a letter to his sister and Jean Crotti in 1952, "a real bitch who cheats some, reinstates others."[24] According to Duchamp, posterity would have the freedom to change its mind every fifty years. It would do with El Greco whatever it wants (Duchamp's repeatedly mentioned precedent). It would distort. Nowhere has Duchamp emphasized this conviction as clearly as in the *American Journal of Arts and Decoration* in 1915 with the example of Rembrandt a few months after the succès de scandale of his *Nude* in the Armory Show: "It is just because Rembrandt is none of the things that posterity has given to him that he remains."[25] It also may be that because Duchamp is none of the things that posterity has given to him that he remains. And it may be because *Étant donnés* is none of the things that posterity has given to it that it remains. Rembrandt, as Duchamp then continued, "could never have expressed all the thoughts found in his work. In the religious age he was the great religious painter, another epoch discovered in him a profound psychologist, another a poet, still another the last one, a master craftsman. This may prove that people give more to pictures than they take from them."[26] Posterity would be "very important since it is in fact what makes history. History is made by people who come afterwards and interpret and also often distort."[27] What would be important for the contemporary observer would be altered by posterity, "by the second onlooker twenty-five or seventy-five years" later.[28]

It is highly interesting to notice that according to his own statements Duchamp himself has sought posterity and its "interpretations" and "distortions." As he explained to James Johnson Sweeney in 1955, posterity would be "the ideal public" for him.[29] His disregard for a broad public, for his contemporary public, would be a way "of putting myself in the right position for that ideal public. The danger for me is to please an immediate public—the immediate public that comes around you, and takes you in, and accepts you, and gives you success, and everything. Instead of that, I would rather wait for a public that will come fifty years—a hundred years—after my death. It is the ideal public—the right public—that I want."[30] In a way, we are the ideal public. We are the public Duchamp wanted, nearly fifty years after his death.

Étant Donnés as a Hermetic Work

Taking into account his statement just quoted, Duchamp expected us (as the ideal, posthumous public) not to be pleased by him, whereas while still living he was in danger of being accepted by his immediate public. As far as I see it, the most important factor concerning the relationship of Duchamp and this ideal public (or to put it more generally of an author and his posterity) is that they are separated. In the postscript of his novel *The Name of the Rose,* Umberto Eco observed that a text produces relations of signification absolutely independent from the author's intentions, and this would become even more manifest, says Eco, the moment the author disappears: "The author should die once he has finished writing. So as not to trouble the path of the text."[31] Even though Duchamp did not, as Eco put it, die directly after having finished *Étant donnés,* his unknown masterpiece was released in the absence of its "author." Duchamp disappeared before *Étant donnés* appeared, which of course leads, as far as the author's intentions and motivations are concerned, to a deprivation of understandability and aggravation of interpretability. Especially after Duchamp's death, *Étant donnés* seems to bear a kind of secret, an enigma, something that seems to be dissolved. And it presents itself as if being fraught with meaning but at the same time appearing as somewhat hermetic, like an unsolvable mystery. In short, Duchamp's calculated abstinence and his self-approved absence causes trouble for everyone who attempts to find out what *Étant donnés* is supposed to mean.

But what does this mean: "Find out what *Étant donnés* is supposed to mean"? This question leads me to the second reason for considering *Étant donnés* to be a hermetic work, directly connected to the first. *Étant donnés* is a work of a highly private iconology. It belongs to Duchamp's own cosmos. With all its connections, all its possible references,

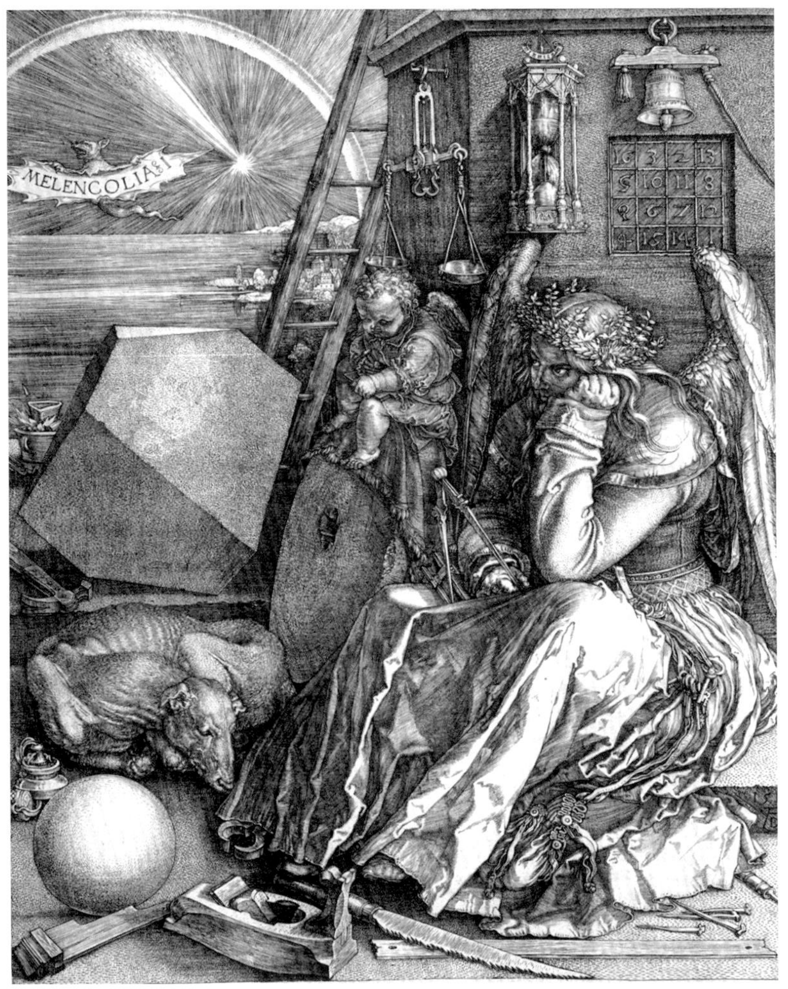

1 Albrecht Dürer, *Melencolia I,* etching, 23.9 x 16.8 cm, 1514. Kupferstichkabinett, Berlin.

all its allusions, *Étant donnés* is part of an infinitely complex semiotic system, a system that is as flexible as it is rhizomatic. One may say that there is an iconography to be found in Duchamp's whole work (i.e., holes, gas lamps, risen arms, nudes, brides, and of course even waterfalls). And one may say that Duchamp's works can be connected to each other through this recurrent iconography. But the point is that the meaning of the iconography used in Duchamp's work is by no means codified. It is not conventionalized. There may have been for Duchamp an intrinsic meaning in his iconographic subject matters, but it is not obligatory.

It is of utmost importance to note that the use and the phenomenon of such a syncretistic iconography and private iconology is by no means new. We only have to look back into Renaissance art to find artworks that could easily be labeled as "hermetic works" in the sense given here. One only has to think about Giorgione's *Tempesta,* Holbein's *Ambassadors,* or Dürer's *Melencolia I.* I suppose it would be worth putting *Étant donnés* into a broader art historical context under the premises of "enigmaticalness," let's say from

Albrecht Dürer's *Melencolia* to Matthew Barney's *Cremaster*.[32] Just to take the *Melencolia I* (fig. 1) into consideration: I think there are principally two opportunities to deal with the complex and complicated iconography in Dürer's etching (and I guess it's the same with *Étant donnés*). The first opportunity is to assume that there is no fixed relation between the signs or symbols in *Melencolia I,* and also to assume that there is no coherent concept regarding the combination of these manifold signs, which would mean that there is no specific, no intended meaning of what we suppose to be an allegory. This opportunity coincides with the point of view that German philosopher Hartmut Boehme took when he wrote about Dürer's etching a few years ago: "The mystery of this print does not lie with the question of which objects and creatures have been gathered, but in what it means that it is precisely these and in the connection between them. The case is that the specific character of Melencolia lies within the fact that the fixed relation between sign and meaning, anchored in theology and philosophy, is abandoned."[33] In this point of view the iconography of *Melencolia I* has no fixed, no specific, no conventionally decodable meaning.

Contrary to this, the second opportunity to deal with the complex and complicated iconography is to assume that the combination of signs follows a coherent concept and that it is intended to have a specific meaning. Whoever is responsible for this concept, he alone holds, as Otto Pächt put it, the "key to decipherment" in his hands.[34] He alone knows about the deeper content hidden in the enigma.

It is of utmost importance to understand that the Archimedean point regarding the decipherment of subject matter in decidedly enigmatic works (be it an enigmatic emblem, be it Dürer's *Melencolia I,* or be it Duchamp's *Étant donnés*) lies neither in the artwork nor in the recipient, but in the author's intention. It lies in what the combination of signs (or more neutral: what the combination of elements) was supposed to mean for the artist or the one in charge of the iconographic program. As far as Duchamp is concerned, his syncretistic iconography is an iconography in the age of art after the end of iconography. And that means: after the end of a conventionalized iconography (if iconography has ever been an issue of strict conventions). It is an iconography and iconology that (maybe) only Duchamp could have explained in its entity and complexity and that after Duchamp's death may only be "cracked" (to quote Grasskamp again) by a "syndicate of decipherers," if it is to be cracked at all.

Notes

1 Walter Grasskamp, "Duchamp als Klassiker" [1998], in *Ist die Moderne eine Epoche?* Munich 2002, p. 140. All translations from the German by LB.

2 Ibid.

3 Rudolf E Kuenzli, "Introduction," in idem. and Francis M. Naumann, *Marcel Duchamp: Artist of the Century,* Cambridge, Mass. 1990, p. 5.

4 Umberto Eco, *The Open Work,* trans. Anna Cancogni, Cambridge, Mass. 1989.

5 Umberto Eco, "Vorwort zur zweiten Auflage" [Preface to the second edition], in *Das offene Kunstwerk,* Frankfurt am Main 1977, p. 11.

6 Eco, *The Open Work (note 4),* p. 39. Every artwork, says Eco, demands from its recipient "a free, inventive response, if only because it cannot really be appreciated," unless it is not reinvented "in psychological collaborations with the author." Every artwork would always enclose "an infinity of possible 'readings.'" Every reception "of a work of art is both an *interpretation* and a *performance* of it, because in every reception the work takes on a fresh perspective for itself." An artwork would even be open "though its author may have aimed at a univocal, unambiguous communication." But even though every artwork

is open, openness (on this level) does not always mean "'indefiniteness' of communication, 'infinite' possibilities of form, and complete freedom of reception." If Eco says that every work of art is open, he proposes an "openness" based on "*mental* collaboration of the consumer, who must freely interpret an artistic datum, a product which has already been organized in its structural entirety (even if this structure allows for an indefinite plurality of interpretations)." Eco, *The Open Work*, pp. 4, 6, 11–12, 24, 39.

[7] Ibid., p. 42.

[8] Ibid., p. 5.

[9] Eco, "Vorwort zur zweiten Auflage" (note 5), p. 8.

[10] Ibid., p. 10.

[11] Eco, *The Open Work* (note 4), p. 39.

[12] Ibid., p. 91.

[13] Ibid., p. 103.

[14] Theodor Adorno, *Aesthetic Theory*, trans. Robert Hullot-Kentor, London 1997, p. 183.

[15] Ibid., p. 159.

[16] Ibid., pp. 160–61.

[17] Ibid., p. 161.

[18] Ibid., p. 162.

[19] Ibid., p. 159.

[20] Ibid., p. 103.

[21] Walter Hopps and Anne d'Harnoncourt, *Étant Donnés: 1° la chute d'eau, 2° le gaz d'éclairage; Reflections on a New Work by Marcel Duchamp*, reprint, Philadelphia Museum of Art 1987, p. 7.

[22] Julian Jason Haladyn, *Marcel Duchamp Étant donnés*, London 2010, p. 4.

[23] Ibid., p. 15.

[24] Marcel Duchamp, letter to Suzanne and Jean Crotti, New York, August 17, 1952, reprinted in Francis M. Naumann, "Affectueusement, Marcel: Ten Letters from Marcel Duchamp to Suzanne Duchamp and Jean Crotti," *Archives of American Art Journal* 22, no. 4 (1982), p. 17.
[25] Marcel Duchamp, interview with *Arts and Decoration*, 1915, reprinted in "A Complete Reversal of Art Opinions" [1915], in *Duchamp: Passim; A Marcel Duchamp Anthology*, ed. Anthony Hill, Singapore 1994, p. 80.
[26] Ibid.
[27] Marcel Duchamp, interview with Pierre Cabanne, 1966, in Pierre Cabanne, *Dialogues with Marcel Duchamp* [1967], trans. Ron Padgett, New York 1979, p. 67.
[28] Marcel Duchamp, interview with Dore Ashton, 1966, in Dore Ashton, "An Interview with Marcel Duchamp," *Studio International* 171, no. 878 (June 1966), p. 246.
[29] Marcel Duchamp, interview with James Johnson Sweeney, 1955, in *Wisdom: Conversations With the Elder Wise Men of our Time*, ed. James Nelson, New York 1958, p. 94.
[30] Ibid.
[31] Umberto Eco, *Postscript to "The Name of the Rose"* [1983], New York 1984, p. 7.
[32] When going through Michael Taylor's superb essays in his book on *Étant donnés*, I was struck by a citation he gives from an essay of Herbert Read, that I did not know up to then. In 1939, Read postulated, "In our decadent society ... art must enter into a monastic phase.... Art must now become individualistic, even hermetic." Quoted in Michael Taylor, *Marcel Duchamp: Étant donnés*, New Haven and London 2009, p. 25. Of course, Read did not lead Duchamp directly into making *Étant donnés* hermetic. But this quotation may indicate that enigmaticalness and "hermeticism" are not only worth exploring in twentieth-century art but also in a broader art historical context.
[33] Hartmut Boehme, *Albrecht Dürer Melencolia I. Im Labyrinth der Deutung* [1989], 2nd ed., Frankfurt am Main 1990, pp. 8–9.
[34] Otto Pächt, *Methodisches zur kunsthistorischen Praxis. Ausgewählte Schriften* [1977], 2nd ed., ed. Jörg Oberhaidacher, Artur Rosenauer, and Gertraut Schikola, Munich 1986, p. 235.

Antje von Graevenitz

Duchamp as a Scientist, Artifex, and Semiotic Philosopher His Notes of the "Infra-mince" (1934/35–1945)

"Everything flows": this motto from antiquity about the seed of all wisdom, ascribed to Heraclitus, just might have been in Marcel Duchamp's mind as he visited the Forestay waterfall near Chexbres on Lake Geneva in 1946. By then, this wisdom had in fact been Duchamp's objective as he sought to make accessible the transitoriness of art: movement and transformation (water, gas, and steam are examples) were the main themes in his art. This also includes sneezing in *Why Not Sneeze Rrose Sélavy?* (1921) (fig. 1),[1] a witty and enigmatic work of sculpture that is, at certain levels of its meaning, about this moist outbreak of the human body, an apparent analogy to an orgasm. A depicted sneeze, however, is not to be seen, but rather only white marble cubes in a small, brightly colored birdcage, in which one finds a thermometer to gauge a fever and a cuttlefish bone on which the absent bird could whet his beak. Sugar, fever, and the imaginary whetting bird beaks, the cage from which one could escape—as with sneezing or during a sexual act, something escapes the body—are all connotations rather well known to Duchamp scholars. A few references in Duchamp's work, however, can be added here. In the posthumously published series of notes to *inframince* from the period of 1934/35 to 1945 we find, under number 26v, the following: "fondage (dans les liquides avec le sucre pax)" (melting [in the liquids with sugar for ex]) (fig. 2). This particular process, or its result, may refer to a love act. The liquids would fit here. But what about the "sucre pax"? This construction does not exist in French. "Pax" is Latin for "peace," and it would be a fitting result for the act of love. While Duchamp always "played" with homophonic words, we can expand this interpretation. "Pax" is also pronounced "pacs," French for pact or agreement, which would point to an erotic liaison. But the word "pacsons" also means parcel or piece, and so the "sucre pax" would indicate pieces of sugar. The English title of the work would translate in French as "Pourquoi ne pas éternuer?" The French for sneezing also invokes "éterniser," in English "immortalize," a paradox to which Duchamp may have referred humorously as he uses marble for his sugar cubes, the principal material in sculptures that were meant to last eternally. "It weighs a ton," Duchamp declared, "and that was one of the elements that interested me when I made it, you see. It is a readymade in which the sugar is changed into marble. It is a sort of mythological effect."[2]

What, however, is the meaning of *infra-mince* in this connection?

We are discussing here at length the desert-like intermediate zone as interval in the interaction of two states, to which Duchamp gave his full attention and which he called the *infra-mince*. It is an almost nothingness that exists between two things, the in-between-ness or the infinitesimal tiny distance between two things that can arise between the seeming and being.

The term cannot be found in any dictionary. Separately, we find in Thibaut's *Dictionary of the English and French Languages* (1897) for "infra" the term "above," and for "mince"

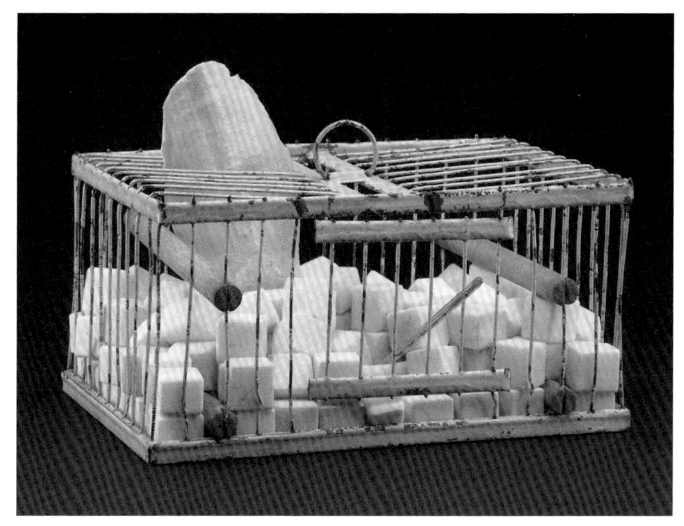

coupage – coupant (massicot,
glissage –
léchage – collage
viscosité – (
cassage.
Brûlage
fondage (
Porosité – imbibage (papier buvard)
Enfonçage (clous, pointe de flèche)
frottage grattage –
ajustage repérage –
séparage (camouflage – ou séparation mécanique
retissage
Adhérence collage –
Empesage –

1 **Marcel Duchamp, *Why Not Sneeze Rrose Sélavy?*,** 152 marble cubes in the shape of sugar lumps, a thermometer, and a cuttlebone in a small birdcage, fitted with four wood bars, 11.4 x 22 x 16 cm, 1921. Philadelphia Museum of Art, Louise and Walter Arensberg Collection. Reconstructed in an edition of 8 in 1964 by Galleria Arturo Schwarz, Milan. 2 **Marcel Duchamp, Infra-mince no. 26**, reproduced in Marcel Duchamp, *Notes*, ed. Paul Matisse, Centre Georges Pompidou, Paris 1980.

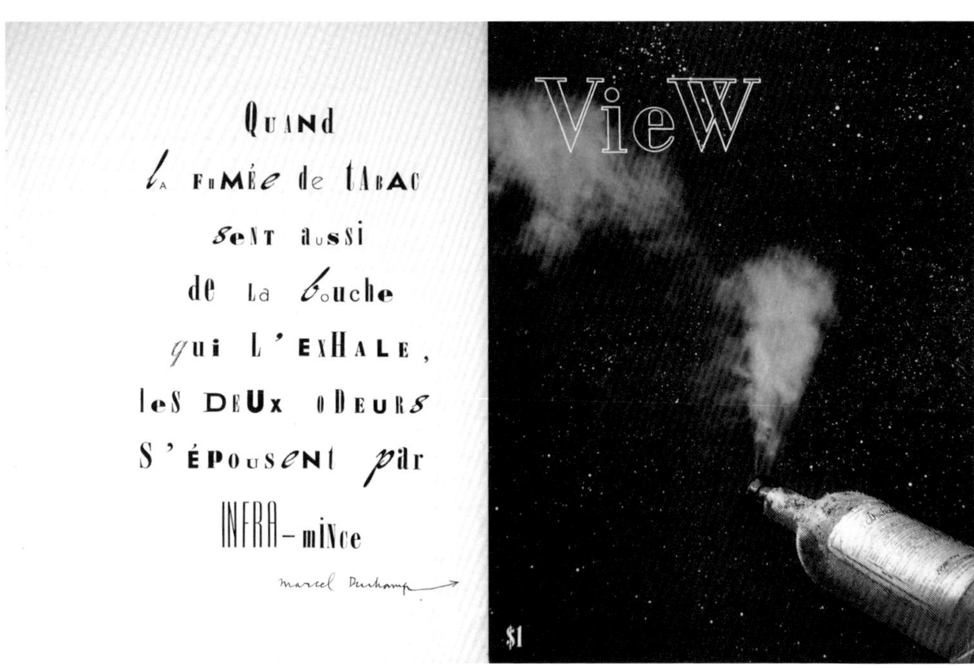

Le possible est
un infra mince. –
La possibilité de plusieurs
tubes de couleur de
devenir un Seurat est
"l'explication" concrète
du possible comme infra
mince.

Le possible impliquant
le devenir – le passage de
l'un à l'autre a lieu
dans l'infra mince.

allégorie sur l'"oubli"

3 **Marcel Duchamp, Covers of *View*** (back and front), March 1945. Photograph by Stefan Banz. 4 **Marcel Duchamp, Infra-mince no. 1,** reproduced in Marcel Duchamp, *Notes*, ed. Paul Matisse, Centre Georges Pompidou, Paris 1980.

we find "thin," "narrow" and "insignificant." Long before Duchamp's notes, Henri Poincaré had thought about the "infinitesimal,"[3] but we are dealing here with a neologism for the hardly noticeable volume of almost nothingness that Duchamp himself had invented. In 1977, Jean Clair had interpreted the term "infra-mince" as a key notion in the transition to the endlessly possible.[4] In addition, the Japanese author Yoshiaki Tono devoted a more general essay to the peculiar neologism a year after the publication of Duchamp's notes, which was published in the catalogues of the Duchamp exhibitions in Barcelona and Cologne in 1984. Tono, challenged by his own infra-mince inventions, declared in the essay, "For Duchamp, who saw eroticism as a fourth dimension, infra-mince could have meant the extremely thin layer between the third dimension—everyday life—and the fourth (the invisible)."[5] Tono went on to state that Duchamp's term should be subjected to thorough research in connection to the Duchamp oeuvre, yet he refrained from starting the process himself.

Duchamp does not define the hybrid notion *infra-mince* in any comprehensive and abstract way, but rather in forty-six different notes published only after his death (why he did not publish them during his lifetime remains unclear), in which number 16 defines the infra-mince as an allegory on forgetting. The numbering of the individual notes is probably not the work of Duchamp, but can rather be attributed to their editor Paul Matisse, who received the packet of paper inscribed "Infra-mince" from his mother Teeny after his stepfather's death, and published them only in 1980.[6] But still, the first note seems to express a kind of program when it states that "Le possible est un infra-mince" (The possible is an infra-mince) (fig. 4).

Duchamp also noted rather sensorily perceptible and dynamic moments,[7] such as when two corduroy-pant legs rub together to produce an infra-mince (9v). Did he mean the resulting warmth? Or is it the mixture of two separate parts in a reciprocal penetration? The possible sparks that fly from the one to the other? Or does Duchamp suggest that both pant legs can also touch and thus seem to love one another after the traditional notion of a chemical marriage? Or is the motto of the humorous intellectual "Rrose Sélavy/Eros, c'est la vie" also applicable to the infra-mince?

The term is only found once in his entire work. In March 1945, Duchamp designed the back and front covers of the magazine *View* (vol. 5, no. 1) (fig. 3), to which the following story is attached. Once, during an evening meal, both Duchamp and the protagonist of the Surrealists André Breton, who had immigrated to New York, drank a bottle of wine and had been smoking. This inspired Duchamp to have a photograph taken of a wine bottle as if a small cloud of smoke or steam escaped from it. He replaced the wine label with a picture of his identity card—this was after all during the American period of Prohibition (1919–33). But it is the steam that is important, an almost nothing. There might have been an association with the genie in the bottle from the fairy tale, who escapes here from a container for spirits as, indeed, a spirit.[8] Then the identity card might point to Duchamp's own spirit. The French also have the metaphoric ghost in the bottle in their language, and this seems to connect nicely with the magazine's title as Duchamp set it for his own cover design: he wrote "VieW," with a capital *W,* a fact that has been largely overlooked in the Duchamp literature. Now, more or less cryptically, this one word produces no less than three others: the French word for life—"vie"—the English word "we" and Double You ("W"). As Duchamp loved playing with words and the way they sounded, which he discovered in the literary work of Stéphane Mallarmé and Raymond Roussel,[9] we can now try and look for meanings ourselves. From the image and the words, the following chain of associations can be formed: view, life, we, twice you, and the spirit—from the bottle. The message on the back cover explains this: "Quand la fumé de tabac sent aussi de la bouche qui exhale, les deux odeurs s'épousent par infra-mince." (When the smoke of the tobacco smells also of the mouth from which it comes, the two smells marry by infra-mince.)[10] So if the tobacco smoke also takes the smell from the mouth it has just escaped from, then both smells join in an infra-mince. The sentence returns in his notes as number 11v and number 33, which very well might be an indication of how important this image was for Duchamp.[11] The reader now stumbles upon some of the key notions: we have here tobacco smoke, something very thin that will dissolve into the air; then there is the mouth, which of course is a hole. But this in itself is not the interval that is so important, but it is rather the space between the smell of the mouth and that of the smoke, both extremely thin substances. The interval resembles a membrane through which both substances come together in a process of osmosis, in which they seem to be married. The word "marry" originates in the erotic life of man, but also served as a metaphor in the "love life" of substances with the "science" of alchemy. In mixing two smells—or the mutual penetration of them—which are the result of cigar smoke, something new and extremely thin has been produced. Duchamp thus defines the spirit not only as *Pneuma,* which in the antique and alchemistic traditions fills man with his spiritual life, but also as a combined penetrating and smelling *Pneumae,* a "Double You." The chemical marriage of two things previously divided results in infra-mince. It is a token of love in the middle of an interval. This explains the remark that Duchamp made to Denis de Rougemont in 1945 that the term "infra-mince" was interesting for him while it was completely overlooked by the natural sciences.[12] "I have chosen 'fine' deliberately because it is a human, emotional word and not a precise laboratory measurement." And he goes on to reveal a secret, that "it is a category which I have been concerned with for ten years now. I believe we can pass from the second and third dimension through the infra-mince."[13] (This interview perhaps took place at the beginning of 1945, so presumably Duchamp began to write his notes on infra-mince in 1934.) Apparently he defined the marriage of extremely thin substances in the interval—not time, as is common, but the marriage—as a fourth dimension. And he also apparently thus chose the infra-mince as a key notion in his oeuvre.

So how can we classify the examples of the infra-mince. I present here my attempt at the classification of these forty-six notes.

First, there is an abstract class of notes: the possible (1), the potential that is within a certain thing is equal in meaning to the infra-mince. This is the text of the first note, of which—as already stated—we do not know whether the numbering stems from Duchamp or from Paul Matisse. As early as 1913, Duchamp engaged himself intensively with the notion of the "possible" and had by then written some texts about it.[14] The possible can be regarded as abstract while it lies before the existence of the real. Additionally, Duchamp writes that

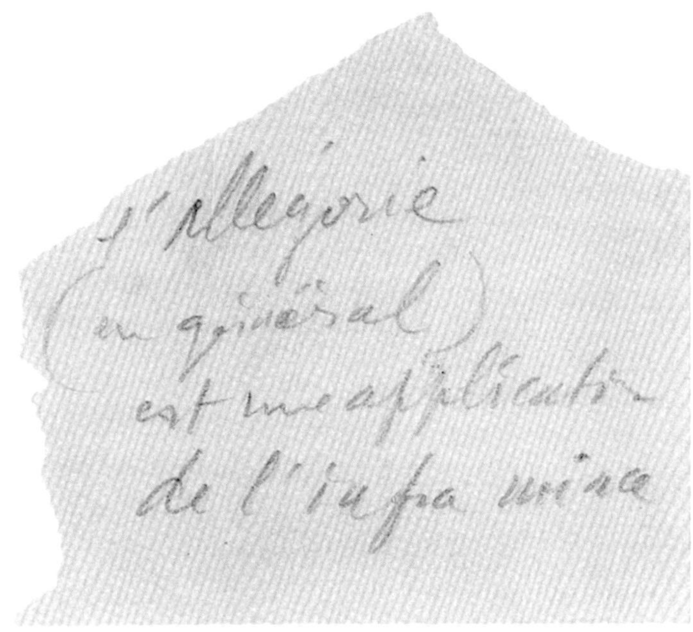
l'allégorie
(en général)
est une application
de l'infra mince

5 Marcel Duchamp, Infra-mince no. 6, reproduced in Marcel Duchamp, *Notes*, ed. Paul Matisse, Centre Georges Pompidou, Paris 1980.

the "allégorie sur *l'oubli*"—the allegory on *forgetting* (1)—is an infra-mince (fig. 5)—so not the forgetting or the forgotten itself but the personification of forgetting, itself a rhetorical strategy of the mind—a metaphorical shifting of an abstract phenomenon that is related to the really forgotten, and therefore in relation to the negation or dissolution of the known. But also the analogy or the allegory in general (2, 6) are infra-minces, the second as *an application*. Intended here is the rhetorical method of the language shifting from abstract meanings toward imaginations—an abstract situation which can be illustrated as follows: to encase beauty in an allegorical way, e.g. as Venus, and then to connect this Venus in comparison with something else again, perhaps indicating the ability to love of this Venus. Also, the difference between similarity and equality (7) is an infra-mince, says Duchamp, as are all matters of identity (35). An example here is when two persons (or things) look the same, as with twins or two drops of water, a note Duchamp wrote down on July 29, 1937 at the Hotel Kongen af Danmark in Copenhagen. Exceptionally, Duchamp added a date here but otherwise we can only guess at the gradual progress in the writing of these notes.

To the second class of infra-mince in the notes belongs the difference between reality and appearance for our perception, as is the case of the colors of the painter Seurat for the Post-Impressionists (1). The same goes for high-gloss paint that when breathed upon shows a patch of vapor on which you can make a drawing. After a little while the vapor disappears, but when one breathes again on the same spot the same drawing appears again! Appearance or being: that is Duchamp's question here.

A third class of infra-mince passages can be mentioned: an example is the doors of underground trains that for a short time are filled with the contours of a passenger (9r) (fig. 6).[15]

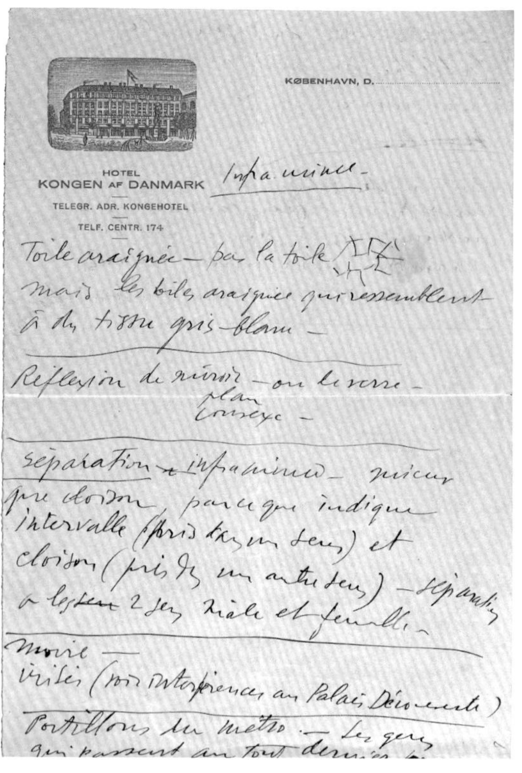

HOTEL
KONGEN AF DANMARK
TELEGR. ADR. KONGEHOTEL
TELF. CENTR. 174

KØBENHAVN, D. ....

Infra mince –

Toile araignée – pas la toile
mais les fils araignée qui ressemblent
à du tissu gris-blanc –

Reflexion de miroir – ou de verre –
plan
convexe –

séparation infra mince – mieux
que cloison, parce que indique
intervalle (pris dans un sens) et
cloison (pris dans un autre sens) – séparation
a le sens 2 sens mâle et femelle –

moiré –
voiles (voir interférences au Palais Découverte)

Portillons du metro – Les gens
qui passent au tout dernier [illegible]

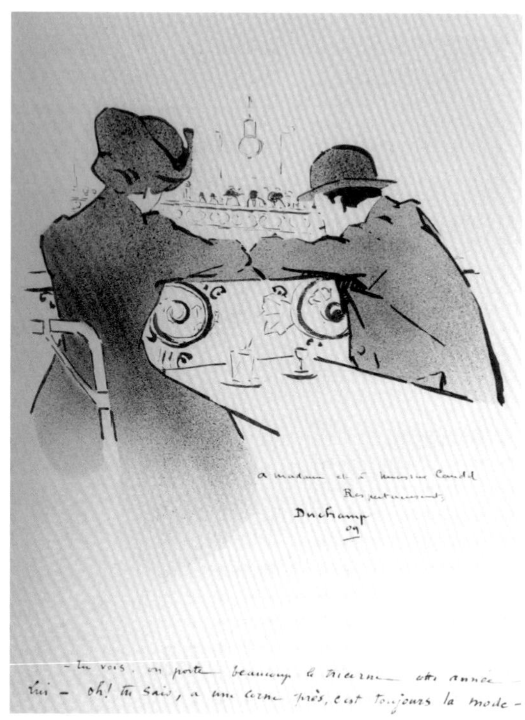

6 Marcel Duchamp, Infra-mince no. 9, reproduced in Marcel Duchamp, *Notes*, ed. Paul Matisse, Centre Georges Pompidou, Paris 1980. **7 Marcel Duchamp, *At the Palais de Glace,*** brush and ink on paper, 43.2 x 30.5 cm, 1910. Metropolitan Museum of Art, New York. Gift of Mrs. William Sisler, 1975.

And also: "Le passage de l'un à l'autre dans l'infra-mince" (The passage from one to the other takes place in the infra-mince) (1). This brings to mind Duchamp's aforementioned remark in a conversation when he said, "I believe we can pass from the second and the third dimension through infra-mince."

In other words, Duchamp here indicates the passing through an interval. This recalls one of his early drawings, *Le roi et la reine traversés par des nus en vitesse* of 1912 (The King and Queen Traversed by Nudes at High Speed),[16] that Duchamp had then found so important he included it in the Armory Show in New York in 1913. In it, an interval between the sexes is being crossed. Again, a reference to the alchemistic tradition can easily be made, in which for centuries a king and queen are an allegory of dualistic substances or even properties like gold and silver, sun and moon, warm and cold, male and female. In alchemistic imagery king and queen embrace each other, both different but still united in a chemical marriage. The theme of Man and Wife can often be found in his work. Although his statement that he never employed alchemy in his work, and when he did, it was without his even knowing it, a statement he made in conversation with Robert Lebel, is often quoted in the Duchamp literature, the last part of the original French sentence, "Si j'ai fait de l'alchimie, c'est de la seul façon, qui soit de nos jours admissible, c'est-a-dire sans le savoir,"[17] has now been translated differently as "without it becoming known." So could it be done in secret, as it would be fitting for a secret science?[18] The artist Robert Smithson did ask Duchamp later, "I see you are into alchemy," upon which Duchamp answered, "Yes."[19] The unification of man and woman is such a fundamental theme for Duchamp that he not only characterizes tenderness in a note (28) as a form of infra-mince, but we can perhaps even say that it is one of the most fundamental principles in his work. One of his early caricatures (dating from 1909) (fig. 7) shows a man and a woman sitting at a table, seemingly eating ice cream, who put their underarms together so that—seen from behind—they form a strange kind of bridge between their bodies, fused together as if they were Siamese twins.[20] In 1942 he adopted the face of a photographed immigrant woman (Compensation portrait),[21] and by transfer and counter-transfer both appear as a third body.[22] The infra-mince here is nothing other than very thin. And further, we may remember that Duchamp is depicted on a perfume bottle as the transvestite *Rrose Sélavy,* a love scent called *Belle Haleine* that fuses itself with other bodies (the cover of Rudolf Ruths' book *Roman de la Belle Helaine,* 1923).

In addition, there are not only other remarks that emphasize Duchamp's affinity with alchemistic knowledge, but there are also works in which he integrated a passage between man and woman as a form of highway or tunnel and in doing so made a connection between alchemy and psychoanalysis. In the period of his notes on the infra-mince he started work on his door *Gradiva* (1937) (fig. 8). The door shows the outlines of a man and woman in a glass wall, and those who walk through it would get the impression that their body would converge with the bodies of the love couple taken from the story "Gradiva" by Wilhelm Jensen. In 1907, Sigmund Freud, in one of his analyses, mentioned Jensen's story as an example of a successful therapy.[23] Gradiva is a girl from Pompeii depicted on a funerary relief who reminded the son of an archeologist, called Hanold, so much of a lover from his youth that had since disappeared, that he could only love the dead girl, thus causing the suppression of his sexuality. Only when he met another girl who resembled the girl on the relief, and when they kissed each other on the threshold of an Apollonian temple in a blistering sun and amidst a swarm of flies, was Hanold able to cure himself; their kiss enabled him to unearth his deeply buried feelings. In the moment of love lies the force of healing, of which the onlooker at the 1937 glass door can take part so that the exhibition might be visited in a reinvigorated way. The glass door not only represents the narrow space between past and present, as told by the Gradiva story, but it is also in its concrete passage an infra-mince between fiction and reality.

As in the glass door *Gradiva,* the dualism of light and shadow is furthermore a decisive source of perception for Duchamp, as the following may prove. The notes of the infra-mince contain many examples, no less than eight, of the theme of light and shadow; so this then is our fourth class. Shadows represent through all sources of light various aspects of the interaction (3). The coincidence with the bearer of a shadow results in a thin interval called infra-mince. In contrast to Plato's parable of the cave (*Politeia,* 514a–517), Duchamp is not so much interested in the relation between the shadow and the invisible object from the outside that causes the shadow to fall in the cave, but he is much more concerned with the reality of the bearer of the shadow itself—the wall of the cave, for example, and the pseudo-reality of the shadow in the interval. It seems as if Duchamp intends to broaden Plato's story of the cave. Also, the difference between the photographed shadow and the real shadow of his readymade *Sculpture de Voyage* (Sculpture for Traveling, 1917–18) is for him an infra-mince (13).

The fifth class of infra-mince is dedicated to temperature. An example is the comic note (4) in which he wrote that "La chaleur d'un siège (qui vient/d'être quitté) est infra-mince" (The warmth of the seat of a chair [which has just been left] is infra-mince).

The sixth class of notes is about looking. Between the things the eye sees and the eye itself Duchamp finds an infra-mince. In addition, he takes as a fact that between the look one offers to somebody and the cold stare an audience directs towards an object, and who immediately afterwards forgets the whole object, lies an ultra-thin interval (10).

Duchamp dedicates the seventh class of notes to a great many calculations of small differences of the weight of things and the way in which one could find them (8, 30r, 30v, 31). But he also considers other types of mass, such as the tiny difference of mass of certain tools that are on offer for both sexes, for example things that are different for female and male hands (9r).

Because he notices in particular the thin interval between reality and appearance, Duchamp dedicates the eighth class of infra-mince to reflections (9r, 43), and all kinds of similar effects that are caused by shining material and draperies, for example the so-called moiré effect (9r) or the changing effects of cloth (11r) that he compares with a dove's throat (44) and also with mother-of-pearl (25). Included also is shining wax in which things are reflected with the effect of presenting a three dimensionality in a two-dimensional surface (36, 42, 43). One is reminded here of a remark by Henri Poincaré, with whose work

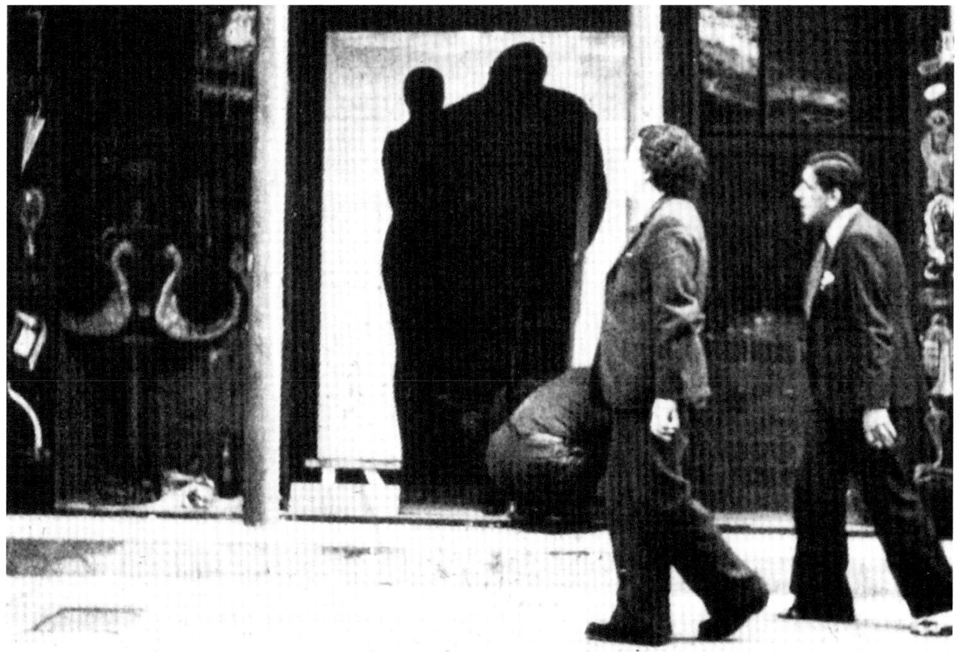

8 Marcel Duchamp, The moment Breton is passing the door *Gradiva* (destroyed). 31, Rue de la Seine, Paris, 1937.

Duchamp was heavily involved and that he therefore might have read. Poincaré describes the relativity of space and considers it a possibility that the third dimension is only a human assumption.[24] Duchamp in his notes is interested at first only with the second and third dimensions, as perceivable fusions only, and presupposes a very small interval between the two, an infra-mince. It could well be that he understood his consideration as the fourth dimension.

The ninth class is about the delay in the perception of a sound and its visible effect, between the sound of a bullet that has been fired and the hole from its impact in a wall (12). In this context, seven photographs of the Forestay waterfall may be remembered, two of which Duchamp took standing at the shooting range. From it, local people were shooting across the waterfall. Although Duchamp speaks in his note (12) clearly of a wall in which the hole can be seen, at the waterfall he may still have been interested in the delay of the shot and its audible sound. Or he may also have been interested in the mixing of the sounds of the shots and the roar of the waterfall, or even in the analogy of shooting a picture and shooting the actual rifles. The delay in the interval would then result in: (1) The view through the camera's lens, (2) Shooting the picture, and (3) The imagined audible shot. Admittedly, this all is a somewhat complicated construct for the photographs that Duchamp had been shooting probably in connection to his notes on the infra-mince. Duchamp took up the theme of delay in other places as well.[25] It is a theme that resembles the uncertainty relation that struck Werner Heisenberg in 1927 during a walk on the island of Helgoland. This physicist was observing the stars, and because of a delay in the perception he was unable to measure an object's position and its impulse at the same time.[26] Henri Bergson, on the other hand, assumed that if something could not be measured it could not be an object of science.[27] Duchamp would probably not have agreed with this at all. Duchamp was interested in delays of any kind. And therefore he noted down various types of viscosity; how, for example, creams or quicksilver slowly move on a surface, or, also, how two different fluids can lay on top of each other in different types of viscosity (14, 24). These thoughts were also expressed by Henri Poincaré, although in a somewhat different way, as he had also dealt with the problem of delay of viscosity.[28]

The tenth class accordingly deals with all kinds of technical acts that make possible various fusions of flat objects, such as gluing, laminating, and relining (24, 26, 26v, 27), and even with dandruff that sticks on a still-moist collar and gives it a kind of pastel color (20). With a little bit of humor one could also include Duchamp's note 28, which states that tenderness might be infra-mince. Well, surely this must be included, for it is also in tenderness that two different bodies are glued together.

Such witty examples are often Duchamp's inventions, as he indeed often finds his scientific observations in everyday life, and unlike Alfred Jarry before him, not in a pre-Surrealistic fantasy world. But still, some of his observations are somewhat Dadaistic, such as note 26, which says that leaded Gruyere is good for bad teeth, and as such it is infra-mince. It would be possible to *hear* this example as well, and should one be a little melancholic about it, the symbolism of the lead for the alchemistic allegory of the artist, or Saturn, would have contributed to it.

We very rarely come across the fact that Duchamp still sees a non-interval as one, so that it is included here as the eleventh class of notes. In it we find a note (15) on observations about the reverse side of glass paintings. We still see a painting there, but it is not the intended one. This difference greatly interests Duchamp, while the intended and the unintended coalesce physically and drift apart only for the viewer in perspective.

From the list of the classes presented so far, we can now deduct some fundamental principles:

1. Abstract definitions (including mathematical definitions)
2. Natural definitions
3. Everyday definitions
4. Human definitions
5. Perceptional definitions

In addition come the following principles:

I. The mixture of objects in a new union, as in the case of tobacco smell and the smell of breath and the sound of the rubbing of corduroy-pant legs.

II. The connection of objects despite a very thin interval, as with a coming together, example tenderness.

III. The coinciding of objects, although no direct mixture will result, as with the polish of wood or the reflection and the fleeting body warmth on a chair.

IV. Differentiating sameness, similarities and differences, divisibility and indivisibility, as in Plato's "Timaeus" (34c–36c), which is broadened with the interval infra-mince here.

Duchamp occupies himself thus with the thought of, the investigated and the experienced duality of meaning, substances, and processes that include an invisible interval which only then makes these correspondences possible. Dualism as such was not typical for the natural sciences in the twentieth century, notwithstanding the earlier relevance of the research into the duality of time and space. Rather it is typical for the alchemistic tradition and its fundamental principle of "solve et coagula" (separate and unite), the natural philosophy of the romantic age, and the pseudo-science that was closely related to symbolism, which, however, are not altogether engaged with the interval.

Not all classes of infra-mince that are mentioned, however, can be compared to the traditional acts of alchemists, but certainly some of them can. For example, the notion of *conjugatio,* as the chemical marriage of substances, qualities, and so forth, is called in alchemy,[29] can be applied to several notes in which Duchamp presents a connection as infra-mince. The same goes for the notion of *inceratio,* or fusion, which he calls fondage/melting, as in the case of the sucre pax. The notion of *reflexio* corresponds with many notes on reflections of the third into the second dimension (compare also Plato's "Timaeus," 46a). The notion of *transmutatio* can be related to notes in which allegories or analogies are mentioned. *Amalgamatio* unites substances that are on top of each other without fusing together, as Duchamp describes the polish and breath, lamination and collaging, as well as the dandruff on the wet collar. *Separatio* corresponds to those notes in which Duchamp ponders upon isolating a light beam or speaks of the viscosity of liquid and their separation walls. But—and that has to be stressed carefully—Duchamp never used the status of *fixatio* in connection with the main aim of alchemists, the *gold* or *philosopher's stone,* by describing phenomena of infra-mince.

One could certainly argue therefore that Duchamp, in his notes to the infra-mince, could have been designing a modern and a-metaphysical alchemy to counter the natural sciences of his day. These were, moreover, presented during his time in the Palais de la Découverte, which opened on May 24, 1937 as part of the larger International Exhibition. Duchamp avoided the larger event,[30] but he probably visited the special exhibition of natural phenomena, such as the "experiences interactives" and the planetarium, as he includes effects he sees on the building in note 9r: "moiré—irisés (voir interférences au Palais Découverte)." He might have been referring to such effects on the steel construction and the colored windows on the dome of the building.

It is also possible, however, that Duchamp wanted to modernize Plato's genesis. Plato describes in his "Timaeus" how each existing interval between the two elements had to be filled, or else the world could not come into existence (58a–61c). Could Duchamp's readymade of a comb, *Peigne* (1916), be a witty representation of this Platonic genesis?

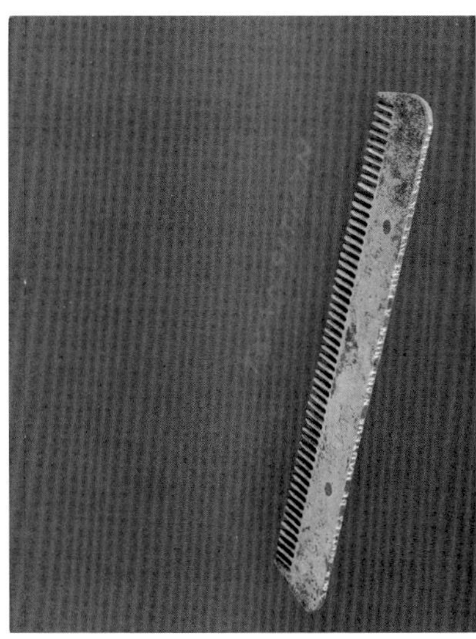

9 Marcel Duchamp, Cover for *Transition,* no. 26 (a reproduction of the readymade *Comb*), 21.5 x 15.5 cm, edited by Eugene Jonas, co-edited by James Johnson Sweeney, New York 1937.

Then only the hair, in its function as a real filler, could be capable of making perfect this *allegorie réelle* about the creation of the world. Duchamp had in addition ordered the comb to be depicted vertically on the cover of the magazine *Transition* (no. 16) (fig. 9),[31] in the same way as his well-known upturned *Urinoir.* Regarding *Étant donnés* (1946–66), a work Duchamp made in connection to the notes to infra-mince (as he had sketched the spread legs of a woman in his note 24) (fig. 10), the four elements in the sense of Plato can be clearly recognized: fire—le gaz d'éclairage; water—the waterfall; and air and earth—the reclining woman as earth waiting to be fertilized. In our world we have to deal with these four elements. In Duchamp's statement, if we can call the work as such, the intervals between the four elements are only "filled in" by the perception of the onlooker. It is the perception that completes not only the work of art itself, but the perception also more generally completes Plato's Genesis. This completion—in its turn—is concurrent with the sixth class of infra-mince, in which, as already noted above, he deals with the interval between looking at things and the things themselves.

If we are left only with a draft of an ontology, then indeed Duchamp's notes with their often torn edges are in no way connected to a finished treatise. The form of the little sheets—their torn edges—reveal a sudden thought, an observation, the still-not-understandable and the not-yet-understood. It is perhaps in the vein of Heisenberg's uncertainty relation, or at least parallel to it. Or did Duchamp want to counter Freud's category of the subconscious, that is also present in the mind a parallel to it in reality? A three-fold interpretation of the infra-mince is proposed here:

1. As the ultra thin-ness in the world between things, that belongs to it although in itself it is an almost nothingness that hardly ever appears, something low, lower even than everything low with which the Surrealists were involved.

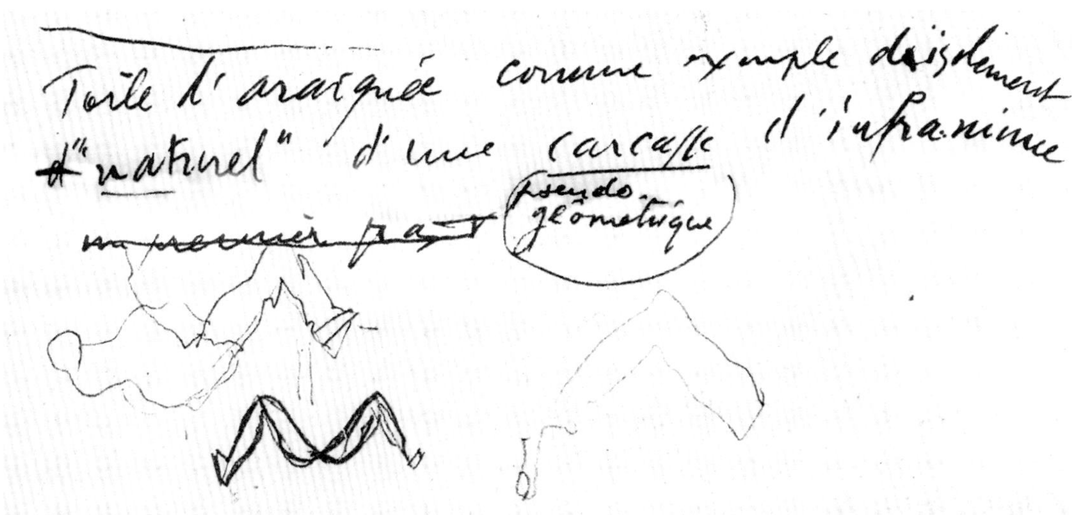

10 Marcel Duchamp, Detail of Infra-mince no. 24, reproduced in Marcel Duchamp, *Notes*, ed. Paul Matisse, Centre Georges Pompidou, Paris 1980.

2. As the finest of the fine processes in the mind—whereby now one would read "mince" as the Latin "mens" (mind); at least both words are homophones.

3. As the insignificant "mince," which in French is commentated upon as "alors" (in English "well?!").

Duchamp did not produce a surrealistic para-science with his notes on the infra-mince, because he was not interested in fiction, except a reflection in a mirror and then this only as a category. His investigations can still be called gnostic, however, because he did find corresponding similarities between ontologically different things, with their intervals, and he set up an order of one thing within the other,[32] for which he even looked for rules; rules that would not necessarily lead to laws.[33] By no means does he mention the soul or even ethical points of view that are so typical for the traditional gnosis. Moreover, gnosis has never separated itself from the transcendental, as Duchamp did. He remained loyal to reality, even in spirit. Anyhow, metaphysics would have never adopted the interval between things and the borders between them. In his attempt, Duchamp succeeded—at least he made a starting point—in finding an experimental kind of physics and a philosophy of everyday life as a parallel for the mind seen from the perspective of an artist and observer, avoiding every form of definition or law, as fully intended.

Translated from the German by Martin Adrichem

Notes

[1] A picture of the work illustrated the cover of Georges Hugnet's book *La septième face du Dé*, in Jennifer Gough-Cooper and Jacques Caumont, "Ephemerides on and about Marcel Duchamp and Rrose Sélavy, 1887–1968" (May 5–7, 1936), in *Marcel Duchamp*, exh. cat. Palazzo Grassi, Milan 1993, unpaginated. The title of the work was left out. The back cover showed two standing cigarettes without their paper wrappings. By the way, friends called Marcel Duchamp "Dee." Was "deus" included in its meaning?

[2] Gough-Cooper and Caumont, "Ephemerides" (note 1), January 15, 1956.
[3] Henri Poincaré, *Science and Methods* [1908], *in The Foundations of Science,* authorized translation by George Bruce Halsted, New York and Harrison, NY 1913, pp. 364–65.
[4] Jean Clair, *Duchamp et la photographie: Essai d'analyse d'un primat technique sur le développement d'une œuvre,* Paris 1977, p. 102; (infra-mince) is "le passage insensible d'une dimension a une autre."
[5] Yoshiaki Tono, "Duchamp und 'infra-mince,'" in *Marcel Duchamp,* exh. cat. Museum Ludwig, Cologne 1984, pp. 65–68.
[6] Marcel Duchamp, *Notes,* preface by Pontus Hultén, translated and edited by Paul Matisse, Centre Georges Pompidou, Paris 1980, no. 1–46; Marcel Duchamp, *Notes,* foreword by Paul Matisse, preface by Pontus Hultén, Paris 1999, pp. 19–36.
[7] Quoted from Dalia Judovitz, *Unpacking Duchamp: Art in Transit,* Berkeley 1995, p. 213. Duchamp points to an interval that contained both meanings of male and female on a projection surface.
[8] C. G. Jung tells the alchemistic fairytale of the genie in the bottle and connects it to the fleeting Greek god Mercury. See his *Studien über Alchemistischen Vorstellungen* [1978], Collected Works, vol. 13, Olten and Freiburg im Breisgau 1982, pp. 211, 216, 221, 223.
[9] Raymond Roussel, *Impression d'Afrique,* Paris 1912. Together with Apollinaire, Picabia and his wife Gabriele, Duchamp visited Roussel's theater piece of the same title in 1912 and was thrilled by Roussel's method of producing sense fusions from the spoken and language. See for this method also: Dario Gamboni, *Potential Images: Ambiguity and Indeterminacy in Modern Art,* London 2002, pp. 142–148.
[10] Antje von Graevenitz, "Das Schweigen brechen, Joseph Beuys und sein 'Herausforderer Marcel Duchamp,'" in *In media res. Festschrift zum 70. Geburtstag von Peter Ludwig,* ed. Rainer Jacobs and Marc Scheps, Cologne 1995, pp. 197–224; see also Juan Antonio Ramirez, *Duchamp: Love and Death, Even,* London 1998, pp. 193–94.
[11] See Breton's explanation in Gough-Cooper and Caumont, "Ephemerides" (note 1), March 15, 1945.
[12] See Theo Steiner, "Duchamps Wissenschaftsbegriff," in *Duchamps Experiment zwischen Wissenschaft und Kunst,* Munich 2006, pp. 218–64.
[13] Denis de Rougemont, "Marcel Duchamp mine de rien," *Preuves* 43, no. 204 (February 1968), pp. 46–47. The interview dated from 1945.
[14] Sandro Zanetti, "Handschrift, Typographie, Faksimile. Marcel Duchamps frühe Schriften—'Possible' (1913)," in *Bilder der Handschrift. Die graphische Dimension der Literatur,* ed. Davide Giuriato and Stephan Kammer, Basel and Frankfurt am Main 2006, pp. 203–38. The author is interested in the conditions that Duchamp assigns to the "possible."
[15] See Ludger Lütkehaus' article "Nichts," in which he explains this definition in such a way that it also contains something coming into existence, in *Big Nothing: Die jenseitigen Ebenbilder des Menschen,* ed. Johannes Bilstein and Mathias Winzen, exh. cat. Staatliche Kunsthalle Baden-Baden. Cologne 2001, p. 37; see also Joseph Hanimann, "'Infra-mince' oder das unendliche Dazwischen," *Pantheon* 44 (1986), pp. 234–40.
[16] Arturo Schwarz, *The Complete Works of Marcel Duchamp,* London and New York 1969, cat no. 187.
[17] Robert Lebel, quoted in André Breton and Gérard Legrand, eds., *L'Art Magique* (Formes de l'art 1), Paris 1957, p. 98. During a conversation with Graham Lanier, Duchamp confirmed that he had been engaged in alchemy in a philosophical way. See Graham Lanier, *Conversations with the Grand Master,* New York 1968, p. 6.

[18] John F. Moffit, *Alchemist of the Avant-Garde: The Case of Marcel Duchamp*, New York 2003, p. 264.
[19] Linda Dalrymple Henderson, *Duchamp in Context: Science and Technology in the Large Glass and Related Works*, Princeton 1989, p. 232.
[20] Illustration in Gough-Cooper and Caumont, "Ephemerides" (note 1), March 26, 1910. A handwritten addition on the right says. "À Madame et à Monsieur Caudel/Respectueusement/Duchamp 1909." Underneath is a conversation: "—tu vois, on porte beaucoup le tricorne cette année—/ lui—Oh! Tu sais, à une corne près, c'est toujours la mode." In *Marcel Duchamp*, ed. Anne d'Harnoncourt and Kynaston McShine, exh. cat. Philadelphia Museum of Art / The Museum of Modern Art, New York 1973, p. 242, cat. no. 31.
[21] In *First Papers of Surrealism*, exh. cat. New York 1942; illustration in Schwarz, cat. no. 486. Duchamp used a photo by Ben Shahn taken in October 1935 for the Farm Security Administration of a client of a resettlement program in the doorway of their home in Boone County, Arkansas; see image at http://secondat.blogspot.com/2009/10/sharecropper-families-of-1930s.html (accessed June 14, 2010).
[22] See Klaus Theweleit, *Übertragung, Gengenübertragung. Dritter Körper. Zur Gehirnveränderung durch die Medien*, International Flusser Lecture, Cologne 2007.
[23] Antje von Graevenitz, "Duchamps Tür 'Gradiva,' eine literarische Figur und ihr Surrealistenkreis," *Avantgarde: Revue interdisciplinaire et internationale / Interdisciplinary and International Review: Marcel Duchamp*, no. 2 (1989), ed. Klaus Beekman and Antje von Graevenitz, pp. 63–93.
[24] Poincaré, *Science and Methods* (note 3), pp. 413–29, 426–27. See also Herbert Molderings, *Kunst als Experiment. Marcel Duchamp und "drei Kunststopfnormalmasse,"* Berlin 2006, pp. 87ff, 94ff; and Hans Belting, *Der Blick hinter Duchamps Tür. Perspektive bei Duchamp, Sugimoto, Jeff Wall*, Cologne 2009, pp. 45–48.
[25] See a quotation of Duchamp in *Marcel Duchamp, Ingénieur du temps perdu: Entretiens avec Pierre Cabanne*, Paris 1977, p. 67; and also a quotation in *Marcel Duchamp. Schriften*, vol. 1: *Zu Lebzeiten veröffentlichte Texte*, translated, annotated, and edited by Serge Stauffer, Zurich 1981, p. 36.
[26] Werner Heisenberg, "Über den anschaulichen Inhalt der quantentheoretische Kinematik und Mechanik," *Zeitschrift für Physik* 43, no. 3 (1927), pp. 172–98.
[27] Bergson quoted by Henri Poincaré in *Dernières Pensées*, Paris 1913, p. 41.
[28] Poincaré, *Science and Methods* (note 3), p. 508.
[29] Claus Prisener and Karin Figala, eds., *Alchemie. Lexikon einer hermetischer Wissenschaft*, Munich 1993.
[30] Gough-Cooper and Caumont, "Ephemerides" (note 1), May 24, 1957.
[31] Ibid., February 17, 1916. See also d'Harnoncourt and McShine, *Marcel Duchamp* (note 20), p. 279, cat. no. 115. It is a simple metal dog's comb. Duchamp had the following text engraved in it: "Trois ou quatre gouttes de hauteur n'ont rien à voir avec la sauvagerie" (Three or four drops of height have nothing to do with wildness). It could also be read as: three or four drops of taste of sublimity have nothing to do with wildness.
[32] See also Gamboni, *Potential Images* (note 9), pp. 142–48.
[33] See also Jacob Taubes, "Noten zum Surrealismus" [1964], in *Immanente Ästhetik. Ästhetische Reflexion. Lyrik als Paradigma der Moderne*, ed. Wolfgang Iser, Cologne and Munich 1966, p. 141.

LOOKING ON THE OTHER SIDE OF THE WATERFALL

Philip Ursprung

The "Spiritualist of Woolworth" Duchamp in the Eyes of Allan Kaprow and Robert Smithson

Amelia Jones has shown in her book *Postmodernism and the En-Gendering of Marcel Duchamp* how Duchamp was installed—and instrumentalized—as a father figure in the realm of postmodernist discourse.[1] Analyzing the patriarchal structure inherent in postmodernist discourse, she argues that Clement Greenberg, as the core reference of a modernist economy of meaning, was replaced by Marcel Duchamp as the center of postmodernist theory. Her book, written shortly after the heyday of the debate about postmodernism during the 1980s and at the peak of Duchamp's fame, sheds light on the power of the art historical canon and the problem represented by the often uncritical reproduction of this canon by critics and theorists. From today's perspective, when Duchamp's star has somewhat faded and been eclipsed by, say, the star of Andy Warhol, Jones's book remains a valid tool to deal with inherent hierarchies guiding historiography.

Duchamp was, in fact, the dominant figure of the discourse from the 1960s to the early 1990s, principally in the United States. Jasper Johns was among those who implicitly and explicitly referred to his work. Duchamp's retrospective in 1963 at the Pasadena Art Museum, curated by Walter Hopps, was widely discussed and established him as the cornerstone of contemporary art history, where he still remains today. Joseph Kosuth insisted on Duchamp's authority when he declared in the late sixties, "all art (after Duchamp) is conceptual (in nature), because art only exists conceptually."[2] In fact, around 1970, most theoreticians agreed that his legacy had informed Conceptual Art. In the words of Ursula Meyer in her seminal book *Conceptual Art,* "Conceptual Art completed the break with traditional aesthetics that the Dadaists, and notably Marcel Duchamp, initiated."[3] In 1989, David Carrier would state, "art which does not acknowledge the pre-eminence of Duchamp and Warhol these days is likely to be misread as positively reactionary."[4]

But Duchamp's reception was not unanimous, and some critics and artists beginning in the early 1960s were very well aware of the ambivalent role played by—or attributed to—Duchamp in the realm of the art world. For instance, Thomas Hess, editor of the then highly influential review *Art News,* ironically called Duchamp "St. Marcel" in an essay his magazine published in the summer of 1960.[5] However, during the sixties and early seventies only a few artists overtly criticized Duchamp, namely Allan Kaprow and Robert Smithson. I had met Kaprow on various occasions in the late nineties in preparation for my book on Happening and Land Art.[6] Since the influence of Duchamp's exhibition installations—notably the *Twelve Hundred Coal Bags Suspended from the Ceiling over a Stove* in the *Exposition Internationale du Surréalisme* in the Galerie des Beaux-Arts in Paris in 1938, and the *Sixteen Miles of String* in the exhibition *First Papers of Surrealism* in 1942—on his environments such as *Yard* (1961) seemed obvious, I asked him about his relation to Duchamp. He told me that he had received a letter from him but had discarded it, so it was now missing in the archive, much to the regret of scholars.[7] (In fact, it is still in his archive, now owned by the Getty Center, and it is about a recommendation for a grant, written by Duchamp to Kaprow in 1962). When I asked him if he and Duchamp had ever met, he told me that he encountered him by chance in a staircase.[8] I am sure that this was a kind of readymade answer, which alluded to Duchamp's famous painting *Nude Descending A Stair Case*. In his biography *Childsplay,* Jeff Kelley quotes Kaprow, who recalls that Duchamp, apparently attending the performance of Kaprow's *A Spring Happening* with Max Ernst, Hans Richter, and Richard Huelsenbeck, was, as he says, "leaping nimbly out of the way."[9]

I mention these anecdotes to indicate that the genealogy many historiographers wish to establish, namely "Duchamp—Cage—Kaprow—Conceptual Art," might be too much of a simplification. For example, Paul Schimmel wrote in the catalogue of the 2006 Kaprow retrospective in Los Angeles, "Marcel Duchamp was also influential, but not as an objectmaker; rather, he was meaningful for his relationship to the found object and for the relationship of his life ... to his art."[10] While I am more interested in differences than in similarities, I believe that the impulse to relate to historical father figures like Duchamp is today less legitimate than in the 1980s. There is no real need to define and defend a neo-avant-garde against what, in the 1980s, was seen as a merely market-driven revival of painting, sculpture, and figurative modes of representation. Furthermore, the position of Duchamp in the art historical realm need not be fought for anymore. Even in the German-speaking academe once reluctant to accept the heritage of Duchamp, he has become part of the art historical canon. He certainly recovered from the banishment by Joseph Beuys, who declared in an early-sixties performance that "the silence of Marcel Duchamp is overrated."

The main differences between Kaprow and Duchamp are, I would argue, the following: first, Kaprow's skepticism toward chance. Unlike Duchamp and later Cage, who was his teacher in the late 1950s, Kaprow was not interested in chance. His Happenings were well planned, carefully outlined in a written "score," and then rehearsed. Their specific beauty lies in composition, so to speak; in other words, in timing, in contrast, in tension. Structurally they are related to play, to experiment, but not to chance. Chance as such was uninteresting to Kaprow because it is rooted in a naturalistic attitude, in the idea that the forces of nature, gravity for instance, or decay over time, can be taken for granted and form a kind of horizon of what happens in the realm of art. A second difference between Kaprow and Duchamp lies in Kaprow's critical relation to authorship. Unlike Duchamp who stood for a pre-modern, quasi-religious, and authoritarian structure of a single artistic master who is interrelated to other masters, to sponsors, and to disciples—a structure typical of romantic artists groups up until the time of the Surrealist groups—Kaprow was interested in the modernist division of labor. He was always engaged in academic teaching at universities, working on educational boards, dealing with grants, positions, and structures of higher education. He advocated the "professionalization" of the artist, or, as he put it in an essay, for the "artist as a man of the world." Unlike Duchamp, he did not believe in the idea that artists will be "discovered" by posterity. In his words: "[The artist] must put up or shut up, succeed in conveying their own vision in reasonably good time or consider giving up the attempt."[11]

A third difference resides in the use of language. Unlike Duchamp's rhetoric based on mystery, on puns, on ambivalence, allusions, metaphors, and various layers of hidden meaning, Kaprow's rhetoric remained transparent and pragmatic. He talked overtly and clearly about his intentions and, as a trained art historian, not only tried to influence interpretation as Duchamp did, but also to insert and contextualize it in a theoretical framework. This was an attitude that many fellow artists such as Claes Oldenburg rejected and that earned him much criticism. After his own retrospective at the Pasadena Art Museum, in 1967, four years after Duchamp's exhibition, *Artforum* published an unusually harsh critique, stating that Kaprow was "less an artist than ... a phenomenon": "The Kaprow phenomenon belongs essentially to the history of art. He has made his objectives not only clear but virtually transparent: he has at every opportunity talked about himself and his intentions, to the point where ... the mystery has gone out."[12]

Robert Smithson, more than Kaprow, liked to polemically criticize his colleagues, be it Donald Judd, Andy Warhol, or Robert Morris. And also, more than any other artist, he chose Duchamp as his prime target. In December 1967 he published his illustrated essay, "A Tour of the Monuments of Passaic" in *Artforum*. While ostensibly a trip to the periphery of New York during which he looks at construction sites as if they were picturesque Roman ruins, it was a critique of a contemporary art in which every monument is transformed into an emblem of an artistic problem. A highlight of his excursion is the description of the "Fountain Monument," which consists of a series of rusty pipes through which water is pumped into the river. Smithson's comment: "The great pipe was in some enigmatic way connected with the infernal fountain. It was as though the pipe was secretly sodomizing some hidden technological orifice, and causing a monstrous sexual organ (the fountain) to have an orgasm. A psychoanalyst might say that the landscape displayed 'homosexual tendencies,' but I will not draw such a crass anthropomorphic conclusion. I will merely say, 'It was there.'"[13]

The "Fountain Monument" is an obvious allusion to Duchamp's *Fountain,* certainly one of the most reproduced works of art in the 1960s. Of course, it is not an interpretation, nor a comment on Duchamp. But is it a general attack on the iconography and especially the rhetoric of Surrealist art and its key figure, Duchamp. "A Tour of the Monuments of Passaic" belongs to a series of trips, both to the suburbs of New York and to more remote places such as the American desert, Florida, and Mexico that Smithson undertook in the late 1960s and turned into works of art. In 1969 he traveled to Yucatan, mainly to Palenque. The results of this trip were presented in a 1972 slide conference at the University of Utah, in Salt Lake City. Smithson served as a visiting professor at the Architecture School—apparently only for one day—and spoke to the students. His conference did not deal with the famous Maya ruins as his audience probably expected, nor did he relate to the Mexican murals, which were widely discussed among artists during that time. Rather he talked about the rundown hotel in the tourist village near the ruins in the jungle. According to Nancy Holt, who reconstructed Hotel Palenque after Smithson's death as an individual work of art—it is now in the collection of the Guggenheim Museum in New York—Smithson had always planned to transform the lecture into a work of art and therefore taped his presentation.[14]

His conference leads the audience through the different states of the building. The snapshots he took with his Instamatic never show the building as a whole. The fragmented view corresponds to its state. Although the hotel is running—Smithson and his company are staying there—it is halfway between a construction site and a ruin. How it is supposed to look when finished and what the original plan was, if such a plan exists at all, remains an open question. Since the construction seems to advance very slowly, some of the unfinished parts are already in decay. Furthermore, a newer part of the hotel seems to be gradually overlapping an older part. Under the already ruinous structures of the construction there are even older remnants, which might have belonged to an earlier building. These parts, which are actually completed, such as the turtle pool in the lobby, look strange in the context of the chaotic surrounding.

Smithson comments on the slides like an expert. He assumes to role of the connoisseur who makes playful associations between the floor pattern and a painting by Frank Stella, an unfinished room and a "Jasper Johnsian simplicity." A pile of garbage looks to him like a floor sculpture by Robert Morris, and a pile of cement bricks reminds him of a "Stack" by Donald Judd. The performance ends with a mysterious green door, obviously the barn door from Duchamp's *Étant donnés: 1. La chute d'eau, 2. Le gaz d'éclairage*. In his words, interrupted on the original tape by the laughter of the students: "This is sort of the door.... The door probably opens to nowhere and closes on nowhere so that we have to leave the Hotel Palenque with this closed door and return to the university of Utah."[15]

At that time, in 1972, Smithson was at the peak of his fame and made some of his most radical statements. Among others, he renounced participating at Documenta 5 in Kassel, and accused the curator, Harald Szeemann, of "cultural confinement." Duchamp was included posthumously in this seminal exhibition, which prepared the ground for his triumphant reception in Europe, marked notably by the retrospective in Paris immediately after the inauguration of the Centre Georges Pompidou, in 1977, curated by Jean Clair. Around that time Smithson was interviewed by Moira Roth, which was published posthumously in 1973 in *Artforum*. Smithson recalled that Duchamp had been a key figure of American discourse since the Armory Show. What Matisse and Picasso were for what he called the "hard-core modernism" of the pre-war area, Duchamp was to the postwar area. It is interesting to note that Smithson used the notion of "postmodernism"—which in the field of visual culture came into general use only in the late 1970s—when he said that "Duchamp is really more in line with post-modernism insofar as he is very knowledgeable about the modernist traditions but disdains them."[16] He ironically disdained the Duchamp cult of the sixties and early seventies as "Duchampitis." And he attacked less the victims of this disease, in his eyes namely Johns and Morris, than Duchamp himself. In his view, Duchamp's art was not about the dematerialization of the object and the critique of the commodification of art, but rather about mystifying the alienated objects, tending "to transcend production itself in the ready-mades when he takes an object out of the manufacturing process and then isolates it."[17] This interpretation moves Duchamp towards an aristocratic conception of art, a conception that disdains the process of work as such. In opposition to his own attitude, an attitude that he conceived as "dialectical," Smithson considered Duchamp representative of just such an aristocratic conception of art, which manifested itself in his predilection for chess, his condescension of the American handicraft tradition and American naiveté, as well as the "French wit," which he differentiated from the English "sense of humor."

In Smithson's view, Duchamp was popular in the art world because he added value to objects—in other words, the very opposite to his own idea that "art should eliminate value, not add to it."[18] For Smithson, Duchamp reactivated the pre-modern illusion, the quasi-alchemistic transformation of dirt into gold. And the readymade played the key role. It was the opposite of, as he put it, Sol LeWitt, who did not turn dirt into gold, but rather gold into dirt, when he proposed "to put a piece of Cellini's jewelry into a block of cement."[19] In Smithson's eyes, Duchamp was perpetuating the religious functions of art that compensated for what Smithson called the "guilt even about being an artist,"[20] which was typical of modernism. Smithson saw Duchamp as an artist who attributed spiritual meaning to consumer objects, as, in his words, "a spiritualist of Woolworth"[21] and as "a kind of priest of a certain sort. He was turning an urinal into a baptismal font. My view is more democratic and that is why the pose of priest-aristocrat that Duchamp takes on strikes me as reactionary."[22]

Smithson's comparison of Duchamp and Greenberg is interesting, especially since it is one rarely made. In his words: "Greenberg is opting for high art or modernism from a more orthodox point of view, but Duchamp seems to want to be playful with that modernism."[23] Smithson's perspective of Duchamp as a playful variety of modernism is in stark contrast to the conventional conception of Duchamp as a radical critic of the modernist canon. Smithson refutes Duchamp's "mechanistic," or "Cartesian," view of the world. "I don't happen to have any mechanistic view of the world so I really can't accept Duchamp in terms of my own development."[24] In conclusion, he compares Andy Warhol, whom he also considers "mechanistic," with Duchamp, by stating "Andy Warhol saying that he wants to be a machine is this linear and Cartesian attitude developed on a simple level. And I just don't find it very productive."[25]

Kaprow and Smithson differed from Duchamp in the sense that they did not adhere to a key element of modernist and postmodernist economies of meaning, namely the transformation of ordinary objects into valuable objects by means of art; or, in other words, what Arthur C. Danto labeled the "Transfiguration of the Commonplace." Both Kaprow and Smithson aimed at reinstalling the function of the artist in society, in articulating specific functions and roles for the artists, not outside, but within society. In their view, Duchamp was not an announcement of the new, but the ghost from the past, not an agent of change, but a screen where anachronistic illusions about the potential of artists were projected.

Notes

[1] Amelia Jones, *Postmodernism and the En-Gendering of Marcel Duchamp,* Cambridge, Mass. 1994.

[2] Joseph Kosuth, "Art after Philosophy," *Studio International,* vol. 178, no. 915 (October 1969), reprinted in Ursula Meyer, *Conceptual Art,* New York 1972, pp. 155–70, here p. 162.

[3] Ibid., p. ix

[4] David Carrier, "Art History and Its Beguiling Fictions," *Art International* 9 (Winter 1989), pp. 36–41, here p. 38.

[5] Thomas B. Hess, "Mixed Mediums for a Soft Revolution," *Art News* 59, no. 4 (Summer 1960), pp. 45, 62; reprinted in Steven Henry Madoff, ed., *Pop Art: A Critical History,* Berkeley 1997, pp. 10–11, here p. 10.

[6] Philip Ursprung, *Grenzen der Kunst: Allan Kaprow und das Happening, Robert Smithson und die Land Art,* Munich 2003.

[7] Allan Kaprow, in conversation with Philip Ursprung, Encinitas, CA, October, 1997.

[8] Ibid.

[9] Jeff Kelley, *Childsplay: The Art of Allan Kaprow,* Berkeley 2004, p. 57.

[10] Paul Schimmel, "'Only memory can carry it into the future': Kaprow's Development from the Action-Collages to the Happening," in *Allan Kaprow: Art as Life,* ed. Eva Meyer-Hermann, Andrew Perchuk, and Stephanie Rosenthal, London 2006, pp. 8–19, here pp. 11, 14.

[11] Allan Kaprow, "The Artist as a Man of the World," *Art News* 63 (1964), reprinted in Allan Kaprow, *Essays in the Blurring of Art and Life,* ed. Jeff Kelley, Berkeley 1993, pp. 46–58, here p. 49.

[12] Jane Livingston, "Allan Kaprow, Pasadena Art Museum," *Artforum,* vol. 6, no. 3 (November 1967), pp. 65–66, here p. 65.

[13] Robert Smithson, "The Monuments of Passaic, Has Passaic replaced Rome as the Eternal City?" *Artforum,* vol. 6, no. 4 (December 1967), reprinted under the title "A Tour of the Monuments of Passaic, New Jersey," in Robert Smithson, *Collected Writings,* ed. by Jack Flam, Berkeley 1996, pp. 68–74, here p. 71.

[14] Nancy Holt, in conversation with Philip Ursprung, Galisteo, New Mexico, October 1997.

[15] Robert Smithson, "Hotel Palenque," *Parkett* 43 (1995), pp. 117–32, here p. 132.

[16] "Robert Smithson on Duchamp, Interview with Moira Roth" (1973), *Artforum,* vol. 12, no. 2 (October 1973), reprinted in Smithson, *Collected Writings* (note 13), pp. 310–12, here p. 310. See also the longer version of the interview: Moira Roth, "An Interview with Robert Smithson (1973)," ed. Naomi Sawelson-Gorse, in *Robert Smithson,* organized by Eugenie Tsai with Cornelia Butler, exh. cat. Museum of Contemporary Art, Los Angeles, Berkeley 2004, pp. 80–94.

[17] Ibid., p. 310.

[18] Robert Smithson, "A Refutation of Historical Humanism," manuscript, 1966–67, Estate of Robert Smithson, in Smithson, *Collected Writings* (note 13), pp. 336–37, here p. 336.

[19] Robert Smithson, "Entropy and the New Monuments," *Artforum,* vol. 4, no. 10 (June 1966), reprinted in Smithson, *Collected Writings* (note 13), pp. 10–23, here p. 12.

[20] Ibid.

[21] "Robert Smithson on Duchamp" (note 16), p. 310.

[22] Ibid., p. 312.

[23] Ibid., p. 310.

[24] Ibid., p. 311.

[25] Ibid.

Herbert Molderings

The Green Ray
Marcel Duchamp's Lost Work of Art

The Green Ray, now lost, formed part of the "Hall of Superstition" in the exhibition *Le Surréalisme en 1947* at the Maeght Gallery in Paris.[1] In October 1946, a few weeks after Duchamp's return to Paris from a holiday trip with Mary Reynolds to Lake Geneva, during which the sight of the Forestay waterfall had inspired a new and labor-intensive work, *Given: 1. The Waterfall, 2. The Illuminating Gas* (pp. 4–5), André Breton asked him to collaborate with him on the concept for a new international exhibition of Surrealism. The theme was to be the visualization of the new myth that had long been germinating in international Surrealist art and, to quote the foreword of the catalogue, "had only yet to be defined and summarized through us."[2] Duchamp suggested prologuing the exhibition with a "salle malgré eux," a room with the works of "Surrealists in spite of themselves," those historical forerunners of Surrealism, such as Hieronymus Bosch, Arcimboldo, Blake, and others, and epiloguing it with a kitchen.[3] Neither of these two suggestions was realized, nor was the suggestion that the main exhibition room be constructed in the form of a labyrinth. What *was* agreed upon were the idea of a "Hall of Superstition," in which the vast multitude of popular superstitions could be visualized, and the concept for a "Rain Room," in which several artificial rain curtains hung down from the ceiling into moss-filled gutters. Duchamp left Paris on January 13, 1947 and returned to New York, where, together with the exhibition designer Frederick Kiesler and Roberto Matta, he immediately began working on a concrete design for the "Hall of Superstition." The result of their brainstorming was to invite various Surrealism-inclined artists living in New York and its environs to design certain figures of popular superstition for this exhibition hall: David Hare, Joan Miró, Max Ernst, Enrico Donati, and Yves Tanguy and his wife Kay Sage.

When it was finally realized, the exhibition hall, which according to several exhibition reviews was immersed in a "mysterious greenish-blue light,"[4] centered around Max Ernst's *Le lac noir, source de l'Angoisse* (The Black Lake, Source of Anguish), out of which grew a *Cascade architecturale* (Architectonic Cascade) of canvas and a transparent picture, on which Miró had painted hieroglyphs of superstition. Hovering alongside the latter was a painting by Tanguy consisting of three interlapping canvases and entitled *L'échelle qui annonce la mort* (The Ladder Heralding Death) (fig. 1). The paintings were accompanied by totem-like sculptures: a skeletal *L'homme-angoisse* (Anguished Man) fabricated by David Hare from wire and plaster of Paris from a sketch done by Frederick Kiesler and posted in sentry fashion on the edge of Max Ernst's *Lake,* Kiesler's *La main blanche* (The White Hand), a tall white plaster of Paris sculpture in the form of an obscene finger gesture that seemed to dominate the space of the exhibition hall (fig. 2) and, lastly, the *Totem des religions* (Totem of All Religions), a piece fabricated by Kiesler and the sculptors Étienne-Martin and François Stahly from driftwood and bearing, instead of a head, "the sign of the hand against the evil eye,"[5] this taking the form of an eye object by Enrico Donati that looked down upon the visitors from the ceiling. Located in several places in the textile outer membrane of the room were cut-out openings in which either a painting

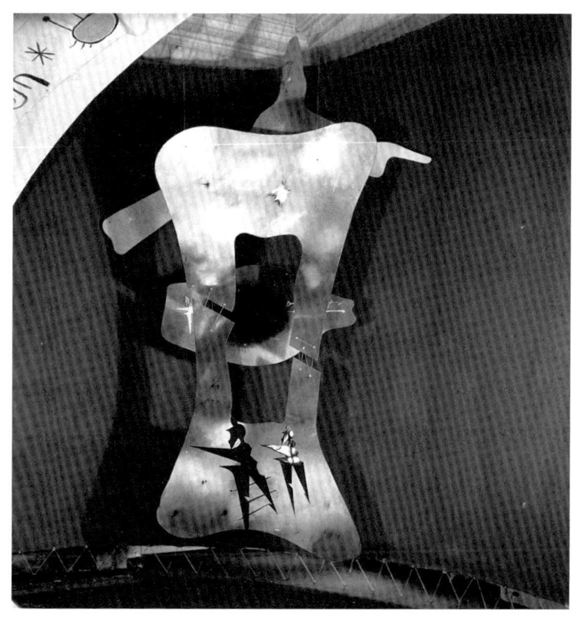

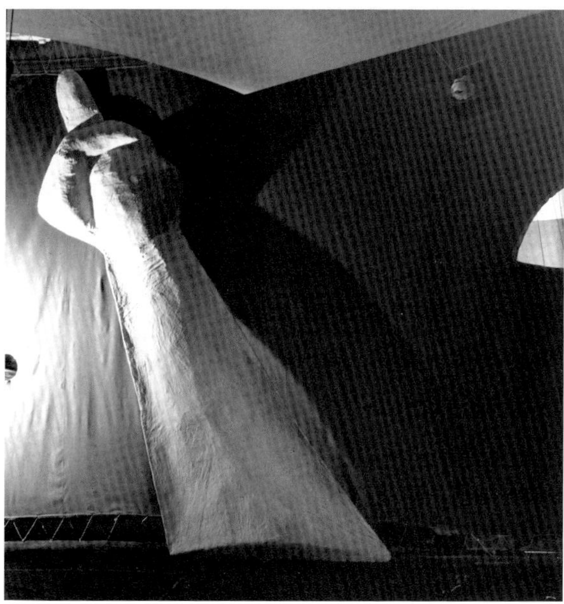

1 Yves Tanguy, *L'échelle qui annonce la mort* (The Ladder Heralding Death), exhibited in *Le Surréalisme en 1947*, Galerie Maeght, Paris 1947. Photograph by Denise Bellon. **2 Frederick Kiesler, *La main blanche. Figue anti-tabou*** (The White Hand: Anti-Taboo Fig). On the right-hand corner *Le mauvais œil* (The Evil Eye) by Enrico Donati, on the left hand *Le Rayon vert* (The Green Ray) by Marcel Duchamp. Exhibited in *Le Surréalisme en 1947*, Galerie Maeght, Paris 1947. Photograph by Denise Bellon.

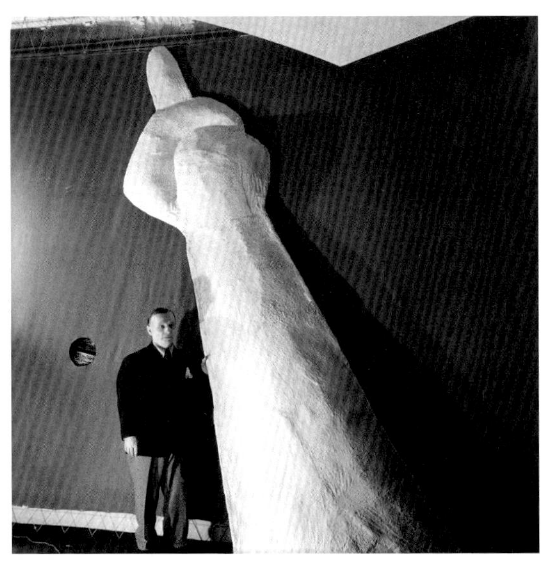

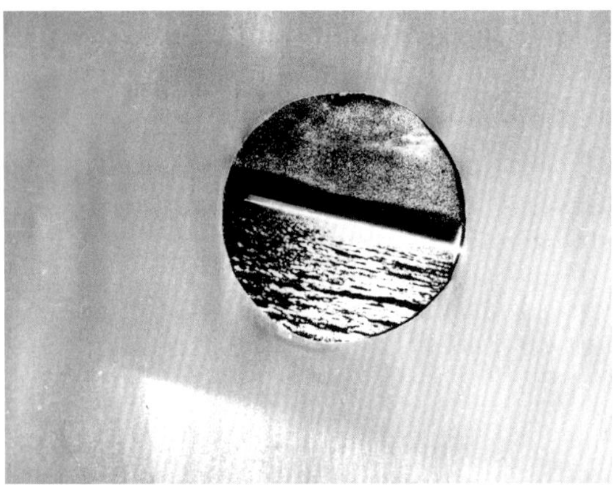

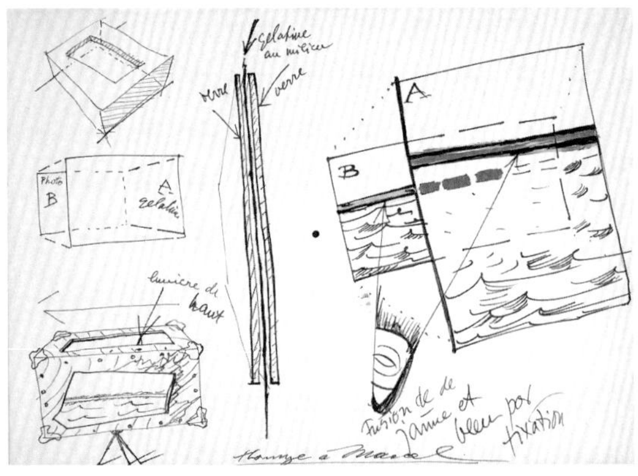

3 **Marcel Duchamp, *The Green Ray*** (next to Frederick Kiesler and his sculpture *The White Hand*). Exhibited in *Le Surréalisme en 1947*, Galerie Maeght, Paris 1947. Photograph by Denise Bellon, © les films de l'équinoxe-fonds photographique Denise Bellon, Paris. 4 **"Un hublot laisse passer *le rayon vert* de Marcel Duchamp"** ("A porthole lets Marcel Duchamp's *Green Ray* pass through it"), exhibited in *Le Surréalisme en 1947*, Galerie Maeght, Paris 1947, destroyed. Photograph by Denise Bellon. 5 **Frederick Kiesler, *Hommage à Marcel,*** study for *The Green Ray* of Marcel Duchamp, ink and opaque watercolor on paper, 25.2 x 35.4 cm, 1947. Philadelphia Museum of Art. Purchased with the Katharine Levin Farrell Fund, 1992.

disappeared in parts, such as Roberto Matta's *Whist,* a painting of a hybrid creature of owl, raven, and woman, or through which a painting exhibited behind it could be viewed, one such painting being Max Ernst's *Euclid* of 1945 as a representation of the superstition of beauty. An opening in the wall next to Kiesler's sculpture *The White Hand* (fig. 2) was described in the exhibition catalogue as follows: "Un hublot laisse passer le *Rayon vert* de Marcel Duchamp" (A porthole lets Marcel Duchamp's *Green Ray* pass through it).[6]

Having disappeared after the close of the exhibition, probably dismantled into its component parts like most of the other installation objects of the exhibition, Duchamp's *Rayon vert* was mentioned in several reviews of the exhibition, though none of the critics described it with any accuracy. It is known to us only through sketches and through photographs of the exhibition.[7]

Clearly recognizable in one of these photographs, to the left of Kiesler and his sculpture *The White Hand,* is the mysterious porthole in the form of a circular cutout in the backcloth that formed the rear wall of the exhibition hall and through which one could see the photograph of a sea view (fig. 3). The sloping horizon suggests the tossing of a boat on a billowing ocean, an impression, however, that is belied by the evidently calm surface of the water. Taking Kiesler's head as a measure of size, the diameter of the circular cutout may be estimated at about sixteen centimeters.[8] In a close-up of the object (fig. 4) one can perceive, roughly on a level with the slightly sloping horizon, above which hovers a strange, dark stratum of air, a brightly flashing streak of light. While the black-and-white photograph naturally does not tell us its color, the streak of light is very probably green. Its appearance can only be explained by the fact that a slit must have been cut in the photograph at the level of the horizon, thus permitting the passage of light from a lamp placed behind it. On some photographs one can clearly make out a white cable that disappears behind the backcloth. Shining through the backcloth is a rectangular shape, slightly wider than it is high, running parallel with the slope of the horizon and measuring approximately twenty-three by twenty-five centimeters. It is evidently a wooden panel or box, onto or into which the "photo object"—the term coined by Marcel Jean in his *Histoire de la peinture surréaliste* of 1959 to describe the "Green Ray"[9]—had been mounted.

But how did the "Green Ray" actually work? How was this "photo object" constructed? An ink and watercolor drawing by Kiesler, which was not published until 1988 and is now in the care of the Philadelphia Museum of Art, makes the reply to this question more difficult rather than easier (fig. 5). It shows a suitcase mounted on a tiny tripod, the front side of which has a cutout rectangular—not circular—window. This window (A) was to be provided with a "gelatine" and the rear inside wall of the case with a photograph of a sea view (B). While on the photograph of the sea view a yellow line was to be painted in watercolor on a level with the horizon, a blue line was to be painted on the "gelatine" at the same height. By bringing the two lines into congruence, the viewer would mix the blue and the yellow together to yield green ["fusion de jaune et bleu par fixation"]. The "gelatine" was to be placed between two panes of glass in order to give it greater stability. What was probably meant by "gelatine" was either a celluloid or an acetate film, materials with which Duchamp was quite familiar, for he had had the reproductions of his glass paint-

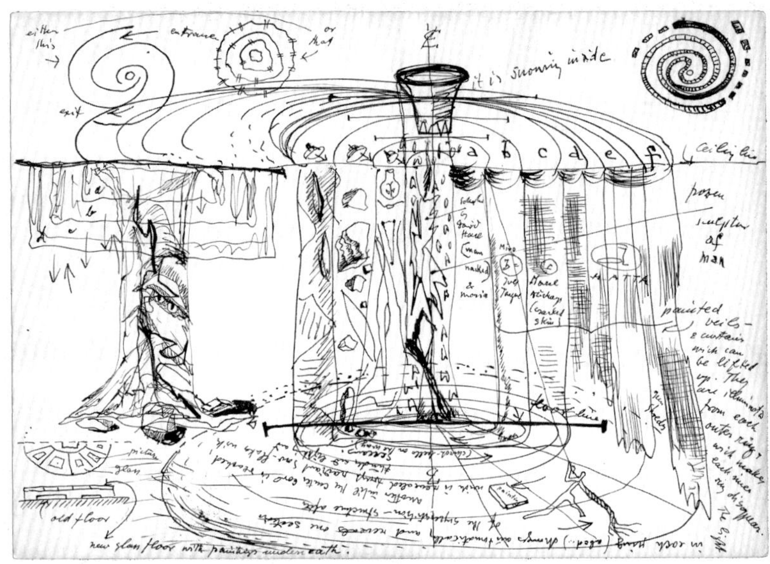

6 Frederick Kiesler, *Study for the Hall of Superstition,* ink on paper, 42.7 x 31.6 cm, February–March 1947. The Austrian Frederick and Lillian Kiesler Private Foundation, Vienna.

ings printed on them for his *Box in a Valise* in 1939. The necessary brightness was to be obtained by shining artificial light into the suitcase through a window cut into its top side ("lumière de haut"). The title "Rayon vert" does not appear anywhere on this 25.2-x-35.4-cm-large drawing. While it bears the dedication "Hommage à Marcel," the drawing is, regrettably, not dated. This drawing is evidently just a sketched idea and not a working drawing, for it is obvious that with a light source from above and an additive color mixing process it is impossible to mix yellow and blue to make green.

There are several pieces of circumstantial evidence that indicate that this drawing belonged not to the first design phase of Duchamp's, Kiesler's, and Matta's "Hall of Superstition," but to a second one. On March 15, Duchamp wrote the following to Breton from New York: "Kiesler and I are very busy. Kiesler has already drawn the main outlines for this hall—most of the things must simply be sent over or found in Paris."[10] As Duchamp wrote these words, he evidently still had in mind a design concept that he was to reject soon afterwards. The "main outlines" mentioned in the letter have survived in the form of a large-format, hitherto unpublished pen-and-ink drawing in the archives of the Kiesler Foundation in Vienna (fig. 6). The drawing, measuring 42.7 x 31.6 cm, clearly shows that the "Hall of Superstition" was originally to comprise a spiral labyrinth, in the center of which was to stand that "nude figure" about which Duchamp wrote the following in another, albeit undated letter to André Breton: "Kiesler thinks the center of the Hall of Superstition should take the form of a transparent pillar in 'plastic,' into which one might place a kind of plaster of Paris sculpture of a nude figure, though more in a skeletal sense (but without looking like a skeleton), and that around this center should be built a labyrinth of transparent tulle or gauze on which certain kinds of superstition could be painted or drawn."[11] Those artists who did in fact produce works in the ultimately realized "Hall of Superstition" have mostly been named already on the pen-and-ink drawing: David Hare (who was to build the nude figure), Matta, Yves Tanguy, Miró, and Duchamp. However, the work mentioned after Duchamp's name is not a "Green Ray" but a "cracked skin." This probably referred to that mysterious piece of leather that can be seen on Kiesler's photomontage *Poème espace dédié a H(ieronymous) Duchamp* of 1945 in the magazine *View* (fig. 7),[12] though it is also possible that Duchamp was already experimenting as early as March 1947 with the covering of plaster of Paris castings with leather. In a letter to his then lover, Maria Martins, on July 11, 1947, for example, Duchamp writes, "The skin is in the press until tomorrow morning."[13] Originally, her works were to be placed next to his in the "Hall of Superstition," for her name appears on Kiesler's drawing next to Duchamp's.[14] In the ultimately realized exhibition, however, Maria's bronze sculptures, *Le chemin, l'ombre, trop longs, trop étroits* and *Impossible,* were not shown in the "Hall of Superstition" but in the central exhibition hall, which was called the "Rain Room" or "Salle des épreuves."[15]

Within the spiral labyrinth "it is snowing," while on the wooden floor a second "glass floor with paintings underneath" was to be laid and, hanging over it, "painted veils and curtains" that would reach up to the ceiling and could be "lifted up. They are illuminated from each outer ring which makes each inner ring disappear. The light in each ring (abcd...) changes automatically and reveals one section of the superstition after another until the center core is reached which is revealed through radiant saw-flakes with thunder and lighting and screams (church-bells on the way)." A ring of "green shreds" was to be suspended close to the floor. As one can see, this sketch dating from the first half of March was far removed from the design of the "Hall of Superstition" as finally realized at the Maeght Gallery during the period from the beginning of June onwards.

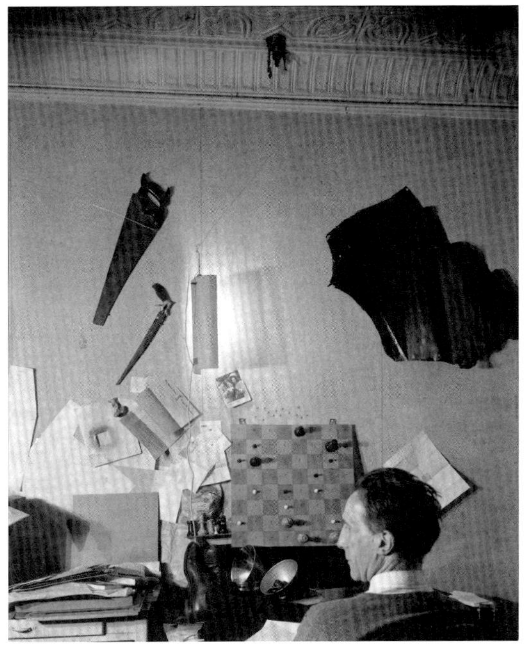

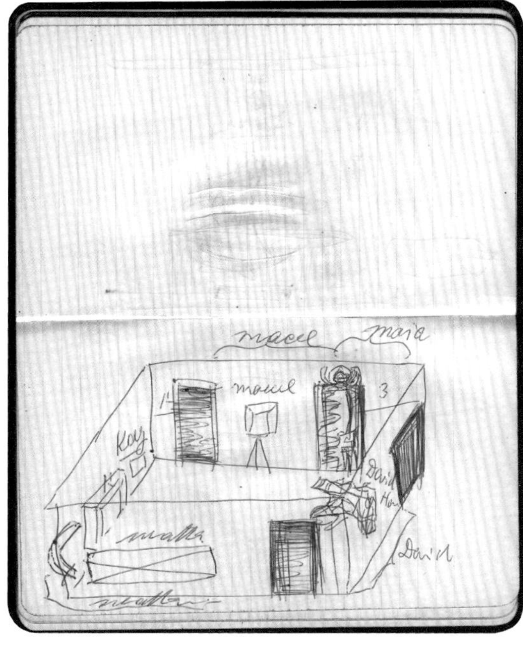

7 Photograph of Marcel Duchamp, used for Frederick Kiesler's photomontage *Poème espace dédié a H(ieronymous) Duchamp* of 1945. **8 Drawing from Frederick Kiesler's notebook, *Voyage à Paris,*** showing an early plan for the "Hall of Superstition," ballpoint pen on paper. The Austrian Frederick and Lillian Kiesler Private Foundation, Vienna.

Note pour Kiesler
the valise will come later—
The black paper cut out is
to go in front of the gelatine
to give a "port hole" effect.
The
will you have the valise
cut roughly in the same
circular shape —
—Light inside the valise
(what about the heat?)
—Distance between gelatine
and the back view 10 cent.
roughly—

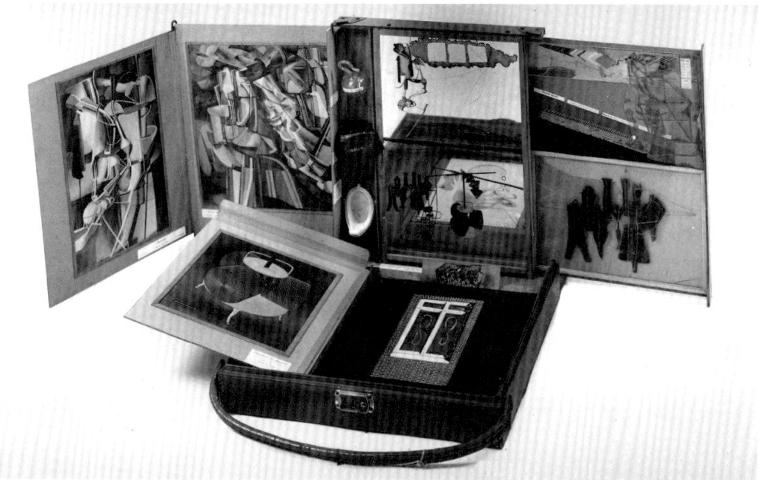

9 Marcel Duchamp, Note pour Kiesler, pencil on paper, 20 x 12.2 cm, 1947. Private collection. **10 Deluxe Edition of *The Box in a Valise (From or by Marcel Duchamp or Rrose Sévaly),*** no. 18/20, 1948. Private Collection. **11 Marcel Duchamp, *Réflection à main*** (Hand Reflection), pencil on paper with collage of a mirror behind a circular cutout of

The tripod-mounted suitcase peepshow sketched by Kiesler in his *Hommage à Marcel* is also depicted in a sketch, likewise hitherto unpublished, in a notebook kept by Kiesler on the journey to Paris and during their work there (now also in the care of the Kiesler Foundation in Vienna) (fig. 8). In this sketch, the exhibition room is outlined as a simple box-like room, in which only the positions of the planned works or groups of works are indicated. Here, too, Matta, Kay Sage, and David Hare are mentioned, and "Marcel" and "Maria" are again to exhibit next to one another, an entire wall having been reserved for them.

In June 2001, the Paris auction house Hôtel Drouot auctioned as part of an ordinary catalogue of *Le Surréalisme en 1947* a "Note pour Kiesler," written by Duchamp, containing more detailed information on the construction of the *Rayon vert* and making mention, for the very first time, of the idea of cutting a circular "porthole" in the front side of the suitcase instead of a rectangular opening (fig. 9). The note, which is written in pencil on one half of a sheet of notepaper, reads as follows: "Note *pour Kiesler* / the valise will come later—The black paper cut out is / to go in front of the gelatine / to give a 'Port hole' effect. / [Here Duchamp makes a sketch of the suitcase with a cutout porthole, in which a line labeled 'rayon vert' marks the horizon] will you have the valise / cut roughly in the same / circular shape - / - Light inside the valise / (what about the heat ?) / - Distance between gelatine / and the back view *10 cent.* / roughly." Drawn in pencil on the back of the sheet is not quite half a circle. The sheet also bears two traces of glue and black paper, the latter being the black paper mentioned in the note. The note had evidently been glued to the "black paper cut-out" at its four corners. Unfortunately the other half of the sheet on notepaper, which probably contained further instructions, has not survived.

How do the two sketches—Kiesler's *Hommage à Marcel* and Duchamp's *Note pour Kiesler*—tally with the visual evidence furnished by the photographs of the *Green Ray*? Evidently Duchamp had indeed planned to provide the suitcase with interior illumination

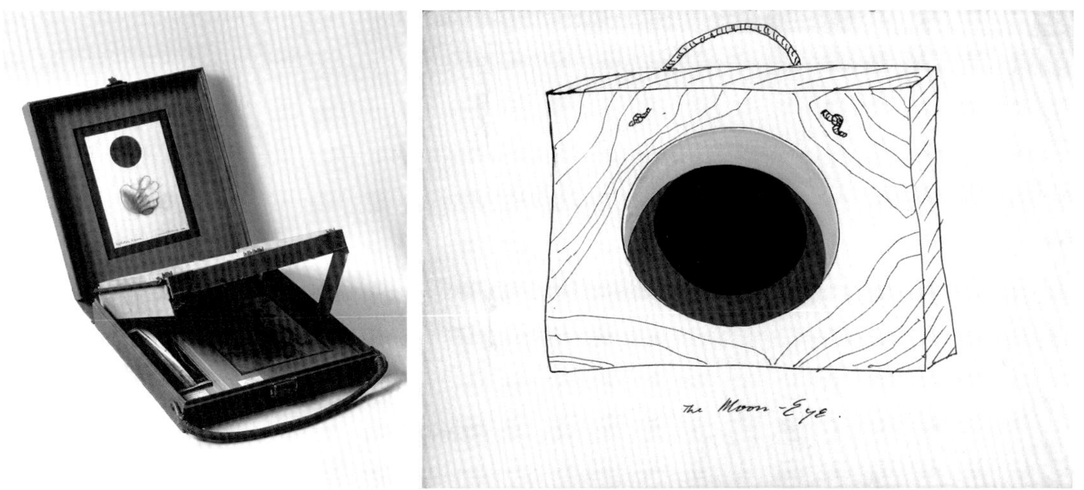

23.5 x 16.5 cm, 1948, in the deluxe edition of *The Box in a Valise (From or by Marcel Duchamp or Rrose Sélavy)*, no. 18/20, 1948. Private Collection. **12 Frederick Kiesler, *The Moon Eye,*** study for the "Hall of Superstition," ink and gouache on paper, 25.5 x 33.9 cm, 1947. The Austrian Frederick and Lillian Kiesler Private Foundation, Vienna.

in the form of a green ray of light on the level of the horizon created by the fusion of a yellow and a blue line. Kiesler's drawing does not show a porthole. This idea evidently did not occur to Duchamp until after Kiesler's departure for Paris on May 27, which meant that he had to send his friend the abovementioned "note" from New York. From his message, "the valise will come later," we may assume that Duchamp did not have any old suitcase in mind, for Kiesler could have purchased such a one on the spot. Duchamp was evidently thinking of an empty specimen of his *Box in a Valise,* the kind of suitcase, in other words, that Kiesler had exhibited five years earlier in a peepshow-like *Vision Machine* in the exhibition *Art of this Century* at the Peggy Guggenheim Gallery. The use of this suitcase as a vehicle for the presentation of new artworks was nothing new for Duchamp in 1947. Since 1941 he had been mounting original works in the lids of the deluxe editions of this leather suitcase (fig. 10).[16] By 1947 Duchamp had already equipped as many as thirteen suitcases of this kind with original works. *Valise* no. 10/20, for example, contained the original design of the back cover created jointly by Duchamp and Kiesler for the issue 2–3 of the magazine *VVV,* the famous "Twin Touch Test."[17] In 1948, Duchamp produced a drawing featuring another circular "paper cut-out," behind which he placed a real mirror in which the viewer could see himself when looking at the drawing (fig. 11).[18] The structural and formal similarity between this drawing, which was titled "Réflection à main," and the *Green Ray,* both being presented in a suitcase as *mises-en-scène* of complex visual phenomena, is obvious. If one opens any one of the leather cases and lifts the miniature, wood-framed *Large Glass* in an upright position, one can look through the transparent cellophane, through the *Large Glass,* onto the respective original work mounted in the inside lid of the case. The depth of the case as indicated in the "note pour Kiesler"—"Distance between gelatine / and the back view *10 cent.* / roughly"—corresponds exactly to the depth of the leather suitcases used for the *Box in a Valise,* namely 10.5 cm. Kiesler was evidently so enthusiastic about Duchamp's "note" that he set about designing a suitcase object of his own: *The Moon Eye,* a work visualizing the ancient superstition that the moon is the eye of a god (fig. 12). As far as I know, the object was never made, probably because space was needed in the "Hall of Superstition" for Enrico Donati's *Evil Eye* object.

As the "note pour Kiesler" clearly proves, the *Green Ray* retained an open, experimental character right up until its ultimate installation. Duchamp's question concerning the light bulb inside the suitcase—"What about the heat?"—suggests that he had not made a prototype of the object while in New York, which meant that important technical questions had yet to be resolved. Once Kiesler had draped the "Hall of Superstition" with fabrics, there was evidently no longer any place in this relatively dark room for a single, easily knocked-over object on a tripod. In his "Manifeste du Corréalisme" of 1949, Kiesler described the aesthetic principle behind his interior design as follows: "In this 'Hall of Superstition' there were no longer any rectangular or oval paintings, no more artworks, *no more spherical or cubic boxes* [my italics].... In the world of Correalism, a picture becomes architecture, a sculpture becomes a picture, and architecture becomes color without losing integrity in the process."[19] This was no doubt the reason why it was decided, probably mutually, to abandon the idea of a suitcase on a tripod and to cut a "porthole" in the backcloth that formed the rear wall of the hall, to mount the photograph of the "back view" behind it and to illuminate it with a sufficiently strong light source. Neither personal recollections nor surviving documents have furnished any information as to how the color of the green ray was created, and from the surviving photographs of the *Rayon vert* it is not possible to tell whether there were in fact two picture planes placed one behind the other or whether only one single photograph was finally installed. Was a green light bulb simply placed behind a slit cut into the horizon line on the photograph? Equally impossible to answer is the question whether the *Green Ray* was permanent or flashed only at intervals. The fact that none of the artists involved in the building-up of the exhibition can remember having seen the *Green Ray* suggests that it flashed only intermittently and very rarely.

Like all of Duchamp's works, the *Green Ray* is a complex work despite its ephemeral nature and is closely bound up in many ways with his biography and with the iconography of his oeuvre as a whole.

Time does not permit me, unfortunately, to deal in detail with the optical phenomenon of the *Green Ray* and with the history of the scientific research it has generated.[20] Suffice it to say the following: The green ray is a rare atmospheric phenomenon that appears after sunset for the duration of no more than the bat of an eyelid. One's best chance of seeing it, whether as a shimmer, a flash or a bundle of rays, is by the sea when the sky is clear and there is absolutely no wind. The rare optical phenomenon is caused by a refraction of the sun's light. This refraction is at its strongest when the sun is close to the horizon, and it is there that the last segment of the setting sun is split into its spectral colors, such that there is a red, a green, and a blue rim of the sun. This splitting increases towards the horizon, but even there it is only a few arc-seconds small. As the red rim is the first one to sink below the horizon, the green and the blue rim remain above the horizon for a very short time. In very good weather conditions, both the green and the blue rims can be seen, but the pollution of the atmosphere normally weakens the blue light, thus rendering only the green rim visible—and for a few seconds only—as a green flash.

With his light-and-photo installation *Le rayon vert* Duchamp attempted neither to reproduce this natural phenomenon as illusionistically as possible nor to analyze and present it in scientific manner. His interest was first and foremost in the legends associated with it, entirely in keeping with the theme of the "Hall of Superstition." This was precisely the theme, too, of Jules Verne's novel *Le Rayon vert,* published in 1882 (figs. 13 & 14).[21] The novel tells the story of a young woman by the name of Helena Campbell who braves every possible danger in order to catch sight of this light phenomenon off the coast of Scotland. A newspaper had reported that it was "a most wondrous green, a green which no artist could ever obtain on his palette, a green of which neither the varied tints of vegetation nor the shades of the most limpid sea could ever produce the like! If there be green in Paradise, it cannot but be this shade, which most surely is the true green of Hope!"[22] This beautiful girl is engaged to a wealthy geologist called Aristobulus Ursiclos, who had studied physics, chemistry, astronomy, and mathematics at the universities of Oxford and Edinburgh. But in order to be sure of her decision, Helena will not marry Aristobulus until she has seen the Green Ray, for the latter "tallied with an ancient legend, which till now she had never been able to understand. It was one of the numerous inexplicable legends of the Highlands, which avers that this ray has the virtue of making him who has seen it impossible to be deceived in matters of sentiment; at its appearance all deceit and falsehood are done away, and he who has been fortunate enough once to behold it is enabled to see closely into his own heart and to read the thoughts of others."[23] For weeks on end, in the company of her uncles and guardians Sam and Sib and her fiancé Aristobulus, Helena sails up and down the coast of Scotland in her quest for the Green Ray. On their travels they meet the painter Olivier Sinclair, who immediately falls in love with Helena and joins the expedition. The story now evolves into a contest between the scientist and the artist for the affection of the young woman. The contest reaches its climax in a heated discussion between the three protagonists about the nature of the Green Ray. While the young woman sees its origin in the mythology of the ancient Scottish bards, interpreting it as "the scarf of some Valkyria with its fringe trailing in the water on the horizon,"[24] the scientist describes it simply as an optical illusion, as "the natural result of the crimson of

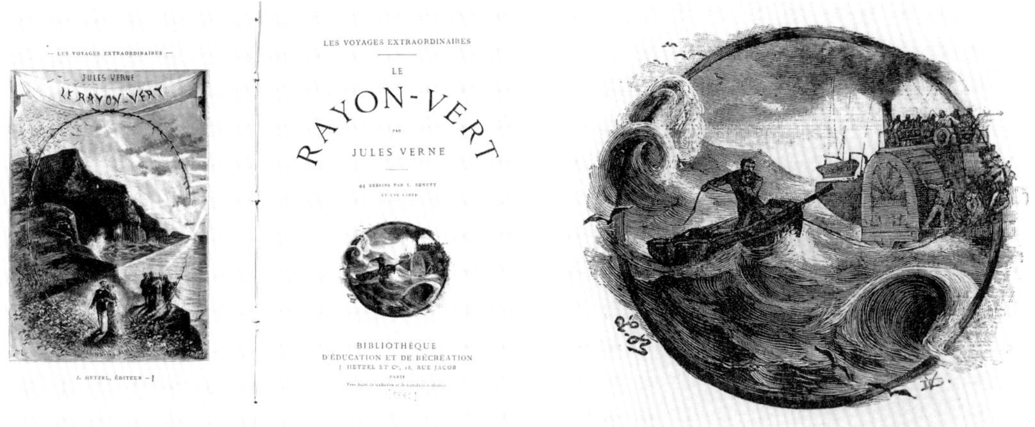

13 Jules Verne, *Le Rayon vert* *(The Green Ray)*, frontispiece and title page, 2 of 44 drawings by L. Benett. Bibliothèque d'éducation et de récréation, Paris: J. Hetzel, 1882. **14 L. Benett, Jules Verne's *Le Rayon vert,*** close-up of the drawing on the title page.

the sun's disk ... which leaves its impression on the retina of the eye, for in optics green is the complementary color of crimson."[25] Helena, beside herself with rage about the scientist's prosaic "physical arguments," is rescued by the artist, who sarcastically recommends that the scientist concern himself with other, as yet unexplored subjects, such as "the question of the influence of fishes' tails on the undulation of the sea" or "the influence of wind instruments on the formation of tempests."[26] After this debate the contest is over and the scientist has lost. "To have stripped her ray of its poetry, to have materialized her dream, to have changed the scarf of a Valkyria into a horrid optical phenomenon! Perhaps she might have forgiven him anything but this."[27] When the Green Ray at last appears, Helena fails to catch sight of it because at that very moment she has eyes only for her new lover, the painter. Perfect happiness reigns, the two marry and the story ends like a Hollywood movie. Asked by her husband whether she regrets not having ever seen the Green Ray, Helena replies, "We have seen something better still!... We have seen the happiness [in the original French novel Jules Verne writes 'le bonheur même'—happiness itself] which the legend attaches to the observation of that phenomenon! And since we have found it, my dear Olivier, let us be content, and leave to those who have never yet known it the search for the Green Ray."[28]

If we now related Jules Verne's novel to Duchamp's biography of the years from 1945 until 1947, we would discover a multitude of resonances. Like Helena Campbell, Duchamp also believed, in 1946 at the age of almost sixty years and after decades of erotic frustration, that he had at last found "happiness itself." A letter written at that time to his lover, Maria Martins, reads as follows: "You must know me well enough by now to realize that for the first time in my life I find myself accepting you completely as you are without my feelings of rebellion of any kind, and it has at least been granted to me to love you simply and purely, i.e. without the vaudeville farce that generally accompanies the trials and tribulations of two lovers."[29]

Jules Verne describes Helena Campbell as a woman with two personalities: "De Maistre has said, 'There are in me two beings: myself and another.' The 'myself' of Miss Campbell was serious and thoughtful, looking upon life from the point of view of its duties rather than of its rights. The 'other' was a romantic being, somewhat prone to superstition, fond of the marvelous tales which sprang up so naturally in the land of Fingal ... The brothers [her guardians] loved Miss Campbell's two personalities equally well, but it must be confessed that if the first charmed them by her good sense, the second occasionally embarrassed them with her unexpected remarks, her capricious flights of imagination, and her sudden excursions into dreamland."[30] It was such a conflict of two beings that Duchamp claimed to have recognized in the personality of his lover, Maria Martins, as we can read in his letters to her. On the one hand there was the "serious and thoughtful being," the woman who conscientiously performed her duties as the wife of an ambassador and the mother of three daughters, and on the other there was the "artistic and romantic being." Between the years of 1946 and 1951 he repeatedly urged her in his letters to liberate herself from the social constraints of her marriage and her entourage and to decide in favor of her true self, as he saw it, her artistic self: "You are condemned and damned to suffer unnecessarily, and that is the tragedy of your situation," was Duchamp's diagnosis. "The net you are caught in is now of such thick rope that not even a razor blade could cut you free. I suffer, my little one, more than you, because I could save myself if I were in your position but can do nothing except talk to you through the holes of the net. I am seized by blind rage every time I think not only of us but just of you as a living being created for a higher destiny, such as you feel it deeply yourself, and whose fulfillment is refused you as when drowning in a dream and *unable* to reach the branch that is near."[31]

The liberation envisaged by Duchamp consisted in Maria's leaving her husband and daughters and renting the studio next to his: "that would really be the beginning of our monastery. You could isolate yourself here with me, and nobody would be aware that this cage away from the world even existed."[32] Trying to convince her that inwardly she felt just as he did, he would ply her with "capricious flights of imagination" and "sudden excursions into dreamland," as Jules Verne put it much less cryptically. "I thought about us a good deal," he writes in one of his love letters. "How simple life is when there is only the inner self to think about. So I took a trip inside your inner self, and I found what I had thought would be there, having guessed by external contact only—I found 'things' that would have no name even in the most poetic language. We must live by these 'things' and these 'things' alone. The rest, mere physical survival, must be reduced to a minimum."[33]

The recognition of such resonances in Jules Verne's novel was naturally reserved for Marcel Duchamp alone. None of the visitors to the *Le Surréalisme en 1947* exhibition could have known anything about them. The hermetic habit of always narrating on two levels, one being closed and private, the other open and publicly accessible, is typical of Marcel Duchamp and runs like a thread through his entire oeuvre. Duchamp's method is an extreme form of *allegoreuein,* of "saying something else." Words said in public are spoken in code. Their private meaning is known only to the author. Outwardly, the installation "A porthole lets Marcel Duchamp's *Green Ray* pass through it" was merely a reference to Jules Verne's popular novel, which, entirely in keeping with the general theme of the "Hall of Superstition," was concerned with, among other things, the superstitious expectations that a young woman had associated with the perception of a rare natural optical phenomenon. Moreover, the contest between the artist and the scientist for the affections of the said young woman—described by Jules Verne in page after page of not unkitschy prose—also reads like the parable of a more general and widespread conflict that has been an ever recurring theme of modern literature and art since the middle of the nineteenth century. Scientific analysis and technological advancement are gaining a grip on ever more areas of life, ousting its mythical traditions and, by the same token, the essentially poetic instincts of life. Duchamp's stance in this conflict was unequivocal. "Art is the only thing left for people who don't give science the last word," he concluded towards the end of his life.[34] Duchamp shared the sarcasm of his fellow artist in the novel, for his art had, after all, always sought to give life back its poetic and playful dimensions and "to discredit [science], mildly, lightly, unimportantly."[35]

As Duchamp explained on several occasions, it was Raymond Roussel's literary method of inventing fictitious events using words having the same sounds but different meanings that in 1912 had inspired his work *The Bride Stripped Bare by her Bachelors, Even.*

Homonyms serve in his notes on the *Large Glass* as "hinge words" that allow the reader's imagination to slide unwittingly from one sphere of meaning into another. One of the most significant resonances in the iconography of the *Large Glass* is based on the homonyms "verre," "vert," and "vers": glass, green, and verse. Glass replaced canvas in Duchamp's painting after 1913, while the *Large Glass* was conceived as a two-part work of "verre" and "vers," of images and words, the happenings graphically represented on the glass being described but not explained.

The color of green played an important role in Duchamp's personal mythology. A "chambre verte" in his parental home in Blainville, a bedroom that was always kept locked and, in keeping with an ancient local tradition, reserved for possible visits from the owner of the house, Baron d'Hachet de Montgascon, had rendered green the color of secrecy and mystery for Duchamp ever since his youth, for the young Marcel's only chance of seeing this bedroom was afforded by peeping through the keyhole. [36] Greenish, too, is the color of the illuminating gas that serves to activate the erotic desire of the Bachelors. Also green is the box of notes and sketches on *The Bride Stripped Bare by Her Bachelors, Even,* which Duchamp published as a limited edition in 1934. A greenish glint appears on the horizon of the *Large Glass.* When Duchamp visited the collector Katherine S. Dreier in 1936 and repaired the *Large Glass,* which had been cracked in transit five years previously, he inserted on the horizon separating the world of the Bachelors from the domain of the Bride three narrow strips of glass, two of which were green, the other one clear. Depending on the angle of view, a green ray of light glints momentarily on the horizon. This horizon is also referred to in the notes in the *Green Box* as the "garment of the Bride,"[37] a reference that cannot but make us think of Helena Campbell's interpretation of the Green Ray in Jules Verne's novel: "the scarf of some Valkyria with its fringe trailing in the water on the horizon." Thus it was that a *rayon verre* had become identical with a *rayon vert* in Duchamp's oeuvre long before he realized his "Rayon vert" in the exhibition of 1947. In Jules Verne's mythography, the color of the Green Ray is the "true green of Hope." For his part, Duchamp hopes that true love has at long last entered his life in the person of Maria Martins, the true love that flashes on the horizon of the ocean viewed through the porthole in the wall of the "Hall of Superstition." "Pour Maria, enfin arrivée" is the dedication written by Duchamp in the *Green Box (The Bride Stripped Bare by her Bachelors, Even)* which he gave to his beloved in Paris in 1946.[38] The similarity in sound between Maria and Mariée is obvious.

The horizon on which, in the repaired *Large Glass,* a green light flashes momentarily also has a part to play in another work of Duchamp's in the exhibition *Le Surréalisme en 1947.* According to his notes and sketches, Duchamp had originally planned to place on this horizon a dancing figure that defied the laws of gravity and would be called "Soigneur de gravité" (Juggler of Gravity) or "Juggler of Centers of Gravity."[39] Breton had selected this figure, which in the end was never featured in the *Large Glass,* as one of the beings "susceptibles d'être doués de vie mythique,"[40] to which an altar ["autel"] had been erected in the "Salle des alvéoles" (Hall of Honeycombs), though it was probably not without some gentle persuasion on Duchamp's part that this had been made possible (fig. 15). The altar, built by Roberto Matta and Frederick Kiesler, was based on a still then unpublished sketch of Duchamp's dating from 1913–14[41] and depicting a bistro table balancing on one of its

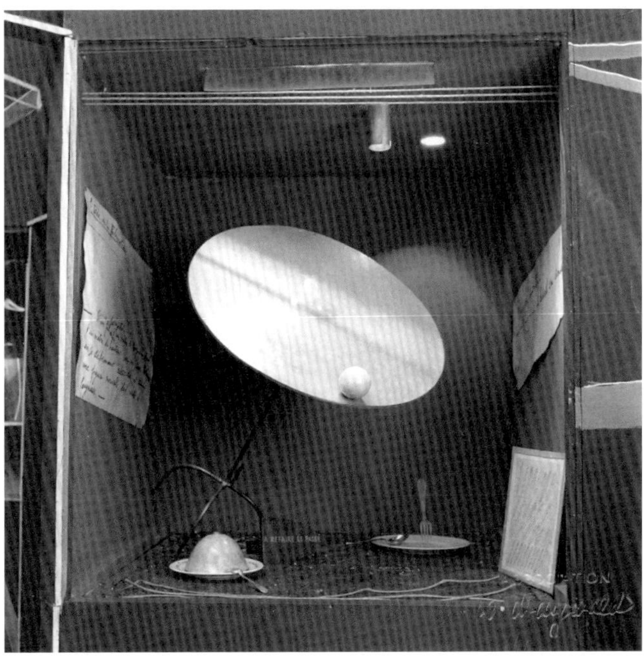

15 Altar of Duchamp's *Juggler of Gravity,* executed by Frederick Kiesler and Roberto Matta, exhibited in *Le Surréalisme en 1947*, Galerie Maeght, Paris, 1947. Photograph by Willy Maywald.

legs and making a white billiard ball roll down its sloping top, but without its dropping over the edge. Standing or lying on the floor of the altar were diverse "dishes" ["mets"] and sacrificial offerings ["offrandes"] for the mythical being:[42] a dessert bowl in the shape of a woman's breast, offered by Henri Goetz,[43] a "golden plate with 5 grams of sunlight" from Jacques Hérold,[44] a mental patient's drawing of several rows of baguettes sacrificed by the painter and psychiatrist Frédéric Delanglade, and a kitchen grater and "golden metal gratings" from Benjamin Peret.[45] By far the most interesting sacrificial object was an iron bearing the inscription "REFAIRE LE PASSÉ" on its base. According to Breton's records this had been contributed by Patricia Matta, Roberto Matta's wife, who in New York had taken part in many of the preparatory discussions for the Paris exhibition.[46] Very probably she had been inspired by Duchamp's play on words[47]—"Le fer à repasser sert à refaire le passé"—and had given the iron, thus inscribed, to her husband to take with him as a sacrificial offering for the altar. The inscription "refaire le passé" definitely originates from Duchamp himself, for at that time no outsider knew anything about what was actually going on in Duchamp's life or in his art. For the past six months or so, Duchamp had already been secretly working on the concept of his "sculptural construction" *Étant donnés: 1° La chute d'eau, 2° le gaz d'éclairage,* in the center of which was to be a "Notre Dame de désirs," based on a casting of the nude torso of his lover Maria Martins. Inspired by their love affair, Duchamp had dug out the notes he had made for the *Bride Stripped Bare by Her Bachelors, Even,* a project he had abandoned in 1923, and begun to extend its concept in a new, three-dimensional, sculptural form, now realizing those intentions that he had failed to implement in the *Large Glass.*[48] One of the most important figures in this regard had been the "Juggler of Gravity."[49]

In 1939 Duchamp had presented in the *London Bulletin* a research project that was suspiciously similar to the one suggested by the painter in Jules Verne's novel to the scientist as a ridiculing comment on his "physical arguments": "Determine the difference between the volumes of air displaced by a clean shirt (ironed and folded) and the same shirt when dirty."[50] Such deliberations were part and parcel of Duchamp's reflections on the "infra-thin perceptions" that had been preoccupying him since 1936. However, unlike the subject matter suggested by the painter to his scientist rival in the novel *The Green Ray,* namely the question of "the influence of fishes' tails on the undulation of the sea" or that of "wind instruments on the formation of tempests," the category of the "infra-thin" ["infra-mince"]

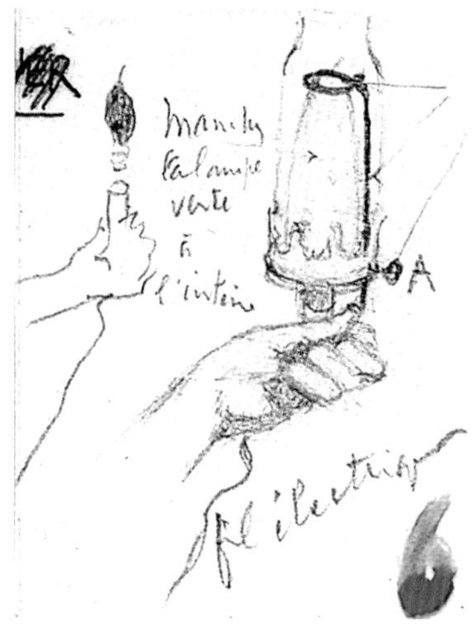

16 Marcel Duchamp, Bec Auer, sketch in *Manual of Instructions for the assembly of Étant donnés : 1° La chute d'eau 2° Le gaz d'éclairage*, Philadelphia Museum of Art 1987 (English re-edition 2009), page 38.

is concerned with barely perceptible phenomena that are nevertheless real, such as, for example, "the warmth of a seat (which has just been left) in infra-thin" or the "infra-thin separation between the detonation noise of a gun (very close) and the apparition of the bullet hole in the target ..."[51] The term serves to designate those differences between identical objects or processes that are virtually imperceptible by our sense organs without the aid of measuring instruments, those infinitely small differences that denote two different individual things, which language, in its generalizing tendency, treats as identical.

Given the fact that the green ray in Jules Verne's novel—as in nature—makes only very rare and extremely short appearances, it may indeed have counted among those "infra-thin perceptions" on the boundary between the visible and the invisible that were preoccupying Duchamp at the time when he was making preparations for the exhibition *Le Surréalisme en 1947,* a likelihood verified not least by Duchamp's design of the back cover of the magazine *View* (1945) and by his conversations with Denis de Rougemont.[52] Thus it is that Thierry Davila, in his thesis "De l'inframince. Brève histoire de l'imperceptible dans l'art moderne et actuel" of 2008, quite rightly relates the "Rayon vert" to Duchamp's speculations on "infra-thin perceptions."[53] This thesis is of course valid only if Duchamp's *Rayon vert* in the "Hall of Superstition" flashed only sporadically and disappeared virtually as quickly as it appeared. While this has not been verified by any contemporary reports furnished by visitors or by fellow artists or by anyone else involved in the exhibition, it is precisely from the absence of such reports that one might deduce that Duchamp's *Rayon vert* flashed only very intermittently and briefly. Among the notes on infra-thin phenomena left by Duchamp there is one that possibly relates directly to his work on the *Rayon vert*. On a—regrettably—undated sheet of notepaper Duchamp had jotted down a whole list of infra-thin phenomena, the first one being "A ray of light (sun) reduced to an infra-thin."[54] Among the other infra-thin phenomena on the list were differences in color when "attenuated" by transparency, and the "Spider web as an example of the 'natural' isolation of a carcass (pseudo-geometric) of infrathin."[55] That Duchamp mentally associated the phenomenon of the green light with his "category of the infra-thin" is proved by one of the creative decisions he took while working on *Étant donnés: 1° La chute d'eau, 2° le gaz d'éclairage*. When in the early sixties he completed the installation of the lighting system for this "sculptural construction," it was a green-painted light bulb that he placed in the yellowish-orange mantle of the bec Auer gas lamp held by the naked woman towards the viewer's peeping gaze (fig. 16). For the viewer, the greenish tinge of the lamplight is an infra-thin perception *par excellence*, for it is so fine that the viewer sees it without perceiving it, that is to say, without being conscious of the nuance of color. Eluding the direct gaze of the viewer, it is the same kind of phenomenon as the "transparency 'attenuating' the colors into infrathin." Thus the historical background of the evolution of *Étant donnés*—from 1946 to 1966—comes full circle, beginning with the first visible manifestation of the *Rayon vert* in 1947 and ending with the apparition of the green light, on the boundary between visibility and invisibility, in the mantle of the bec Auer gas lamp.

Translated from the German by John Brogden

Notes

[1] This paper consists of extracts from my essay "Le bonheur même. À la recherche du *Rayon vert* de Marcel Duchamp" published in the magazine *Retour d'y voir*, no. 3 & 4 (2010), pp. 9–55, of the Musée d'art moderne et contemporain in Geneva.

[2] *Le Surréalisme en 1947. Exposition internationale du surréalisme. Présentée par André Breton et Marcel Duchamp*, Paris 1947, p. 19.

[3] See letter from Marcel Duchamp to André Breton of July 18, 1947, in *Affectionately, Marcel: The Selected Correspondence of Marcel Duchamp*, ed. Francis M. Naumann and Hector Obalk, London 2000, p. 169.

[4] Described by Charles Estienne in his exhibition review "Surréalisme et peinture," in *Combat*, July 8, 1947. Archives of the Austrian Frederick and Lillian Kiesler Private Foundation.

[5] Quoted from Kiesler's description on the back of a photograph of the "Totem of All Religions," the Austrian Frederick and Lillian Kiesler Private Foundation, Inv. No. PHO 935/2.

[6] Exhibition catalogue, p. 1. Not to be confused with the catalogue *Le Surréalisme en 1947*, in which the work is mentioned only by its title as part of the Salle de Superstition in a footnote to Kiesler's essay (note 2, p. 134).

[7] The photographs were first published in Herbert Molderings, *Marcel Duchamp. Parawissenschaft, das Ephemere und der Skeptizismus*, Frankfurt am Main 1983, pp. 85–86, and not in 1987 as erroneously stated by Arturo Schwarz in *The Complete Works of Marcel Duchamp*, 3rd revised and expanded edition, New York 1999, vol. 2, p. 789.

[8] The diameter of 28 cm as indicated by Arturo Schwarz, ibid, p. 788, is much too large if we compare the size of the porthole with Kiesler's head.

[9] Marcel Jean, *Histoire de la peinture surréaliste*, Paris 1959, pp. 342–43.

[10] Quoted from auction catalogue *André Breton 42, rue Fontaine*, Calmels Cohen, vol. "Manuscrits," Paris, April 11–12, 2003, no. 2282, p. 204.

[11] Ibid, p. 207–8.

[12] *View*, "Marcel Duchamp" issue, series 5, no. 1, 1945, pp. 26–28. See also Michael Taylor, *Marcel Duchamp: Étant donnés*, exh. cat. Philadelphia Museum of Art, Philadelphia and New Haven 2009, p. 402.

[13] Quoted from Taylor, *Marcel Duchamp* (note 12), p. 404.

[14] In Kiesler's essay "L'Architecture magique de la salle de superstition" in the exhibition catalogue (note 2, p. 134), Maria Martins is also named among those artists who contributed to the "Hall of Superstition."
[15] See exhibition review by Denys Chevalier in *Arts*, July 11, 1947. Archives of the Austrian Frederick and Lillian Kiesler Private Foundation.
[16] See *Marcel Duchamp Die große Schachtel: De ou par Marcel Duchamp et Rrose Sélavy*, ed. Ecke Bonk, Munich 1989. pp. 258–97.
[17] Ibid., pp. 280–81.
[18] First published in Molderings, *Marcel Duchamp. Parawissenschaft* (note 7), p. 77.
[19] Frederick Kiesler, *Manifeste du Corréalisme ou Les états unis de l'art plastique*, Paris 1949, n.p.
[20] See in particular Marcel Joszef Minnaert's book, *Light and Colour in the Open Air*, London 1940 (republished under the title *The Nature of Light & Colour in the Open Air*, New York 1954), which had been reviewed in that very year—1947—in *The Meteorological Magazine*, no. 76, pp. 67–69. For further reading see my essay "Le bonheur même. À la recherche du *Rayon vert* de Marcel Duchamp" (note 1), pp. 35–36.
[21] Jules Verne, *Le Rayon vert*, 44 dessins par L. Benett et une carte, Paris 1883.
[22] Ibid, pp. 17–18. Both this and the following quotations in English have been taken from Jules Verne, *The Green Ray*, trans. M. de Hauteville, Holicong, PA 2003.
[23] Ibid., p. 18.
[24] Ibid., p. 115.
[25] Ibid., p. 116.
[26] Ibid.
[27] Ibid., p. 117.
[28] Ibid., 172.
[29] Taylor, *Marcel Duchamp* (note 12), p. 404.
[30] Verne, *The Green Ray* (note 22), p. 13.
[31] Taylor, *Marcel Duchamp* (note 12), p. 418.
[32] Ibid., p. 412.
[33] Ibid., p. 406.
[34] Dore Ashton, "An Interview with Marcel Duchamp," *Studio International*, vol. 171, no. 878, June 1966, p. 245.
[35] Pierre Cabanne, *Dialogues with Marcel Duchamp*, New York 1971, p. 39.
[36] See Patrice Quéréel, *Prendre Duchamp (Marcel) ... à R(r)ouen*, Rouen 2000.
[37] See *The Writings of Marcel Duchamp*, ed. Michel Sanouillet and Elmer Peterson, New York 1989, p. 67.

[38] See Francis M. Naumann, *Étant donnés: 1°Maria Martins 2°Marcel Duchamp,* Paris 2004, pp. 25–26.
[39] See *Marcel Duchamp, Notes,* presentation and translation by Paul Matisse, Centre national d'art et de culture Georges Pompidou, Paris 1980, n.p., notes 149 and 152.
[40] Quoted from *Le Surréalisme en 1947* (note 2), p. 136.
[41] See *Marcel Duchamp, Notes* (note 39), note 149.
[42] Arturo Schwarz wrongly assumes in his catalogue raisonné (note 7) that the "offerings" in Duchamp's "altar" were selected by Duchamp himself and thus interprets them with reference to Duchamp's notes for the *Large Glass.* However, Breton's notes in his dossier on the 12 "altars" give us to understand that these objects were in fact chosen by other artists. See auction catalogue *André Breton 42, rue Fontaine* (note 10), no. 2282: "12 chemises titrées par André Breton des 12 autels de l'exposition surréaliste à la Galerie Maeght en 1947," p. 206.
[43] Ibid., p. 2006.
[44] See Sarane Alexandrian, *Jacques Herold,* Paris 1995, p. 83.
[45] See *Le Surréalisme en 1947* (note 2), p. 140.
[46] See auction catalogue *André Breton 42, rue Fontaine* (note 10), p. 2006.
[47] Another spontaneous pun with "faire/fer," made by Duchamp in 1945, is mentioned in Denis de Rougemont's memoirs: "Nous avons fini hier par un petit jeu de questions et réponses écrites simultanément. Ma première question était: '*Qu'est-ce que le génie?*' Marcel lit sa réponse: '*L'impossibilité du fer*'. Et il ajoute: 'Encore un calembours, évidemment.'" Denis de Rougemont, "Marcel Duchamp mine de rien," *Preuves,* no. 204 (February 1968), p. 45.
[48] For further reading see Herbert Molderings, "Un cul-de-lampe: Réflexions sur la structure et l'iconographie d'*Étant donnés,*" *Étant donné Marcel Duchamp,* no. 3 (2001), pp. 92–111.
[49] Regarding the semantic connection between the horizon of green glass, the "garment of the Bride" on the *Large Glass,* and the *3 Standard Stoppages,* which play a central role in the "Altar" of the "Juggler of Gravity," see Herbert Molderings, *Kunst als Experiment. Marcel Duchamps "3 Kunststopf-Normalmaße,"* Munich and Berlin 2006, pp. 64–66 and idem: *Duchamp and the Aesthetics of Chance. Art as Experiment,* New York 2010, pp. 54–56.
[50] Marcel Duchamp, *London Bulletin,* no. 13 (April 15, 1939), p. 12.
[51] *Marcel Duchamp, Notes* (note 39), note 4.
[52] De Rougemont, "Marcel Duchamp mine de rien" (note 47), pp. 45–46.
[53] Thierry Davila, "De l'inframince. Brève histoire de l'imperceptible dans l'art moderne et actuel," thesis directed by Eric Michaud, funded by the EHESS, Paris, June 24, 2008, pp. 63–64.
[54] *Marcel Duchamp, Notes* (note 39), note 24.
[55] Ibid.

Stanislaus von Moos

The Missed Encounter with Le Corbusier

Duchamp probably did not know about the little house Le Corbusier built in 1923–24 for his parents in Corseaux (figs. 2, 7, 15). Moreover, given his "intrepid and unwavering despise" of the architect,[1] a disdain that is variously documented and that arguably culminated in his somewhat moody characterization of Le Corbusier as:

> un cas de ménopause masculine précoce sublimisée en coït mental,[2]

he would have had no wish to visit it when he stayed at Lake Geneva near Chexbres and in Chardonne in 1946. As to Le Corbusier, whose perception of Duchamp was no less distant (though slightly less vicious), he considered the *petite maison* and the modifications it had undergone in the then thirty years of its lifetime topical enough as to make it the subject of a little book (*Une petite maison,* published in 1954).

The opening spread underscores the house's model character, so that even the hastiest of readers understands that what is at stake is not the house as such but what it stands for (see fig. 7). On the one hand, the issue is the "machine à habiter" whose conception is allegedly independent from the contingencies of time and place ("Le plan en poche, on a longuement cherché le terrain. On en retint plusieurs. Mais un jour, du haut des coteaux on découvrit le vrai terrain").[3] And on the other, it is the "landscape" offered from the shores of the Léman and whose spectacular "view" [vue] is the core theme around which the little house was in fact built, fusing in such a way the concept of the "machine à habiter" with that of the "machine à voir"—the dwelling with the camera.

Not by coincidence, on one of the house's emblematic photographs a pair of binoculars is randomly placed on the windowsill, as if the horizontal strip window were not enough to highlight the view across the lake as the trump of the site (fig. 2). That object, together with the centrally placed watchmaker's lamp, the spartan folding table in the middle of the picture, let alone the factory-type sliding window itself that defines the field of vision, highlights Le Corbusier's fascination with anonymous products of modern industry. Industrial "readymades" of sorts, these objects are set off against the equally anonymous presence of certain items borrowed from traditional handicrafts: a Serbian vase, two traditional peasants' chairs from his parents' household as borrowings from the world of "folklore." As documented in this photograph, the *petite maison* thus displays an inventory of objects that can't help recalling notions of industry that one could easily associate with the universe of Duchamp as well as (perhaps even more so) of Picabia.

Granted that Duchamp's verdict against what he called a "case of anticipated male menopause sublimated as mental coitus" suggests a thorough annoyance on the side of Duchamp with the architect, what then are its premises?

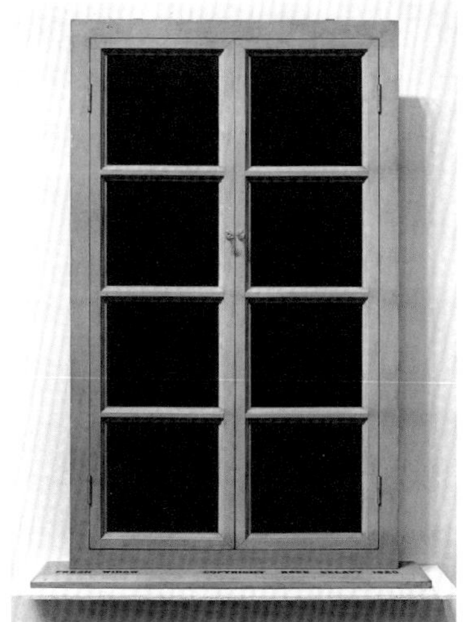

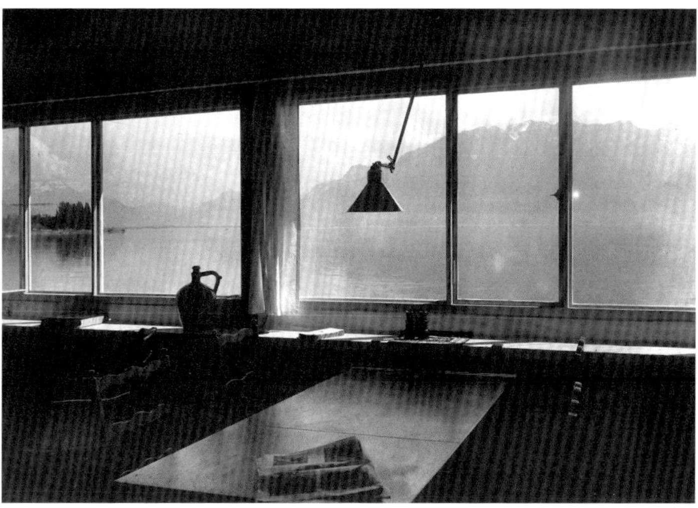

1 Marcel Duchamp, *Fresh Widow,* miniature French window, painted wood frame and eight panes of glass covered with black leather, 77.5 x 45 cm, on wood sill (1.9 x 63.3 x 10.2 cm), 1920. Museum of Modern Art, New York. Bequest of Katherine S. Dreier. **2 Le Corbusier, Villa "Le Lac," Corseaux, Switzerland,** view from the living room. Fondation Le Corbusier, Paris.

Two of them are relatively easy to spot. First, the simple traditionalism of Duchamp's views on architecture; second, the annoyance regarding the fact that the media campaign championed by Le Corbusier and Ozenfant in the 1920s so blatantly drew on certain among Duchamp's key formal and conceptual inventions, recycling them in what resembled nothing so much as a campaign of lifestyle marketing. In fact, the *Esprit Nouveau* and the many books by Le Corbusier that were assembled from its contents (*Vers une architecture, Urbanisme, L'Art décoratif d'aujourd'hui*) didn't fail to leave their impact on their contemporaries:

> .... with which it guarantees artistic pleasure and homey comforts in exchange for submitting to a few simple rules (André Thirion).[4]

Needless to say that all this hardly coincided with the role of machines and everyday objects in art as it had been practiced by Duchamp.

Duchamp's annoyance with Le Corbusier may have been all the more troubling as concepts of architectural draftsmanship—in fact: emphatically *traditional* concepts of architectural draftsmanship—had long begun to play a considerable role in his work (figs. 3 & 5).[5] While his drawing style explicitly refers to classical concepts of "perspective," the way he mounts his "objets" notoriously plays with classical notions of furniture design (the Louis XV legs of the *Chocolate Grinder* are merely an example among many). Time and again even the *objets* themselves are defined as emblematic illustrations of age-old architectural types—most blatantly so in the case of his windows and doors. With *Fresh Widow* (fig. 1), Duchamp even involuntarily anticipates Auguste Perret's critique of Le Corbusier that was indeed based on the "non-architectural" character of the *fenêtre en*

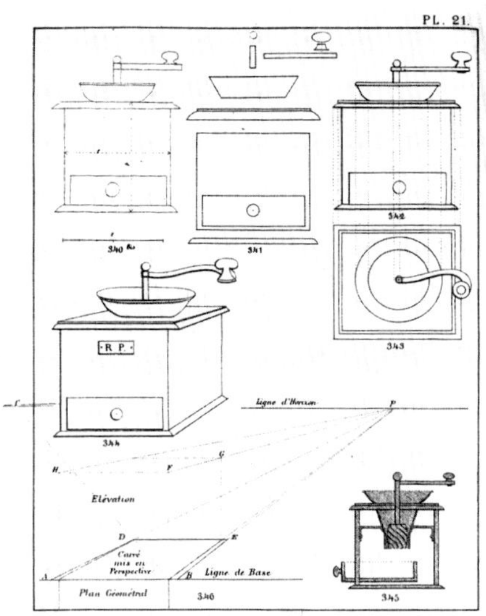

3 Plate from Ris-Paquot, cours préparatoire aux examens pour les brevets de capacité de l'enseignement primaire, Paris 1887. From Molly Nesbit, "The Language of Industry," in *The Definitely Unfinished Marcel Duchamp*, ed. Thierry de Duve, Cambridge, MA and London 1991, p. 370.

longueur which in turn is one of the principle assets of Le Corbusier's architectural program.[6] No wonder that he developed an increasingly violent opposition to what he called Le Corbusier's "Nudisme."[7]

Duchamp's view of the matter was probably not so different from the commonsense view of the vast majority among his contemporaries for whom Le Corbusier's fantasies of architecture's power to change the world were either too megalomaniac or too "childish" to be taken seriously—certainly so in the case of Le Corbusier's Plan Voisin of 1925, which proposed the wholesale demolition of the center of Paris (see fig.6).[8] Note that this occurred the very year when Duchamp and Man Ray were content to play chess on the roof of the Théatre des Champs Elysées (in Picabia's and René Clair's film *Entr'acte*). The immediate precedent and model of the Plan Voisin, the "ville contemporaine pour 3 millions d'habitants" of 1922, is nothing so much as an urbanistic extrapolation of factory production and factory efficiency seen as a goal in itself—combined with the logic of capitalism and fueled by an irritating rhetoric of *grande nation* ("grande," but "sans bras ni tête"[9]). What may have annoyed even more was the fact that the *Esprit Nouveau*'s edifying gospel reflected so many of the preoccupations Duchamp and his friends had heralded ten years previously, in their own discovery of the "New World." By the time Apollinaire's visionary statement of 1912 regarding the "iron constructions—machines, automobiles, bicycles and airplanes" as the true signs of a "style moderne" was re-proposed in the *Esprit Nouveau* under such headings as "Eyes That Do Not See" ["Des yeux qui ne voient pas"], showing ocean liners, automobiles, and airplanes as models for contemporary architectural form-giving, something essential appeared to have fallen by the wayside (fig. 9).[10] Worse: in the light of Le Corbusier's grandiloquent "Reminders to the Architects" to take seriously the advice of American engineers, but to beware of American *architects*, Duchamp's erstwhile

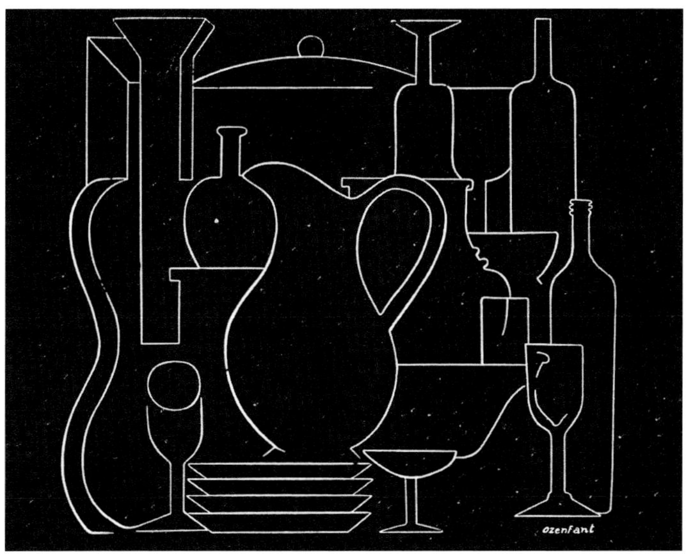

4 Amédée Ozenfant, *Still Life,* drawing, 1921, shown in the negative. From Sigfried Giedion, *Mechanization Takes Command,* New York 1948, p. 358.

statement that the plumbing and the bridges are "the only works of art America has given" seems long forgotten.[11] Moreover, the statement had come along with works that aimed at thoroughly subverting the congruency of function, name, and object, whereas Le Corbusier and Ozenfant seemed eager to reaffirm it—admittedly with a whiff of irony. The *Esprit Nouveau's* closest nudging with Dada if not with Duchamp's *Fountain* (1913) probably occurred with "Further Icons: The Museums" ["Autres icônes. Les musées"] (fig. 10).

Not only had Le Corbusier and Ozenfant long ago evicted the *Esprit Nouveau's* founding co-editor, the Dadaist poet Paul Dermée, from the board of directors, they had steered the enterprise towards more edifying goals, in fact into what must have looked more and more like an agency for lifestyle marketing, thus compromising (or so it appeared) the paternity of Guillaume Apollinaire.[12] Duchamp's collage *Sapolin Enameled* can be interpreted in multiple ways, yet with *L'Esprit Nouveau* in view one can't help reading it as an anticipation of some topical themes in Le Corbusier's own later promotion of "La loi du Ripolin" (the law of whitewash) as the key to a new architecture.[13] One of the best-known spreads from *L'Esprit Nouveau* is altogether symptomatic in this context. The montage illustrates Le Corbusier's version of Marinetti's comparison of the racing car and the Nike of Samothrace—or perhaps even more authentically the enthusiasm experienced by Duchamp's brother Duchamp-Villon, Léger, and Brancusi as they peaked behind the curtain that separated the 1912 *Salon d'automne* from the purely technical *Salon de l'aviation.* But then, Le Corbusier's prostration in front of the machine not only lacked any sarcasm, it occurred with a time lapse of almost a decade with respect to the prewar avant-gardes (fig. 9).[14]

Admittedly, Duchamp's metaphysical impatience with Le Corbusier is compensated for by a somewhat patronizing attitude towards Dadaism's relative artistic virtues on the side of Le Corbusier and—even more so—Amédée Ozenfant. Once the Dadaist footprints had been successfully removed from the *Esprit Nouveau*'s record, the two ideologues of "Purism" turned out to have no problem admitting some shared areas of interest. Speaking of "les nouveaux 'Surréalistes' (anciens Dadaistes)" and the "rapports suprêmement élégants de leurs métaphores" (the supremely elegant relationship of their metaphors), Le Corbusier cannot not have had Duchamp on his mind. While drawing a borderline between what he considers a "nouveau romantisme byronien" and serious art, he nevertheless insists that

> these emotive relationships will continue to be based on objects, and the only possible objects are objects with a function.[15]

Ozenfant, in turn, in his *Mémoires* confesses his annoyance around 1915 with the Dadaist magazines he received from Zurich and New York, saying of Duchamp and Picabia:

> For them, society and its bourgeois art was rotten, and they turned their backs on the era and its lingering romanticism. Their judgmental patter, spitting and pissing on everything man believes good, annoyed me.[16]

Yet earlier, in 1930, he had not hesitated to grandiloquently state (in *Foundations of Modern Art*):

> It will be perceived at some future date, that from 1914 on, all artistic activity falls into two living collective trends, Dadaism and Purism. These two movements, though apparently in opposition to each other, were equally sickened by the glib and stale productions of art, and sought to restore it to health: the former by ridiculing time-worn formulas, the latter by emphasizing the need for discipline.[17]

In fact, he even introduced the chapter with a reproduction of one of Duchamp's variations on the "Glass" (see fig. 5).[18] Since Ozenfant's days, much has been done to elucidate the various schools of technical drawing exploited by Duchamp/Picabia on the one hand and by Ozenfant/Jeanneret on the other in their respective courtships of "common sense."[19]

Yet the first to have insisted on the broader cultural implications of Dada's as well as Purism's insistence on everyday iconography was probably Sigfried Giedion when he compared the project of Purism (represented by one of Ozenfant's line drawings of around 1920, fig. 4) with Henry Cole's program for elementary drawing classes to be taught at English schools, as an attempt at securing a basic grammar of understanding both for the construction and for the practice of "common sense."[20]

*

The "landscape" as a pictorial genre is not part of the techniques of applied geometry that make industry work. Yet nevertheless it ranks among the skills an architect needs to be

4

PAINTING

(continued)

DADAISM: PURISM: SURREALISM

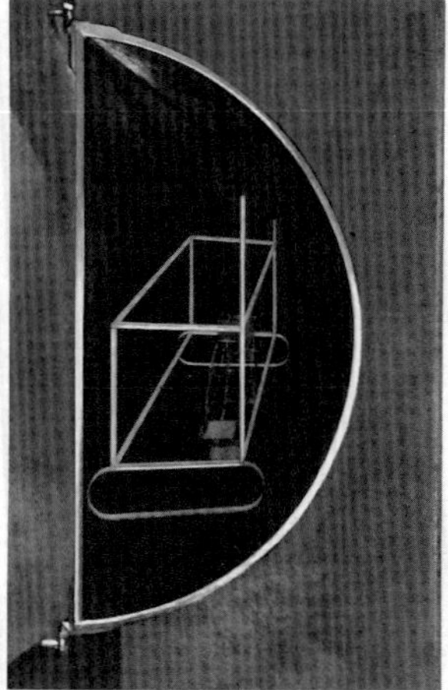

Object in Glass and Zinc.

Marcel Duchamp, 1914.

IT will be perceived at some future date, that from 1914 on, all artistic activity falls into two living *collective* trends, Dadaism and Purism. These two movements, though apparently in opposition to each other, were equally sickened by the glib and stale productions of art, and sought to restore it to health: the former by ridiculing time-worn formulas, the latter by emphasising the need for discipline.

116

INAUGURATION

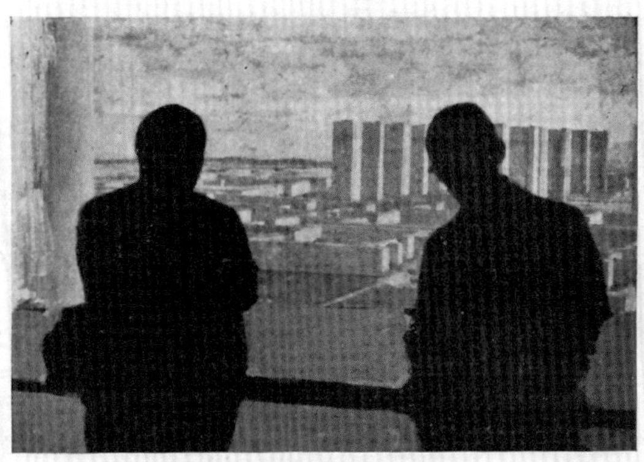

M. de Monzie.

5 Page from Amédée Ozenfant's book *Foundations of Modern Art,* 1931, with Marcel Duchamp's *Water Mill within Glider,* 1913–15, here referred to as "Object in Glass and Zinc," New York 1952 (1st ed. 1931). **6 Le Corbusier and Pierre Jeanneret, Ville contemporaine pour 3 millions d'habitants** (Modern City for 3 Million Habitants), with Le Corbusier (right) and the housing minister de Monzie contemplating the diorama shown at the Pavillon de *L'Esprit Nouveau,* Paris, 1925. From *Almanach d'architecture moderne,* Paris 1925, p. 136.

familiar with in order to practice his job, certainly so according to the idea of the architect in the tradition of the Grand Tour as it was institutionalized in nineteenth-century architectural and art education—and as it was practiced at the Art School in La Chaux-de-Fonds, where Le Corbusier had come of age. When, in 1921, coming from Paris, he visited his parents who spent the summer months in a rented chalet in Châbles, the Alps that frame the *bassin lémanique* couldn't fail to capture his curiosity. Possibly encouraged by Ozenfant, who had accompanied him, he began to fill a large album with views alternatively using pencil, color pencil, pastel, or watercolor. Despite his annoyance with his father's Alpinist passions he even indulged in picturing some Alpine sites, though undeniably that subject as all others interest him most when it conformed to the *Esprit Nouveau*'s taste for Platonic solids—such as in an intriguing and arguably rather conceptual color pencil drawing of the Weisshorn.[21] A similar taste for the abstract and the ideal is at play in a panoramic pencil drawing that represents the mountain chain looking south across the lake, a drawing made in 1921 and thus *not* from the *petite maison,* but from its predecessor, a chalet Le Corbusier's parents had rented in the summers preceding the building of the house (see fig. 12).[22] It must be said that otherwise the dramatic mountain scenery is difficult to picture as a classical landscape, especially if as seen towards the east, with the Dents du Midi on the horizon (fig. 11).

The album was later donated to the banker Raoul La Roche, Le Corbusier's first important client in Paris, in memory of a short trip to Venice the two had undertaken in 1922 (in the meantime, in 1923–24, Le Corbusier and Pierre Jeanneret had built the house that ultimately served as envelope for La Roche's important collection of Cubist and post-Cubist art).[23] In fact, one year after his visit to les Châbles, Le Corbusier returned to the region, this time only to continue towards Venice, together with La Roche. The better part of that album is thus filled with crayon and watercolor studies of Venice.[24] If the artist were a Sunday painter in the tradition of late Impressionism, the subject matter of these *vedute* might be called predictable, even banal; though since they were made by one of the key

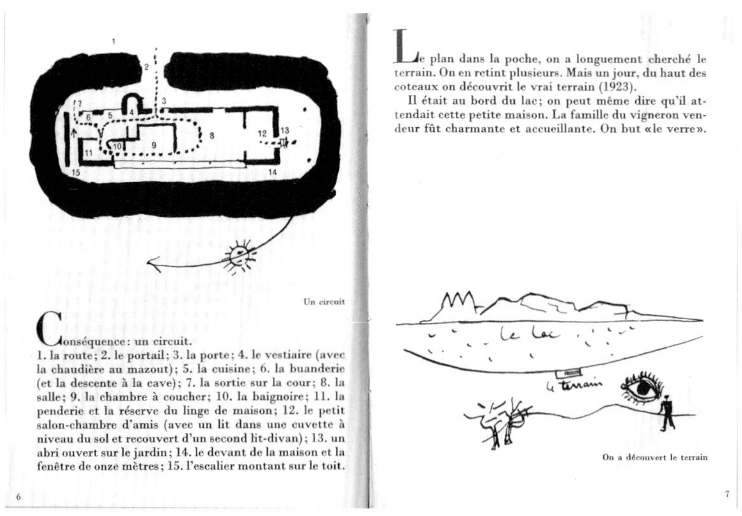

Conséquence: un circuit.
1. la route; 2. le portail; 3. la porte; 4. le vestiaire (avec la chaudière au mazout); 5. la cuisine; 6. la buanderie (et la descente à la cave); 7. la sortie sur la cour; 8. la salle; 9. la chambre à coucher; 10. la baignoire; 11. la penderie et la réserve du linge de maison; 12. le petit salon-chambre d'amis (avec un lit dans une cuvette à niveau du sol et recouvert d'un second lit-divan); 13. un abri ouvert sur le jardin; 14. le devant de la maison et la fenêtre de onze mètres; 15. l'escalier montant sur le toit.

6

Le plan dans la poche, on a longuement cherché le terrain. On en retint plusieurs. Mais un jour, du haut des coteaux on découvrit le vrai terrain (1923).

Il était au bord du lac; on peut même dire qu'il attendait cette petite maison. La famille du vigneron vendeur fût charmante et accueillante. On but «le verre».

7

7 Spread from Le Corbusier's *Une petite maison* (A Small House), Zurich 1954, pp. 6–7, showing the plan of the little house Le Corbusier built for his parents in Corseaux, Switzerland, 1923–24, and the view from the site across Lake Geneva .

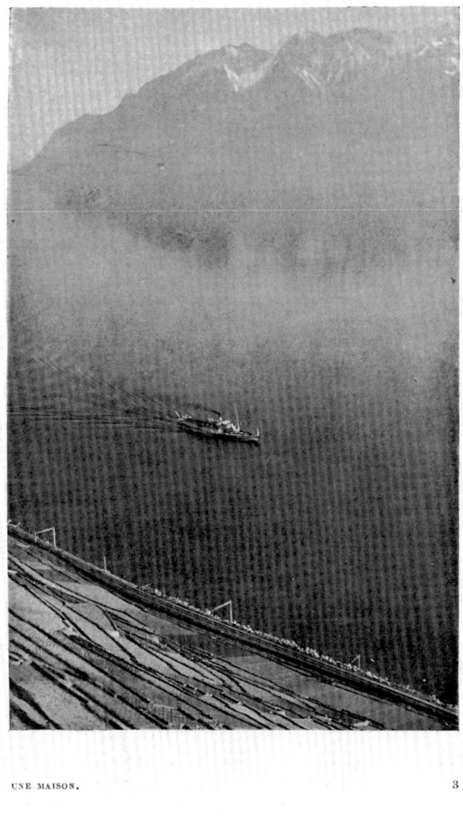

8 View of the slopes of the Lavaux with its vineyards structured by its system of retaining walls. From Le Corbusier, *Une maison–un palais*, Paris, n.d. [1928], p. 27.

ideologues of architectural modernism (the album also contains some studies related to the ideal city project referred to earlier), they may at least challenge preconceived ideas about what modernism is about.

*

It is in this context that the *petite maison* enters the stage as a highly significant laboratory experiment. Here is the story in detail:

> 1922, 1923, I boarded the Paris-Milan express several times, or the Orient Express (Paris-Ankara). In my pocket was the plan of a house. A plan without a site? The plans of a house in search of a plot of ground? Yes.[25]

The idea that the house should be "parachuted" onto the land, complete in itself, in no way depending on the contingencies of a site, is obviously part of the myth of the "house as

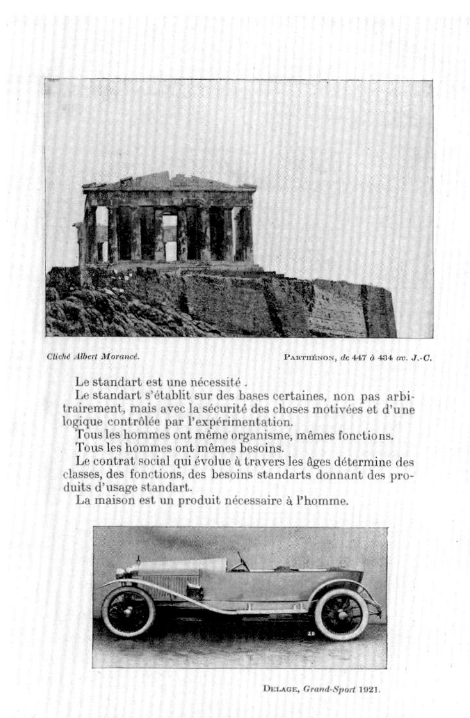

Cliché Albert Morancé. PARTHÉNON, *de 447 à 434 av. J.-C.*

Le standart est une nécessité .

Le standart s'établit sur des bases certaines, non pas arbitrairement, mais avec la sécurité des choses motivées et d'une logique contrôlée par l'expérimentation.

Tous les hommes ont même organisme, mêmes fonctions.

Tous les hommes ont mêmes besoins.

Le contrat social qui évolue à travers les âges détermine des classes, des fonctions, des besoins standarts donnant des produits d'usage standart.

La maison est un produit nécessaire à l'homme.

DELAGE, *Grand-Sport* 1921.

9 Page from Le Corbusier, "Des yeux qui ne voient pas: III. Les automobiles," in *L'Esprit Nouveau*, no. 10, Paris, n.d. [July 1921], unpaginated.

machine" (fig. 7). As to the story of the pre-existing plan, it is pure fiction. In fact, there exists a considerable number of studies of houses in various shapes and sizes, some related to the sites from where some of the *vedute* in the album were made, others related to the site that was ultimately purchased: a small plot of land between the *route cantonale* and the lake outside of Corseaux.[26] In the 1954 book, Le Corbusier went on telling the story of the vintner's family who sold him the land ("La famille du vigneron vendeur fut charmante et accueillante, on but 'le verre'")[27]—a bucolic image that serves to establish the roots of the house in the history of the region and its age-old farming tradition. In actual fact, rather than to a vintner the land belonged to the French painter Gaston Vaudou, who had purchased it only a few years previously, etc.

Une petite maison thus offers a fairly romanticized version of the little house's genesis. The text begins with a description of the mythological character of the *coteaux* as a landscape constructed by human labor:

> The region—the Lake Léman where the terraced vines rise one above the other. If you were to place the walls that support them end on end, they would total 30,000 kilometres (three quarters of a trip around the world!). The vine growers certainly know their job! There work is meant to last for centuries, perhaps for a thousand years.[28]

The Lavaux countryside is thus seen as made by retaining walls girding the slopes that run down to the lake, breaking it up in a myriad of terraces so as to facilitate the vintners' work. Rather than as a mere postcard stereotype, this archetypal "landscape of industry" is seen as an authentic witness to human intelligence—equivalent, in this respect, to the straight lines of the railways that opened it to modernity (fig. 8).

> The perception of such harmony produces the ineffable moments of life. Are these pleasures the greatest wealth?[29]

It is in one of the early sheets in the series of drawings of Lake Geneva that Le Corbusier comes closest to his conception of a "pure" landscape (fig. 12). Springing out of nowhere, the Savoy Alps appear to turn their sharply outlined, multifaceted morphology towards the sky, offering the viewer from across the lake a panorama without even a trace of foreground. Given the *ingresque* magic of this panorama, it seems only logical that the architect should have ended up choosing for his parents' house a spot of land immediately bordering the lake so that the Alps rise directly from the sheet of water, as from the sea.

In such a way, the *petite maison* is built to frame the "an unparalleled view, which cannot be spoilt by building, of one of the finest horizons in the world," as Le Corbusier put it. In a number of lectures given first in Paris, then in Lausanne, Basel, and Zurich, Le Corbusier,

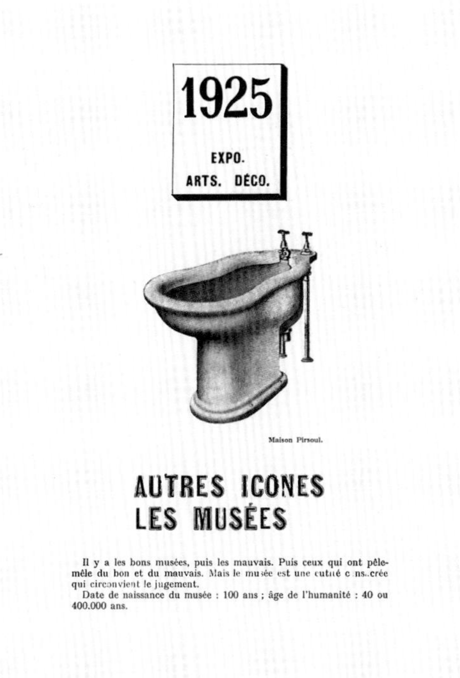

1925

EXPO.
ARTS. DÉCO.

Maison Pirsoul.

AUTRES ICONES
LES MUSÉES

Il y a les bons musées, puis les mauvais. Puis ceux qui ont pêle-mêle du bon et du mauvais. Mais le musée est une entité consacrée qui circonvient le jugement.

Date de naissance du musée : 100 ans ; âge de l'humanité : 40 ou 400.000 ans.

10 Title page from Le Corbusier, "Autres icônes. Les musées," in *L'Esprit Nouveau*, no. 20, n.d. [January/February 1924], unpaginated.

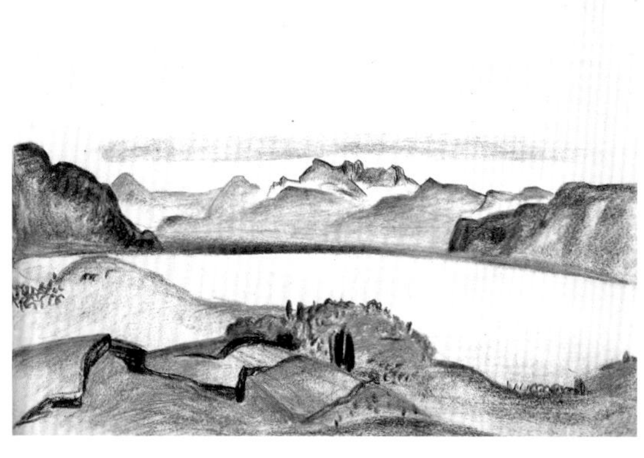

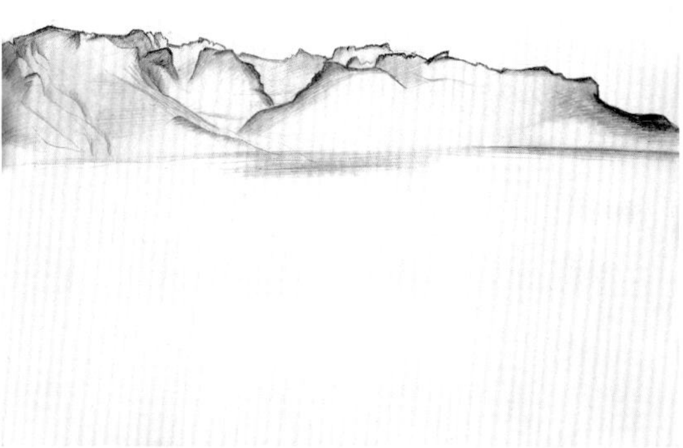

11 Le Corbusier, View of Lake Geneva towards the East from around Châbles, with the Dents du Midi on the horizon, color pencil and pastel drawing, 24 x 31.5 cm, 1921 or 1922, fol. 18r of the *Album La Roche*. Private Collection, Berlin. **12 Le Corbusier, View of the Savoy Alps as seen from Châbles,** pencil drawing, 24 x 31.5 cm, 1922, fol. 14r of the *Album La Roche*. Private Collection, Berlin.

speaking at length of the views from the *Côtes vaudoises,* couldn't resist the temptation to offer a maverick theory of the sublime as opposed to the beautiful (or the merely picturesque) landscape, thus linking the appreciation of landscape to the theories on the platonic bodies exposed earlier in the *Esprit Nouveau* (figs. 13, 14). The predictable result is a vigorous rebuttal of the sublime as claimed by the Swiss eighteenth-century ideologues of the Alpine landscape ever since Albrecht von Haller and Caspar Wolf in favor of a unequivocally neoclassical view. The bottom line being that a broken, jigsaw line seen in a landscape is troubling, unpleasant, whereas a wavy contour—and let alone a straight horizontal line—is calming and therefore pleasant:

> ... this broken line is unpleasant (Le Corbusier says); this continuous line is pleasing; this jumble of lines disturbs us; this rhythmic composition calms us (fig. 13).

As there exists a transcript of the lecture first given at the Salle Rapp in Paris, in 1924, we can quote him literally. The main point was that "the new aesthetic" he championed "needed some fundamental principles if it is to gain currency":

> A useful point of departure is the physiology of sensations. This physiology of sensations is our sensory reaction in response to a given optic phenomenon. My eyes transmit to my senses the spectacle before them. Confronted by these various lines, which I am drawing on the blackboard, different sensations are generated. The difference between a broken or continuous line is enough to stimulate the heartbeat, in response to the shocking or soothing effect produced by the forms.[30]

That forms, either "pure" like the Platonic solids or "chaotic" like a configuration of Alpine peaks, automatically trigger a standard set of emotions had been part of Purist aesthetics to begin with. As far as Le Corbusier is concerned, it may even reflect an early awareness of Wilhelm Worringer's ideas about abstraction and empathy (*Abstraktion und Einfühlung,* 1907).[31] Given Le Corbusier's habit to extend such psychological codings to architecture and more specifically to the styles of architectural history, it comes as no surprise that, in another sketch done in view of that lecture, he explicitly linked the Alpine sublime of the Dents du Midi to the "bad," "Germanic," and ultimately "gothic" architecture of the late nineteenth century, synonymous for him with the bad influence of the English and the Swiss Germans on the landscape of the Romandie. That influence, we understand, can only be overcome by reconfiguring architecture in a new, purified kind of classicism that would be in harmony both with the sober outline of the Grammont and with the remnants of the "useful past" as embodied by the retaining walls of the Lavaux (fig. 8).[32]

In the final analysis, the raison d'être of the little house is thus its view of the lake panorama. Though ruled by a rigorous discipline of domestic functions, the house, barely larger than a trailer, is defined architecturally by nothing so much as a tool for cutting views out of the landscape (figs. 7, 15). As if to illustrate an archetypal dichotomy, those views fit into two categories: the almost square (in fact horizontally rectangular) "hole" in the garden wall overlooking the lake that corresponds to the "classical" proportions of a landscape painting, and the *fenêtre en longueur* of the living room that corresponds to the panorama.

Though the rhetoric of modernism of course focused on the *fenêtre en longueur,* considerable space in the book is spent on the garden wall and the quasi "marina" it frames. Perhaps even more than in the strip window, architecture is here defined as a tool for

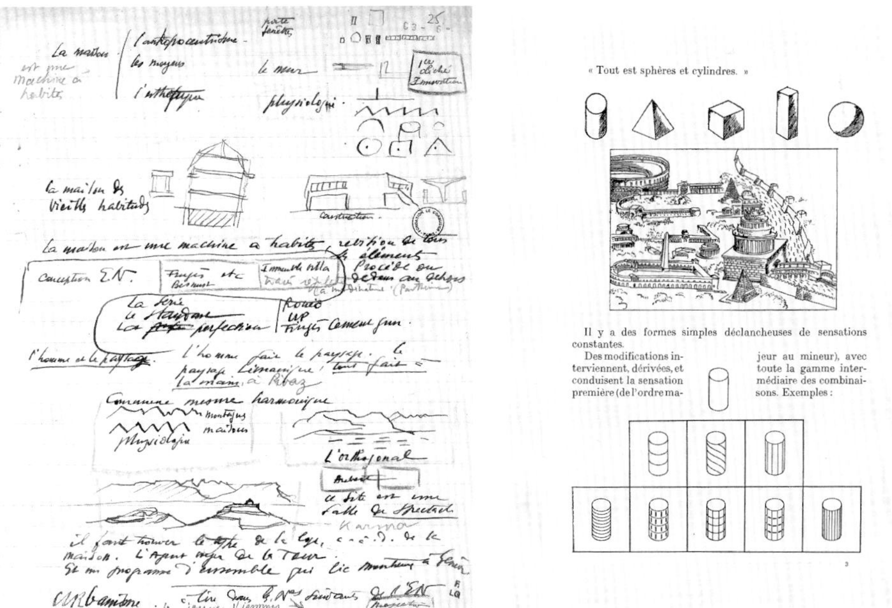

« Tout est sphères et cylindres. »

Il y a des formes simples déclancheuses de sensations constantes.

Des modifications interviennent, dérivées, et conduisent la sensation première (de l'ordre majeur au mineur), avec toute la gamme intermédiaire des combinaisons. Exemples :

13 Le Corbusier, Notes for a lecture given in Lausanne, February 1924. Fondation Le Corbusier, Paris, C3(6)25. **14 Illustration from Le Corbusier, "Sur le plastique,"** in *L'Esprit Nouveau*, no. 1 (1919), p. 43.

cutting views out of the landscape—granted that the picture chosen for *Une petite maison* is heavily retouched with the help of a rough screen to highlight the surface of the lake (the sailboat that appears on the horizon is evidently a fake, fig. 15).

Things were different with the strip window of the house itself, which runs nearly the entire length of the facade. Here, architecture is put at the service of a radically *modern* type of view—that of the panorama. Typical of turn of the century World's Fairs, the panorama (or rather its miniature form, the diorama) had been very much on the architect's mind as a strategy of display at the moment the *petite maison* was under preparation, i.e., around 1922. Had not the first presentation of the *Ville contemporaine* in the Salon d'automne of 1922 been in the form of a diorama to be seen through a narrow horizontal slit? Three years later, a twin version of that arrangement formed the *parti* of the Pavillon de *L'Esprit Nouveau* at the Decorative Arts Exhibition of 1925 (figs. 6, 16). Apart from strangely prefiguring Duchamp's similar fascinations with the diorama—fascinations that ultimately crystallized in the *Étant donnés*—all this also parallels the architect's interest in the Alpine panorama as revealed on the decks of steamboats (and most spectacularly so on the Lake of Geneva; fig. 17).[33] One may recall at this point that the type of the panorama partly originated as a form of representing the chains of the Swiss Alps.

Radically attacked by Le Corbusier's erstwhile master Auguste Perret for being an offense to the traditional concept of the window, the strip window is an *idée fixe* of Le Corbusier's program. Perret argued that it reduces the ability to perceive the landscape, preventing an "integral" spatial impression by cutting out precisely what is necessary to any illusion of depth: the foreground and the sky. Only the vertical "French" window was able to offer a

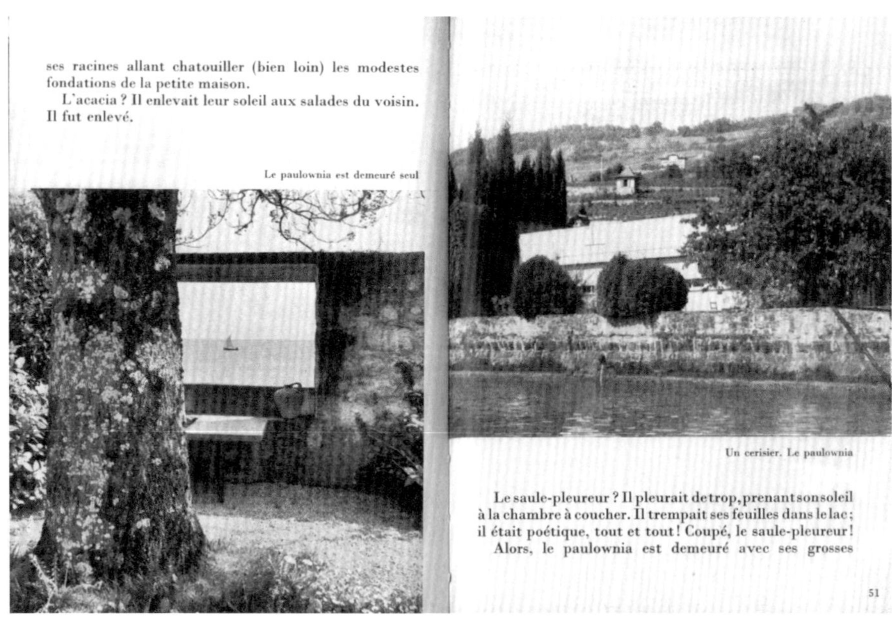

ses racines allant chatouiller (bien loin) les modestes fondations de la petite maison.

L'acacia ? Il enlevait leur soleil aux salades du voisin. Il fut enlevé.

Le paulownia est demeuré seul

Un cerisier. Le paulownia

Le saule-pleureur ? Il pleurait de trop, prenant son soleil à la chambre à coucher. Il trempait ses feuilles dans le lac; il était poétique, tout et tout! Coupé, le saule-pleureur!

Alors, le paulownia est demeuré avec ses grosses

51

15 Spread from Le Corbusier's *Une petite maison* (A Small House), Zurich 1954, pp. 50–51, with the garden wall of the villa "Le lac" with its window framing a heavily retouched "marina" (left) and the villa itself with its strip window (right).

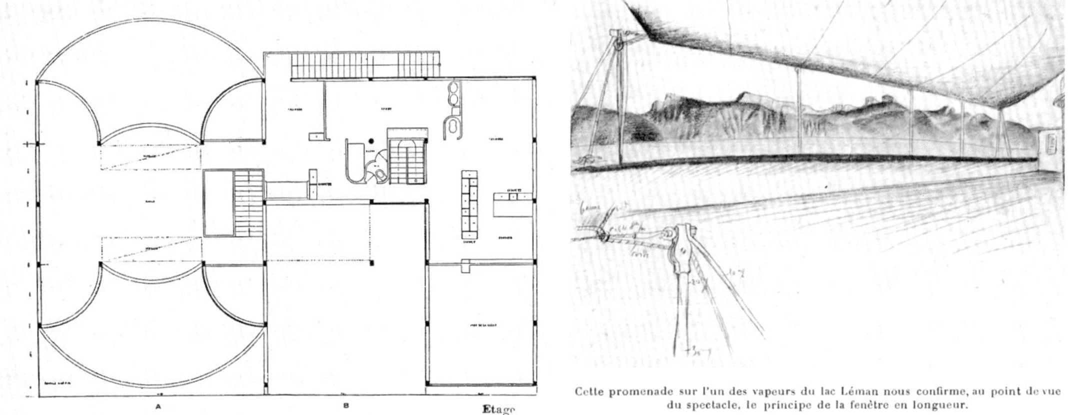

16 Le Corbusier and Pierre Jeanneret, Pavillon de *L'Esprit Nouveau* with twin dioramas at the *Exposition internationale des arts décoratifs,* Paris, 1925, ground plan, *Le Corbusier. Oeuvre complète*, Zurich 1937, p. 100. **17 Le Corbusier, Sketch of the Savoy Alps as seen from the passenger deck of a steamboat on Lake Geneva,** c. 1922, as reproduced with caption in *Une maison–un palais*, Paris, n.d. [1928], p. 99.

"complete" perception of space, a true effect of perspectival depth, in that it allowed the eye to range from the foreground to the middle distance, and from there to the background.[34] Needless to add, that the very blindness of Duchamp's *Fresh Widow* underscores those properties of the "French Window" that Perret was to canonize; see fig. 1).

As to Le Corbusier, he remained unconvinced by these explanations and left no stone unturned in order to demonstrate the superiority of the *fenêtre en longueur* with respect

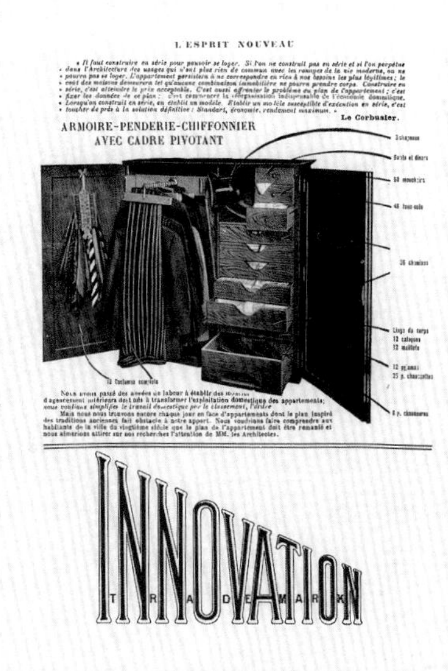

18 Advertisement for "Innovation" trunk, designed by Le Corbusier (or Amédée Ozenfant?) and published in *L'Esprit Nouveau*, no. 18, n.d. [November 1923], unpaginated.

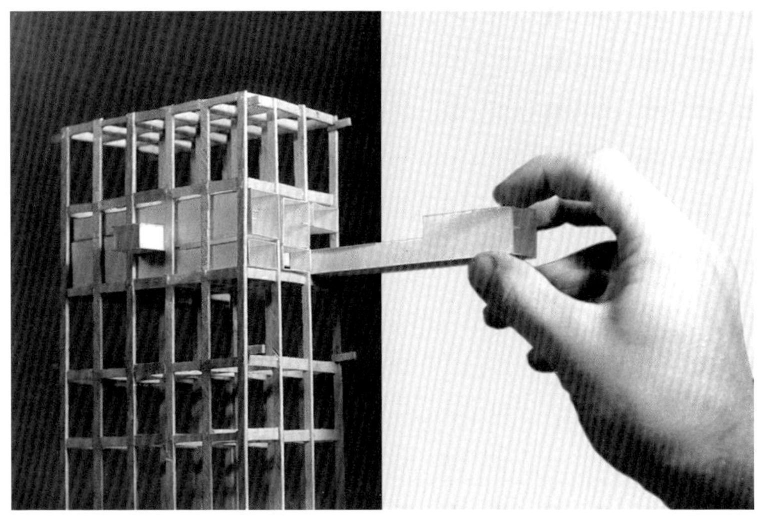

19 Le Corbusier, Typical dwelling unit as inserted into the "bouteiller" (bottle rack) of the Unité d'habitation, c. 1950. From *Le Corbusier. Textes et planches,* Paris 1960, p. 161. Photograph by Robert Doisneau, modified by Le Corbusier.

to the traditional type. Not surprisingly, it was the machine—in this case, the photographic camera—that ultimately brought the "scientific proof" of the strip window's superiority.[35]

*

Returning, finally, to the *Riviéra lémanique,*[36] one may wonder whether Duchamp's and Le Corbusier's views of the machine and of industry need to be upheld as radically opposed, mutually exclusive conceptions of modernity—justifying Duchamp's clinical diagnosis of the "ménopause masculine précoce sublimisée en coït mental"—or whether what ultimately survives are two in some ways not so dissimilar variations within the spectrum of Cartesian modernism, or rather as two personifications of the "dry modernism" [modernisme sec] proposed by Bernard Marcadé.[37]

Though I assume that most Duchamp admirers would probably insist on the categorical differences of the positions embodied by these two alpha animals of modernism, and though my insistence on Le Corbusier as a *vedutista* and his celebrations of the *finestra sul mondo* appears to massively support such a view, I suspect that an alternative case could also be made, i.e. a case for a considerable parallelism of interests, based on the existence of a number of shared themes, themes that imply—yet do go beyond—the merely formal. Among these, it may suffice to recall both men's embrace of traditional, classical graphic styles, caught in the very moment of their becoming old fashioned, and in this connection, their shared quasi proto-pop-obsession with what one might call the "commercial sublime" (see figs. 9 & 10). Not to mention a pervasive interest in objects and instruments that pertain to operations for collecting fluids and solids, for controlling, ordering, cleaning up: the urinal, the shovel, the cage, the box, the *boîte,* the *valise,* the bottle rack...

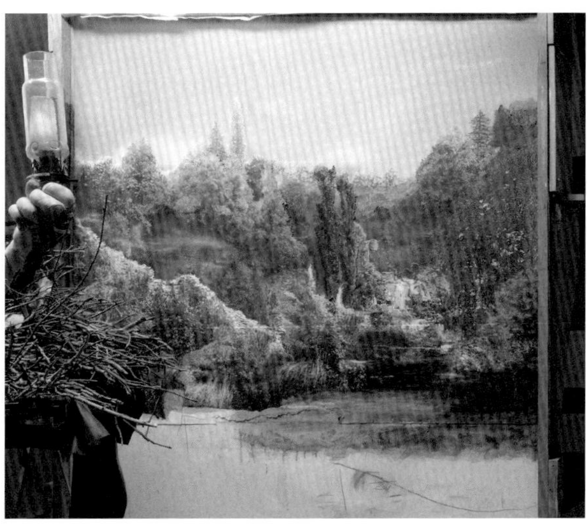

20 Marcel Duchamp, Le Forestay, in *Étant donnés: 1° La chute d'eau 2° Le gaz d'éclairage*, colored print (collotype) of a photo-collage, 63 x 89 cm, 1959. Philadelphia Museum of Art. Photograph by Philadelphia Museum of Art.

The issue, obviously, is not historical precedence: while the ads for the "Innovation" trunk in *L'Esprit Nouveau,* designed by Le Corbusier in 1923, predate the *Boîte-en-valise,* the didactic renderings of the bottle-like *appartements-tiroirs* inserted into the "bouteiller" of the legendary Unité d'habitation in Marseille can't help recalling Duchamp's *Bottle Rack* of 1914, etc. (figs. 18, 19). Moreover, both men have proverbially located the "New World" in an idealized America at important moments in their careers. And, by the way, both have returned to the *Riviéra lémanique* as the locus of alternative views of the natural sublime.

Both have, in their own ways, made an issue of the fabricated nature of the given landscape, its character, in fact, as a *paysage industriel.* Whereas for Duchamp the waterfall is a function of the watermill and vice versa, Le Corbusier explains the location of the *petite maison* as determined by the international railway connections available in Lausanne (not by coincidence, the opening spread of *Une petite maison* follows the rhetoric of the conventional travel brochure[38]). Both understand the landscape as a site of production, of productive rationality, yet both end up framing it, oddly enough, as a romantic site, emptied of all traces of human hubbub—or almost. As he practices the *veduta,* Le Corbusier makes us forget that the *Riviéra lémanique* is anything but the bucolic paradise described in Rousseau's *Julie ou la nouvelle Héloise,* but rather a heavily urbanized stretch of land. He simply disregards the built reality that makes up that landscape, the totality of what an architect today would have to be preoccupied by and/or be dealing with.[39] Duchamp, in turn, chooses to literally turn his back on everything that attracted him to the site in the first place, and to proceed to his somber meditations on the forgotten waterfall near Chexbres. Not without, however, subjecting it too to a radical cleansing operation that sacrifices the cultural and architectural "étants donnés" of the site—the mill, the distillery, the shooting range—in favor of a melancholic, almost Art Nouveau landscape consisting of a waterfall surrounded by a few weepy trees (fig. 20).[40]

Notes

*The present essay is partly based on some earlier remarks on Le Corbusier and the Léman region (see "The 'Riviéra lémanique,'" in Stanislaus von Moos, ed., *Album La Roche* (Facsimile and commentary), Milan and New York 1997, pp. 63–78. I am grateful to Stefan Banz for the occasion to review my earlier understanding of that "case" in the light of Marcel Duchamp.

1 Robin Middleton, "Foreword," in Philippe Duboy, *Lequeu: An Architectural Enigma*, Cambridge, Mass. 1986, pp. 6ff.
2 Quoted after Jean-Louis Cohen, *Le Corbusier. La planète comme chantier*, Paris and Geneva 2005, p. 7.
3 Le Corbusier, *Une petite maison*, Les carnets de la recherche patiente, no. 1, Zurich 1954, p. 7. The cited English edition was published in Basel et al. 2001 in a multilingual edition.
4 "... à qui il garantissait des joies artistiques et le confort domestique moyennant la soumission à quelques règles simples." André Thirion, in *Révolutionnaires sans révolution*, Paris 1972, pp. 72–73. The preceding line by Thirion is no less interesting. It characterizes the *Esprit Nouveau's* campaign as "un cours d'esthétique pour écoles primaires ... où militent, pêle-mêle, en faveur d'un ordre préétabli, les divagations sur le nombre d'or, la réduction des cathédrales en triangles isocèles et en demi-cercles et la lutte contre les taudis." I am grateful to Roxana Vicovanu for having signaled me Thirion's book (see her "Modernité rêvée, modernité vécue. La revue *L'Esprit Nouveau* (1920–1925) et les enjeux du modernisme dans la France des années 20," unpublished PhD thesis, Johns Hopkins University, Baltimore 2010. On the parallels and the "subterranean dialogue" between Le Corbusier and Duchamp see Beatriz Colomina, *Privacy and Publicity: Modern Architecture as Mass Media*, Cambridge, Mass. 1994, pp. 170–83; and Molly Nesbit, *Their Common Sense*, London 2000; and Françoise Ducros, "Amédée Ozenfant. frère puriste. Essai sur sa contribution" in Serge Lemoine, ed., *L'Esprit Nouveau. Le purisme à Paris, 1918-1925*, pp. 73–97. As to Philippe Duboy's lengthy discussion of the Le Corbusier vs. Duchamp case in *Lequeu: An Architectural Enigma* (note 1), and in particular his "Demolishing an Architect: Le Corbusier," ibid., pp. 89–103, it is too eccentric to be taken at face value—despite perceptive insights.
5 See Molly Nesbit, "The Language of Industry," in Thierry de Duve, ed., *The Definitely Unfinished Marcel Duchamp*, Halifax and Cambridge, Mass. 1991, pp. 351–94; and Linda Dalrymple Henderson, *Duchamp in Context: Science and Technology in the Large Glass and in Related Works*, Princeton, NJ 1998, pp. 58–68 and passim. The key study however is Molly Nesbit's *Their Common Sense* (note 4).
6 See Le Corbusier, "Petite contribution à la naissance d'une fenêtre moderne," in idem., *Almanach d'architecture moderne*, Paris n.d. [1925], pp. 91–101 and Bruno Reichlin, "La 'petite maison' à Corseaux. Une analyse structurale," in Isabelle Charollais and André Ducret, eds., *Le Corbusier à Genève*, Lausanne 1987, pp. 119–34, here p. 128.
7 See Duboy, *Lequeu* (note 1), pp. 9, 91.
8 When Molly Nesbit says in 2000, referring to "the pages of *L'Esprit Nouveau* publications," that "they look childish," Duchamp might have used similar terms 75 years earlier. Nesbit, *Their Common Sense* (note 4), p. 162.
9 Amédée Ozenfant had introduced the Nike of Samothrace ("without arms nor head") as a symbol of wartime France on the cover of *L'Élan*, no. 5 (June 1915), and in 1922 Le Corbusier placed colossal reproductions of the Nike on the four corners of the Ville contemporaine's triumphal gates.
10 See Le Corbusier, "Des Yeux qui ne voient pas," in *L'Esprit Nouveau*, nos. 8, 9, and 10. Apollinaire's essay "La renaissance dans les arts décoratifs" had appeared in *L'Intransigeant*, June 6, 1912.
11 Le Corbusier, "Trois rappels à MM. les architectes," *L'Esprit Nouveau*, no. 2 (November 1920), pp. 195–99; and Anonymous, "The Richard Mutt Case," *The Blind Man*, no. 2 (1917). Often attributed to Duchamp, the unsigned text was possibly written by Beatrice Wood or by Louise Norton; see William A. Camfield, *Marcel Duchamp: Fountain*, Houston 1989, pp. 37–38.
12 The magazine's name had in fact been borrowed from Apollinaire's 1917 lecture on "*L'Esprit Nouveau* et les poètes." See Jean-Marie Roulin, "Paul Dermée et *L'Esprit Nouveau* ou le difficile héritage d'Apollinaire," in S. von Moos, ed., *Le Corbusier et l'industrie, 1920-1925*, Berlin and Strasbourg 1987, pp. 152–59.
13 See Le Corbusier, *L'Art décoratif d'aujourd'hui*, Paris 1925, pp. 187ff.
14 On the topical role of the prewar Parisian avant-garde for *L'Esprit Nouveau*, see Reyner Banham, "Architecture and the Cubist Tradition," in *Theory and Design in the First Machine Age*, London 1960, pp. 202–13.
15 "Les points d'appui des rapports émouvants seront des objets, et seuls possibles, des objets qui fonctionnent." Le Corbusier, *L'Art décoratif* (note 13), p. 190.
16 "Pour eux la société et son art bourgeois étaient pourris, il refusaient donc l'époque en bloc—en bons romantiques attardés. Leur bagout, genre tribuns irréductibles crachant et pissant sur tout ce que l'humanité a créé de mieux, m'agaçait." Amédée Ozenfant, *Mémoires 1886-1962*, Paris 1968, p. 99.

[17] Amédée Ozenfant, *Foundations of Modern Art,* New York 1952 (orig. ed. 1931), p. 117. Ozenfant continues by attributing Duchamp the topical role in the history of Dadaism.
[18] Ibid., p. 116. See in this context Françoise Ducros, Amédée *Ozenfant,* Paris 2002, pp. 129ff.
[19] See Molly Nesbit, *Their Common Sense* (note 4); Françoise Ducros, "Amédée Ozenfant" (note 4), pp. 100–1. and passim. Some remarks relative to this issue also in von Moos, *Album La Roche* (note *), pp. 52–55.
[20] Sigfried Giedion, *Mechanization Takes Command,* New York and Oxford 1948, pp. 357ff.
[21] Von Moos, *Album La Roche* (note *), fol. 4, comments pp. 100–1.
[22] Ibid., fol. 14, comments pp. 103. A similar drawing has later been published by Le Corbusier in *Une petite maison* in an effort to appropriate the landscape as part of his private mythology. *Une petite maison* (note 3) p. 18.
[23] The best discussion of this project is by Tim Benton, "'Villa La Rocca'. Die Planungs- und Baugeschichte der Villa La Roche," in Katharina Schmidt und Hartwig Fischer, eds., *Ein Haus für den Kubismus. Die Sammlung Raoul La Roche,* exh. cat. Kunstmuseum Basel, Ostfildern 1998, pp. 227–43.
[24] The most beautiful ones are *Album La Roche,* fol. 28, 30, 32, 36, and 37; for comments see my "La leçon de Venise" in von Moos, *Album La Roche* (note *), comments, pp. 24–40.
[25] "1922, 1923, je prends à plusieurs reprises le rapide Paris-Milan ou l'Orient-Express (Paris-Ankara). J'emporte un plan de maison dans ma poche. La plan avant le terrain? Le plan d'une maison pour lui trouver un terrain? Oui." Le Corbusier, *Une petite maison* (note 3), p. 107 [p. 9].
[26] Adolphe Stiller, "Une descente sur les lieux: construction et détails techniques de la 'petite maison,'" in *Le Corbusier à Genève* (note 6), pp. 135–42. Stiller's detailed version of the "story" arguably is not the last word on the issue, however. See also Françoise Vaudou, *La petite maison de Le Corbusier,* Geneva 1991 and some additional details in my "The 'Riviéra lémanique'" (note *).
[27] "The vine-grower and his family who sold it were very obliging and agreeable. The sale was toasted." Le Corbusier, *Une petite maison* (note 3) p. 11 (p. 108).
[28] "La région, c'est le lac Léman où s'étagent les vignes en terrasses: la longueur des murs de soutènement alignés bout à bout totaliserait trente mille kilomètres (les trois quarts du tour de la Terre!). Les vignerons vont fort! Oeuvre séculaire, peut-être millénaire." Ibid., p. 107 [p. 9].
[29] "La perception d'une telle harmonie fait les heures ineffables de la vie. Est-il plus grande richesse que de telles joies?" Le Corbusier, *Une maison–un palais,* Paris n.d. [1928?], pp. 26f. Several landscape studies in the *Album La Roche* also highlight the retaining walls of the côtes du Lavaux (fol. 18, 19, 21, 23 among others).
[30] Quoted in Tim Benton, *The Rhetoric of Modernism: Le Corbusier as Lecturer,* Basel et al. 2009, p. 81.
[31] No later than 1911, during their trip to Turkey and Greece, August Klipstein and his travel companion appear to have discussed Worringer's theory of empathy. See Adolf Max Vogt, "Die 'verkehrte' Grand Tour des Charles Edouard Jeanneret," *Bauwelt,* no. 38–39 (1987), pp. 1430–9. Note that the theory of empathy was topical in the studies on the psychology of perception published in *Esprit Nouveau* that served as references for Purism's aesthetic theory, and in particular in the writings of Victor Basch and Charles Henry.
[32] With these thoughts Jeanneret-Le Corbusier ties up with earlier ideas about the culture of the Romandie and its indebtedness to a Mediterranean "classicism." The ultimate reference for such concepts is Alexandre Cingria-Vaneyre, *Les Entretiens de la Villa du Rouet. Essais dialogués sur les arts plastiques en Suisse romande,* Geneva 1908.
[33] The drawing of the steamboat-panorama is reproduced in *Une maison–un palais* (note 29), p. 99. For further references regarding the "petite maison" and the particularities of its design see my "The 'Riviéra lémanique" (note *).
[34] See above, note 6.
[35] See Le Corbusier's "Five Points of a New Architecture," 1925/27. For the details and the respective literature see my *Le Corbusier: Elements of a Synthesis,* revised ed., Rotterdam 2009, pp. 84ff.
[36] The term "Riviéra lémanique" has been introduced by Gilles Barbey and Jacques Gubler in *Werk-Archithese,* no. 6 (June 1977), special edition edited by Barbey/Gubler under this title.
[37] See Bernard Marcadé's essay, "Water Leaking on All Floors" in this volume (pp. 98–109).
[38] Le Corbusier, *Une petite maison* (note 3), pp. 12–13; see my "The 'Riviéra lémanique'" (note *), pp. 64ff.
[39] Ibid.
[40] See Stefan Banz's description of the Forestay waterfall in his essay "Paysage fautif: Marcel Duchamp and the Forestay Waterfall" in this volume (pp. 26–57).

DRINKING BLACK COFFEE

Molly Nesbit

The Hinge at the End of the Mind
Duchamp's Work in Progress

Marcel Duchamp found himself being interviewed more and more frequently after World War II. In 1952 Winthrop Sargeant made him the news for *Life Magazine,* spurred by Rose Fried's show of Duchamp's work and that of his brothers and sister, and fueled by the publication of Robert Motherwell's anthology of the *Dada Painters and Poets.* In *Life* everything would appear in translation. The *Box in a Valise* got a double-page spread, the *Rotoreliefs'* titles a loose, and probably unwanted, translation. It was on a par with the kind of treatment that Duchamp saw being given by American museums, writing that year to his sister Suzanne and her husband Jean Crotti, that they were hoping to teach modern art by means of "chemical formula."[1] He did not approve. Duchamp too was photographed for *Life* and found himself there sitting between the ad pages, pointed out. The art directors were sharing ideas, clearly, with the art directors for the Arrow shirt company and all of them were savvy. With their kisses, the Arrow men called up an inside memory of *La révolution surréaliste,* specifically the lip-stained page of the Second Surrealist manifesto; with the arrow, they called up the Duchamp number of *View.* One arrow became an homage to another, a tip and a slip of the arrow that had once shot forth to connect the *infra-mince* to the Milky Way.

Something of what had been lost in translation by *Life* came across on the last line of the story there, where Duchamp was quoted saying, "What would you consider the proper solution? Obviously there can be no solution when there is no problem. Problems are inventions of the mind. They are nonsensical."[2] It was something that Sargeant had fished out of the Motherwell book.[3] Or perhaps Duchamp had repeated it for him. Sargeant calls it dialectic but it is not really; it stems from another kind of thinking that is not formal; it involves instead a condensation, a change of state, the kind of thinking that had initially led Duchamp to the *infra-mince,* a term Sargeant did not bring up. Meanwhile, unbeknownst to *Life,* Duchamp had taken the idea of the arrow through the experience of a Swiss waterfall. The *infra-mince* was now only words and it had joined the other words he had summarily put aside.

The putting aside of the problem, like the putting aside of words, gives most people pause. Duchamp's interviewers were forced to hurdle over this as best they could. Every long interview Duchamp ever gave had its hurdles. The last long one, the book-length interview Duchamp did in 1966 with Pierre Cabanne, was no different. At the end Cabanne asked Duchamp if he believed in God (never mind that Duchamp had already told him that he did not subscribe to the word belief). Duchamp told him that God was another of man's inventions, that for him the question did not exist, and then he turned the tables.[4] He liked to outfox. "Do you know," he asked Cabanne, "the story of the Viennese logicians?" Cabanne did not.

"The Viennese logicians," Duchamp explained, "worked out a system wherein everything is, as far as I understood it, a tautology, that is, a repetition of premises. In mathematics, it goes from a very simple theorem to a very complicated one, but it's all in the first theorem. So, metaphysics: tautology; religion: tautology: everything is tautology, except black coffee because the senses are in control! The eyes see the black coffee, the senses are in control, it's a truth; but the rest is always tautology."

This combination of tautology and coffee was itself a work in progress. It too had been an idea he liked to repeat. It was not the first time it had come up in conversation: in 1958 when Lawrence Gold came to see him for an interview during his research on his senior thesis, Duchamp had said to him:

> (1) Breathing is a problem whether we regard it as one or not. There are certain physical problems that we are victims of. We should concentrate on these, but putting them in logical terms does not help us. Problems of the mind reduce to tautologies. Our talk about them adds nothing.
>
> (37) There is no finality; we build tautologically and get nowhere.
>
> (38) I once read part of a book by a Viennese group of mathematicians. They showed that all conceptions of reality were tautological except for black coffee. It was the only reality. I found that a very pleasing and amusing conception, and thought it showed a great deal of intelligence.
>
> (39) Logic may be necessary to communication, but it reflects only part of man. I see no reason for discarding it completely, but we should not have too great a reliance on it.[5]

Lawrence Gold went back to his room and wrote all this down from memory. His thesis circumvented these honest problems as best it could and focused elsewhere. For Duchamp these problems had for a long time been alive and would continue to be.

Duchamp had been fascinated by the abyss of tautology since the time of the *Large Glass.* Underneath an early note about its waterfall, he jotted down a phrase—"tautologie en actes"—for use in thinking about the Bride; it was a note held back from both the Green and the White Boxes.[6] It might have been touched off by something in Henri Poincaré, who had written a critique of logic as nothing more than an immense tautology in *Science et méthode,* a book Duchamp had been mining, along with *Science et hypothèse,* while working on the *Glass.*[7] But tautology was not a word that was otherwise very active in his thoughts. It seems to have come around again during World War II in New York. Duchamp went to see Denis de Rougemont at Lake George in the summer of 1945. Because of the new *View,* de Rougemont had asked him about the *infra-mince* and other things, and in reply Duchamp brought up tautology not as the example, but instead the favorite Surrealist concept, myth, attaching it to science, specifically physics and mathematics.[8] Much the same turns of conversation had already been taken that

QUAND
lA FUMÉe de tABAC
seNT aUSSi
de La bouche
qui L'EXHALE,
leS DEUx ODEURS
S'ÉPOUSENt par
INFRA-miNce

marcel Duchamp →

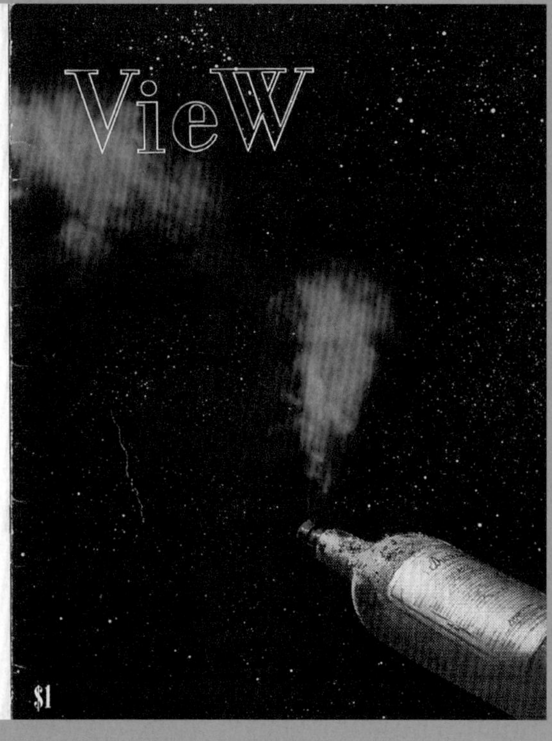

1 Marcel Duchamp, Covers of *View* (back and front), March 1945. Collection Molly Nesbit, New York.

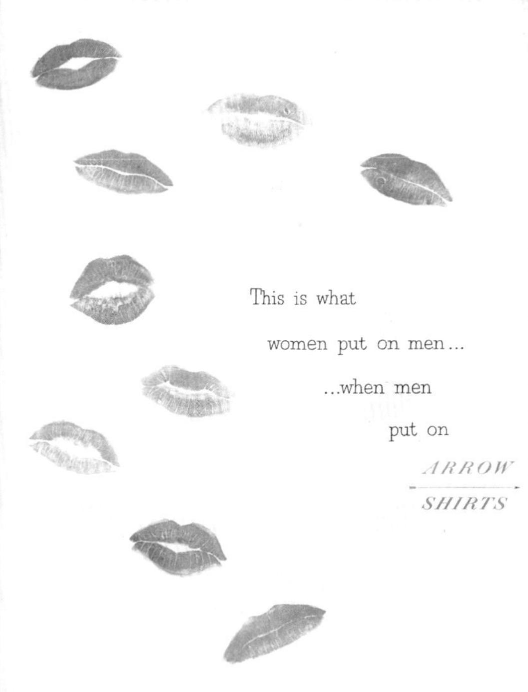

DADA'S DADDY CONTINUED

want to get in touch with him can do so by sending telegrams. His studio is dominated by its chess table. Here Duchamp sits by the hour, sometimes actually playing against an opponent. But "chess has become a drug," he feels, and he is even able to outwit his tendency to become addicted to it. This he does by not playing chess too well. When he finds himself getting too ambitious, Duchamp stops playing and takes stock of himself. Ambition, as he well knows, is a trap, and might threaten his individuality by entangling him in competitive activity.

He practices the avoidance of such traps with wily agility. He was once married long ago for a period of a few months. But any such entanglement as domesticity is far from his thoughts today. "I can't understand domesticity," he explains. "You can go without food or umbrellas alone, but with a wife and children you can't." He is about to become a U.S. citizen. But one thing about his future civic functions disturbs him, and that is the danger of being entrapped in jury duty: "Who am I and who is any man that he can bring judgment on another man? I just don't want to do it." To Duchamp even art itself is a trap. "I have always had a horror," he explains, "of being a 'professional' painter. The minute you become that, you are lost." Besides, he adds thoughtfully, "I was never passionate about painting. I never had the olfactory sensation of most artists. They paint because they love the smell of turpentine. Personally, I used to paint for two or three hours a day, and I couldn't get away fast enough." Despite his position as an oracle of the avant-garde, Duchamp takes a very dim view of contemporary painting. "In my estimation," he says, "there is no hope for the future of art at least for the next 25 years."

Sitting quietly in his studio, smoking pipeful after pipeful of strong Cuban tobacco, Duchamp can talk interestingly by the hour, allowing an amazing stream of esthetic, philosophical and purely Dada ideas to filter through his detached, ironic mind. But no sooner has he ventured into a definite statement than, like a true Dadaist, he retreats from it under a smoke screen of ridicule. Around him lie piled the materials with which he carries on his present task, that of stuffing his life work into small suitcases. It is, rationally considered, a rather mad process, calculated to astound the onlooker. The onlooker naturally seeks an explanation: Why a suitcase? It is obviously ready to be carried off somewhere. Is he implying an ironic thrust at his own art? If so it is obviously an ironic thrust at an ironic thrust, for his own art is pure irony. Wheels within wheels. Are there deeper meanings to all this? Try and find them. You will only find that Marcel Duchamp, within the frame of his own elusive dialectic, has you outwitted. "What would you consider the proper solution?" he asks, smiling intelligently. "Obviously there can be no solution when there is no problem. Problems are inventions of the mind. They are nonsensical."

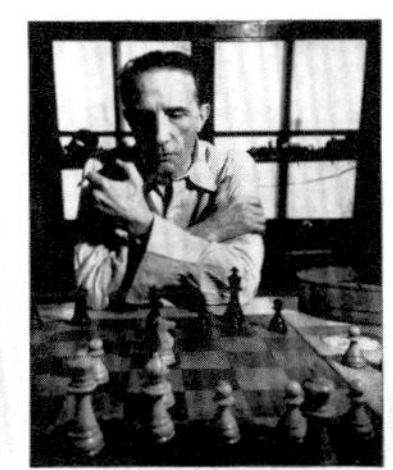

RETIRED TO HIS CHESSBOARD, Duchamp plays by the hour at a table with a clock that keeps track of the time between moves.

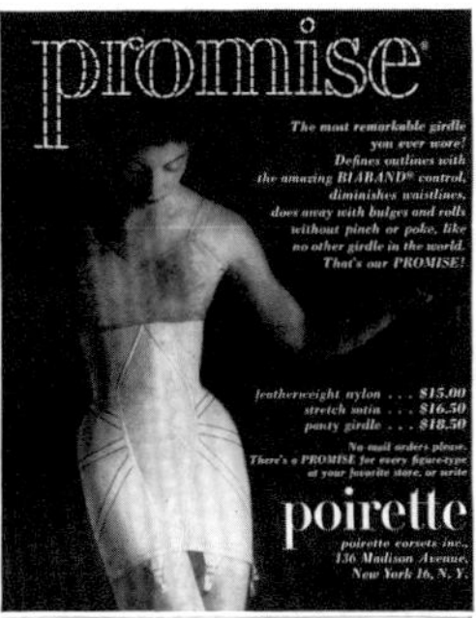

announcement from LIFE

about an important political event on television

Presidential candidates Estes Kefauver, Robert S. Kerr, Harold Stassen, Earl Warren and, speaking for General Eisenhower, Mr. Paul Hoffman, will meet together in Cincinnati on May 1. There they will reply to the important issues raised in some 350 public forums which have been held throughout the country during the past two weeks, under the sponsorship of LIFE and The League of Women Voters.

Because of the nationwide interest in the candidates' replies, their appearance in Cincinnati, before the National Convention of the League of Women Voters, will be covered in an hour-long television program, from 8 to 9 P.M., E.D.T., over the American Broadcasting Company's network.

Watch the candidates reply to the Citizens' View of '52, Thursday night, May 1.

111

2 Winthrop Sargeant, "Dada's Daddy," *Life*, vol. 22, April 28, 1952, pp. 110–11. Collection Molly Nesbit, New York.

spring when Duchamp was being interviewed at length by James Johnson Sweeney, who was hoping to write a Duchamp book.[9] It was only in the late fifties that Duchamp yoked tautology to the Viennese. He was repeating something that he had not only read, but pondered and continued to ponder. The path of that pondering, the kind of thinking that becomes a way, will be the subject now. It is important that it remain nameless.

As for the Viennese idea about tautology, it has a time and a place. It dates from the very first years of the Vienna Circle, from 1929, when an impressive group of scientists, logicians, mathematicians, philosophers, and social scientists imagined themselves in all their diversity to be producing a collective breakthrough in knowledge that they themselves would call a Second Enlightenment and would lead to an international movement they baptized the Unity of Science. Their idea about tautology appeared right away in 1929 when they formally announced themselves and their project to the scientific community at large in an unsigned pamphlet entitled "The Scientific Conception of the World: the Vienna Circle" ["Wissenschaftliche Weltauffassung: der Wiener Kreis," Vienna 1929]: it was written collectively but anonymously by the sociologist Otto Neurath, the logician Rudolph Carnap, and the mathematician Hans Hahn. They opened with an attack on metaphysics and theology, allied themselves with Bertrand Russell in England, William James in America, and what they were calling the new Russia; they saw themselves working in the tradition of the physicist Ernst Mach; they claimed to be working, scientifically, on a total system of concepts.

"The scientific world-conception knows no unsolvable riddle," they wrote. "Clarification of the traditional philosophical problems leads us partly to unmask them as pseudo-problems, and partly to transform them into empirical problems and thereby to subject them to the judgment of experimental science. The task of philosophical work lies in this clarification of problems and assertions."[10] For this they settled upon the method of logical analysis. This enabled them to separate statements made by empirical science from all the others. They pointed to what they felt were the basic errors of metaphysics:

> ... the notion that thinking can either lead to knowledge out of its own resources without using any empirical material, or at least arrive at new contents by an inference from given states of affair. Logical investigation, however, leads to the result that all thought and inference consists of nothing but a transition from statements to other statements that contain nothing that was not already in the former (tautological transformation). It is therefore not possible to develop a metaphysic from "pure thought." ... For us, something is "real" through being incorporated into the total structure of experience.[11]

They reset priorities:

> A scientific description can contain only the structure (form of order) of objects, not their "essence." What unites men in language are structural

> formulae; in them the content of common knowledge of men presents itself. Subjectively experienced qualities—redness, pleasure—are as such only experiences, not knowledge; physical optics admits only what is in principle understandable to a blind man too.[12]

The new logic they proposed would use what they were then calling *logical analysis* on this immediate material. It right away provoked controversy in philosophical and scientific circles for it questioned how to handle *the givens*, which they saw to be always already empirical, or physical, in nature.[13]

In 1959 some of the early essays of Carnap and his colleagues (but not the manifesto of 1929) would be anthologized and translated for the first time into English by A. J. Ayer in a book entitled *Logical Positivism*. Here the Viennese were presented as a school of logicians, the way Duchamp himself summarized them to Cabanne. And there sits Carnap's early essay on the old and new logic, written in 1931:

> The tautological character of logic shows that all inference is tautological. The conclusion always says the same as the premises (or less), but in a different linguistic form.... From this follows the impossibility of any metaphysics which tries to draw inferences from experience to something transcendent which lies beyond experience and is not itself experiencable; e.g. the "thing in itself" lying behind the things of experience, the "Absolute" behind the totality of the relative, the "essence" and "meaning" of events behind the events themselves.[14]

Carnap went on to say that if a sentence was neither tautological or contradictory (contradiction being the negation of a tautology), it was then demonstrably an empirical sentence, reducible to the given and capable of being ascertained true or false. He wrote these essays in 1931 and 1932. These lines were part of his bold definition of a new logic based on the latest discoveries in physics: this logic would be empirical and would cleanse science of its illusions and its sentimentality. If one proceeds from a statement to a phenomenon, one cannot logically deduce another phenomenon, Carnap began. So, what *can* a statement do in relation to other statements?

Let us turn then from the idea, or statement, about tautology to the idea about coffee. The Viennese logicians' idea about coffee lay elsewhere and is obscure; it only became generally known after Duchamp's death and did not accompany a discussion of tautology. It is nothing more than an aside that appeared in Neurath's book *Empirische Soziologie* in 1931 during a critique of Max Weber: "Empathy, understanding and the like may help the research worker, but they enter the totality of scientific statements as little as does a good cup of coffee which also furthers a scholar in his work." The cup of coffee internalized a reference to Poincaré's famous example in *Science et méthode* of his own inspiration, late at night, after having drunk black coffee but it summarized a line of thinking present everywhere in the Circle's first work.[15] It is the kind of one-liner that could well have been passed along for years in conversation, arriving somehow to Duchamp. The idea about coffee interferes with the standard machinery of logic; it introduces a break—it is another way of saying that in the beginning, there were givens that escaped.

Still, these were distant ideas, coming when they did into the interviews in 1958 and again in 1966. The idea about tautology had run through Carnap's early writing and in the early summaries being written for the English-speaking reader, but it was not a formulation that Carnap retained for long, nor does the idea figure in the work on the Circle's collective Encyclopedia that would be published both before and after the war, nor does it animate the series of annual international conferences in Prague, Paris, and Copenhagen organized in order to build momentum. The Unity of Science movement was something of an event in the thirties. Max Horkheimer felt their work worth following closely and sent Theodore Adorno, the man with whom he would write *Dialectic of the Enlightenment,* to write a critical report on the 1937 Paris conference. Adorno called Walter Benjamin out of Italy to come help. Benjamin came away more than skeptical, "*Molière n'a rien vu*" (Molière had not seen anything), he wrote to a friend.[16] The war would interrupt them all. Much of the Circle's work came to be done in England and the United States during and after the war, and it would become identified with the scientific successes of the war effort, including the atomic bomb and cybernetics. As for the idea about tautology, it is present no more in the books in the 1950s aiming to summarize the group's accomplishments, which were multiple and included the foundational work in semantics by Carnap, mathematics by Kurt Gödel, and physics by work of Nils Bohr.[17] In other words, the Vienna Circle was celebrated but their idea about tautology was an anachronism, stale beer, when Duchamp trotted it out.

Duchamp, his friend François Le Lionnais later explained, liked to discuss mathematics and tried to keep up with all the new advances; Le Lionnais being a Dada poet, champion chess player, and professional mathematician, and good friend of Duchamp since the 1920s, they had many topics.[18] Mathematics and chess demanded similar turns of mind. Le Lionnais would, along with his and Duchamp's equally good friend, mathematician-writer Raymond Queneau, go on to found OuLiPo in 1962 and Duchamp became an associate American member, interested from afar in this poetry that proposed to take its directions from mathematics, imagining anaglyph-poems and texts transformed through projection.[19] At his death Duchamp was working on an anaglyph for his Cadaqués fireplace. Duchamp did not, however, *study* mathematics; no matter what decade, he followed these things at some distance, from the corridors and with a delay. As with the talk around the *Rotoreliefs* in 1935, which Duchamp showed to "scientists (optical people)," as he put it to Katharine Dreier, Duchamp liked to learn through conversation.[20]

There would be similar conversations with mathematicians; there was some reading. Le Lionnais emphasized that Duchamp kept up by means of second-hand accounts,

Next double page. On the left: **3 Marcel Duchamp, *Rotorelief No. 11 – Éclipse Totale,*** 1935 (second edition, 1953), offset lithography on cardboard. The Frances Lehman Loeb Art Center, Vassar College, Poughkeepsie. Gift of Jane C. and Leon A. Arkus, 1991. On the right: **4 Marcel Duchamp, *Rotorelief No. 12 – Spirale Blanche*** – Modèle déposé, 1935 (second edition, 1953), offset lithography on cardboard. The Frances Lehman Loeb Art Center, Vassar College, Poughkeepsie. Gift of Jane C. and Leon A. Arkus, 1991.

describing them as books of essays written by the great minds of his time, which had been collected together for the general reader. It was probably Duchamp who persuaded Le Lionnais himself to translate *Mathematics and the Imagination,* a popular and spirited but intellectually sharp book written in 1941 by the American mathematician Edward Kasner and his student James Newman. Kasner was someone Duchamp had met in New York during the war and with whom he also talked.[21] Le Lionnais's translation of *Mathematics and the Imagination* came out in 1950.

Le Lionnais himself had already compiled such a book collecting the work of great minds, *Great Currents of Mathematical Thought,* immediately upon his release from the concentration camp at Dora.[22] It did not include the Viennese school of logicians. Le Lionnais' compendium was grounded in distinctly French debates, favoring the titanic dispute mounted in the 1920s between the formalists who followed the theses of David Hilbert and the intuitionists who followed the theses of L. E. J. Brouwer. Duchamp, Le Lionnais explained, had not gone that far: he was "stuck at Henri Poincaré," who had died in 1912. He named Poincaré's *Science and Theory* [*sic*] as a book that had particularly influenced Duchamp. But Poincaré was not being cited by Duchamp when after the war the subject of mathematics was raised by his interviewers.

Between Le Lionnais and Duchamp the mathematics debates collapsed into their own personal, private competition between the Hilbertian group writing since 1935 in France under the name Nicolas Bourbaki and the old lineage that stopped at Poincaré, neither abandoning their side, as if this too were a chess match. In 1960 Georges Charbonnier tried to draw out Duchamp on the subject of Bourbaki during the set of interviews they did for the French radio, but to no avail. Duchamp maintained a public modesty about his own grasp of mathematics and its evolution and had done so for years; already in 1934 he had made the decision to hold back the mathematical notes for the *Large Glass,* as well as those on the readymades and language, from the *Green Box,* a sign that he was aware by then that the mathematics of the continuum had a new frontier.[23] Meanwhile the history of twentieth-century mathematics had always had a third term, which by the late twenties was commonly held to be Viennese.[24] In the early thirties Gödel's two incompleteness theorems had by most accounts undermined the foundations of the Hilbertians' formalism. Kasner and Newman's book, partial to the Viennese, summarized the situation in a note.[25] Brouwer's intuitionism was the step in the debate that Duchamp did not, at least overtly, take. The proofs involved the mathematics of infinity; the disputes hinged on something Duchamp had upended for himself using different means—the Principle of the Excluded Middle, one of the givens of classical logic and the guardian of the principle of pure contradiction. Duchamp did not refer to mathematics when he worked on the *infra-mince.* He would agree already with Brouwer's declaration that "there are no non-experienced truths."[26] Was the *infra-mince* launching its own pile of counter-examples? Truth could proceed, then, to expand like the warmth left by someone else on the seat of a chair.

Duchamp's own work in progress came and went. He contributed to the Da Costa Encyclopedia after the war, the stakes of its work more apparent if one has the Unity of Science Encyclopedia in mind; his Da Costa entries, like the others, were designed to push logic

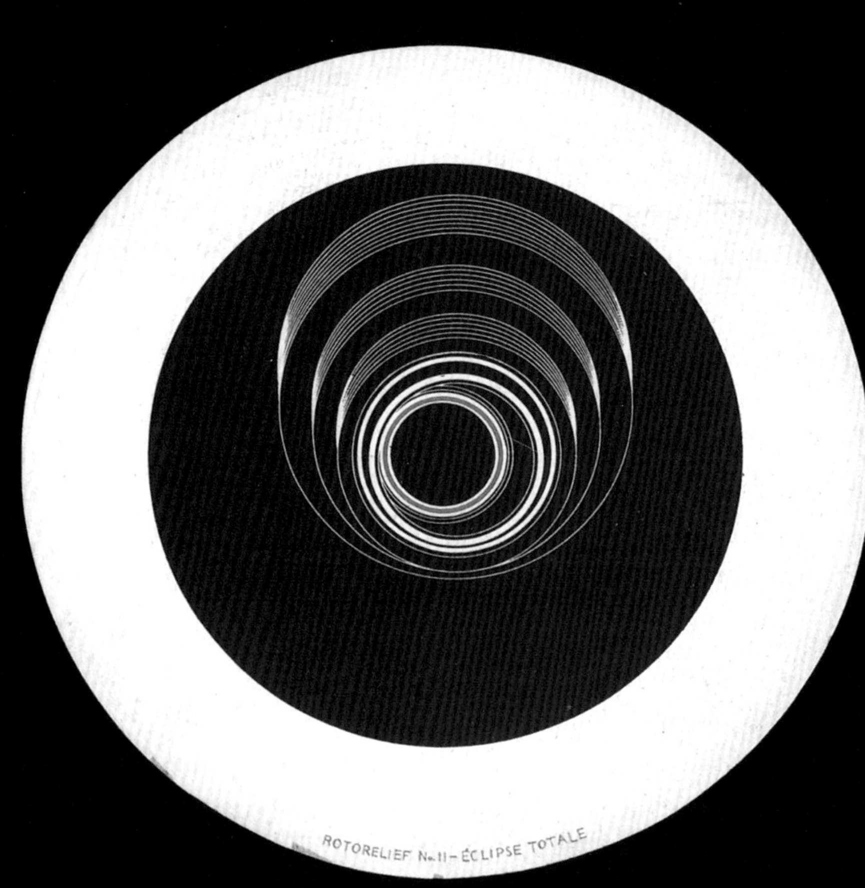
ROTORELIEF No. 11 – ÉCLIPSE TOTALE

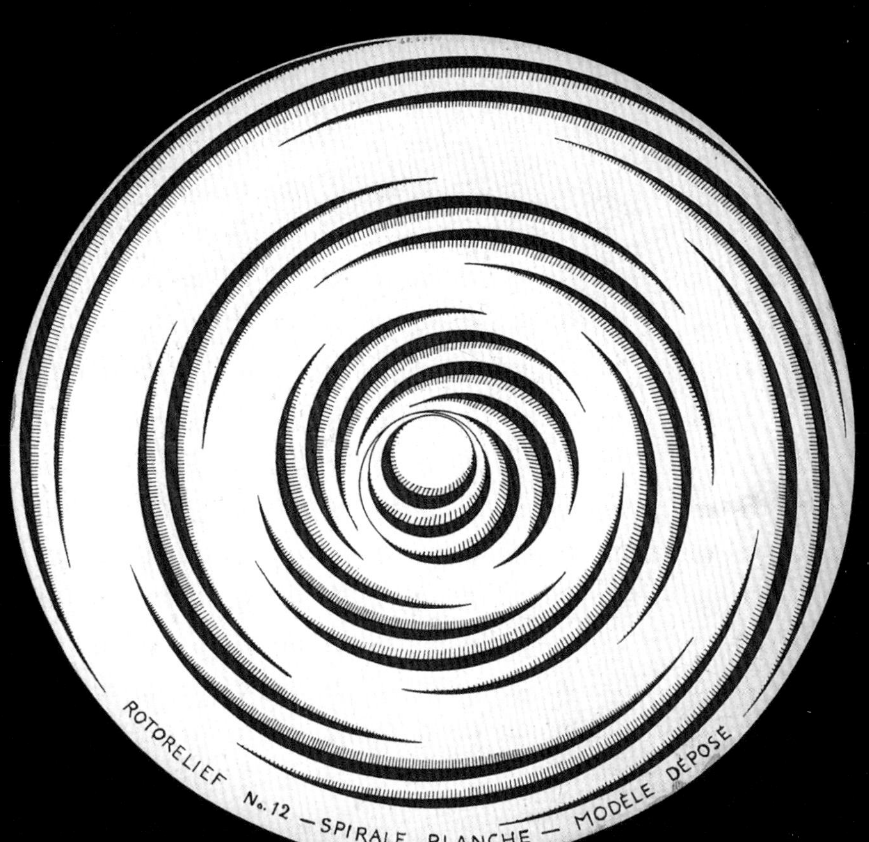
ROTORELIEF No. 12 —SPIRALE BLANCHE— MODÈLE DÉPOSÉ

over the edge. There and elsewhere Duchamp did not choose to think through tautologies or by pondering aesthetics. He liked to announce his distrust in logic. All the same, there were periods when he became more organized about refining his own ideas. One came around 1957, when he was preparing his lecture for the symposium in Houston on the Creative Act, a symposium that sought to collect great minds of the time and have them address *its* topic. Duchamp's talk stuck to the *propos,* but this was the year when he read more widely, when Kasner and Newman's book became his and Teeny's *livre de chevet* and C. K. Ogden and I. A. Richards' *The Meaning of Meaning* was read by them with great interest.[27]

The Meaning of Meaning came up now and then in his subsequent interviews. When explaining his ideas in 1959 to Anthony Hill, who was asking him about the problems and solutions line, hoping to hear about Wittgenstein, Duchamp first demurred, but when pressed about the philosophy, implied he admitted to having tried to read Ogden and Richards' book.[28] To Serge Stauffer in 1960 he lamented the limits to language and gave him the example of black coffee, this time uncredited, explaining that he had these ideas on his mind and hoped to use them in his series of radio interviews with Charbonnier, where they took another form.[29] When in the spring of 1965 Duchamp complained about language to Calvin Tomkins, he added that he'd been interested "in that group of philosophers in England, the ones who argue that all language tends to become tautological and therefore meaningless. I even tried to read that book of theirs on *The Meaning of Meaning*. I couldn't read it, of course, couldn't understand a word. But I agree with their idea that only a sentence like 'the coffee is black' had any meaning—only the fact directly perceived by the senses. The minute you get beyond that into abstractions, you're lost."[30]

When *The Meaning of Meaning: A Study of the Influence of Language upon Thought and of The Science of Symbolism* appeared in 1923, it was ground-breaking: it undertook to chart all the new modern developments in linguistics, philosophy, logic, and the sciences; it foreshadowed the kind of work the Vienna Circle would propose. In Duchamp's mind it probably existed as one of those anthologies that Le Lionnais remembered. It contains no coffee sentences but the same point is made by examples like "I have a sensation of yellow" or a match breaking into flame or a chicken offended by the taste of a black and yellow caterpillar.[31]

What to do with ideas? The idea about tautology had packed many of his thoughts about the insufficiency of language into a nutshell; an idea about black could be siphoned into the idea about black coffee. This work in progress on his ideas, condensing them differently, refining sugar from molasses by various means, producing the hurdles that would enable others to grasp something they did not understand yet, was dynamic. But black coffee was not, during these years, the only example Duchamp would use to conjure up the sensations that escaped understanding. He had other piles of examples building up elsewhere, quietly.

In 1963, when preparing the text of his long interview for *Vogue* with William Seitz, Duchamp struck eighteen pages from the transcript, cutting to the marrow, he explained, for reasons of length and because "many of the points I took away would have had to be completely reworked."[32] It is not the work we have come to expect from him, but it was not unusual. During the early sixties he made a practice of asking his audience for questions in advance of his lectures; presumably he had been doing the same with his interviewers. This way of working triggered another phase of notes, new notes: black examples came forward again, not always coffee now. In one of these new notes he considered using what he called the black sun of David Hume, a sketch done perhaps in anticipation of his filmed interview for French television later that fall with Jean-Marie Drot. He was unsure about the black sun, not certain the idea was really coming from Hume or, maybe, Herbert Spencer. But he saved it:

> "Le Soleil noir ou même pas noir—suivant un raisonnement simpliste et subjectiviste à la Hume?"
>
> Si on accepte le passage forcé à travers chacun des 5 sens d'un monde soi-disant extérieur, on ne peut s'empêcher de conclure que le soleil que nous voyons n'est ce que nous voyons que par le truchement de l'oeil et qu'en réalité, il n'est ni brillant ni jaune ni éblouissant et qu'il n'est même pas noir dans ce monde extérieur dépouillé de nos 5 sens. Il semble aussi que ce qu'on appelle conscience est la manifestation intime du concept être, ce qui revient à énoncer une tautologie. En face de ce mirage tautologique, je me permets de mettre en accusation le verbe être pour les crimes commis en son nom. D'ailleurs, l'école logistique de Vienne a depuis 1920 accusé de tautologisme les grandes vérités humaines comme les mathématiques, la religion, la métaphysique.
>
> appliquer à la peinture et à l'art
>
> ramener à la condition actuelle de surproduction, médiocrité—/ Phila le génie de demain prendra le maquis[33]
>
> ("The Black Sun or not even black—according to a reasoning, simplistic and subjectivist, à la Hume?"
>
> If one accepts the forced passage of a so-called exterior world across each of the 5 senses, one cannot help but conclude that the sun such as we see it is what we see only through the trick of the eye and that in reality it is neither shining nor yellow nor dazzling and that it is not even black in this exterior world deprived of our 5 senses. It also seems that what one calls consciousness is the intimate manifestation of the concept "to be," which brings us back to the statement of a tautology. In front of this tautological mirage, I allow myself to accuse the verb "to be" of crimes committed in its name. Besides, the logistical school of Vienna has since 1920 accused the great human truths, like mathematics, religion, metaphysics, of tautologism.

apply to painting and to art

take back to the current condition of over-production, mediocrity—/Phila[delphia] the great artist of tomorrow will go underground)

This idea about black set the matter into the sun; it was not Hume's trope exactly, it called to Gérard de Nerval. Hume had ended the first book in his *Treatise of Human Nature* in 1748 with a reflection on the place to which he had come, having cast off the received ideas of metaphysics, religion, mathematics, and logic. Hume was brooding. He had relied upon the principles derived from experience and habit, resigned himself to the impossibility of knowing anything for certain beyond his own senses; this meant that knowledge beyond oneself could be chimerical; this could lead to black thoughts, of shipwreck and melancholy, or not. It was certainly solitary.[34] Nerval, for himself, had launched melancholy into the image of the black sun in "El Desdichado," one of his poems he called *Chimères* in 1853. The disinherited knight from *Ivanhoe* follows the second descent of Orpheus down and cries:

Ma seule *étoile* est morte: et mon luth constellé
Porte le *Soleil noir* de la *Mélancholie*.

(My only *star* is dead: and my lute, star-strewn,
Bears the *Black Sun* of *Melancholia*.)[35]

For Duchamp the condensation and extensions in the black were perhaps the point. All of these examples together were giving Duchamp the grounds, the resistant's *maquis*, or underground, to take another step in his work in progress. His underground also conjures with the shadows, political ones, market critiques. These things were much on his mind in the years before he died. For he was now concluding that the abyss was not only to be found in the vicious circles of tautology; another, equally dangerous abyss was to be found in the illusions spun by the senses—being itself, whether a word or not, was small, beside some larger point, doomed *and* light.

This was an ever-expanding black. Black intuition had taken the place of the *infra-mince*, the word that had fallen from discussion after 1945.[36] The blacks in his examples now all moved beyond the simply retinal, or optical experience of a color: they occupy the space between the senses, they pull. *They* make a hinge at the end of the mind. It swung outward and never closed.

The *Rotoreliefs* had always accompanied this way of thinking. The idea of the *infra-mince* had come to Duchamp just after he'd finished them, as he expanded his thinking about just what had happened optically, scientifically with the play toy. At first he began to make lists of other possible examples of sense extension and, as he did, the *infra-mince* opened up in the space between all the senses, to be known only through examples; it exceeded even the words that described it. But while the word *infra-mince* was eventually put aside as Duchamp's sense of language's dangers grew, he kept the *Rotoreliefs* going.

There were five editions made overall—in 1935, 1953, 1959, 1963, and 1965. The *Rotoreliefs* do their work, turning viciously against a field of black velvet. That black suddenly opens up into the experience of objects and phenomena, as would the black coffee and the black sun. But were the senses in control? The last in the series of disks pushed the problem of apprehension to its extremes: first darkness falls, the total eclipse of the sun? of the moon? and then the next occludes everything with a spiral, like a blizzard's tail, spinning into white. And that would be enough. Now we *see* the hurdles. Was this Duchamp's treatise on human nature? There is no progress, no solution offered, in any of this work. As if to underscore the point once and for all, after his death he left us looking through black velvet into the work he called, like a provocation to all future minds, *Givens*. We do not know when exactly he'd come up with that name for this work. It too came from this way of thinking outside words, into infinity. Just like the waterfall, just like the illuminating gas, nothing about it is logical.

Notes

[1] "*Affectueusement, Marcel*: Ten Letters from Marcel Duchamp to Suzanne Duchamp and Jean Crotti," *Archives of American Art Journal*, vol. 22, no. 4 (1982), letter dated August 17, 1952, pp. 16–17. Given in French in *Affectionately, Marcel: the Selected Correspondence of Marcel Duchamp*, ed. Francis M. Naumann and Hector Obalk, Ghent 2000, pp. 318–22.

[2] Winthrop Sargeant, "Dada's Daddy," *Life Magazine*, vol. 22 (April 28, 1952), pp. 100–11.

[3] Quoted by Harriet and Sidney Janis, "Marcel Duchamp: Anti-Artist," which first appeared in the March 1945 Duchamp number of *View* and was reprinted in 1951 in *The Dada Painters and Poets: an Anthology*, ed. Robert Motherwell, 2nd ed., Boston 1981, p. 313. *Life* has given the quote a line edit, it seems. See also Rudi Blesh, *Modern Art USA: Men, Rebellion, Conquest, 1900–1956*, New York 1956, quoting Duchamp on p. 76: "Problems? There are no problems; problems are inventions of the mind."

[4] Marcel Duchamp, *Entretiens avec Pierre Cabanne*, 2nd ed. Paris 1995, pp. 129–31: "Vous connaissez l'histoire des logisticiens de Vienne? Les logisticiens de Vienne ont élaboré un système selon lequel tout est, autant que j'ai compris, tautologie, c'est-à-dire une répétition des prémisses. Dans les maths, cela va du théorème très simple au très compliqué, mais tout est dans le premier théorème. Alors, la métaphysique: tautologie; la religion: tautologie, tout est tautologie sauf le café noir parce qu'il y a un contrôle des sens! Les yeux voient le café noir, il y a un contrôle des sens, c'est une vérité; mais le reste, c'est toujours tautologie." Duchamp attacks the idea of belief on p. 111. I have used the translation from the English edition, *Dialogues with Marcel Duchamp by Pierre Cabanne*, trans. Ron Padgett, New York 1971, p. 107.

[5] From the Appendix in Laurence Gold, *A Discussion of Marcel Duchamp's Views on the Nature of Reality and Their Relation to the Course of his Artistic Career*, senior thesis, Dept. of Art and Archaeology, Princeton University, May 1958, pp. i–xiii.

[6] *Marcel Duchamp, Notes*, ed. and trans. by Paul Matisse, Paris 1980, n.p., note 91.

[7] Henri Poincaré, *Science et méthode*, Paris 1918 (first edition 1908), pp. 210–11. He reports his conclusions regarding analytic logic: "Une démonstration vraiment fondée sur les principes de la Logique Analytique se composera d'une suite de propositions; les unes, qui serviront de prémisses, seront des identités ou des définitions; les autres se déduiront des premières de proche en proche; mais bien que le lien entre chaque proposition et la suivante s'aperçoive immédiatement, on ne verra pas du premier coup comment on a pu passer de la première à la dernière, que l'on pourra être tenté de regarder comme une vérité nouvelle. Mais si l'on remplace successivement les diverses expressions qui y figurent par leur définition et si l'on poursuit cette opération aussi loin qu'on le peut, il ne restera plus à la fin que des identités, de sorte que tout se réduira à une immense tautologie. La Logique reste donc stérile, à moins d'être fécondée par l'intuition." On Duchamp and Poincaré, see especially Herbert Molderings, *Duchamp and the Aesthetics of Chance: Art as Experiment*, trans. John Brogden, New York 2010.

[8] Denis de Rougemont, *Journal d'une époque*, Paris 1968, pp. 563–64, entry dated August 3, 1945 and p. 569, entry dated August 9, 1945.

[9] James Johnson Sweeney interview notes, Archives of the Philadelphia Museum of Art, Alexina and Marcel Duchamp Papers, series III, box 3, folder 5 (February 1945?).

[10] "The Scientific Conception of the World: The Vienna Circle," first translated into English in 1973 in *Empiricism and Sociology*, ed. M. Neurath and R. S. Cohen, Dordrecht 1973, p. 306. See Thomas Uebel, "Writing the Revolution: On the Production and Early Reception of the Vienna Circle's Manifesto," *Perspectives on Science*, vol. 16 (2008), pp. 70–102; p. 306.

[11] "The Scientific Conception of the World" (note 10), p. 308.

[12] Ibid. pp. 309–10.

[13] Ibid., p. 309.

[14] Rudolph Carnap, "The Old and the New Logic," in *Logical Positivism*, ed. A. J. Ayer, New York 1959, p. 145. Originally appeared as "Die alte und die neue Logik," *Erkenntnis*, no. 1 (1930–31), pp. 12–26. In the early thirties Carnap's essays were

being translated and circulated in France: *L'ancienne et la nouvelle logique*, trans. General Ernest Vouillemin, reviewed and updated by the author; introduction by M. Marcel Boll, Paris 1933; *La science et la métaphysique devant l'analyse logique du langage*, trans. General Ernest Vouillemin reviewed and updated by the author, introduction by M. Marcel Boll, Paris 1934; *Le problème de la logique de la science; science formelle et science du réel*, trans. General Vouillemin, Paris 1935. In this context, it is worth pointing out that these ideas find their root in Wittgenstein's *Tractatus Logico-Philosophicus*, trans. C. K. Ogden, London 1922, p. 165, "6.124 The logical propositions describe the scaffolding of the world, or rather they present it. They 'treat' of nothing. They presuppose that names have meaning, and that elementary propositions have sense. And this is their connexion with the world. And it is clear that it must show something about the world that certain combinations of symbols—which essentially have a definite character—are tautologies. Herein lies the decisive point. We said that in the symbols which we use something is arbitrary, something not. In logic only this expresses : but this means that in logic it is not *we* who express, by means of signs, what we want, but in logic the nature of the essentially necessary signs itself asserts. That is to say, if we know the logical syntax of any sign language, then all propositions of logic are already given."

[15] It appears in Neurath, *Empirische Soziologie*, Vienna 1931, first translated into English in 1973 in the anthology of his writings, *Empiricism and Sociology*, p. 357. Meanwhile, Karl-Otto Apel, "Communication and the Foundations of the Humanities," *Acta Sociologica*, vol. 15 (1972), p. 16, translated the passage and called it "the cup of coffee theory of understanding": "Empathy, understanding and the like may help the researcher, but it enters into the system of statements of science as little as does a good cup of coffee, which helped the researcher to do his work." This was not a formulation Neurath continued to use; Apel's work has revived it. Poincaré, in *Science et méthode*, Paris 1918 (first edition 1908), p. 51, told the story of his breakthrough with Fuchsian functions coming, spontaneously, after drinking coffee late one night, a story which has become legend.

[16] See the Chronology in Walter Benjamin, *Selected Writings*, vol. 3, ed. Howard Eiland and Michael W. Jennings, trans. Edmund Jephcott, Howard Eiland, et al., Cambridge, Mass. 2002, p. 438. About the proceedings of "the Viennese logistical school," as he called it, Benjamin wrote to Gershom Scholem, "Molière n'a rien vu."

[17] The Circle's journal, *Erkenntnis*, like most of its other publications, was published in German, a language Duchamp could read, but they became increasingly aware of the need to circulate their ideas in other languages. Some of its articles were translated into French in the early thirties by General Vouillemin. Carnap's book, *Der Logische Aufbau der Welt*, 1928 (translated in 1967 as *The Logical Structure of the World: Pseudoproblems in Philosophy*, trans. Rolf A. George, Berkeley 1967), contains many of the formulations for the attack on metaphysics and it drew the attention of the Bauhaus, where he was invited to speak, and did so memorably, in October 1929. Neurath published an article, "Physicalism: the Philosophy of the Viennese Circle," *The Monist*, vol. 41 (1931), pp. 618–23. For English-language readers, A. J. Ayer, *Language, Truth and Logic*, 2nd ed., London 1946, became the chief means of dissemination of these ideas when it appeared in 1936; Philipp Frank's book, *Between Physics and Philosophy*, Cambridge, Mass. 1941, pp. 86ff, summarizes Carnap's argument in the Aufbau about tautology; the 1949 edition of Frank's book was titled *Modern Science and its Philosophy* was also important for continuing to register the contributions of the Circle in the 1930s, as was his later meditation on their subsequent work, *Modern Science and its Philosophy*, Englewood Cliffs 1957. Viktor Kraft wrote a general account of the group's work in 1950 that appeared in English as *The Vienna Circle*, New York 1953. Duchamp's reference to his reading of the Viennese school however specifies a *collectively written* book. As far as the collective work goes, after 1929 it was really done through individual contributions to the *International Encyclopedia of Unified Science*, ed. Otto Neurath, Rudolph Carnap, and Charles Morris, and begun in 1938, vol. 1, no. 1, Chicago 1938. The *Encyclopedia* drew upon the international colloquiums the group had organized in Prague (1934), Paris (1935 and 1937), and Copenhagen (1936); later numbers came out in journal installments. These were collected in 1955 into two volumes published by the University of Chicago Press. Neurath's introduction, written in 1938, already revises the 1929 pamphlet in favor of the pursuit of an incomplete knowledge, rather than a system, that will become this ongoing encyclopedia. The mathematics colloquium of the Vienna Circle published small specialized pamphlets of essays in the thirties and Kasner and Newman give one in the bibliography of *Mathematics and the Imagination:* Mark, Thirring, Nöbeling, Hahn and Menger, *Krise une Neuaufbau in den exakten Wissenschaften*, Vienna 1937, with an annotation that points to their work on the revolutionary aspects of modern science. In 1956 James Newman put together a much more accessible, four-volume set of essays called *The World of Mathematics*, New York 1956, which contained a good sample of the new work of the Vienna Circle, then largely dispersed in England and the United States. In 1959 Ayer put together an anthology of Vienna circle articles from all periods in his book, *Logical Positivism*, New York 1959, which has become the standard anthology for an overview of the work of the Circle. For an understanding of the evolution of the Vienna Circle's work, see especially Peter Galison's two articles: "Aufbau/Bauhaus: Logical Positivism and Architectural Modernism," *Critical Inquiry*, vol. 16 (Summer 1990), pp. 709–52, and "The Americanization of Unity," *Daedalus*, vol. 127 (Winter 1998), pp. 45–71. Friedrich Stadler, *The Vienna Circle: Studies in the Origins, Development, and Influence of Logical Empiricism*, Vienna 2001, remains the key reference.

[18] François Le Lionnais interviewed by Ralph Rumney, "Marcel Duchamp as a Chess Player and One or Two Related Matters,"

Studio International, vol. 189 (January 1975), pp. 23–25, includes the championship game played by Duchamp and Le Lionnais in Paris 1932 with commentary by Ksawery Tartakower (in French as Xavier Tartacover). Reprinted in *Duchamp: Passim; A Marcel Duchamp Anthology*, ed. Anthony Hill, Singapore 1994, pp. 127–28.

[19] See the first Oulipo manifesto written by Le Lionnais, in *La Bibliothèque Oulipienne*, vol. 2, Paris 1987, pp. III-VI.

[20] *Affectionately, Marcel* (note 1), p. 206, letter dated January 1, 1946 to Katherine Dreier.

[21] Edward Kasner and James Newman, *Mathematics and the Imagination*, New York 1940. Duchamp told Sweeney about Kasner and gave him Kasner's address. James Johnson Sweeney interview notes, Archives of the Philadelphia Museum of Art, Alexina and Marcel Duchamp Papers, series III, box 3, folder 10 (interview dated April 14, 1945) and folder 24 (undated note).

[22] François Le Lionnais, *Les grands courants de la pensée mathématique*, Paris 1948 (2nd expanded ed., Paris 1962).

[23] On this modesty see Calvin Tomkins, *Duchamp: a Biography*, New York 1996, pp. 444–45.

[24] See for a more recent set of assessments *History and Philosophy of Modern Mathematics*, ed. William Aspray and Philip Kitcher, Minnesota Studies in the Philosophy of Science, vol. 11, Minneapolis 1988.

[25] "The Scientific Conception of the World: the Vienna Circle" (note 10), p. 311, laid out the divisions between the new mathematicians plainly enough in one sentence: "Besides the logicism of Russell and Whitehead [with which the Vienna Circle had allied], there is Hilbert's 'formalism' which regards arithmetic as a playing with formulae according to certain rules, and Brower's 'intuitionism' according to which arithmetic knowledge rests on a not further reducible intuition of duality and unity." In *Mathematics and the Imagination* (note 17), pp. 221–22, the situation is mapped at slightly more length: "there are the Intuitionists, led by Brouwer and Weyl, who reject the axiom and whose skepticism about the infinite in mathematics has carried them to the point where they would reject large portions of modern mathematics as meaningless, because they are interwoven with the infinite; and there are the formalists, led by Hilbert, who, while opposed to the beliefs of the Intuitionists, differ considerably from [Bertrand] Russell and the Logistic school. it is Hilbert who considers mathematics a meaningless game, comparable to chess, and he has created a subject of metamathematics which has for its program the discussion of this meaningless game and its axioms."

[26] Brouwer's work did not have a general audience and was not easily accessible to non-specialists. See Dirk van Dalen, *Mystic, Geometer and Intuitionist: the Life of L. E. J. Brouwer, 1881–1966*, vol. 2, Oxford 2005. His student and mathematics professor Max Euwe was world chess champion in the 1930s and someone known to Duchamp. The passage cited appeared in an excerpt, "Consciousness, Philosophy, and Mathematics" [1948], published by Paul Benaceraff and Hillary Putnam, *Philosophy of Mathematics: Selected Readings*, Oxford 1964, p. 90. Jean van Heijenoort, secretary to Leon Trotsky in the thirties and part of André Breton's circle in New York during the war, became a mathematician and settled in the United States, producing a source book that also included some of Brouwer's work, *From Frege to Gödel: A Source Book in Mathematical Logic, 1879–1931*, Cambridge, Mass. 1967.

[27] Marc Décimo, *La bibliothèque de Marcel Duchamp, peut-être*, Dijon 2002, pp. 135–36, 207.

[28] Anthony Hill, "The Spectacle of Duchamp," *Studio International*, vol. 189 (January 1975), p. 21. As for the idea at the end of the *Tractatus Logico-Philosophicus*, trans. C. K. Ogden, London 1922, p. 187, proposition 6.5ff., it had entered philosophical conversation by the late 1920s. Hill made his first visit to L. E. J. Brouwer in 1959 and in 1968 he would publish his own excerpts from Brouwer's essay, "Consciousness, Philosophy and Mathematics," in his anthology *DATA: Directions in Art, Theory and Aesthetics*, London 1968, but he seems not to have discussed Brouwer's intuitionist mathematics with Duchamp, who is not present in the anthology. See instead Hill's *Duchamp: Passim* (note 18).

[29] Serge Stauffer, "Du Coq à l'Ane mit Marcel Duchamp" [1960], in *Marcel Duchamp. Die Schriften*, Zurich 1994, pp. 299–305. The interview with Georges Charbonnier has been published: Georges Charbonnier, *Entretiens avec Marcel Duchamp*, Marseille 1994.

[30] "Not Seen And/Or Less Seen," *The New Yorker*, vol. 41 (February 6, 1965), pp. 31–32.

[31] C. K. Ogden and I. A. Richards, *The Meaning of Meaning: a Study of the Influence of Language upon Thought and of The Science of Symbolism*, London 1923, p. 49ff. The 1948 edition is in the collection of books from Marcel and Teeny Duchamp's library at the Duchamp archive in Villiers-sous-Grez.

[32] William Seitz papers, Archives of the Museum of Modern Art, New York, box 1, series III, folder III, IA, letter from Marcel Duchamp dated January 5, 1963.

[33] Most of this note was published by Bernard Marcadé, *Marcel Duchamp: la vie à credit*, Paris 2007, pp. 458–59. It is to be found with the new group of notes in the Archives of the Philadelphia Museum of Art, Alexina and Marcel Duchamp Papers, series II, box 2, folder 29. Translated by MN.

[34] David Hume, *A Treatise of Human Nature*, vol. 1, New York 1911, see the conclusion, p. 249ff.

[35] Gérard de Nerval, "El Desdichado," *Les Chimères*, Paris 2005, p. 29. Translated by MN.

[36] *Les Quatre vents*, no. 8 (1947), p. 7, would publish the *infra-mince* back cover from *View* as a page layout with a different array of typefaces. It did not seem to produce much reaction.

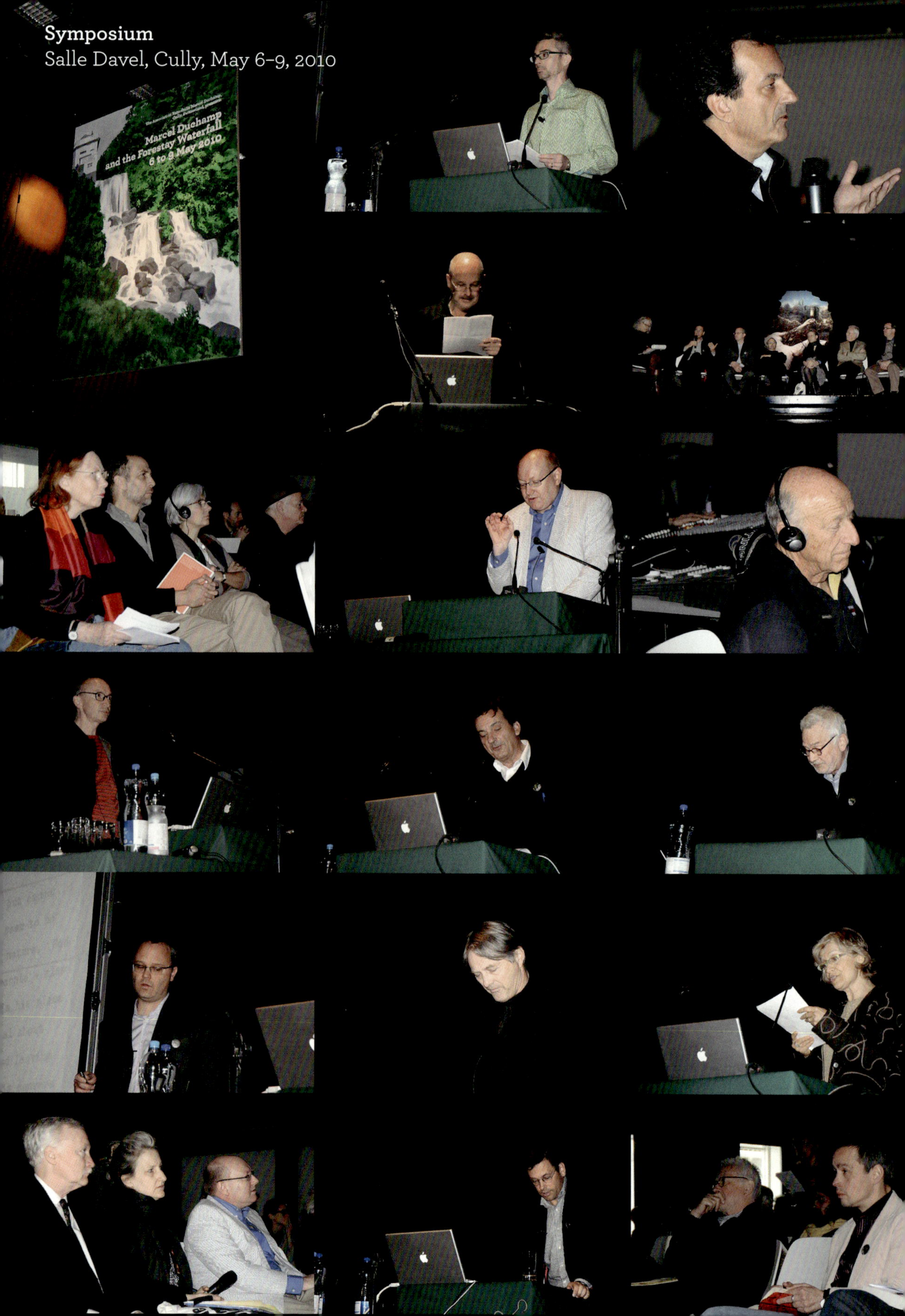

Symposium
Salle Davel, Cully, May 6–9, 2010

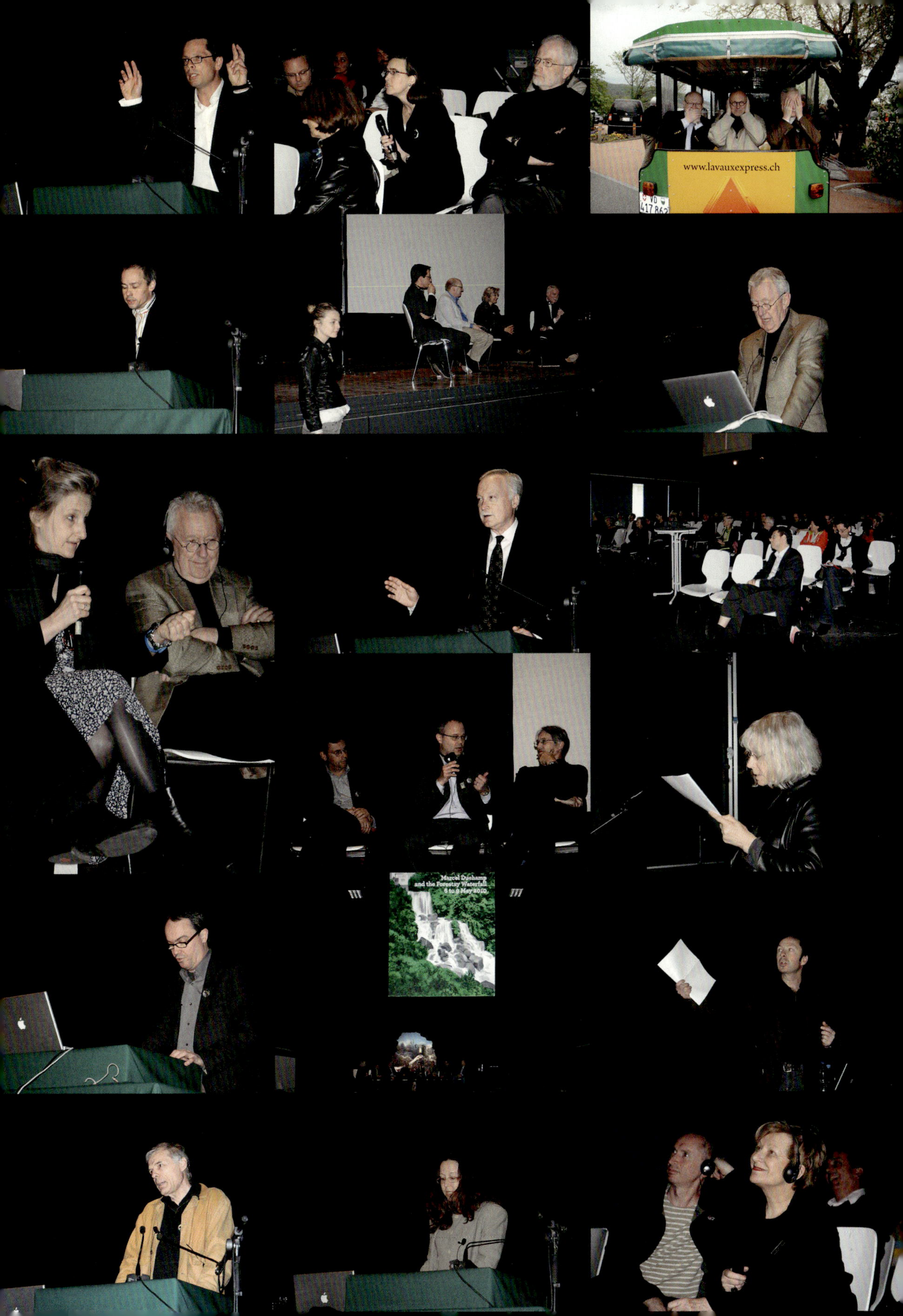
www.lavauxexpress.ch
Marcel Duchamp
and the Forestay Waterfall
6 to 9 May 2010

CONCERT – INTERVENTION – EXHIBITIONS

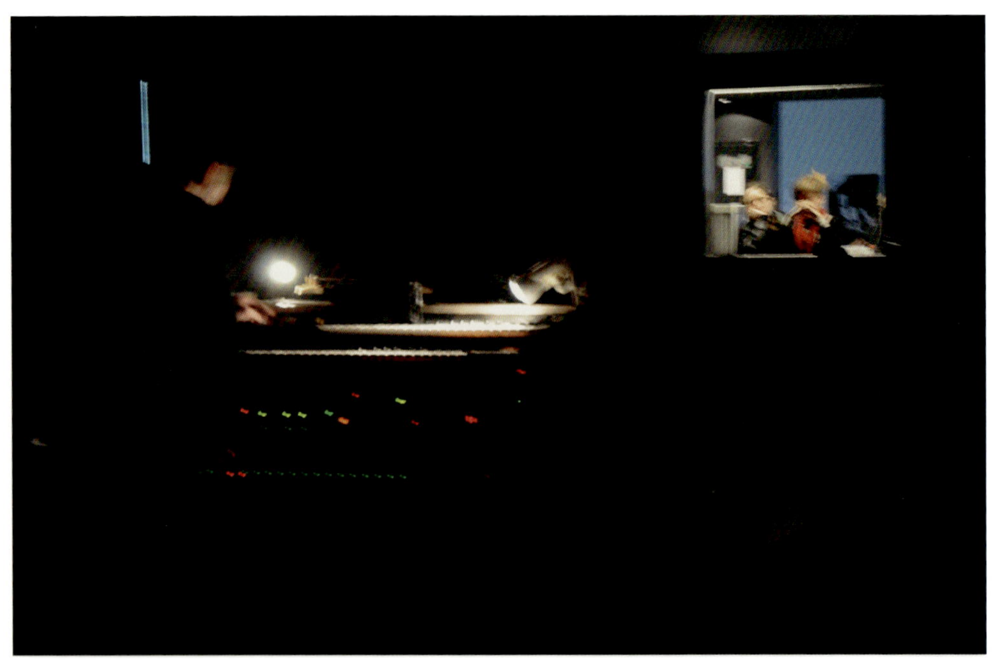

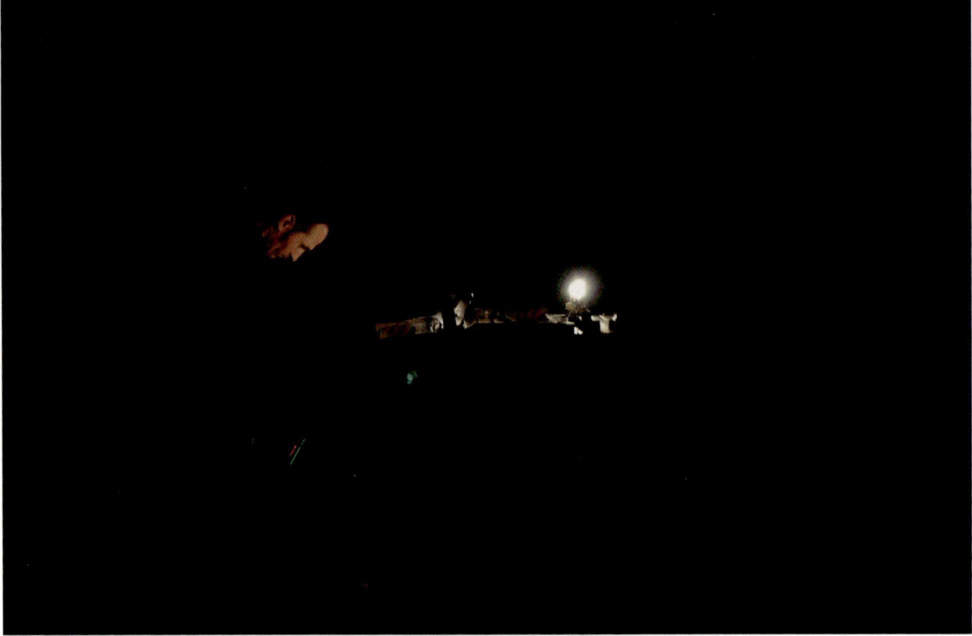

Andreas Glauser
Plays *Sonitus Errans* after Marcel Duchamp's *Musical Erratum*
Salle Davel, Cully, Thursday, May 6, 2010, 18:00

In his interpretation of Marcel Duchamp's only piece of music, *Musical Erratum,* Andreas Glauser works with the elements of random and instant composing. Instead of using the classical notation of music, he works with short, electronically generated compositions using devices that he himself developed. Based on sounds (*sonitus*—tone,

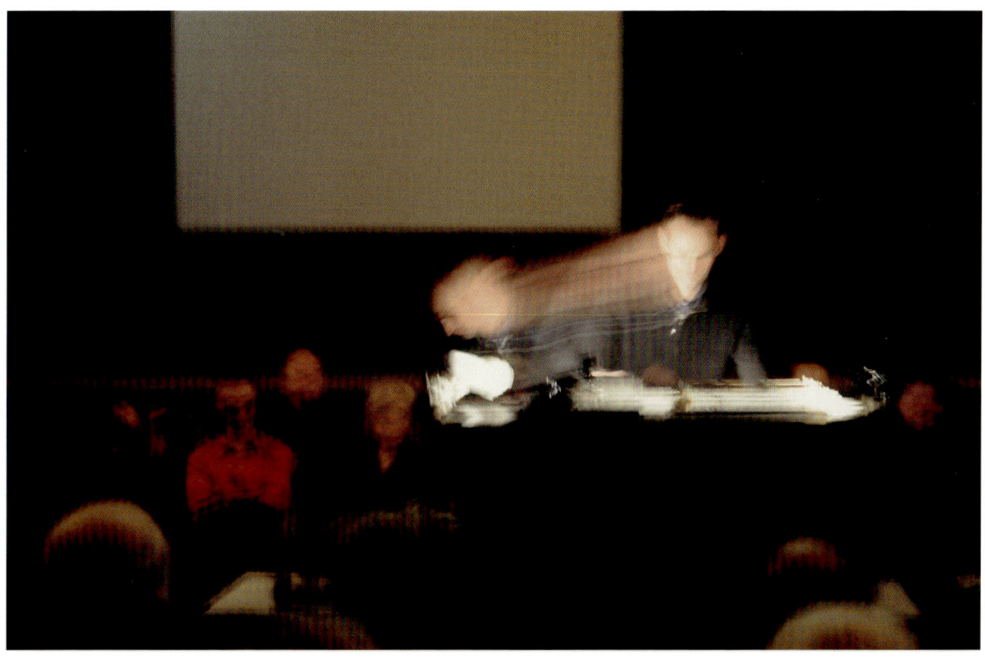

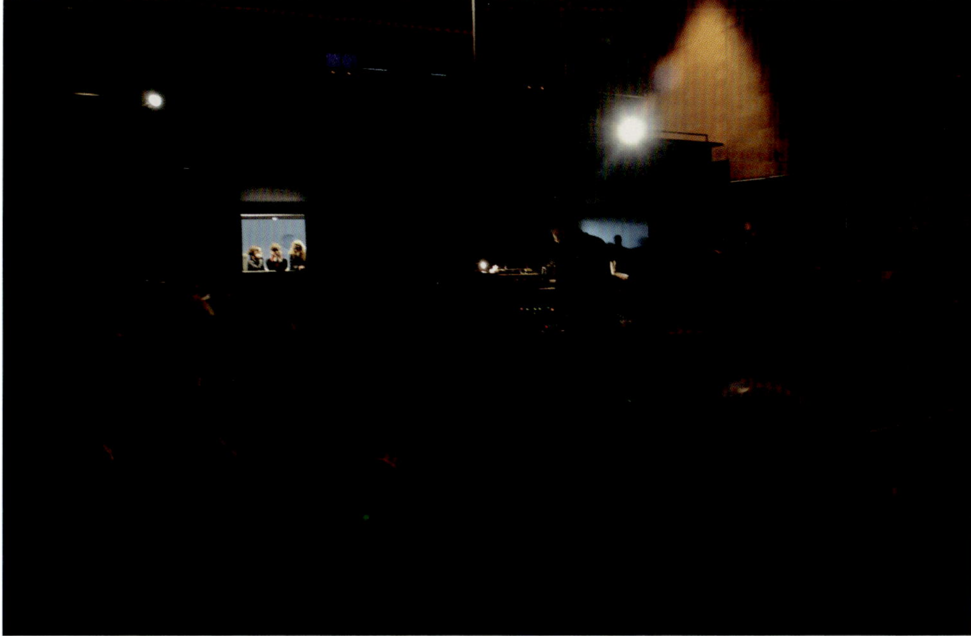

resonance, sound, racket, noise), these elements are the acoustic foundation of *Sonitus Errans*. Like Duchamp, who based the composition of his piece on the random combination of twenty-four notes, Glauser makes reference to the number 24. Programmed in random mode, twenty-four short compositions are heard on four players (*errare*—to make mistakes, get lost, wander, stray). Countless superimposed noises emerge, forming brief collages of sound to which the artist reacts live and spontaneously with his electronic mixer. What the audience perceives is randomly controlled instant composing. (S.B.)

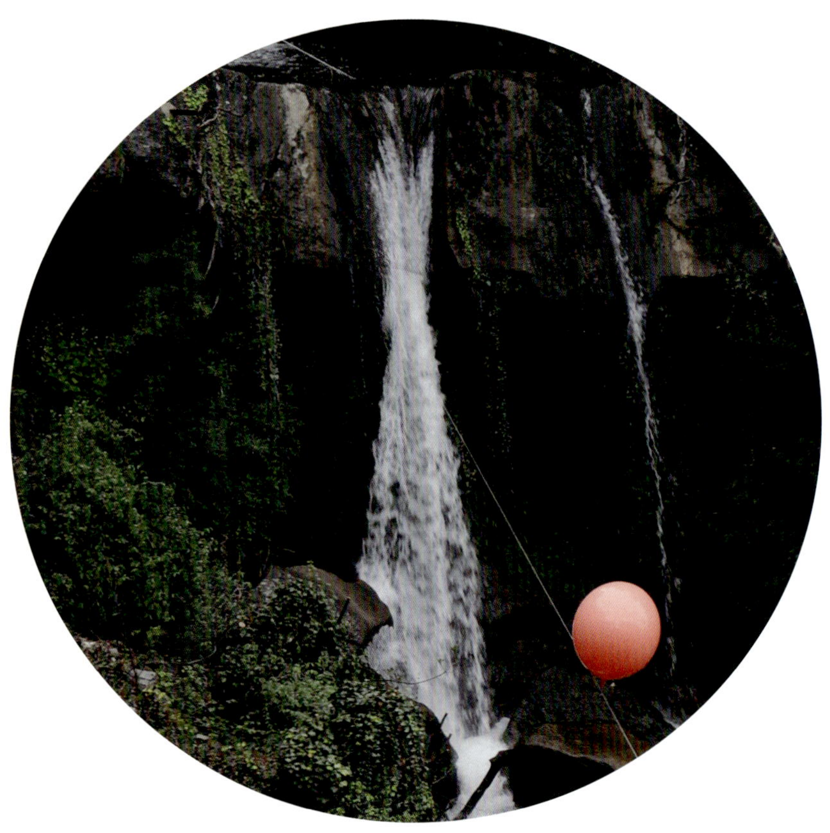

Roman Signer
Installation: Intervention in the Forestay Waterfall, Bellevue-Chexbres
Friday, May 7, 2010, 18:00

The *Installation,* as Roman Signer has titled his work for the Forestay waterfall, can be described as a loving and humorous homage to Marcel Duchamp's *Eau et Gaz à tous les étages* (Water and Gas on all Floors). A large red, helium-filled balloon attached to a thin rope is climbing up the cascading falls. Underneath a boulder it makes contact with the waters that are tumbling down. The wedding of gas and water, to use Duchamp's vocabulary, does not lead to a chemical reaction; instead—because the helium is enclosed in the protective, condom-like covering of a balloon—the fleeting and shapeless substance has acquired a form, and a physical reaction results: the balloon is bombarded with water and begins to quiver. For a brief instant the rushing waters change direction, but

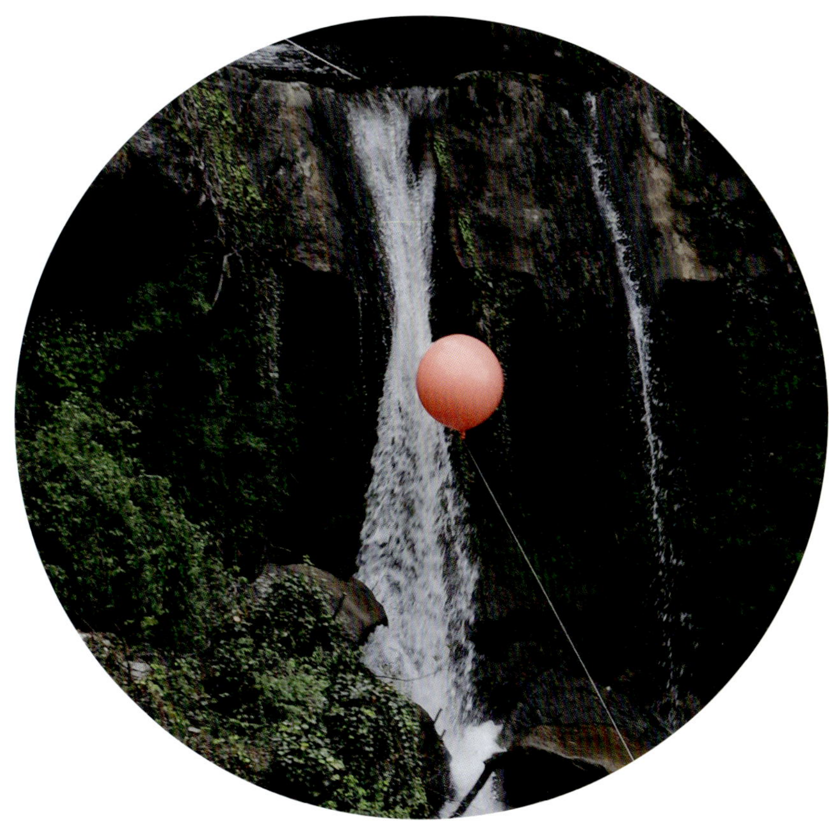

the pressure of the water is so great that it pushes the balloon away until it is out in the open again where it continues floating inexorably upward on the rope. Due to the steady uplift of the gas, the drama soon repeats itself. Again and again, the balloon tries to touch, displace, surrender to, or copulate with the water. The Sisyphean process is ceaseless, an incessant back and forth with no end in sight (as in Duchamp's idea of the runners and the love pistons in the *Large Glass*). Roman Signer's *Installation* demonstrates how senseless and attractive futility is, or, to put it differently, how precarious and poetic physis (Greek: nature) can actually be. (S.B.)

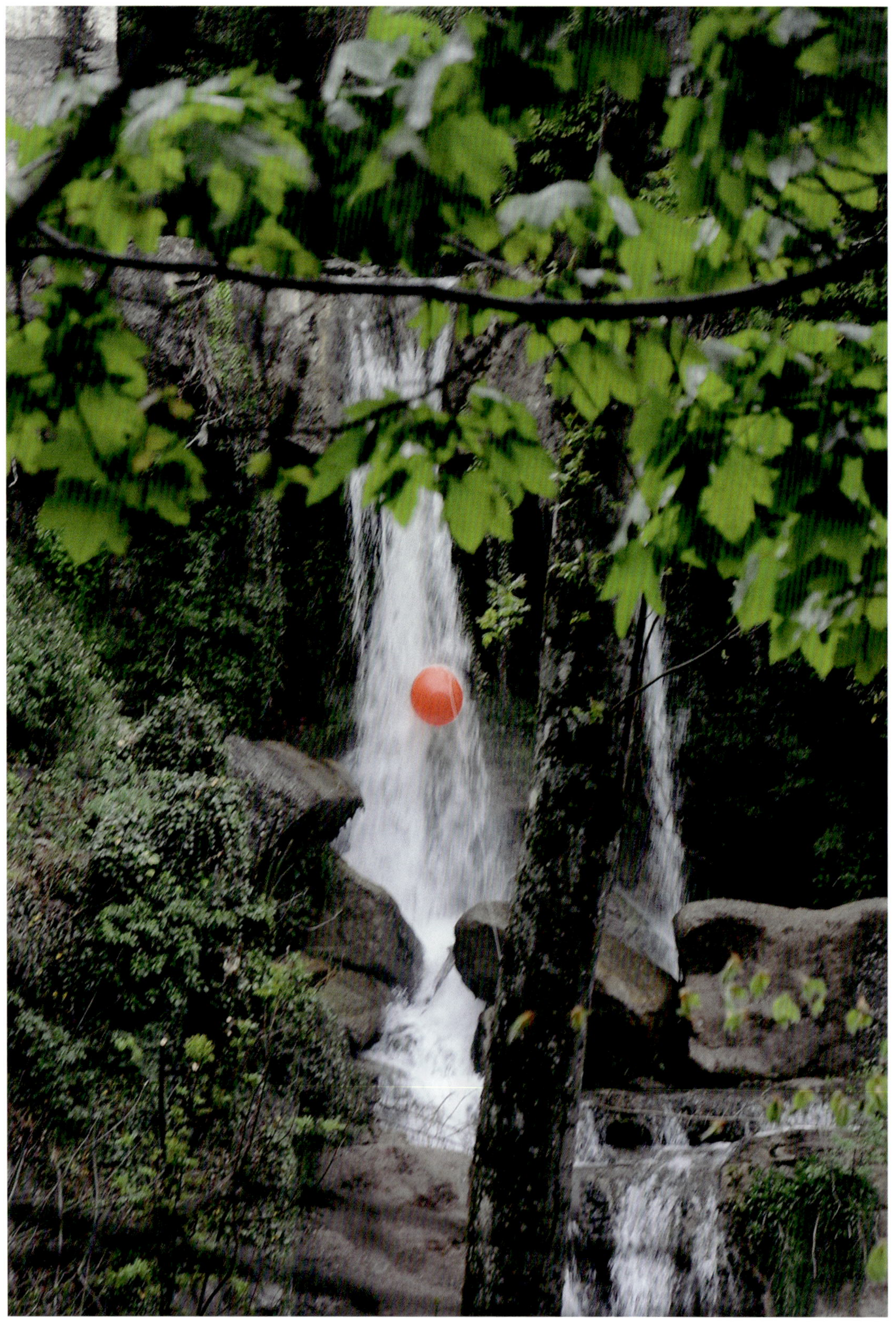

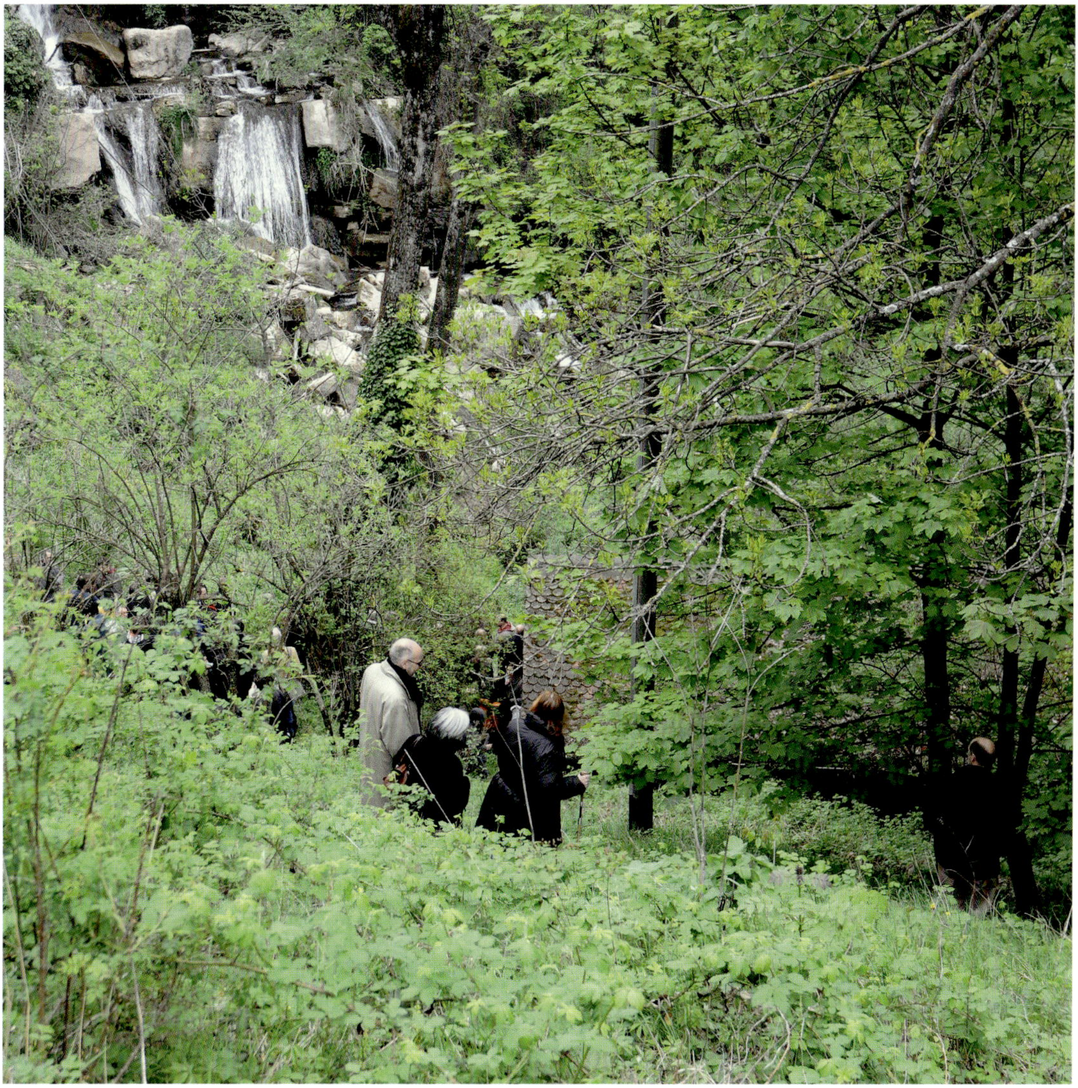

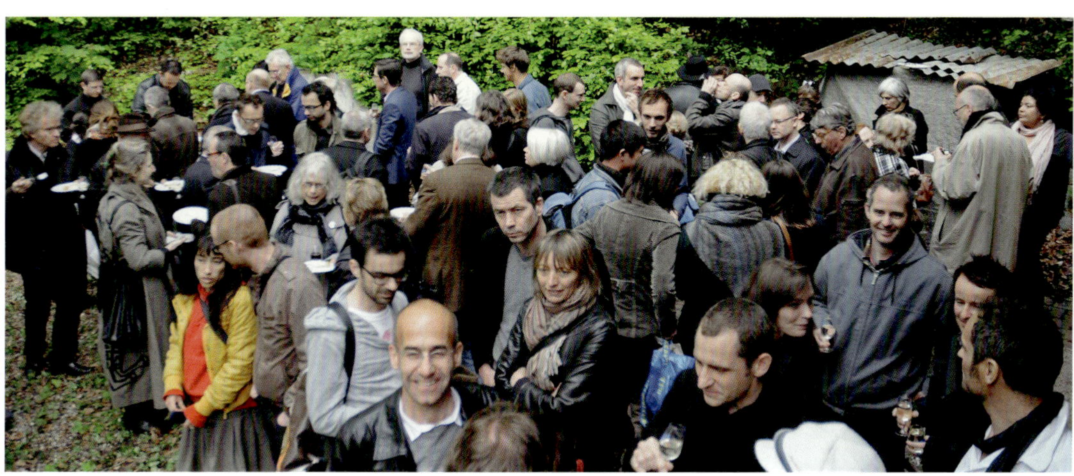

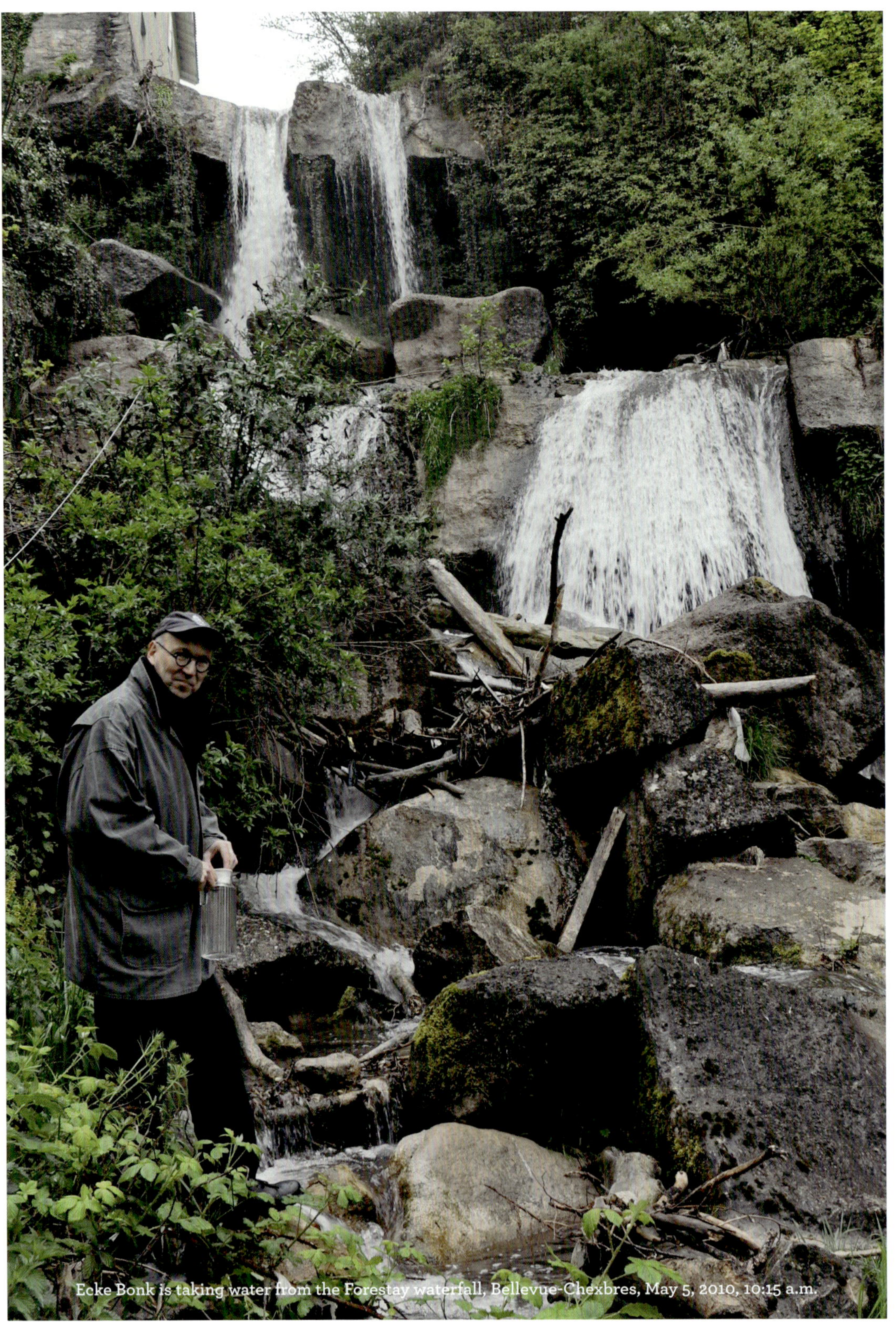

Ecke Bonk is taking water from the Forestay waterfall, Bellevue-Chexbres, May 5, 2010, 10:15 a.m.

Ecke Bonk – *50cc Eau de Forestay, 110gr Auer von Welsbach*
... et quelques rayons cosmiques

Inaugural exhibition at Kunsthalle Marcel Duchamp, Cully
Architect: Melanie Althaus

Opening: Thursday, May 6, 2010, 19:00
Exhibition: May 7–June 13, 2010

Adeena Mey

Cosmic Diagram

On Ecke Bonk's Exhibition and Melanie Althaus's Architecture

Eau et gaz. Let me reiterate and borrow Ecke Bonk's own *formula:* "50cc Eau de Forestay, 110gr Auer von Welsbach." Here, Bonk traces two of the coordinates of the Duchampian space. These two elements—which have traversed Duchamp's economy of fluxes to gain their most explicit significance in *Étant donnés*—are resorted to by Bonk to produce an intervention that both re-enacts and extends a Duchampian gesture and which recasts it within a different plane where the French artist's life stories and his work collide and intertwine with the technological artifacts of Carl Auer von Welsbach (the gas mantle or "Welsbach mantle") and their cultural histories. In this regard, Bonk's formula functions as a re-formulation—that is, following the etymology of the word, both a method *and* a form—of Duchamp's and Welsbach's principles. As a matter of fact, the author of *The Portable Museum* and amateur of the epistemology of science has literally placed within the modular rooms of the *Kunsthalle Marcel Duchamp* "50cc Eau de Forestay" and "110gr Auer von Welsbach." Thus, if the first part of the title of Bonk's work sounds like the name of a perfume, it is—similarly to Duchamp and his *Belle Haleine*—a means of drawing one's attention to the importance of the olfactory. The water of the Forestay waterfall, in its tiny glass container, and the gas lamp both manifest themselves through their smells. Yet here a first chiasm must be noted. Indeed, in the way they were displayed, these idiosyncratic drops of water and flow of gas first appeared as objects to be viewed. Hence, if the title rather points at their smell, this is only to produce a twist within the economy of senses through which one comes to apprehend Bonk's intervention as well as to de-encapsulate the invisible and unsayable thresholds that divide up language, the senses, objects, and the worlds they inhabit.

* * *

50cc Eau de Forestay, 110gr Auer von Welsbach ... et quelques rayons cosmiques is the first exhibition to take place in the newly built Kunsthalle Marcel Duchamp (KMD). Designed by Swiss architect Melanie Althaus, the building of approximately 40 x 40 x 40 cm combines a modernist approach to surface, structure, and function with a playful set of references to Duchamp as well as with different approaches to opticality and viewing modalities. All vertical surfaces of the KMD and its top are equipped with viewfinders that double-function as windows. Since they are projecting, not only do they enable the viewer to engage in singular optical experiences with the works displayed, but they can also act as exhibition spaces themselves. Moreover, thanks to their almost anamorphic nature, these telescopic devices mimic the very bodily action of viewing: the KMD gazes at those who gaze through it, and engaging with the works consequently requires particular corporeal movements. But the kind of optical regime enabled by this structure does not merely revolve around such a simplistic dualism (viewing/being viewed). For one can see through it and must break with one's viewing habits, and because viewership becomes a process of constant framing and re-framing, the visual ontology of the KMD oscillates between opacity and transparency, appearance and disappearance, thus highlighting the importance

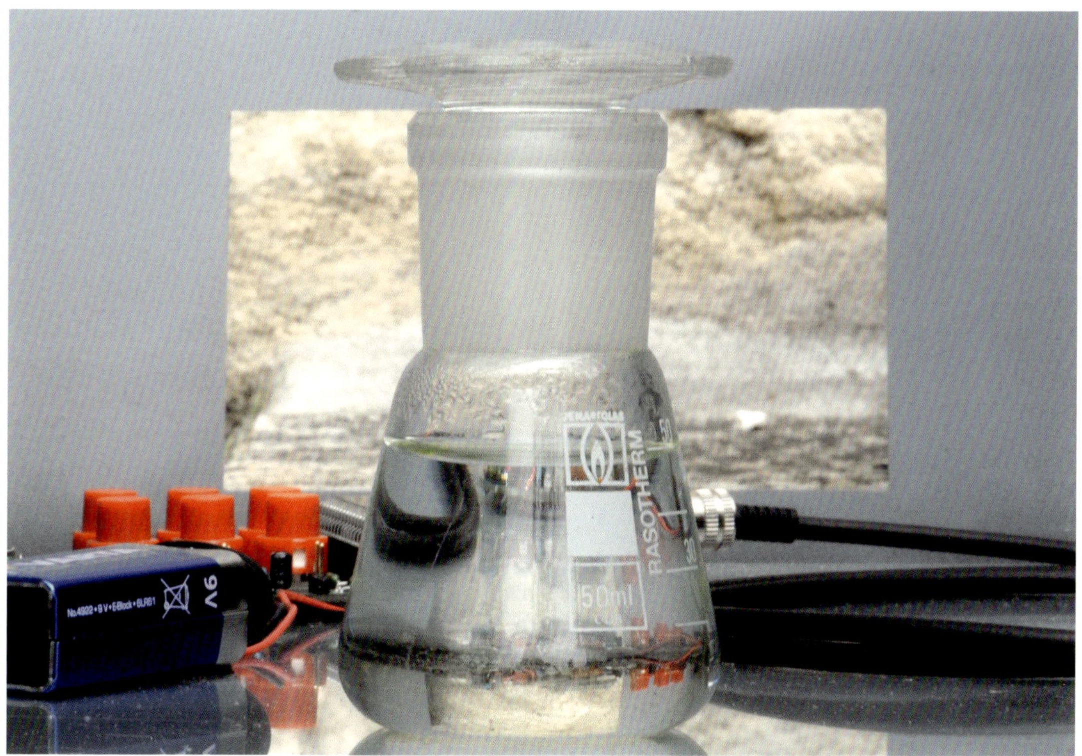

Ecke Bonk, *50cc Eau de Forestay,* Erlenmeyer bottle, 50cc of water from the Forestay waterfall, Geiger counter, battery, live wires, Kunsthalle Marcel Duchamp, Cully, 2010.

of its location—Cully on the shores of Lake Geneva—and producing a kind of evolving kaleidoscopic space within the very spatial setting that "Duchamp abandoned for the waterfall" (Bachmann and Banz). Hence if by its size it literally is a model—a miniature "kunsthalle"—from the point of view of curatorial practices, the KMD is also a model for the type of experiments in exhibition-making aimed at other Kunsthallen, which attempt at the creation of "a state of permanent constructive conflict within contemporary art production" (Ruf).

* * *

This little detour through questions of space and vision now allows me to go back to *50cc Eau de Forestay, 110gr Auer von Welsbach ... et quelques rayons cosmiques.* In his graceful analysis of Vittore Carpaccio's *Sacra Conversazione,* philosopher Michel Serres resorts to that painting to tell us that space is protean in that it multiplies *sites* and *graphs.* In other words, it generates more spaces and, at the same time, tracings of the latter. Alongside the water taken from the Forestay waterfall and the Welsbach mantle, Bonk has installed two Geiger counters that measure the radiations of the site where they are located. These radiations are different in each and every location and the Geiger counter allows for such subtle measurements, which emphasize the highly specific location of each place within the cosmos; it is as if it could actually draw lines circumscribing the location of the KMD and its multiple ties that connect it to the latter. But again, in an analogous chiasmatic

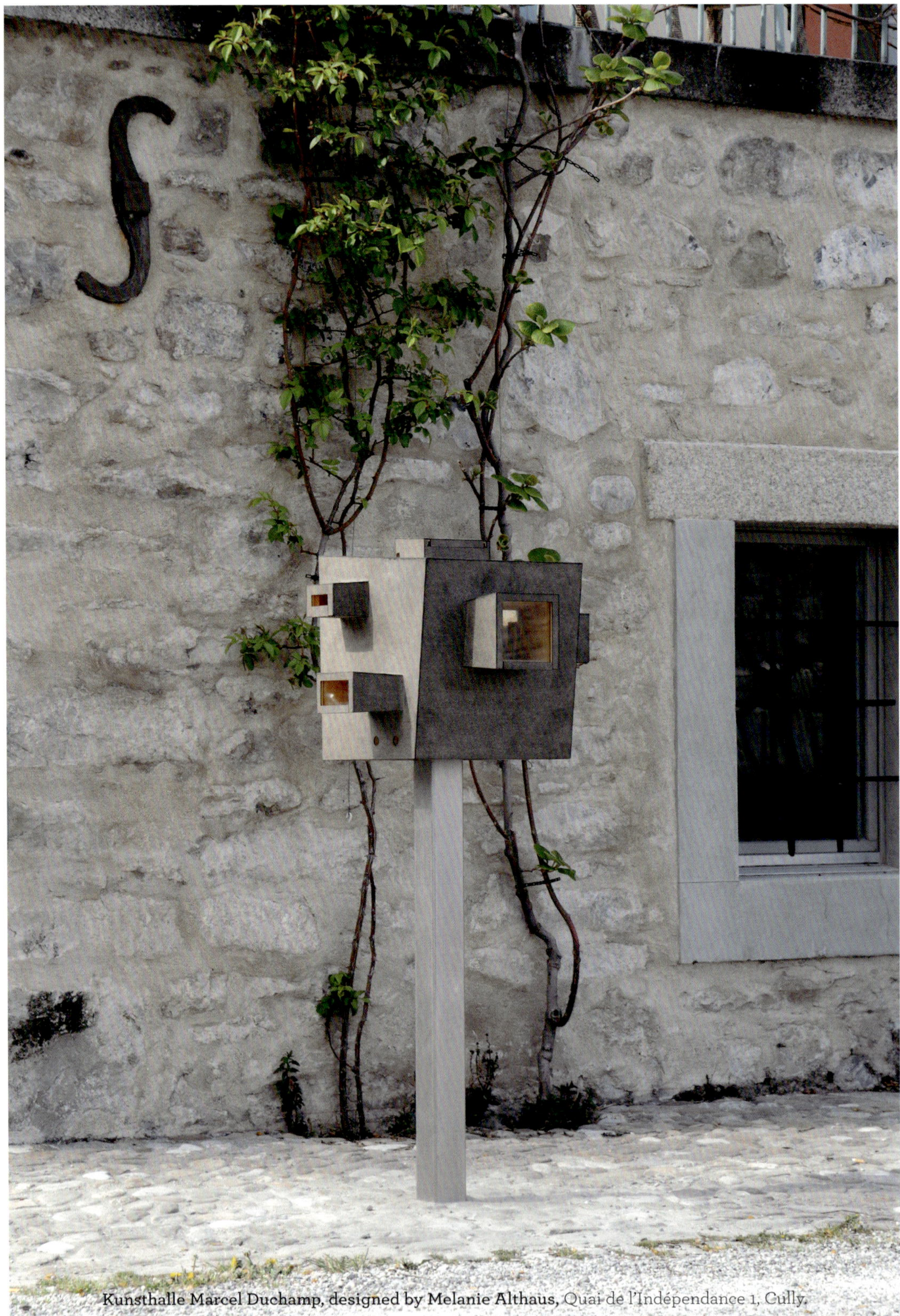

Kunsthalle Marcel Duchamp, designed by Melanie Althaus, Quai de l'Indépendance 1, Cully.

movement to that consisting of inviting the viewer through the invocation of the linguistic manifestation of the olfactory dimension of his work, radiations do occur, but one can only perceive them through the *mediation* of the Geiger counter, which, for Bonk, doubles the events. In this sense, he uses this device as a technological metaphor for perception. Let's remind ourselves that the recording instrument developed by Hans Geiger itself functions by provoking *cascades* of ionization. Radiations are thus pervasive and, unlike physical spaces, do not have ends. They are limitless. Hence, within such a continuous flow, how and when do they come to be experienced and how and when does experience translate into an object of thought and consciousness? Radiations *per se* do not reveal their point of saliency. However, real-time measurements of the passages of radiations provide data for a chart yet to be drawn and the presence of the counter within the KMD pinpoint at their localization (one that actually overflows its material boundaries): *graph* and *site*.

* * *

Duchamp's name sits as comfortably in aesthetic narratives as in epistemological ones. From the point of view of the second, his method can be seen as one that—thanks to a historically constituted specific declension of authorship—wittily manages to grant objects unprecedented ontological status. Such an assertion is hardly enunciable in the case of Carl Auer von Welsbach. His biographical data often state that he is both a "scientist" or "discoverer" *and* an "inventor." This sums up the great anxiety of modern science: if things are invented—that is man-made—they are not objective, whereas scientists supposedly reveal and describe phenomena that have been waiting to be discovered. Historical, epistemological, and aesthetic reasons all play their part in this segmentation of the world's phenomenal realities, the way we perceive them and the modalities through which we apprehend them. The assemblage resulting from the encounter between the constellation of Bonk's objects and the KMD acts as a machine that re-reads the histories of Duchamp and Welsbach, explores the interstitial spaces left out by scholarship, circumscribes their territories, and convokes the artifacts (the water from the waterfall, the gas) that symbolize these stories (Duchamp's stay at the Forestay waterfall and the heterogenesis of both *Étant donnés* and Auer von Welsbach's lamp) and in which they are embodied. Bonk has thus produced a "diagram" (Deleuze) in that his assemblage maps all these components to create, by the same token, a whole new constellation in which thresholds between non-knowledge (Maharaj) and perception are re-negotiated, with this permanent concern as event-horizon: acknowledging the heterogeneity of positions within diverse chaosmologies (Joyce/Bonk).

References

Caroline Bachmann and Stefan Banz, *What Duchamp Abandoned for the Waterfall*, Zurich 2009.
Ecke Bonk, *Monte Carlo Method: A Typosophic Manual*, Munich 2007.
Gilles Deleuze, *Foucault*, Paris 1986.
Beatrix Ruf, "The Kunsthalle Format" in *The Exhibitionist: Journal on Exhibition Making*, no. 1 (2010), pp. 37–39.
Michel Serres, *Esthétiques sur Carpaccio*, Paris 1975.

Ecke Bonk, *50cc Eau de Forestay,* Erlenmeyer bottle, 50cc of water from the Forestay waterfall, Kunsthalle Marcel

Ecke Bonk, *... et quelques rayons cosmiques,* Geiger counter, battery, live wires, light, Kunsthalle Marcel Duchamp, Cully, 2010.

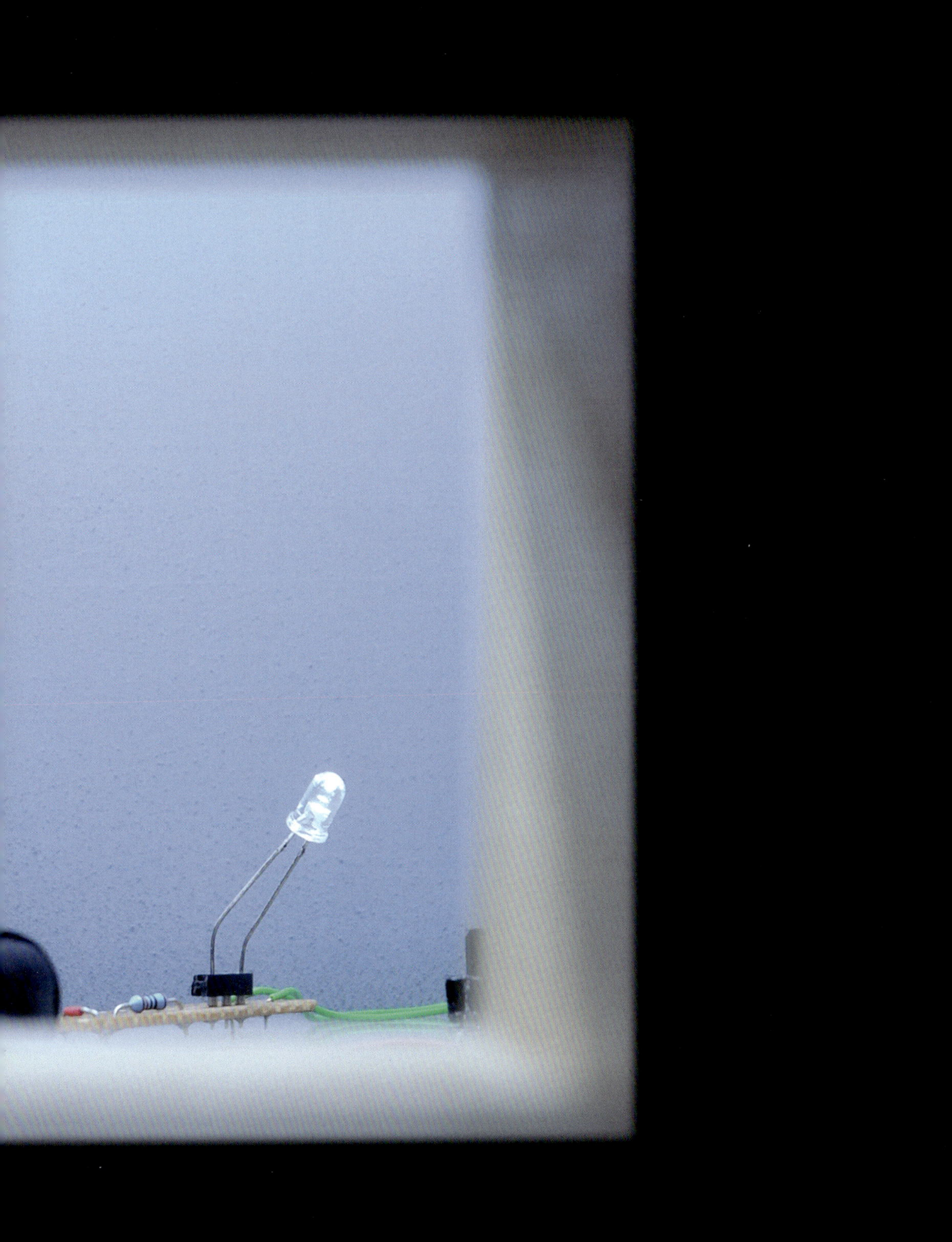

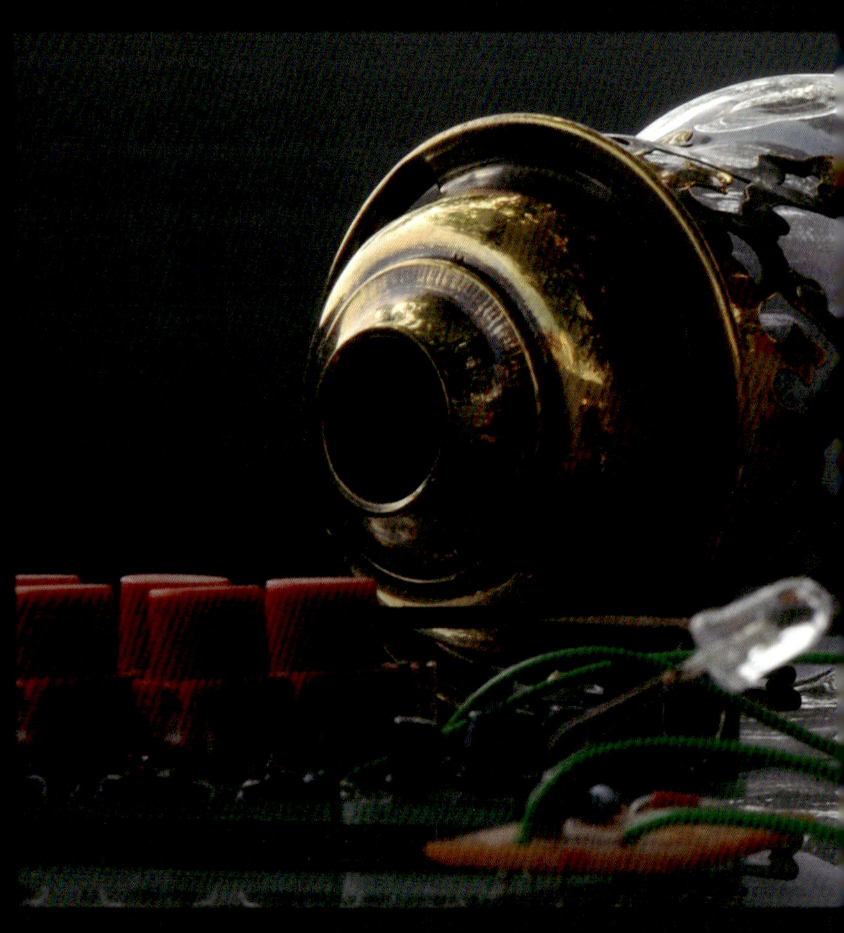

Ecke Bonk, *110gr Auer von Welsbach ... et quelques rayons cosmiques,* bec Auer glass, metal fittings, bec Auer gas mantle, Geiger counter, battery, live wires, light, Kunsthalle Marcel Duchamp, Cully, 2010.

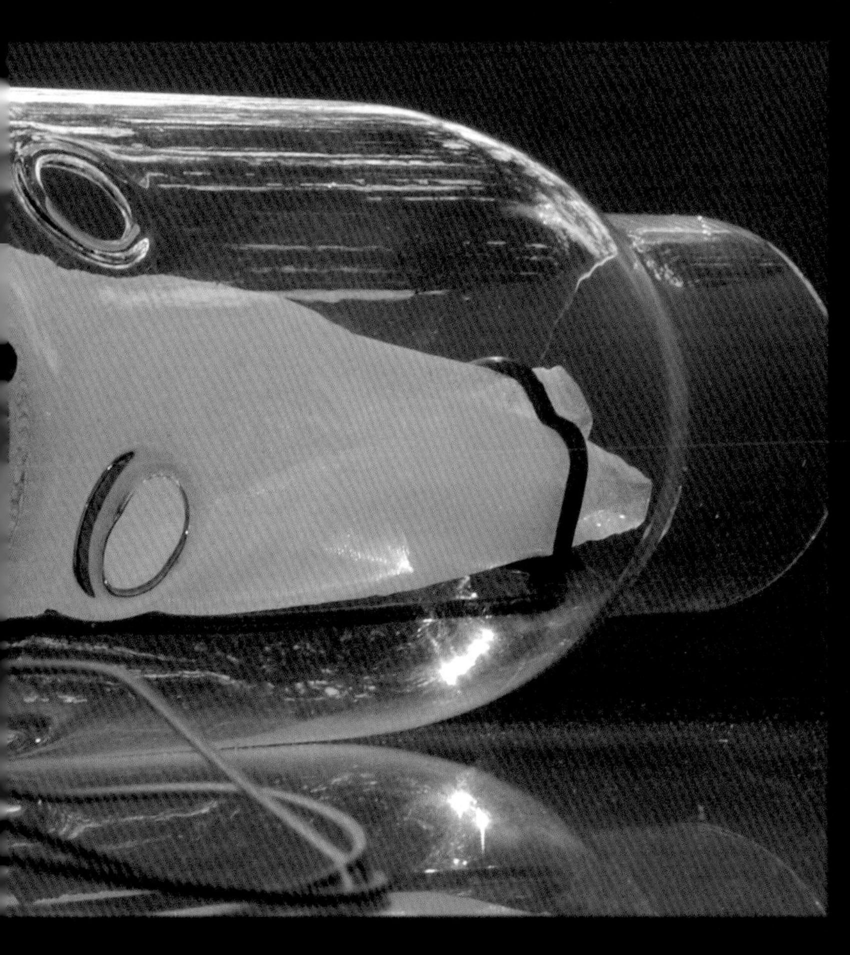

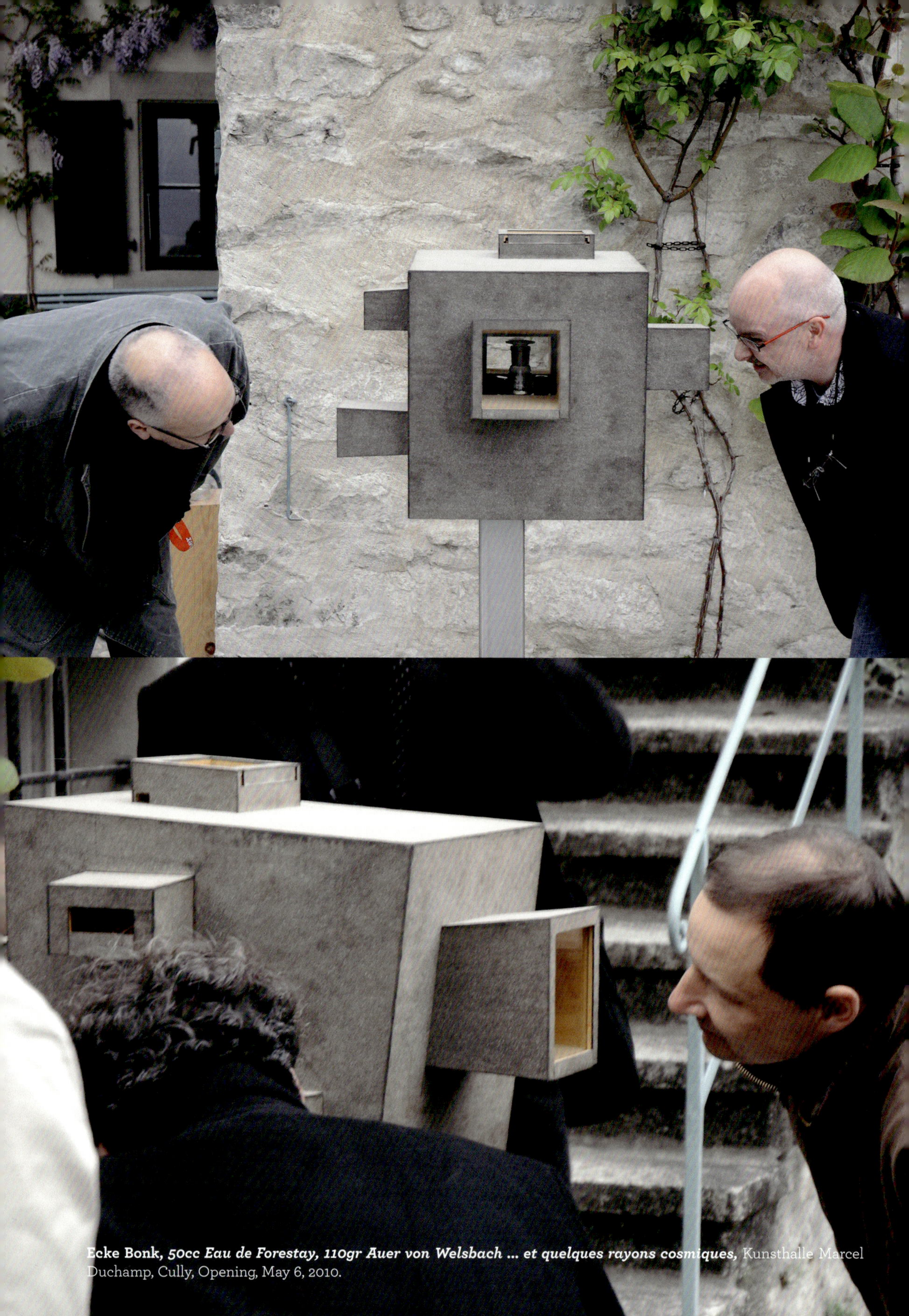

Ecke Bonk, *50cc Eau de Forestay, 110gr Auer von Welsbach … et quelques rayons cosmiques,* Kunsthalle Marcel Duchamp, Cully, Opening, May 6, 2010.

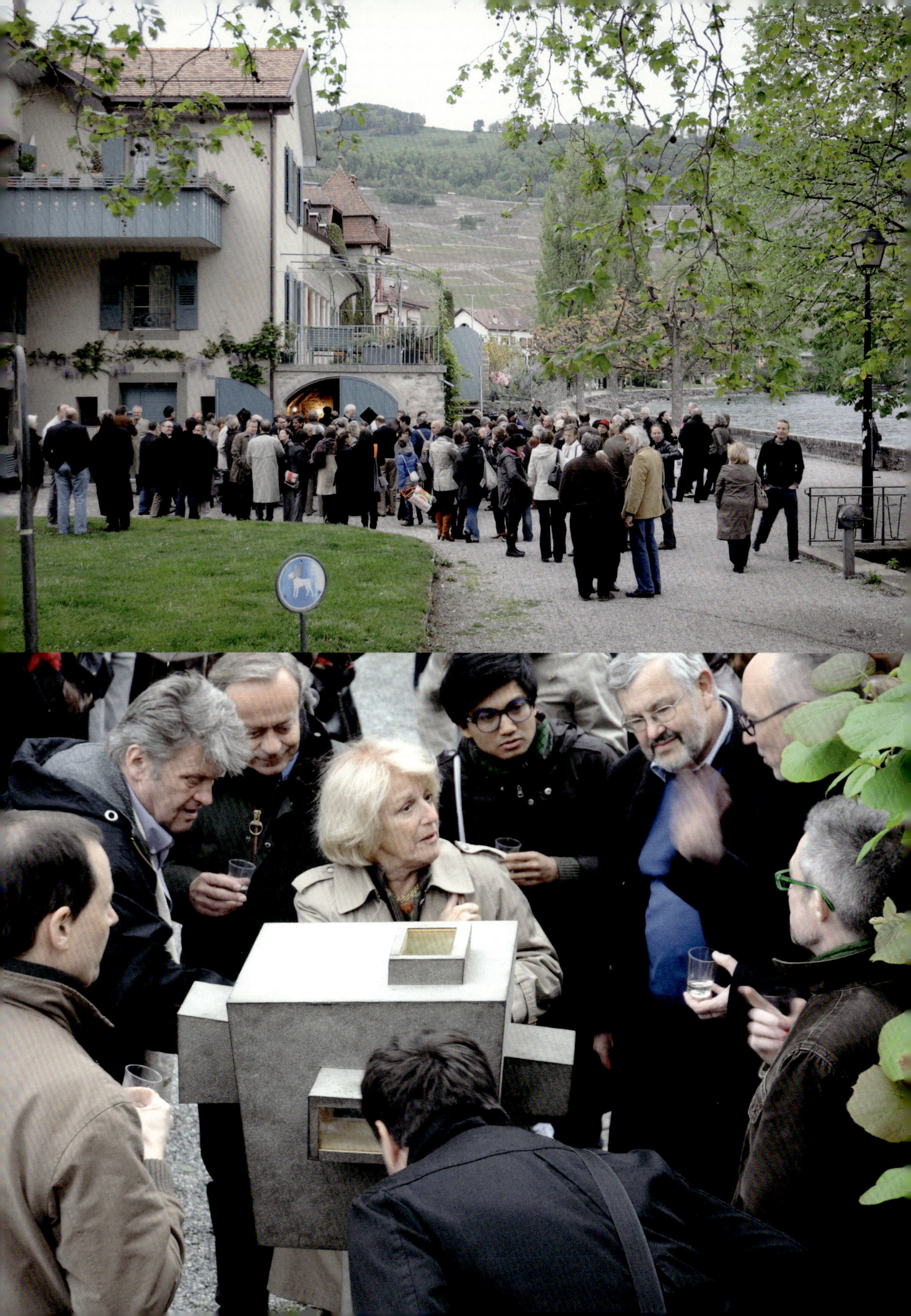

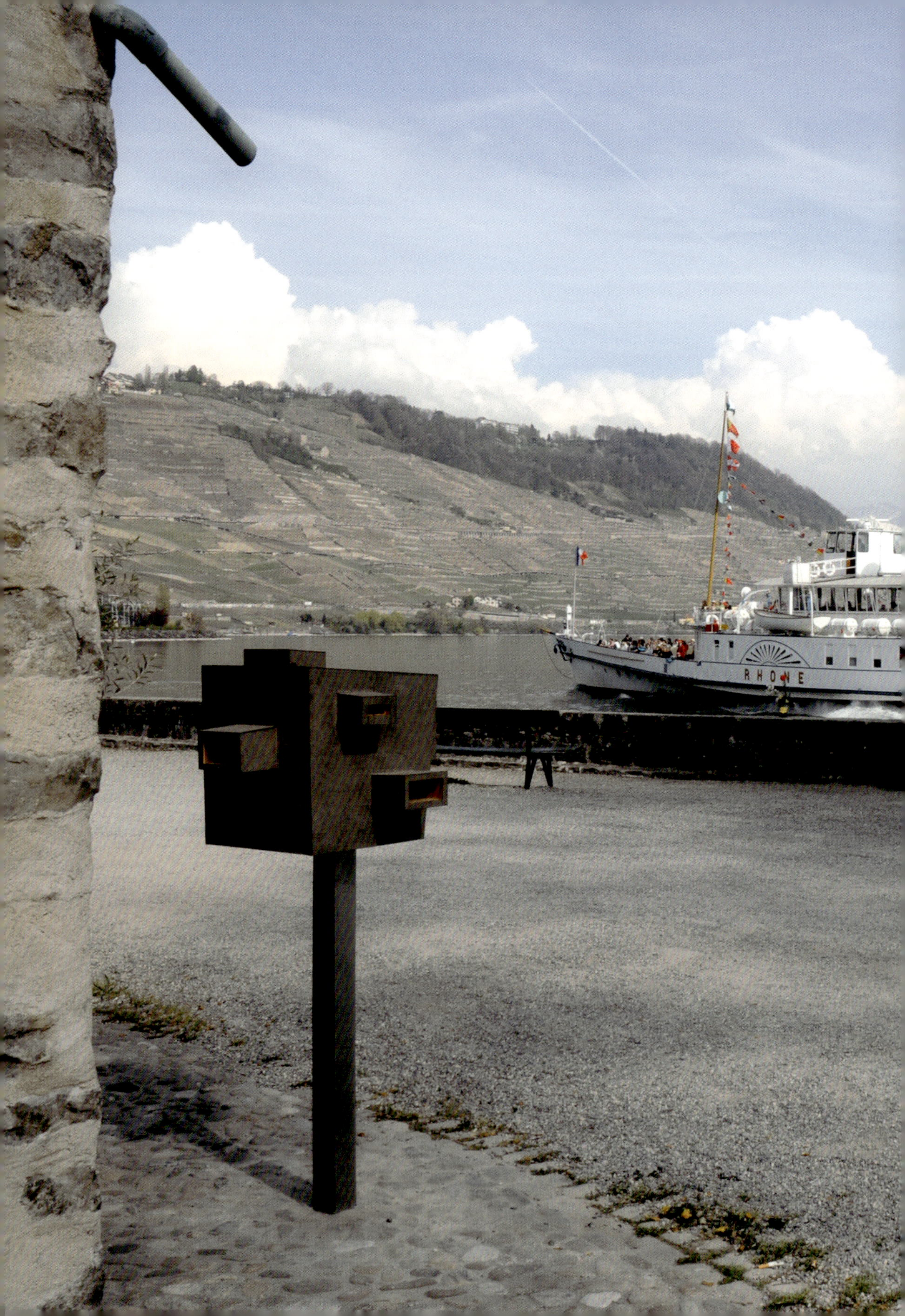
RHONE

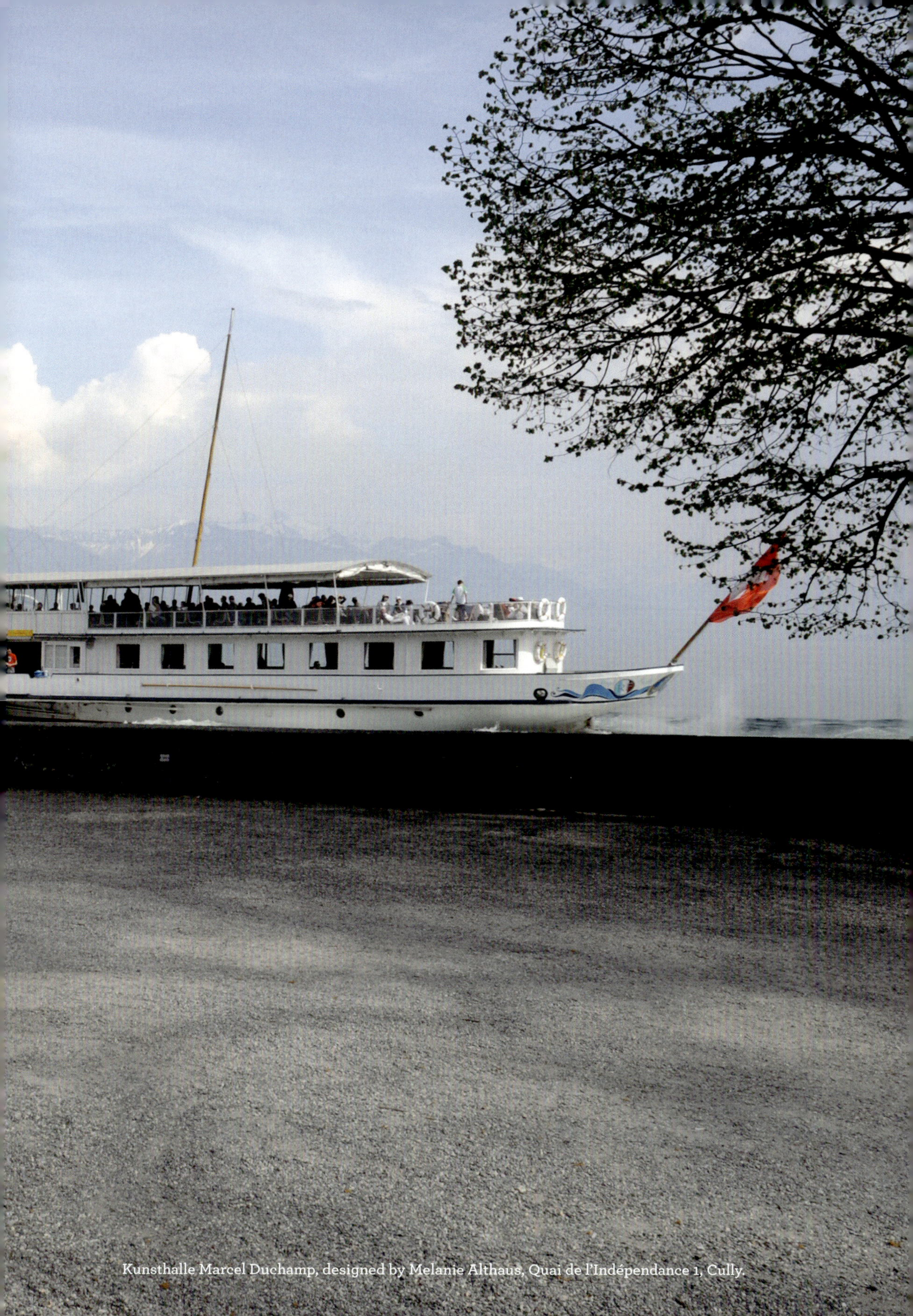

Kunsthalle Marcel Duchamp, designed by Melanie Althaus, Quai de l'Indépendance 1, Cully.

I Want to Grasp Things with the Mind the Way the Penis is Grasped by the Vagina

Exhibition with works and documents by John Zorn, Tadanori Yokoo, Stephan Wittmer, Rolf Winnewisser, Martin Widmer, Wang Xingwei, Aldo Walker, Michael R. Taylor, Harald Szeemann, Denis Savary, Jukka Rusanen, Sam Rosenthal, Peter Roesch, Jason Rhoades, Jean-Michel Rabaté, Céline Peruzzo, Mimosa Pale, Mark Nelson/Sarah Hudson Bayliss, Olivier Mosset, Charles Moser, Gudrun Meier, Line Marquis, Le Forestay, Konrad Klapheck, Pierre Keller, Felix Kälin, Bert Jansen, Jing Wei, Richard Jackson, Fabrice Hyber, Erwin Hofstetter, Herzog & de Meuron, Erwin Grünenfelder, Goldfrapp, Jean-Claude Forest, Étant donnés, Marcel Duchamp, Anke Doberauer, Jacques Derrida, Basil Debraine, Jacques Caumont, Rosemary Cel, Monica Bonvicini, Ecke Bonk/Antoine Monnier, Rudolf Blättler, Georg Baselitz, Fritz Balthaus, Francis Bacon, Caroline Bachmann/Stefan Banz, and Ai Weiwei. Curated by Stefan Banz

Galerie Davel 14, Cully
Opening: Thursday, May 6, 2010, 20:00
Exhibition: May 7–June 13, 2010

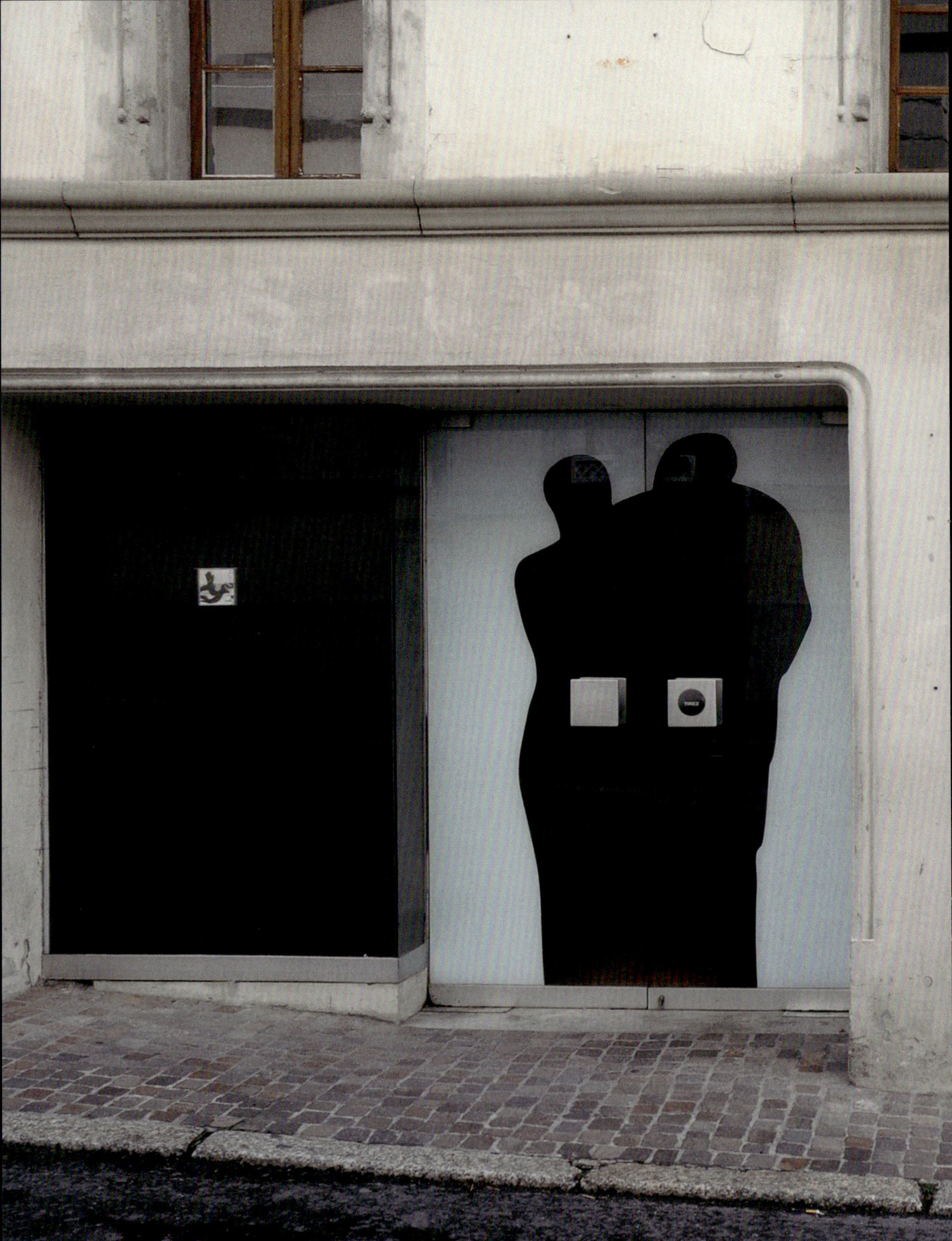

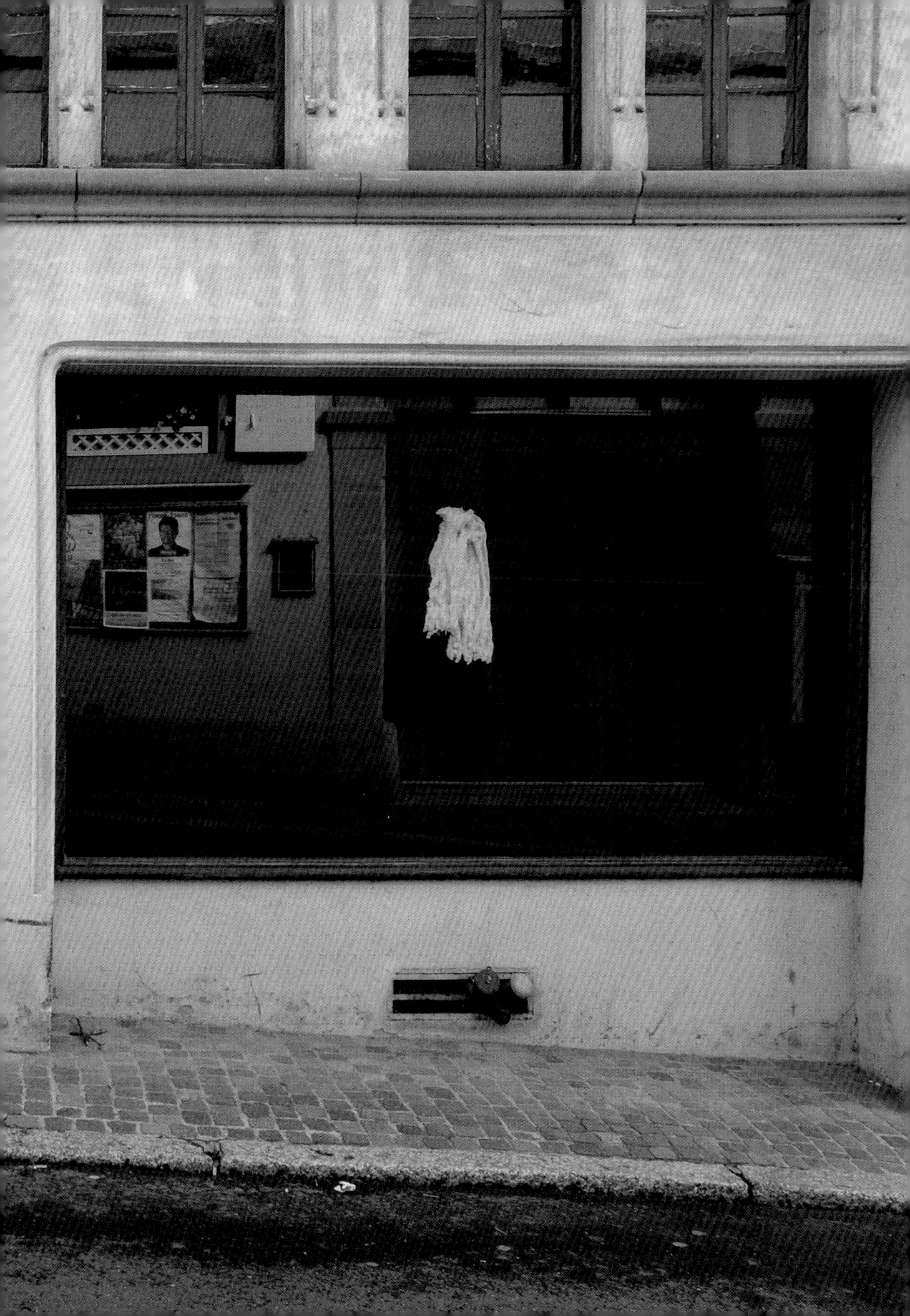

Caroline Bachmann

Gradiva on the Trail

On the Exhibition at Galerie Davel 14

The exhibition *I Want to Grasp Things with the Mind the Way the Penis is Grasped by the Vagina* accompanied the "Marcel Duchamp and the Forestay Waterfall" symposium. We entered the exhibition by walking through a replica of the door Duchamp created in 1937 for the Gradiva Gallery André Breton founded that same year. The name was likely chosen in homage to "Gradiva," the 1903 short story by Wilhelm Jensen, whose eponymous heroine, a walking female figure carved in bas-relief, is the source of the Lover's obsessive desire, which he eventually succeeds in transferring to a real person. But it may also be a nod to his friend Salvador Dalí, considering that the outline of the embracing couple uncannily resembles the one in the foreground of *Gradiva encuentra las ruinas de Antropomorphos* from 1931. Gradiva, the walking woman, plays the role of an active muse for these prewar artists and, following Freud's 1907 analysis of Jensen's story, a figure facilitating the passage from dreams to reality. This notion of a martial woman, both feminine and masculine (Gradiva is thought to be the feminine form of the Latin Gradivus, another name of the god Mars), contains the contradictory terms presented under various guises in Duchamp's work. *Étant donnés: 1° la chute d'eau, 2° le gaz d'éclairage* (1946–66, pp. 4–5) presents the confrontation of water and gas, life and death in a single body, and the state of the watcher being watched.

And desire is indeed the force powering creative energy and leading us towards a more complete understanding of the visible and the invisible. Such are the ways into the exhibition, a kind of accumulation of clues collected by the organizers of this investigation around *Étant donnés* and its waterfall.

The black vitrines of the gallery establish the parameters of the inquiry: the Forestay waterfall, a three-dimensional replica of the waterfall from *Étant donnés* by Caroline Bachmann and Stefan Banz, and *Duras/Duchamp,* a CD by John Zorn. Between these two homages to Duchamp, the door of Gradiva opens onto a large mural painting by Peter Roesch showing purple water ribbons with a green body surrounded by wide-open orange eyes floating at the surface. This depiction of flux forms the background for various works, including *Piston de courant d'air,* a silkscreen on plexiglas by Duchamp; *Thomas,* a Wang Xingwei work from the 1990s showing an incredulous vandal between two impassible guards with Joseph Beuys's and Andy Warhol's features; a naked cowboy reclining on a couch by Anke Doberauer; and a rifle for shooting in the corners by Jason Rhoades. The exhibition space is filled with paintings, drawings, art reviews documenting works inspired by *Étant donnés,* a facsimile of Duchamp's instruction manual, Michael Taylor's book, CDs in their sleeves, photographs, vitrines containing various objects, and a wall of waterfall postcards collected over the last thirty years by Tadanori Yokoo. Also included are prints of seven photographs taken by Duchamp of the Forestay in 1946, as well as documentation of Felix Kälin's efforts between 1979 and 1981 to find the forgotten location of these photographs.

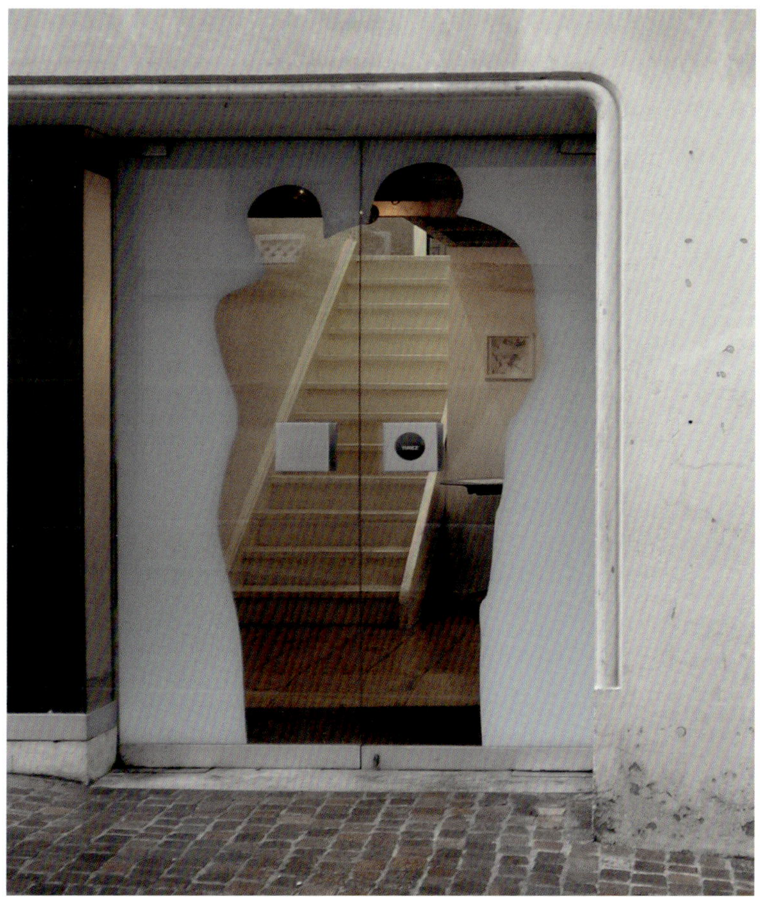

Marcel Duchamp, The door *Gradiva* (destroyed), Paris, 1937. Replication for the exhibition *I Want to Grasp Things with the Mind the Way the Penis is Grasped by the Vagina*, Galerie Davel 14, Cully, 2010.

A video work recalls the scintillating waterfall in the PMA's installation of *Étant donnés,* another documents Roman Signer's contribution during the Forestay colloquium: a red balloon released in the waterfall. All of this takes place under the enlightened gaze of *Alma,* a passive version of Gradiva reinterpreted by Denis Savary based on the mannequin made in 1918 by Oskar Kokoschka with his lost lover Alma Mahler's measurements. Spread out on a table, a selection of antique postcards show the surroundings of the Forestay as Duchamp probably found them during his stay in Chexbres. Finally, through a slit cut across a wall of fabric, we catch a glimpse of a painting of the interior of the *Étant donnés* installation, along with a diptych about the themes of the visible and the invisible by Caroline Bachmann and Stefan Banz.

Original works and copies, readymades and documentation, all these works tell us a story of appropriation, continuity, and *détournement.* The true and the false blend together, the inquiry peters out. The field of questions tends to grow larger just as you think you're holding the glimmer of an explanation, and Gradiva, our immutable guide, leads us towards unknown shores with always reinvigorated, fascinating shapes.

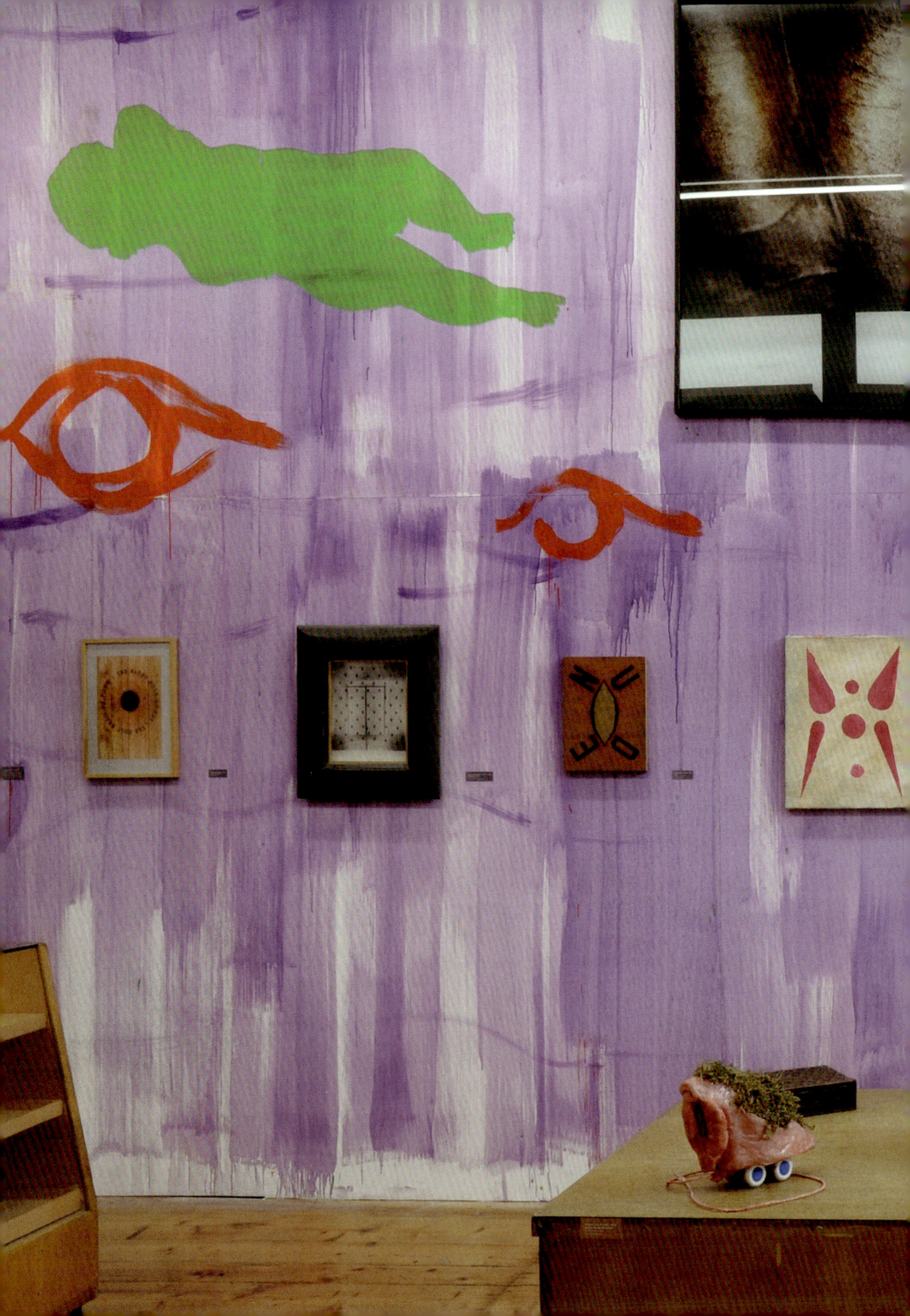

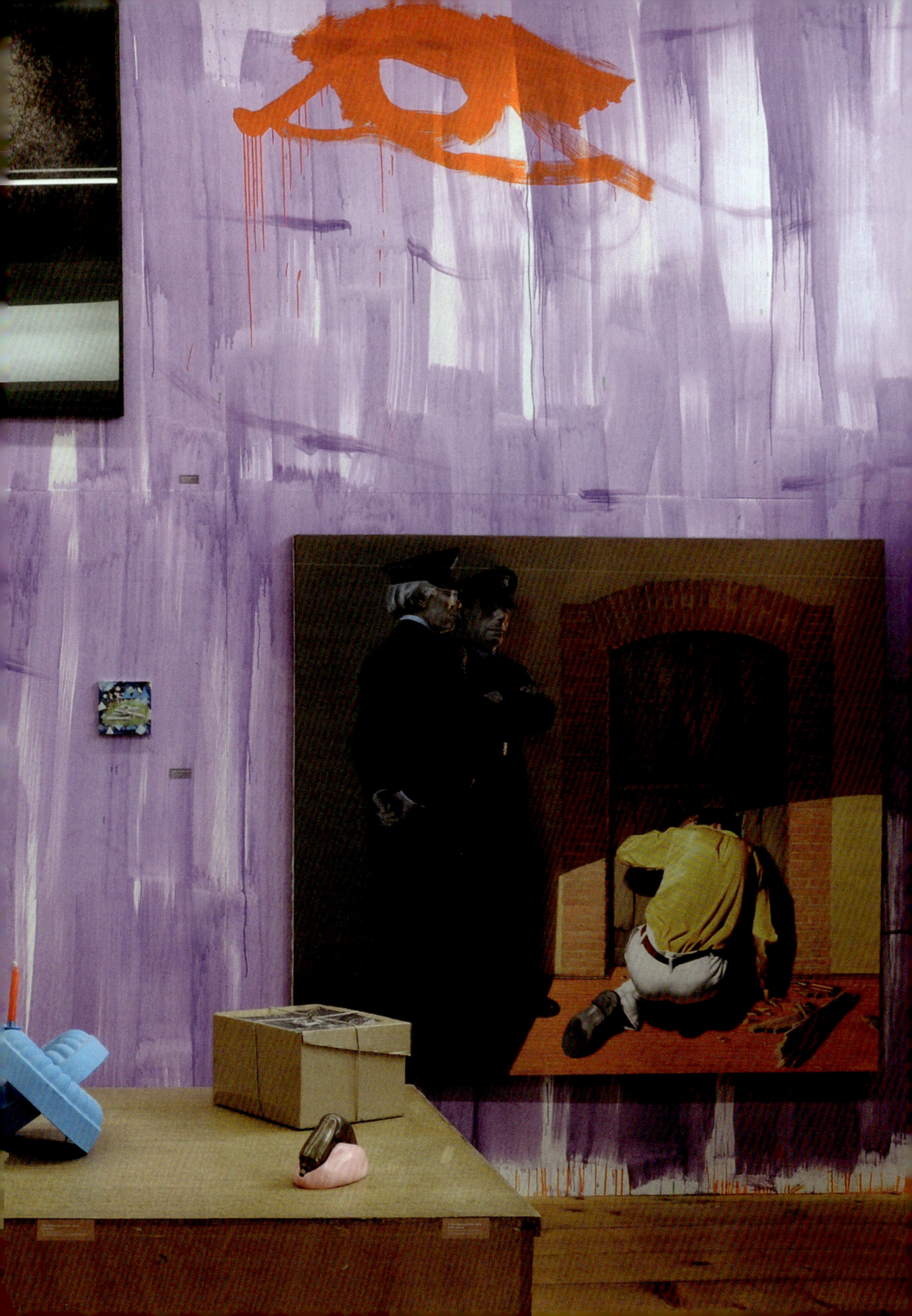

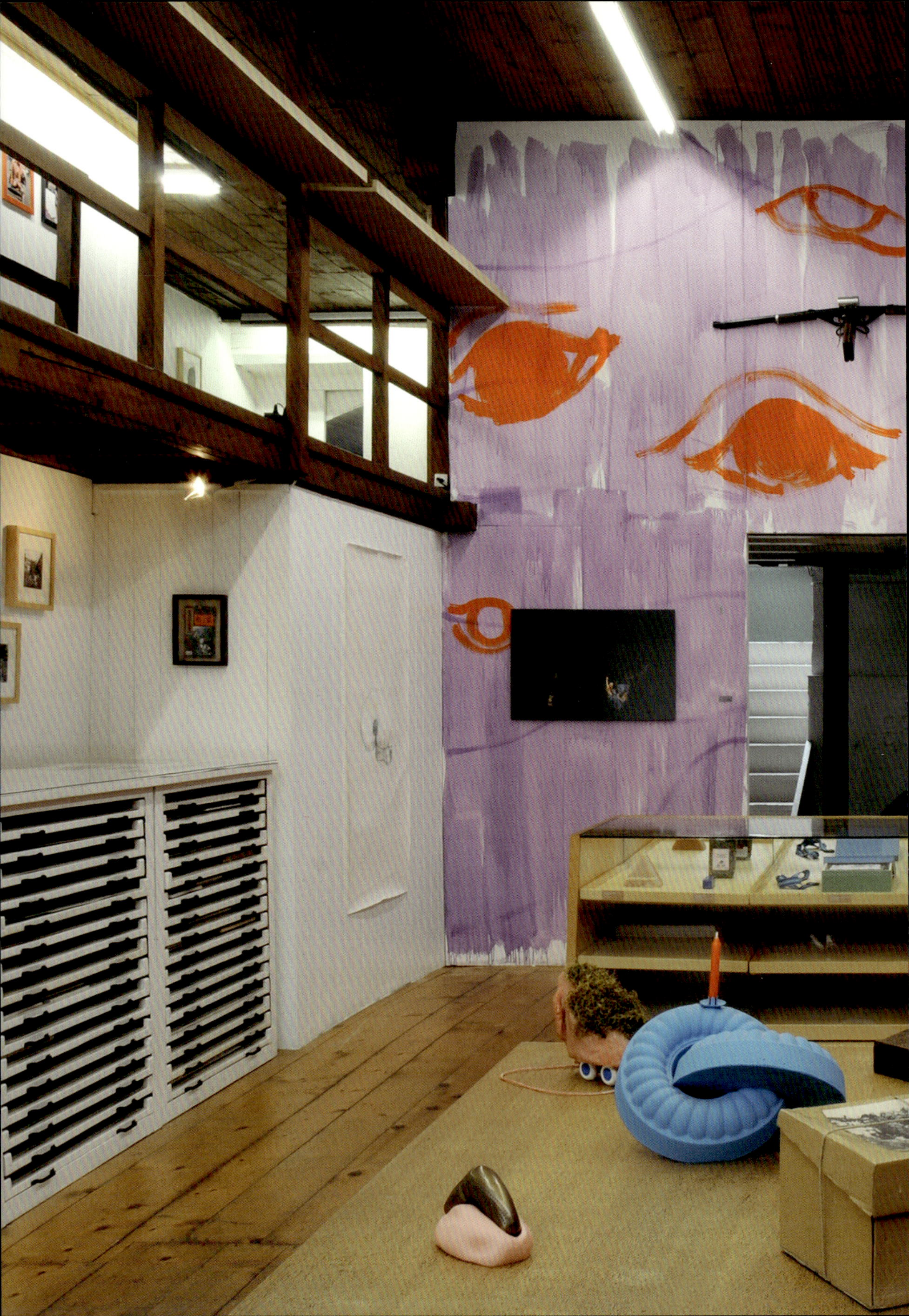

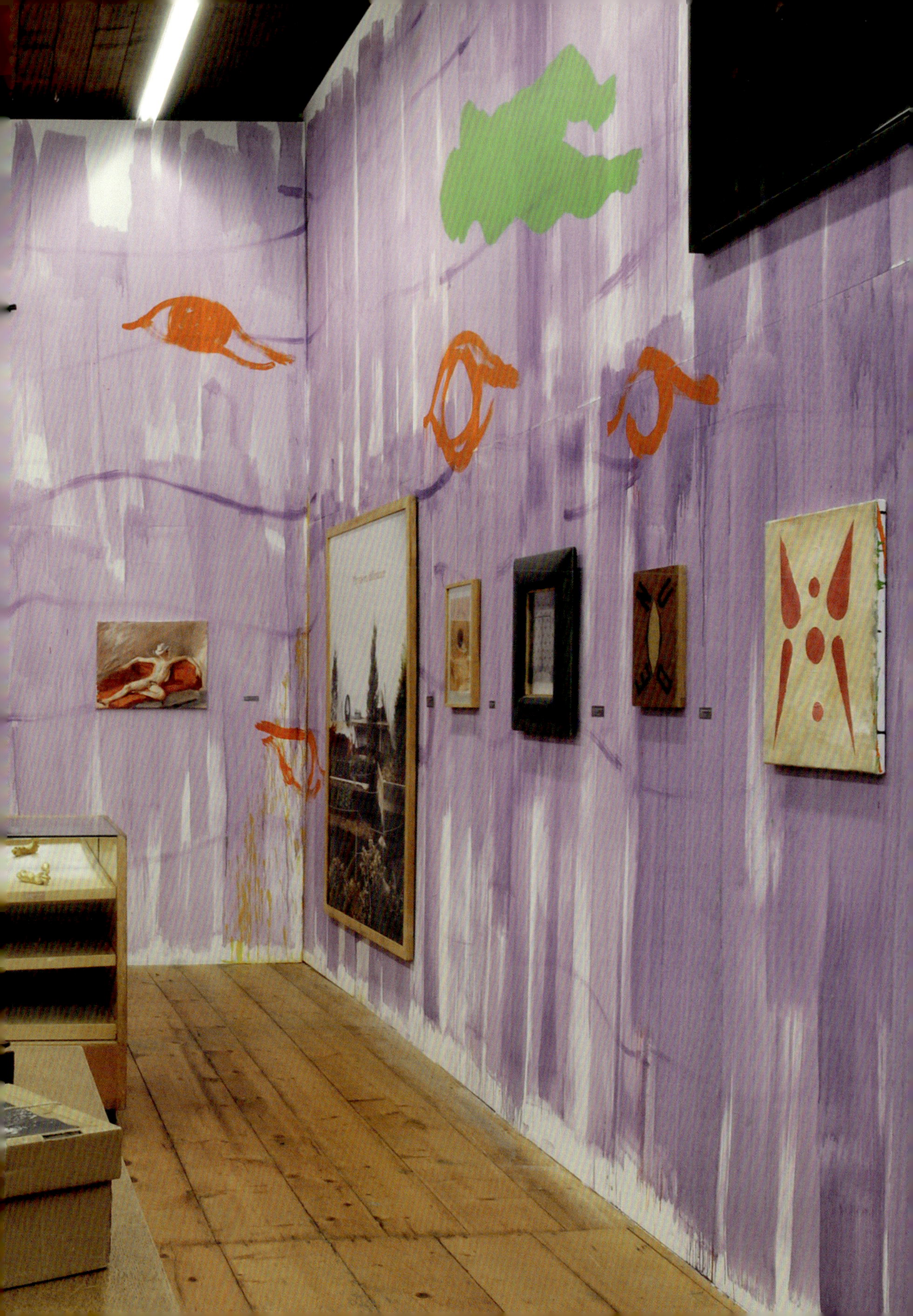

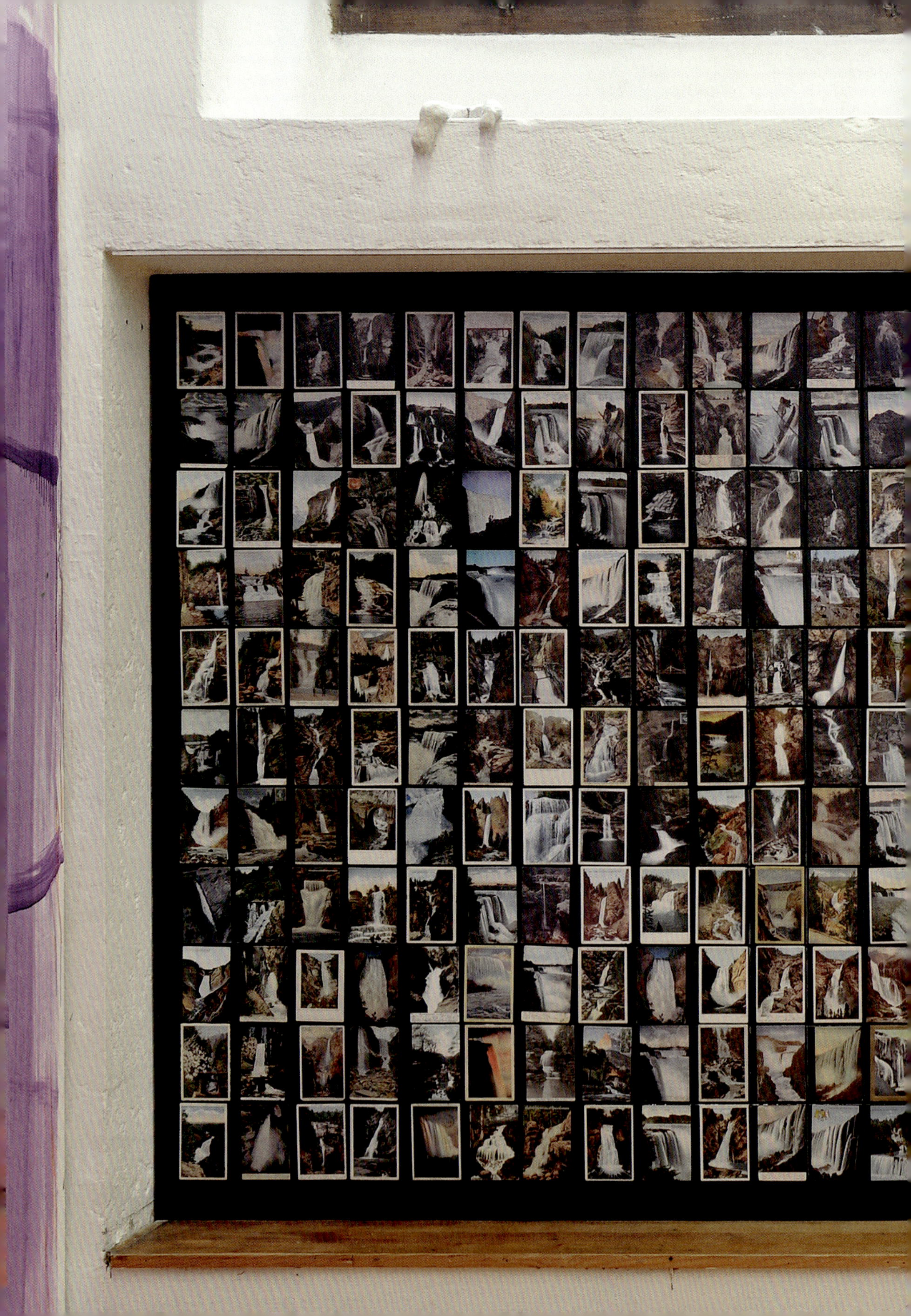

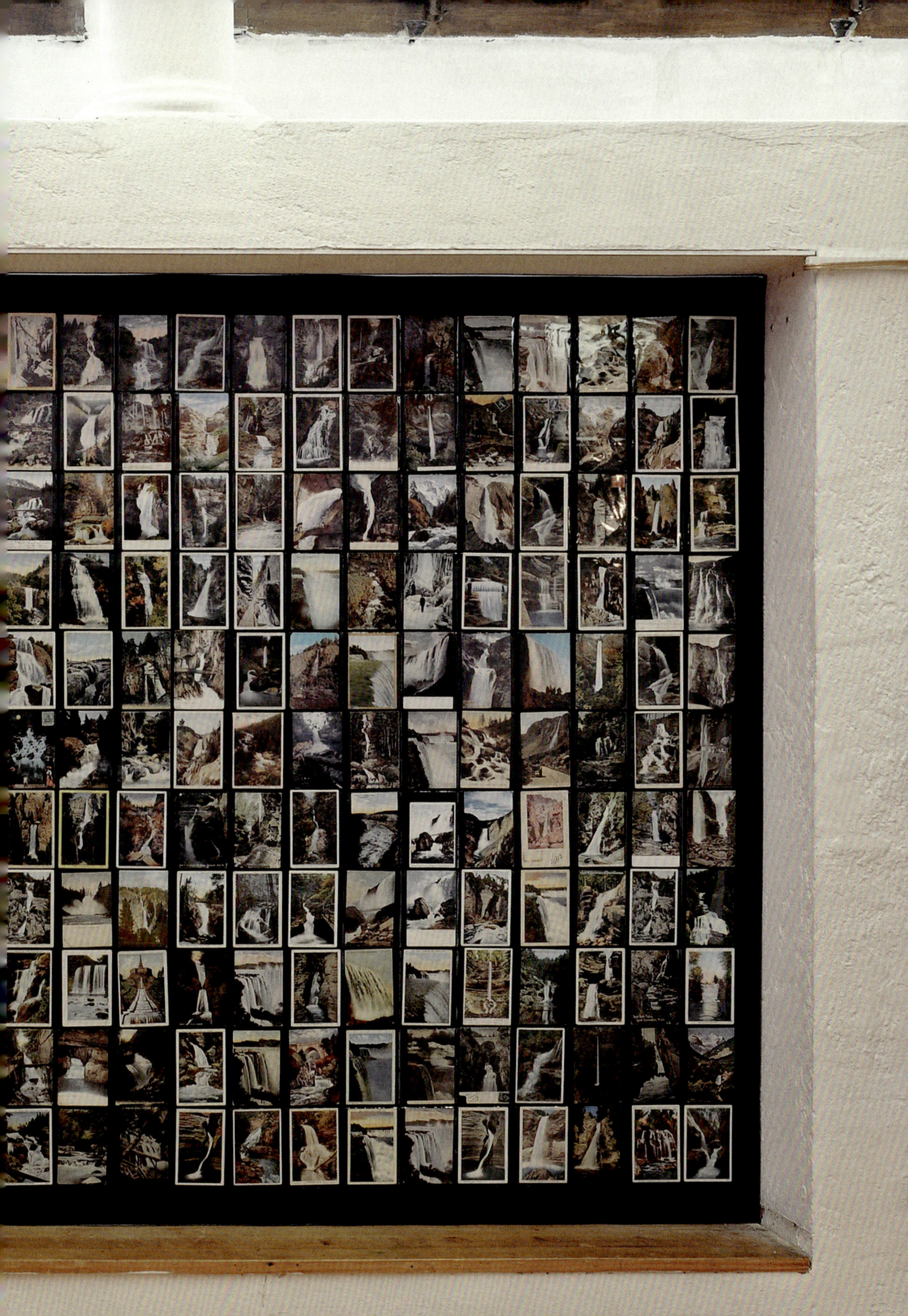

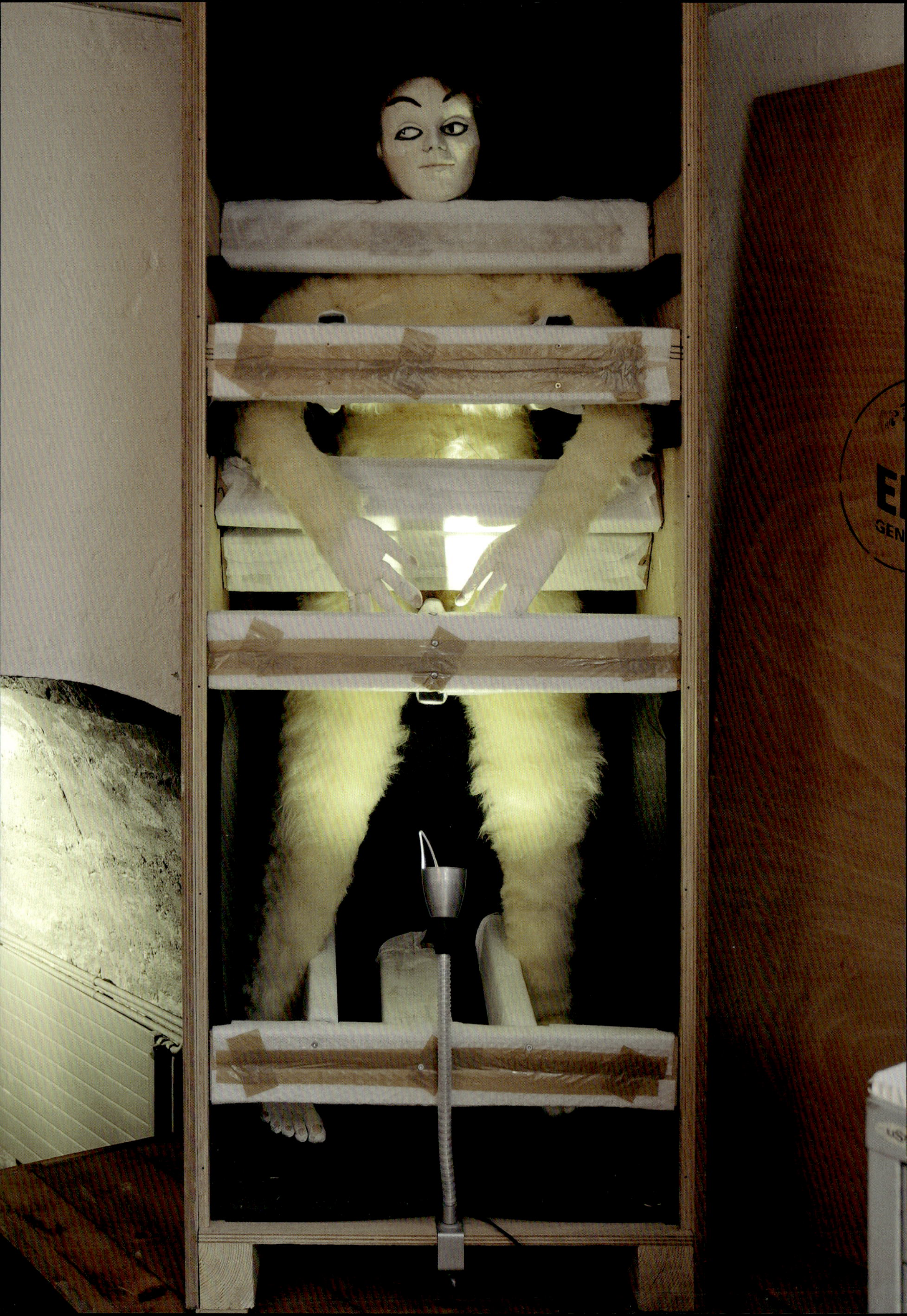

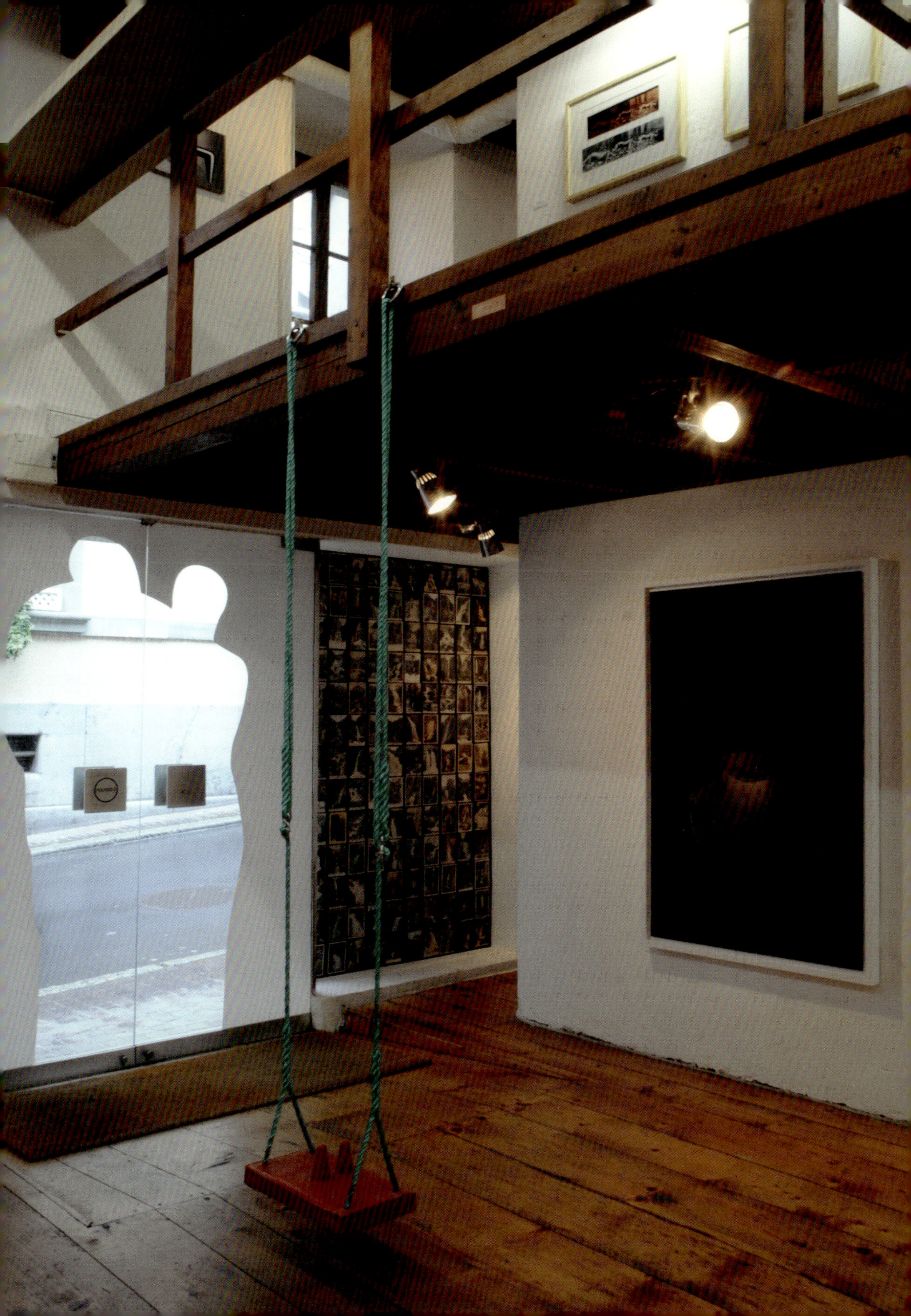

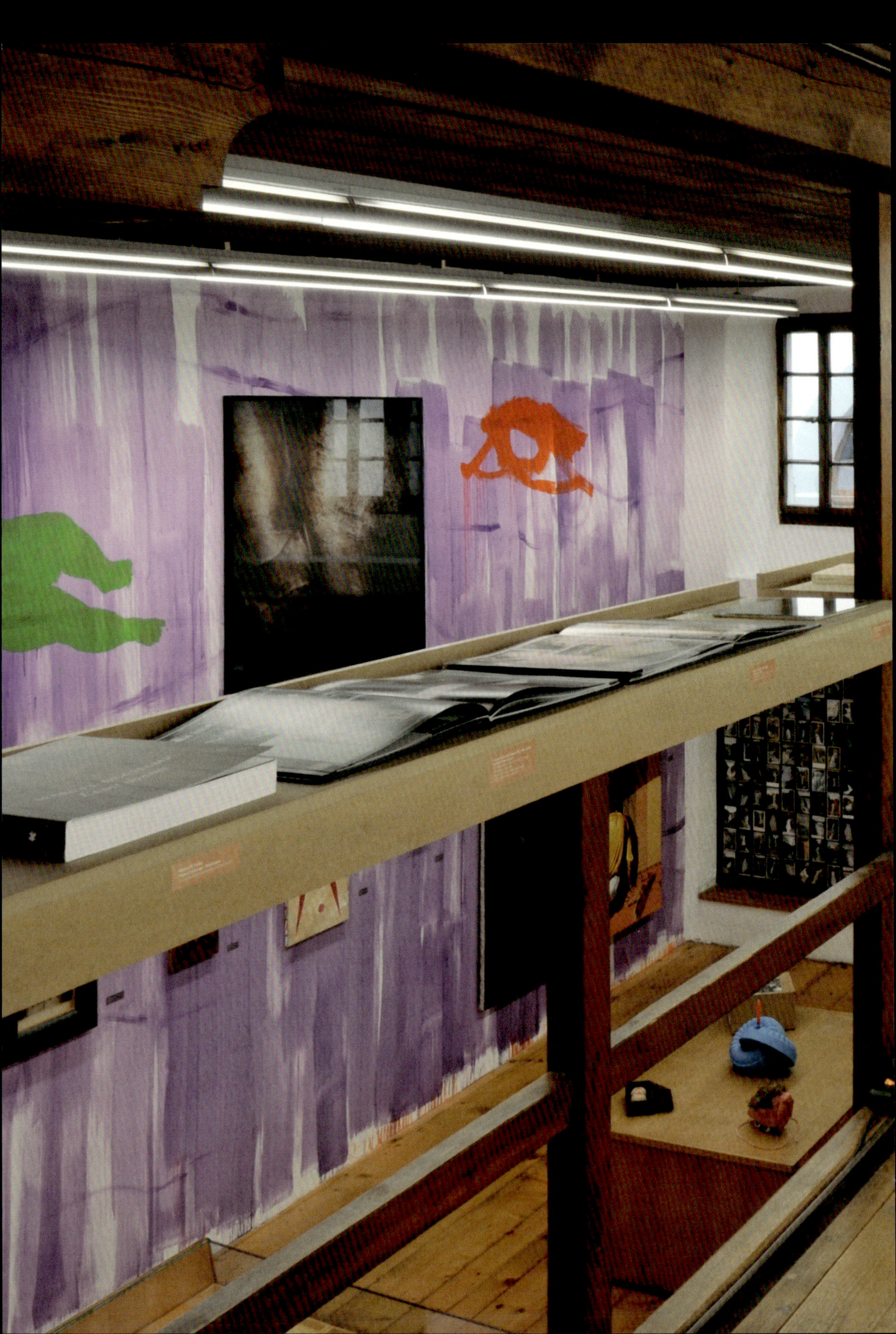

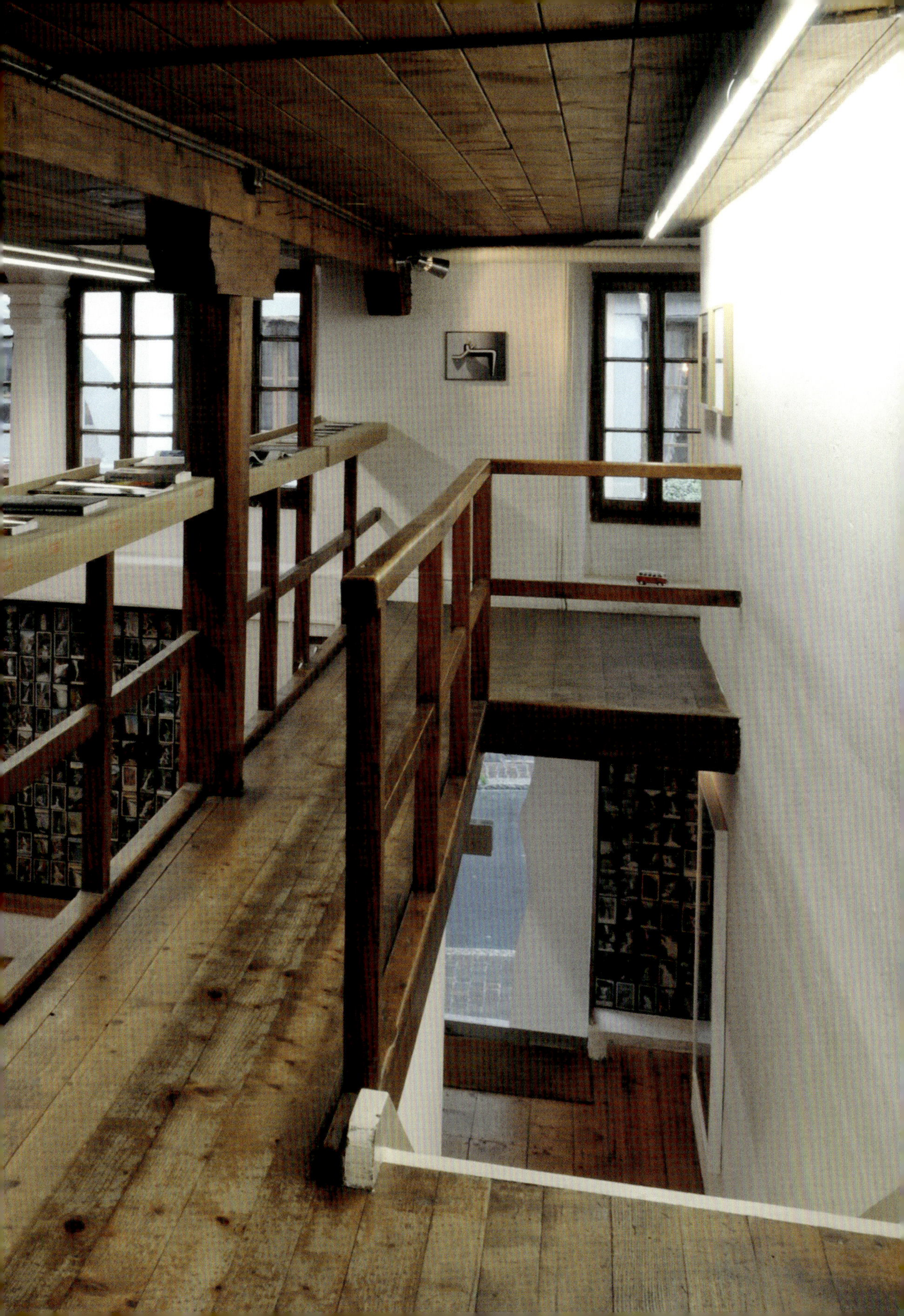

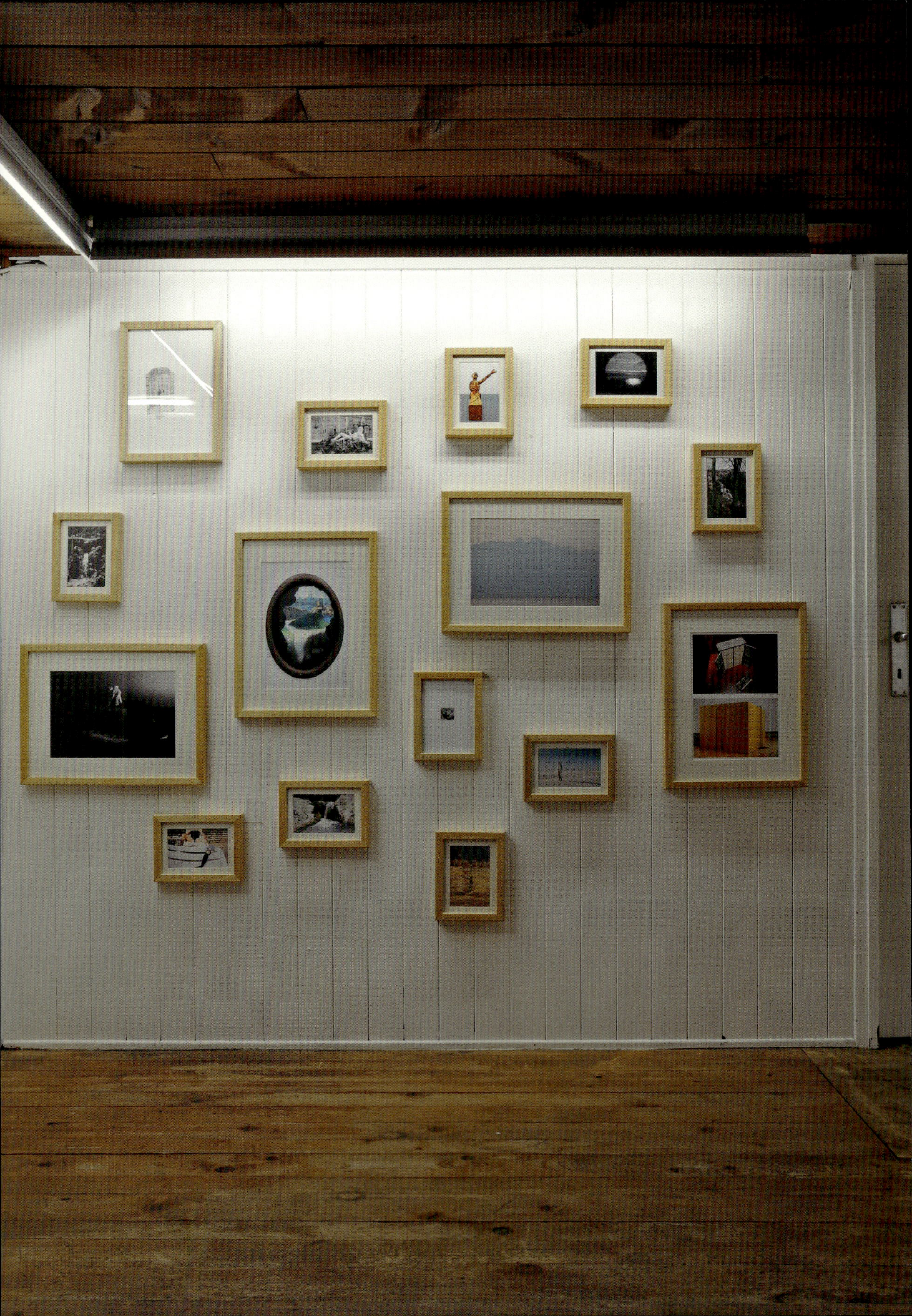

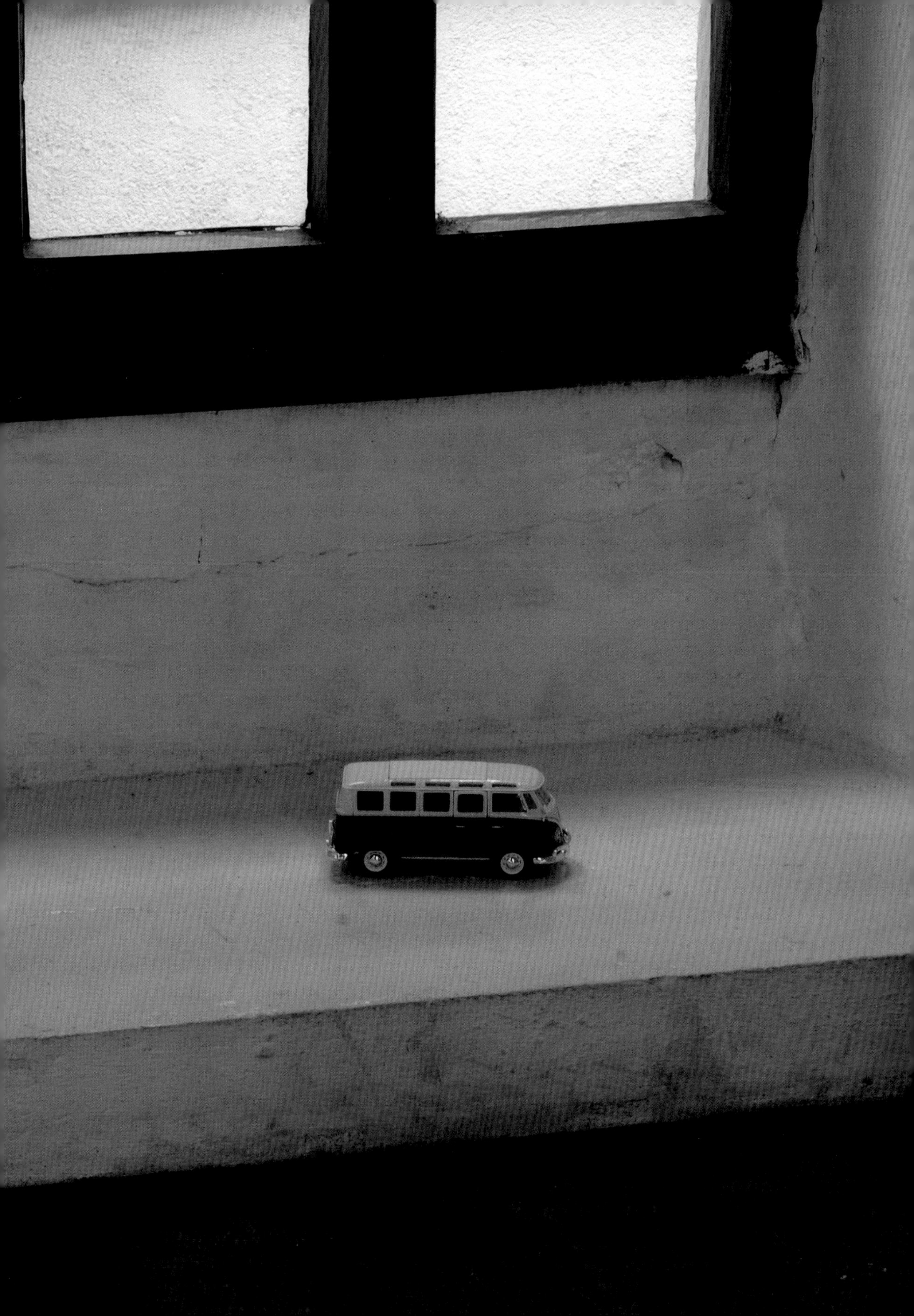

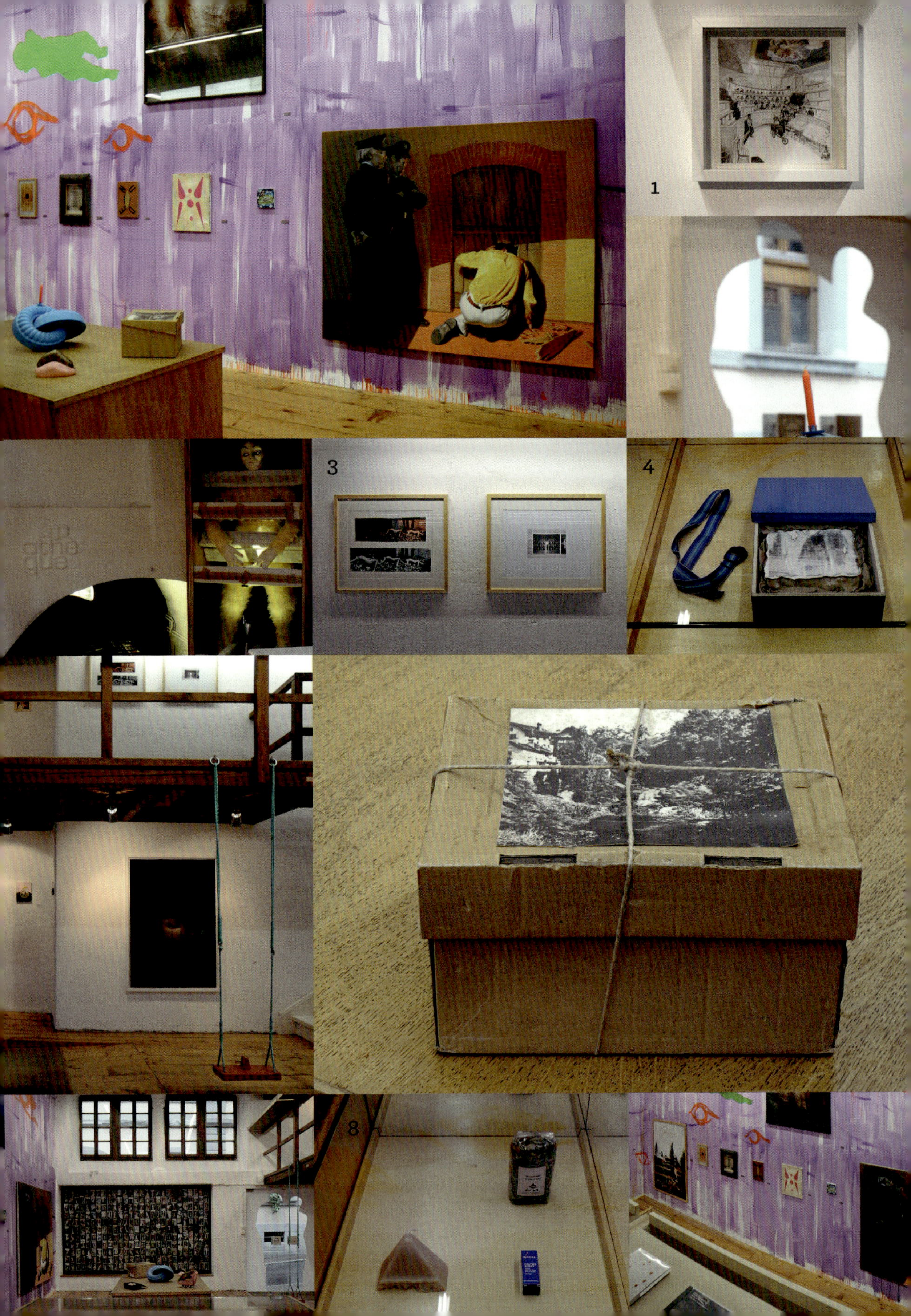
1
3
4
8

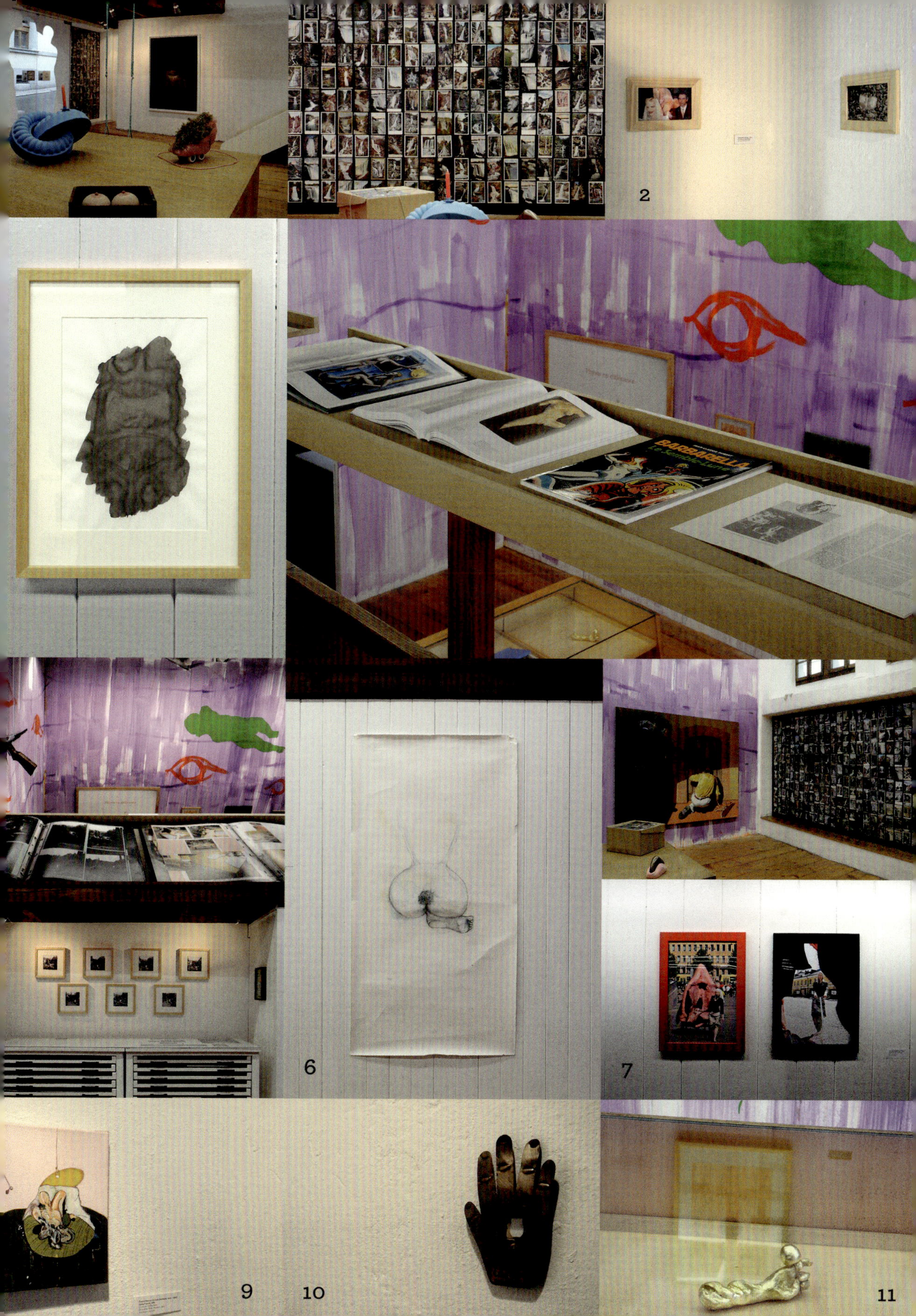
2
BARBARELLA
6
7
9
10
11

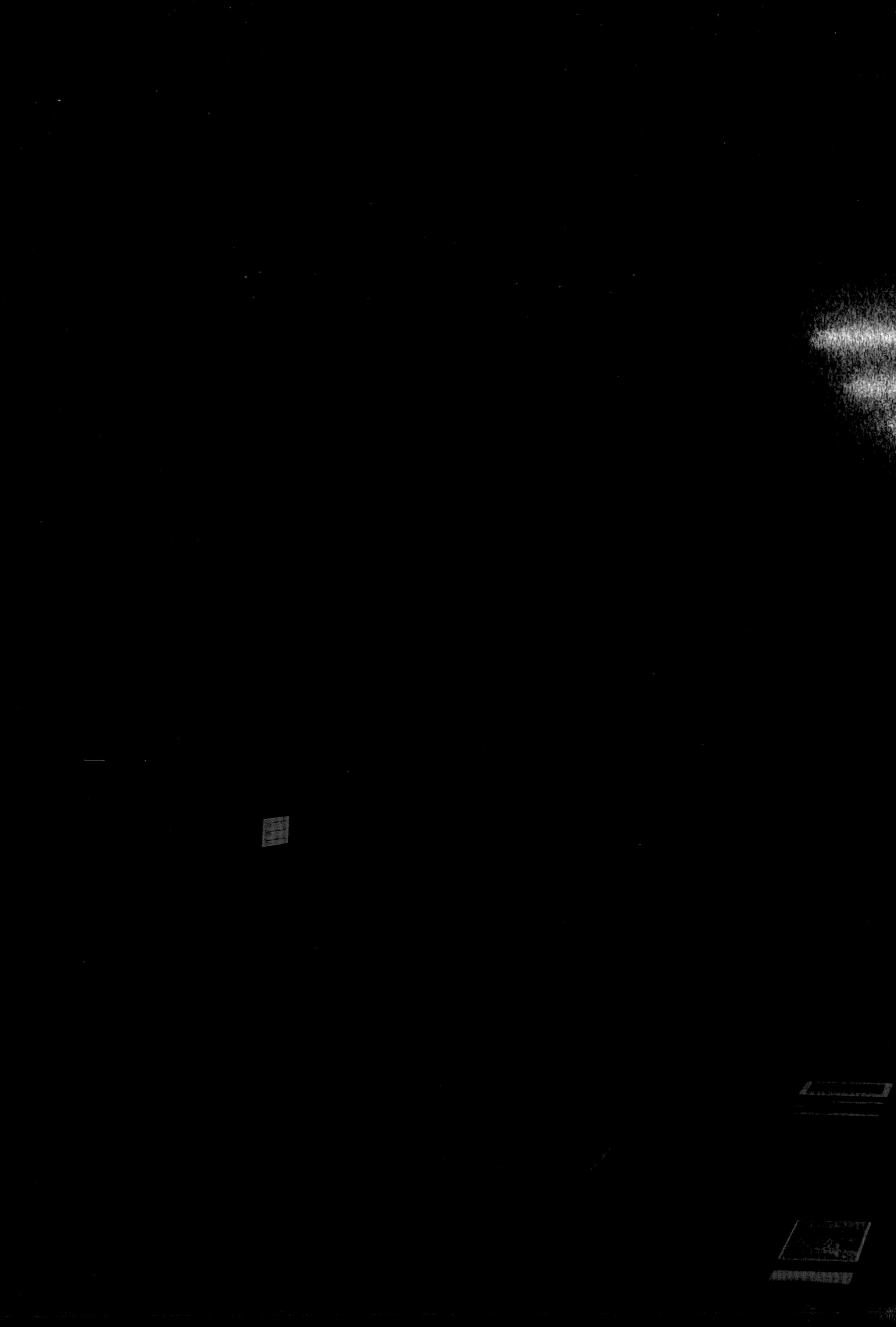

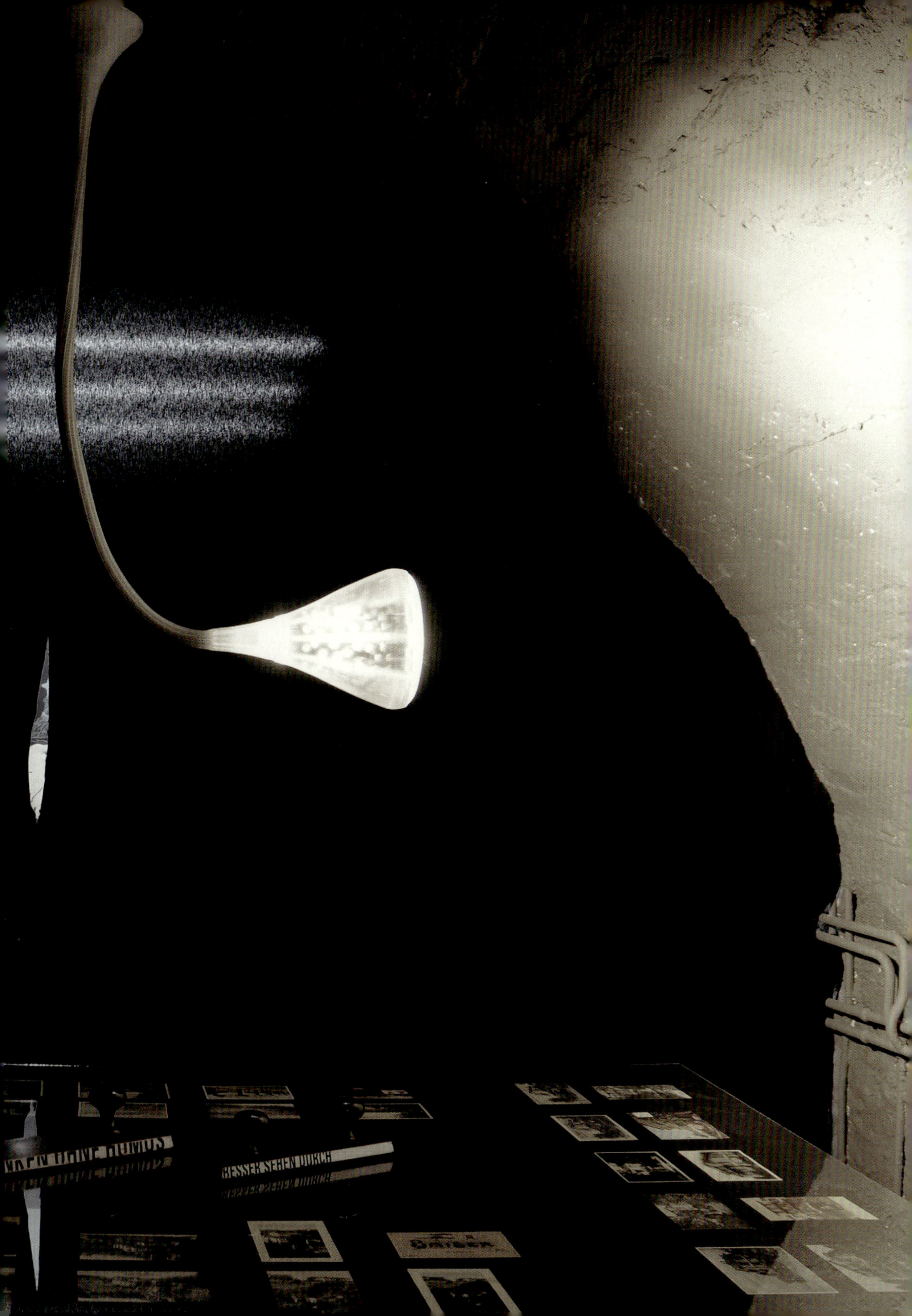
BESSER SEHEN DURCH

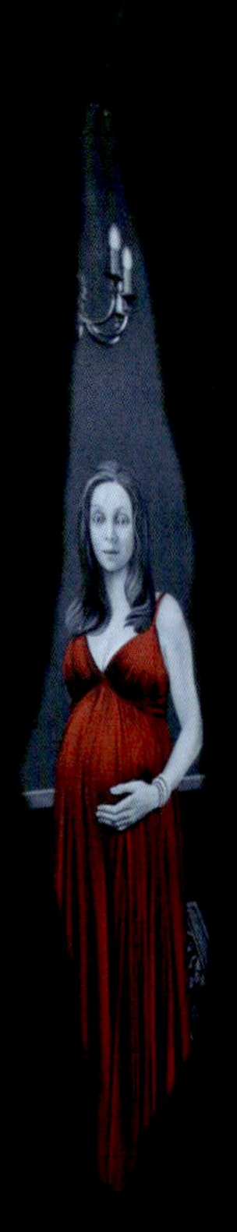
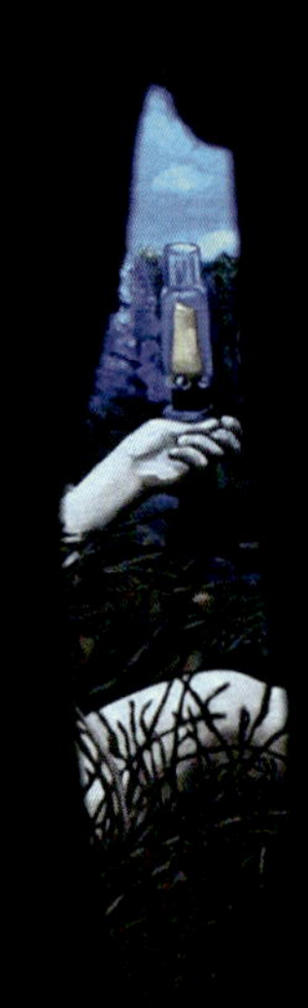
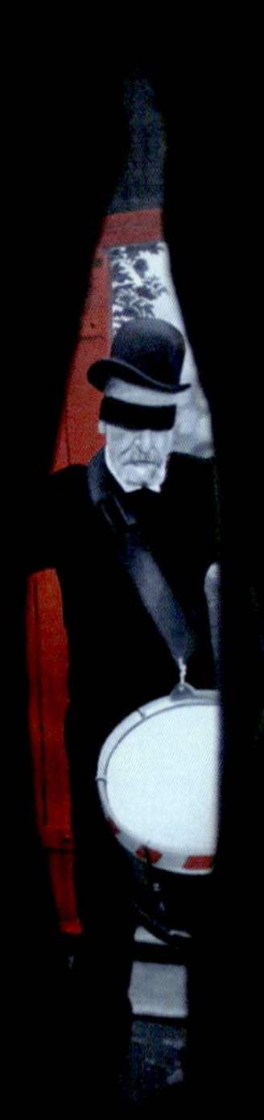

Exhibited Works and Documents

Page 321
Ai Weiwei
Untitled
Wood, color, shoes, 1986/87
Uli Sigg Collection, Mauensee

Page 322–23
Small showcase (on the left)
John Zorn
Duras: Duchamp
CD, 1997

Entrance (in the middle)
Marcel Duchamp
The door *Gradiva*
Installation for the Galerie Gradiva, Paris, 1937 (destroyed)
(Reproduction after a photo of a 1968 reproduction)

Big showcase (on the right)
Caroline Bachmann/Stefan Banz
The Waterfall
(After Marcel Duchamp's *Étant donnés: 1° La chute d'eau*)
Latex, 1/3, 2009–10
Philadelphia Museum Art

Pages 326–27
Wallpainting
Peter Roesch
Untitled (Hommage à *Étant donnés*)
Acrylic on wood, 2010
Courtesy the Artist

On the wall, from left to right
Charles Moser
The Gloryhole of Art
Photograph, digital image processing, 2010
Courtesy the Artist

Marcel Duchamp
Draft Piston
Positive Print, 1965
Musée Jenisch, Vevey

Stephan Wittmer
Nude
Acrylic on wood, 1984
Private Collection

Peter Roesch
Untitled (Fallen Angels)
Oil on canvas, 2009–10
Courtesy the Artist

Rolf Winnewisser
Untitled
Oil on canvas, 1984
Private Collection

Wang Xingwei
Thomas
Oil on canvas, 1998
Uli Sigg Collection, Mauensee

Above
Pierre Keller
Queue de cheval
Photograph, 1984
Courtesy the Artist

On the pedestal, from left to right
Mimosa Pale
Mobile Female Monument
Latex, grass, 2007
Private Collection

Rosemary Cel
Prière de fermer (Please Close)
Mixed media, 2008
Private Collection

Aldo Walker
Untitled
Styrofoam, 1 of 5, 2000
Ruth and Jürg Nyffeler Collection, Erstfeld

Felix Kälin
Box with documents of the Forestay waterfall research
Cardboard, string, 1982
Courtesy Felix Kälin, Basel

Monica Bonvicini
Drill 4 Chastity
Two-part cast, bronze, resin, 2004
Courtesy Parkett Verlag, Zurich

Pages 328–29
On the furniture
Felix Kälin
Documents from the Forestay Waterfall research, 1979–82
(Not visible in the photograph, see chapter
"Excerpts from the Archive of Felix Kälin" in this volume)
Courtesy Felix Kälin, Basel

Marcel Duchamp
The Forestay Waterfall (Swiss Landscape)
7 photographs, 1946
Philadelphia Museum of Art
(Reprints for the exhibition)

Jing Wei
***The Forestay Waterfall* (2 for 3)**
Painting and mixed media
Private Collection

Céline Peruzzo
Untitled
Pencil and color pencil on paper, 2010
Courtesy the Artist

On the violet wall: from left to right
Jukka Rusanen
Swing
Color photograph, 2006
Courtesy the Artist

Jason Rhoades
Brunopetgun
Two rifles, 1 of 2, 1998
Bruno Weber Collection, Zurich

Anke Doberauer
Cowboy
Oil on canvas, 2010
Courtesy the Artist

First work on the violet wall on the right
Jacques Derrida
Physis en différance
Intervention for the exhibition *Cultivating the Museum*, Kunsthalle Luzern, 1992, curated by Stefan Banz,
Private Collection

Pages 330–31
Above
Rosemary Cel
On the Ledge
Alumina, 2008
Private Collection

Center
Tadanori Yokoo
Waterfalls
Installation with postcards, 2010
Courtesy the Artist

Page 332
Image on the left
Denis Savary
Alma
(After the doll of Oskar Kokoschka from 1918)
(Exposed in its crate with a lamp)
Mixed media, 2007
Musée Jenisch, Vevey

Page 333
Illustration on the right, work in the center
Fabrice Hyber
Swing
Wood, latex, 1995
Bruno Weber Collection, Zurich

Work on the right
Martin Widmer
325'200.-
Photograph mounted on aluminum, 1 of 5, 2010
Courtesy the Artist

Pages 334–35
Documentation on the shelf
Michael R. Taylor
Marcel Duchamp: Étant donnés
Book, 2009
Private Collection

Marcel Duchamp
Manual of Instructions for the assembly of Étant donnés: 1° La chute d'eau, 2° Le gaz d'éclairage
Facsimile, 1987 (new English edition 2009),
Philadelphia Museum of Art
Private Collection

Richard Jackson
The Maid's Room
Book after Duchamp's *Manual of Instructions*, 2007
Private Collection

Marcel Duchamp
Le surréalisme, même
Art magazine, 1956
Private Collection

Jacques Derrida
Donner le temps, 1. La fausse monnaie
Book, 1991
Private Collection

Jean Michel Rabaté
Given: 1° Art, 2° Crime
Book, 2006
Private Collection

Mark Nelson/Sarah Hudson Bayliss
Exquisite Corpse: Surrealism and the Black Dahlia Murder
Book, 2006
Private Collection

Jean-Claude Forest
Barbarella: Le Semble-Lune
Comic, 1977
Private Collection

Gudrun Meier
Josef Schröder: Durchhalten
Book cover, 2009
Private Collection

Konrad Klapheck
The Bathroom, 1968
In Arturo Schwarz, *Klapheck*
Book, 2003
Private Collection

Bert Jansen
Van Waterfall tot Flessenrek
In *Kunstbeeld* 6, June 16, 2002
Courtesy the Author

Jacques Caumont
Rrosopopées
Publication, January 1981
Dominique Radrizzani Collection, Vevey

John Zorn
Filmworks XXI, Belle de Nature
CD, 2008
Private Collection

John Zorn
Femina
CD, 2009
Private Collection

Étant donnés
Offenbarung und Untergang by Georg Trakl
with Michael Gira
CD, 1999
Private Collection

Étant donnés
Re-Up
with Alan Vega, Lydia Lunch, and Genesis P-Orridge
CD, 1999
Private Collection

Painting in the back
Konrad Klapheck
The Motherly Friend
Oil on canvas, 1966
(Copied by Eric Vuille, 2010)
Private Collection

Page 336
Illustration on the left: from left to right, from up to down
Basil Debraine
The Door
Pencil on paper, 2010
Private Collection

Rosemary Cel
Vater Rhein (Neptun)
Photograph, 1 of 5, 2009
Private Collection

Georg Baselitz
Model for a Sculpture
Wood, 1985
Documentation, image reversed
Private Collection

Stefan Banz
Le Léman (The Green Ray)
Photograph, 1 of 10, 2006
Private Collection

Caroline Bachmann/Stefan Banz
Waterfall
Photograph, 1 of 10, 2009
Private Collection

Wang Xingwei
Color photograph of *Beacon*
Oil on canvas, 1998
Private Collection

Stefan Banz
Les tours d'Aï
Photograph, 1 of 12, 2004
Courtesy the Artist

Stefan Banz
The Forestay Waterfall
Photograph, 1 of 10, 2008
Courtesy the Artist

Rudolf Blättler
Black House II
Documentation of the making of the installation at Kunstmuseum Luzern, 2004
Courtesy the Artist

Anonym
Tree (Vagina)
Photograph from the Internet, 2009
Private Collection

Caroline Bachmann/Stefan Banz
The Ballad of Badwater (White Sands)
Photograph, 1 of 10, 2009
Courtesy the Artists

Caroline Bachmann/Stefan Banz
Bellevue
Detail of the installation in the exhibition *Éclairage*, Musée cantonal des Beaux-Arts, Lausanne, 2008
Photograph, 1 of 5, 2008
Courtesy the Artists

Stefan Banz
The Doll
Photograph, 1 of 10, 1997
Courtesy the Artist

Stefan Banz
Waterfall
Photograph, 1 of 10, 2008
Courtesy the Artist

Rosemary Cel
Scar
Photograph, 1 of 5, 2009
Private Collection

Page 337
Illustration on the right
Rosemary Cel
Volkswagen (Faux vagin)
Model car, 2009
Private Collection

Pages 338–39

1
Line Marquis
La leçon d'autonomie
Pencil, color pencil, collage, 2010
Courtesy the Artist

2
Stefan Banz
Cicciolina and Jeff Koons
Photograph, 1 of 10, 1992
Courtesy the Artist

Rosemary Cel
Spade
Photograph, 1 of 5, 2009
Private Collection

3
Sam Rosenthal
This Lush Garden Within
2 photographs, 1993
Courtesy Sam Rosenthal, Brooklyn

Fritz Balthaus
48 Porträts
Taken from the newspaper *FAZ*, September, 4, 1999
(Photograph: Barbara Klemm)
C-Print, 3 of 3, 2007
Courtesy the Artist

4
Erwin Hofstetter
The Waterfall
Mixed media, 2010
Courtesy the Artist

5
Rudolf Blättler
Untitled
Gouache on paper, 1990
Private Collection

6
Céline Peruzzo
Untitled
Pencil and color pencil on paper, 2010
Courtesy the Artist

7
Mimosa Pale
Mobile Female Monument
Performance, 2007
Documentation, two photographs
Courtesy the Artist

8
Olivier Mosset
Toblerone
Wax, 2004
Private Collection

Erwin Grünenfelder
Waterfall
Biological herbs of the Swiss mountains, 2009
Private Collection

Ecke Bonk/Antoine Monnier
Innoxa (Blue Drops)
Eyedrops, 2010
Courtesy Ecke Bonk

9
Francis Bacon
Lying Figure, 1969
Copy by Stefan Banz
(From his series *Baby Bacons*, 1999)
Acrylic on canvas
Courtesy the Artist

10
Rosemary Cel
The Light
Mixed media, 2009
Private Collection

11
Céline Peruzzo
Untitled
Alumina, gold, 2009
Private Collection

Pages 340–41
On the ceiling
Herzog & de Meuron
Pipe Ceiling Lamp
Mixed media, 2009
Zap Design Collection, Cully

On the table
The Forestay Waterfall
9 postcards, 1910–45
Association du Vieux Lavaux, Chexbres

Hotel Bellevue, Bellevue-Chexbres
10 postcards, 1910–45
Association du Vieux Lavaux, Chexbres

View from Hotel Bellevue-Chexbres
10 postcards, 1910–45
Association du Vieux Lavaux, Chexbres

Hotel Bellevue, Chardonne
6 postcards, 1910–45
Association du Vieux Lavaux, Chexbres

Harald Szeemann
Besser sehen durch Agentur für geistige Gastarbeit
Giant stamp made for the exhibition *Cultivating the Museum,* Kunsthalle Luzern, 1992, cur. by Stefan Banz
Private Collection

Harald Szeemann
Gedanken ohne Humus sind Blumen ohne Farbe
Giant stamp made for the exhibition *Cultivating the Museum,* Kunsthalle Luzern, 1992, cur. by Stefan Banz
Private Collection

In the back, behind the black curtain, on the left (see also p. 342)
Caroline Bachmann/Stefan Banz
Electric Ladyland
Oil on canvas, 2009
Courtesy the Artists

In the middle (see also p. 342)
Caroline Bachmann/Stefan Banz
Golden Slumbers
(After Marcel Duchamp's *Étant donnés*)
Oil on cotton, 2007
Musée Jenisch, Vevey

On the right (see also p. 342)
Caroline Bachmann/Stefan Banz
The Drummer
Oil on canvas, 2009–10
Courtesy the Artists

Exhibited but not visible on the photos
Caroline Bachmann/Stefan Banz
Un image nous regarde (An Image Watches Us)
Pastel on canvas, 2009
Courtesy the Artists

Caroline Bachmann/Stefan Banz
The Forestay Waterfall in Marcel Duchamp's *Étant donnés: 1° La chute d'eau, 2° Le gaz d'éclairage*
Video, 2008
Courtesy the Artists

Caroline Bachmann/Stefan Banz
The Forestay Waterfall
Photograph, 1 of 10, 2007
Courtesy the Artists

Roman Signer
Installation
Intervention in the Forestay waterfall
Documentation, video, May 7, 2010
Courtesy the Artist

MATERIALS

The Forestay Waterfall

In Postcards

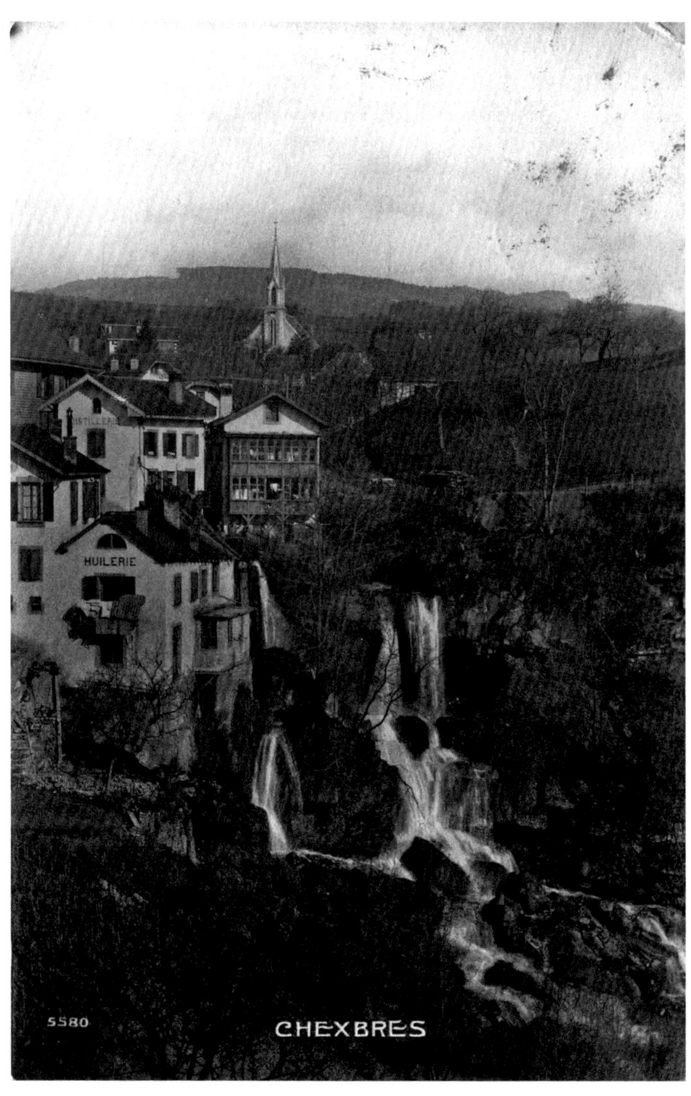

5580 Chexbres. The Forestay waterfall seen from the hillside of the Corniche near Hotel Bellevue (Municipality of Puidoux), postcard, before 1924. Photographed and edited by Edition Art. Perrochet-Matile, Lausanne. Collection Association du Vieux Lavaux, Chexbres.

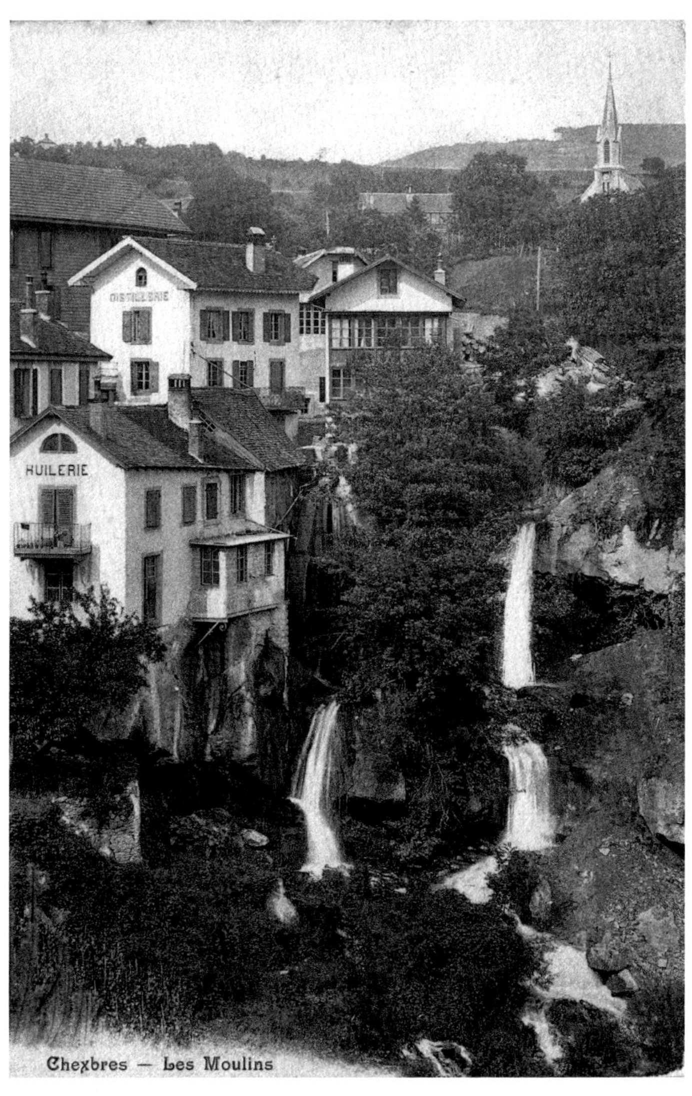

Chexbres – Les Moulins. The Forestay waterfall seen from the hillside of the Corniche near Hotel Bellevue (Municipality of Puidoux), postcard, between 1913 and 1928. Photographed by Charnaux frères & Co., Genève. Collection Association du Vieux Lavaux, Chexbres.

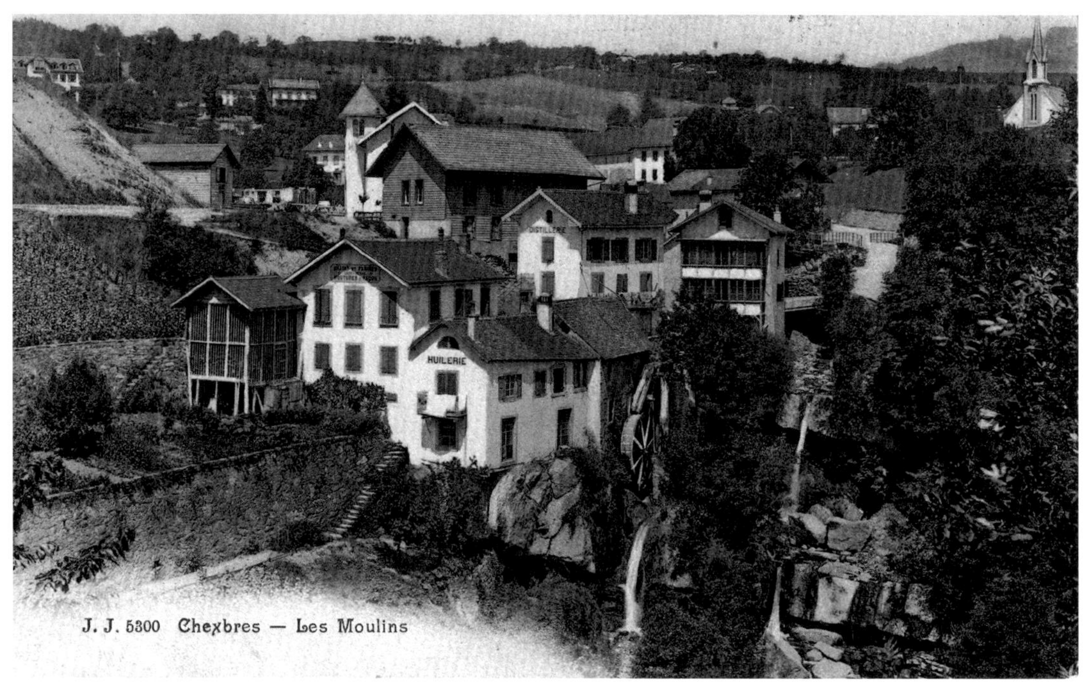

J.J. 5300 Chexbres – Les Moulins. The Forestay waterfall seen from the hillside of the Corniche near Hotel Bellevue (Municipality of Puidoux), postcard, c. 1908. Photographed by Julien frères, Genève. Collection Association du Vieux Lavaux, Chexbres.

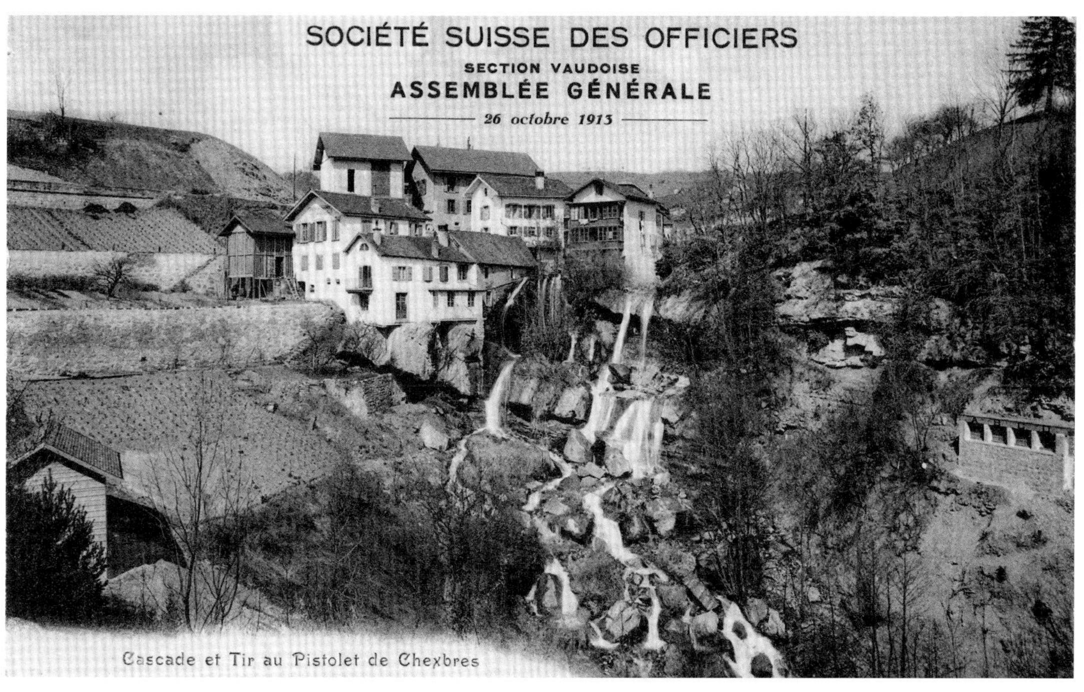

Cascade et Tir au pistolet de Chexbres (Cascade and Shooting Range of Chexbres). The Forestay waterfall seen from the hillside of the balcony of Lake Geneva near Hotel Bellevue (Municipality of Puidoux), postcard, 1913. Photographed by Julien frères, Genève. Collection Association du Vieux Lavaux, Chexbres.

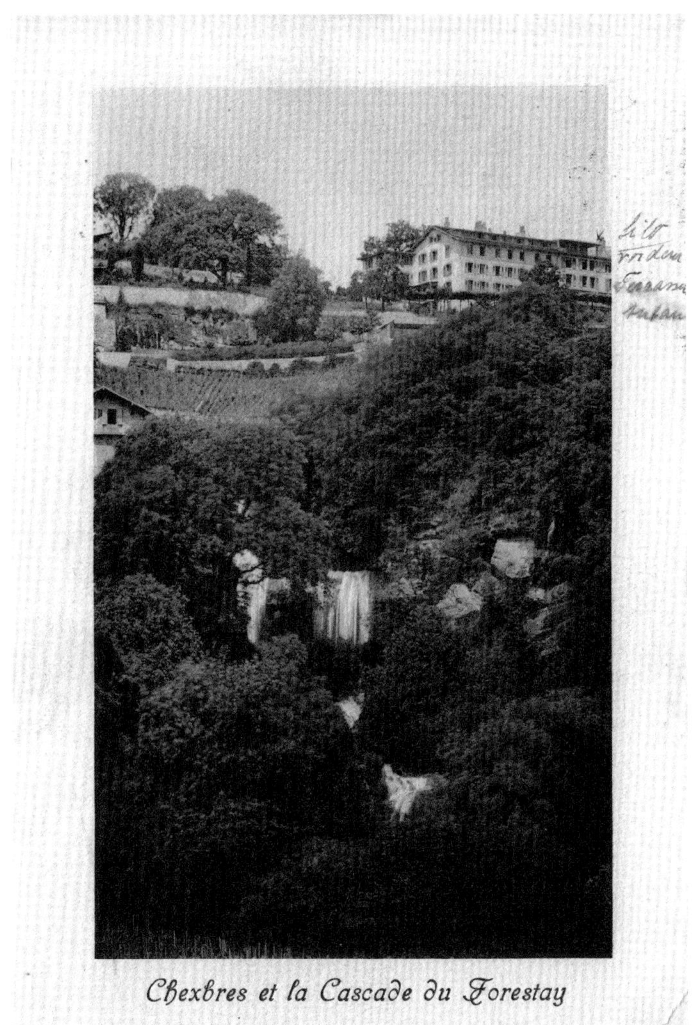

Chexbres et la Cascade du Forestay. The Forestay waterfall seen from the hillside of the Corniche near Hotel Bellevue (Municipality of Puidoux), postcard, between 1910 and 1928. Photographed by Charnaux frères & Co., Genève. Collection Association du Vieux Lavaux, Chexbres.

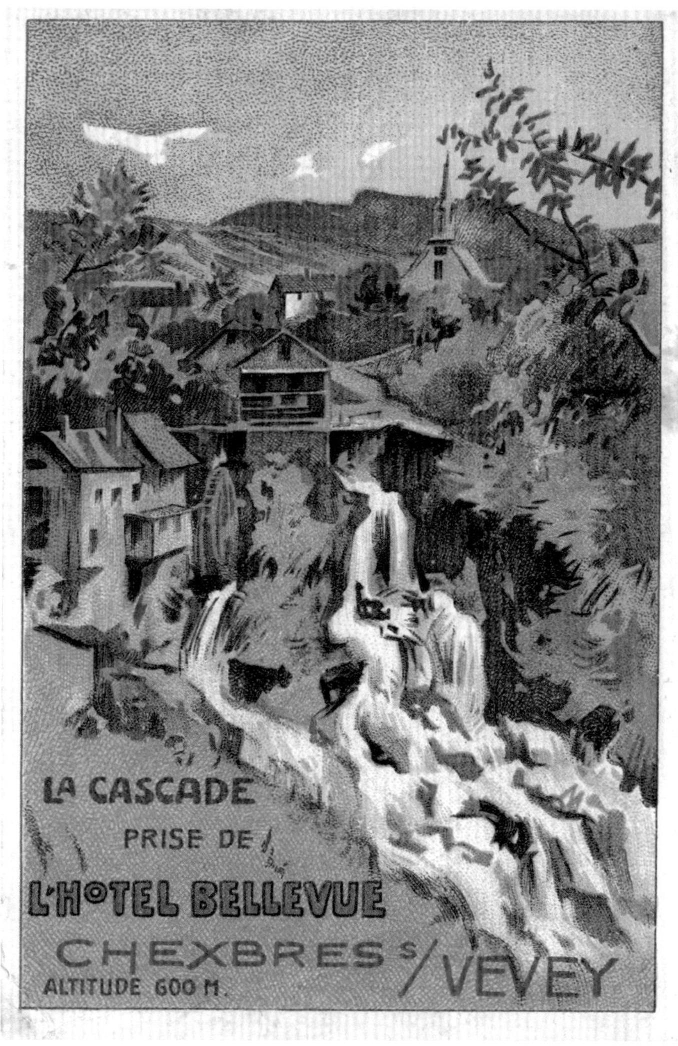

La cascade prise de l'Hôtel Bellevue Chexbres s/Vevey. Altitude 600 m (The Forestay waterfall seen from Hotel Bellevue, Bellevue near Chexbres. Altitude 600 m). Postcard, c. 1930. Collection Association du Vieux Lavaux, Chexbres.

Hotel Bellevue in Bellevue near Chexbres

In Postcards

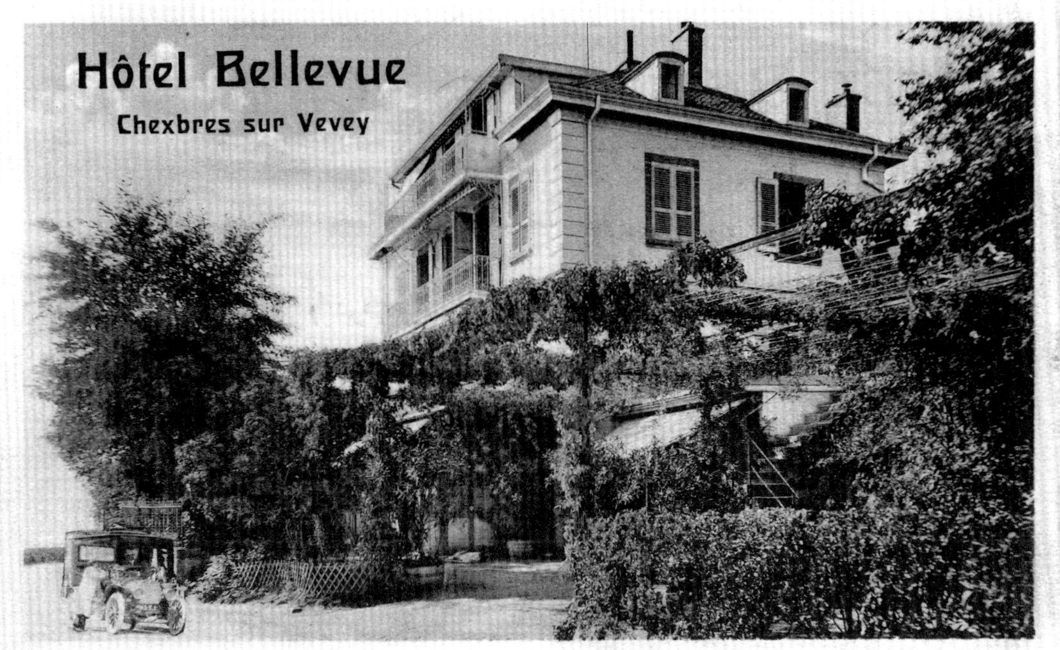

Hôtel Bellevue – Chexbres
sur Vevey (Altitude 600 mètres)

A 5 minutes de la Gare et du village. Point de vue unique de toute l'étendue du Lac Léman, des Alpes et du Jura. Vastes terrasses ombragées.
L'Hôtel, par sa situation splendide au haut de la Célèbre Corniche vaudoise, est exposé au midi et de chaque chambre on jouit d'une vue superbe.

Hôtel Bellevue, Chexbres sur Vevey. Hôtel Bellevue, Bellevue (Municipality of Puidoux), Balcon du Léman near Chexbres, postcard, c. 1910. The text is from the backside of the postcard. Collection Association du Vieux Lavaux, Chexbres.

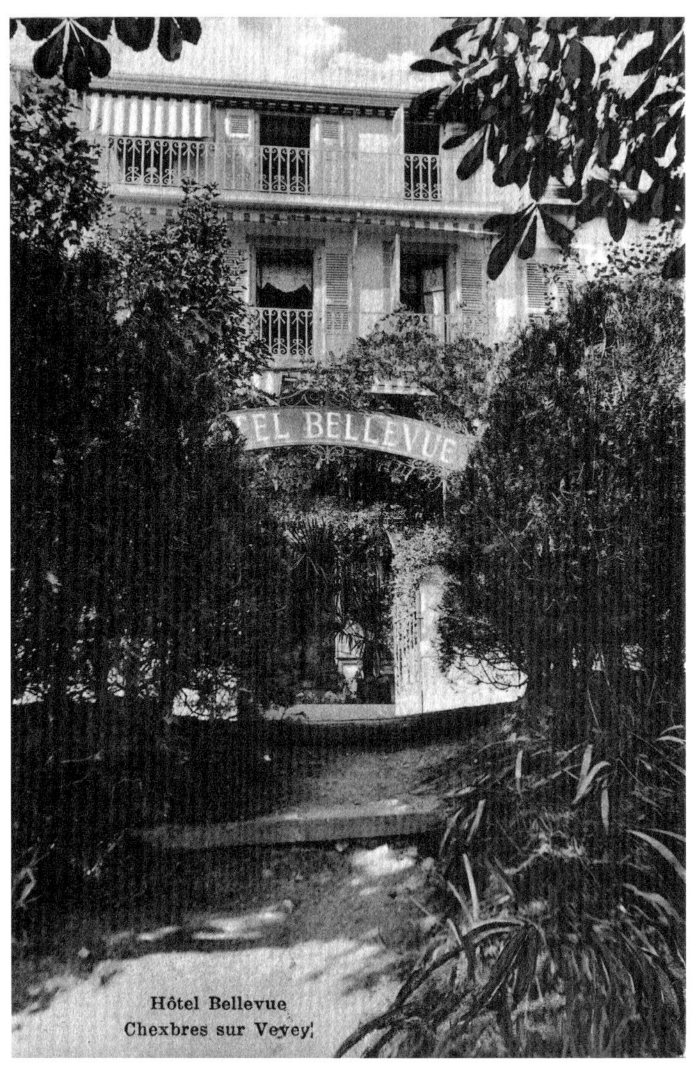

Hôtel Bellevue, Chexbres sur Vevey. Hôtel Bellevue, Bellevue (Municipality of Puidoux) Balcon du Léman near Chexbres, postcard, c. 1913. Photographed by E. Würgler, Lausanne. Collection Association du Vieux Lavaux, Chexbres.

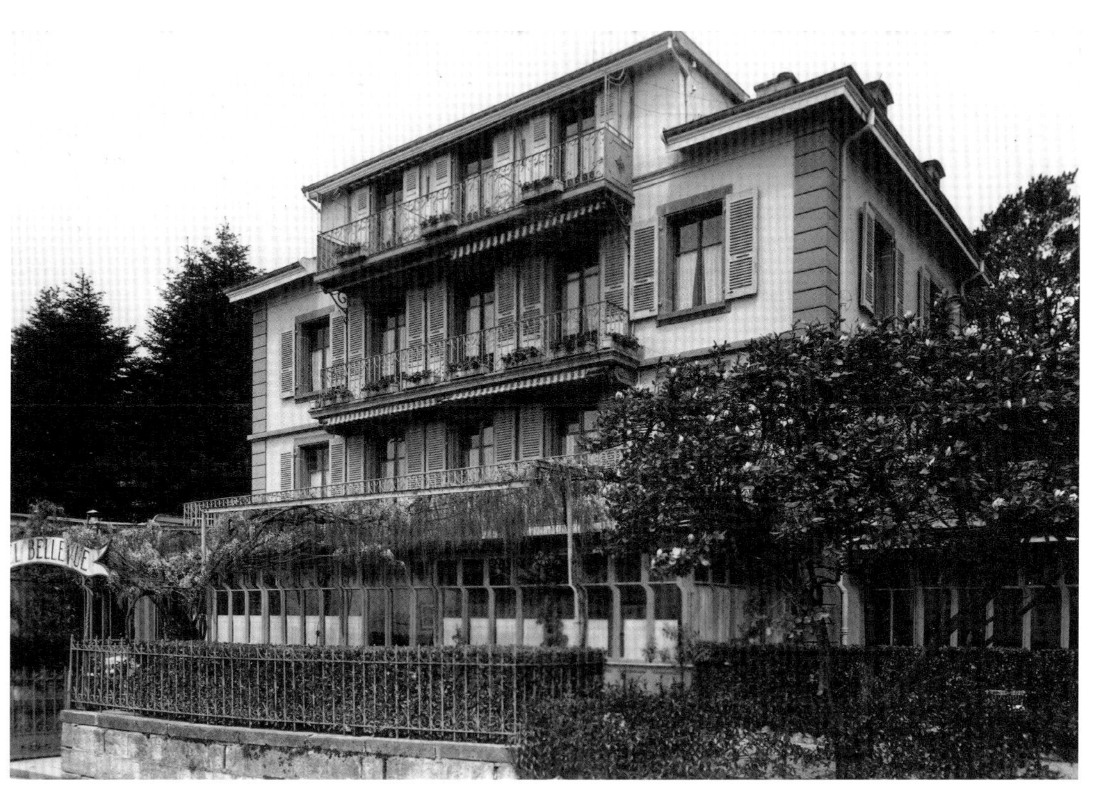

Hôtel Bellevue, Balcon du Léman, Chexbres. Hôtel Bellevue, Bellevue (Municipality of Puidoux), Balcon du Léman near Chexbres, postcard, c. 1940. Les Editions Seal, Lausanne. Collection Association du Vieux Lavaux, Chexbres.

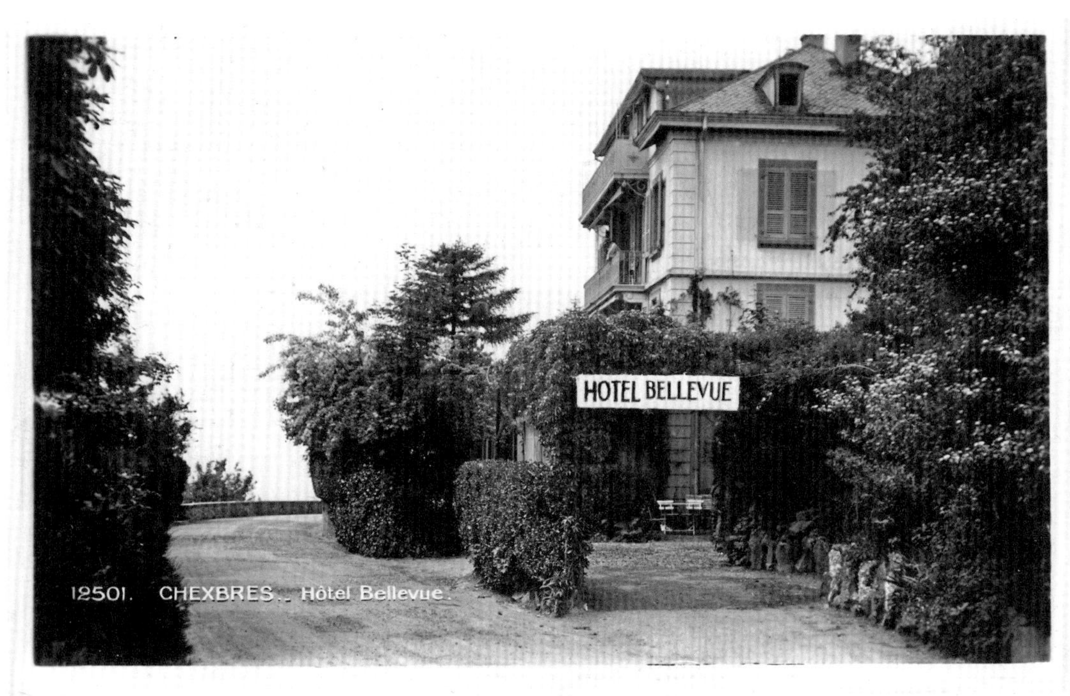

12501. Chexbres, Hôtel Bellevue. Hôtel Bellevue, Bellevue (Municipality of Puidoux), Balcon du Léman near Chexbres, postcard, c. 1940. Seal Edit. d'Art R.E. Chapallaz fils, Lausanne. Collection Association du Vieux Lavaux, Chexbres.

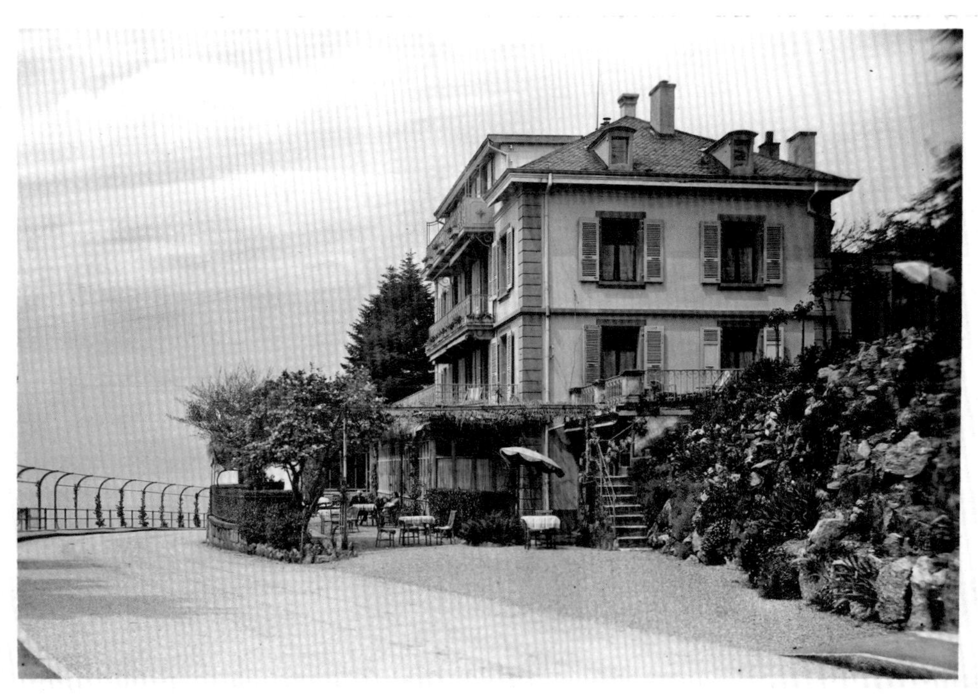

Hôtel Bellevue, Balcon du Léman. Hôtel Bellevue, Bellevue (Municipality of Puidoux), Balcon du Léman near Chexbres, postcard, c. 1945. Les Editions Seal, Lausanne. Collection Association du Vieux Lavaux, Chexbres.

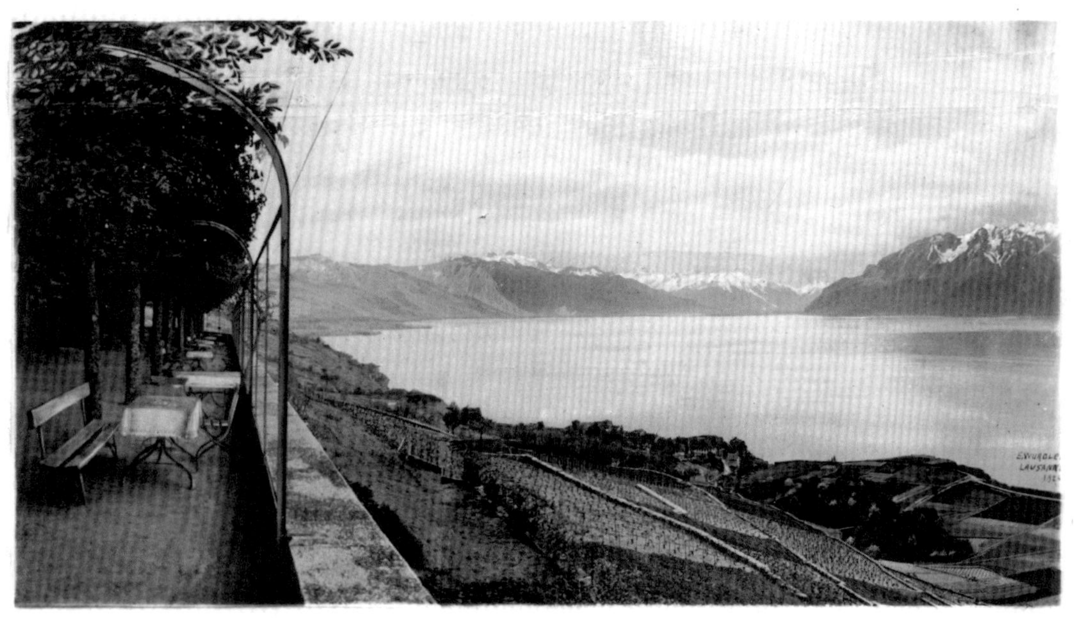

Terrasse de l'Hôtel Bellevue à Chexbres. Terrace of the Hotel Bellevue, Bellevue (Municipality of Puidoux), Balcon du Léman near Chexbres, postcard, c. 1930. Photographed by E. Würgler, Lausanne. Collection Association du Vieux Lavaux, Chexbres.

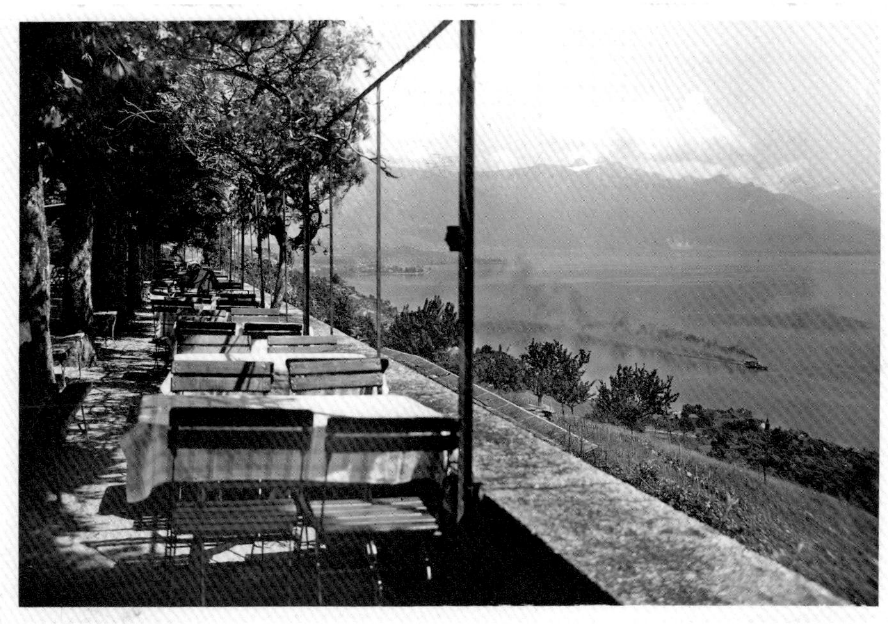

Terrasse de l'Hôtel Bellevue à Chexbres, Balcon du Léman – J. Butticaz, prop. Terrace of the Hotel Bellevue, Bellevue, Bellevue (Municipality of Puidoux), Balcon du Léman near Chexbres, postcard, c. 1935. Les Editions Seal, Rob. E. Chapallaz, Lausanne. Collection Association du Vieux Lavaux, Chexbres.

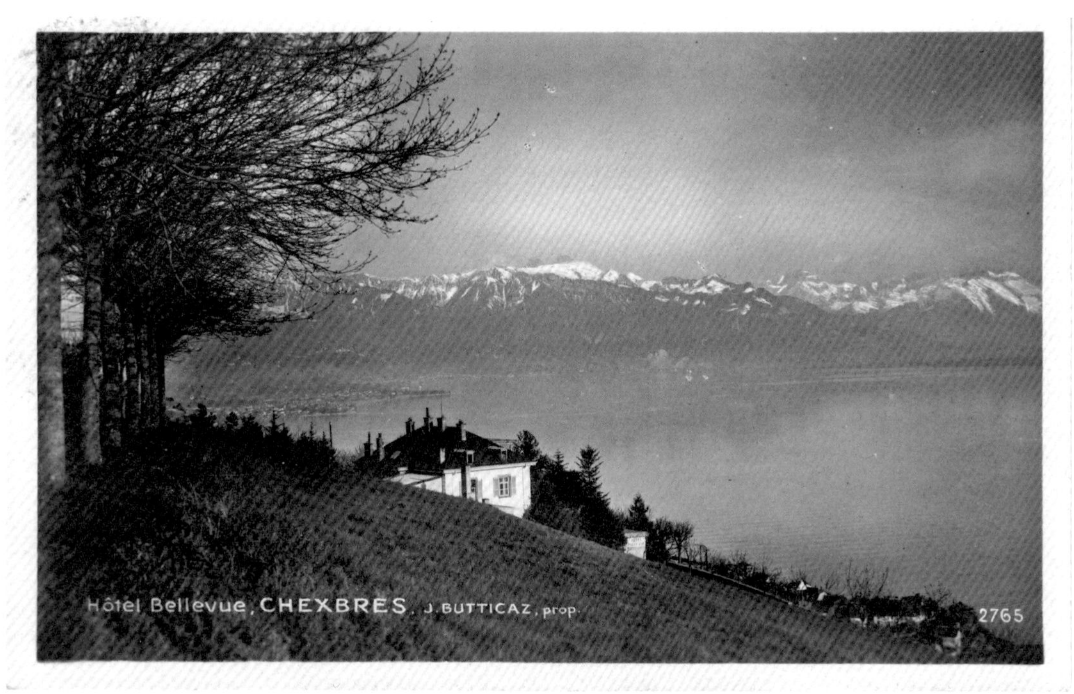

Hôtel Bellevue. Chexbres. J. Butticaz, prop. View of Hôtel Bellevue, Bellevue (Municipality of Puidoux), Balcon du Léman near Chexbres and on Lake Geneva with the peninsula of La Tour-de-Peilz (where Gustave Courbet died) and the two mountains Les tours d'Aï (a.k.a. La tour de Mayen and La tour d'Aï) above, postcard, c. 1928. Edition Art. Perrochet-Matile, Lausanne. Collection Association du Vieux Lavaux, Chexbres.

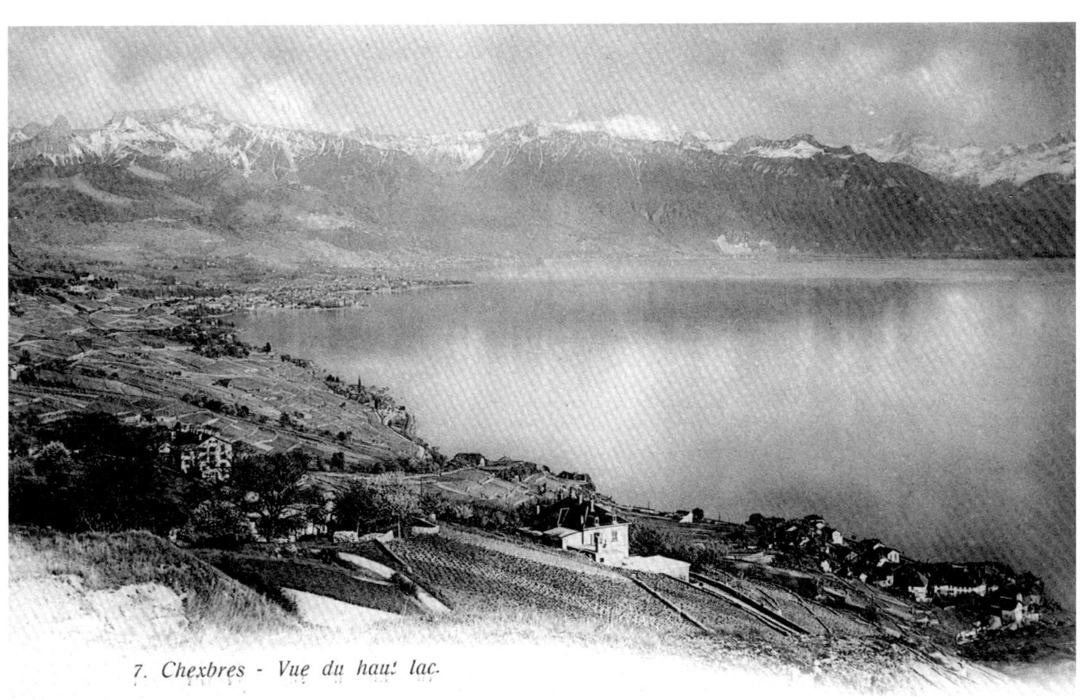

7. Chexbres – Vue du haut lac. View from Chexbres on Lake Geneva with the peninsula of La Tour-de-Peilz and from left to right the mountains La dent de Jaman, Le rocher de Naye, Les tours d'Aï, Le grand Mouveran, and Le petit Mouveran, postcard, c. 1910, A. Schwendimann, Edit., Chexbres. Collection Association du Vieux Lavaux, Chexbres.

Hotel Bellevue in Chardonne (razed)
In Postcards

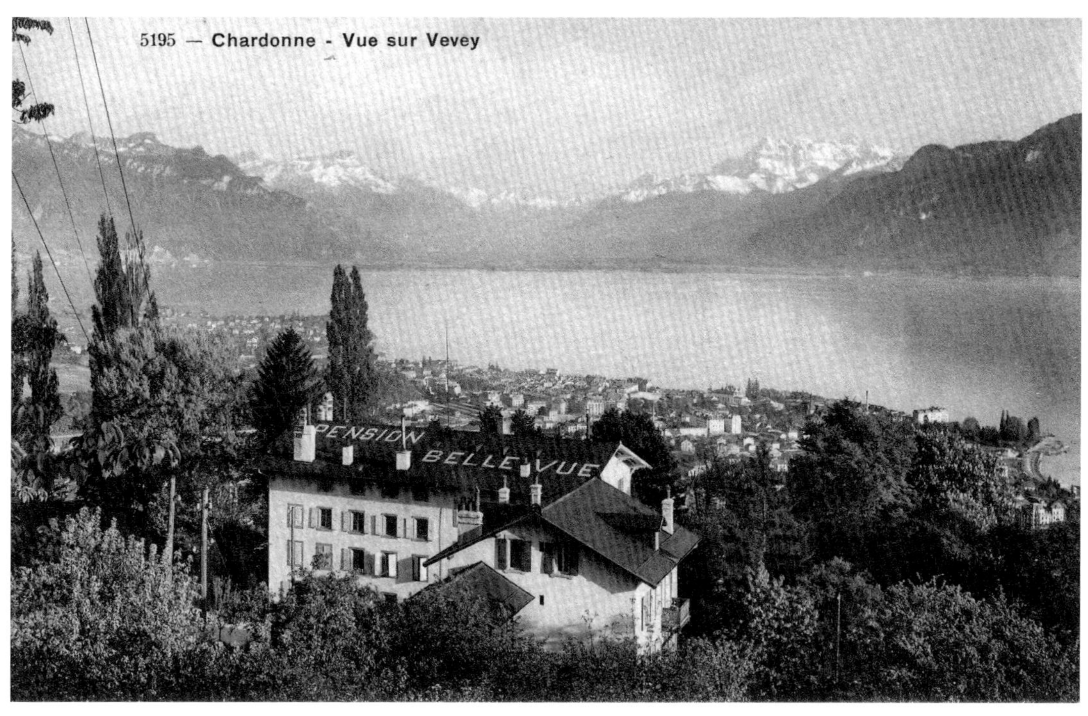

5195 – Chardonne - Vue sur Vevey. View of Pension Belle-vue, Chardonne, and the town of Vevey, postcard, c. 1925. Phototypie Co., Neuchâtel. Collection Association du Vieux Lavaux, Chexbres.

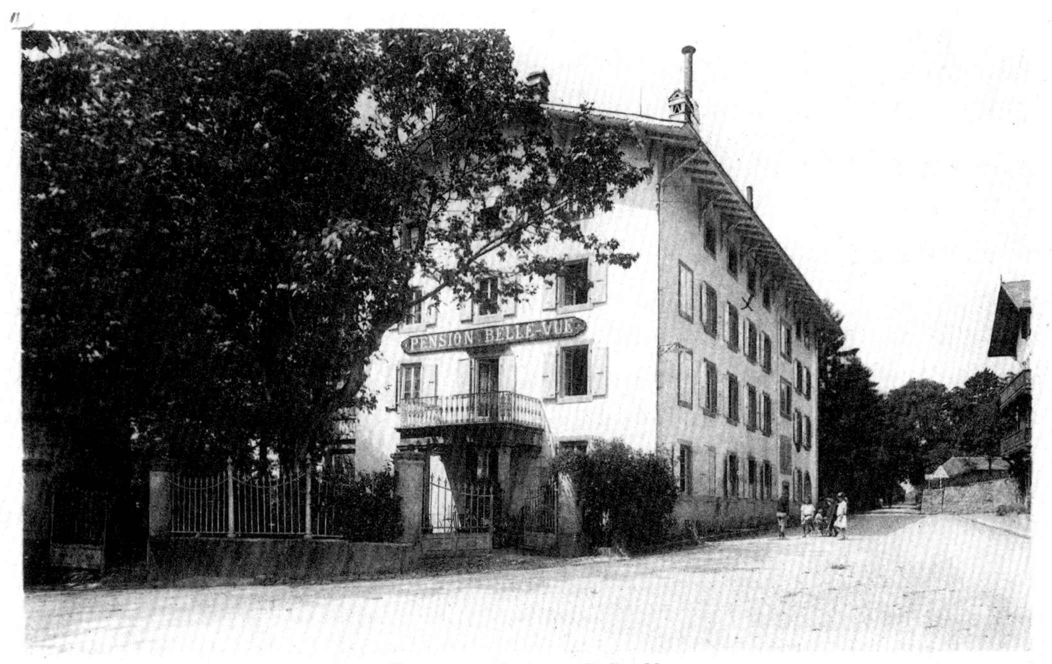

Chardonne Pension Belle-Vue

Chardonne Pension Belle–Vue. Photographed c. 1925. Re-used by Seal Edit. d'Art R.E. Chapallaz fils, Lausanne. Collection Association du Vieux Lavaux, Chexbres.

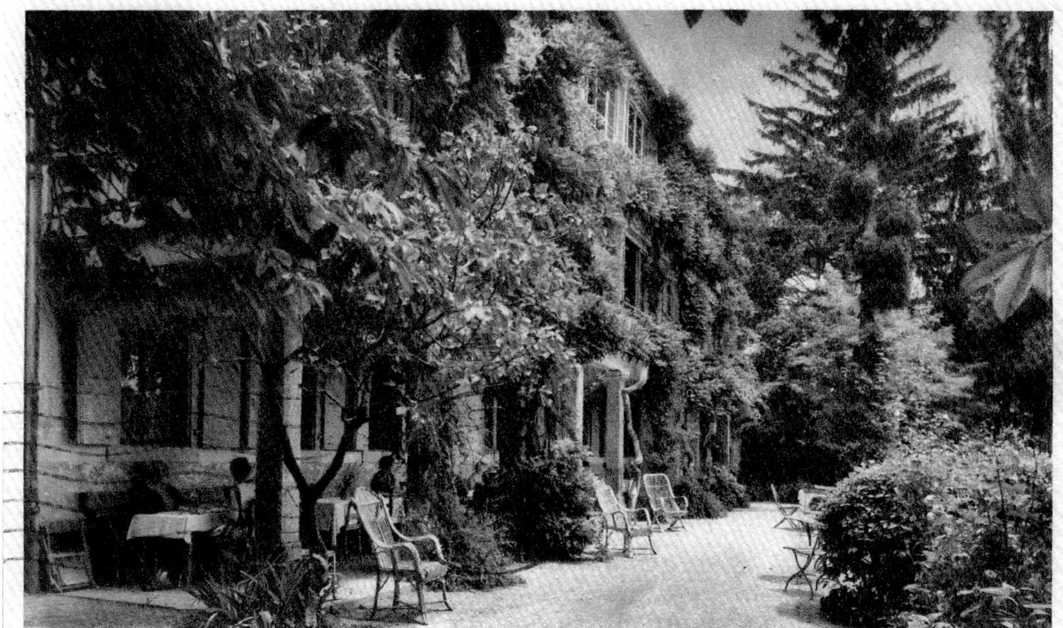

Une terrasse de la pension Bellevue, Chardonne sur Vevey. Postcard, c. 1933. Photographed by de Jongh, Lausanne, printed by Roto-Sadag S.A., Genève. Collection Association du Vieux Lavaux, Chexbres.

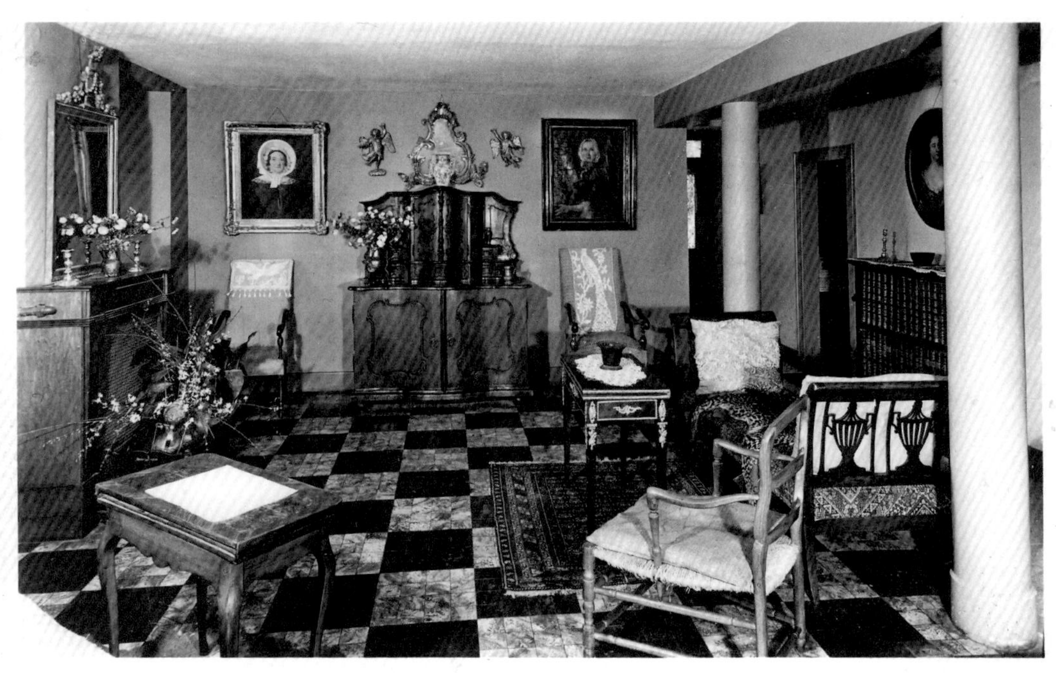

Hôtel Bellevue, Chardonne s/Vevey, Le Hall. Postcard, c. 1940. Säuberlin & Pfeiffer, S.A., Vevey. Collection Association du Vieux Lavaux, Chexbres. The floor in this hall might have inspired Duchamp to use the same floor in *Étant donnés.*

Excerpts from the Archive of Felix Kälin

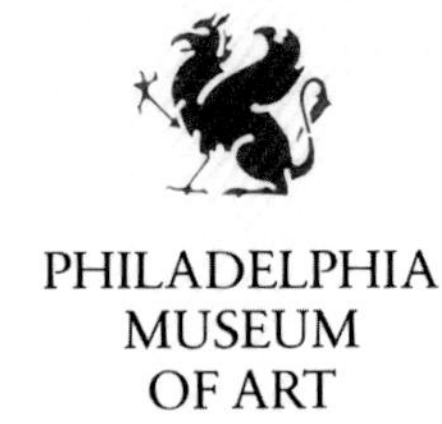

PHILADELPHIA
MUSEUM
OF ART

Benjamin Franklin Parkway, Box 7646, Philadelphia, Pennsylvania 19101 · Telephone: 215 763-8100 · Cable: Philmuse

July 18, 1979

Mr. Felix Kälin
Zeughausgasse 22
9000 St. Gallen
Switzerland

Dear Mr. Kälin,

Thank you for your letter regarding Marcel Duchamp's Etant Donnes. I am afraid we are not sure of the exact location of the waterfall in Switzerland. There is no written record and Madame Duchamp cannot remember. If you find the answer, please let us know.

With best wishes,

Yours sincerely,

Anne d'Harnoncourt

Anne d'Harnoncourt
Curator of 20th Century Art

Letter from Anne d'Harnoncourt, July 18, 1979. Collection Felix Kälin, Basel.

ARTURO SCHWARZ

20129 MILANO - VIA M. GIURIATI, 17

TEL. (02) 71.77.73

27/8/79

Dear Mr. Kälin,

Sorry, I do not know where this landscape is, as a matter of fact, I was always curious about it. If you ever find out, please let me know,

Warm regards,

Arturo Schwarz

Postcard from Arturo Schwarz, August 27, 1979. Collection Felix Kälin, Basel.

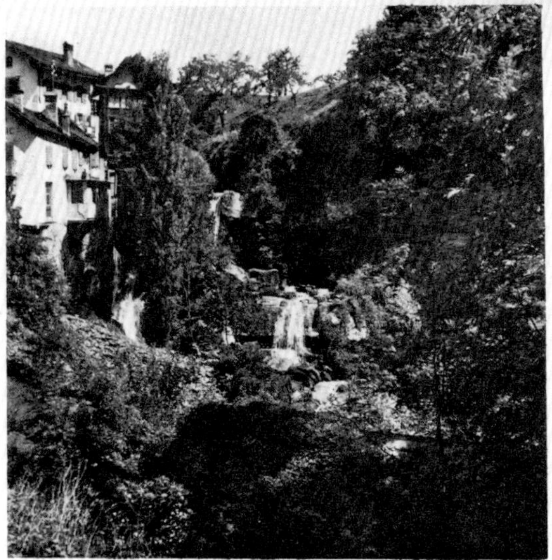

Reprinted from the Philadelphia Museum of Art Bulletin,
Volume LXIV, numbers 299 and 300, april-september 1969.

Liebe Gemeinde,

*Seit einigen Jahren beschäftige ich mich mit dem Leben und Werk des Künstlers Marcel Duchamp (1887 - 1968). Zurzeit interessiere ich mich für seine letzte Arbeit, das sogenannte *Etant donnés: 1° la chute d'eau 2° le gaz d'éclairage*. In einer amerikanischen Publikation fand ich obige Photographie (entstanden ca. 1950), welche ergänzt wurde durch den Hinweis, dass sich diese Landschaft irgendwo in der Schweiz befinde. Marcel Duchamp übertrug diese Landschaft in den Hintergrund seines letzten Werkes.*

Meine Frage:Kennen Sie den genauen Platz dieser Landschaft?

Für alle Hinweise und Informationen danke ich Ihnen im voraus.

Caro Commune,

*Da alcuni anni mi occupo della vita e dell'opera dell'artista Marcel Duchamp (1887 - 1968). Adesso mi interesso della sua ultima opera, dal titulo *Etant donnés: 1° la chute d'eau 2° le gaz d'éclairage*. In una publicazione americana trovavo la fotografia (ripresso 1950), qui sopra allegata, completata con l'indicazione che questo paesaggio si trova in qualche luogo della Svizzera. Marcel Duchamp trasferiva questa cascata nello sfondo della sua opera.*

La mia domanda è: Sapete voi, dove si trova questo paesaggio?

Per indicazione e risposta ringrazio tanto in anticipo.

Chère Commune,

*Il y a quelques ans que je m'occupe de la vie et l'oeuvre du Marcel Duchamp (artiste 1887 - 1968). Pour ce temps je m'interesse son dernier objet d'art qui s'appelle *Etant donnés: 1° la chute d'eau 2° le gaz d'éclairage*. Dans une publication américain j'ai trouvée la photographie ajoutée (née un peu près 1950) avec l'indication que ce paysage se trouve en Suisse.*

Ma question: Connaissez-vous la place précise de ce paysage?

Pour toutes les indications et informations je vous remercie en advance.

Wollen Sie bitte Ihre Zuschrift richten an:	Felix Kälin
Si prega da spedire le risposte all indirizzo:	Zeughausgasse 22
Veuillez adresser votre réponse à:	9000 St. Gallen

Circular from Felix Kälin sent to 2,034 municipalities in Switzerland, September 1979–May 1980. Also sent as the eighth page in the letter to Anne d'Harnoncourt, June 11, 1980. Courtesy Felix Kälin, Basel.

THE BUREAUCRATIC PHASE'S BOOK-KEEPING

name of canton	number of communities	cost accounting	number of replies
Aargau	242	sFr. 48.80	25
Fribourg	180	36.20	4
Glarus	26	5.40	3
Graubünden	290	58.40	15
Jura (incl. Jura-Bern)	151	30.60	10
Neuenburg	89	18.20	11
Nid-Obwalden	35	7.20	2
Solothurn	118	24.—	8
Schwyz	55	11.—	6
Ticino	266	53.60	34
Uri	26	5.40	3
Vaud	368	74.—	15
Valais	188	38.—	10
Total of mailing	2034	sFr. 410.80	146

other costs:	
- printing-press	200.60
- envelopes	30.40
Total of costs (without body-heat)	sFr. 641.80

The Bureaucratic Phase's Book-keeping, May 1980. Also sent as the sixth page in the letter to Anne d'Harnoncourt, June 11, 1980. Courtesy Felix Kälin, Basel.

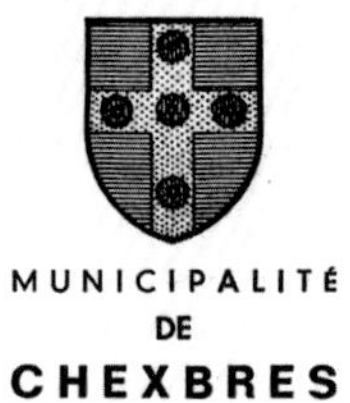

MUNICIPALITÉ
DE
CHEXBRES

1605 Chexbres, le 5 mai 1980

Monsieur
Félix KALIN
Zeughausgasse 22
9000. ST GALL

Monsieur,

Après avoir examiné la photo ci-jointe nous pouvons vous dire qu'il s'agit de Chexbres "Sur le Moulin". Les chutes d'eau sont celles du ruisseau "Le Forestay".

Le premier bâtiment à gauche était un moulin.

Espérant avoir satisfait à votre demande, nous vous présentons, Monsieur, nos salutations distinguées.

Au nom de la Municipalité
le Syndic: Le Secrétaire

CHS BORGEAUD C. BIAVATI

Response from the municipality of Chexbres, May 5, 1980. Collection Felix Kälin, Basel.

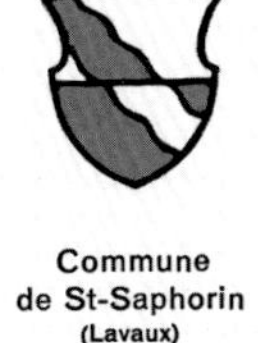

Commune
de St-Saphorin
(Lavaux)

Avec nos compliments

Monsieur Félix Kälin
Zeughausgasse 22

9000 St Gall

t.s.v.pl.

Le 8 mai 1980

Monsieur,

Nous avons soumis votre demande à la Municipalité lors de sa dernière séance. La photographie que vous nous soumettez représente les chutes du Forestay, près de l'ancienne huilerie. Cet endroit se situe à la limite des communes de Chexbres et Puidoux, le ruisseau faisant frontière. Il est possible que l'une de ces communes vous communique également ce renseignement.

Nous précisons que le territoire de notre commune commence très rès de ce lieu.

Nous espérons vous avoir ainsi rendu service et vous présentons, Monsieur, nos salutations distinguées.

SECRÉTARIAT MUNICIPAL ST-SAPHORIN (LAVAUX)

Response from the municipality of St-Saphorin, recto and verso, May 8, 1980. Collection Felix Kälin, Basel.

Anne d'Harnoncourt
P. O. Box 7646
Philadelphia, Penns. 19101
U S A

St. Gallen / June 11, 1980

Dear Anne d'Harnoncourt,

Finally I can answer your letter from july 18, 1979.
The following pages should give you an impression of my effort to find the exact location of the waterfall in Marcel Duchamp's Etant Donnés.

Yours sincerely

F. Käl

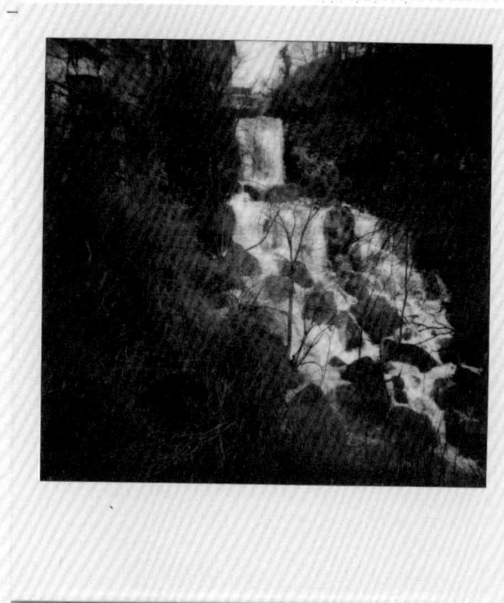

Copy of the first page of the letter from Felix Kälin to Anne d'Harnoncourt, June 11, 1980. In this letter he explains how and where he found the Forestay waterfall. Courtesy Felix Kälin, Basel.

Dear Anne d'Harnoncourt,

I'm sure you notice that I didn't tell you the name and the exact location of the landscape/waterfall I have found.
I think you should remunerate the work I have treated.
So please hear my offer:

I would like to work as a keeper in the Duchamp-part of the Philadelphia museum of Art from first of october 1980 till end of march 1981. My payment has to be the same as a keeper gets in your museum.

Now I'm working as a bookseller (I made an apprenticeship of 3 years) and I'll quit my job end of august 1980. I'm 28 years old, célibataire and elsewhere.

So soon I receive your agreement I'll send you a) copies of all five replies b) a detail map of the location c) some more and better photos (Mr. Serge Stauffer will help me in this case).

Once more my address: Felix Kälin
Zeughausgasse 22

9000 St. Gallen / Switzerland

I hope you can accept my offer and I can meet you in autumn

best wishes

F. Käl

Copy of page 18 of the letter from Felix Kälin to Anne d'Harnoncourt, June 11, 1980. On this, the last page, he explains what he wants in return from the Philadelphia Museum for providing the name and exact location of the waterfall. Courtesy Felix Kälin, Basel.

Exp. Felix Kälin
Felsenstr. 36

9000 St. Gallen
Suisse

St. Gallen/12/5/1981/

Dear Jennifer & Jacques

the last time I was a little bit occupied with the search for the *chute d'eau* in reality which Duchamp transformed in his last work the *Etant donnés*. As you can see from the including papers (re-copies from my report to Anne d'Harnoncourt) I found the place. It's in a village called Chexbres (to find near Lausanne).
Also I include this package a bigger photo made by Serge Stauffer who gave me your address too.
I know you are working on a biography of M.D. so that's why I have some questions:

Are there any connection between Chexbres and Marcel Duchamps' lifelines?

Has he been once in Chexbres? and when?

Serge Stauffer told me that Teeny Duchamp can't remember a place called Chexbres at all otherwise she gets an old photo (around 1915) of this waterfall on the wall.

Hoping you get the picture and can give me some more informations:

thanks & merci in advance

F. Kä[illegible]

Copy of the letter from Felix Kälin to Jennifer Cough-Cooper and Jacques Caumont, in which he writes that he has found the waterfall, May 12, 1981. **Opposite: Three photographs from Felix Kälin's first visit to the waterfall** (with Katharina Heusser). Above and bottom: The targets of the shooting range (now destroyed). Middle: Felix Kälin standing on the small bridge which crossed the Forestay river (destroyed). Photos by Katharina Heusser. Courtesy Felix Kälin, Basel.

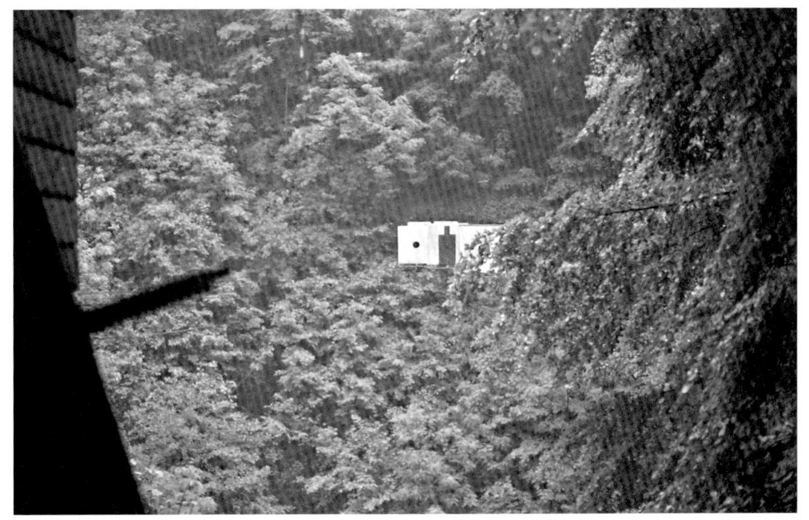

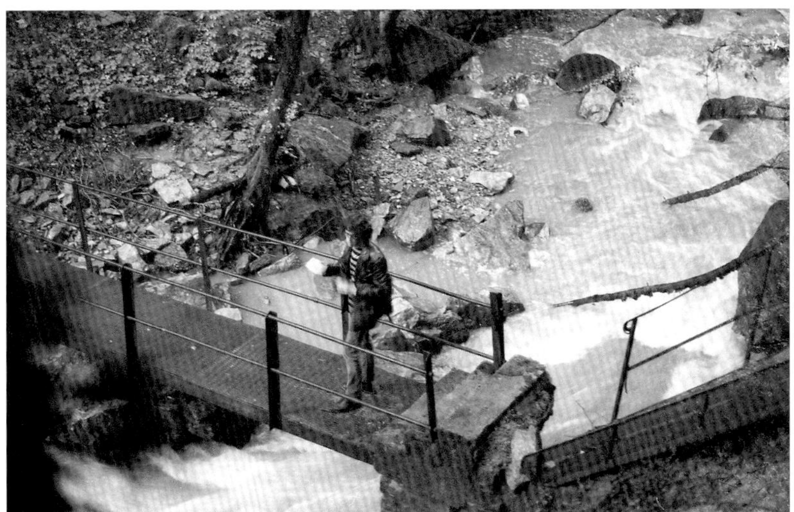

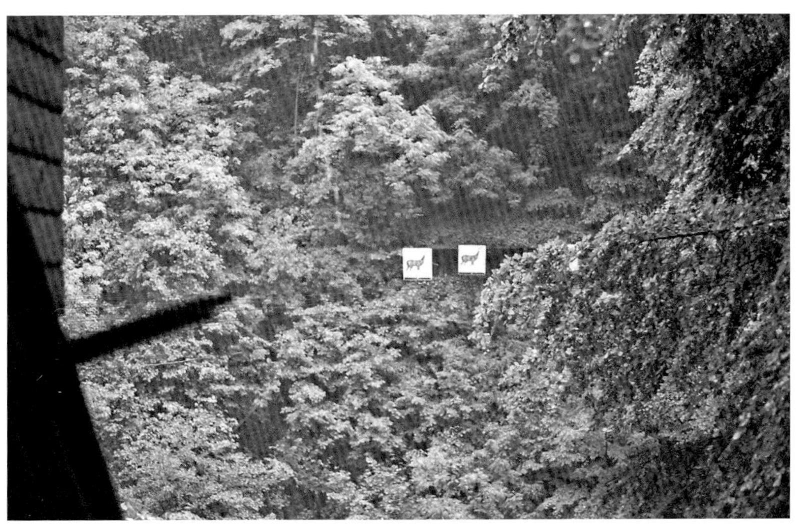

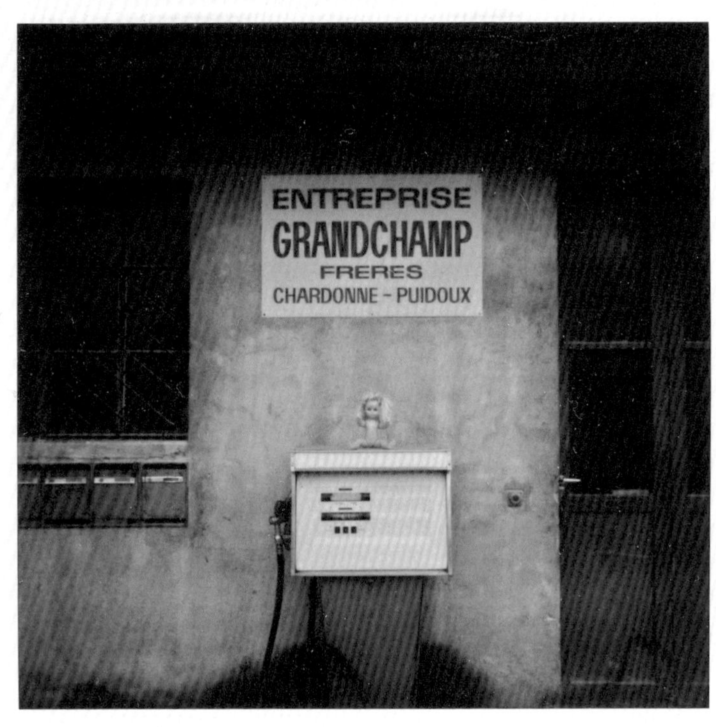

Felix Kälin, Entreprise Grandchamp frères, Chardonne-Puidoux, Polaroid, 10.4 x 10.1 cm, June 8, 1980. The photograph was taken at the gas station just beside the waterfall. Courtesy Felix Kälin, Basel.

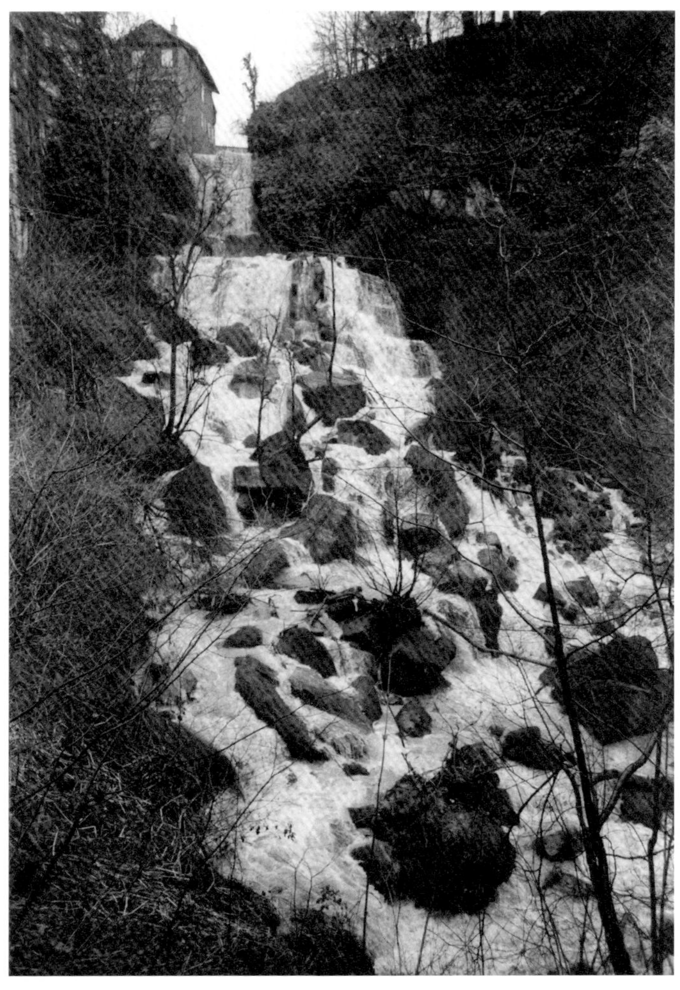

Serge Stauffer, The Forestay Waterfall, color photograph, 9 x 13 cm, March, 1981. One of a series of more than 40 photographs taken during a visit with Felix Kälin and Wolfgang Steiger one year after Kälin discovered the location of the waterfall. Collection Felix Kälin, Basel.

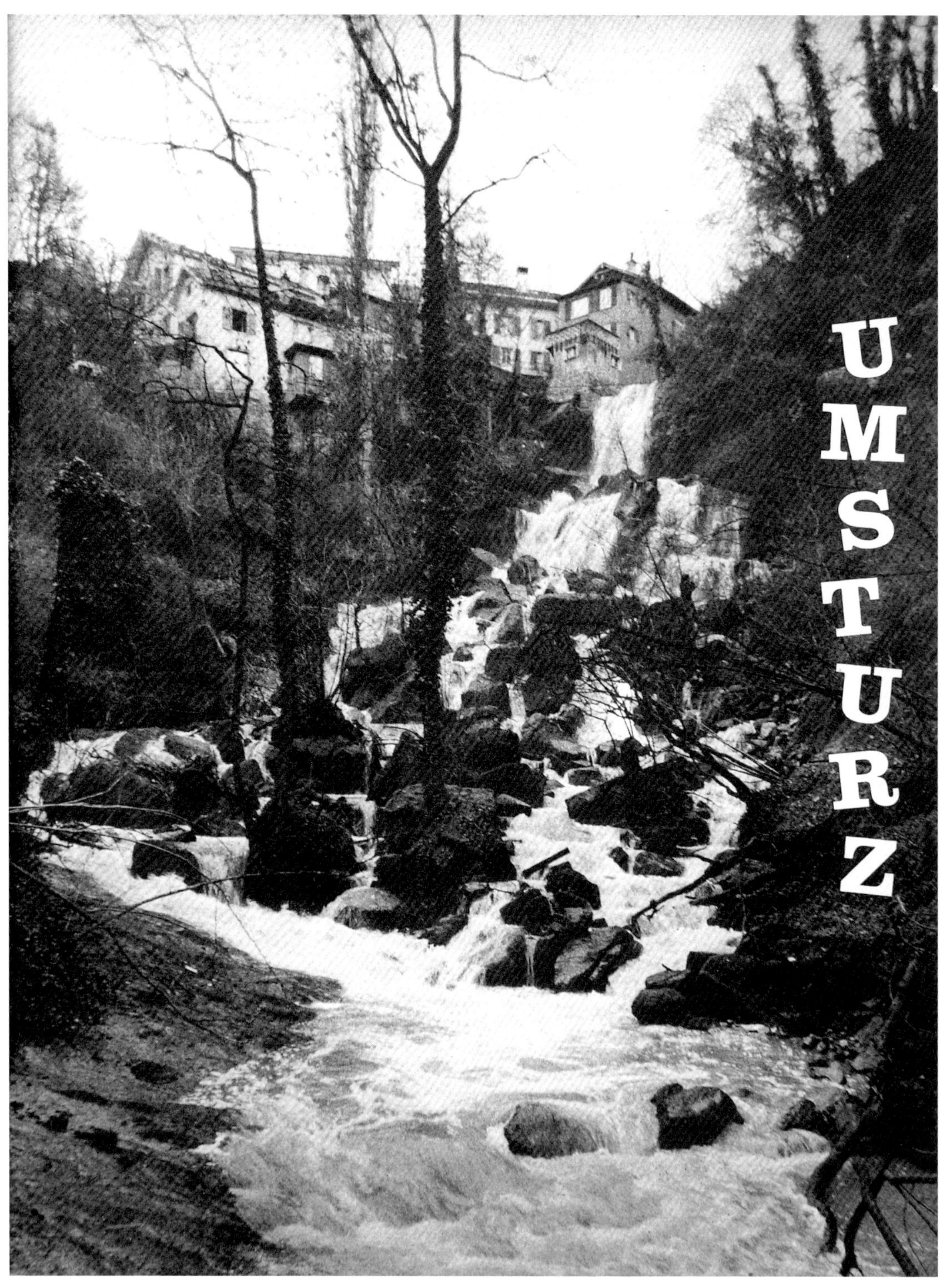

Felix Kälin (with Wolfgang Steiger and Serge Stauffer), front cover of the "overground" magazine *Umsturz*, black and white, 28 pages, 38 x 28 cm, edited by Regenbogenverlag Zürich, Autumn 1981. Photograph of the Forestay waterfall by Serge Stauffer. Collection Stefan Banz, Cully.

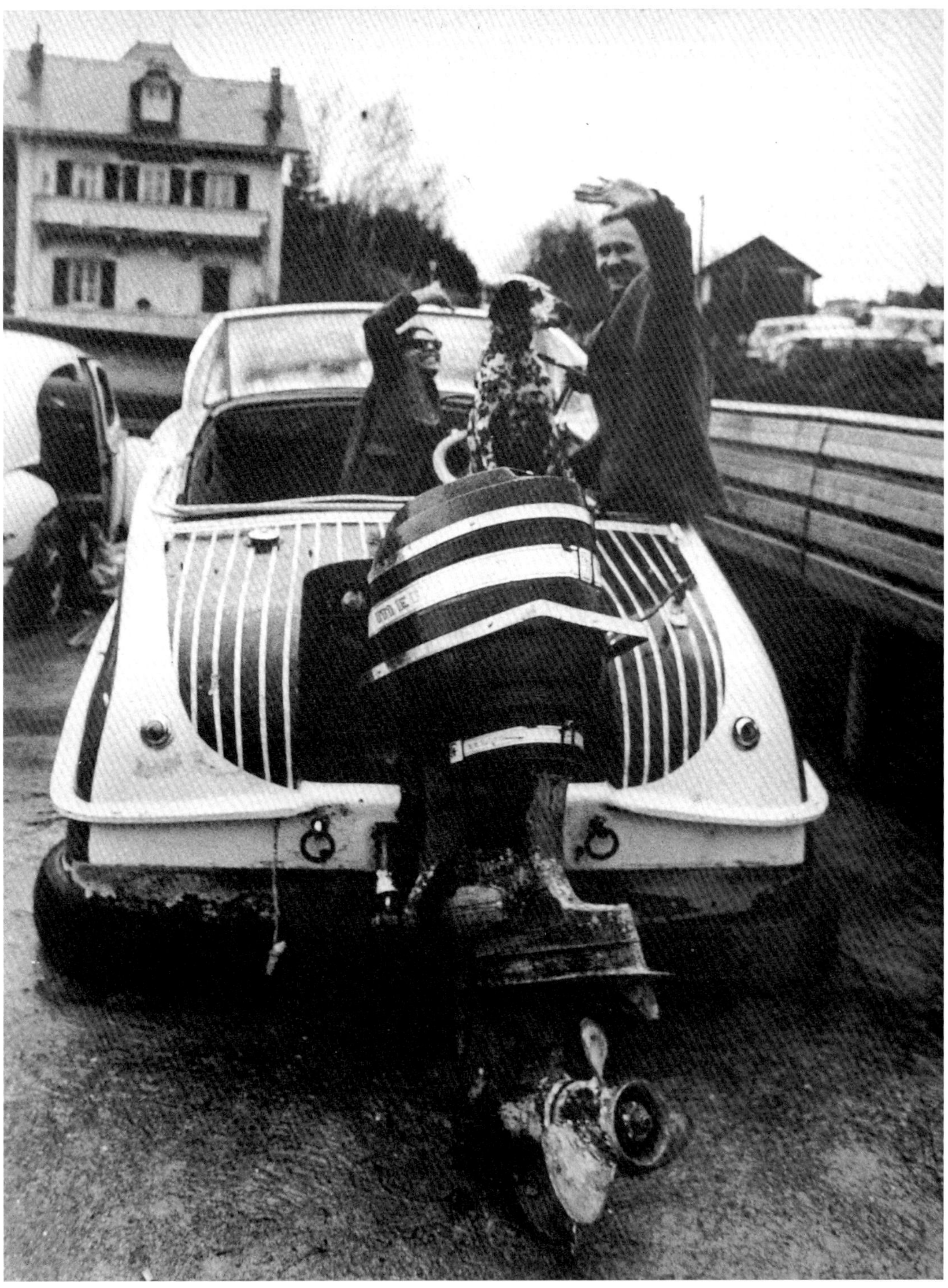

Felix Kälin (with Wolfgang Steiger and Serge Stauffer), back cover of *Umsturz* (facing page for details). Photograph by Serge Stauffer taken just behind the Forestay waterfall in Chexbres. On the left: Felix Kälin; on the right: Wolfgang Steiger with his dog.

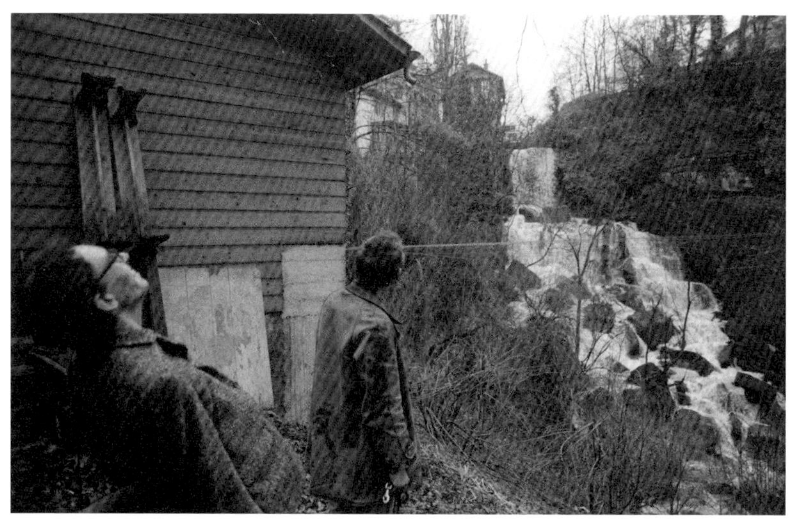

Serge Stauffer, The Forestay Waterfall (with shooting range, Felix Kälin and Wolfgang Steiger), color photograph, 9 x 13 cm, March 1981. Collection Felix Kälin, Basel.

Marcel Duchamp's Visits to Switzerland, 1946 and 1968

The following descriptions are taken from Jennifer Gough-Cooper and Jacques Caumont, "Ephemerides on and about Marcel Duchamp and Rrose Sélavy 1887–1968," in *Marcel Duchamp*, Milan 1993, unpaginated.

Paris, Monday, July 29, 1946
Mary Reynolds and Marcel Duchamp set off for a holiday in Switzerland, taking the night train for Bern, which departs at ten minutes past eleven from the Gare de Lyon.

Chexbres, Monday, August 5, 1946
After several days enjoying the warm hospitality of the Hoppenots at the French embassy in Bern, Mary and Marcel are staying at the Bellevue, a small hotel built on the ledge, recommended to them by Hélène Hoppenot, who stayed there as a child. Dominating the steep vineyards of Lavaux, the hotel has a stupendous view across Lake Geneva to the mountains of Savoy.

Within a stone's throw is the deep ravine of the Forestay, the mountain stream dividing Puidoux from Chexbres. There, where its racing waters drive the millwheels belonging to the cluster of rural industries clinging to the rocky slope, as it plunges with a roar on its precipitous course to the lake below, is the waterfall which Marcel wants to photograph, finding it perfect for the décor of the new piece burgeoning in his mind.

During the day, Mary and Marcel explore Vevey and are captivated by the romantic lakeside market town with its memories of Jean-Jacques Rousseau, Lord Byron, Gustave Courbet, Hodler and Vallotton. For the Hoppenots, they ask an estate agent, M. Flouck, about houses for sale in the area.

Chexbres, Tuesday, August 6, 1946
Mary writes a spirited thank-you letter to Henri and Hélène Hoppenots, declaring that she and Marcel "are still travelling under their star from Bellevue to Bellevue." Mary finds the Hôtel Bellevue at Chexbres "a very pleasant introduction to Bellevue-Chardonne," situated on the hillside just a few kilometres east, which they "anticipate as perfection."

Marcel writes a paragraph expressing his enthusiasm for the "ideal" holiday, thanks to the French ambassador and his wife. As for the view: "The weather has a hand in it and every hour the lake changes her gown."

Chexbres, Wednesday, August 7, 1946
From the Hôtel Bellevue Mary and Marcel make an excursion to Lausanne where they hope to meet Henri and Hélène Hoppenot, their hosts at the embassy in Bern.

Chexbres, Friday, August 9, 1946
Writes to thank Ettie Stettheimer for the surprise case delivered to him on the *Brazil* (May 3, 1946). He kept several bottles "for the family," Marcel recounts, "who, on my arrival in Paris, drank the champagne to your health."

Of Europe after the war: "… there is no famine," says Marcel, "many impoverished or poorly paid people who subsist with difficulty—the prices, the salaries and the black market—you know the story. In Paris the trees are greener than ever," he explains, "because car fumes and chimney smoke have not stopped them growing in their own way during the war."

Very distressed at the death of Alfred Stieglitz, Marcel remarks: "New York without Stieglitz is no longer our New York," and he asks Ettie to send his condolences to Georgia O'Keeffe. Providing he can get his visas without delay on his return to Paris, Marcel still hopes to be back in New York for Florine's exhibition which is due to open on October 1.

Chardonne, Thursday, August 22, 1946

In the afternoon, Mary Reynolds and Marcel manage to catch the estate agent, M. Flouck, and visit the property in Chexbres, less than five minutes walk from the railway station, which may be of interest to the Hoppenots.

Mary finds it "beautiful, with an abundance of fruit trees apples pears peaches plums all loaded with fruit …" The house is too small and the conservatory too large, but Mary is interested in the hen house: "not quite a semicircle built in the hill with a tiled roof," which she thinks would make a very nice summer living room. "In fact," she considers, "there are all sorts of possibilities and I wish I were rich."

Chardonne, Saturday, August 24, 1946

Mary and Marcel leave their second Hôtel Bellevue situated on the hillside with a funicular down to Vevey and the lake, and take a train up the Rhône Valley to Sion. The ancient see and historic town is dominated, rather like Le Puy, by two rocky promontories.

Zug, Tuesday August 27, 1946

Mary and Marcel travel to Zurich, where they plan to stay a few days.

Bern, Saturday, August 31, 1946

Returning from Zurich on the last stage of their holiday in Switzerland, Mary and Marcel spend two days at the French ambassador's residence with their friends Henri and Hélène Hoppenot.

Bern, Monday, September 2, 1946

At the station in the afternoon, prior to the departure of the 5:12 train bound for Paris (for which they have reservations), a young man from the French embassy arrives bearing letters for the customs officials with the result that none of the pieces of luggage belonging to Mary and Marcel is opened for inspection.

Paris, Wednesday, September 4, 1946

A couple of days after their return from Bern, Mary and Marcel are invited to dine with Violaine, the Hoppenots' daughter. They recount all the "activities at the embassy and *ailleurs*" including, no doubt, dinner the previous weekend at the Hôtel de la Croix Blanche in a village near Fribourg. With the staff off duty at the ambassador's residence, the *maître d'hôtel* Louis was asked to reserve a table. Returning perplexed, he announced that the speciality of the establishment was *pis de vache* or cow's udder. When the astonished ambassador enquired, "Is it good?" Louis, with dignity but evidently shocked, replied: "I have never served anything of the sort yet! I don't commit myself in that way!"

Paris, Thursday, September 5, 1946

Marcel's hopes of obtaining a visa rapidly for his return to the United States are dashed when he learns that he must wait a month.

It is Marcel's "night off," but before going out he has asked Mary, who doesn't want to delay writing to their friends any longer, to pass on his warm regards and "a thousand things" for Henri and Hélène Hoppenot.

Lucerne, Saturday, June 1, 1968

On a card illustrated with a view of the lake and the alps in the distance, Marcel writes to Brookes Hubachek: "We left Paris a week ago with just enough gas to make Basel …" He and Teeny have been staying in Lucerne, far from the turmoil reigning in Paris. "We hope that France will be all right again soon."

On a excursion in their Volkswagen one wet day to Lake Geneva, Marcel searches unsuccessfully for the waterfall at Chexbres, which inspired him for the setting of *Étant donnés*. But although he would like to have shown it to Teeny, the landscape of the water mill is now hidden in its overgrown ravine by all trees.

Lucerne, Tuesday, June 4, 1968

After ten days in Switzerland, Teeny and Marcel travel to Zurich airport and fly to London.

Étant donnés in Marcel Duchamp's Letters to Maria Martins

The following excerpts are taken from Duchamp's letters to Maria Martins, published in Michael R. Taylor, *Marcel Duchamp: Étant donnés,* Philadelphia 2009, pp. 404–25.

New York, Friday (July 11, 1947)
The skin is in the press until tomorrow morning. When it is wet and taut it looks like fine quality marble but I fear that in drying it will yellow.
I had lots of ideas to make the job simpler. (405)

Edicott, September 6, (1948)
I am returning tomorrow and will go back to my dry skin under its steel rods—only you can understand this sentence.
I have even started to draw the woman. (In pencil.) (409)

October 12, (1948)
Tomorrow and the following days I will be putting my skin under the nails and will make a test, which will be more or less definitive, before starting on the full-scale plastilene. (409)

April 7, (1949)
Besides which, as we have always said, the way out is your sculpture and my woman with the open pussy.
But the main thing is to repeat it like a litany, or more like a prayer, every morning and every evening. Before leaving I had very nearly finished my woman's hand.
When I left her, she did not look too "wooden." (409)

Hollywood, April 22, (1949)
I often think about your hand, which I have never hurt and which has given me more joy than any lover could wish for. (411)

May 6, 1949
(P.S.:) The hand has been cast. (411)

June 20, (19)49
My plaster cast is back home and I am working on the sterile surface of the intractable plaster, with the inevitable little mishaps. What is ugly about plaster is the impression it gives of having been molded; that very thin top layer has to be removed by reworking the contours and then you have another original. (412)

June 30, (1949)
I am back to working 8hrs a day, retouching the plaster cast, i.e., redoing it completely. I find that the surface produced by the plastilene gives me more or less what I am looking for, namely, the epidermis and not the sculpture of the bones or the volumes. In any case this plaster cast was only made with a view to the skin that will go on it and that changes the whole conception.
I have high hopes for the end of July.... (415)

Tuesday evening (November / December 1949)
For a start, my experiments with the skin are turning out to be very disappointing. The cast is fine but the skin *won't* follow the shape of the cast. In short, I am writing for you to speak to you more about it. (417)

March 19, (1950)
Please write me a line or 2 with your left hand to tell me when you will be able to write with your right hand.—I would like to know more or less when. This isolation hurts.

As for the white orchid, I am preparing my third coat, which will be slightly pink! A skin color that will be as natural as possible.
But with each new coat, I have regrets and alter certain details because I would like to keep for you this unique example of direct sculpture; for as the photo already shows, it no longer has anything to do with the plastilene mode I had cast less than six month ago. With the skin I can look forward to many happy days with difficult problems on my hands. (417)

April 3, (1950)
(P.S.:) Our Lady of Desire is now flesh-pink: I am struggling against an overly fondant candy color. (419)

October 17, (1951)
I am hard at work on the paraffin and it works. It molds perfectly and keeps its shape while remaining very firm—and it is much less sensitive to heat than the much-vaunted wax, of which I have 55 pounds sent me by Socony-Vacuum.
Naturally I am molding 10 separate pieces of paraffin that I will join with the plaster on top. (423)

October 25, (1951)
As for Our Lady of Desires, I can manage to soften the paraffin and apply it to perfection (while still a little hot); I have obtained a mold that is perfect enough for what I want to do with it. I only have 5 or 6 pieces (molds) to do to cover the whole.

... My studio has become one big pig trough full of plaster and bits of paraffin—impossible to clean. (423)

November 9, (1951)
The paraffin molding is coming along; I hope to finish the upper half soon—it is time consuming but fun. The paraffin as tangible matter, is like a kind of soft opal and remains quite hard at room temperature, in the apartment....
P.S. I have also put the severed leg under the skin. It is marvelous—it is your leg and of such beauty!! (423)

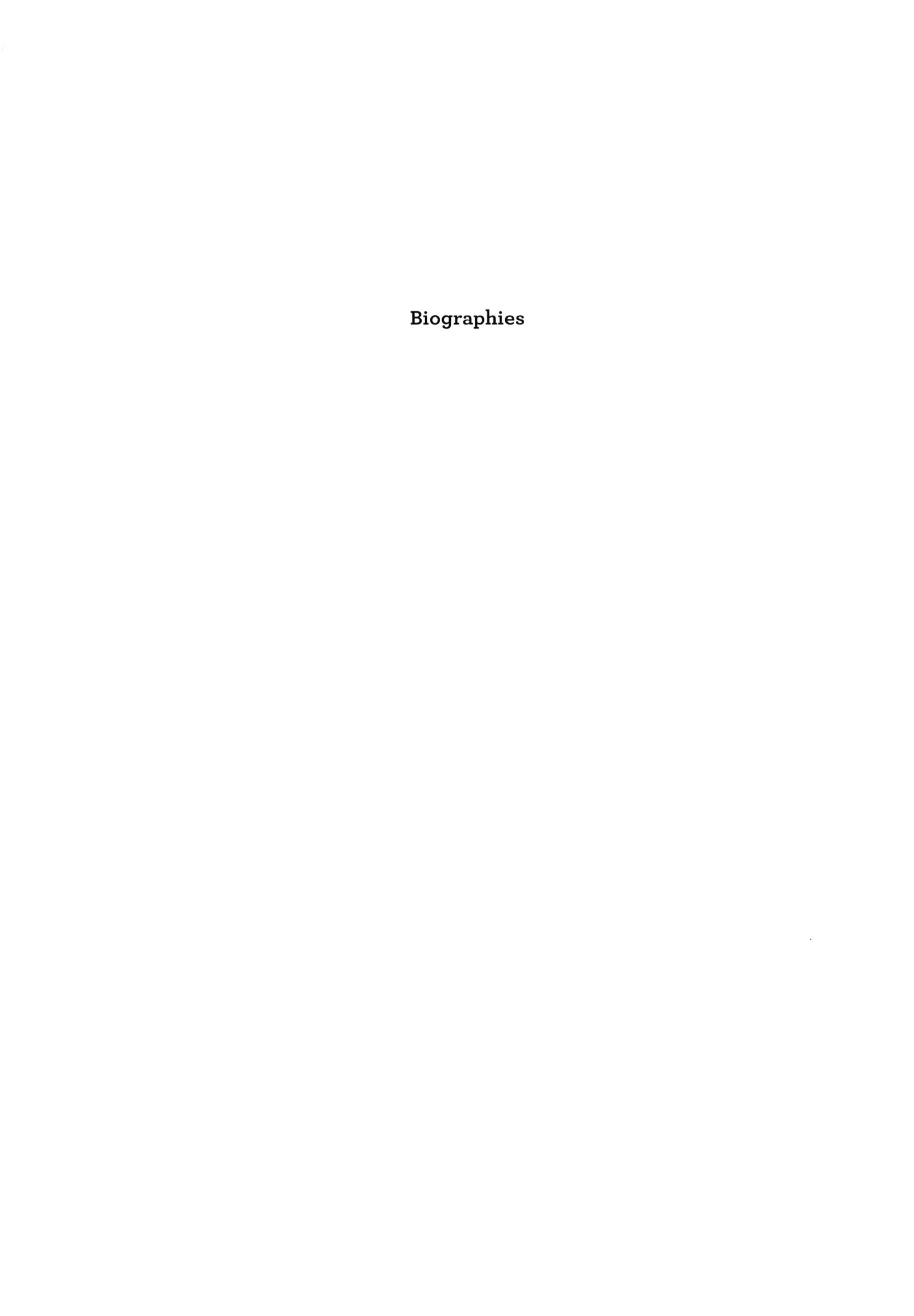

Biographies

Melanie Althaus studied human sciences in Lausanne and Paris and has been a lecturer in Media Studies and Visual Culture at the University of Lausanne and Fribourg. She is currently completing her MA in architecture at the EPFL (Swiss Institute of Technology, Lausanne). She explores intermediate territories and hybrid spaces. She's been involved in several editorial projects for more than ten years.

Caroline Bachmann is a painter and professor of painting and drawing at the HEAD in Geneva, Switzerland. She grew up in Cully, Switzerland. From 1983 to 1987 she studied at the Academy of Arts and Crafts in Geneva. From 1987 to 1990 she worked in the studio of internationally acknowledged Spanish graphic artist Peret in Barcelona. From 1991 to 2002 Bachmann lived in Rome. She took part in the ORESTE Projects, featured, among the other venues, in the Italian Pavilion of the 48th Venice Biennale curated by Harald Szeemann. She has been collaborating with Stefan Banz since 2004. Together, they published the artist book *What Duchamp Abandoned for the Waterfall* and founded the Association Kunsthalle Marcel Duchamp, both in 2009. They are the organizers and curators of the event "Marcel Duchamp and the Forestay Waterfall." Website: www.bxb.ch.

Stefan Banz is a conceptual artist and curator. He studied art history, German literature, and literary criticism at the University of Zurich. In 1989 he co-founded the Kunsthalle Lucerne and was its artistic director until 1993. He was a member of the Swiss Commission for the Arts (2001–7), received the Manor Art Prize and the Recognition Award of the city of Lucerne (2000), and was the curator of the 2005 Swiss Pavilion at the Venice Biennale. He has been collaborating with Caroline Bachmann since 2004. Together, they published the artist book *What Duchamp Abandoned for the Waterfall* and founded the Association Kunsthalle Marcel Duchamp, both in 2009. They are the organizers and curators of the event "Marcel Duchamp and the Forestay Waterfall." Websites: www.banz.tv and www.bxb.ch.

Étienne Barilier is the author of approximately forty novels and essays. While most of his writings deal with music, he is also passionate about the visual arts. His latest book is devoted to the great baroque architect Francesco Borromini (2009).

Lars Blunck is a full visiting professor at the Institute of Art History and Urban Studies at the Technical University Berlin since September 2008. After an MA in 1998, Blunck obtained a PhD in 2001 with a dissertation on performative assemblages in American Art of the 1950s and 60s. From March 2002 to September 2008, he was assistant professor at the Technical University Berlin. In 2005 he was the recipient of a Deubner Award for effective art historical research. In November 2007 he wrote his habilitation thesis on Duchamp's precision optics (published 2008).

Ecke Bonk was born in Cairo and educated in Germany where he studied history of science (Heidelberg and Tubingen) and typography with Herbert Bayer (Aspen). In the 1980s he was the director of the Ernst Mach Archive in Hamburg. He founded the Typosophic Society in 1994 and Typosophes Sans Frontières in 2001. Exhibitions include: Kunstmuseum Winterthur (1993); Documenta X (1997); Venice Biennale (1999); Documenta 11 (2002); Venice Biennale (2003); Neue Galerie Graz (2005); 3rd Guangzhou

Triennale (2008); Biennale Sao Paolo (2010). Publications include: *Marcel Duchamp: The Portable Museum; Inventory of an Edition* (1989), *The White Book / In the Infinitive* (1999, with Richard Hamilton), *Monte Carlo Method: A Typosophic Manual* (2007). Currently working on "On Clocks and Clouds," a re-enactment of a lecture by Karl Popper. Lives and works in Fontainebleau, France, and Whangaroa, New Zealand.

Hans Maria de Wolf is the general coordinator of the arts platform in Brussels, an interdisciplinary institute that brings together academics and artists. He studied art history at the Free University of Brussels and Columbia University in New York. He obtained a PhD degree in 2002 with an in-depth study of Marcel Duchamp's *Large Glass*. Before being appointed as a professor for art history at the Free University of Brussels, he collaborated as a curator at the Nationalgalerie im Hamburger Bahnhof in Berlin.

Paul B. Franklin is the editor in chief of *Étant donné Marcel Duchamp,* an acclaimed scholarly journal devoted to the life and work of the artist. He also works closely with Duchamp's heirs in managing the artist's estate.

Andreas Glauser is an artist, musician, and organizer, and is engaged with sound performances and exhibitions. He studied at the School of Art and Design in Lucerne and graduated with a degree in fine arts. In his audio studio, he experiments with computer and converted equipment such as organs, mixing consoles, and tape machines. Together with Julia Kälin, he is the director of the art production label Brainhall.

Antje von Graevenitz, retired, born in Hamburg in 1940, lives in Amsterdam, a former lecturer in modern art history at the University of Amsterdam, was professor of art history of the 20th and 21st century at the University of Cologne (1989–2005). From 1975 until 2006 she worked for editorial teams of the Museumjournaal, Kunstschrift OKB, Vrij Nederland, Archis, and Wallraf-Richartz-Jahrbuch. From 1972 to 1985 she wrote art criticism for the *Süddeutsche Zeitung* as a correspondent and published widely in books, museum catalogues, and art journals, mainly about anthropological and intertextual subjects in classical modern and contemporary art, such as performance art and the art of alchemy. In two articles she analyzed Duchamp's door *Gradiva* and compared Duchamp's and Joseph Beuys's works.

Dalia Judovitz is National Endowment for the Humanities Professor of French at Emory University. Born in Transylvania, Romania, she was educated in the United States and France. Her publications in the field of modern art and postmodern aesthetics include: *Unpacking Duchamp: Art in Transit* (1995), *Déplier Duchamp: Passages de l'art* (2000), and *Drawing on Art: Duchamp and Company* (2010). Her other area of research is focused on the relation of philosophy and literature in early modern texts and she has authored, among others: *The Culture of the Body: Genealogies of Modernity* (2001) and co-edited the book series The Body, in Theory: Histories of Cultural Materialism (1994–2004).

Michael Lüthy studied art history and history at the universities of Basel and Berlin. He graduated in Basel with a thesis on "Image and Gaze in Manet's Painting." Since 2003, he is the coordinator of the Collaborative Research Centre "Aesthetic Experience and the Dissolution of Artistic Limits" at Freie Universität Berlin. He specializes in 19th- and 20th-century French art, postwar American art, and the theories of modern art.

Bernard Marcadé is an art critic, independent curator, and professor of aesthetics and art history at the Ecole Nationale Supérieure d'Arts de Paris-Cergy. Recent publications include: *Les 53 Oeuvres qui m'ébranlèrent le monde* (2009) *Fabrice Hyber* (2009), and *Marcel Duchamp, une vie à credit* (2007). He has curated several shows, which include: *Libertad, Igualdad, Fraternidad* (Zaragoza, Madrid, and Pamplona, 2009–10, with Isabel Duran); *On dirait le Sud, Cartographies sentimentales et documentaires* (C.R.A.C, Sète, 2007), and *Je ne crois pas aux fantômes, mais j'en ai peur,* "La Force de l'art" (Grand Palais, Paris, 2006).

Adeena Mey is a writer and researcher. He studied art theory at Goldsmiths College, University of London, and anthropology at the University of Lausanne, Switzerland. His writings and translations have appeared in *Nowiswere, Sang Bleu, FlashartOnline,* as well as in diverse independent editorial initiatives. He has published a booklet entitled "Christian Marclay's Christmas Tales" (Helvetic Centre Editions).

Herbert Molderings is a freelance writer and professor of art history at the Ruhr-University in Bochum. He has published extensively on Marcel Duchamp, Man Ray, László Moholy-Nagy, Umbo, and the history of photography. Books on Duchamp: *Marcel Duchamp. Parawissenschaft, das Ephemere und der Skeptizismus* (1983, 1987, 1997), *Duchamp and the Aesthetics of Chance: Art as Experiment* (2010). Major essay on *Étant donnés* in the review *Étant donné Marcel Duchamp,* no. 3 (2001). He was co-curator of the exhibition *Re-Object: Marcel Duchamp, Damien Hirst, Jeff Koons, Gerhard Merz* (Kunsthaus Bregenz, 2006).

Stanislaus von Moos is an art historian. He has published monographs on Le Corbusier (1968 and 2009), Italian Renaissance architecture (1976), the architecture of Venturi, Scott Brown & Associates (1987 and 1999) and the history of industrial design in Switzerland (1992). Recent publications include *Le Corbusier: Album La Roche* (1998), *Fernand Léger: "La Ville"* (1999), and *Le Corbusier Before Le Corbusier* (2001, with Arthur Rüegg). His current research involves the history of modern architecture in Switzerland and the cross-pollinations between architecture and the visual arts since 1970. He has been professor of modern art at the University of Zurich and is presently serving as Vincent Scully Visiting Professor at Yale University.

Francis M. Naumann is an independent scholar, curator, and art dealer specializing in the art of the Dada and Surrealist periods. He is the author of numerous articles and exhibition catalogues, including *New York Dada 1915–25* (1994), considered to be the definitive history of the movement, and *Marcel Duchamp: The Art of Making Art in the Age of Mechanical Reproduction* (1999). He has curated several exhibitions in New York. He is currently in the process of gathering his articles and lectures on Duchamp for a book entitled *The Recurrent, Haunting Ghost: Essays on the Art, Life and Legacy of Marcel Duchamp.*

Mark Nelson is a partner at McCall Associates in New York City where he designs books for museums, galleries, and artists. He has worked closely with many leading contemporary artists including Richard Serra, Jenny Holzer, David Hammons, Tom Friedman, and Mitch Epstein. Recent book designs have included *Bauhaus 1919–1933: Workshops for Modernity* (2009) for The Museum of Modern Art, and *Roni Horn aka Roni Horn* (2009) for the Whitney Museum of American Art. Mr. Nelson is the author, with Sarah Hudson Bayliss, of *Exquisite Corpse: Surrealism and the Black Dahlia Murder* (2006). His next book, currently underway, is a visual reconstruction of the Hollywood home of Walter and Louise Arensberg.

Molly Nesbit is a professor of art history at Vassar College and a contributing editor of *Artforum*. Her books include *Atget's Seven Albums* (1992) and *Their Common Sense* (2000). *Midnight: The Tempest Essays,* a collection of her essays on contemporary art, will be published by Periscope Press. Since 2002, together with Hans Ulrich Obrist and Rirkrit Tiravanija, she has been organizing "Utopia Station," an ongoing book, exhibition, seminar, website, and street project.

Dominique Radrizzani is an art historian. He co-founded the Colloque de la relève Suisse in 1997 and produced several catalogues based on public collections in Vevey, Lausanne, and Geneva. Since 2004 he is the director of the Musée Jenisch in Vevey, where he created the National Drawing Centre in 2005. His curatorial and editorial work include: Pierre Alechinsky (Malraux Prize 2004), Balthus (with Jean Clair), François Bocion, Christian Boltanksi, Francesco Borromini, Cesare da Sesto, Circuit, Alberto Giacometti, Alexander Hahn, Alain Huck, Oskar Kokoschka, Denis Savary, and Théophile-Alexandre Steinlen.

Roman Signer is a sculptor and performance artist. He was born in Appenzell, Switzerland. He studied at the Schule für Gestaltung, Zurich (1966); the Schule für Gestaltung, Lucerne (1971–72); and the Academy of Fine Arts, Warsaw, Poland (1971–72). He lives and works in St. Gallen, Switzerland. Selected solo shows include: Swiss Institute, New York (2010); Hamburger Kunsthalle, Hamburg (2009); Hauser and Wirth, London (2008); Helmhaus, Zurich (2008); and Bonnefanten Museum, Maastricht (2008).

Michael R. Taylor is the Muriel and Philip Berman Curator of Modern Art at the Philadelphia Museum of Art. His most recent exhibitions at the Museum include *Marcel Duchamp: "Étant donnés"* (2009), *Arshile Gorky: A Retrospective* (2009), and *Salvador Dalí: The Centennial Retrospective* (2005). He studied at the Courtauld Institute of Art in London, where he wrote a masters thesis on Richard Hamilton and a doctoral dissertation on Marcel Duchamp's readymades. In 2009 he co-curated with Carlos Basualdo the Bruce Nauman exhibition at the American Pavilion for the 53rd Venice Biennale (winner of the Golden Lion award for best national pavilion). Future projects include an exhibition on Surrealism in the 1940s that focuses on myth, magic, and eroticism.

Philip Ursprung is a professor of modern and contemporary art at the University of Zurich since 2005. He was born in Baltimore, MD, in 1963. He received his PhD from the Freie Universität Berlin. In 2007 he was visiting professor at the Graduate School of Architecture,

Planning and Preservation of Columbia University, New York. He was a visiting curator at the Canadian Centre for Architecture in Montréal where he curated *Herzog & de Meuron: Archeology of the Mind* (2002–3). Recent publications include *Images: A Picture Book of Architecture* (2004, with Ilka and Andreas Ruby), *Grenzen der Kunst: Allan Kaprow und das Happening, Robert Smithson und die Land Art* (2003), and *Die Kunst der Gegenwart, 1960 bis heute* (2010).

I Want to Grasp Things with the Mind the Way the Penis is Grasped by the Vagina
Galerie Davel 14, Cully. Exhibition with works, books, CDs, and documents by:

Ai Weiwei, one of China's most respected artists, lives and works in Beijing. **Caroline Bachmann and Stefan Banz,** conceptual artists, live and work in Cully, Switzerland, and Berlin, Germany. **Fritz Balthaus,** conceptual artist, lives and works in Berlin, Germany. **Francis Bacon,** born October 28, 1919 in Dublin, Ireland, and died April 28, 1992 in Madrid, Spain, one of the most important painters of the 20th century. **Georg Baselitz,** one of the most influential German painters and sculptors of his generation, lives and works in Inning at Ammersee, Germany, and in Imperia, Italy. **Rudolf Blättler,** a sculptor lives and works in Lucerne, Switzerland. **Ecke Bonk and Antoine Monnier,** conceptual artists, live and work in Fontainebleau, France; Whangaroa, New Zealand; and Villiers-sous-Grez, France. **Monica Bonvicini,** an installation artist, lives and works in Berlin, Germany. **Jacques Caumont,** a widely known Duchamp biographer and scholar, lives and works in France. **Rosemary Cel,** a conceptual artist, lives and works everywhere she is. **Basil Debraine,** a student, born in 1992, who wants to become an artist. **Jacques Derrida,** born July 15, 1930 in El Biar, Algeria, and died October 8, 2004 in Paris, France, one of the most influential French philosophers of the 20th century and founder of what is today called deconstructivism. **Anke Doberauer,** a painter and professor at the Akademie of Arts, Munich, lives and works in Munich, Germany and Marseille, France. **Marcel Duchamp,** born July 1887 in Blainville-Crevon, France, and died October 2, 1968 in Neuilly-sur-Seine, France, one of the most important and influential artists of the 20th century. Between August 5 and 9, 1946 he photographed the Forestay waterfall for his last masterpiece *Étant donnés: 1° La chute d'eau, 2° Le gaz d'éclairage* (1946–66, Philadelphia Museum of Art, Gift of the Cassandra Foundation). **Étant Donnés,** an experimental/industrial duo formed in Grenoble, France, in 1980 by brothers Eric and Marc Hurtado, originally from Rabat, Morocco. **Jean-Claude Forest,** born September 11, 1930 in Le Perreux-sur-Marne, France, and died December 29, 1998 in Paris, France, a writer and illustrator of comics and the creator of character Barbarella. **Goldfrapp,** an electronic pop band from Bristol, England, consisting of Alison Goldfrapp (voice) and Will Gregory (keyboards). **Erwin Grünenfelder,** a biological farmer, lives and works in Switzerland. **Herzog & de Meuron,** a Swiss architecture firm, founded in 1978 and headquartered in Basel, Switzerland, perhaps best known for its conversion of the giant Bankside Power Station in London for the new home of the Tate Modern and the Beijing National Stadium for the 2008 Olympic Games. **Erwin Hofstetter,** a sculptor and painter, lives and works in Lucerne, Switzerland. **Fabrice Hyber,** a conceptual artist, lives and works in Paris, France. **Bert Jansen,** an art critic, lives and works in Amsterdam. **Jing Wei,** a painter lives and works in Lucerne, Switzerland. **Richard Jackson,** an installation artist, lives since 1993 in Sierra Madre, California. **Felix Kälin,** a bookreader and bookseller, and the discoverer of the Forestay waterfall for Duchamp research in 1980, lives in Basel, Switzerland. **Pierre Keller,** an artist and the director of ECAL /University of Art and Design, Lausanne, lives in St. Saphorin, Switzerland. **Konrad Klapheck,** one of the most significant German painters of his generation, lives in Düsseldorf, Germany. **Le Forestay,** the waterfall between Bellevue (commune of Puidoux) and Chexbres, which was seven times photographed by Marcel Duchamp between August 5 and 9, 1946. **Line Marquis,** a draftswoman, lives and works in Lausanne, Switzerland. **Gudrun Meier,** a freelance translator specializing in texts about classical music, lives in Glinde near Hamburg, Germany. **Charles Moser,** an artist and professor at Lucerne's University of Applied Sciences and Art, lives in Menziken, Switzerland. **Olivier Mosset,** a minimal and conceptual painter lives and works in Tucson, Arizona and Geneva, Switzerland. **Mark Nelson and Sarah Hudson Bayliss,** the authors of *Exquisite Corpse: Surrealism and the Black Dahlia Murder,* New York 2006, both live in Brooklyn, New York. **Mimosa Pale,** a sculptor and performance artist lives and works in Berlin, Germany, and Pori, Finland. **Céline Peruzzo,** an artist lives and works in Zurich. **Jean-Michel Rabaté,** a professor of English and comparative literature at the University of Pennsylvania and author of *Given: 1° Art, 2° Crime,* Sussex 2006. **Jason Rhoades,** an installation artist, born July 9, 1965 in Newcastle, California, and died August 1, 2006 in Los Angeles, one of the most significant artists of his generation. **Peter Roesch,** a painter, lives and works in Lucerne, Switzerland. **Sam Rosenthal,** a composer, musician, founder and leader of Black Tape For a Blue Girl and Projekt Records, lives in Brooklyn, New York. **Jukka Rusanen,** a painter and photographer, lives and works in Helsinki, Finland. **Denis Savary,** an artist, lives and works in Lausanne, Switzerland. **Harald Szeemann,** born June 11, 1933 in Bern, Switzerland, and died February 18, 2005 in Tegna, Switzerland, one of the most internationally respected curators and a specialist on Marcel Duchamp's work. **Michael R. Taylor,** the Muriel and Philip Berman Curator of Modern Art at the Philadelphia Museum of Art, lives in Philadelphia, Pennsylvania. **Aldo Walker,** born November 6, 1938 in Winterthur, Switzerland, and died March 17, 2000 in Lucerne, Switzerland, a conceptual artist, who lived and worked in Lucerne, represented Switzerland in 1986 at the Venice Biennale together with John Armleder. **Wang Xingwei,** a painter, lives and works in Beijing, China. **Martin Widmer,** an artist, lives and works in Geneva, Switzerland. **Rolf Winnewisser,** a painter, draftsman, and writer who took part at Documenta 5 in Kassel at the age of 22, lives and works in Ennetbaden, Switzerland. **Stephan Wittmer,** an artist and professor at Lucerne's University of Applied Sciences and Art, lives and works in Adligenswil, Switzerland. **Tadanori Yokoo,** one of Japan's most successful and internationally recognized graphic designers and artists, is based in Tokyo, Japan. **John Zorn,** a famous American avant-garde composer, arranger, record producer, saxophonist, and multi-instrumentalist, lives in New York.

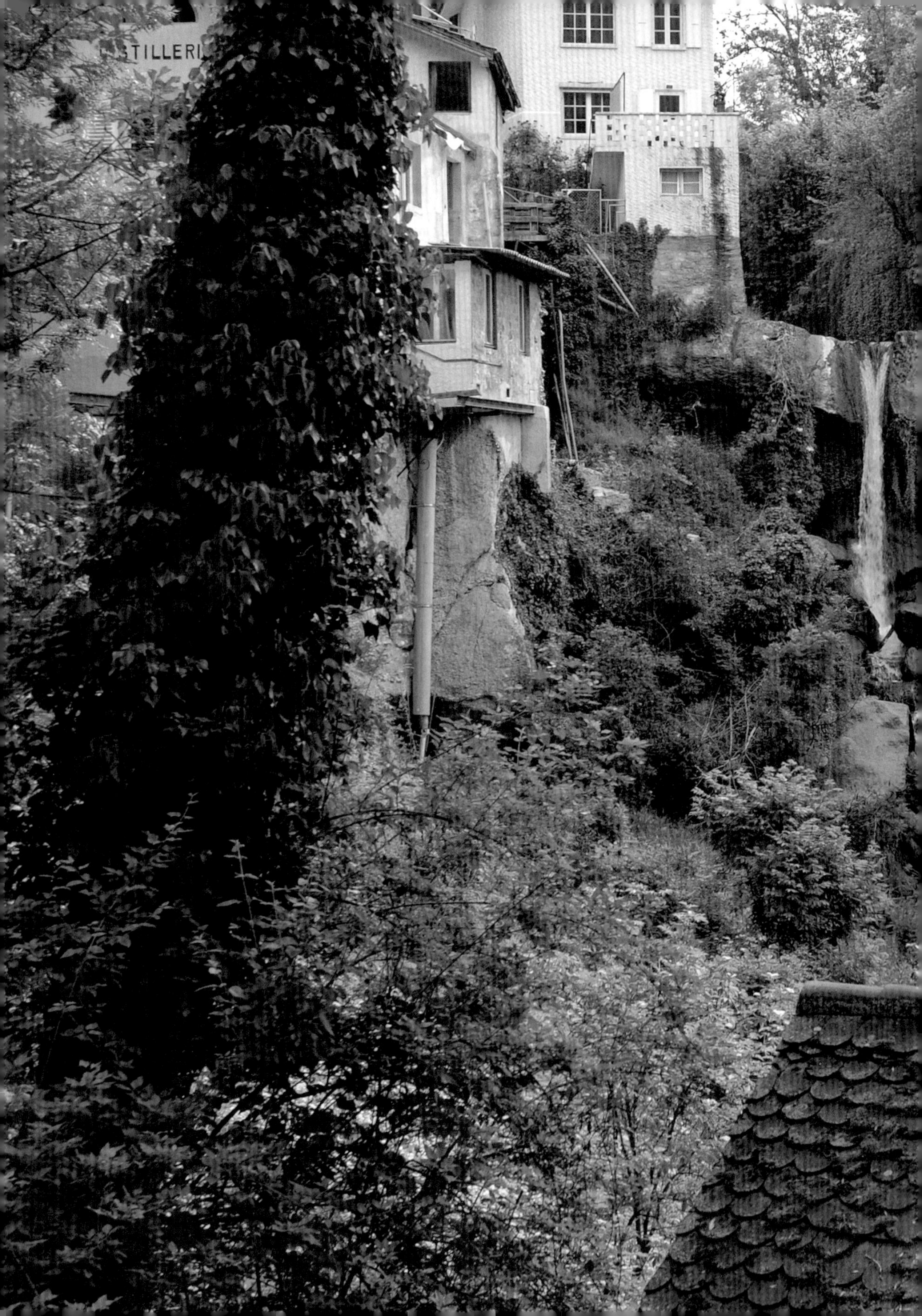
STILLERI

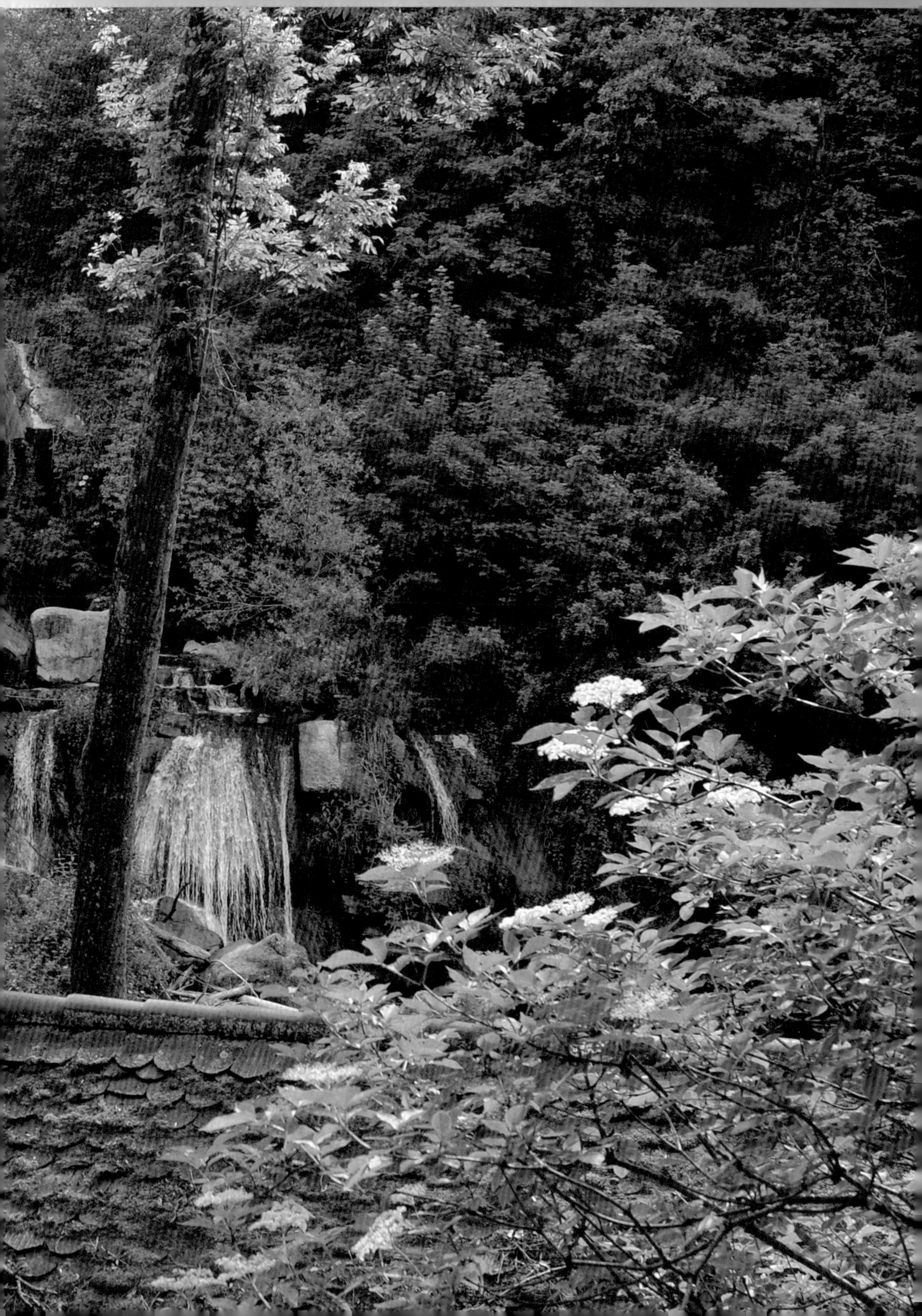

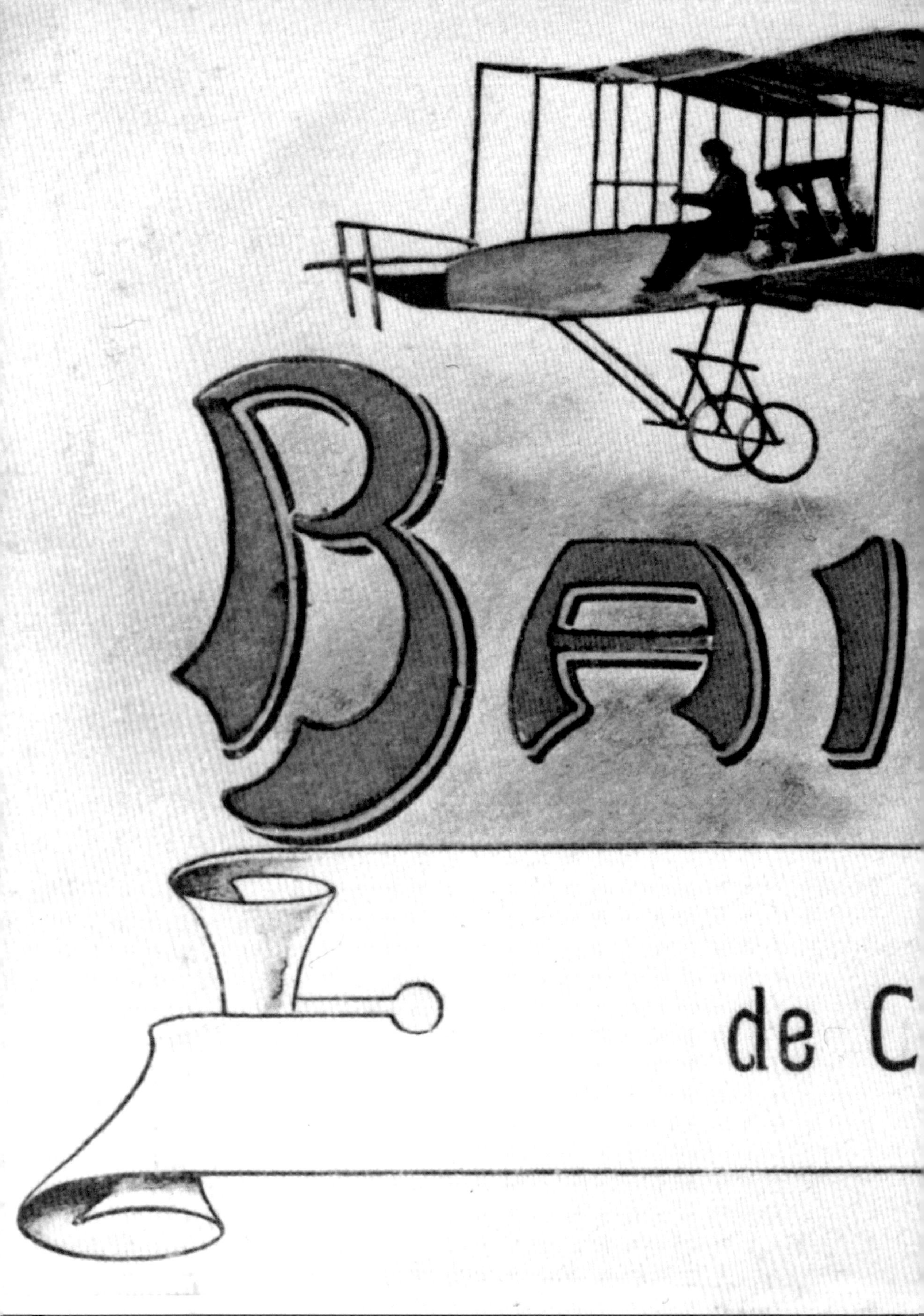
Bai
de C

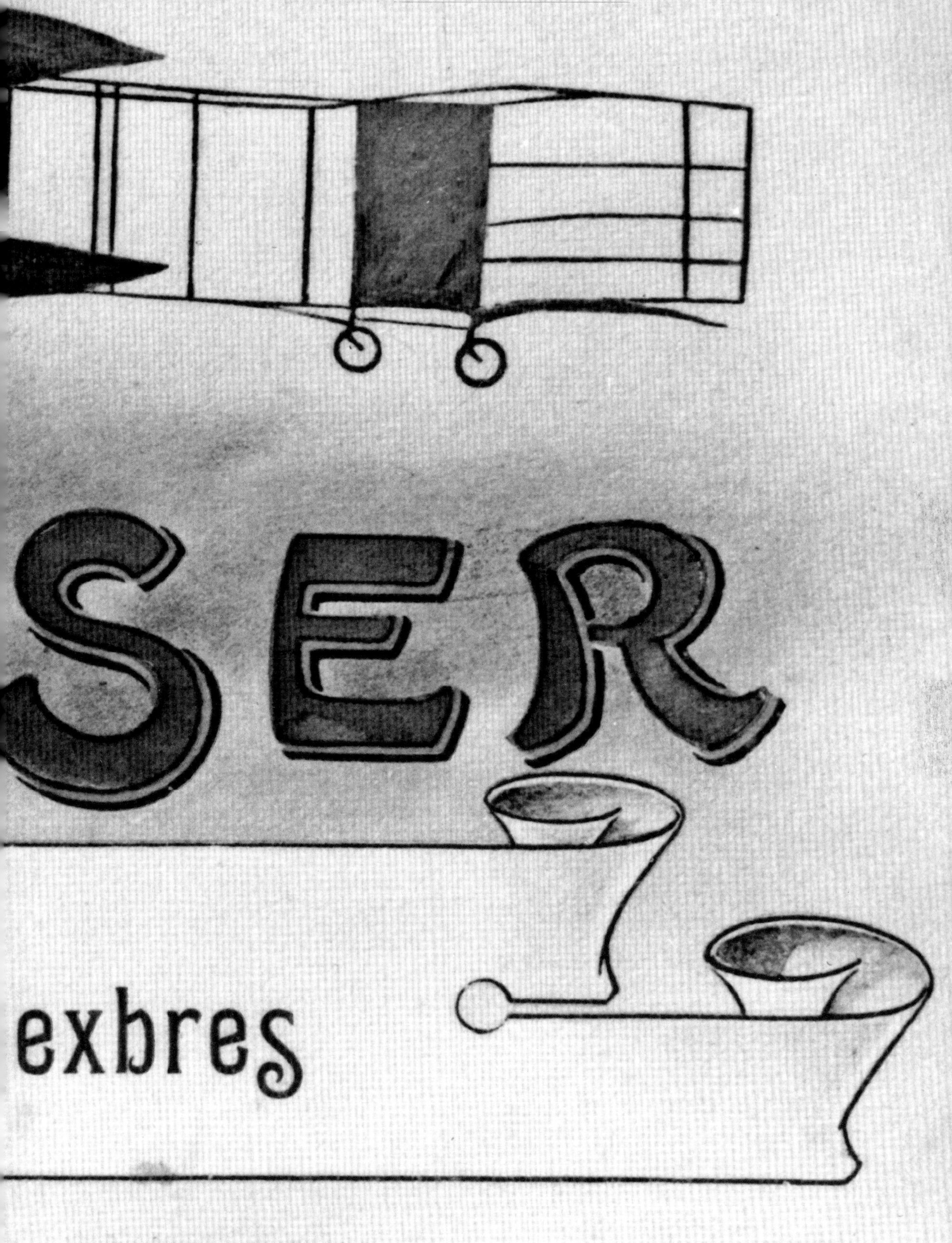
SER
exbres

Edited by
Stefan Banz for the Association Kunsthalle Marcel Duchamp, rue de l'Indépendance 2, CH-1096 Cully, kmd@bxb.ch, www.bxb.ch/kunsthalle

Translations by
Martin Adrichem (Antje von Graevenitz), Anthony Allen (Caroline Bachmann, Excerpt from Eric Muller's *Puidoux, une commune au coeur du Lavaux*), Gaston Bertin and Jonathan Fox (Étienne Barilier, Bernard Marcadé), John Brogden (Herbert Molderings), Daniel Hendrickson (Michael Lüthy), Suzanne Kobine-Roy and Amélia Tarzi (Dominique Radrizzani), Hugh Rorrison (Introduction, Acknowledgments), and Catherine Schelbert (Stefan Banz, Concert Andreas Glauser, Installation Roman Signer).

Copyediting by
Jonathan Fox with Catherine Schelbert

Concept, layout, and digital image processing by
Stefan Banz

Lithography, printing, and bookbinding by
DZA Druckerei zu Altenburg GmbH, Altenburg, Germany

Photography by
Stefan Banz and Caroline Bachmann (if not otherwise indicated). The concert of Andreas Glauser and the opening of Ecke Bonk's exhibition at the Kunsthalle Marcel Duchamp by Erwin Hofstetter, and *The Waterfall's Photographer* on the front end-paper by Christian Selig. Photographs also by Hans Bellmer (p. 53); Denise Bellon (pp. 65, 194, 241, & 242); René Clair (p. 101); Steven Crosset (p. 124); D. James Dee (p. 152); J. C. Ducret (p. 31); Dorothee Fischer (p. 137); Katharina Heusser (p. 381); George Hodel (p. 201); Felix Kälin (pp. 378 & 382); Glen Kearns (p. 191); Gerard Malanga (p. 148); Willy Maywald (p. 253); Francis M. Naumann (p. 157); Dominique Radrizzani (p. 68); Man Ray (pp. 89, 194, 195, & 197); Serge Stauffer (pp. 383–86); Bert Stern (p. 186); and Joel Sternfeld (p. 37). *Baiser de Chexbres* (pp. 406–7), postcard, c. 1915, Collection Association du Vieux Lavaux, Chexbres.

Photography credits
Association Marcel Duchamp, Villiers-sous-Grez; Association du Vieux Lavaux, Chexbres; Jutta Niemann, Association Willy Maywald, Paris; Austrian Frederick and Lillian Kiesler Private Foundation, Vienna; Art Institute of Chicago; Barnes Foundation, Merion; California Historical Society, San Francisco; Comité André Masson, Paris; Estate of William N. Copley/ Copley LLC, New York; Fondation Le Corbusier, Paris; Enrico Donati Papers, Getty Research Institute, Los Angeles; Eric Le Roy, les films de l'équinoxe-fonds photographique Denis Bellon, Paris; Luhring Augustine, New York; Metropolitan Museum of Art, New York; Musée cantonal des Beaux-Arts, La Chaux-de-Fonds; Musée cantonal des Beaux-Arts, Lausanne; Musée d'Orsay, Paris; Museum of Modern Art, New York; Philadelphia Museum of Art, Philadelphia; Szépmuvészeti Múzeüm, Budapest; Museo Thyssen-Bornemisza, Madrid; Galerie Konrad Fischer, Düsseldorf; Ubu Gallery, New York and Galerie Berinson, Berlin; Vito Acconci, New York; Stefan Banz and Caroline Bachmann, Cully; Steve Hodel, Los Angeles; Felix Kälin, Basel; Francis M. Naumann, New York; Uli Sigg, Mauensee; and Christian Selig, Zürich.

ISBN: 978-3-03764-156-9

Distributed by
JRP|Ringier, Letzigraben 134, CH-8047 Zurich, T +41 (0)43 311 27 50, F +41 (0)43 311 27 51, E info@jrp-ringier.com, www.jrp-ringier.com. JRP|Ringier publications are available internationally at selected bookstores and from following distribution partners: Switzerland: Buch 200, AVA Verlagsauslieferung AG, Centralweg 16, CH-8910 Affoltern a.A., buch2000@ava.ch, www.ava.ch. Germany and Austria: Vice Versa Vertrieb, Immanuelkirchstrasse 12, D-10405 Berlin, info@vice-versa-vertrieb.de, www.vice-versa-vertrieb.de. France: Les presses du réel, 35 rue Colson, F-2100 Dijon, info@lespressesdureel.com, www.lespressesdureel.com. UK and other European Countries: Cornerhouse Publications, 70 Oxford Street, UK-Manchester M1 5NH, publications@cornerhouse.org, www.cornerhouse.org|books. USA, Canada, and Australia: D.A.P./Distributed Art Publishers, 155 Sixth Avenue, 2nd Floor, USA-New York, NY 10013, dap@dapinc.com, www.artbook.com.

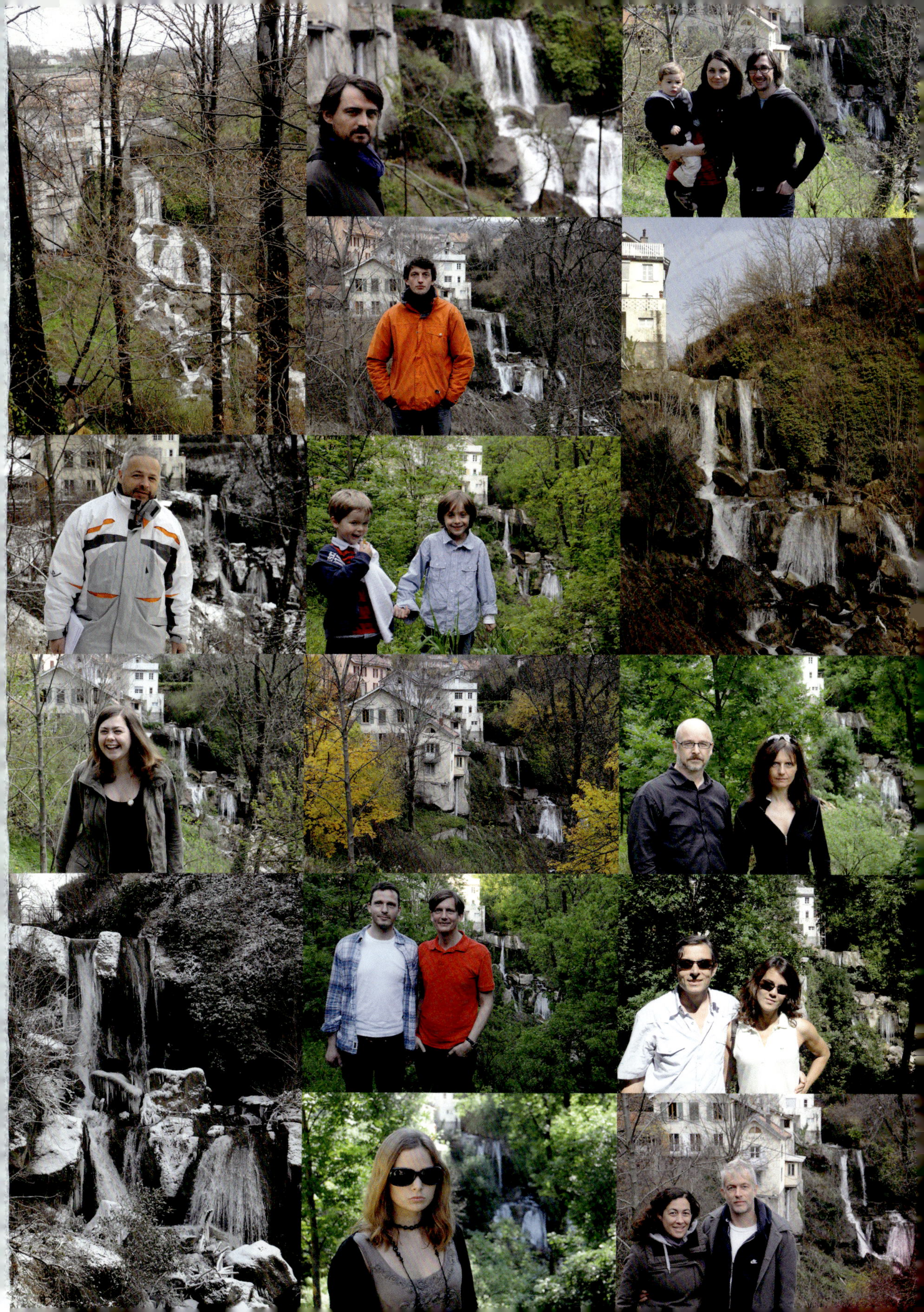

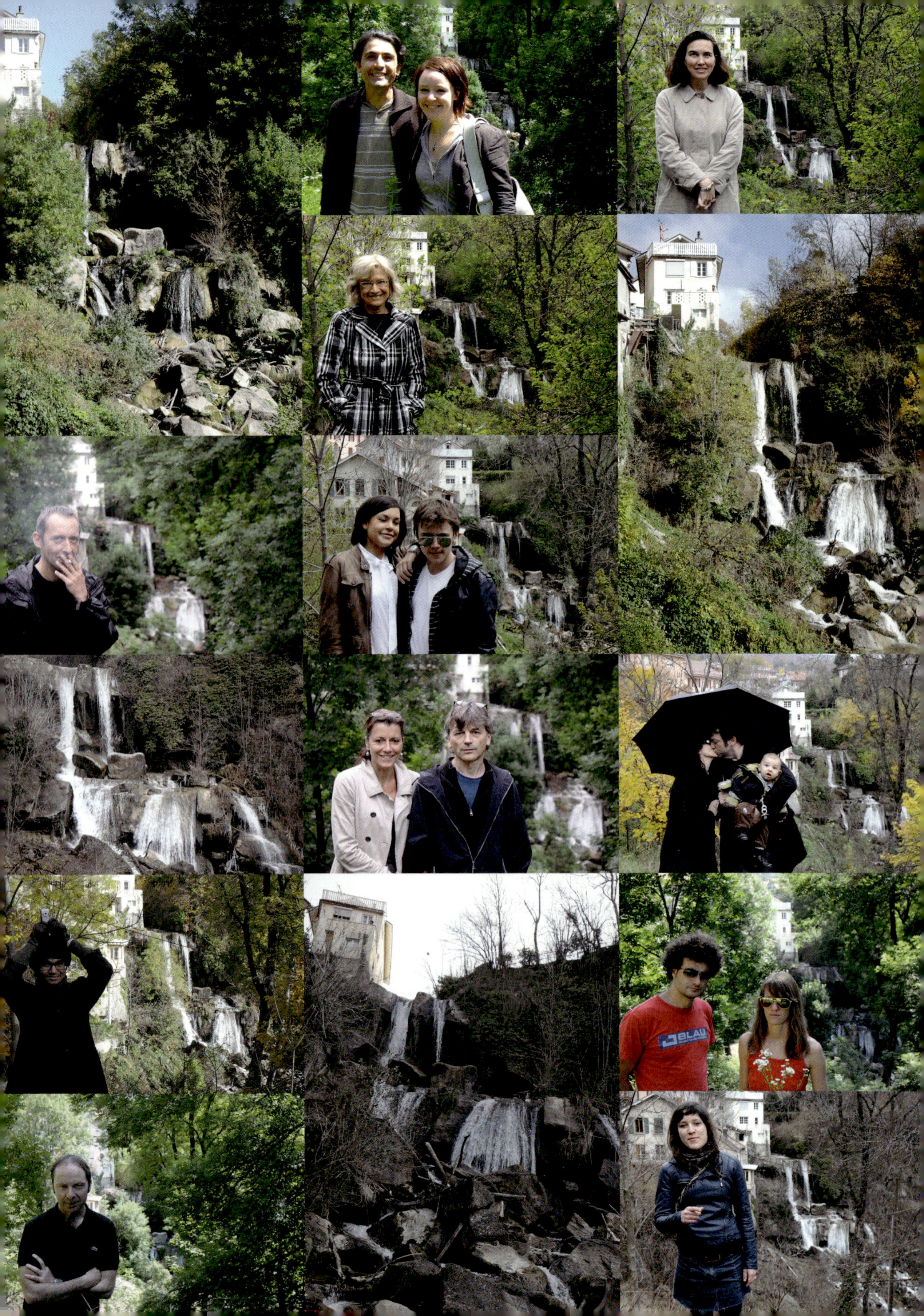
BLAU